The Fundamentals of Video Game Literacy

This book posits a novel framework for sense-making and meaning-making in the play of video games. Extending a modern, process-oriented, audience-inclusive philosophy of artistic meaning generation, this book grapples with the question of how to personally and critically examine video games as artistic artifacts that do not have set, predetermined, standardized forms until live play is enacted. The resulting artistic product, live gameplay, expresses both the game's developers *and* its players.

This book argues that players hold three separate, concurrent perspectives during play: the embodied avatar within the simulated space, the role-playing participant in the narrative fantasy, and the external strategist manipulating the game's software affordances. The exciting dynamics that arise from live gameplay are the result of the tensions and harmonies between these three parallel layers of play.

Video games are systems with designed behaviors capable of a great diversity of instantiated expressions. Players are brought into that system of instantiated generation to produce truly emergent and personal gameplay. As such, players directly impact the shape and form of the gameplay artifact itself. This creates a relationship between the art, the player, and its meaning radically different from all previous art forms.

This book builds around this central premise with examinations of related subjects pertaining to video game meaning-making, such as the ways in which video games facilitate play that is expressive of their players and the ways in which it is appropriate to compare and contextualize the differences in players' instantiated play activities. These subjects are designed to give readers an in-depth understanding of the dynamics of gameplay in order to facilitate richer, more meaningful encounters with video games as cultural artifacts.

This book:

- Provides a useful framework for enriching players' experiences with video game play.
- Helps players identify and distinguish aspects of their own and game developers' expression in gameplay.
- Posits a novel framework examining the role of player as embodied avatar, role-player, and strategist.
- Gives players appropriate questions to better interrogate the generation of meaning from within and surrounding the system of gameplay.

Ryan Zhao is an independent researcher and lecturer specializing in video game literacy. After achieving his MS in the psychological sciences, he has worked for almost a decade in the video game industry, performing research and marketing roles for Nintendo and Xbox, and he has more than a decade of critical work through podcasts and publications *Cane and Rinse*, *Sound of Play*, and *Play;Write*.

The Fundamentals of Video Game Literacy
Theory, Practice, and Aesthetics

Ryan Zhao

CRC Press
Taylor & Francis Group
Boca Raton London New York

CRC Press is an imprint of the
Taylor & Francis Group, an **informa** business

Designed cover image: Ryan Zhao

First edition published 2025
by CRC Press
2385 NW Executive Center Drive, Suite 320, Boca Raton FL 33431

and by CRC Press
4 Park Square, Milton Park, Abingdon, Oxon, OX14 4RN

CRC Press is an imprint of Taylor & Francis Group, LLC

ISBN: 9781032871127 (hbk)
ISBN: 9781032869278 (pbk)
ISBN: 9781003530961 (ebk)

DOI: 10.1201/9781003530961

Typeset in Minion Pro
by codeMantra

Access the Support Material: www.routledge.com/9781032869278

Contents

Acknowledgments, vii

CHAPTER 1 ▪ Introduction 1

CHAPTER 2 ▪ Key Terms 26

CHAPTER 3 ▪ Reading Game Design 65

CHAPTER 4 ▪ Interfacing with Games 95

CHAPTER 5 ▪ Other Models of Meaning-Making for Video Games 127

CHAPTER 6 ▪ Layered Literacy, Part 1: Diegesis, Mimesis, and Methexis 158

CHAPTER 7 ▪ Layered Literacy, Part 2: Sense-Making 169

CHAPTER 8 ▪ Layered Literacy, Part 3: Meaning-Making 203

CHAPTER 9 ▪ Narrative 239

CHAPTER 10 ▪ Perspective-Taking 254

CHAPTER 11 ▪ Instantiation and Characterization 267

CHAPTER 12 ▪ Expressivity 306

CHAPTER 13 ▪ Glitches, Cheating, and Metagame 321

CHAPTER 14 ▪ Ideology and Ethics 345

Appendix: Ludography, 363

INDEX, 405

Acknowledgments

I would like to extend great, personal thanks to Aaron Schlichting for graphic design support, Jesse Fuchs for academic guidance, and to Leon Cox, Joshua Garrity, and the rest of the *Cane and Rinse* team for granting my first opportunity to engage in published, critical discourse around video games.

CHAPTER 1

Introduction

FRAMING

The slow but pronounced evolution of human thought and society lurches ever forward but can feel invisible, or at least inscrutable, to those who experience it from within. Often easier to diagnose and categorize in retrospect, we can observe bouts of collective progress, moments of regression, and cyclical patterns that characterize the unsteady, chronological journey through time as a collective experience.

Far from being a sum of all individual actors within the culture, societal attitude and philosophy do seem to operate as a collective (though certainly not united) whole of sorts, amorphously congealing around particular subjects of curiosity, celebration, or derision at particular times and in particular places.

Sometimes the collective consciousness is guided by top-down mechanisms of communication and control; the mandates of important figures, whether in government, information, or business, occupy a disproportionate significance in the public eye. Other times, the defining philosophies of an age bubble up from the common people, whether reacting to unbearable circumstances, such as those that motivate civil rights movements, or collectively celebrating a new flavor of expression that uniquely speaks to the dreams and frustrations of a new generation.

Nowhere is the metaphorical mind—the pulse—of a culturally situated collective more thoroughly observable than in a culture's arts and other expressive artifacts. Whether we wish to untangle the narrative of our developmental history or gain predictive insights into our present age, the arts are an invaluable domain through which the soul of a people group can be glimpsed. Such is the objective of the culturally curious, intentionally literate observer.

Each artwork is produced within a cultural context by someone deeply affected by their unique contextual situation. Every work is as political as it is psychological, whether explicitly commenting upon the existential experience situated in a particular time and place or implicitly and unintentionally reflecting the assumptions and value-ethics the artist has drawn from her situated experience within the culture. Furthermore, works of note are elevated and celebrated because they connect with people in a manner that directly speaks to an unmet need. Any work that becomes truly beloved does so through the acceptance of individuals embedded in a particular cultural situation. Such that we can conclude that, for a work to truly resonate, it must speak a "language" that the culture's ear needs to hear. From the most abstractly simple to the most situationally specific artwork, every work contains aspects of both the personal and the collective within it.

Human society has always been shaped by a dense web of interacting systems. Much of human life is spent navigating the push-and-pull of institutional powers, social allowances, and natural circumstances. Each of these factors intersects and interrelates. Political decisions affect the economy. Economic circumstances affect religious institutions. Religious institutions affect value attitudes. Value attitudes affect social prejudices. Social prejudices affect political landscapes... This is not to say that this is a linear, unidirectional chain of dependencies; each of these factors and dozens more like them affect every other factor in the circumstantial web that constitutes collective living.

DOI: 10.1201/9781003530961-1

Citizens of modern society, now more than at any other point in history, are aware and critical of the systems that constitute society. Modern technologies like the internet and other electronic media elucidate these systemic forces and enable participation within domains to which those in past generations had limited access. It is increasingly obvious how the actions within one domain ripple through others.

An intersectional awakening is evidenced in many avenues of modern society. Conditions like the COVID-19 pandemic of 2020 and global climate change prompt us to consider humanity's most pressing issues as complex interworking of international politics, societal attitudes, and capitalistic forces that affect the whole of the global environment. International barriers are dissolved on the perpetually interconnected internet, and the spread of goods and culture between distant peoples has never thrived to such a degree. Even our modes of social connection are increasingly globalized and perversely "gamified" through the metrics and often-inscrutable dynamics of social media networks, prompting systemic consideration of even the tools that recreationally connect us. Modern philosophies surrounding our social responsibilities to one another emphasize the intersections between aspects of identity, background, and circumstance (Crenshaw, 1989) encouraging an understanding of society rooted in an awareness of systemic dynamics at play in the myriad of these relationships.

Humans have always lived in the context of systemic interrelationship—from the tribal groups that developed practical ethics to maintain group harmony to the evolution of society and the laws and social contracts that serve that function in a larger context. The scale of the systems in which we are now embedded and the proliferation of available information make the systemic structure of our now *global* society unavoidably present. This is reflected in our language, social practices, and even our entertainment. We cannot understand our individual places in the world *but* through the intersections of increasingly complex systems. It is only natural that this systemic perspective is reflected in the arts and cultural artifacts produced within such a time and place. For this reason, video games—designed simulations within which player-agents systemically operate—may just be the medium that best speaks the language of our modern world.

Before fully diving into the topic of video games, it should be noted that more traditional media are becoming increasingly systemic themselves. Rare is the wholly self-contained artistic work in modern culture. Our culture's stories are increasingly transmedial. *Star Wars* is not a self-contained story told through a trilogy of films as it was in the 1980s; *Star Wars* (Lucas, 1977) is an ever-expanding cinematic catalog, a growing slate of episodic "television" series, countless video games, theme park experiences, novels of fluctuating canonicity, toys, a recognized religion, comic books, and *at least* one embarrassing holiday special. All of these distinct instances are to be held in consideration when understanding all others. Characters from the video games are referenced in the theme parks, events from the animated series are referenced in the live-action series, and events from the embarrassing holiday special are integral to the comic books… The story of *Star Wars* is not *one* thing or even told through one *artistic medium*; it is the collective whole of a perpetually remediated *library* of texts, each in systemic balance of tension and harmony with one another.

In fact, I argue that the primary artistic project of the 20th century was the reframing of the relationship between artists, their works, and audiences. The artistic work is no longer viewed as a static artifact from which audiences must studiously extract meaning that the artist has unidirectionally imbued. Rather, art today is created with a greater priority towards observer-subjectivity, such that the artist "collaborates" with the audience to construct indeterminant, dynamic meaning through thoughtful affordances of ambiguity and even formic plurality.

To *briefly* summarize more than a century of artistic-philosophical development (with an admittedly narrow focus on western artists), we can consider as an example the division between the Realists and Impressionists of the late 19th century. The Realists, following the tradition of artistic development to that point in history, sought to masterfully reproduce the world as-it-was, while the Impressionists forewent exact likenesses for a more subjective perspective of their subjects. They sought to illustrate the world as it was *experienced* by the mind, by the memory. This makes a subtle, philosophical plea to audiences: think not only of *what* you see but *how* you see it. Consider the *process* of seeing. In a sense, the subject of each painting was deprioritized, instead privileging the *experience* of observing.

Going beyond the depiction of subjectivity to elucidating the subjectivity of production, many 20th-century movements rejected singular form for ambiguity and process. The Surrealists of the 1920s–1950s, inspired by the philosophies of the subconscious put forward by Sigmund Freud and Carl Jung, developed methods of artistic production that intentionally removed the conscious agency of the artist(s). This includes *automatic drawing*, in which the artist would produce a series of non-formic squiggles from which she would elucidate forms afterward, and nominally collaborative art in which multiple artists would contribute pieces of a drawing or text that would later compose a whole without knowing the context of what the others had drawn or written. This suggests that humans have capacities beyond conscious agency from which meaning can be produced, whether it is in a Jungian, collective sense or simply the pleasurable experience of divining meaning from what appears to be nonsense. Again, an appeal to process over product.

Abstract and expressionist arts forego representation for evocative ambiguity. The artist creates an experience of *seeing* rather than something to be *seen*. Avant-garde artists like John Cage, famously in his composition *4'33* (1952), demonstrated that meaning from a work of art can be attributed to the context and circumstance in which it is witnessed to a greater degree than the content of the work itself. Environmental artists often produce art that will change or be destroyed over time, arguing that art can be *meaningful* even if it does not present *consistently* to every observer. The artist admits that the formic specificity of her production is not as important to the construction of meaning as the observer's circumstance of encounter and subjective experience of an indeterminate gestalt.

More radically, the Dadaists of the 1910s–1920s and the pop artists of the 1950s bridged the gap between commercial culture and high arts. In an increasingly post-religious world, natural beauty was no longer the *de facto* pinnacle of aesthetic standards. As demonstrated by Andy Warhol's famous *Campbell's Soup Cans* (1962) series, there is a primal power in the collective experience of "low" culture. The ubiquity of experience and memory of the can of tomato soup proves to be powerfully evocative despite its utilitarian and aesthetically unremarkable subject. It is unconcerned with capturing a *thing of beauty* and rather interested in stirring a deeper well of feelings, attached to nostalgia, security, and collective experience.

These artists and many, many others demonstrate a shift in the philosophy of art from *product* to *process*; from *instructional* to *involving*; from *meaning-laden* to *meaning-latent*; and from *determined* to *diverse*. Fundamentally, this is a radical reclamation of the concept of a "living text", as it opens the door to artworks meaning different things in different contexts. Specifically, it embodies a philosophy of proceduralism and generativity even in "static" works.

Naturally, as this philosophy is more fully embodied by the culture, emerging and preferred art forms trend toward greater proceduralism and generativity as well. Video games are the prime example of this kind of procedural expression, but we can observe similar trends in other popular art forms that matured in parallel, such as interactive theatre, immersive art exhibits, theme parks that present immersive role-playing experiences, and formalized remediation of past works in dub, hip hop, and electronic music through sampling and remixing.

Even beyond the arts, procedural indeterminacy pervades the practical aspects of our lives. Public and commercial spaces are rapidly being "gamified", utilizing the design language and reward/feedback structures of games to (charitably) make engagement with these spaces more compelling and intrinsically motivating, or (realistically) tapping into the compulsive and sometimes addictive power of game systems to ingrain our engagement with capitalist structures at baser, less critical levels of human cognition.

Workplaces are increasingly gamifying labor with scores, leaderboards, and achievements, practices that make evident corporate micromanagement that some workers call "the electronic whip" (Lopez, 2011; Gabrielle, 2018). Health apps are framed with competitive leaderboards to incentivize daily exercise (Wood & Reiners, 2015). Social media and dating sites encourage the sharing of personal information with progress bars toward profile "completion" (Huotari & Hamari, 2012). Purchases are "rewarded" with increasingly complex loyalty programs (Zichermann & Cunningham, 2011, p. 6).

Increasingly, our political, social, and commercial systems are being framed and understood as "games" of sorts. The language and logics of games serve to make the interdependencies and behaviors of systemic institutions more obvious and predictable. In our modern world, the threads of interconnection between systems are more evident, accessible, and consequential than ever before. The same internet that serves as a primary ground for social, cultural, and playful engagement also serves as the structure that maintains our systems of finance, government, and business. Actions from one domain—from one actor, no less—are no longer localized events; actions ripple outward to the world and to other domains of the system faster and more radically than ever before.

It becomes increasingly apparent that a functional understanding of the modern world requires a systems-based approach. Likewise, the products and artifacts of such an interconnected culture will naturally trend toward more procedural forms that reflect the experience of participating in a culture of this sort. It is no wonder that video games have become a cornerstone form of cultural expression and exploration over the past half-century. More than any other expressive medium, video games communicate the embodied experience of navigating dense systems. Video games are an appropriately procedural and generative art for a complex time.

Beyond providing a useful metaphor and cipher for the operations and logics of the modern world, video games have become an important mode of cultural production in and of themselves. Standout titles are not only rightly celebrated within the enthusiast community, but the influences of these works can be felt throughout other media as well. The immersive theatre production *Sleep No More* (Barrett & Doyle, 2003–2025) drew heavily from the visual and audio aesthetics of *BioShock* (2007), a legacy it shares with the 2016 television series remake of *Westworld* (Abrams et al., 2016–2022). Furthermore, it not only harnesses these surface-level similarities but also orients its spatial, exploratory storytelling around the operational logics of video gaming. Cinema has adopted cues from games, pertaining to the ways in which spaces are presented and the perspective and movement of the camera. For example, *John Wick: Chapter 4* (Stahelski, 2023) frames a standout action scene from a bird's eye perspective, as the camera follows Wick from room to room situated like dollhouse dioramas, utilizing visual logics unmistakably in the lineage of the action game *Hotline Miami* (2012) (or, more specifically, *Hotline Miami*-inspired successor *The Hong Kong Massacre* (2019), per the director's comments on the subject).

Video games have become preferred social spaces for new generations of players. Though the earliest online games (typically MUDs [multi-user dungeons] and MOOs [multi-user dungeons, object-oriented]) were strictly enthusiast spaces due to technical and practical requirements to access, online games have become increasingly easy to access and have drawn larger and larger player bases over the years. MMORPG (massively multiplayer online role-playing game) *World of WarCraft* (2004) hosted over 12 million users at its peak. There are (at the time of writing) over 400 million registered *Fortnite* (2017) players, with that game benefitting from being free-to-play and from ease of access from multiple devices (including dedicated game consoles, personal computers, smartphones, tablets, and cloud-based endpoints, which, themselves, can be accessed through a wide range of consumer devices). *Fortnite*, along with competitors like *Roblox* (2006), regularly hosts social events separate from the competitive game at its core, hosting virtual concerts and movie screenings that players from all over the world can virtually attend together.

Regardless of the friendliness of interactions within these spaces, it is worth considering how the ludic framing of these spaces may contribute to differing social outcomes for those for whom virtual spaces are their primary locations of interaction. These spaces are not only often competitive (much research has already been performed on the types of attitudes and social outcomes that can be observed from those who play competitive sports; Mangan, 1986; Furley, 2018) but also often entail the adoption of a virtual identity separate from (or loosely emulating) the individual's real-world identity. We will return to these considerations in great detail later in the book; these are the kinds of considerations that benefit from games-literate examination.

Games also regularly drive and exhibit the capabilities of emerging technologies. From the integration of cutting-edge, ray-traced, real-time lighting models into three-dimensional games to early experiments run with generative artificial intelligence (AI) language models, games have always been an exciting and eye-catching place to exhibit future directions for tech and computing. If this represents an appetite to drive tech forward and go *larger*, a similar urge to go *smaller* drives innovative hackers to find ways to play games through ever more unconventional technological endpoints. Seminal first-person shooter *DOOM* (1993) has been made playable on devices as unusual as calculators (Guinamard & Siryani, 2002), ATMs (Tucker, 2021), and pregnancy tests (Keane, 2020).

In these ways and many more that we will encounter throughout this exploration, games are being deeply woven into the fabric of the modern world, such that being an informed citizen or even a context-curious lover of the arts requires at least a basic literacy of the language and logics of games.

Games, despite their proximity to other art forms in the popular culture, exhibit fundamental differences from those other art forms that may leave even those deeply studied in more traditional arts and media lost in unproductive engagements with them. Despite often telling stories in manners that will be familiar to most gaming newcomers, the primary expressive language of games is in their capacity to communicate and weave narratives through spatial, kinesthetic, and/or logic-oriented interactions with reactive systems. Being able to read meaning and even ideology into the aspects of games that seem purely operational or kinesthetic requires a type of literacy that is not often taught—frankly, even experienced game players may not recognize that this separate level of meaning *exists* and that a games-specific literacy should be *sought*.

Even more so, games differ from other media and art forms in their requirement of active engagement from the audience. No other medium makes such a strong claim to audience co-authorship as games, which are formally incomplete until the point at which they are *enacted* by each audience member through active play. Players have agency to make decisions that affect the *fundamental text* of their experience with the game. Games require non-trivial *effort* to complete (Murray, 1997). In a sense, games, as cultural artifacts, are not only expressive of their creators but also of their *players*, who play an active role in the happenings of each unique narrative.

The purpose of this book is to help new and experienced players alike develop this specialized capacity for meaning-making in ludic experiences. Along with learning *how* to "read" the implicit and systemic "texts" of games, I seek to answer *why* to analyze games by drawing games into the context of the wider history and present landscape of culture and the arts from which games are too often wrongfully excluded.

Disciplinary Categorization

As you have surely noticed already, I have (perhaps controversially) framed video games as artistic artifacts and have compared and contrasted games against other more established, traditional media and art forms. Any exploration of this nature requires a framing by which the subject can be contextually examined. Whether or not this framing of video games as *capital-A "Art"* is appropriate is an important matter to justify, for an incorrect framing would lead us down a counterproductive path.

This is just one, non-exclusive framing, chosen for the purposes of this exploration, specifically. Games can be viewed as works of art, tools of education, means of casual recreation, marvels of technical engineering, commercial products, and means of sustained capital extraction. For the purpose of this exploration, there will be times in which each of these frames is situationally explored, but the primary framing is determined by the objective and target audience. As noted above, my primary interest in games is the manner in which they communicate and transform culture and the ways in which we can draw from and impart into them narrative, ideology, and messages about the human experience. This objective may differ from those who wish to improve their technical understanding of games from an operational perspective or increase their skilled play from a competitive perspective.

This exploration will primarily engage with games as artistic artifacts. This framing centers games as an expressive medium and serves the benefit of elucidating insights about culture and humanity through our engagement with games as a novel art form. I believe that the largest and least-obvious step toward truly understanding games is the push past uncritical play toward the intentional recognition and engagement with the designed systems and mechanics that guide the simulation. A narrative-artistic framing of game literacy not only prompts this intentional design curiosity but also pushes further into discerning the underlying messages and humanity of games as intentionally designed and expressive objects. Furthermore, it necessitates reading games not only in terms of internally relevant objectives (such as winning or setting a high score) but also in the broader context of the culture in which they were developed and the cultures in which they are later consumed.

Video games certainly *contain* art (no one will argue against the artistic categorization for the elements of games that reproduce existing art forms, such as their musical soundtracks, visual composition, and written stories), but video games are also *functional* and *recreational* objects. Surely, if this book argued that plumbing pipes were to be *primarily regarded* as artistic objects, we would be ill-prepared for utilizing them for their primary purpose: the transportation of water. Despite occasional, undeniable aesthetic charm, plumbing pipes serve a clear, utilitarian purpose. The same is often argued about video games.

As video games have developed a cultural niche, there has been much debate about whether or not they can be cleanly categorized as "art" (a slippery term that means many things to different people, as we will explore further below). This debate often becomes emotionally charged and personal, as classification as "art" often confers or implies an intrinsic value. The label can "elevate" a craft into something important and enlightening, and, as often bubbles under this discussion as an unspoken undercurrent, can justify time spent with a hobby as somehow more valuable than pure recreation.

Famously, late film critic Roger Ebert claimed that "video games can never be art" (Ebert, 2012), citing examples of then-recent, critically acclaimed titles that failed to emotionally resonate with him in ways that even early and crude examples of art in other mediums (such as his beloved cinema) accomplished. In the cited essay in which he defends his point, he seems to endorse a definition of art dependent upon quality or effectiveness in communicating a narrative message, saying that a well-written book is art while a poorly written book falls short of the definition. This seemingly affirms the value judgment associated with the "art" label that I mentioned above. His is a definition with which I personally disagree (and will later argue against). His argument, though, represents well a common cultural perspective on games; they are recreational objects that encourage *thoughtless distraction* rather than *enlightening engagement*, so they should not be considered amongst the fine arts, or they may generously be considered "low art".

Yet, when considering how games are read, contending with their adjacency to other cultural artifacts is crucial and *unavoidable*. In the same way that it would be foolish to read romantic poetry and furniture installation instructions, in the same way, the miscategorization of games can burden our interactions with them with incongruent interpretive frameworks. It is important to ask whether video games should be understood more like films, baseball, or slot machines. Looking for specific types of meaning in areas where it is domain-inappropriate would not only be frustrating but may also lead to drawing harmful and inconsistent conclusions based on illusory patterns. To determine how to properly activate appropriate literacies for examining games, we have to seriously contend with the questions: how do we functionally define art, and is it productive to utilize an artistic framework in the examination of video game artifacts? To emphasize: I am not, at this time, arguing against Mr. Ebert's claims that video games *are* not art; rather, I ask the simpler question of whether or not "art" is a *useful framework* to guide this specific analysis.

Defining "Art"

Some argue that the primary way to appreciate art is in its aesthetics. If a work primarily serves a practical purpose, it becomes a craft or tool, which is why we do not typically consider a pair of scissors to be a work of art, though scissors can have an undeniable aesthetic quality about them. Immanuel Kant calls art "a kind of representation that is purposive in itself and, though without an end, nevertheless promotes the cultivation of the mental powers for sociable communication" (Kant, 1790).

Those who cite this definition may differentiate video games from other mediums with the argument that games serve a primarily practical purpose: hijacking our psychological reward centers through the feedback of metrics and graphics rather than through the engagement of critical thought—in other words, we play games to feel good or have fun rather than to cultivate our mental powers for sociable communication. It is satisfying to clear the enemies from a level in a video game in the same way it is satisfying to organize a messy pile of clothes into clean stacks.

Unlike literature or cinema, in which satisfaction requires empathetic engagement with a presented fiction, video games are pleasurable on a pre-linguistic level, seemingly ambivalent to capital-M "Meaning" (this point will be heavily caveated later). This can be evidenced by the existence of games (often with a satirical edge, like *Universal Paperclips* [2017]) that pare back presentation and narrative to absolute basics to demonstrate how we need little more than a steady increase in numbers to create compelling and/or compulsive experiences. This framing posits that video games *can* tell stories, but it seemingly disproves that they *must*.

In fact, some within the game studies literature argue that narrative within games serves a primarily ornamental purpose, providing the necessary context to help players understand and invest in a game's behaviorally engaged systems (Aarseth, 1997). After a player gains fluency with the systems from a behavioral perspective, she may disregard the narrative content altogether and engage on a purely non-meaning-oriented level. For this reason, some scholars and lay people categorize video games alongside other mediums optimized for practical use, such as pornography, which, despite its similarity to traditional photography and filmmaking, is often not considered an artistic pursuit because it is intended to be used to evoke a base, physiological reaction rather than encouraging critical and thoughtful engagement (despite how fervently one may claim to be interested in reading the articles).

Excluding mediums that serve practical uses creates a definitional space too narrow for most conceptualizations of art, though. We would have to exclude architecture, culinary arts, fashion, propaganda, ceremonial or religious artifacts, and a great deal of other mediums that most would argue are definitionally artistic, or at least can be considered so in the proper context. Abstract art is also primarily engaged with on a non-representational, non-semiotic level. There must be a more comprehensive and consistent theory of art.

Some argue that art requires artist intention in its communication of themes and ideas. Art is a medium of communication of abstract ideas and emotions, and it should come from a carefully crafted vision that guides its narrative and aesthetic peaks and troughs toward intentional conclusions. This is why a baseball game would not be considered a work of art, but a film about a baseball game would. A story requires a teller, or, in the absence of a teller, a chooser (or curator), as in the case of photography where the artist does not create her subject as a sculptor would but instead chooses a scene and guides a reading of it through the inclusions and exclusions of the photograph.

Those who endorse this definition may be uncomfortable with how much of a video game's content and pacing is directed by the audience rather than the artist. Games are formally indeterminant and can vary wildly in the experiences they create for each player. When the player is in a significant level of control of what happens and does not happen in a playthrough, the artists' authorial intentions are too loose to classify games as a viable medium for unidirectional artistic communication. It becomes more akin to a children's jungle gym: a set of structures amidst which recreational experiences may occur, but it has little capacity for guided storytelling.

Not all art is intended to be such a closed loop, though. Increasingly over the past century, it has become more widely accepted for art to involve artist-audience collaboration or embrace elements of randomness, as we have already discussed. In the communication of ideas and experiences, it is not always appropriate for all aspects of art to be within the control of the artist. Improv theatre is reactive to the input of audiences. Immersive art, such as the self-directed but narratively suggestive exploration of designed spaces like theme parks, surrenders control of pacing and occurrent happenings to visitors. In these cases, artists provide a "shape" of possible experiences and allow each audience member's experience to differ and become individually unique. As we will explore in later chapters, video games, in the affordances and freedoms endowed upon players, are directed and curated by way of agency and constraints.

Still, others believe that art is decreed by institutional authority. A medium, or works within a medium, may *become* art once they are "canonized" by an academic or popular representative. A craft is not inherently artistic (at least in the *fine arts* sense) until it is pulled into conversation with existing artistic works by a liminal figure or institution. Such a brief description may sound like a deliberately uncharitable framing of the argument or even a conspiratorial accusation, but there is merit to this perspective. It expresses an understanding that the essential qualities of what we may consider art are shared with that which we would not. Instead, it benefits us to take a practical approach to our definition and framing of art.

Some boundaries are arbitrary, determined by the indirect "conversation" between cultural artifacts situated within a time and place. The boundaries of art and craft may expand or contract in response to cultural shifts. For example, the tenants of Rococo art and architecture are very clearly reflected in the furniture and even the silverware of that time period, but there were periods before (and periods since, probably including the present day) in which furniture and silverware are not quite as closely linked to the culture's artistic explorations. These shifts are not *essentially* true, but they are useful patterns, recognized and named by those who study and influence culture, either in retrospect or contemporaneously.

There is no central governing body that determines what is and is not considered art, but the confluence of opinions for how cultural artifacts are contextualized can lend a sense of artistic credibility. Academics, art historians, tastemakers, museum curators, fellow artists, professional critics, and members of specialized sub-cultures make these independent determinations, typically trending toward consensus over time. Rather than asking whether something is *essentially* art, this position asks if it is *useful* to consider something art and whether it is useful in the inspiration and production of further art. Does it enhance our understanding of the cultural appetite of a time and place, of the psychology and soul of a generation of people? Does it give us better context with which to understand other cultural artifacts, contemporary or future?

This definition can be paralyzingly subjective, though. As in the previously cited Roger Ebert essay, he, as a studied and respected tastemaker and critic, argues for and against the classification of individual works as art on the merits of effectiveness rather than by matter of form, intent, or definitional attributes. When reading low-quality poetry, though, does it not still require the engagement of our poetic literacy? May a bad novel still teach us about the cultural appetite of its time? Certainly, Ebert did not fundamentally alter the discipline by which he wrote about great movies and poor movies alike.

If art is definitionally contingent upon what academics or tastemakers find emotionally stirring, one would presume that works created in known, culturally familiar forms would more readily resonate than works from outsider groups or works that express unfamiliar philosophies. Coupled with the reality that those in positions of cultural influence are often advantaged by demographic inequality, we must also consider the inevitability that outsider art may only be recognized as significant or worthy of elevated status long after more culturally congruent art is canonized. This can lead to the under-representation of diverse voices within the cultural conversation and a self-perpetuating system of narrowing perspectives. While the curated approach can be a useful way of narrativizing art history, it leaves too many blind spots and inconsistencies to be sufficient for guiding the consumption and education of art contemporaneously.

Ultimately, why is it important whether or not something is considered art? When considering art from an academic perspective, we should not think of the label as one of aggrandizement or flattery. Rather, it informs how we interact with certain categories of cultural artifacts: the modality of interpretation and contextualization. Art is evocative of the intangible. Art is the communicative language used to express the feelings and concepts that we cannot express directly with plain language. My operational definition is dependent upon this difference between artistic and non-artistic communication. That which can be said directly is information, whereas that which must be evoked indirectly necessitates *artful* communication. Through plain language, I can present to you the information necessary to assemble a lamp, but if I want to communicate the feeling of falling in love, I *must* approach it evocatively, indirectly, poetically.

The process of beholding and interpreting art can be metaphorically likened to a machine. It is an imprecise mechanism, though. The artist wishes to evoke a mental reality (an emotion, a sense of place or being, an intuitive understanding, and an empathetic disposition). The "piece of art" is the raw material fed into this metaphorical machine, which exists within the mind of each beholder. These raw materials are processed by the various mechanisms within the machine: audiences' sense memories, episodic memories, emotional temperament, knowledge stores, innate evolutionary cues, associations, traumas, cultural symbology, and other such influencing factors. Each individual has a different constellation of these mechanisms. On the other side, the machine outputs an emotional or cognitive state: a feeling, an idea, or a philosophy. It will never match the artist's intended emotional or cognitive state one for one. Great artists create works that allow for and celebrate these differing resultant realities. This is what makes art compelling. We can draw complex takeaways from even simple works, and the differences between our resulting realities remind us of our vital and beautiful differences as humans and challenge us to expand our processing capacities and empathy.

My definition of art, and the framework that informs our objectives and parameters throughout this book, follows. *Art is the means of intentional communication of intangible, indirectly accessible (or second-order) emotional, empathetic, or conceptual states through representational/presentational craft or contextualization, designed to produce a range of reactions through the intersection with an individual's memories, emotions, temperament, and associations.*

By this definition, all artistic meaning-making is collaborative, as a work of art does not have a singular, essential meaning until it is processed by its audience. The artist does not imbue a singular meaning as much as she allows and guides audiences toward a desired range of reactions. This definition is amongst the most inclusive of definitions that I have encountered, though the communicative basis excludes craft that was not created or curated with the intention of conveying any kind of mentally transportive shift. Art *may* still serve a practical purpose or convey useful information, but it should be done in such a way that evokes a second-order state.

To draw meaning from the artistic interchange, audiences must employ appropriate literacies. Reading a work of poetry like one would read an instructional booklet or legal document would be deeply confusing. We must prepare ourselves to engage beyond a surface level and take away an experience rather than information or utility. To this end, we construct prescriptive literacies to aid in the meaning-making process.

Wide-reaching cultural literacies help us contextualize these works within the wider narrative of history and place, and domain-specific literacies give us the necessary "vocabulary" to better ascertain details of communicated meaning. Like with spoken language, we can only process that which we have language to mentally represent. For example, I have very poor understanding of baseball; a low domain-specific literacy for the sport of baseball. If a pitcher throws 20 pitches, they may all look identical to me, whereas a friend literate in the domain of baseball may notice all of the various types of pitches being thrown. I do not have the language to read, let alone describe, these variances, so I do not perceive the differences. Just as one may be able to perceive additional crucial details with a stronger baseball literacy, we may also improve our literacy for various artistic domains and truly notice more than we would have otherwise.

Additionally, greater domain-specific literacy will give us the ability to more fluently and fruitfully converse with other knowledgeable beholders, and we can even be more helpfully specific to non-knowledgeable audiences. Surely, my baseball-literate friend could tell me what types of pitches are being thrown, how each differs, and what strategic considerations may cause a pitcher to throw one type or another. I still may not be able to intuitively see the differences myself, but my experience can be enriched by proxy.

So… Are Video Games Art?

With a working definition established that describes the artistic dynamic, we return to the question of whether or not it is useful to "read" and analyze video games through an artistic framework. Again, this question is distinct from whether or not video games *are* art—that, even with the above context, is a question with a more complicated answer to which we will return in Chapter 11 after further context has been established.

With regard to the pressing question of analytical framework, I argue that it is, indeed, reasonable to read video game artifacts through the lens of expressive artistry. Using our process-oriented definition, video games have the capacity to evoke the second-order feelings or cognitive states that serve as the end products of artistic transformation, and it does so via indirect evocation rather than the straightforward communication of these states through plain language, sign, or symbol.

Before I justify that position, though, I must be more specific with regard to what elements of the video game *artifact* constitute its unique, expressive language. As mentioned above, video games inarguably *contain* art. No one will argue against the classification of the elements of past arts that video games have repurposed and incorporated, from written story to musical accompaniment to acted performances to environmental design. Arguing artistic semantics with regard to these elements is not contentious. The argument around *games as art* instead centers around the elements of video games that are not shared with other mediums, such as systemic design, dynamics of multi-linear narrative, designed constructs that shape the agency and interactability of the player, and, generally, what I will refer to as *non-semiotic* elements of the simulation (I will define this shortly). These are the elements that *uniquely* constitute video games, and these are the elements that are the most controversial in making an art/non-art classification.

Even within the working definition I established above, reasonable arguments could be made against using an artistic framework to understand these elements. It can be argued that they lack *intentionality* and *second-order transformation*.

Video games, being interactive to a greater degree than any other medium, give their audience (players) a great degree of control over the shape of the experience. A video game may structure a story around a potentially infinite combination of possible occurrences that take place in free gameplay. There are other art forms that take a somewhat similar approach to a much more limited degree. A stage play contains within its script a structured story but allows actors to make significant decisions with regard to how lines are delivered and how performances are conveyed. Similarly, consistent sheet music structures the performances of orchestral music, but the dynamics of each performance may vary depending upon the arrangement and live guidance of the conductor. In each of these cases, the script or sheet music can be understood as "instructions" that inform and guide the instantiated enactment of an artistic product.

A performance of *Death of a Salesman* (Miller, 1949) will always be recognizable as *Death of a Salesman*, though. Any orchestra that performs Mozart's *Symphony No. 40 in G Minor* (1788) plays what is *essentially* the same symphony, even if intonations differ. Play of any particular video game, though, offers a *much greater* degree of potential variance, though, to the degree that it can seem like two players are playing a particular game in a *fundamentally different* manner. Someone who plays the 3D exploration platformer game *Super Mario 64* (1996) in a careful and thorough manner, cautiously approaching each obstacle and searching out each secret, plays a very different "game" than the expert player who has memorized the structure of the game and seeks a world-record pace through the game by planning minimally viable routes through the game and exploiting design ambiguities to shave seconds off of her fastest time. Can we still argue that the designers of *Super Mario 64* (or any video game) have "intentionally" communicated an artistic experience?

In both manners of playing *Super Mario 64*, certain elements unite both approaches. Though the events that constitute each game's "narrative" are starkly variant, both players experience the "inhabitation" of Mario as a vector of expression within the fictional world. Both players experience and interface with the structural logics that constitute the world of *Super Mario 64* and differentiate it from its genre peers. To understand video game art, we must release ourselves from the expectation that a game's "narrative" lies in its linear progression of events and embrace that the artistry of games lies in their procedural dynamics. If the intended artistic experience of the game is not "a series of specific events occurs in a particular order" like it is for most other narrative mediums and is *instead* the evocation of a particular state of being or the demonstration of beautiful logics in a systemic world, the objection against games' necessary "intentionality" dissolves. The variance is *the point*, and it strengthens these procedural goals.

Secondly, one may question whether or not a *second-order* state is brought about through the play of games. One may argue that games serve only the primary, practical purpose of being "fun" and that all of a game's non-semiotic dynamics ultimately serve that purpose alone. Are video games optimized for simple amusement through the flattery of our cognitive pleasure centers via the regular deployment of rewards?

To argue against this point, we can cite examples of games that evoke reactions other than "fun", such as the intentionally stressful and tedious *Papers, Please* (2013), a game about checking passports at a border-crossing checkpoint during a time of political unrest, or *Darfur Is Dying* (2006), which is a documentary-like game intended to express and bring attention to the suffering of the people of Darfur during a time of war. Even in light of those counter-examples, though, it could be argued that they simply replace the primary byproduct of "fun" with another type of primary mental state, such as the "pleasure" of challenging emotional ambiguity or educational self-betterment.

In that case, we can go back to the "second-order" element from our working definition. A second-order change of state, what we might classify as a *transportive* or *transformative* state, is an evocation of a differentiated state of being beyond aesthetic pleasure or displeasure. An impressionist painting is artistically compelling not because of *what* it depicts but because it evokes a feeling and espouses a philosophy of what it is like *to see*. A film not only communicates the *information* about a sequence of events but also creates empathy for its characters and draws the audience into a feeling of being in another world or another circumstance throughout its runtime, and it uses ambiguity in performance and plotting nuances to invite inferences from viewers, creating rich subtext utterly involving of the audience.

Certainly, in that context, video games meet and exceed the "second-order" requirement. Beyond just being "toys" that convey aesthetic or kinesthetic pleasure, video games involve empathetic, projective "inhabitation" of imagined characters in evocative worlds. The empathetic posture is different, of course; it is a matter of practical necessity for taking action within the game space by acting *as* and *through* an avatar (the term I apply to the player-controlled character; see Chapter 4) rather than the unidirectional, detached emotional investment we direct toward characters of film and literature. One can argue that it is a less refined attachment, perhaps best illustrated by the uncritical perspective some players take toward immoral actions taken within the game space, self-justifying as necessary for the progression of the story (Gee, 2003), framed not as the damnable decisions of a morally compromised character, as we might attribute to the anti-heroes of many Martin Scorsese films, but as intrinsically rewarding actions taken within an ideologically neutral simulation space. Indeed, recognizing and wrestling with ideologies and ethics in game systems is a difficult task and one that is less obvious than it might be in more traditional narrative mediums. It is the focus of this book's Chapter 14.

Despite the differences, the mechanical expression of "becoming" another character in a virtual game world *is* similar to the ways in which traditional arts invoke second-order projective perspectives. In fact, arts theorist and philosopher Kendall L. Walton, in his seminal *Mimesis as Make-Believe* (1990), frames engagement with the arts as a kind of game. Walton argues that works of representational art are observed *de se*, inherently (though not explicitly) imagined as ourselves from our own perspective:

> The viewer of Meindert Hobbema's *[The] Water Mill with the Great Red Roof* plays a game in which it is fictional that he sees a red-roofed mill. As a participant in the game, he imagines that this is so. And this self-imagining is done in a first-person manner: he imagines seeing a mill, not just that he sees one, and he imagines this from the inside.
>
> *(Walton, 1990, p. 293)*

Or, more succinctly, "To imagine seeing a rhinoceros is to imagine *oneself* seeing a rhinoceros, not just to imagine an instance of rhinoceros seeing" (Walton, 1990, p. 31). To participate in the "game" suggested by a work of art, we not only internalize its subject factually but also imaginatively project a perspective by which the subject is observed on its own terms within the fictional "world" of the piece. Thus, we see a mill with a red roof instead of seeing only oils haphazardly arranged on a canvas *because* we implicitly imagine ourselves temporarily becoming an observer within that fictional space. To "participate" with the fictionality of something fictional, we must instantiate ourselves as an observer *within* that fictionality. In the same way, the video game avatar is a necessary conduit within the virtual world not only for observation but also for *agency* and *exploration*.

Thus, a work of art may invoke the *feeling* of falling in love or a sense memory of the simple comfort of going to grandma's home through the imaginative exploration and reflection of this fictionally instantiated "double" of the self projected into the fiction. And just as the fictional double relays the feeling of what it is *like* to see a red-roofed mill, so too does the video game avatar reflect an expressive statement on what it is *like* to *be* Mario or the Prince of All Cosmos or a world-class athlete within the fictional world of the game. Further exploration of the role of the projective avatar in meaning-making will be conducted in Chapter 4.

Furthermore, the evocative potential of "second-order" meaning can be richly layered into games' virtual environments themselves. To play within a game world is not only to observe it but also to be able to test it, act upon it, and witness it acting upon the instantiated quasi-self of the avatar. It is a world not only of suggestive aesthetic detail but also of suggestive operation, and surprisingly complex ideologies can be communicated in the dynamics of these living simulations. A haunting example is noted by writer Tauriq Moosa in a profound analysis of the open-world crime drama game *Mafia III* (2016). Reflecting on the manner in which the operational systems of the game reflect systemic racism, Moosa writes:

> Officers walking by Lincoln question what he's doing there. A white woman clutches a bag to her chest when Lincoln passes by. As you progress through the game, the Italian mob becomes flustered, wavering between disbelief and anger at how 'some [n****r]' could be tearing apart their empire.
>
> *(Moosa, 2016)*

Clearly, video games can communicate surprisingly complex second-order transportive and transformational states of mind in their operations. With both objections addressed, I can say without reservation that, for the purpose of this exploration into literacy, an artistic framework is wholly appropriate. This only concludes our search for an appropriate framework, though. This is not yet a conclusive justification of whether or not video games *are* works of art, in refutation of Roger Ebert's earlier claim. As noted already, that final conclusion is surprisingly complex and will be addressed once additional groundwork has been established in Chapter 11.

Video Games and Semiotics

Above, I noted that this exploration specifically involves the elements of artistic communication specific to video games. Though a video game domain literacy includes a cinematic literacy, as video games often make use of short, film-like *cutscenes* to establish narrative context between interactive segments, such literacies will only be *taught* in this book insofar as they differ from their typical expressions due to the unique nature of video games. I will not teach textual literacy just because video games contain text, because I can presume that all readers have an understanding of textual literacy already.

While video games *contain* such remediations of existent forms, it is necessary, to guide this study, to identify the aspects of ludic communication that are *unique* to video games, the central pillar around which all other elements will be built around. Such aspects can be broadly classified as *dynamics*: systemic design, structuring of player agency, kinesthetics, and the projective embodiment of avatars in virtual spaces. These elements will be referred to throughout the book as *non-semiotic*.

Semiotics is the study of the communication of meaning through signs, symbols, language, and denotation. For example, there are several semiotic conventions that allow us to recognize a police officer walking down the street. The officer has a distinctive uniform; in the United States, it is often black or blue and fitted with a visible badge (iconography) and a distinctive hat. The word "POLICE" is written across both sides of the uniform, using written language (itself a system of representative symbols) to communicate the officer's role. In the United States, officers carry handguns, recognizable by their shape; a shape that is only perceived as threatening because of convention and prior knowledge (a gun shaped like a hand fan would not be immediately threatening because its shape would not denote its deadly purpose). Finally, aspects of non-verbal communication, such as the authoritative posture of the officer or the meticulous cleanliness of the uniform, may communicate status or authority. And, of course, all of these symbols are heavily context-dependent. An officer on television "reads" very differently than an officer knocking on your own front door, and the perceived threat of violence inherent in the visible weaponry may "read" very differently for white Americans and Black Americans.

Semiotics is a powerful framework through which representative arts of all kinds can be explored, but video games have a distinctively non-semiotic layer that must be considered as well. A car in a video game may be semiotically recognizable in its visual representation; even a heavily iconographic abstraction, such as the collections of rectangles we imaginatively understand to represent cars in the early racing game *Pole Position* (1982), has inherent properties of action that function in particular ways regardless of whether or not their semiotic representations are recognized.

Because a video game simulates a system of rules with which the player may interact, we can consider ludic elements not only for their representational, semiotic properties but also for their essential properties within the fictional world. The non-semiotic layer includes the shapes of virtual spaces, the movement within virtual spaces, the interactions of virtual objects, the dynamic interplay of mechanics, etc. Ultimately, it is unimportant if the player "reads" the vehicles of *Pole Position* to represent cars or mobile neoplastic paintings, besides the ways in which proper representational recognition cues particular behavioral properties within the interactive simulation (such as the acceleration curve of a race car).

Thus, in the formation of a video game literacy, this exploration privileges the non-semiotic elements of the simulation above the representational or semiotic aspects. In practice, both inform and provide context to one another, but for the purpose of this study, it is my belief that each serves as primary "languages" in their own rights through which meaning and even ideology can be communicated. I return to the semiotic/non-semiotic divide in Chapter 2.

Purpose and Audience of This Exploration

This book is intended to elucidate the processes of decoding and meaning-making in the play of video games. Specifically, decoding (which has nothing to do with the code or computer language that constitutes games on an operational level) is analogous to reading. It is the process by which players perceive, react to, and see reflected their actions in the sensory information video games provide (primarily visuals on a video display, though audio and haptic feedback are other common forms of game-to-player sensory communication/feedback).

Meaning-making is the process by which we construct narrative, value, message, or ideology from play experiences, influenced by personal, cultural, or broader philosophical context. Decoding (or sense-making) is the process by which we understand *what* happens, and meaning-making is the process by which we construct narrative or higher-order representation to understand or hypothesize *why* something happens or *what significance* a happening has.

Video game literacy is not likely to be a familiar concept to most reading this. In fact, most likely do not consider *types* of literacy; we, rather, tend to refer to "literacy" as a holistic term describing our ability to read and write or otherwise communicate linguistically. But, of course, reading and writing are not contextually ambivalent skills. One can expertly interpret the pages of a financial journal but be completely unable to derive meaning from poetry.

We engage multiple literacies daily. While most are familiar with the broader domain of "textual literacy" necessary for, say, understanding the meaning of this very paragraph, that broader categorical domain can be broken down into smaller, more specific domains in any number of ways, as illustrated above. Beyond that which we read, we engage domain-specific literacies to understand the significance of goal attempts in football, to recognize the genre of a song and what it may signify about the purpose of that song, to follow the events of a reality television competition, and so on. One can become "literate" in just about any area of life.

As we intend to explore in this book, one can improve her domain-specific literacy of video games by attuning to design "grammars" and derive greater meaning from that which happens during gameplay. Literacy extends far beyond just the parsing of written text. Just as dance communicates meaning through action rather than spoken or printed words, so too can personal, cultural, and human stories and messages be communicated through the actions of designed gameplay. Through the intentional study of game design and its communicative capacities, we can improve our ability to draw rich meaning from gameplay experiences, critically communicate about these experiences, and generalize this working knowledge to related domains of gamified experiences throughout life.

This book is written primarily to benefit those who wish to improve their critical thinking and meaning-making capabilities as they pertain to the domain of video games. This can apply to new players, who may not know how to parse complicated gameplay scenes and lack the context through which they can discern greater meaning from non-semiotic interactions, as well as experienced players, who may not have yet formalized their intuitive knowledge of gameplay into critical structures through which they can reflect, contextualize, and communicate gameplay experiences precisely. This book is also intended as an educational aid to provide structure and context to the education, exhibition, and historical contextualization of games.

Many (though not all) video games are skill-based activities, to differing degrees. Most games pose challenges that new (and even experienced) players may have difficulty overcoming. Though, in a sense, I aim to make readers of this book into "better" players, my focus and concern is in the improvement of skills pertaining to meaning-making and value-orientation. This book is *not* intended to make players more competitively viable or skillful per the parameters of the ludic challenge. One *may* improve in their ludic successes and survivability as a matter of being more acutely aware of design cues within the simulation, but this book should not be read with the intent of becoming an "expert" player; I only wish to produce *thoughtful* players. In fact, many valuable insights can be gleaned through "poor"/unskilled play. Our greatest awareness of systemic design parameters often occurs at the moments of greatest friction, after all. I would rather someone lose thoughtfully than win absentmindedly.

As previously alluded, this book has several potential audiences at differing levels of familiarity with games. Most obviously, this book is intended to appeal to those who lack experience with video games altogether. Whether one wishes to begin one's journey into the somewhat intimidating and alien world of video games or whether one simply wishes to be a better-informed observer from the outside of the hobby group, this book will provide the necessary context and instruction to kickstart a lifelong relationship with the new and exciting art form.

A fluency in the language and logics of games can bridge gaps between players and non-players. This will be a useful exploration for those inexperienced with games who have video game enthusiasts in their lives, such as parents, community leaders, or therapists. Players and non-players alike will be familiar with controversies and worries pertaining to the effects violent or otherwise antisocial content within video games may have on young players. A major part of what prompted these concerns, particularly in gaming's earliest decades, was how generationally isolating the hobby had become. Parents in the 1980s and 1990s largely had not grown up with as ubiquitous exposure to video games as their children's generation had. They had not developed a familiarity with the language of games, much less the practical skill required to participate in gaming activities along with their children. Video games were these novel, scary objects of seemingly alien origin, utterly baffling in their function and seemingly chaotic in their virtue.

With a functional literacy of video games, this type of disconnect can be rectified. Those spanning generational gaps, or even chronological peers who simply have differing levels of interest in the hobby, can converse deeply and productively regardless of skill or experience level. Ultimately, appeals for greater shared understanding tend to lead to better results than the incitation of further moral panics.

Beyond that specific concern, the primary value of this book is in one's own productive betterment. A new player should be able to play a novel game and be able to derive valuable insights from her experience. As an increasingly foundational mode of cultural expression, everyone deserves to have the necessary context and language to understand what any game expresses through its ludic enactment.

Experienced players have much to gain from this exploration as well. Those who have always played games as recreation and now wish to better understand games as a narrative art form will find their experience deepened. A fluency with the operations of games does not necessarily mean that one is thoughtfully aware of the dynamics at work during gameplay. Experienced players will become aware of additional layers of meaning in gameplay systems that they might not have previously considered and will be able to more productively communicate their insights and experiences with others.

Experienced players may also wish to introduce video gaming to non-gaming acquaintances or loved ones or even just productively communicate about a gameplay experience with someone unfamiliar with gaming lexicon and tropes. This book will illustrate a path to productive introduction for those who lack gaming experience. The book will also help to "deprogram" ingrained communicative patterns, allowing experienced players to communicate about games in a manner that is not insular or exclusionary due to an over-reliance on domain-specific terminology. We will learn how to effectively speak about games without utilizing "gamer-speak", which can be alienating to those outside of the subculture.

This book is also intended to help video game developers. Though it is written from the perspective of the player (decoding/deconstructing the gameplay experience to discern and construct meaning) rather than from the perspective of designers (encoding/constructing the gameplay experience to impart meaning), it is useful to understand how and why specific design dynamics affect gameplay aesthetics, and it will enhance meaningful, expressive communication about such design considerations.

Gameplay is a medium that achieves its prevailing experiential aesthetic through the agential interactions of players. The artistic value of a game is dependent upon the degree to which it is able to effectively involve its audience in the procedural construction of meaning, which is just as much of a feat of cognitive transformation as technical performance. As such, a greater understanding of the ways in which players (new or experienced in the medium) read and interpret the dynamics systems of play can help steer design thought from the purely technical to the experiential.

Furthermore, this exploration may elucidate "tools in the toolbelt" that designers may not know are available to them, or that they may recognize in the games of other designers but not have the words or context to properly implement into their own games. This book will not provide technical instruction on the design of games, but it does deconstruct and lay bare the means by which games express complex and valuable ideas.

As illustrated already, I have a personal interest in where games fit in the broader cultural and artistic context. Those who study, teach, or curate cultural artifacts may be interested in the exhibition and understanding of games on such terms. Those with institutional opportunities to curate and educate about such topics may not always be experienced or deeply knowledgeable about games themselves, though. Rather than excluding games from such curricula, deferring a vital stream of cultural and anthropological expression to a future generation, this book can serve as a guide to establish a necessary knowledge and framework with which games can be properly discussed and exhibited alongside peer and antecedent media. Video games are an extension of the ongoing story of art history and cultural development, and those in positions of educational influence should be well-equipped to contend with this new evolutionary step.

Finally, this book is written as an extension of and in conversation with the academic discipline of games studies. A great deal has been written about the discipline of game design, but a holistic theory of the player-centered process of sense- and meaning-making is yet underdeveloped. Most works in the field are production-oriented rather than analysis-focused, though some works, like Clara Fernández-Vara's *Introduction to Game Analysis* (2014), have recently expanded the field. Resources such as the website Critical Distance (Lawrence et al., 2009) and the proliferation of insightful writers and creators on platforms such as YouTube have made good game analysis more plentiful than ever before, but the study of how to *arrive at* such useful analysis remains underexplored.

What Is a Video Game?

This book primarily concerns the study of video games. A detailed definition of the term will be explored in Chapter 2, but a basic definition and a justification about terminology and boundaries should be established upfront as well.

The purpose of this exploration is not to define a comprehensive and rigid ontology but rather to identify mechanisms of expression. Video games, to a greater degree than the social, card, board, and tabletop games before them, are expressions of their host technologies, and as digital technologies and human interactions evolve, so too will the varieties of games that these technologies enable. Methods of interaction with modern video games, such as touchscreen interfaces and immersive virtual reality (VR) displays, would have been completely alien to any definitions of video games that would have developed in the early 1980s, and we should anticipate that the novel affordances of upcoming technologies will similarly diversify the types of games we can expect to encounter decades from now.

For our purposes, a definition of the medium serves to benefit us in three ways:

- **Outlining formic consistencies informs the tasks that our domain literacy must accomplish**. To illustrate this, we define video games as fundamentally interactive, and this necessitates that the literacy model developed in this exploration must account for interactivity. Conversely, the boundaries drawn around the medium of interest limit our literacy model from becoming unnecessarily broad and unwieldy. To illustrate this, we establish that video games and board games are similar but distinct mediums; helpful parallels may be drawn, but any consideration that applies *only* to board games and *not* to video games (such as the negotiability of "house rules" and physical techniques used to manipulate outcomes of dice rolls) does not need to be incorporated into our study.
- **Identifies lineage, legacy, and interconnectedness between works**. To understand an artwork is not only to understand it in isolation but also to see it as an extension of and comment upon the works that have come before. A careful definition of medium is a delineation of lineage. It is useful and manageable to consider each work as a series of small steps away from median conventions rather than as wholly separate constructs that have to be analyzed from scratch in isolation. This kind of differential framing elucidates specific choices rather than losing crucial artistic statements amidst the noise of complex systems.
- **Prompts the type of language needed to interact with this medium**. Theories of literacy prompt methods of both consumption and production—of reading and writing. In the context of video games, gameplay can be thought of as a combination of the two: a consumption-production act, as it involves the elucidation of information from a designed system as well as the active participation in the construction of the ongoing, enacted story. Gaining clarity on the specific phenomenological and interpretive "tasks" players undergo during active play allows us to "read", "produce", and play games in a manner optimal to the instillation and inference of meaning.

Our definition guides us from a perspective of what provides the most useful insights rather than establishing concrete, binary boundaries. There are many fringe and closely related mediums that we may not consider video games, but we may still find that it is helpful to utilize aspects of our framework to explore these works. *Choose Your Own Adventure* books (Granger, 1979–1998), for example, are not digital and will not "react" to readers with the nuance and sensitivity of simulation-situated games, but insights and methodology of the model established in this exploration can still be useful in a limited capacity.

Throughout this book, the term "video game" is used to describe our medium of interest. This is not the only term used to describe the medium, particularly within academic works. Other terms I have encountered in the literature include *digital game*, *computer game*, *virtual environment*, and *interactive digital narrative (IDN)*. Sometimes video games are folded into parent or sister classifications; Espen Aarseth's studies, for example, follow a philosophy of multilinear design to combine several interactive mediums as "cybertexts" and "ergodic literature" (Aarseth, 1997).

"Video game" is used not necessarily as the most *comprehensively and consistently accurate* descriptor for our medium of interest (I will highlight exceptions to both "video" and "game" components of the name in Chapter 2) but is rather a term of colloquial usefulness. An element of any domain literacy is being prepared to fruitfully engage with others about the domain in question. Despite the development of more *technically inclusive* terms, most community discussion and even formal research around the medium predominantly uses the term "video game" (or "videogame"). An increase in precision brought about by a more "correct" yet esoteric term would only linguistically isolate my readers from the wider community. Sometimes, it is preferable to accept an unpretentious, colloquial name rather than each writer and researcher creating bespoke *cul-de-sac* variations.

Ultimately, it is worth remembering that "video game" is a term derived from marketing copy near the inception point of the medium's evolution. It was not developed by ontologists with decades of design precedent to reference in an effort to craft the most comprehensive terminology. This is comparable to the terms "movie" and "film" used to describe cinematic works; the fact that they *move* and (used to be) captured on *film* are no longer the most accurate or identifiably unique aspects of the medium. Formal definitions have evolved around these more-or-less static terms rather than upending the colloquial language.

For the purpose of this exploration, we will identify "video games" simply as games operated by and within a computer or computational aggregate that communicates visual feedback to players through a video display (often amongst other forms of sensory output). "Games" obviously holds a lot of meaning within that definition that needs to be elucidated as well. Briefly, we will define "game" as a reactive information system designed for the interaction between at least one interactor with a series of rules that constrains the agential operations necessary for the pursuit of formalized objectives.

This definition will be discussed in much greater detail in Chapter 2. In that same chapter, we will contend with examples of artifacts that we may still classify as video games even though they fall outside of the definitional boundaries. As a reminder, no definition perfectly encapsulates the full diversity of the video game lineage while perfectly excluding all inappropriate examples. I frame this as a useful starting point around which marginal examples can be appended.

GAMES LITERACY

To some, it may seem strange to assign a term like "literacy" to the act of playing games. Most will rarely encounter the word "literacy" outside of materials relating to the educational development of small children ("practice reading and writing to gain literacy") or population-wide policy statements ("the pursuit of universal literacy"). While the development of reading and writing abilities is a form of literacy, it does not fully describe the meaning of the word. These refer to only a fraction of functional literacies and narrow its definitional scope to an outdated construct of generalized literacy with the implication that "literacy" describes one's ability to read and write generally.

This definition came from a time at which basic literacy was uncommon or reserved for members of the upper class only. The general trajectory of history has been toward the democratization and decentralization of information, though. Traditionally, formal education was reserved for those predetermined to be in positions of leadership (children and adults of the upper socioeconomic classes or members of religious leadership). Technological advancements (like the invention of the printing press, which made informational materials much easier to reproduce and distribute) and cultural advancements made mass literacy more of a tenable achievement. Widespread literacy helped propel the economic and cultural advancement of nations that invested in educational infrastructure during the Industrial Revolution and Information Age by preparing a large workforce equipped for more technical work than was expected of the working class during the Feudal and Pre-Industrial Ages. The ability to read and write proved to be a powerful tool for class mobility, contributing (in part) to the emergence of a middle class with financial agency.

As more of the population gained basic literacy (in this context, the ability to understand and produce written language), the study of literacy shifted its focus to specialized domains of literacy. We can see how definitions of literacy have evolved over the decades, with UNESCO stating in 1958 that "a literate person is one who can, with understanding, both read and write a short simple statement on his or her everyday life". By 1970, UNESCO adopted a definition that took into account the social context of literacy, stating that:

> a functionally literate person is one who can engage in all those activities in which literacy is required for the effective functioning of his or her group and community and also for enabling him or her to continue to use reading, writing and calculation for his or her own and the community's development.

Finally, we see nods to a plurality of literacies in 2003:

> Literacy is the ability to identify, understand, interpret, create, communicate and compute, using printed and written materials associated with varying contexts. Literacy involves a continuum of learning in enabling individuals to achieve their goals, to develop their knowledge and potential, and to participate fully in their community and wider society.
>
> *(UNESCO, 2004)*

To summarize, "literacy" has steadily shifted away from narrowly describing the ability to read and write generally toward a broader definition describing the ability to ingest, interpret, utilize, and communicate ideas in a multitude of ways. This definition accounts for a more functional view of literacy, acknowledging that a reader who can understand and interpret a message is more functionally literate than one who can only recognize words but is unable to contextualize the information within frameworks of outside information. Furthermore, the definition hints at (though falls short of explaining) a context-sensitivity in literacy.

In the time since UNESCO's latest definition was penned, our understanding of functional literacy has become more nuanced, and their definition is no longer sufficient. Though it hints at context sensitivity, it falls short of explaining the domain specificity of literacy. Additionally, it does not account for the rapid diversification of methods of communication in quantity and form during the Information Age.

The concept of generalized literacy is no longer a helpful framework. James Paul Gee (2003) notes, "We never just read or write; rather, we always read or write something in some way". One who is able to read a novel may not have the necessary skills or experience to read a legal tract. One who is able to write academic papers may struggle to produce a compelling superhero comic. This is complicated further by the multimodality of modern communication. More so than ever before, text is juxtaposed with images, video, sound, music, symbols, gestures, etc., any of which can carry meaning entirely separate from the meaning that the text communicates in isolation. Reading the text alone is not sufficient for extracting all of the communicated meaning. Many of these modes feature internal languages of their own—some formalized (like the meaning conveyed by differently shaped panels in comic books or types of scene transitions in films) and some memetic and ever-shifting (like the meaning associated with particular emojis or the use of specific songs in films). True literacy (in the sense of being able to fluently extract meaning from and communicate within culturally relevant modes of communication) requires a definition that takes into account this multimodality.

As implied in my examples above, the ability to effectively communicate in the modern age requires an understanding of how to communicate across culturally relevant mediums, how to utilize multimodality to convey intended meaning, and how to ascertain and adapt to different or conflicting meanings across mediums and contexts. James Paul Gee (2003) calls these contexts "semiotic domains". Simply put, a semiotic domain is a context in which one or more modes of communication have specialized formal or informal conventions through which meaning is communicated in ways distinct from other domains. Specialized knowledge can be communicated within a domain using language and symbols that should be near-universally recognized and understood by participants within that domain but may not be understood by those outside of the domain's social group. For example, a hunter may brag about "bagging a ten-point buck", a phrase easily understood within that semiotic domain but nearly meaningless to someone unfamiliar with it. Semiotic domains can include identities (football fans, software engineers, boy scouts, Caribbean immigrants), settings (church services, microbiology labs, Twitter, Alcoholics Anonymous meetings), mediums (academic articles, cubist paintings, progressive rock concept albums, first-person shooter games), and any other subset of people in which specialized knowledge and language evolve.

A person can be literate or illiterate (or partially literate) in a semiotic domain separate from literacy in any other domain. When we incorporate this multiplicity of literacies into our broad conceptualization, we quickly realize that it is inappropriate to regard functional literacy as simply the ability to read and write. In the context of modern communication in which people regularly receive and create meaning across dozens of modalities, the test of true literacy is the ability to quickly adapt to new modalities and learn the ever-changing rules for extracting and communicating meaning. This is a test of adaptability rather than stored knowledge.

This book uses the term "literacy" throughout, though it should also be noted that the related term "electracy" is relevant as well. "Electracy" is a term developed by constructivist Gregory L. Ulmer in his 1998 text *Teletheory*. It specifically studies the production and deduction of meaning in electronic media. Though highly relevant to our subject matter, I have elected to use the more traditional "literacy" for its colloquial ubiquity. Readers have pre-existing notions associated with literacy from experiences with other media, and it is more useful to frame the understanding of video games as a continuation of that practice than to frame it as something qualitatively separate.

Game literacy differs from literacies associated with more traditional artistic domains. While each involves aspects of consumption and production (reading and writing, for example), one only *needs* to be proficient in one or the other to meaningfully interact with other art forms. One may be able to read but not write and still have a fruitful relationship with a book. Video games are interactive systems, though, dependent upon player interaction; to a degree, consumption and production are concurrent.

A player does not need to be able to know how to *program* a video game in order to play, but the player must make active contributions to the system in which gameplay operates for play to continue. Whereas a book is a static object that is encountered by a human reader, a video game is a dynamic system that *includes* the player, such that without the player, the game will produce no gameplay "text". This is a fundamental difference that we will explore in greater depth in Chapter 7. In short, the code of a video game is not analogous to the text of a book; the text of a book is, instead, analogous to the *live enactment* of gameplay within the simulation. As such, while books only involve their readers at the interpretive and analytical levels, video games *also* involve players at a pre-interpretive level that runs in concurrence with and is affected by interpretation and analysis.

This means that, while a book can be considered *in abstract* as the sum of its textual data, video games *must* be considered postphenomenologically as a system that transcends the technology to include the human player and the play environment. While *To Kill a Mockingbird* (Lee, 1960) remains *To Kill a Mockingbird* even when sitting idle on a shelf, *Marvel vs. Capcom 3* (2011) does not "exist" as an ergodic "text" until the triune elements of technology, player, and environment come into contact.

Thus, this exploration will extend beyond an *in-abstract* reading of video games and instead frame game literacy as postphenomenological, embodied experience. Message, ideology, ethic, and experience expressed through video games will be framed as expressions of systemic design, not traditional authorship, for video game developers do not "author" a singular text in the manner that the writer of a book might; they design a system, dependent upon embodied enactment, that will *bring about* the game's "text" procedurally.

To the degree that we are comfortable with the framing of video games as expressive artifacts alongside other art forms, a compelling novelty of the medium is a reappraisal of who is the object of expression. Traditional arts are foremost thought to be expressions of the artist(s) or author(s) that create the work. Beyond this, artworks are also largely expressive of the broader cultural context in which they were created and into which they were accepted.

An interpretation of a work can also be thought of as expressive of its beholder in an abstract sense. Like proponents of psychological Rorschach Tests posit, it may reveal something about a beholder if she interprets an ambiguous inkblot as threatening and predatory while another beholder sees it as calming and reassuring. Certainly, a work of art can be interpreted through differing philosophical and political lenses, and beholders who encounter a work without a particular philosophical disposition may surprise themselves with the types of thoughts, feelings, and associations that a work evokes.

Video games are unique, though, in that they *always* express aspects of the player along with aspects of the creator(s) and culture. It is impossible to play a game and not express *something* about the self in the process. Not only in a Rorschachian *interpretive* sense, but manifested in the behaviors and happenings that can be observed on-screen. Video games are systems that require active involvement, so the player not only provides a standard, detached interpretation of what they witness, but that interpretation (along with elements of the player's personality, disposition, beliefs, and temperament) also *affects* all further proceedings.

This dual role of the player as beholder and performer—of observer and creator—makes gameplay a fundamentally *self-reflective* activity. The sophistication of the elements of the self expressed through the act of gameplay increases as players improve in their gameplay abilities and in the refinement of their games literacy. At a basic level, one can easily observe behaviors within a game that indicate someone being flustered, over-confident, or oblivious to systems of rules, but more nuanced and educated readings can reveal ideology and ethical thinking in the participation in gameplay systems that are surprisingly deep and revealing.

Throughout the book, I will continually re-emphasize that games literacy entails not only an understanding of the video game object in isolation but also of the whole system that produces active gameplay—including the game software and the rules, systems, and mechanics therein, the context in which it is played, and, crucially, the *player* herself.

Ultimately, literacy describes our relationship with meaning. Whether having a conversation, interpreting street signs, or writing a newspaper article, the act of meaning communication involves steps of transformation. The producer has an image or idea that she wishes to communicate, but to externalize it, she must transform it into a "message-form", a linguistic representation descriptive of the idea but ultimately unmoored to it in any specific way (as there is nothing fundamentally "true" about the words we assign to describe objects or concepts; they are arbitrary, socially defined, and shift over time). This is the act of encoding. The encoded message is decoded by the receiver via mechanisms of knowledge, definitions, assumptions, and cultural contexts unique to each receiver. As such, there is distortion during decoding that leads to an imperfect and asymmetric transmission of ideas. Distortion is not the correct word, though, as distortion implies an obfuscation or dilapidation of an essential, central truth. Within the arts, though, decoding reveals a diversification of meanings, "true" and useful to varying degrees within a wide range of responses. Improvement in domain-specific literacies can produce more useful insights as medium-specific language empowers a common framework. Better understanding of the language of the medium means greater (or more complex) understanding of the messages within.

With that in mind, the reason I have written this book is to help readers develop a specialized literacy in video games. Like any other medium or semiotic domain, video games are created and experienced using specialized language. I am not referring to the programming languages that literally instruct the moment-to-moment functioning of each game; rather, I am referring to the experiential language through which players and the game communicate. This is an unusually verb-heavy language composed of mechanics and systems, experienced through player-initiated action and feedback. In this book, I create a framework through which readers can efficiently and effectively extract meaning from video game play experiences and produce meaning within the semiotic domain of video games (perhaps not literally *creating* video games, as that requires technical skills beyond what this book is scoped to teach, but at least being able to speak about games with others within the semiotic domain in insightful and novel ways).

ABILITY BARRIER

Detouring briefly from the subject of literacy, it is worth taking some time to address some of the unique challenges to access that video games can present. If you are a new player or are looking to introduce someone new to games, these may be helpful considerations to ensure you're making the most of your effort and avoiding roadblocks where they can be anticipated. This section will be mostly practical advice, and it can be skipped by anyone who already has regular avenues for playing games.

One of the challenges in gaining literacy in video games is the barrier to their use for some players. Though playing games is not the only way to learn about games, having some hands-on experience will help the concepts take root. Like cooking, one can read cookbooks and watch cooking videos and have a solid functional knowledge of how to assemble certain entrées, but that knowledge cannot be truly complete until she has felt the ingredients with her own hands and tasted the resulting meal.

Even more than other art forms, video games have accessibility, approachability, availability, and affordability issues that can leave certain audiences unable to play and enjoy them fully.

Accessibility

Within the fields of game design and game criticism, the term "accessibility" usually refers to ways in which games interface with players who have disabilities. In fact, this narrow definition is protected by members of the community, as broadening its scope to include challenges to access for reasons other than disability dilutes the term's usefulness for those who rely upon accessibility warnings in reviews and those who advocate for greater accessibility in gaming. In keeping with this best practice, I will use "accessibility" to refer to game design catering to overcoming access interference due to disabilities and "approachability" to refer to game design catering to overcoming access interference due to other factors such as inexperience with genre conventions or control methods.

Due to the expansive multimodality of video games, several types of disabilities can interrupt play:

- Motor disabilities, particularly fine motor control disabilities of the hands, can make it difficult to hold controllers, access all of their buttons, adjust analogue controls like thumbsticks with the required sensitivity, or perform repetitive actions like repeatedly hammering the same button.
- Visual disabilities such as blindness and colorblindness can make it difficult to distinguish important on-screen information when shapes and colors are not adequately differentiated.
- Auditory disabilities such as deafness can cause players to miss vital audio cues and information communicated in dialogue if they are not accompanied by complimentary visual cues and/or subtitles.
- Mental health problems each manifest and interact with gameplay differently. ADD/ADHD can manifest in difficulty focusing on necessary information when other on-screen elements are moving; trauma and phobias can be triggered by certain types of imagery or situations; and so forth.

Some players have multiple forms of disabilities, which can have a compounding effect on the disruption of play when games are not built with adequate accessibility measures. As this book is primarily focused on playing games rather than developing games, I will not spend a great amount of time detailing best practices for creating accessible games, but I highly recommend reading The AbleGamers Society's groundbreaking Includification guide (Barlet & Spohn, 2012).

If you are affected by a disability that may affect your ability to engage with games, or if you are trying to introduce others with disabilities to games, it is advisable to research the accessibility accommodations in the game you choose to play. Sites like Can I Play That? (www.caniplaythat.com), Game Accessibility Nexus (www.gameaccessibilitynexus.com), and the Accessible Games Database (www.accessiblegames-database.com) provide reviews and detailed explanations of accessibility features available in thousands of games. These can be invaluable resources for appropriately choosing games that suit each player's personal level of ability.

Though accessibility features are becoming more common and expected within modern games, there are still many modern and older games that have shamefully few, if any, accommodations for players with disabilities. In cases in which players wish to play games that do not have adequate in-built accessibility features, there are some options external to the games themselves that may help ease the experience.

- Choice of controller: Some motor disabilities make full operation of a standard game controller difficult, but there are often several types of controllers available that may suit a particular player's needs. Microsoft's Adaptive Controller is a modular hub into which many different types of external inputs (buttons, joysticks, foot pedals, etc.) can be connected. Arcade sticks, or fight sticks, emulate arcade control setups, featuring bigger buttons and a single, larger joystick, which may be more comfortable for some players to operate than a standard controller (though arcade sticks are typically limited to one joystick without the kind of analogue control that controller thumbsticks typically have). Though options for controller types may be somewhat limited on consoles, players can use a much wider variety of control options very easily on PCs.
- System-level button remapping: Sometimes, all it takes to overcome a fine motor obstacle to play is the ability to move vital functions to other buttons or triggers on the controller. While most games produced these days include button remapping options within the software, those that do not might still be playable with system-level button remapping. Most modern consoles offer this feature in the settings menus. Steam (the PC platform's most prominent storefront and launcher)

offers extensive per-game button remapping through its interface, even allowing users to map multi-button combinations and PC system features (like volume adjustment or taking a screenshot) to any button on the controller or keyboard.

- Co-Pilot mode: Modern Xbox consoles include an option called Co-Pilot Mode, allowing two controllers to control the action on-screen, with the intention being for a second player with a separate controller to be able to assist with actions that the primary player cannot perform without the inconvenience of passing one controller back and forth. Like having a passenger-side brake pedal in a driving instructor's car, this can be a great way to provide gentle assistance in a non-disruptive way.

Approachability

Approachability is a catch-all term for considerations of any number of things that might be an obstacle to pursuing or persisting with a game. For the purposes of this introductory chapter, I will focus on the "skill barrier", the obstacle presented by the player being unable (or at least unable to the individual's threshold for frustration) to overcome a game's challenges, either due to the challenges being too steep or due to general inexperience with the genre or gaming as a whole.

This can be a massive hurdle for new players to overcome. As we will explore in later chapters, games typically provide challenge (formally, "resistance") to give players something to overcome. It is what drives the experiential narrative of the game and is what makes players' victories satisfying. Appropriate challenge levels wildly vary from player to player, though, and a game well-balanced for players experienced with games in the same genre may be excessively difficult for someone new to the paradigm. When players experience nothing but defeats, a player may conclude that she doesn't have what it takes to succeed—that she is missing some essential element of skill or knowledge that is necessary to play the game. Amongst older players, especially, they may believe that they are too old to learn and master a "young person's technology". After all, you can't teach an old dog new tricks, right?

I disagree with this sentiment. I believe that motivated people can learn how to play video games at any age. The amount of time I have dedicated to writing this book is staked on that belief! Even so, though, the intention of this book is not to teach people how to play video games to a competitive level; my goal is to help people extract meaning from games and have meaningful experiences with games. In that vein, let's restructure the negative experience that has driven these hypothetical players away.

If a player feels like a failure for being unable to achieve the goal that the game has set out for them (make it to the end of the level, solve the puzzle, defeat the opponent…), begin by rejecting the paradigm. Find the joy in movement (or whatever the game's "verbs" might be). One does not compete in a bicycle race the first time she gets onto a bicycle; first, she must find the joy in riding.

HOW TO READ THIS BOOK

Throughout this book, I will make specific references to many different games. I will always try to provide a brief description of what kind of game is being referenced and why it is a relevant example, but I empathize that, for readers just now engaging with video games for the first time, these references may not be immediately meaningful. I think it is important to make reference to relevant games, though, for a number of reasons:

1. The medium of video games is uniquely action-oriented when compared to other mediums (not in the sense that it contains more gunfights, though that is probably also true, but rather that games are experienced through audience-initiated action rather than passively observed). As we get into the nuances of how game systems are *felt* and experienced, correlations with other passively consumed media fall short of communicating all of the necessary ideas.

2. One goal of this book is to prepare readers to not only be able to extract meaning from games but also to produce meaningful insights regarding games in conversation. Insights and observations about video games are more valuable when situated within the context of the medium and its history. Gaining literacy also means gaining at least a cursory understanding

> of the medium's history and major touchpoints. The conventions and symbols of a medium are shaped in real-time as the medium emerges in conversation with itself.

Artistic choices cannot be considered in isolation. Imagine someone who had never seen another film describing the artistic choices of Mel Brooks' *Young Frankenstein* (1974). She may lack the necessary context to understand why the film was presented in black and white. She may misunderstand elements of the story that are intentional parodies of earlier Universal horror films. Her recounting of the film (though doubtless fascinating) would not be terribly useful from a critical perspective when not situated within the historical context of the medium.

To prepare readers with relevant examples, I will speak about video games utilizing the language of video games. Perhaps a reference to a particular game prompts no further curiosity, but maybe it becomes squirreled away in the back of your mind, and when you encounter, for example, a combat racing game in the future, my mention of the *Burnout* series (2001–2018) will provide a breadcrumb towards relevant context.

It is my hope that you can use the titles of relevant games that I mention to look further into games that interest you. Even spending a few minutes playing a game can help contextualize references and arguments. Sometimes, though, even that can be difficult to accomplish.

I empathize with the fact that arranging to play the games that I mention may prove untenable, as playing games not only requires purchasing the game itself but also often requires owning specific game consoles, a powerful, gaming-capable PC, and/or specific controller types. For new games, modern consoles, controllers, VR headsets, and accessories can become very expensive, and older games are often difficult to obtain due to poor preservation of older titles and changes across evolving hardware making previous-generation games incompatible.

A ludography is included as an appendix at the end of the book listing each game I reference (the ludography is better introduced in Chapter 2). Be forewarned that these portions of the book will likely be the first to age past their relevancy, as the availability of specific games is in a perpetual state of flux, especially as more and more games are being pulled into subscription services rather than being sold as standalone products.

It is possible to play older games on PC through emulators (software that emulates the workings of older consoles, handhelds, and arcade cabinets that can play older games as if they were running on original hardware, with varying levels of fidelity and success). This is a legal gray area, and as such, tracking down emulators or ROMs (the games themselves transformed into sharable files) can lead you into potentially untrustworthy corners of the internet. For that risk, I will stop short of recommending the use of emulators, but if you feel internet-savvy enough to safely put together a robust emulation collection, it is an excellent way to experience older games (though we will explore the effects that emulation has on the artwork as opposed to playing it on the original hardware for which it was built in Chapter 4).

Even if specific games cannot be purchased or found, there is a near-limitless amount of video data that can be easily referenced for just about any game you are interested in. Reviews (in video or written form) can be immensely informative, but my preferred method of research is to watch portions of a recorded playthrough as pure, unedited gameplay. Searching just about any game's name on YouTube will return results that feature gameplay with commentary, which can serve as a useful insight into the thought processes of someone actually playing the game. If you would prefer to watch gameplay without commentary (which, honestly, is my preferred method, as the ratio of insightful commentators to obnoxious yelling skews unfavorably on YouTube), you can add terms like "longplay" or "no commentary" to the search.

As I cite games throughout the book, I will use examples from throughout the breadth of gaming history rather than privileging contemporary games (or, contemporary as of the time of writing). This holistic approach not only shields the book from becoming rapidly outdated (as it would if all of my examples were uniformly from the early 2020s) but also presents a more coherent narrative of the lineage of games and their ideas over time. As an industry and culture, those involved in gaming tend to have a future-facing perspective that discourages revisiting games from the recent and distant pasts. I believe that understanding the lineage and evolution of ideas, mechanics, and technology through time greatly enriches the gameplay experience. To build a discipline of approaching games from an art history perspective, my examples will be unmoored from particular time periods.

Archetypical Framing

One additional note that I would like to communicate upfront applies throughout the book. There is a multitude of types and forms that video games take. Some games feature a fully explorable 3D world, some are constrained to two dimensions, and some are presented only in text. Some games feature controllable protagonists (avatars), while others do not have any centralized, personified presence within the game space. Some games simulate worlds while others are more abstract, using only numbers, letters, cards, or tokens.

The theory that I outline throughout the book is written in such a way that presumes both a *diegetic game world* and a *controllable avatar within and exposed to that game world*. Much of the language that I use in descriptions and examples will implicitly assume that both of these conditions are met in the game analyzed. This is not to say that the methodology that I put forward is *incompatible* with non-avatar-based games or games that do not posit fantasy game worlds. Rather, this is only a convenience of writing style to have an archetypical model from which non-conforming games can be thought to deviate. Rather than say, "the player explores the game world (or non-figurative space) as the avatar (or other locus of focus and manipulation of the simulation)", I leave the assumed counter-examples unstated for the sake of efficiency.

When there are substantial differences in the manner in which games are interpreted, based on these factors, I call those out, specifically. For the sake of reducing repetitive writing, though, please read all following explanations with the understanding that they apply to all forms of video games, perhaps with some intuitive adaptation.

REFERENCES

Aarseth, E. J. (1997). *Cybertext: Perspectives on ergodic literature*. The Johns Hopkins University Press.

Abrams, J. J., Nolan, J., Joy, L., Weintraub, J., Burk, B., Lewis, R. J., … Schapker, A. (Executive Producers). (2016–2022). *Westworld* [TV series]. HBO Entertainment; Kilter Films; Bad Robot; Jerry Weintraub Productions; Warner Bros. Television.

Barlet, M. C. & Spohn, S. D. (2012). *Includification: A practical guide to game accessibility*. The AbleGamers Foundation.

Barrett, F. & Doyle, M. (Directors). (2003–2025). *Sleep no more* by Punchdrunk [Play]. London.

Brooks, M. (Director). (1974). *Young Frankenstein* [Film]. 20th Century Fox.

Cage, J. (1952). 4'33" [Song].

Crenshaw, K. (1989). *Demarginalizing the intersection of race and sex: A black feminist critique of antidiscrimination doctrine, feminist theory and antiracist politice*. University of Chicago Legal Forum.

Ebert, R. (2012). *Video games can never be art*. RogerEbert.com. https://www.rogerebert.com/roger-ebert/video-games-can-never-be-art

Fernández-Vara, C. (2014). *Introduction to game analysis*. Routledge. doi:10.4324/9781003355779

Furley, P. (2018). What modern sports competitions can tell us about human nature. *Perspectives on Psychological Science*, 1–18. doi:10.1177/1745691618794912

Gabrielle, V. (2018). *The dark side of gamifying work*. Fast Company. https://www.fastcompany.com/90260703/the-dark-side-of-gamifying-work

Gee, J. P. (2003). *What games have to teach us about learning and literacy*. St. Martin's Press.

Granger, P. (1979–1998). *Choose your own adventure* [Book Series]. Bantam Books.

Guinamard, A. & Siryani, R. (2002). *Doom for Ti 83*. ticalc.org. https://www.ticalc.org/archives/files/fileinfo/238/23843.html

Hobbema, M. (1665). *The watermill with the great red roof* [Painting]. The Art Institute of Chicago. https://www.artic.edu/artworks/869/the-watermill-with-the-great-red-roof

Huotari, K. & Hamari, J. (2012). Defining gamification: A service marketing perspective. *MindTrek 2012*, 17–22.

Kant, I. (1790). *Critique of judgment*.

Keane, S. (2020). *Programmer makes original Doom playable on pregnancy test*. CNET. https://www.cnet.com/culture/programmer-makes-original-doom-playable-on-pregnancy-test/

Lawrence, C., Alexander, Z., & Filipowich, M. (2009). *Critical distance*. https://critical-distance.com/

Lee, H. (1960). *To kill a mockingbird*. J. B. Lippincott & Co.

Lopez, S. (2011). *Disneyland workers answer to 'electronic whip'*. Los Angeles Times. https://www.latimes.com/health/la-xpm-2011-oct-19-la-me-1019-lopez-disney-20111018-story.html

Lucas, G. (1977-present). *Star wars* [Media Franchise]. Lucasfilm, Disney.

Mangan, J. A. (1986). *The games ethic and imperialism*. Frank Cass.

Miller, A. (Writer). (1949). *Death of a salesman* [Play]. Morosco Theatre, New York City.

Mozart, W. A. (Composer). (1788). *Symphony no. 40 in G minor, K. 550* [Song].

Murray, J. H. (1997). *Hamlet on the holodeck: The future of narrative in cyberspace*. The MIT Press.

Moosa, T. (2016). *Mafia III is just a game, but it shines a spotlight on the reality of racism*. The Guardian. https://www.theguardian.com/commentisfree/2016/oct/20/mafia-iii-videogame-racism

Stahelski, C. (Director). (2023). *John Wick: Chapter 4* [Film]. Summit Entertainment; Thunder Road Films; 87Eleven Entertainment.

Tucker, J. (2021). *Game developer gets 'Doom' running on an ATM*. NME. https://www.nme.com/news/game-developer-gets-doom-running-on-an-atm-3073133

Ulmer, G. L. (1998). *Teletheory: Grammatology in the age of video*. Routledge.

UNESCO (2004). *Literacy*. UNESCO. https://uis.unesco.org/node/3079547

Walton, K. L. (1990). *Mimesis as make-believe: On the foundations of the representational arts*. Harvard Press.

Warhol, A. (1962). *Campbell's Soup Cans* [Paintings].

Wood, L. C. & Reiners, T. (2015). Gamification. In M. Khosrow-Pour (Ed.) *Encyclopedia of information science and technology*, 3rd ed. IGI Global. doi:10.4018/978-1-4666-5888-2.ch297

Zichermann, G. & Cunningham, C. (2011). *Gamification by design: Implementing game mechanics in web and mobile apps*. O'Reilly.

CHAPTER 2

Key Terms

To begin this exploration, we must define the area of study. The methods and considerations posed throughout this book are systemic and procedural—they intend to elucidate the methods of meaning construction in the uniquely procedural medium of video games. As discussed in the introductory chapter, though, all art can be read from the lens of systemic meaning-making, and as a whole, this is the direction that critical art interpretation has trended over the past century. So while the methods proposed are written to assist with the interpretation of video games, specifically, it can be useful to consider these methods when examining other artworks or systemic, non-artistic experiences, though understanding that the fine details may not always align. Identifying the areas in which the method strains its goodness of fit when applied to other experiences may even reveal some of the qualities of games as unique systems.

This chapter will identify the elements that are necessary to be able to identify an artifact as a video game and detail some of the core aesthetics that video games produce as an art form. I then position those aesthetic experiences in the context of other arts. I reiterate the distinction between the semiotic and non-semiotic (or procedural) elements of games that will inform point of focus for most of the chapters following. Finally, the chapter concludes with definitions of key terms and genres that will serve as a helpful reference section throughout the rest of the book.

DEFINING A VIDEO GAME

In this section, I will attempt to build a working definition for "video game". Like most definitions of similar mediums, "you know it when you see it" will typically suffice in non-critical environments, but it is useful to have some kind of definitional framework for more deliberate study like this. More useful than establishing boundaries for the purpose of excluding non-video game artifacts, though, this definitional exercise may provide more use in expanding what we may include within it.

Anecdotally, it is common for people who, by self-report, "do not play video games" to admit to *some degree* of regular video gaming habits upon closer inspection, due to the ubiquity of games-ready devices. Some games, like digitized versions of crosswords and sudoku puzzles, translate with relatively high fidelity the experience of playing such games in a non-digital context; even these non-self-identifying video game players often admit to enjoying some gaming pastimes that are unique to the digital form, such as tile-matching games like *Candy Crush Saga* (2012) and *Bejeweled* (2001) or socially oriented games like *Heads Up!* (2013) and *The Jackbox Party Pack* (2014). Though these games do not put forward sprawling and involving fantasies or inspire the same kind of fervent, long-session play as what people might more typically define as "video games", they hold many of the same design constructs and procedural aesthetics. It is necessary to have a theory and practice of literacy that can account for both the games that are pulled up as momentary distractions while waiting in line as well as the 100+-hour epics to which devotees dedicate entire weekends.

My hope, with this book, is to encourage people at every level of knowledge and investment in video gaming as a hobby to have language and context to be able to derive greater meaning from the video

DOI: 10.1201/9781003530961-2

game experiences that they encounter wherever and at whatever scale that might be.

What Is a Video Game?

In a sense, a definition for "video game" seems straightforward. In its name alone, it makes two cogent arguments about its ontology. A video game is presumably "like video, but game" and "like game, but video"; or, to expand upon that, a video game is presumably "similar to video-based media like film and television but transformed through the objective-based interactivity of gameness" and "like traditional games like Chess and Monopoly, but played through and with digital images". These intuitive arguments will lead audiences *close* to a useful definition, but they are neither sufficient nor wholly accurate. A more carefully considered definition is required.

Throughout this book, I will refer to the subjects of our exploration as "video games", though there are several other terms that are used in colloquial and academic settings, such as "computer games", "digital games", and "interactive digital narratives (IDN)", to name only a few. Some of these alternate names seek to address controversies or shortcomings of the term "video game". Though this is an academic exercise and should exercise specific, controlled language for clarity and accuracy, instruction in literacy should prepare readers for practical engagement with the studied objects within the context of cultural use and conversation. Wholly accurate or not, "video game" is the term by which these cultural texts are most commonly known. Colloquial conversation usually employs that term. Paratexts are discoverable with that terminology. Professionals within the industry refer to their work as video games. It is more practically useful to utilize and caveat the imperfect, existent term than to devise something more accurate but isolating in utilization outside of this context. This is not an uncommon practice. A painting may employ non-paint pigment, and a film may not be captured on film stock.

It is worth noting before continuing that the term "video game" likely originated from trade or marketing copy in the 1970s. It became ubiquitous because of its primacy rather than its categorical accuracy. "Video game" is a term that results from a colloquial evolution rather than a hard, etymological manifesto. As the medium has grown beyond that which 1970s electronics marketers envisioned, we need not artificially constrict our understanding of the medium and community to conform to that early terminology. Let us instead consider the usefulness of our definitional boundaries. It is more useful to group categories of media that share essential design grammar and interpretive frameworks, created in conversation and community with more definitionally traditional "video games", than to arbitrarily exclude works on the basis of honoring 50-year-old marketing copy.

Review of Historical Definitions of "Game"

Addressing both "video" and "game" separately, I begin the definitional exercise by identifying what is meant by "game". Numerous writers have offered compelling definitions of games. Some detailed and specific, others more abstract, aiming to convey an emotional or experiential truth about playing games, such as Sid Meier's oft-quoted idea that a game is "a series of meaningful choices" (Rollings & Morris, 2000).

An early definition that makes more specific claims about the mechanisms of gamic behavior comes from philosopher Roger Caillois (1958), who defines a game as "and activity which is [...] *free* [...] *separate* [...] *uncertain* [...] *unproductive* [...] *governed by rules* [...] *make-believe*" (pp. 9, 10):

> *Free* refers to players' voluntary involvement. This is a reflection of the arbitrariness of games. Games are not contests for survival, they are activities that players enter into through social contract, taking on a cooperative attitude of maintenance of its rule-based structure. This is an element of what Bernard Suits (1978) calls the *lusory attitude*: players accept their roles and voluntarily ascribe to the rules and means of play in order to maintain the structure of the game (p. 38).
>
> *Separate* is an extension of this; the idea that games have defined boundaries that separate the activities of play from the activities of life. This corresponds with what Johan Huizinga (1938) defined as the *magic circle*, the "temporary worlds within the ordinary world, dedicated to the performance of an act apart" (p. 10); the semi-penetrable social boundary in which the actions of play are privileged and separated from the world without.

Uncertain refers to the necessity for a game's results to not be determined beforehand. A fixed boxing match is more of an act of theatre than sport, as it progresses towards a predetermined conclusion. For any contest to be exciting, uncertainty of result even takes precedence over fairness of rules, such that more skilled players may adopt handicaps to ensure that a contest between them and less-skilled opponents maintains the necessary uncertainty of result.

Unproductive requires that games create "neither goods, nor wealth, nor new elements of any kind" (Caillois, 1958, p. 10). This is perhaps the most controversial element of Caillois' definition, as it calls into question the definitional status of professional sports for which athletes are paid. It reinforces the *free* and *separate* mandates, though, by noting that games are separate from work and from the concerns of the world from which the magic circle separates its players. Any *productive* or *compensated* game has the risk of becoming *necessary* and losing its *free* and *voluntary* pretext. While it is perhaps useful to separate slot machines and other gambling activities into a category of questionable playfulness, surely most players have experience with attaching some friendly stakes to a game in order to increase the drama of play.

Governed by rules maintains that it is definitionally-necessary for games to be structured by socially-maintained constraints. Rules are often held as the distinguishing quality between "games" and "free play". I go into greater detail into rules in a later section.

Make-believe states that games have an element of fantasy, simulation, or representation, "a second reality or [...] a free unreality" (Caillois, 1958, p. 10). This may be true of games of Cops and Robbers, Chess, or Chutes and Ladders, but I argue that many games, like bowling, tag, or sudoku, do not require an allegorical reading beyond their own mechanics of play. I do not believe that this should disqualify such activities from being games.

Another well-considered definition comes from researcher Jesper Juul (2005):

> a game is a rule-based formal system [...] with variable and quantifiable outcomes [...] where different outcomes are assigned different values [...] where the player exerts effort in order to influence the outcome [...] the player feels attached to the outcome [...] and the consequences of the activity are optional and negotiable.
>
> *(pp. 6, 7)*

A rule-based system aligns with Caillois' definition and is a through-line between most definitions of games.

With variable and quantifiable outcomes refers not only to Caillois' principle of uncertainty but also to the idea that it is necessary to be able to clearly quantify and differentiate a game's outcomes.

Where different outcomes are assigned different values, which Juul calls *valorization* (*ibid*, p. 35). It is necessary for games to not only have possible outcomes; those outcomes must be valued as *good* or *bad*. Players should be compelled to achieve positive outcomes.

Where the player exerts effort in order to influence the outcome; the valorized outcome causes players to strive for its achievement. It becomes definitionally-necessary for games to be effortful activities, to require active participation.

The player feels attached to the outcome rides a line with Caillois' *unproductiveness*. For both to be true, the player must internalize the motivation of pursuit of the valorized outcome, but this "attachment" should not be motivated by the production of goods or wealth outside of the context of play. The achievement of the valorized outcome should be an end in-and-of itself.

And the consequences of the activity are optional and negotiable hints at rules (*including objectives and rewards*) being subject to social contract. This also reinforces Caillois' *free* and *separate* by asserting that participants

> agree to the terms of their own involvement. A contest between those who have no ability to negotiate consequences or opt out of the activity is not a *game*.

Game designer Chris Crawford (1982) outlines what may be the first formal definition in the games studies canon written specifically to apply to video games. He lists as necessary qualities of games:

> *Systemic, subjective representation*: a ruleset, in accordance with other definitions of games. These rulesets model phenomena or relationships existent in the real world. Crawford differentiates games from simulations as reflections of their relationship with fidelity and abstraction. "The simulations designer simplifies reluctantly and only as a concession to material and intellectual limitations. The game designer simplifies deliberately in order to focus the player's attention on those factors the designer judges to be important" (Crawford, 1982, p. 8). I am reluctant to accept the assertion that games *must* point to something beyond themselves in a metaphorical manner, but we can observe a level of substantification that takes place between a game's abstract rules and its instantiated play. If we can boil down a game's *essence* to its *rules*, it is clear that play of those rules involves translating the rules into something non-abstract.
>
> *Interaction*: Specifically, Crawford requires competition; intelligent reaction to player inputs. "A cube puzzle does not actively respond to the human's moves; a high jump pole does not react to the jumper's efforts. In both tic tac toe and basketball the opposing players acknowledge and respond to the player's actions" (Crawford, 1982, p. 10). This distinction is troublesome, though. He is correct to note that a cube puzzle only *reflects* player manipulation rather than *reacting* to it; in changing "state", it presents players with a "new" puzzle that represents either a step closer to or farther away from the ultimate solution of the puzzle. We can question how different his tic-tac-toe counter-example is, though. As other theorists have reported (Jesper Juul in almost excruciating detail on multiple occasions; Juul, 2003; 2005), tic-tac-toe does not present "choices" at each step during play as much as it presents single "logical" next-steps (often mirrored in the symmetrical grid). The other player only "reacts" to a tic-tac-toe move insofar as she recognizes the one "correct" move and chooses it (almost always resulting in a stalemate competition) or against her best interest chooses an "incorrect" move that leads to the game's termination. In the case of tic-tac-toe, are the players *really* interacting with one another, or do they only follow a prescriptive sequence of actions, deviation from which entails *not really playing* the game? One could easily write a booklet in which an optimal response was given to any tic-tac-toe game state, and following these prescriptive branches would not be significantly different from playing a live game. Crawford writes, "the player is actively pursuing some goal. Obstacles prevent him from easily achieving this goal. If the obstacles are passive or static, the challenge is a puzzle or athletic challenge. If they are active or dynamic, if they purposefully respond to the player, the challenge is a game. However, active, responsive, purposeful obstacles require an intelligent agent" (Crawford, 1982, p. 13).
>
> This leads us to the intersection of greatest interest: if Crawford purports that games require *active, intelligent* response to player actions rather than inert and mechanical reflection of game state which proceeds logically into the next, sequential axiom of play, does this not disqualify all single-player video games as being games? Staying within Crawford's definition, the argument that one could make to assert that single-player video games *do* produce challenge is that the mechanical system that manages the events of play is so complex that its logical behaviors produce unexpected and exciting feedback that feels like intelligent response (what I will later refer to as *emergence*; see Chapter 3). In that sense, the game's systems stand-in for the intelligent game designer by proxy. But this supposes that a sufficiently-complex Rubik's Cube could also be

read as "intelligent", if it was designed in such a way that each action a player could perform results in a satisfyingly-engrossing puzzle. My point is that inert, prescriptive, mechanical change always trends towards the illusion of intelligence with (well-applied) complexity, and *actual* intelligence can always be broken down into simpler, mechanical binaries as the variables and constraints of a system are better understood.

Ultimately, I am not able to offer a solution to that problem. One can spend a tremendous amount of time mapping the behavior of a game's systems to determine which games are sufficiently "game-like" or "puzzle-like", to use Crawford's dichotomy. Salen and Zimmerman (2003) cite puzzle and game designer Scott Kim, who distinguishes puzzles from games because puzzles have single, correct answers while games have multiple outcomes at every moment during play. However, even though puzzles have singular "solved" states, there are usually multiple fruitful strategies to reach these points, a "play" in approach. Conversely, games that take on a narrative structure, as most video games do, tend to resolve to one (or a handful of) predetermined outcome(s); the "play" of a game is also an indeterminacy of strategies and approaches to the (valorized) outcome.

Safety: following on from Crawford's assertion that games are representational systems, he notes that games are "safe" ways to confront and overcome the types of challenges that might pose dangers in life (or their fantastical contexts). This reflects the *separateness* of Caillois' definition and the *optional and negotiable consequences* of Juul's. This reflects an essential nature of play activities as opportunities for learning about aspects of life that might be restricted or dangerous otherwise – children play-acting certain professions or domestic roles, for instance.

Katie Salen (Tekinbaş) and Eric Zimmerman, in their seminal *Rules of Play* (2003), define a game as "a system in which players engage in an artificial conflict, defined by rules, that results in a quantifiable outcome". Most elements of their definition look familiar: "system", "artificial conflict", "defined by rules", and "quantifiable outcome". Crucially, they elaborate on the measure of ludic conflict to a greater degree than Crawford had, noting that conflict can be found in players "competing" against game systems. To the degree that "competition" implies a bilateral directionality, they seem to be more comfortable with de-personified conflict than was Crawford.

A final definition I would like to highlight is that of game designer David Kanaga. He begins by acknowledging the diversity of objects, theorems, and activities we call "games", positing a generalized starting point for his definition, "*played form*, no goals, optima, etc. required" (Kanaga, 2015). Of course, this is more poetic than definitional; one may recognize that a violin would qualify as a game under that definition (a claim that Kanaga probably would not resist, as he has claimed before and does so again in the quoted article, "games are music").

Kanaga is interested in games as the intersection of two sets of "invariants" that constrain play: *rules* and *forces*. Rules effect "an abstract legal system that play must abide by if it is to be considered lawful" (Kanaga, 2015) while forces "compose a system of material-energetic tendencies which are fully actual and not abstract". In other words, baseball is subject to certain invariant forces that constrain actions performed within it by way of the forces of physics, and its rules are written to play off of these forces to create interesting challenges. The distance between home plate and the back fence makes for an interesting challenge in the context of Earth's gravity and atmospheric inertia. One can negotiate the rules if it does not produce interesting play (a children's league will make the threshold for hitting a home run closer to home plate than in a Major League game), but one cannot negotiate "house rules" for the forces of play (the children's league does not negotiate away gravity).

This confronts us with an uncomfortable question (and one that I more fully explore in Chapter 13): if rules are negotiable social contracts that shape play via players' investment (lusory attitude) in the roles of maintaining play, and forces are employed as matter-of-fact, do video games *have* rules at all, or is it only bounded by nonnegotiable conditions as impersonally applied as the physics of a baseball game?

Rules vs. Mechanics

This question has been approached, but it is far from being resolved. In his book *The Beauty of Games* (2023), Frank Lantz quotes game designer and teacher Doug Wilson, "videogames are not a subset of 'games.' Both the 'video' and 'game' parts of the word are vestigial, like your appendix" (p. 21), a provocative statement Wilson wrote in what appears to be a since-lost tweet.[1] Lantz puts this statement in the context of a statement made by Malcolm Gladwell (2005):

> videogames are not games in the sense of those pastimes—like Monopoly or Gin Rummy or Chess—which most of us grew up with. They don't have a set of unambiguous rules that have to be learned and then followed during the course of play.

Stephanie Boluk and Patrick LeMieux (2017) take this sentiment even further:

> despite their colloquial designation and sale as games, videogames do not have rules. Rules are voluntary constraints and social contracts. They are pacts between players not to peek or move outside invisible boundaries. Mechanics, on the other hand, are ontological operations. Players have no choice but to work within the limitations of these involuntary systems.
>
> *(p. 8)*

The definitions of "game" reviewed in the previous section (and endless more in the literature beyond) regularly name rules as conditions for considering activities *games.* Following Boluk and LeMieux's quote, we can differentiate *rules* from *mechanics. Rules* are elements of design. They are abstract, negotiable, and socially enforced. The rules of Monopoly can, thus, be modified in a particular play session; *house rules* can be adopted to reshape the experience of play. Computers are logic-based machines, though. They cannot apply subjective judgment nor entertain spontaneous negotiation. As such, the abstract *rules* envisioned and designed by game developers must be *translated* into *mechanics* when the game is programmed into code. The software executes purely operational procedures based on the variables programmed into its system. The degree to which a system can be "intelligent" is only a reflection of the complex contingencies programmed into it.

So if almost all definitions of "game" insist that the form is "bound by rules", and it is questionable to what degree applying "rules" to video games is appropriate, does that jeopardize our ability to call video games "games" at all? If so, it rides dangerously close to the primary formalist principle of "walking and quacking like a duck". Intuitively, we *recognize* video games as games; surely this nit-picky distinction is only of interest to strict ontological formalists and the least interesting person in any room at any given time. Were this vector of exploration to end here, I would agree, but Boluk and LeMieux put forward an essential conclusion that reframes the discussion entirely. "Rather than continue to conflate mechanics with rules and videogames with games, what if videogames were not considered games in the first place, but equipment for making metagames?" (Boluk & LeMieux, 2017, p. 9).

Metagames are a focus of Chapter 13, but to briefly define them here, *metagames* are the personal and communal games that players singularly and collectively play within and around the structure that a video game's rigid mechanics enforce. In the same way that a curb on a street "invites" the metagame of challenging oneself to balance on its edge, video games provide a concrete structure in which abstract metagames can flourish. So whether or not video games **ARE** games in the most formal, nit-picky sense, gameplay occurs within them and around them.

This is an exciting development because it reframes the tasks of the developer and the player. The developer is not a *storyteller* in as much as she is a *systems designer*, producing a fertile ground from which stories emerge, reflecting aspects of her vision and the personality of the participating player. It also repositions the player as *game designer*, structuring her own metagame, consciously or unconsciously, and participating in the group task of communal metagame creation by way of her input into the cumulative cultural context of a game. It also repositions our area of interest in our examination of video games as artistic artifacts. Whereas a painting is an evocative object designed to elicit artistic interpretations and aesthetic experiences from its beholders, video games—used here to mean the designed software distributed as commercial products—are not, themselves, aesthetic objects that directly engage the players. Video games (commercial software) are sets of instructions that *produce* live, enacted gameplay—and it is *live gameplay* that is the aesthetic object and artistic artifact of our study. Players do not interpret code; code does not stir the player's emotions—gameplay performs this task. The commercial software only gives gameplay its shape. As such, game developers design far more *indirectly* than do artists in other mediums, in a manner far more collaborative with the audience.

So where does this leave us? Defining "game" within the "video game" name has already proven more challenging than expected. Using the best pieces of the historical definitions examined above and operating with the metagame caveat discussed, I land on the following definition: the word "game" in the compound name "video game" is an interactive system, given shape and direction by rules of design and mechanics of computational operation, in which players express constrained agency and form metagames in pursuit of intrinsically valued objectives.

Defining "Video"

Video games set themselves apart from other types of games, such as board games and card games, by incorporating a video element as the primary mode of information exchange. Implicit in that definition is that video games are *digital*; interaction is facilitated by a computer, and the player interfaces with the computer by digital means to control the game, with the locus of interaction being represented within the digital space.

All games can be thought of as "state machines". At their most formal level, they do not flow continuously like organic movement; they exist as a sequence of discrete states. A basketball game can be reduced to the sequence of the teams' scores; every time a team makes a basket, the game state updates. There are continuous elements—position of the ball on the court, time remaining in each quarter—but the scores represent the essence of the game. Players' performance is in service of altering this game state, and the scoreboard serves as the game state's "memory", impartially reflecting the current state. In the same way, the arrangement of pieces on a Chessboard serves as the game state's "memory". Chess can be played without a board—by mail or even verbally, provided the players can keep the game's state in their own memories in such a way that will not result in dispute. Chess' rules are abstract and transferable.

Video games, as digital technologies, are able to maintain much more complex "memories" than can a Chessboard. As such, the game state of a video game is much less "knowable" (for its complexity) at any moment than that of Chess, but a similar principle applies. Video games are supremely complex *state machines*, an idea to which I return in Chapter 7. As such, the actions that resolve into digital state changes must either originate within or be translated to the digital space.[2]

This means that, even though controller inputs are physical actions (the player's thumb physically presses a button or physically moves a thumbstick), the action is read and processed as a digital signal before being transmitted to the central computer, which tracks and updates the game state in response to player input. The primary source of state-tracking and maintenance of ludic operations is digital.

This sets video games apart from primarily physical games that incorporate peripheral video elements, such as pinball tables. Pinball tables share many qualities with video games—the player has limited, representational input into a system tracked and scored by a computer that visualizes necessary feedback and elements of the gameplay on a screen. Where it differentiates itself is that the locus of interaction (what we will later call the "avatar"; the representation of the player in the game world or systemic structure; see Chapter 4) exists on the pre-digital layer; it is the physical mechanism of the machine (the manipulatable paddles) or arguably the ball (though interaction with the ball is indirect, mediated through the directly controlled paddles).

The primary interchange of action and reaction takes place on the physical layer, whereas video games primarily concentrate interaction within the digital space. How is that different from motion-controlled, first-person VR games in which the player's physical body is used to interact with the virtual world? In actuality, there is no direct interaction between the physical body and the virtual world. The game creates a digital double (the avatar), aligned as closely as possible to the physical presence of the player, that interfaces with the virtual world. An avatar is still being embodied, and all interaction remains a digital exchange. In the context of state change, according to the mechanics of the game, it is only the proprioceptive "state" of the avatar that constitutes mechanically relevant action; player state, if it becomes detached from avatar state by way of tracking error, becomes irrelevant.

To review, video games are set apart from other types of games due to the privileging of the *digital, computational* maintenance, and manipulation of the game state. This is slightly unsatisfying as a definitional condition of "video game", though, since the *digital*-ness of the experience is only (in this context) relevant because of its inferential link with "video". How do we grapple with the word "video" itself? I have a flexible tolerance for what may represent a game's video element, with one major restriction: it must be an electronic visual display, but any number of electronic displays are acceptable.

Though modern players will be most familiar with various types of screens that display moving images through rapidly changing constellations of colorful pixels (made possible by a number of different methods, such as illuminated LEDs or liquid crystals), other types of visual interfaces may be assimilated within our category of "video games" as well. Some early video games were built for vector displays. If someone programs a controllable character that could snake her way through color-changing Christmas lights, I would consider that an unconventional video game, as the electronic lightbulbs create a visual interface functionally identical to that of a traditional screen, only with far fewer and less densely packed points of iteration.

I would exclude games in which the locus of game state manipulation resides outside of the digital space, though, such as grip test machines (often styled as "love tests") at carnivals, in which feedback may be given with arrangements of colorful lightbulbs (analogous to pixels on a screen), but the primary gameplay verb is exercised in the physical space. No avatar or digital locus of control is required as a digital in-between, much like the game of Operation. Theoretically, a computer-operated game that feeds back visual information to the player using a mechanically operated arrangement of physical tiles (such as a game of mechanical tic-tac-toe against a robot) would also not be considered a video game, since game state manipulation (and memory) also primarily occurs outside of the digital space.

As noted above, all video games require some form of controller interface, since the virtual world simulated by the computer cannot be directly, physically manipulated. This can be a handheld controller, a computer mouse and/or keyboard, a touchscreen, a camera, a microphone, etc. There has to be some kind of interface to translate the physical inputs of the player into digital signals that can be virtually represented within the game world. Just as the player needs a controller with which to interface with the computer (a *threshold object*, as Janet H. Murray [2012] terms it), the computer requires a threshold object with which to interface with the player in the realm of the physical. So, though the digital game state "lives" within the processor and memory of the computer itself, the game state and ludic action are communicated to the player through audio, haptic, and—yes—*video* interfaces.

As such, video is not *wholly* necessary as a component of the video game system—it only informs the player; it *reflects* the game state rather than interfacing with it. This is evidenced by particularly skillful players within the community surrounding "challenge running" games, such as those who exhibit the astounding ability to play *Mike Tyson's Punch-Out!!* (1987) while blindfolded (Summoning Alt, 2022) or the genre of "audio games" that will be explored in the next section. There are also avid players within the community who are blind as a matter of physiological fact, and they are able to thrive and excel despite receiving no or little of their game state feedback from the video element of the system of play.

Again, I am inching toward an unsatisfying conclusion with this portion of the definition. I may reflect Doug Wilson's quote from before—perhaps he is correct that both "video" and "game" elements of the name *are* vestigial. "Game" is a complicated meta-element buried a layer deep, and "video" may not be *necessary* at all. I am inclined to respect the "video" adjective, though, as a matter of *convention* if not *absolute necessity.* Video might not be a load-bearing element of games' construction, but it has a long tradition of being the system's primary mode of feedback/output, and it remains the most recognizable element of games' presentation. To keep the "video" in the name is to express an identifiable element of design tradition. Besides, rock music contains very few actual rocks.

"Games" That Resist Categorization

Earlier, I wrote that rules are abstract and must be translated into concrete mechanics when implemented into video games. While this is true, echoes of rules in their abstract form still echo strongly throughout the experience of play. A *victory condition* is one of the most important types of rules, as it orients the player toward a goal and directs the sub-objectives that she sets for herself working toward that macro-level goal. Rules of play are interesting only in the context of how they interact with the player's pursuit of the macro- or micro-objectives, as defined by the game's rules.

A victory condition translates well into the logical operations of computational mechanics. A condition is fulfilled to transition the game state from "not won" to "won", crudely speaking. In that sense, most video games do have a victory condition, or at least an ending, such that some valorized action cues the credits roll or the high-score screen.

Despite the presence of an "ending" condition, there are some games that are commonly cited as not being sufficiently "game-like" to satisfy the strictest (and most literal) definitions of "video game". *Dear Esther* (2012), an exploration adventure game by The Chinese Room, puts players in the perspective of an anonymous character walking through a sparsely inhabited island. Throughout his journey through rocky hillsides, abandoned buildings, and beautiful caves and cliffs, poetic narration is read aloud, seemingly unconnected to the stroll through the island. The player must draw her own conclusions about the connections and meaning of the seemingly unrelated experiential and narrative layers of *Dear Esther*. Though *Dear Esther* has all of the contextual cues of being a video game (it is sold on video game storefronts, it is controlled using standard video game control methods, it was built in a video game engine…), the mechanics that bound play do not obviously interface with the abstract win condition. It does not require mastery over skill-based systems to complete. While it is inarguably a vehicle for interactive storytelling, it is a game.

Similarly, an increasing number of "live service" experiences prioritize repeatable play loops with no progression toward a definitive ending. Platforms like *World of WarCraft* (2004) are play spaces in which players can congregate, compete, and cooperate, though these open-ended spaces do not draw players toward a conclusive state of having "finished" the game. Though smaller victories can be achieved throughout the adventure (such as completing boss battles, clearing dungeons, or reaching the level cap), there is no point of ultimate culmination—a single, ultimate "victory condition"—comparable to most games. Like the real world, players can continue playing in these spaces for as long as they would like. Again, these experiences have all of the contextual cues of being games, but do their overarching structures require us to categorize them as some other kinds of avenues for play rather than formal games?

These two examples approach the problem from opposite directions. *Dear Esther* has the structure of a game without many of the mechanics and systems that we typically associate with games, while *World of WarCraft* is stuffed to the gills with mechanics and systems, but lacks aspects of games' typical structure. *Dear Esther* inarguably provides a narrative puzzle to be solved, but so do mystery books. Games require mechanical feedback, and one could reasonably argue that, without the game mechanically tracking and feeding back on progress toward solving this narrative mystery, *Dear Esther* has more in common with an audiobook in which new passages will not be read until players walk a few hundred virtual yards. Similarly, *World of WarCraft* inarguably features gameplay—engagement with mechanics and systems that reward and punish player choices, tracking and feeding back on player inputs within a fictionalized setting. But one could reasonably argue that *World of WarCraft* is instead a platform in which gameplay experiences take place, not dissimilar to software like *Roblox* (2006), while lacking key definitional parameters at the highest level.

Instead of arguing against specific objections one by one, I instead encourage an inclusive perspective centered around usefulness rather than discriminatory criteria. Though categorization in art is useful to ensure that like objects are being compared and discussed with accurate language and context, it is often more useful to consider adjacency than form. Ultimately, the purpose of artistic categorization is to help us ascertain context and determine how to talk about pieces of art rather than draw hard lines around archetypical forms. Regardless of where a member of the audience falls in the categorical debate around *Dear Esther* or *World of WarCraft*, it is useful to acknowledge that these works are at least *in conversation* with more traditional video games. They are made by video game developers, adopted by video game players, celebrated within video game communities.

By treating these as an art form wholly different from video games, we do not gain any additional clarity when trying to understand or contextualize these titles. These works have their influences and legacy within the lineage of games. Many, many games are in direct conversation with these titles, either extending or imitating the things that they did well or responding to and expanding upon shortcomings. Removing these titles from the categorical lineage of video games would make a less comprehensible historical narrative when viewed holistically.

Consider an additional form that breaks our organizational taxonomy: the aforementioned category of audio games. Audio games operate similarly to video games, with simulated environments generated and tracked by the computer, but they feature no (or incidental) video output. Games like *The Vale: Shadow of the Crown* (2021), *Dark Echo* (2015), *A Blind Legend* (2015), and *Papa Sangre* (2010) operate in a manner familiar to players of more traditional video games, except all cues come from the audio layer of the experience. In these games, players tend to inhabit the roles of blind characters, or sometimes these games simulate technology that is not accompanied by visual feedback in real life, like deep-sea probes. In a sense, the absence of information on the screen is still representational. While it is useful to have the "audio game" descriptor to delineate lineage within this small, ultra-specific sub-group of games, it is also useful to consider these alongside and in conversation with more conventional video games. They are designed to be consumed and understood utilizing our developed video game domain literacy, and we can expect that advancements made within this small field are likely to be adopted by the closely-adjacent realm of video games before they are adopted by less proximal mediums.

In conclusion, the term "video game" is, as Doug Wilson suggested, a largely vestigial term that was adopted to distinguish the early console and computer-based games from other types of electronic games, such as handheld electronic toys with lights but no imaging display. It is a commercially-driven category and a legacy term that has only become primary due to its primacy. In the decades since its adoption, it no longer adequately describes the breadth of experiences offered by artists creating in community with one another. Whether this means that the medium of "video games" has expanded beyond its terminological scope or additional mediums have grown up alongside video games, that is up to each individual's theory of art history to determine. Others have suggested more accurate and inclusive terms, like "interactive digital narratives", but it is unlikely that these will ever replace the familiar terminology in the cultural vocabulary. As such, let us consider the term a starting point rather than a strict set of definitional boundaries. Consider that "video games" refers not only to the products but also to the industry (which also produces non-traditional game experiences), a non-professional or extra-industry professional community of creators (who very often push on definitional boundaries), a means and philosophy of production, as well as the culture of fans and consumers.

Video Game Ontology

Though we have established a working definition of video games, we must acknowledge that, in practical convention, "video game" bears a complicated ontology that can describe numerous aspects of any referenced property. When someone refers to a specific game, what do they mean? Researcher and professor Ian Bogost (2009a) explores this complicated ontology in an insightful portion of his 2009 Digital Games Research Association (DiGRA) keynote (later transcribed and expanded as a blog entry entitled *Videogames Are a Mess*; Bogost, 2009b). This section is indebted to his framing but draws some different conclusions and explores different aspects of the question.

A video game is its digital data. When a player purchases a game from a digital marketplace, a set of files transfers to the host machine. The data of a game contain (roughly) everything that a game needs to run (though, increasingly, a portion or all of a game's data may be accessed remotely through the cloud rather than being stored wholly on a player's local machine; even in such cases, the data must still live on *a* computer, even if it is not the player's). This data includes all of the art assets, sounds, engine architecture, code, 3D models, etc. from which the game draws to populate, animate, and execute its simulation. This data represents the "presence" of a digital game. *American McGee's Alice* (2000) is made of 962 MB of data, and once that data has been loaded onto a player's machine, it's reasonable to say that the machine contains *American McGee's Alice*. If that data is deleted, that machine no longer contains *American McGee's Alice*. Reasonably, the presence or absence of the data corresponds to the presence or non-presence of the game, regardless of whether the game can be played. If, for example, the player's computer is not technically capable of playing *American McGee's Alice* (if it does not have a video card capable of rendering 3D graphics) or if the game requires a serial number to activate as a piracy deterrent that the player no longer has, it is still reasonable to say that the computer contains *American McGee's Alice*, even though the player cannot play it.

This is complicated by the fact that digital data can be manipulated by the player, developer, or publisher. Most modern games are "patched" post-release to fix glitches and exploits, add (or sometimes remove) content, and make other changes to the way that a game plays. Once a game is updated, older "versions" of the game (referring to incremental versions of the same software) are usually completely unavailable. Some games, such as fantasy action role-playing game (ARPG) *Dark Souls II* (2014), undergo significant design changes when patched, constituting fundamental shifts in identity and player experience. Right now, the version of *Dark Souls II* that players bought at the launch of that game is completely unavailable for download from digital storefronts. Those interested in the original experience of *Dark Souls II* may still satisfy their curiosity by tracking down a copy of its original Xbox 360 or PlayStation 3 versions on disc (and not allowing the console to apply patches, which it will attempt to do automatically), but incremental versions between that which is on-disc and the modern iteration may be impossible to preserve. This introduces interesting questions around identity, aura, and authenticity. If *Dark Souls II* is its data, is it fundamentally more or less *Dark Souls II* once it has been updated?

Certain online games, dubbed "live service" games, not only add content through post-release patches, but content is sometimes removed or is only included within the game for a short amount of time during an event or "season". 100-player online battle royale shooter *Fortnite* (2017), for example, regularly updates and changes its world, such that the map in which the 100-player battles take place is fundamentally different in layout and content today than it was in 2019. Is it fair to call it the same game? Is there a degree to which a game's data can be altered, after which it can no longer be considered the same game? Hypothetically, if a first-person shooter (FPS) game slowly evolves over the years to introduce vehicles that can be used during combat, then is further patched to add lengthy vehicular sections in between gun battles, then is patched to spin its driving into a separate mode of play, then is patched again to remove the gunfights entirely and wholly become a racing game—is it fundamentally the same game? Conversely, if a game's data are optimized and replaced entirely with more efficiently constructed files that are imperceptibly different, is the game—experientially unaltered—the same or different from before?

Furthermore, players can often themselves modify (mod, in the parlance of the gaming community) a game's digital data. If a player replaces specific files within a game's data structure to replace the game's cast with talking horses, is it still fundamentally the same game? It is reasonable to say that it is, with the caveat. It may not fully represent the developers' intended vision any longer, but it is reasonable to say that play still occurs in the same "game space". This is a matter of degree, though. Some modifications are so extensive that they can only be referred to as their own entity. For example, an ambitious mod called *The Forgotten City* (2015) was released for the fantasy ARPG *The Elder Scrolls V: Skyrim* (2011). It contains a complex story within a brand new location featuring new characters, new voice acting, and new gameplay mechanics developed specifically for the mod. Though it executes within the *Skyrim* engine and uses much of the structural *Skyrim* data and runtime code, it would not be wholly accurate to describe playing *The Forgotten City* mod as just "playing *Skyrim*".

A video game is its physical media. If a player goes to a store and purchases *Chrono Trigger* (1995) for the Super Nintendo Entertainment System (SNES), it is reasonable to say that the cartridge that she receives **is** *Chrono Trigger*. From a commercial perspective, physical media, whether it is a cartridge, disc, or other type of media, can be bought, sold, and traded to wholly bestow and transfer ownership and access to the play of a specific game. If the *Chrono Trigger* cartridge is lent to a friend, she can put the cartridge into her own SNES and begin playing *Chrono Trigger* as well. Damage to the cartridge means damage (or destruction) to the game in its play. Once someone snaps her

Chrono Trigger cartridge in half, she no longer owns *Chrono Trigger.* There seems to exist a strong link between the physical media's presence and the presence of the game.

A video game is its code. In the real world, games are not fundamentally bound to particular physical "containers". Any deck of cards can be used to play Solitaire, because Solitaire is, in its core essence, a set of rules and parameters. Similarly, any sufficiently large space can become a football field. A large group of friends can outline a grid on the ground, playact as chess pieces, and play a full game of chess without any equipment whatsoever. As these real-world games are fundamentally constructions of social convention, video games are constructions of code. Whereas any group of people can play Tag by following the rules of Tag, one cannot play *PAC-MAN* (1980) outside of its digital environment. One can play-pretend as *PAC-MAN*, and a group can play an approximation of *PAC-MAN* with sufficient knowledge of the operation of the game's components, but it is not fundamentally a game of *PAC-MAN* when executed outside of the digital context. Just as social games are engineered around the physicality and constraints of the real-world setting (the children's game Ring around the Rosie is only fun because of how its spinning and falling over interact with human physiology and the dizziness sensation that such actions cause), video games are built in a manner absolutely dependent upon their digital simulation.

As such, a video game's code (which Bogost rightly notes can be conceptualized in terms of its raw binary operands that directly command processor functions or its human-legible source code; Bogost, 2009a) functions as the instructions that construct the simulation and the actions therein. As rules are the instructions that guide social play, code (instantiated into mechanics) guides digital play. From a historical perspective, the moment at which a game's rules are formalized is the moment at which it first exists. Similarly, it may be fair to say that *PAC-MAN* did not exist until its code was finalized.

Furthermore, code preserves a sense of aura and authenticity, such that the gaming community uses different terms to describe later re-releases of games built with and without the original code base of the game in question. Typically, "remaster" and "remake" both describe later productions of older games that employ technological advancements not available at the time of the original productions to improve the aesthetics or dynamics of play. Crucially, though, a *remaster* runs the original code (even if other assets within the game are changed), while a *remake* operates from new code. Experientially, a remake may mimic the original game's play very closely, but there is still the perception that a different (though closely related) game is being played.

Code is so fundamental to a game's identity that some games in the 1980s were distributed through code as printed text. Game magazines aimed at owners of early PCs like the Commodore 64 and ZX Spectrum would print code in long form in their pages. Readers would meticulously type the code into their PCs to re-program these games from scratch. Though players often experienced problems, as even the slightest mistyped text could lead to execution failure, successful reproduction of the code in its entirety would produce what is inarguably an instance of the game being distributed. In this sense, it seems that authentic code, whether shared digitally or in long form, constitutes the essential being of a game.

Though this answer may be accurate, it is neither satisfying nor useful. If the operational code of *ELDEN RING* (2022) was printed in a massive tome, the average reader would find it neither identifiable nor particularly engaging. Certainly, the experience of playing *ELDEN RING* cannot be reduced to the execution of its code any more than the experience of listening to a song can be reproduced by studying its waveform.

A video game is the live execution of its code. Whereas a video game's code contains all of the necessary parameters for the game to operate, it is not identifiable or communicative of the experience of play outside of its execution. Even if the code is translated into a set of human-legible instructions mirroring the presentation of the rules of social games, video games are almost *definitionally* too complicated to be mentally simulated outside of the digital context, for each rule not only imposes specific affordances and limitations on gameplay but also interacts with every other rule simultaneously executed within the simulation. Social games that incorporate comparable levels of complexity, like *Dungeons & Dragons* (Gygax & Arneson, 1974) and other tabletop RPGs, tend to be played very slowly with dice rolls and hand calculations modeling each action and frequent references back to guidebooks to determine interactions between actions. Video games utilize the power of the computational machines on which they are played to perform these calculations and checks in real-time, capable of producing a more action-oriented aesthetic of play than comparably complex social or tabletop games.

Code can execute without player involvement. An observer can watch a programmed machine complete a game but never truly have the experience associated with that game as an interactive artwork. Once gameplay is recorded (whether through video capture of the on-screen events or pre-recording of a program that can execute a game's necessary commands in real-time), it transforms into another linear medium. It becomes video; it becomes performance art, but it is no longer a video game in the truest sense, for the play and interaction with a game is definitionally core to the medium. In the same way that a visually indistinguishable plastic reproduction of a meal is not *food*, a recording of gameplay is not, in itself, a video game.

Ultimately, video gaming is a reactive medium. It is designed as a question-and-answer machine: the player submits questions (inputs) to which the game replies with answers (outputs) in logical but often surprising ways. The core aesthetic experience of video games is in this surprise, just as the core aesthetic experience of the Roman Colosseum is in its scale. One can view a photograph of the Colosseum and admire surface-level aesthetic details, but the experience of standing in its center and being utterly overwhelmed by its imposing architecture is only available in its physical presence, in exposing ourselves to the building. Similarly, we are exposed to the divergent happenings within video game simulations—logical yet exciting. To observe a game from afar is not to truly engage with a game. As such, we must factor in a level of player involvement in our understanding of video games.

A video game is the live execution of code, involving a human player. Player participation is crucial to video games; I argue it is definitionally contingent upon this aspect. Unlike the previous ontological claims, though, this differs in that it does not intuitively signal a game coming into presence from absence. The acquisition of data or physical media intuitively corresponds with the arrival of a game where none was before. Similarly, the writing and execution of its code correspond with a game completing its design process and being enacted in real time on a computer, respectively. The final step is less intuitive: to consider that code execution is not fundamentally a video game until a human player initiates her participation through controller inputs. Am I to argue that a video game left idle temporarily becomes some kind of non-game until a player returns to the controls? Surely anyone would intuitively point to an empty arcade cabinet and identify, "that is a video game".

This is where I must reassert the ontological grounding of this book. If we view video games as software, we are inclined to consider their data, opcodes, source code, system manipulations, and operational presence within HDD and RAM. If we view video games as commercial products, we are inclined to consider their physical media, marketing-constructed brand identity, and intellectual property. If we view video games as an extension of social games, we are inclined to consider the rules and mechanics that structure play. This book is a narrative and artistic exploration, though. As such, the core of a video game lies at the catalyzing moment of artistic transformation: the presentation to the player of novel and directed forms of agency.

Returning to our theoretical model of art, the process of transformation that results in the artistic experience is catalyzed by an artwork as raw material, around which the observer's mind constructs meaning. The observation of a painting, for instance, initiates the process by which meaning is made in the mind of the observer. Video games are not like paintings, though. Paintings are static objects that manifest in a particular way to all observers, even if they individually take away different impressions. Video games are not even like live theatre, which changes in minor or major ways with each performance. A theatrical performance becomes a static object upon its completion. Again, everyone in the particular performance's audience may be struck with different interpretations, but they all fundamentally experienced the same artistic product. The core raw material of the video game artistic experience is the play itself. It is the experience of vicariously existing within a fictional space, making decisions, and experiencing the game's intelligently designed systems react and change around those decisions. It is the experience of exploring a designed and directed system.

So, returning to the question at hand, speaking about a video game as software, a commercial product, or a set of rules and contingencies designed and programmed to be experienced in a particular way; yes, we may designate something a video game apart from player participation. Considering video games as expressive artistic works, though, for the purpose of narrative and interpretive analysis, our definitional framework must center around enacted play. This framework even informs how we read and consider developer intent. Whereas a painter designs a painting to induce a range of reactions in her audience, a game developer sets the parameters by which the audience produces metagames within the artistic work (to which the audience *also* reacts). Both painter and game developer design around an element of uncertain audience interpretation, but the painter produces a singular statement whereas the game developer designs the *grammar* with which the player makes a statement of her own. This is not to say that players are wholly free to make any kind of statement within the systems of a video game or that the game developer is unable to impart specific meaning in the construction of a game due to the freedom of the player; rather, the artistry of game design comes from choosing the grammar that will lead the player toward certain types of statements.

AESTHETICS OF PLAY

The study of any artform benefits from identification of the form's core aesthetics. The aesthetics of an artistic object involve the experiential quality of beholding it. Beyond the description of form, how does it present as an object of beauty, or what deeper sensations does it arouse in the beholder?

> The object has certain properties (colors and shapes). On account of these properties, it is capable of arousing a certain complex of sensations and feelings. On the assumption that this resulting experience is valuable, we can say that this capacity is a kind of value: aesthetic value.
>
> *(Beardsley, 1966, p. 32)*

In fact, an aesthetic object has an effect and a value to the beholder before it is interrogated for meaning and practical purpose. That which it inspires is attributable to its aesthetic properties.

Though aesthetics are experienced pre-critically, it does not preclude us from examining aesthetics from a critical perspective. One can train oneself to "deeply" experience the sensory qualities of a work in order to derive greater meaning from it in part by understanding how it reliably acts upon our pre-critical capacities as beholders (Oliveros, 2005). Just as one does not discount the importance of the ingredients that constitute a meal, so too must we take notice of the "ingredients" of the experience of the arts. Perhaps this metaphor is apt, because sensitivity to aesthetics also leads one to greater artistic "taste". "Kant argues that an intelligent and autonomous exercise of taste is one that fathoms internal movements excited in the subject, especially in connection with the sublime" (Kirkpatrick, 2011, p. 28).

Beyond being mere ingredients, though, aesthetics can also be ends unto themselves—the reasons why people engage with particular artworks. For that reason, consider the exploration of aesthetics below to constitute both takeaways of experiences with games as artistic artifacts *and* constructive elements that compose a greater (aesthetic) experience, holistically.

As C. Thi Nguyen (2020) identifies, discussion of the aesthetics of video games typically reduces games to formal components for which we already have aesthetic categories to understand. We are comfortable discussing the aesthetic qualities of a game's music, visuals, or embedded narrative, but we do not yet have formalized methods and language for examining the aesthetics of striving and play (p. 12). It is *these* qualities that good game design aims to evoke, so to become literate game players, we must recognize the aesthetics of gameplay in order to discern how design pushes toward those ends.

I deviate from some categorizations of aesthetic qualities by not exclusively focusing on the elements that players find *beautiful* (a quality some hold as definitional to aesthetic theory) but also on what we find *repellant, discordant,* or *challenging,* for these are experiences that occur in much the same way as the experience of beauty, and they can be used to similarly meaningful ends in aesthetic practice.

In the sections below, I have privileged one examination of aesthetics that has compiled a very useful list. In their MDA model (see Chapter 5), Hunicke et al. (2004) compile a collection of nine aesthetics of gameplay. In addition to their nine, I have myself identified and pulled from other sources five additional aesthetics that I find to be useful descriptors of experience. I break the aesthetics into two categories: *pre-reflective aesthetics* (the aesthetics that occur before and separate from conscious thought) and *critical aesthetics* (the aesthetics involved in conscious thought about the experience).

Pre-Reflective Aesthetics

Sensation. The aesthetic of sensation involves two elements of sensory pleasure: the sensory experience of the player viewing the screen, hearing the audio, and feeling the haptics of the game, and the *vicariosensory* experience of the avatar experienced through projective embodiment (see Chapter 4). The former involves all of the sense pleasures of games as visual and aural artifacts: art style, animation, lights and colors, music, sound effects, voices, controller vibration, and the resting pleasure of feeling the texture of the controller in hand.

The vicariosensory aspect is an extension of what film theorists know as "visual touch". Summarizing the etymological study on the subject by Vivian Sobchack (2004, pp. 54–56); Soviet filmmaker and theorist Sergei Eisenstein was interested in the "synchronization of the senses", a cinematic synesthesia. The concept was further explored with the Payne Studies (Charters, 1933), examining the "galvanic responses" evoked by cinematic experiences. Walter Benjamin describes filmgoers' "mimetic faculty"—embodied perception of cinematic images (Benjamin, 1935/1968). Siegfried Kracauer stressed the ability to sensually stimulate its audience as "corporeal-material being" (Hansen, 1993, p. 458). Linda Williams investigates "body genres" (Williams, 1991). Jonathan Crary identifies the "carnal density" of film viewership (Crary, 1992). Steven Shaviro writes *The Cinematic Body* on the subject of the viscerality of cinema (Shaviro, 1993). Laura U. Marks studies the "haptic visuality" that connects the audience to the "skin of the film" (Marks, 1999; 2002). Elena del Río advanced the concept of embodied viewing, breaking the "rigid boundary demarcations of externality and internality" (del Río, 1996; 2000). And, of course, in the chapter from which this past research is summarized, Sobchack draws connections between the textual and textural in film, speaking of cinematic audiences as "cinesthetic subjects" engaging in "transmodal cooperation and translation within and across the sensorium" (Sobchack, 2004).

Video games push this particular aesthetic further, due to the projective perspective that the player takes during play. Through the instrumental connection that the player has with the avatar, as a locus and focus of manipulative capacity within the game world, the player cognitively incorporates the avatar into their sensory model of the world (which extends into the virtual space). Thus, particular actions, textures, and materials within the virtual space can appear sensually pleasing or abrasive. Greater exploration of this topic is given in Chapter 4.

Vertigo. Related to the first category is my own addition. Vertigo describes the sensation of proprioceptive peril or disorientation. Because of the projective quality of embodied avatar play, the player can experience a version of the sense of falling, being at a great height (see *Grow Home* [2015]), or being in a confined space. These uncomfortable feelings form an aesthetic quality of their own, and not always an unpleasant one—they also contribute to the sense of grandiose scale, as observed in many VR games (such as *A Fisherman's Tale* [2019]) and even non-VR games (like *Shadow of the Colossus* [2005] and *Manifold Garden* [2019]).

Presence. Another of my additions to the list, presence describes the sense of *being* in a virtual space. As Peter Bayliss eloquently describes it, "the sense of experiencing mediated space as unmediated" (Bayliss, 2007). Embodied presence within video games is also sometimes called *telepresence*, a term that originally referred to remote operation of technological devices that impart a sense of vicarious instrumental presence, such as Earthbound scientists using remote tools to work on satellites in orbit (McMahan, 2003, p. 72).

We might also consider not only presence within the "physical" (virtual) space that games represent but also the "social space" that multiplayer games evoke. The sense of being "with" a friend even though interactions are mediated through avatar representatives. Ruth Aylett (1999) researched the sense of "social presence" that can emerge as a part of cooperative and competitive play.

Challenge. The aesthetic of challenge is evoked by facing and overcoming the objectives that the game sets out for the player. The pleasure of facing off against obstacles. This contributes to the sense of *flow* (see Chapter 7).

Progress. Another of my additions to the list, *progress* is the aesthetic pleasure of making incremental advances toward a goal. Separate even from the aesthetic associated with victory, incremental, sustained progress is a reward in and of itself. It valorizes patience. This is one of the appeals of *grinding* in RPGs (performing repetitive, trivial tasks in order to receive incremental, long-term efficiencies; for example, engaging in dozens of easy battles in order to level up the avatar). As Naomi Clark notes, grinding, though typically pejorative as a term, can be a pleasurable exercise of players' "patience, efficiency, and optimization" (Anthropy & Clark, 2014, p. 147).

Ontological upset. This is a term that I use to describe the moment of horror—the moment our gut turns—when thrown from our immersion within a game by a glitch or other sudden reminder of the unreality of the virtual space:

> In media accidents like these, the void involves the unknown – that which cannot be described or planned for. These empty spaces of non-understanding trigger a *horror vacui*: a fear of voids to which nothing else can be compared and that is beyond all possibilities of calculation, measurement or imitation.
>
> *(Menkman, 2011, p. 30; referencing the horror vacui that was named by Kluitenberg, 2008)*

Expression. Playing a game "to make choices that teach you something new about yourself or to explore new parts of your character, preferences, or personality" (Leone, n.d.). Pre-reflective expression is about the joy of interacting with reactive systems and feeling free to inscribe one's personal touches within moment-to-moment play. Beyond the pleasures of presence and avatar control, there is a separate pleasure that arises from feeling as though the avatar behaves uniquely because *I* am in control—I am performing in a manner no one else would. I see myself reflected in the actions on-screen. Expressivity is the primary focus of Chapter 12, and this form of expression is what that chapter terms *micro-expressivity*.

Compulsion. Another of my additions to this list, compulsion is not necessarily a *positive* aesthetic trait, but it does have an aesthetic effect. It is the experience of being *driven* to play or play in a certain way, bordering upon addictive behavior. Particularly in instances of play regularity, there is an aesthetic quality to performing a repetitive task day after day. It is not quite a *pleasure*, but it satisfies an itch. Many games are built to be *compulsive*, as detailed thoroughly in the seminal *Addiction by Design: Machine Gambling in Las Vegas* (Schüll, 2012).

Submission. This is the aesthetic of returning to a comfortable and familiar hobby as a way of relaxing. It is a pastime of choice that allows players to de-stress.

Critical Aesthetics

Progress. A category shared with the pre-reflective set, there is a reflective aspect to progress as well. This is a pride in how far the player has come. A reflection on the journey that has been undertaken. This can include narrative or statistical progress in-game, but it also reflects the player's own sense of improvement of skill.

Fantasy. The pleasure of role-playing; of becoming someone else within a fantasy world. This is included in what I call the *mimetic perspective* in Chapter 6.

Narrative. The pleasure of partaking in a well-told story. One can enjoy the aesthetic of narrative from both an embodied (role-playing) perspective or as a detached observer, simply interested in the events of the game's fiction.

Fellowship. Interfacing with other players is one of the key aesthetics of multiplayer gaming. Engaging in jolly cooperation or friendly competition can all contribute to the sense of fellowship, as can asynchronous or "parallel play", partaking in a broader *community* of play, even if the player does not, herself, directly interface with others in-game.

Competition. The urge to surpass and dominate those with whom the player competes. This does not necessarily have to be other players—the player is "in competition" (or conflict, more accurately) with the design of a single-player game's challenges (and, by proxy, the game's developers). Games give an opportunity for safe competition and conflict, as Chris Crawford notes, eliminating the risks of danger and harm inherent in engagement with competition and conflict elsewhere in life (Crawford, 1982, p. 13).

Discovery. The sense of discovery can involve uncovering surprising secrets in the diegetic world of the game or being driven to discover what comes next in the game's story. As explorable simulations, games offer a tremendous amount of satisfaction for the curious. For those who feel that they have exhausted all that a game has to see, additional discoveries might be made within the game as a technological object through hacking, modding, glitching the play space, or further dissecting the code (see Chapter 13).

Expression. Critical expression involves the reflective pleasure of noticing the ways in which the player's individual choices and manner of play affected the direction of the journey. Expressivity is the focus of Chapter 12, and this form of expression is what that chapter terms *macro-expressivity*.

KEY TERMS

Throughout this book, I will try to use language that does not exclude those who are not familiar with the culture surrounding video games. A few pieces of common jargon will prove to be very useful, though, so I will define those necessary terms here and trust that this can be used as a reference.

Since the terms are colloquial amongst a subculture, their definitions are subject to morph and change over time, so perhaps this section will date the book. This also serves as a reference for how I use these terms *in this particular moment in time*.

The terms below are presented alphabetically. Genre and subgenre definitions will be presented in the next section.

- **2D/3D**: Two-dimensional and three-dimensional games represent different methods by which game worlds are simulated or presented. A "2D" game is that which allows movement on two axes (or to a very limited degree on a third axis, such as the minimal in-and-out-of-the-screen movement in *Streets of Rage* [1991]) and is typically presented from a side view (such as *Super Mario Bros.* [1985]) or overhead (such as *Advance Wars* [2001]), though some 2D games are purely abstract and do not posit a diegesis (such as *Tetris* [1985]). A "3D" game allows or presents movement along three axes (X, Y, Z). It either presents as an explorable, 3D space (such as in *Super Mario 64* [1996]) or moves automatically through spaces, making use of all axes of motion (such as *Pokémon Snap* [1999]). 2D games are often made with flat, painting-like *sprites*, and 3D games are often made with 3D polygonal assets, but the opposite can also be true, and the presence of sprites or polygons is not enough to classify a game as 2D or 3D. For example, *Donkey Kong Country Returns* (2010) features fully 3D characters and environments, but action is constrained to a typical side-scrolling view of its linear spaces. It is a 2D game. Conversely, *Out Run* (1986) is composed of 2D sprites moving in such a manner that presents an illusion of 3D play. Sometimes 2D and 3D can be combined in complicated arrangements, such as in *Marvel vs. Capcom 2: New Age of Heroes* (2000), in which the characters are 2D *sprites* integrated into 3D environments presented in a 2D perspective.
  - *Note*: Within the gaming hobby, there are other ways in which "2D" and "3D" are used. In the context of VR, "3D" refers to the immersive worlds experienceable through the visor display, while "2D" refers to any game played on-screen, outside of VR, so you could say, "you can play a 2D version of *Walkabout Mini Golf* (2020) on smartphone". Similarly, sometimes "3D" refers to games that feature actual three-dimensional technology, such as those played on Nintendo's Virtual Boy or 3DS devices. You could say, "you can play *Rhythm Heaven Megamix* (2015) in 3D or in 2D if you turn off the 3D feature". For the purpose of this book, "2D" and "3D" will only refer to the perspective by which gameplay is presented.
- **Achievement**: Unless otherwise contextualized, "achievements" refer to rewards for in-game tasks that are presented extradiegetically—typically at the layer of the computer's operating system. Video game consoles (such as Xbox and PlayStation) have achievement systems (Achievements and Trophies, respectively) in their native user interfaces that track and accumulate the achievement of specialized challenges across games, such that long-time players can reference their cumulative score or trophy list to represent their achievements across all games played within that ecosystem.

- **Analog**: Typically used in the context of controllers. Contrasted to *digital controls.* Refers to controls or inputs that are continuous rather than discrete or binary. For example, pressure-sensitive triggers, articulated thumbsticks, and motion controls.

- **AR**: Abbreviation of *alternate reality.* Like *VR*, AR presents an "immersive" view of virtual assets, but typically utilizing a device's camera, such that it looks like elements of the virtual are embedded into the player's actual surroundings (when viewed through the screen of the device hosting the AR experience). Smartphones and tablets are often used like "windows" through which virtual elements can be viewed, though a multitude of devices can create AR experiences, like Meta Quest 3 VR headsets, Nintendo 3DS handhelds, and Xbox Kinect sensors. AR can be used in interactive games (such as *Face Raiders* [2011] and *Pokémon GO* [2016]) or in non-interactive contexts (such as some concert experiences in which audiences can see AR animations play on and around the stage when they look through their phone's camera).

- **Avatar**: A general term for a controllable entity within a game. Specifically, the avatar is contextualized as being *within* and *exposed to* the simulated game world (as opposed to a cursor or pointer, which similarly directs attention and intention but does not interact with the simulated physicality or topology of the game world). The avatar is a primary focus of Chapter 4.

- **Button**: Refers to a feature of an input device that is depressed to actuate and is not better described as a *trigger* or *pedal*, based on its shape or usage. Almost always a *digital* control (a control with binary, discrete states), though *analog* buttons (with continuous or pressure-sensitive states) exist, such as on the PlayStation 2 and PlayStation 3 controllers. *Types of buttons*:
  - **Face button**: The two to six (usually four) buttons on the right-hand face of a handheld game console controller. Typically labeled with letters (A, B, X, and Y) or symbols (cross, circle, square, triangle). Sometimes distinguishable by color (Xbox 360 controllers) or shape (GameCube controllers). Face buttons are typically used for primary in-game actions, so system-level buttons (such as Start, Select, Guide, Menu, Share, etc.) are not called "face buttons".
  - **Interface button**: Small buttons that reside on the face of the controller but typically serve purposes peripheral to gameplay, either pausing, navigating interfaces, or calling functions of the computer's user interface (such as returning to the operating system or taking a screenshot). They are contrasted to *face buttons*, which are the primary methods of interaction. These buttons include varying combinations of Start, Select, Guide, Menu, Share, and more.
  - **Shoulder button/bumper**: Long, roughly rectangular buttons positioned on top of game console controllers, typically activated by the pointer fingers rather than the thumbs. Typically placed above *triggers.* Almost always named for the side of the controller on which they reside (L1/R1, LB/RB, and L/R).

- **Computer**: Used in this book to not only refer to *personal computers* but to also refer to all systems on which video games are played.

- **Console**: In gaming lexicon, "console" is typically contrasted to "computer" to represent specialized game systems that are plugged into a television for the express or primary purpose of gaming rather than personal computing. For the purpose of this book, the distinction is rarely needed, so all systems that play video games will be classified under the umbrella term "computers".

- **Controller**: A handheld input device that translates player impulses via physical manipulation of buttons, triggers, sticks, etc. into digital signals interpretable by the game software. Colloquially, it is usually used to describe the types of controllers built to operate game consoles (Xbox, PlayStation, etc.), but this book will use the term generally to include any game input device (keyboard, mouse, specialty controllers such as

Guitar Hero (2005) guitars, etc.). Also sometimes called a *gamepad* or *joypad*. *Related specialized terminology*: see button, d-pad, motion control, thumbstick, and touchscreen.

- **D-pad**: An abbreviation of *directional pad*. The often cross-shaped input on the left-hand side of a game controller into which the player can input cardinal directions, typically for avatar movement or menu navigation. The D-pad is typically a *digital* control (inputs are on/off binaries and discrete), as opposed to *thumbsticks*, which are continuous and sensitive to multiple degrees of manipulation in any direction.
- **Digital**: In the context of "digital games" or similar phrases, "digital" simply means "computer-enacted". In the context in which it is contrasted against *analog*, though, digital refers to something discrete or binary, as opposed to continuous. For example, while the sensitive, continuous degrees of input are possible with a controller's *analog* thumbstick, most controllers' buttons are *digital controls*: on/off switches that are either depressed or released with no degrees in between these states.
- **Free-to-play/F2P**: This categorization is typically applied to games that can be played for free (without purchase) but contain purchasable elements within them. These purchases can include unlocking more of the experience (perhaps World 1 is available at no cost within the free-to-play software, but Worlds 2–7 require a one-time "full unlock" purchase, such that the free-to-play portion behaves like a demo) or infinitely purchasable consumables/microtransactions. For example, the third-person shooter *Fortnite* (2017) is free-to-play and features within it purchasable "skins" (costumes) for avatars, items, weapons, in-game currencies, and a "battle pass" that acts as a seasonal reward structure for frequent players. Games that can be obtained at no cost but *do not* feature any in-game purchases are most often just called *free* rather than *free-to-play*. As such, *free-to-play* and *F2P* terminology are primarily used derisively in corners of the player community to describe games that are particularly predatory in their microtransactional structure.
- **NPC**: An acronym for *non-playable character* or *non-player character*. This refers to any artificial being within a game simulation that presents as intelligent (performs motivated action). In colloquial usage, it typically refers to friendly or neutral members of the game world rather than enemies, but it is more accurate to call enemies a sub-division of NPCs.
- **Remake/Remaster/Port**: Remake, remaster, and port describe three categories of subsequent versions of video games on platforms other than that on which they originally released.
  - A *port* describes a version of a game developed for a platform other than the one(s) on which it originally launched that does not undergo *significant* technological rework. For example, the game *BioShock* was released on Xbox 360 and PC in 2007, and it was *ported* to PlayStation 3 in 2008. Though the PS3 version required developer work to optimize it for the new system, it is roughly technologically equivalent and is generally considered to be an equivalent version of the game. Games that require full rebuilds when being made for other systems, such as *Tony Hawk's Pro Skater* on PlayStation (1999) and Game Boy Color (2000), are typically considered *separate* (but related) games.
  - A *remaster* describes a later release of a game in which significant work has gone into modernizing the technology or adding quality-of-life features, aided by advances in technology or the evolution of design best practices. Crucially, a remaster executes a large proportion of the *same code* in the *same engine* of the original release, such that a remaster is typically considered to be "the same game" as the original release (as most of the executed code is the same) but may look or run better than it originally did. For example, a remastered version of *BioShock* was released on PlayStation 4, Xbox One, and PC in 2007. The game plays almost exactly like the original release but with a better frame rate, clearer visuals, and new technology powering its simulation of liquid physics.

    - A *remake* entails a *from-the-ground-up* reproduction of a game (with varying levels of fidelity). Crucially, while a remaster runs most of the *same code* in the *same engine*, a remake is *rebuilt entirely* and most often adopts a *different engine*. Some remakes are radically different from the original game upon which they are based, such as *FINAL FANTASY VII REMAKE* (2020), which features a heavily rewritten story and significantly different gameplay than the 1997 original, while other remakes aim to recreate an experience as close to the original as possible, such as the 2018 remake of *Katamari Damacy* (2004), which aims for high fidelity to the 2004 original while, under the hood, being rebuilt in the Unity engine instead of the custom engine of the original.
- **Score**: Used to describe the accumulative number given to in-game actions as an evaluative measure, such that skillful play results in a "high score". Beyond occasional bonuses at particular intervals (an extra life every 1,000 points, for example), score is generally a measure separate from diegetic, consequential feedback. As such, skillful players can challenge themselves to achieve high scores in games that they have mastered, while less skillful players can usually ignore the score system without consequence.
    - *Note*: "Score" is sometimes also used, in the game community, to describe the musical accompaniment of a game's soundtrack. It is not used in this way in this book. Score will always refer to the evaluative metric.
- **Sprite**: A sprite is a two-dimensional image that represents an entity within a scene. Games presented in a 2D format featuring 2D assets typically have "background layers" which are relatively static (though there may be multiple background layers to introduce an effect of parallax perspective-based movement) and *sprites*, which can be moved around in those scenes. Early video game consoles had limits on how many sprites could be on-screen at one time, so developers had to be clever about how they presented the illusion of numerous or especially large entities. Sprites can also be integrated into 3D spaces, such as in *Tinykin* (2022), though static 2D objects in 3D spaces tend to be called *billboards* instead. Unlike polygons, which can be repositioned and reshaped in real-time by the computer, sprites are all pre-drawn, like the cells of a hand-animated cartoon. Characters will typically have a limited set of poses that can combine into animations.
- **Thumbstick**: A component of many types of video game controllers. Like the *joystick* of earlier video games, the smaller, thumb-operated *thumbstick* offers 360-degree inputs with varying degrees of sensitivity. Modern game controllers typically include two thumbsticks (one for each thumb), with the left thumbstick typically controlling avatar movement and the right typically controlling camera perspective (in 3D games).
- **Trigger**: A type of button on a game controller that usually sits on top/back of the controller below the shoulder buttons. Manipulated with the player's pointer finger, they typically have a concave shape, like the trigger of a gun (for which they are named). They are typically *analog* controls, such that they can be lightly squeezed or more fully depressed, most useful in racing games in which they often serve like the gas and brake pedals of a car. On modern controllers, they are typically labeled RT/LT, R2/L2, or ZR/ZL.
- **VR**: An abbreviation for *virtual reality*. Used to describe *all* immersive digital simulations in early games studies writing and popular reporting, it now *only* applies to helmet/visor-based immersive displays that position one screen in front of each eye (refracted through lenses) to simulate the sense of being within a virtual space. In this book, "VR" will be used exclusively to describe this kind of over-the-eyes display technology, such as the Oculus Rift, Meta Quest, Apple Vision Pro, and PlayStation VR headsets. See *AR* for a similar but distinct technology.

GENRE

Throughout the book, I reference a very large number of games. I often include a small amount of contextual information in-line with the mention, and I include a standardized set of metadata in the book's ludography (see the next section). For the sake of efficiency, though, I most often use genre and subgenre names instead of laboriously describing the gameplay conventions of every game I mention. For that reason, I list here the genres that I will name throughout the book and a description of how each is distinguished and examples of games that fit into each category. Within each genre group, I also list and define subgenres.

Genre classifications are not standardized, though there are some efforts to work toward standardized classifications (Lee et al., 2013; 2014; Clarke et al., 2015; Jett et al., 2016). What I list below is only the *division of genres as I personally group them.* I am certain that others will disagree with my definitions and some game attributions because each person's genre judgments are personal reflections of how *they* read and associate particular conventions of design. I do not claim that my organizational system is any more *correct* or *valid* than any other's, nor do I put it forward as a model upon which others should be built within the games studies literature—I defer to the rigor of study performed by actual information science experts. This collection of genres *only* serves to provide reference and transparency for how *I* use genre classifications in this book, based on my experience and opinions.

Genre definition is admittedly messy. Classifications draw from social conventions, formulas of design, marketing descriptors, academic recognition... Genres also evolve and shift over time, encompassing both the literal tropes of stories told within them and the structural conventions of those tellings. Jim Kitses (1970) calls genre "a varied and flexible structure, a thematically fertile and ambiguous world of historical material shot through with archetypal elements which are themselves ever in flux" (p. 19).

Kitses studied the Western genre of film, which has, itself, undergone significant transformations in meaning over the decades. Cinematic stories of sheriffs, cowboys, and outlaws shared material conditions of production, and their success invited others to create similar films (aided by the availability of sets, appropriate locations, procedures for filming Western-appropriate activities, availability of trained horses...). Whether by choice or deterministically as a product of those material conditions, conventions of theme, tone, philosophy, and "stimmung" (Sinnerbrink, 2012) set audience expectations for the types of stories that they could expect to see in Western movies. Shifts in the economics of filmmaking made the Western an easy genre to export; to make on the cheap in Italy, and elements of that shift embedded into the "language" of the genre (or more literally the lack of; "Spaghetti Westerns", as they became known, developed a trend of stoic quietness that is now definitive of the genre, doubtlessly prompted by the large proportion of non-English speakers in the Italian casts and crews. Finally, the *mechanics* of the Western superseded their material preconditions, such that works as diverse as *Firefly* (Wheadon & Minear, 2002), *Yojimbo* (Kurosawa, 1961), *No Country for Old Men* (Coen & Coen, 2007), and *Tampopo* (Itami, 1985) are recognizable for employing Western plot structures and thematic conventions, even removed from the practical trappings of horses and six-shooters.

In fact, genre boundaries are in perpetual flux. Steve Neale (1990) writes:

> the process-like nature of genres manifests itself as an interaction between three levels: the level of expectation, the level of the generic corpus, and the level of the 'rules' or 'norms' that govern both. [...] the elements and conventions of a genre are always in play rather than being, simply re-played; and any generic corpus is always being expanded.
>
> *(p. 56)*

As such, the definition of genre at any moment is a reflection of a moment in time rather than something ontologically fundamental about classified works.

That said, genre is still important to consider. Rick Altman (1998) outlines four purposes genre classification holds:

- "genre as *blueprint*, as a formula that precedes, programmes and patterns industry production" (p. 14), referring to the efficiencies of production that come from developing within formulas with which artists have experience (or access to experience) and resources.
- "genre as *structure*, as the formal framework on which individual [works] are founded" (p. 14),

referring to plotting efficiencies and conventional schemas of reference.

- "genre as *label*, as the name of a category central to the decisions and communications of distributors and exhibitors" (p. 14), referring to efficiencies of marketing and informational cues to prompt a primed audience's attention without explaining each work from scratch.

- "genre as *contract*, as the viewing position required by each genre film of its audience" (p. 14), referring to the implicit experiential priming for which audiences prepare when entering a film in an understood genre space. It models for the beholder *how* to perceive and relate with a work and cues particular avenues of meaning-making.

To that list, I would add genre as a *statement of lineage and history*, implicitly identifying the historical works that give it context and engaging in conversation with its contemporaries. Additionally, genre introduces the notion of an approximately understood *archetypal mean* against which an individual work can deviate. Any narrative or artistic work makes meaning not only from that which is depicted but also from its negative space as well; what it is not. To consider a film or a game only for what it is—its positive attributes—is to miss important context. One must also consider the specters of expectations it left tactfully unfulfilled: its generic tensions and restraint. *The Babadook* (Kent, 2014) impresses not only as a standalone story but also for the ways in which it exists in tension with and subverts particular tropes of Horror filmmaking. In the video game space, *Gone Home* (2013) became renowned and even controversial at the time of its release for how its design conventions inferred a type of experience that its mechanics actively rejected. This type of context is additive to the meaning that can be made from artworks.

Types of Genres

As genres have many sources of inception, there are also many *types* of genres that develop around different aspects of convention. Most tend to originate as *mechanical* or *aesthetic* genres. *Mechanical* genres are based on the active "mechanics" of a story. For instance, *When Harry Met Sally...* (Reiner, 1989) is a Romance movie (or romcom: romantic comedy) because the story is galvanized by two people falling in love. Romance serves as the central "mechanic" of the story. This can be opposed to the Western genre, which inherited mechanical and structural conventions but was recognized and named originally for its aesthetic wrapper: being set in the Old West.

In video games, mechanical genres describe more than just story mechanics; video games are interactive systems, so the mechanics at their core are interactive, systemic mechanics of software operation. Mechanical genres in video games describe what the player *does*, or rather, how the player *can interact* with a particular type of system. Many video game genres are named after verbs: Shooter, Platformer, Racing, Fighting... Due to their active nature, these are the details for which experiential cueing is paramount.

Video games do possess some aesthetic genres, though. The Horror genre, for instance, does not identify the necessary player action (besides "be scared", I suppose) but instead identifies an audience and design philosophy. Since games are fundamentally interactive, though, calling a game purely by an aesthetic genre is usually unsatisfactory—the player still does not know what is expected from her within the game. As such, games within the Horror genre tend to either explicitly or implicitly fit within mechanical genres as well. For example, *Resident Evil* (1996) is Horror *and* a Third-Person Shooter. *Doki Doki Literature Club!* (2017) is Horror *and* a Visual Novel. *Little Nightmares* (2017) is Horror *and* a 2D Platformer. In the case of Horror (or other aesthetic categories like Erotic Games), the genre label signals an intended emotional experience and prepares players for the type of material that they will encounter rather than the methods by which they encounter it.

Video games have a third category of genre that is not *truly* aesthetic but is more contextually grounded. It identifies a lineage of design and games with which it is in conversation. It is heavily convention-oriented, such that classifications may *only* be useful to those with contextual knowledge of those design conventions. For instance, the Adventure genre is not named because its characters always *go on adventures*; it is named for the progenitor of a particular modality of design: *Colossal Cave Adventure* (1976), a text-based game that involves the exploration of the winding passages of Mammoth Cave in Kentucky. As the genre iterated—augmenting its text querying approach with graphics, ultimately foregoing text entry and sentence construction altogether in favor of purely graphical environmental interactions that still maintained environmental exploration and semantically structured interactions with that environment—it maintained its conventional name as a (perhaps not *knowing* but *vestigial*) tip of the cap back to the genre's point of origin. As such, games as diverse as *Phoenix Wright: Ace Attorney* (2001) and *Everybody's Gone to the Rapture* (2015) can be considered Adventure games not because they tell particularly *adventurous* stories but because they sit at the distal end of a long line of evolution that began with *Colossal Cave Adventure.*

This category of contextual genre is particularly common as new genres form. When a game does something novel, it is difficult to foresee the shape of what the games in its lineage will ultimately entail; thus, following iterations are most often related back to a design convention's point of origin or point of popularization as the only known reference point. Even once the genre develops further, these colloquial, referential names often persist, frequently to the frustration of particular members of the community who fear that tying a genre of games to a single origin point limits what developers can do in that space.

Such genres (and subgenres) include Metroidvanias (which genre purists prefer calling Exploration Platformers or Search Action), games that follow in the tradition of *Super Metroid* (1994) and *Castlevania: Symphony of the Night* (1997), resulting in a clumsy portmanteau (of titles that Rivera [2019] humorously points out are *also* portmanteaus of "metro"/"android" and "castle"/"Transylvania", respectively). DOOM Clones was the colloquial name for what we now know as FPSs, referencing not the originator but the popularizer of the mechanics, *DOOM* (1993). There is a trend of giving genres (and conventions) names like Rogue-like (named for *Rogue* [1980]) and Souls-like (named for *Demon's Souls* [2009] and *Dark Souls* [2011]), which serve the purpose of identifying design trends on which the game iterates and positioning themselves for audiences invested in the development of a particular community or philosophy of design.

I sparingly use the contextual genre Arcade not to trace a lineage to any particular game but to acknowledge a design trajectory with its origin in a set of material and commercial conditions: games designed for video arcade settings. Design for this setting was constrained by commercial considerations (these publicly exhibited games cost money per play, so the games were designed around single-session play, either through short but emergent linear structure or infinitely replayable games without formal conclusions, designed to draw additional coins from their players with frequent failures and tantalizing possibilities of victory being just one more push away) and material conditions (arcade cabinets were in competitively crowded spaces, so they incentivized design that was flashy, attention-grabbing, and immediately easy to understand for passersby). I use the descriptor to identify games with similarity to the types of experiences that resulted from the conventions developed in response to the above preconditions: games in which action takes place on a single screen, games with abstract aesthetics but intuitive action, or games that feature a collection of or rapidly switch between minigames of different forms.

There are some contextual labels that are frequently used by the gaming community in a manner like genres, but I feel that they fall short of the descriptive purposes of genres. These labels typically reflect the mode or means of production or audience for which a game is intended. Some games are labeled "Casual" or "Hardcore" to signal that they may appeal to those not deeply immersed in the hobby or those who take the hobby more "seriously", respectively. I do not like these labels, because they have an air of unbecoming determinism that feels more limiting than categorically helpful. Hidden Object Games and certain types of puzzle games, such as Tile Matching (or Match Three), games are frequently labeled "Casual" not because they possess any formal difference from "non-Casual" games but because they *tend to* be played by people the community deems "non-standard" in some way. In these ways, it acts as a form of gatekeeping, evidenced by its frequently derisive use ("You only play Casual games, you're not a real gamer"). While it can be useful to identify a game's target audience and its model for monetization, progress, intended length of play session, etc. It is more useful to examine these trends separate from a totalizing categorization like "Casual" that pulls into it details that are unhelpful or destructive to forming a more literate and well-rounded understanding of a tradition of design and play.

Similarly, it can be useful to identify the scale and resources of particular games, but treating labels like "Indie" (games made by small teams separate from the resources of an established, large-scale commercial company) or "AAA" (games made within "the industry" by large, well-resourced studios with access to cutting-edge technologies and employee counts in the hundreds or thousands) like *genres* creates unhelpful expectations. Because Indie games are typically made for a lower cost than AAA games, certain design and aesthetic conventions are common (heavy stylization rather than photorealistic graphics, text dialogue instead of professional voice acting, manageable length instead of sprawling, epic structures). While it is useful to recognize these contextual details, drawing firm divisions between the categories is messy. Games built by small teams can produce games that feel cutting edge, and enormous studios can choose to produce smaller, simpler games that might otherwise conventionally have more in common with trends in the Indie space, despite emerging from within the commercial industry, such as *Katamari Damacy* (2004) and *Valiant Hearts: The Great War* (2014). While there is *useful* information that can come from recognizing the scale and funding of a production (such as the singularity or dilution of vision as team size increases), it is more useful to draw these categories at levels higher than genre.

Ultimately, game genres tend to evolve naturally as conventions develop in the production, consumption, or contextualization of games. As such, genres reflect not only aspects of their formal design but also their use and acceptance within pockets of the gaming community. They also inform design, such that developers create games with certain assumptions in place, operating against known expectations from players. Genre labels identify *patterns* of design. Like artistic movements, they can be useful in identifying sources of shared inspiration and conversation rather than fundamental differences.

Genre Index

In the section below, I identify and define 17 primary genres. Within each, I list and define subgenres that I will name throughout the book. Examples are provided at each level. Rather than reading this section from start to finish, I recommend instead bookmarking it and referring back to it when you encounter a genre or subgenre label of which you are not familiar when reading the book. This is intended as a reference section for how *I* (and I alone) classify games and is not intended as an argument that this book is written to advance.

- **Action**: Games that present players with challenges of real-time control, testing reflexes or improvisational play. Action is regarded as an umbrella genre into which *all* real-time genres (shooters, rhythm, racing...) fit by some classifications, but I prefer to elevate each of those contained genres to the same primary level due to the hierarchy of subgenres within them, instead using "action" only to refer to a subset of games that are not better categorized elsewhere. "Action" as a descriptor is nonspecific, so the genre titles typically grouped under "action" better stand on their own.
    - **Examples**: *Shadow of the Colossus, Batman: Arkham Asylum, Marvel's Spider-Man 2, Gunpoint*
- *Sandbox*: Action games that allow loosely structured interactions with typically large, open worlds in a manner that produces highly emergent results and highly expressive play.
    - **Examples**: *Grand Theft Auto V, Sleeping Dogs, Just Cause 2, Saints Row: The Third, Red Dead Redemption 2*
- *Stealth*: Games that require sneaking or blending into hostile areas without being discovered.
    - **Examples**: *HITMAN, Mark of the Ninja, Thief: The Dark Project, Metal Gear Solid, Tom Clancy's Splinter Cell*
- *Survival*: Games that require survival on scarce, scavenged resources, typically on large, procedurally-generated maps. Some feature zombies or other hostile forces, while others simply focus the challenge on realistic nature survival.
    - **Examples**: *Rust, Grounded, Subnautica, Valheim, ARK: Survival Evolved, State of Decay 2*

- **Adventure**: Games in which the primary focus involves involvement in an interactive fiction, typically through simple interactions, puzzle-solving, or game world exploration. Less systems-based than other genres, they tend to have fixed, puzzle-like solutions to challenges put forward or may not feature puzzles at all, instead allowing players to simply explore an immersive world.
  - **Examples**: *Outer Wilds, To the Moon, INDIKA, Spiritfarer, Hypnagogia 無限の夢 Boundless Dreams.*
  - *Cinematic adventure*: A descendant of the point-and-click adventure that de-emphasizes puzzle-solving for consequential dialogue- and story-branch choices not associated with "challenge" as much as narrative agency. Typically presents in a film-like manner with fully voice-acted characters and more limited interactivity than other genres.
    - **Examples**: *The Walking Dead, Life Is Strange, Detroit: Become Human, Dragon's Lair, IMMORTALITY.*
  - *Dating sim*: Games that simulate romantic relationships. Typically involving a sense of time management and a balance between spending time with a romantic interest and bettering oneself to be a more attractive potential partner. Some involve chaste Romance while others feature explicit erotic material.
    - **Examples**: *Tokimeki Memorial, Dream Daddy: A Dad Dating Simulator, Monster Prom, HuniePop, LovePlus, Hatoful Boyfriend.*
  - *Exploration adventure/walking simulator*: Games that involve the exploration of environments, sometimes with light puzzle-solving, often without. These games can be audio-visual experiences, or they can tell a story prompted forward by movement or simple environmental investigation/interactions alone. "Walking simulator" originated as a derisive term for the minimal "gameplay" that the genre presented, but it was quickly adopted by the community of creators and fans of the genre and is now used quite affectionately.
    - **Examples**: *Everybody's Gone to the Rapture, Gone Home, Dear Esther, The Stanley Parable, The Norwood Suite.*
  - *Point-and-click adventure*: Originating on PCs, these games typically feature a mouse cursor (or touchscreen interface) that directs the avatar's attention to areas of interest within the environment rather than the player assuming direct control over the avatar. These games, typically narrative-heavy and often humorous, typically involve picking up items from environments and using them to solve puzzles. This subgenre is in the lineage of the text adventure, and early point-and-click adventures similarly structure their challenges around sentence construction, with verbs being literalized and acted out by an on-screen protagonist. Later point-and-click games do away with the explicit sentence construction but retain a similar logic in their design.
    - **Examples**: *The Secret of Monkey Island, King's Quest, Kentucky Route Zero, Botanicula, Later Alligator.*
  - *Text adventure*: Games that feature *only* or *primarily* text, in which players' inputs are entered via text entry (processed by a verb-noun parser or natural language processor). Modern text adventures are often called interactive fiction games.
    - **Examples**: *Colossal Cave Adventure, Zork, The Hitchhiker's Guide to the Galaxy, Counterfeit Monkey, 80 Days, Roadwarden.*
  - *Visual novel (VN)/light novel*: A descendent of the text adventure, VNs tell stories primarily through text but are accompanied by some graphical elements, such as on-screen character illustrations and environments. Sometimes the text-based storytelling section is broken up by other forms of gameplay,

such as environmental exploration, relationship management, or puzzle-solving.

- **Examples**: *Phoenix Wright: Ace Attorney, Steins; Gate, Zero Escape: Virtue's Last Reward, Danganronpa: Trigger Happy Havoc, 428: Shibuya Scramble, Doki Doki Literature Club!*

- **Arcade**: An informal genre of games that endorse an "arcade-like" sensibility, typically favoring abstraction over reality, simple vicariosensory pleasures over complex simulation, or featuring a multitude of mechanically diverse challenges rather than a singular, coherent interaction structure. Games in this genre sometimes reflect design practices that were common in games designed for video arcade settings, such as single-screen gameplay and high-score chasing.
  - **Examples**: *Katamari Damacy, Libble Rabble, WHAT THE GOLF?, Joust, DIG DUG.*
  - *Anthology*: Collections of games, minigames, or microgames.
    - **Examples**: *Atari Vault, WarioWare, Inc.: Mega Microgames!, UFO 50, Rare Replay*
  - *Maze*: Games that involve navigation of or within a maze.
    - **Examples**: *PAC-MAN, Kuru Kuru Kururin, Devil World.*
  - *Paddle games/ball games*: Games that involve the bouncing or redirection of balls, often with paddles and often to clear blocks or other such tokens. Informally descend from activities such as air hockey and pachinko.
    - **Examples**: *Breakout, Pong, Peggle.*
  - *Pinball*: Games that simulate pinball tables.
    - **Examples**: *Sonic Spinball, Pinball FX 3, Metroid Prime Pinball, 3D Pinball for Windows—Space Cadet.*
- **Brawler**: Games that involve combat, either hand-to-hand or using short-range weapons, against large groups of enemies. A sister genre to the fighting game; whereas fighting games typically focus on one-on-one, evenly matched bouts, brawlers typically feature one-against-many battles in which the player's avatar outclasses enemies apart from their quantities.
  - **Examples**: *Hades, Bloodroots, Marvel: Ultimate Alliance.*
  - *Beat-em-up*: Games featuring a start-stop rhythm of spatial progression halted by battles against groups of enemies. Often viewed in a side-on perspective, though 3D beat-em-ups exist. This subgenre title is used interchangeably with "brawler" in some classifications.
    - **Examples**: *Streets of Rage, River City Ransom, Teenage Mutant Ninja Turtles: Shredder's Revenge, Double Dragon.*
  - *Character action*: A type of brawler closely related to the hack and slash in which combat focuses on skillful and expressive execution of stylish combos, often given scores at the end of each battle.
    - **Examples**: *Bayonetta, Devil May Cry, God of War, No More Heroes, Hi-Fi RUSH*
  - *Hack and slash*: Brawlers in which combat is primarily (blade) weapons-based, sometimes foregoing the stop-and-start, progressive pace of beat-em-ups.
    - **Examples**: *Golden Axe, Strider, Muramasa: The Demon Blade, Dragon's Crown.*
  - *Musou*: A form of brawler in which the player's avatar fights enemy armies by the hundreds, often making a stylish spectacle of dozens of enemies being cut down at once. Impressive in scale and spectacle, these games often include management of the entire battlefield in addition to the handling of immediate threats, requiring players to disengage from present concerns to protect or capture points of interest elsewhere on the battlefield. Named for the *Dynasty Warriors* series of games.
    - **Examples**: *Dynasty Warriors 8, Hyrule Warriors, EARTH DEFENSE FORCE 6.*

- **Fighting**: Games centered around combat between evenly matched combatants, most often in a one-on-one duel structure.
  - **Examples**: *The King of Fighters XIII, GUILTY GEAR Xrd -SIGN-, UNDER NIGHT IN-BIRTH, ARMS, GAROU: MARK OF THE WOLVES.*
  - *2D fighting*: Fighting games that take place on a 2D plane, most often viewed from the side with combatants always facing one another.
    - **Examples**: *Street Fighter II: The World Warrior, GUILTY GEAR -STRIVE-, Mortal Kombat, DNF DUEL, Skullgirls.*
  - *3D fighting*: Fighting games that take place within a 3D space. Sometimes action is primarily confined to a 2D plane with occasional "sidesteps" into the foreground or background, while other games feature free movement in three dimensions.
    - **Examples**: *DEAD OR ALIVE 6, SoulCalibur II, NARUTO SHIPPUDEN: Ultimate Ninja STORM 3, GigaBash.*
  - *Airdash fighting*: An informal classification of 2D fighting games in which characters move quickly around the arena, oftentimes being able to perform quick dash movements in the air. Combat involves challenges of positioning and momentum more than executing intricate attack combinations.
    - **Examples**: *MELTY BLOOD: TYPE LUMINA, BlazBlue Centralfiction, DRAGON BALL FighterZ.*
  - *Platform fighting*: Games that pair fighting game-style combat with platformer-like free and expressive movement. Though popularized by *Super Smash Bros.* (1999), earlier examples, like *The Outfoxies* (1995), established conventions. Following *Super Smash Bros.*, many platform games since 1999 feature casts of characters from other games or media properties, causing some categorization systems to label this subgenre "mascot fighter", even though mascots are not necessary to the category and examples exist that do not feature pre-existing mascots.
    - **Examples**: *Super Smash Bros. Ultimate, Nickelodeon All-Star Brawl, Brawlout, Rivals of Aether, Power Stone 2, Samurai Gunn.*
- **Horror**: An aesthetic genre describing games that are designed to be scary or utilize horror archetypes. Horror warrants genre-level classification for its proliferation and cohesiveness as a lineage of design. Despite not being a mechanics-oriented genre, particular systemic tropes have emerged that are inherently identifiable with horror games.
  - **Examples**: *Resident Evil Village, Deadly Premonition, Until Dawn, Year Walk, The Static Speaks My Name, Haunted House.*
  - *Exploration horror*: Horror titles, typically presented in a first-person perspective, that minimize combat for a greater focus on environmental exploration, puzzle-solving, or stealth-based survival.
    - **Examples**: *P.T., Outlast, SOMA, The Complex: Found Footage.*
  - *Survival horror*: Horror games with action elements (typically shooting) in which the avatar is under-equipped to face the dangers that plague the environment. Often involves scavenging resources from the environment and avoiding conflict altogether to conserve scarce resources. Related to the *survival* subgenre of the *action* genre, but with a greater emphasis on scares.
    - **Examples**: *Resident Evil, Silent Hill 2, Dead Space, Alien: Isolation, Dead Rising, Fatal Frame, The Last of Us, Sweet Home.*
- **Party**: Games typically played in groups that feature play in short sessions rather than prolonged campaigns, featuring easy-to-approach gameplay forms rather than being mechanically dense. Most often designed with a heavy emphasis on luck, humor, or esoteric skills that are intended to elicit social cohesion rather than exhibit skillful play.
  - **Examples**: *Mario Party, Fall Guys, Overcooked!, Use Your Words, Among Us.*
  - *Physics competition*: Games that involve competitions structured around manipulation of

(often clumsy) physics systems. Most often intended to elicit comedy rather than test mastery.

  - **Examples**: *Mount Your Friends, Gang Beasts, Moving Out, Boom Blox.*

- *Quiz/game show*: Party games structured as quizzes or gameshow formats. Sometimes based on television game shows.

  - **Examples**: *The Jackbox Party Pack, You Don't Know Jack, Buzz!: The BIG Quiz.*

- **Platformer**: Games of traversal in which avatars navigate obstacle course-like environments with exaggerated and expressive movement affordances. Named for the near-ubiquity of jumping between perilous "platforms".

  - **Examples**: *ASTRO BOT, Conker's Bad Fur Day, Yellow Taxi Goes Vroom, Orbo's Odyssey, FEZ, Donkey Kong.*

- *2D platformer*: A platformer presented in a 2D perspective, typically viewed from a side-on perspective.

  - **Examples**: *Donkey Kong Country, Super Mario Bros., Rayman Legends, Shovel Knight, Mosa Lina, Pizza Tower.*

- *3D platformer*: A platformer presented in a 3D perspective. The perspective most often follows the avatar from behind, though there are some 3D platformers with fixed camera perspectives and some that are viewed from the first-person perspective (like *Mirror's Edge* [2008]). Because of the 3D perspective, there are often multiple valid routes to each goal, offering more capacity for exploration than most 2D platformers, which prescribe a singular way forward.

  - **Examples**: *Banjo-Kazooie, A Hat in Time, Super Mario Galaxy 2, Jumping Flash!, Neon White, Psychonauts, Tinykin.*

- *Cinematic platformer*: Platformers, typically presented from a 2D perspective, typically featuring "heavy", elaborately animated (often rotoscoped) movements, with a greater emphasis on puzzle-solving (often requiring trial-and-error memorization of sequences of challenges) rather than improvisational and zippy acrobatics.

  - **Examples**: *INSIDE, Another World, Prince of Persia, Flashback, Heart of Darkness, Oddworld: Abe's Oddysee.*

- *Marble game*: Heavily physics-dependent games in which the player navigates a spherical object around perilous courses, typically managing accumulation of speed and navigation of sloped surfaces rather than the more precise control of character-based platformers.

  - **Examples**: *Venineth, Super Monkey Ball, Marble It Up!, Marble Madness.*

- *Metroidvania/exploration platformer/search action*: Games that present large, interconnected worlds in which progress is blocked by different types of barriers that require avatar ability upgrades to pass. For instance, earning the ability to fire missiles may allow metal barriers to be destroyed, so the player must remember all of the instances of metal barriers that she had previously seen and could not pass before. Since these maps eschew linearity, players spend much of the game backtracking through familiar passages, recontextualized through the new abilities the avatar has since collected.

  - **Examples**: *Super Metroid, Castlevania: Symphony of the Night, Ori and the Blind Forest, Hollow Knight, ANIMAL WELL.*

- *Precision platformer*: Platformers that involve exacting, precise movement through challenging obstacle courses, often aided by very generous checkpoints such that only a short sequence of demanding jumps must be completed before moving onto the next room and the next checkpoint. These games typically incentivize clearing these challenging room as quickly as possible.

  - **Examples**: *Celeste, Super Meat Boy, n++, Downwell, Ultimate Chicken Horse.*

- *Puzzle platformer*: Platformers that feature a greater emphasis on puzzle-solving than acrobatic obstacle overcoming.

- **Examples**: *Trine 2, Captain Toad: Treasure Tracker, Toki Tori 2, Braid.*

- **Puzzle**: Games in which puzzle-solving is the core focus. Puzzles are characterized by (usually) having singular correct answers rather than rewarding creativity of approach (though the singular correct answer may require lateral thinking). Puzzle games typically operate at a relaxed pace, giving players as long as needed to consider and work out the puzzles in front of them.
  - **Examples**: *Portal, Return of the Obra Dinn, Storyteller, Gorogoa, Chants of Sennaar.*
  - *Exploration puzzle*: Puzzles contextualized within explorable environments in which, typically, deducing the manner in which the puzzle fits into the environment is crucial for solving it.
    - **Examples**: *Myst, The Witness, The Talos Principle, The Room, Lorelei and the Laser Eyes.*
  - *Falling block puzzle*: An action-oriented form of puzzle game, these are sorting-based puzzles in which the player must manage the placements of blocks that fall from the top of the screen, often fitting odd-shaped pieces into sensible arrangements or matching groups of colors together.
    - **Examples**: *Tetris, Panel de Pon, Dr. Mario, Puyo Puyo, Lumines: Puzzle Fusion, Suika Game.*
  - *Hidden object game*: Puzzle games that involve searching visually dense images or environments for particular items or characters of interest.
    - **Examples**: *Hidden through Time, Hidden Cats in New York, i commissioned some bees, Crime O'Clock, Tiny Lands.*
  - *Number or letter / word puzzle*: Like crosswords or sudoku puzzles, these are puzzles that combine letters, words, or numbers into spatial puzzles.
    - **Examples**: *Knotwords, Picross DS, Wordle, Hexcells.*
  - *Physics puzzle*: Puzzles that rely upon physics systems, either to build structures, form Rube Goldberg machines, or trigger sequences of events using physics interactions.
    - **Examples**: *The Incredible Machine, Job Simulator, World of Goo, Cut the Rope.*
  - *Sokoban*: Puzzles that involve grid-based navigation in confined spaces, typically pushing boxes or other objects into specified locations. The challenge comes from determining the sequence of moves that put the objects where they are supposed to go without stalemating the system.
    - **Examples**: *Sokoban, Boxyboy, Patrick's Parabox, Handshakes, Baba Is You, Stephen's Sausage Roll, Chip's Challenge.*
  - *Tile-matching game/match three game*: Puzzle games in which the player is presented with a grid of tiles, with which she must match combinations of three or more in a row by swapping the positions of two at a time.
    - **Examples**: *Bejeweled, Grindstone, Puzzle & Dragons.*

- **Racing**: Games that involve the speedy navigation of a course, often in competition to reach a designated point before opponents. Some classifications use the term "driving", though I do not prefer this term, as it excludes games that involve racing on foot or using non-motored vehicles. The term "driving" also implies the inclusion of non-speed-oriented vehicle simulations such as *Euro Truck Simulator 2* (2012), which I instead classify as a *simulation* game, as it has a significantly different incentive and decision structure than a competitive race.
  - **Examples**: *F-Zero GX, Driver: San Francisco, Inertial Drift, Beetle Adventure Racing!*
  - *Arcade racing*: Racing games that have a looser, exaggerated, or more forgiving system of vehicle-handling physics rather than simulating realistic vehicle operations, typically to create games of greater action, speed, and competitive chaos than simulation racers.

  - **Examples**: *Burnout Paradise, blur, Crazy Taxi, Split/Second, Cruis'n USA, Ivan "Ironman" Stewart's Super Off Road, Excitebike, Sonic R.*
- *Kart racing*: Games that simulate go-kart racing, typically with mascot characters, over-the-top environments, and cartoony weapons and items. Typically balanced to produce chaos and drama rather than wholly fair tests of mastery.
  - **Examples**: *Mario Kart 64, Crash Team Racing, Sonic & All-Stars Racing Transformed, Diddy Kong Racing.*
- *Simulation racing*: Racing games that extensively simulate the operation and handling of real cars with great fidelity to mechanical and physical specificities. For this reason, races are often slower with higher consequences for crashes than *arcade racing* counterparts.
  - **Examples**: *Gran Turismo 7, Assetto Corsa, Forza Motorsport.*

- **Rhythm**: Games featuring rhythm- or music-based challenges. These games typically test mastery, demanding perfect reproduction of sequences of notes that correspond with controller inputs, but sometimes they allow for unstructured improvisation and music construction.
  - **Examples**: *Rock Band 4, Rhythm Heaven Fever, PaRappa the Rapper, VOEZ, Aaero, Elite Beat Agents, Thumper.*
- *Dancing game*: Rhythm games in which the player performs full-body movements. Movements are registered via "dance pads" on which players step in rhythm, motion inputs, or camera tracking.
  - **Examples**: *Dance Dance Revolution, Just Dance, Dance Central.*
- *Music-making game*: Rhythm games that enable the production or remixing of new music. Often nondemanding, challenge-wise, in favor of free creative expression.
  - **Examples**: *FUSER, Mario Paint, Disney Fantasia: Music Evolved, MTV Music Generator.*

- **RPG (role-playing game)**: Games designed in the tradition of *Dungeons & Dragons* (Gygax & Arneson, 1974) in which grand stories are told while avatar abilities and actions are managed by numerical statistics that can be "weighted" through point allocation. For example, a player may choose to allocate her character-building resources between attributes like strength, dexterity, intelligence, luck, and charm, each of which make relevant tasks more likely to succeed. As the player progresses, the avatar "levels up", granting additional points that can be invested into advantaging the character further, keeping up with or pulling ahead of the curve of the game's progressive difficulty and demand. As implied by the name, the player typically adopts a role as a character embedded within the fantasy narrative rather than inhabiting a more flexible or blank character through whom she can personally express. That said, a great deal of personalization can go into building each character's specialties, managed by choice of equipment or character skills. RPGs often (but do not always) involve building a party of adventurers that persist throughout the course of these extensive journeys. When games in other genres are said to have "RPG systems", this refers to the incorporation of upgrade paths for characters or items, progressed through the allocation of earnable points.
  - **Examples**: *Thirsty Suitors, The Legend of Zelda: Ocarina of Time, Paper Mario: The Thousand Year Door, West of Loathing.*
- *ARPG (action role-playing game)*: RPGs that feature real-time combat within the game world using the "verbs" available to the avatar at all times rather than issuing battles into separated spaces with turn-based ordering or battle-specific sets of character verbs.
  - **Examples**: *Dark Souls, The Elder Scrolls V: Skyrim, The Legend of Zelda: A Link to the Past, Bloodborne, The Witcher 3: Wild Hunt, Diablo IV, Ōkami.*
- *CRPG (computer role-playing game)*: RPGs that simulate the rules of *Dungeons & Dragons* (Gygax & Arneson, 1974) and other tabletop RPG systems the closest, these games

are typically viewed from an isometric perspective, typically feature cursor-based indirect character control, and typically involve turn-based combat embedded within the overworld environment (rather than breaking into separate battle screens and systems like Japanese role-playing game (JRPGs). These games are typically heavily-dependent on weighted chance, simulating or showing dice rolls to determine success or failure of actions (weighed against character point allocations).

  - **Examples**: *Baldur's Gate 3, Disco Elysium, Planescape: Torment, Fallout 2, STAR WARS Knights of the Old Republic.*

- *Dungeon crawler*: RPGs in which parties of characters explore often-procedurally-generated environments (dungeons) in a grid-based layout. Movement and combat is turn-based. Often viewed from a first-person perspective with an ever-present map, or viewed from simultaneous first- and iconographic-third-person perspectives.

  - **Examples**: *Etrian Odyssey, Legend of Grimrock, Dungeon Master, Persona Q: Shadow of the Labyrinth.*

- *JRPG (Japanese role-playing game):* RPGs in which world exploration and battle encounters are separated. While actions available to the avatar and partied characters in the overworld are typically sparse, a separate set of combat verbs becomes available during battles. Battles are often presented as "random encounters", chance-based ambushes. In-combat actions are typically chosen from a menu rather than executed in real time; as such, battles are often turn-based. The name "Japanese RPG" does **not** mean that all JRPGs are made in Japan; rather, it means that they are made in the Japanese *tradition*, in the design lineage pioneered by the early RPGs made by Japanese developers. Think of it like cuisines; it is possible to have Mexican-inspired dishes by employing techniques and ingredients traditional in Mexican foods without the dish originating from Mexico.

  - **Examples**: *DRAGON QUEST XI: Echoes of an Elusive Age, FINAL FANTASY VI, Yakuza: Like a Dragon, Undertale, Pokémon.*

- *MMORPG (massively multiplayer online role-playing game)*: RPGs set in large worlds concurrently inhabited by large populations of players online. Players can form factions and accomplish challenging feats cooperatively, or they can choose to do battle with other players. Though other genres of games can be "MMO", it is most common for such massively multiplayer games to be RPGs.

  - **Examples**: *World of WarCraft, STAR WARS Galaxies, Black Desert Online, EverQuest, Guild Wars 2, EVE Online, FINAL FANTASY XIV, Genshin Impact.*

- *Roguelike/roguelite*: Games that follow in the tradition of *Rogue* (1980), these games present players with random upgrades and enhancements (from large pools of available items), many of which have interesting synergies with one another. Crucially, progress resets upon avatar death, meaning that each "run" of the game starts from the very beginning of the game. Because each run is unique and upgrades are randomized, the player never knows what upgrades and challenges she will encounter with each run and what interesting synergies those upgrades might have with one another. Upgrades can quite often rewrite the rules of the game altogether, meaning that players have to be ready to adopt highly-improvisational patterns of play at a systemic level rather than at the executional level more typical in other genres. "Roguelike" is used when *all* progress is reset upon death and each run is truly "fresh" (with the only progress that carries over between runs is the player's acquired knowledge and familiarity with game systems). "Roguelite" is used when some elements of progression persist between runs, such that, even if a run does not successfully reach the end of the game, the player's avatar is mechanically empowered to push a little further next time.

- **Examples**: *Balatro, Slay the Spire, Hades, The Binding of Isaac, Spelunky 2.*

- **Shmup (shoot-em-up)**: Games that involve ranged combat from a usually third-person (most often 2D) or in-vehicle-cockpit perspective using one of a variety of conventional control methods (detailed in the subgenres below). Whereas *shooters* tend to organize gameplay around more "realistic" models of gun-based combat, shmups tend to be more abstract, iconographic, and exaggerated, featuring large "bullets" that form dense patterns through which avatars must carefully navigate while firing back. Shmups originated with science-fiction spaceship combat games, so the manner in which shmup avatars move and shoot tends to feel more vehicle-like than organic, even when the avatar is not presented as a spaceship. Though most classification systems group this and the *shooter* genre (as both have closely related lineages), I prefer to keep shmups separated due to the richness and specificity of design traditions that exist within it.
  - **Examples**: *Jet Lancer, PixelJunk Shooter, LUFTRAUSERS, STAR WARS X-Wing vs TIE Fighter, Sinistar, Asteroids.*
  - *Bullet heaven/survivor game / reverse bullet hell*: Popularized by *Vampire Survivors* (2022), like the bullet hell, these games feature dense patterns of projectiles, but they are fired by the avatar instead of being aimed at the avatar. Instead, the avatar navigates environments filled with hundreds of enemies (making these games similar to *musous*) that are quickly dispatched, leaving behind XP (experience points), which can be cashed in to earn additional weapons or upgrade existing weapons. The avatar quickly becomes incredibly powerful, but so too do the numbers and strength of enemies build, requiring constant attention to gaining XP and leveling to stay ahead of the challenge curve.
    - **Examples**: *Vampire Survivors, 20 Minutes till Dawn, Brotato.*
  - *Bullet hell*: Shmups that feature dense, intricate patterns of slow-moving enemy bullets through which the player must navigate the avatar, like the field of bullets was a dynamic labyrinth. Avatars are typically destroyed in one hit, making careful navigation through the hypnotically patterned projectiles the top priority.
    - **Examples**: *Crimzon Clover, Ikaruga, DoDonPachi.*
  - *Fixed shmup/stationary shmup*: Shmup games in which the avatar (typically a shapeship or military vehicle) moves on one axis (or within a very limited two-axis space). Thus, these games are typically presented as if the avatar is defending a line she does not want the enemy to cross rather than flying into enemy territory.
    - **Examples**: *Space Invaders, Missile Command, GALAGA, Gorf, Centipede.*
  - *Run 'n' gun*: Games presented from a side-on or top-down perspective that involve an avatar running or driving through a ground-based environment, often with platforming-type challenges. All combat is performed using shmup-like projectile weapons.
    - **Examples**: *Contra, Gunstar Heroes, Sunset Riders, Super Time Force, Cuphead, Metal Slug.*
  - *Scrolling shmup (horizontally/vertically)*: Shmups (typically featuring spaceships or other vehicles) that fly on *either* a horizontal or vertical access. It is called "scrolling" because the screen's perspective moves with the avatar, meaning that it appears as if the environment and enemy planes are moving toward the avatar as the avatar stays (mostly) still, relative to the direction that the screen scrolls. Often paired with *bullet hell* elements.
    - **Examples**: *1942, Defender, TwinBee, Dragon Spirit, Schildmaid MX.*
  - *Twin-stick shooter*: Shmups presented from overhead or isometric perspectives in which the player has full, 360-degree control over the direction of movement and the direction of projectile fire. Often involves "herding"

large groups of enemies into manageable patterns using the relatively unrestrained navigational affordances not common in other subgenres of shmups. Named for the conventionally "twin stick" control scheme, with one thumbstick (or arcade joystick) controlling movement and the other stick controlling the direction of fire.

  - **Examples**: *Smash TV, Geometry Wars: Retro Evolved, Nex Machina, Enter the Gungeon, Assault Android Cactus.*

- **Shooter**: Games that feature primarily gun- or projectile-based combat. Distinct from the closely related *shmup* for being less abstract and more grounded in "realistic" models of embodied proprioception. Since the divergent "speciation" point between shmups and shooters occurred after the advent of 3D game rendering technology, most *shooters* are in 3D, while most subsequent shmups adopt a retro-stylization and present in 2D.

  - **Examples**: *El Paso, Elsewhere, Half-Life: Alyx, TimeSplitters 2, Xybots, Wolfenstein 3-D.*

  - *Boomer shooter*: Modern shooters designed to evoke the retro stylization and pace of classic FPSs like *DOOM* (1993) and *Quake* (1996). Often featuring over-the-top weaponry, fast-paced movement, abstractly designed maps, and comical amounts of gore and viscera, these games eschew the realism made possible by modern engines in favor of immediate and explosive fun. The name is a playful pun, evoking the explosiveness of the stylized gameplay and evoking the "oldness" of the retro sensibilities in reference to the "baby boomer" generation.

    - **Examples**: *Prodeus, Ion Fury, Devil Daggers, DOOM Eternal.*

  - *Extraction shooter*: Shooters that incorporate tactical and survival-oriented mechanics with (often team-based) objectives that require the extraction of a particular object or accomplishment of a particular goal within the game world rather than simply facing enemies in combat.

    - **Examples**: *Escape from Tarkov, Helldivers 2, Hunt: Showdown.*

  - *First-person shooter (FPS)*: A shooter from the first-person perspective, as if the game world is being seen through the eyes of the character.

    - **Examples**: *Half-Life 2, DOOM, Call of Duty 4: Modern Warfare, Titanfall 2, Oddworld: Stranger's Wrath.*

  - *Hero shooter*: Competitive, team-based shooters (first- or third-person) in which players play as designated characters or classes with unique abilities and vulnerabilities. Knowledge of each character's abilities and other characters' counters to those abilities comprises the *metagame* (or "meta") of playing these games.

    - **Examples**: *Overwatch, Paladins, Apex Legends, VALORANT.*

  - *Immersive sim*: Though not always shooters, immersive sims are a subset of action games in which objectives are held within worlds that simulate extensive, overlapping systems of physics and behavior in a manner that produces a high level of *procedural emergence* and encourages creative, expressive play using highly flexible tools and weapons. Often coupled with RPG-like character leveling systems, these games encourage nearly endless valid play styles.

    - **Examples**: *Deus Ex, Prey, System Shock 2, Ultima Underworld: The Stygian Abyss.*

  - *Light gun shooter*: Shooters in which objects on-screen are "shot" with a gun-like controller held by the player. Most often presented in static, shooting gallery-like scenes.

    - **Examples**: *Time Crisis 4, The House of the Dead, Duck Hunt, Point Blank*

  - *Rail shooter/on-rails shooter*: Shooters in which the player does not control (or has limited control over) the movement of the avatar through the environment. Instead, the player focuses on aiming and shooting while avatar movement is either continuous and predetermined or stop-and-go as the avatar moves between static shooting gallery-like encounters.

  - **Examples**: *Space Harrier, Pokémon Snap, Dead Space: Extraction, Sin & Punishment: Star Successor, Rez, Sayonara Wild Hearts.*

- *Tactical shooter*: Shooters that incorporate realistic, tactical coordination between players or players and NPCs. They most often simulate military operations and often feature extensive affordances for giving orders to allies and planning out coordinated strikes ahead of their execution.
  - **Examples**: *Tom Clancy's Rainbow Six, Tom Clancy's Ghost Recon, SOCOM U.S. Navy SEALs, Insurgency: Sandstorm.*
- *Third-person shooter*: Shooters presented from a third-person perspective, typically behind or over-the-shoulder of the avatar.
  - **Examples**: *Fortnite, Vanquish, Control, Gears of War, Sunset Overdrive, STAR WARS Battlefront, Splatoon 2.*

- **Simulation**: Games that simulate systems or particular activities. The challenge in these games typically stems from coming to understand the operations of the systems and relationships between systems that drive the simulation (see the exploration of the *black box* in Chapter 3).
  - **Examples**: *Planet Coaster, Papers, Please, Tiny Glade, SPORE, Stardew Valley, Nour: Play with Your Food.*
  - *Business management (tycoon game)*: Games that involve the commercial operation of a business, often involving an amount of creative control over the business' identity and output.
    - **Examples**: *RollerCoaster Tycoon, Planet Zoo, Two Point Hospital, Game Dev Tycoon, The Movies.*
  - *City builder*: Games that simulate building and managing a city, often requiring the management of city zoning (balancing residential, commercial/retail, and industrial needs), infrastructure, transportation, environmental resources, safety, and happiness of the citizenry. Though some city sims focus on the joy and creativity of building rather than the stresses of management, allowing players to build freely without regard for mayoral tasks.
    - **Examples**: *Cities: Skylines, SimCity, Manor Lords, Townscaper, Frostpunk.*
  - *Clicker game/idle game/incremental game*: Games of patience and incremental progress rather than narrative, action, or strategy demands. These games begin by simply requiring the player to increment her score by clicking on an object until she quickly earns tools that can perform this "clicking" task on her behalf. Further unlocks upgrade the rate at which these automatic clicks occur and the value of each click, causing resources to grow at exponential rates with every purchase. These quickly become games of absurd and astronomical growth, often rewarding complete resets of progress with carryover upgrades that can push resource gain even higher. Often derisively called Skinner Box systems of "number go up" appeal, these games are appreciable for discerning an undeniable aesthetic appeal in the rate at which these mathematical increases occur.
    - **Examples**: *Cookie Clicker, Cow Clicker, Clicker Heroes, Universal Paperclips.*
  - *Flight sim*: Games that simulate the realistic operation of aircraft.
    - **Examples**: *Microsoft Flight Simulator.*
  - *Job sim*: Games that simulate the performance of what might otherwise be termed a normal or mundane job, often not significantly streamlined to increase their entertainment value—these games typically revel in their slow and deliberate pace, forming an

aesthetic around doing a repetitive task with care and excellence.

- **Examples**: *Farming Simulator 22, PowerWash Simulator, Euro Truck Simulator 2, 911 Operator.*

- *Life sim*: Games that simulate the social or animal systems of life, sometimes played in a dollhouse-like fashion in which characters' lives can be directly played and meddled with, and sometimes played from a removed perspective in which the player has light influence over the conditions by which life may flourish.
  - **Examples**: *The Sims 2, Animal Crossing, Viva Piñata, SimAnt, Little Computer People, Façade.*
- *Photography sim*: Games that simulate the act of taking photographs.
  - **Examples**: *Pokémon Snap, Afrika, Umurangi Generation.*

- **Sports**: Games that simulate sport activities. These can be either real-world sports or fictional sports.
  - **Examples**: *The Climb, Triple Play 2000, OlliOlli, 720°, NBA Jam.*
  - *Fishing/hunting game*: Games that simulate fishing and/or hunting.
    - **Examples**: *SEGA Bass Fishing, Ridiculous Fishing, theHunter: Call of the Wild.*
  - *[Individual sport] game*: Games that simulate real-world sports (golf, cricket, basketball, football) or fictional sports (*Windjammers* [1994], *Lethal League* [2014]). Spans from realistic simulations to "arcade"-style exaggerated play.
    - **Examples**: *EA SPORTS FC 25, Golden Tee Golf, Mario Tennis, Walkabout Mini Golf, Rocket League, Kirby's Dream Course, Pong.*
  - *[Extreme sport] game*: Games that simulate extreme sports, such as skateboarding, skating, and bicycling.
    - **Examples**: *Tony Hawk's Pro Skater 1 + 2, Lonely Mountains: Downhill, Jet Set Radio.*
  - *Wrestling*: Games that simulate professional wrestling or wrestling-like combat. Distinguished from fighting games by typically having a greater emphasis on grapples, holds, and environmental/prop-based improvisation.
    - **Examples**: *WWE SmackDown! vs. Raw 2006, Def Jam Vendetta, Fire Pro Wrestling World.*

- **Strategy**: Games that present players challenges of strategic and tactical planning. These can involve civilization management, warfare, or abstract strategic tasks.
  - **Examples**: *Gears Tactics, Desperados III, Pikmin 4, 13 Sentinels: Aegis Rim, Project X Zone, Into the Breach, Rome: Total War.*
  - *4X (explore, expand, exploit, exterminate)/grand strategy*: Strategy games that involve building a civilization or empire in a competitive setting against other civilizations growing in parallel. Typically, there are several courses of play that can lead to victories of different forms, some not involving conflict or combat altogether.
    - **Examples**: *Crusader Kings, Europa Universalis IV, Sins of a Solar Empire, Victoria 3*
  - *Artillery*: Strategy games (usually presented in a 2D, side-on perspective) that involve turn-based operation of projectile weapons/vehicles with limited or no movement capabilities in which players must fire physics-affected projectiles at enemy units. Usually, these games involve destructible environments that can reshape the field of battle throughout play.
    - **Examples**: *Worms Armageddon, Scorched Earth, Angry Birds.*
  - *Auto battler/auto chess*: Competitive strategy games in which unit types of limited pools are placed around grid-based fields during a preparation phase. Once the battle phase initiates,

the units act independently, playing out their operational behaviors until all of one or the other players' units have been defeated.

  - **Examples**: *Dota Auto Chess, Dota Underlords, Teamfight Tactics.*

- *Card game/board game/tabletop game*: Video games that simulate real card, board, or tabletop games or games that utilize the types of materials and tokens that *would* feature in these kinds of games in real life, even if the result is something that could only exist within a video game.
  - **Examples**: *Balatro, Carcassonne, Solitaire, Inscryption.*
- *Civilization sim/god game*: Games in which the player takes on the perspective of a supernatural god, overseeing a civilization, often in competition and conflict with rival civilizations and their gods.
  - **Examples**: *Populous, Black & White, From Dust, Doshin the Giant.*
- *MOBA (multiplayer online battle arena)*: Competitive strategy games in which two teams of players select powerful hero units with unique abilities and work together to destroy the opponent team's base on the opposing side of the map. The map is typically divided into three "lanes" (top, middle, and bottom lanes) that players can traverse, separated by "jungles", which are hostile to both teams. Each player's heroes are assisted by computer-controlled "minions", weaker characters that can provide assistance or distraction during conflict. MOBAs provide highly symmetrical and structured conflict between teams, kept interesting by the expansive set of unique hero characters from which players can choose.
  - **Examples**: *Dota 2, League of Legends, Pokémon Unite, Herzog Zwei.*
- *Real-time strategy*: Games in which strategic tasks are performed in real-time, whether it is building a civilization and rushing to gather resources to expand or performing single-character actions.
  - **Examples**: *Age of Empires II: The Age of Kings, StarCraft.*
- *Tactics/tactical RPG*: Turn-based strategy (TBS) games that typically present as puzzle-like, crafted encounters rather than the emergent, unpredictable conditions of a standard TBS encounter. Often presented in a grid-based format featuring turn-based movement and combat and character-based abilities.
  - **Examples**: *Advance Wars, Fire Emblem Awakening, Disgaea 4, XCOM 2, Valkyria Chronicles, Mario + Rabbids Kingdom Battle*
- *Turn-based strategy (TBS)*: Strategy games in which players (or computer-simulated opponents) take turns performing actions in a board game-like fashion. Information is often withheld from players when opponent forces are not within range of sight, hiding the consequences of opponents' turns.
  - **Examples**: *SteamWorld Heist, Sid Meier's Civilization VI, Age of Wonders.*
- *Tower defense*: Strategy games, often with preparation and action phases, in which the player must prevent enemies from reaching a point on the map or destroying a particular structure by setting a number of autonomous defenses; typically in the form of turrets and walls. Enemies usually approach in waves from predictable directions, proper battlefield management involves creating winding routes through which the enemies must pass (to slow them down) lined with turrets and defenses that will pick them off as they advance. During the battle phase, most of the action is automatic, apart from the player's ability to buy additional defenses with resources picked up during the defense. The player usually does not take an active role (as an avatar) in performing direct combat.
  - **Examples**: *Rampart, Bloons TD6, Plants vs. Zombies, Kingdom Rush, Star Fox Guard, Five Nights at Freddy's.*

READING THE LUDOGRAPHY

As other books and articles referenced in this volume are detailed in each chapter's citation section, metadata for referenced games is included in the ludography appendix. The formatting of this section does not follow an established academic standard, because I wish to give more information than a typical APA video game citation would allow.

The intention of the ludography is to not only serve as a reference list but to aid discovery of unfamiliar games and provide technological, business, and genre context for each game. Platforms on which the game is available to play are listed to aid the reader in finding the games for herself (current as of the time of writing). Video games are expensive, numerous, time-consuming, and often require specialized hardware, so in lieu of playing all of the referenced games, readers might find it easier to seek out videos of these games being played instead. Videos labeled "longplays" provide the most representative samples of games being played, as opposed to trailers, which are marketing videos cut to be exciting rather than representative, and "speedruns", which are exhibitions of skillful metagame play, typically exploiting glitches and unintended affordances.

Games in the ludography follow the format below:

Game title (year the game first released)
Developer(s) separated by commas; publisher(s) separated by commas
Genre (subgenre)
Platforms on which the game was released. The [...] symbol represents a delay of at least two years in the time in which a game was ported to further platforms. Platforms will only be listed *once*, even after time skips, even if new editions such as remakes or remasters release on a previously-mentioned platform. In (parentheses), I will note if a later release is a *remaster* or *remake*.

For example:

PaRappa the Rapper (1996)
NanaOn-Sha; Sony Computer Entertainment
Rhythm
PSX [...] PSP (remaster) [...] PS4 (remaster)

Platform list *excludes* streaming or subscription services such as Xbox Game Pass, Google Stadia, Amazon Luna, PlayStation Plus, and Nintendo Switch Online.

Platform abbreviations:

2600: Atari 2600 (1977)
3DO: 3DO (1993)
3DS: Nintendo 3DS (2011)
5200: Atari 5200 SuperSystem (1982)
7800: Atari 7800 ProSystem (1986)
AND: Google Android mobile OS (2008)
ARC: Used here to refer to all video arcade cabinets regardless of form factor
AVP: Apple Vision Pro (2024)
CD-i: Philips Compact Disc-Interactive (1990)
DC: SEGA Dreamcast (1998)
Flash: Macromedia Flash / Adobe Flash (1993)
G&W: Nintendo Game & Watch (1980)
GB: Nintendo Game Boy (1989)
GBA: Nintendo Game Boy Advance (2001)
GCN: Nintendo GameCube (2001)
Gear: Samsung Gear VR (2015)
GEN: SEGA Mega Drive / SEGA Genesis (1988; *includes 32X and SEGA CD games*)
GG: SEGA Game Gear (1990)
iOS: Apple iOS mobile OS (2007)
iQue: iQue Player (2003)
ITV: Intellivision
JAG: Atari Jaguar (1993)
Lynx: Atari Lynx (1989)
Mobile: Various mobile devices not using Android or iOS operating systems
N64: Nintendo 64 (1996)
NDS: Nintendo DS (2004)
NES: Nintendo Entertainment System / Family Computer (Famicom; 1983)
NG: Neo Geo Multi Video System (1990)
NS: Nintendo Switch (2017)
PC: Used here to include all personal computers, such as computers running Windows, Mac, Linux, as well as specialized classic home computer systems such as the Commodore 64 and ZX Spectrum.
PS2: Sony PlayStation 2 (2000)
PS3: Sony PlayStation 3 (2006)
PS4: Sony PlayStation 4 (2013)
PS5: Sony PlayStation 5 (2020)
PSP: Sony PlayStation Portable (2004)
PSV: Sony PlayStation Vita (2011)
PSX: Sony PlayStation (1994)
Quest: Oculus Quest / Meta Quest series of standalone VR headsets (2019)
SMS: SEGA Master System (1985)
SNES: Super Nintendo Entertainment System (Super NES) / Super Famicom (1990)
SS: SEGA Saturn (1994)
VB: Nintendo Virtual Boy (1995)
Wii: Nintendo Wii (2006)
WU: Nintendo Wii U (2012)
X360: Xbox 360 (2005)
XB: Xbox (2001)
XBO: Xbox One (2013)
XS: Xbox Series (2020)

NOTES

1 Much of value has been lost from what once was Twitter, a grim reminder of the ephemerality of online discourse, but I trust that Lantz quoted Wilson correctly.

2 I examine in Chapter 7 the fact that video game representation is not *wholly* digital, and the state changes enacted in the player's mind or even the context of play all feed into the system that produces gameplay, but for now, I use a simpler framing.

REFERENCES

Altman, R. (1998). *Film/genre*. British Film Institute.

Anthropy, A. & Clark, N. (2014). *A game design vocabulary: Exploring the foundational principles behind good game design*. Addison-Wesley.

Aylett, R. (1999). Narrative in virtual environments. *AAAI Technical Report FS-99-01*.

Bayliss, P. (2007). Beings in the game-world. *Proceedings of the 4th Australian Conference on Interactive Entertainment, 4*, 1–6.

Beardsley, M. C. (1966) The aesthetic problem of justification. *The Journal of Aesthetic Education*, 1(2), 29–39. doi:10.2307/3331311

Benjamin, W. (1968). The work of art in the age of mechanical reproduction (H. B. Jovanovich, Trans). In H. Arendt (Ed.), *Illuminations* (pp. 217–252). Schocken Books Inc. (Original work published 1935).

Bogost, I. (2009a). *On videogames and ontology* [Conference presentation]. Digital Games Research Association (DiGRA) 2009.

Bogost, I. (2009b). *Videogames are a mess*. Ian Bogost. https://bogost.com/writing/videogames_are_a_mess/

Boluk, S. & LeMieux, P. (2017). *Metagaming: Playing, competing, spectating, cheating, trading, making, and breaking videogames*. University of Minnesota Press.

Caillois, R. (1958). *Man, play, and games*. Librairie Gallimard.

Charters, W. W. (1933). *Motion pictures and youth: A summary*. Macmillan.

Clarke, R. I., Lee, J. H., & Clark, N. (2015). Why video game genres fail: A classificatory analysis. *Games & Culture*, 12(5). doi:10.1177/1555412015591900

Coen, J. & Coen, E. (Directors). (2007). *No country for old men* [Film]. Miramax Films; Paramount Pictures.

Crary, J. (1992). *Techniques of the observer*. The MIT Press.

Crawford, C. (1982). *The art of computer game design*. McGraw-Hill Osborne Media.

del Río, E. (1996). The body as foundation of the screen: Allegories of technology in Atom Egoyan's *Speaking Parts*. *Camera Obscura, 13*(2(38)), 37–38. doi:10.1215/02705346-13-2_38-92

del Río, E. (2000). The body of voyeurism: Mapping a discourse of the senses in Michael Powell's *Peeping Tom*. *Camera Obscura 15*(3(45)), 115–149. doi:10.1215/02705346-15-3_45-115

Gladwell, M. (2005). *Brain candy*. The New Yorker. https://www.newyorker.com/magazine/2005/05/16/brain-candy

Gygax, G. & Arneson, D. (1974). *Dungeons & Dragons*. TSR, Inc.

Hansen, M. (1993). 'With skin and hair': Kracauer's theory of film, Marseilles 1940. *Critical Inquiry, 19*(3), 458.

Huizinga, J. (1938). *Homo ludens: A study of the play element in culture*. Beacon Press.

Hunicke, R., LeBlanc, M., & Zubek, R. (2004). MDA: A formal approach to game design and game research. *Proceedings of the AAAI Workshop on Challenges in Game AI, 4*(1), 1722.

Itami, J. (1985). *Tampopo* [Film]. Toho.

Jett, J., Sacchi, S., Lee, J. H., & Clarke, R. I. (2016). A conceptual model for video games and interactive media. *Journal of the Association for Information Science and Technology* (JASIST*)*, 67(3), 505–517.

Juul, J. (2003). *255,168 ways of playing tic tac toe*. The Ludologist. https://www.jesperjuul.net/ludologist/2003/12/28/255168-ways-of-playing-tic-tac-toe/

Juul, J. (2005). *Half-real: Video games between real rules and fictional worlds*. The MIT Press.

Kanaga, D. (2015). *Intro to ludic ecologonomy (pt. 1)*. https://wombflashforest.blogspot.com/2015/04/intro-to-ludic-ecologonomy-pt-1.html

Kent, J. (Director). (2014). *The babadook* [Film]. Umbrella Entertainment.

Kirkpatrick, G. (2011). *Aesthetic theory and the video game*. Manchester University Press.

Kitses, J. (1970). *Horizons west: Directing the western from John Ford to Clint Eastwood*. Indiana University Press.

Kluitenberg, E. (2008). *Delusive spaces: Essays on culture, media and technology*. NAi Publishers.

Kurosawa, A. (Director). (1961). *Yojimbo* [Film]. Kurosawa Production; Toho.

Lantz, F. (2023). *The beauty of games*. The MIT Press.

Lee, J. H., Karlova, N., Clarke, R. I., Thornton, K., & Perti, A. (2014). Facet analysis of video game genres. *Proceedings of the iConference 2014*, 125–139.

Lee, J. H., Tennis, J. T., Clarke, R. I., & Carpenter, M. (2013). Developing a video game metadata schema for the Seattle *Interactive Media Museum*. *International Journal on Digital Libraries, 13*(2), 105–117.

Leone, A. (n.d.) *Aesthetics of play*. Aesthetics of Play. https://aestheticsofplay.com/about

Marks, L. U. (1999). *The skin of the film: Intercultural cinema, embodiment, and the senses*. Duke University Press.

Marks, L. U. (2002). *Touch: Sensuous theory and multisensory media*. University of Minnesota Press.

McMahan, A. (2003). Immersion, engagement, and presence: A method for analyzing 3-D video games. In M. J. P. Wolf & B. Perron (Eds.) *The Video Game Theory Reader.* Routledge.

Menkman, R. (2011). *The glitch moment(um).* Institute of Network Cultures.

Murray, J. H. (2012). *Inventing the medium: Principles of interaction design as cultural practice.* The MIT Press.

Neale, S. (1990). The question of genre. *Screen, 31*(1), 45–66.

Nguyen, C. T. (2020). *Games: Agency as art.* Oxford University Press.

Oliveros, P. (2005). *Deep listening: A composer's sound practice.* iUniverse.

Reiner, R. (Driector). (1989). *When Harry met Sally...* [Film]. Columbia Pictures.

Rivera, J. (2019). *Stop calling games 'metroidvania'.* Kotaku. https://kotaku.com/stop-calling-games-metroidvania-1836051152

Rollings, A. & Morris, D. (2000). *Game architecture and design.* Coriolis.

Salen, K. & Zimmerman, E. (2003). *Rules of play: Game design fundamentals.* The MIT Press.

Schüll, N. D. (2012). *Addiction by design: Machine gambling in Las Vegas.* Princeton University Press.

Shaviro, S. (1993). *The cinematic body.* University of Minnesota Press.

Sinnerbrink, R. (2012). Stimmung: Exploring the aesthetics of mood. *Screen, 53*(2), 148–163. doi:10.1093/screen/hjs007

Sobchack, V. (2004). *Carnal thoughts: Embodiment and moving image culture.* University of California Press.

Suits, B. (1978). *The grasshopper: Games, life and utopia.* Broadview Press.

Summoning Alt. (2022, March 10). *Blindfolded Punch-Out in 18:03.54 (world record)* [Video]. YouTube. https://youtu.be/jc9XE6zns7A

Wheadon, J. & Minear, T. (Executive producers). (2002). *Firefly* [TV series]. Mutant Enemy Productions; 20th Century Fox Television.

Williams, L. (1991). Film bodies: Gender, genre, and excess. *Film Quarterly, 44*(4), 2–13.

CHAPTER 3

Reading Game Design

ANY STUDY OF LITERACY involves aspects of both consumption and production. All communicative media, be it artistic or informational, serve three primary functions: inscription, transmission, and representation (Murray, 2012, pp. 13–16). *Inscription* is the process of manipulation of an object with a capacity for "memory" (a retention of its manipulated form) for the purpose of encoding a message or meaning on or within that object. Writing on a note, carving a marble slab into a statue, or capturing images onto frames of film allow the transformation of something ephemeral—a thought or a moment in time—to be preserved within an object that can "hold" that information for however long is needed.

Once something has been intentionally inscribed upon a medium, the information it contains can be *transmitted* to someone else. A photograph can be viewed, a record can be listened to, a shopping list can be read. Per Charles Sanders Peirce's theory of semiotics, the inscribed *signs* are received by the beholder and translated back into the ephemerality of sensory experience and human memory. The raw sensory information is interpreted into a message or experience through the process of *representation*. The novel experience of beholding the inscribed object is compared to that with which the beholder is familiar in order to de-abstract a meaning amidst *codes* and *schemas* of social, cultural, and experiential origin. Depending on the purpose and context of the inscribed signs, the signs may refer to something specific per properties of their production (*indices*), they may represent something identifiable by their shared characteristics (*icons*), or they may denote something through convention (*symbol*).

In the case of video games, the relationship between inscription and representation is complicated. Game developers hold the role of the inscribers. That which they wish to transmit is inscribed into digital code, but this code is not read directly by the audience. Another interpretant plays an intermediary role. The code is interpreted by a computer, which enacts the code's instructions in real-time, creating a runtime environment that is both expressive of the design of its creators and sensitive to determined forms of interaction from the audience (the player). The code's executed runtime behavior produces representations—abstractions of the systemic operations of the code—that are readable by players: video, audio, and haptic signals.

To illustrate the manner in which the "message" of a game transmits: the developer programs code, the code transmits the developer's instructions to the computer, the computer executes the code, the processes it enacts are represented on the computer's output devices, those sensory signals are transmitted to the player, and the player forms a representational interpretation of the signals. Even this is a simplification (programming code is translated into a much more basic machine code that configures elements of the behavior and relationships between a computer's components, etc.), but even this abbreviated journey demonstrates that there are several more steps of abstraction and mediation between the developer and the player than between, for example, the painter and the beholder or the chef and the consumer.

As such, how many layers of mediation are *necessary* to understand for a literate player? The player is typically only able to behold the outermost representational layer. Might she simply utilize her cinematic

DOI: 10.1201/9781003530961-3

literacy to interpret the video and audio signals she receives from the system? That will not suffice, for she also *interacts* with the runtime code through mediated, coded behaviors of her own through the interface of the controller, making her an agent within the system similarly capable of inscription. But certainly, we cannot argue that one *cannot* play video games without understanding the programming language that underlies its operation. Apart from specific hobbyist subgroups like hackers and modders (see Chapter 13), the compiled code of the game is not likely to be accessibly readable by the player even if she wants to see it. So how do we identify the skills necessary to be able to derive rich meaning from games as digital simulations, and how does this inform how we understand games as designed objects capable of carrying meaning inscribed by both developer and player?

FROM DESIGN TO CODE TO EXPERIENCE

The multiple layers of mediation between the game developer and the player described above are similar to the layers of mediation between the playwright and the theatre audience. The playwright's mode of inscription is the theatrical script, and while some audiences will read this written work directly, most will see it performed by a troupe of actors who interpret the script into another form as they make adaptations for the stage. Before going into greater depth with regard to reading and understanding game design conventions, it is useful to trace the journey a game goes through as an artifact in between the intention of the developer and the experience of the player.

In Chapter 2, we grappled with the question of "what is a game?" and came up with many possible ways to answer the question based on the context in which it is asked. From one perspective, a game is its live, enacted gameplay. *Crazy Taxi* (1999) does not exist *as a game* until someone plays it and engages with its exchange of information and its structure of emergent decision-making opportunities. In another sense, a game is the commercial product that one can purchase digitally or at retail locations and perhaps even hold in her hands as a disc or cartridge. After all, the moment of purchasing the *Crazy Taxi* disc is the moment one transitions from "not owning *Crazy Taxi*" to "owning *Crazy Taxi*". This can be reduced to the data *on* that disc, cartridge, or download. If one's *Crazy Taxi* disc is scratched beyond what the Dreamcast can read, one no longer owns (has the ability to play) *Crazy Taxi*. Or maybe a game is not its specific codebase but is the set of logics that the code represents. *Crazy Taxi* is available for multiple systems and settings, each with different hardware architecture that requires different code to execute properly. If it is true that *Crazy Taxi* on Dreamcast and *Crazy Taxi* on Xbox 360 are essentially the same *game* despite their code-level differences, the essence of a game must exist at a level deeper than its digital DNA.

This is an abbreviation of the exploration in Chapter 2, and it leads us to a conclusion about the process of artistic production of video games. A game does not *begin* its "life" as programming code. Substantial intentional design is applied before a single line of code is written. Game developers do not aspire to write beautiful code; they wish to create meaningful experiences, and the digital simulation is simply the medium by which the experience is actualized.

Design Language

So, before a programming language is ever utilized, a different kind of language is used to plan the structure of the play experience: design language. The term "game design" typically refers to the design of rules, goals, and variables. The design of the systems and mechanics of gameplay may be iterated upon using the tools of tabletop or social play (such as cards and tokens). There are many specialties within game design in a development studio: combat design, technical design, puzzle design, competitive design, mechanics design, economy design, UI/UX design, etc. The organizing principles that drive game logic are planned ahead of their codebase implementation.

Narrative design intermingles with this type of pre-production design as well. Narrative is important to the manner in which players contextually understand gameplay, and the aims of the narrative will influence the types of structure of mechanics deemed appropriate to enact them. For instance, if the developers wish to explore a narrative of mannered negotiations, it would be unwise to heavily invest in systems of violent conflict. Narrative design includes not only writing the story of a game (in fact, *narrative designer* and *writer*, *quest designer*, or *story designer* are typically separate specialties in game development teams; the former concerned with large-scale systems design and the latter with embedded story content), it also involves making decisions about player perspective, information flow between game and player, experiential pacing, characterization, and player direction.

Level design is also considered during this preproduction phase. Most video games are inherently spatial, so the layout of spaces can determine or influence the types of choices that players can make and will necessitate certain types of choices from a mechanical perspective. Level designers determine how players will move through a space and how to best shape the game's spaces to pace the experience and encourage the desired forms of player behavior. The discipline of level design may be divided, depending on the type of game, between *level design* (regarding the spatial arrangement of topology, challenges, and information for small or contained spaces, managing the players' moment-to-moment navigational experience) and *world design*, considering the navigation and flow between large, interconnected spaces, typically those that are navigated across the *whole* of a playthrough, particularly in open-world games (Yang, 2025).

These and many other specialized forms of design precede the implementation of code and continue through the development process. The considerations and work done at this stage are examples of design language. Design language is based on the conventions of production but is not the specifically codified technical language of implementation. Design language pertains to vision-setting and structure of the intended audience experience. Specialized language develops as a matter of convention rather than being strictly codified. For example, a developer may say, "I want my game to have a roguelike structure", understood by other developers to mean "a structure of shorter, discrete play sessions that reset player progress completely after avatar deaths rather than being a structure of continual progression along a game-long narrative trend".

It is not *necessary* for video game players to learn design language, but its proximity to the experiential qualities of play means that players will likely pick up on some of the conventions through re-exposure across multiple games and engagement with the community. In fact, the task of forming practical strategies in-game will require design-oriented thinking, even if the player does not need to internalize design-oriented *vocabulary*.

The video game player, in this regard, sits between the film audience and the board game player. An avid film watcher may recognize conventions of cinematic design language, but unless she specifically reads about design techniques or engages with paratexts such as film commentaries or interviews, she may never naturally encounter terms like "ADR" and "Dutch angle". These design techniques (such as staging, camera movements, and sound design) engineer aspects of the experience of watching the film, creating certain moods or narrative beats, and they may become familiar with repetition, but it is only *necessary* that she *feel* the effects of these techniques at a gut level rather than understanding them at an intellectual level.

The card game player, on the other hand, *must* internalize design-oriented patterns of thought. Since players self-direct play and are responsible for the enforcement of rules, players must engage directly with the game's design layer—more likely than not, utilizing the specific vocabulary of design.

The video game player does not bear the responsibility of rule maintenance that the card game player does. Video game rules are enforced and enacted by the computer, so the player can take a much more embodied role within the game rather than having to understand and enact the specificities of design. But the video game player also cannot surrender to the more passive, experience-led mode of the film watcher, as the player is required to act and make choices within the game systems in order to play. A greater grasp of the strategic affordances within a video game will lead to a deeper engagement with its design layer, but not necessarily to the same degree that the card game player will experience. For example, to inform a video game player's strategy in an role-playing game (RPG) battle system, she may benefit from knowing that water attacks are strong against fire enemies, but she will not need to understand the specifics to the same degree. So, whereas a card game player might have to calculate by hand (base damage * [elemental advantage – level difference]), the video game player can understand the broad strokes of the rules and let the computer work out the specificities.

In Chapter 6, I will introduce three perspectives a player takes during video game play: the diegetic perspective involves the embodied experience of presence and movement through the virtual world, the mimetic perspective involves role-playing and otherwise engaging with the fiction a game simulates, and the methectic perspective involves manipulating game elements as logical variables and software affordances in order to form productive strategies for metagame-level play. It is this third perspective that encourages engagement with design language. As one de-abstracts the representational aspects of play into mechanical logics and operations, the player moves from the experiential language toward design language.

As such, explorations within this book will hop between experiential and design languages. An understanding of the logical qualities of video games enriches the experience of play to a greater and more necessary degree than an understanding of the technical operations of play. There are situations in which it is useful to call upon *some* technical language, though. As a computational medium, the algorithmic logics at the basis of code execution *unavoidably* inform the design-level logics that developers can implement. The design goals that developers wish to fulfill must be able to be instantiated by a computer, lacking the flexibility and negotiability of human-administered play or fantasy. To a great degree, the digital nature of the video game medium is a deterministic factor that shapes the kinds of stories that can be told and the types of experiences that can be explored. As such, deepening one's understanding of games' technical language and capacities *will* lead to richer play.

Technical Language

While a game's rules and mechanics are planned at the design level, they are inscribed into a digital system using technical language. This is not simply a process of literalizing design, though. Further experiential creation occurs at this level. Due to the complexity of the systems that games simulate—particularly involving physics or artificial intelligence (AI) systems—elements central to ludic experience and identity are "found" during technical implementation. In fact, the most exciting behavioral elements of games—their ability to produce unpredictable yet logical emergent behaviors through interactions between complex or multi-sequential mechanics—often emerge from fortuitous technical synergies rather than pre-planned design.

Technical language is the language of games' inscription. Unlike card games, in which players internalize and act upon and within the designed rule systems, video game players *only* interface with games' technical layers and *not* their design layers. In other words, developers may envision the series of rules and choices that constitute a game, but players can only ever interface with those rules in their digital form, *after* they have been translated from design language to technical language. For instance, in a game about painting like *Passpartout: The Starving Artist* (2017), the developer may design a rule that says, "patrons pay more for beautiful paintings than ugly paintings", but she can only enforce this rule to the degree that she can create a systemic methodology for programmatically recognizing "beauty" and "ugliness" in the paintings that the player creates. If the developer programs the rule to recognize beautiful paintings as "only those that use colors contained to 90-degree segments of the color wheel", then *that* is the *effective* rule at the technical level. If the player comes to understand *that* technical specificity, she only needs to obey *that* rule and can disregard the *abstract* design rule concerning "beauty" and "ugliness".

As illustrated above, technical language requires that any abstractness or subjectivity of rules be made concrete and quantifiable. The preservation of abstract principles must be simulated through adequate complexity or (semi-)randomness of variables. So, for example, if a developer wanted to create a simulation that evoked the abstract and undefinable experience of falling in love (something poorly suited to the kinds of binary, logical operations computer prefer), she might program an attraction mechanic that queries 50 different character variables in order to obscure the logical, deterministic nature of the calculation, or she might choose to attach or modify the attraction variable with a random number generator to give it a sense of spontaneity (though computers are unable to generate *truly* random numbers; in actuality, this is similarly another level of "obscuring the pattern through complexity" at a technical level).

The technical language of games involves their operational code. Even this has multiple layers of abstraction. Developers program in semantically parsable programming languages (such as Java, Python, or C#), which are more specific, logical, and ordered than conversational language but still easily readable by those who are familiar with that programming language. This human-oriented programming language is compiled into an assembly language, which is still semantically parsable but more specifically oriented to the machine operations of computer architecture. It is more difficult for humans to efficiently read because it foregoes the linguistic logics of higher-level programming code. That language is assembled into binary (the language of 0s and 1s), which corresponds to the on/off states of the billions of transistors within the computer. Binary is purely optimized for machine operation and holds no semantic similarity to natural language, so while humans can *decode* binary, it is a slow and inefficient process, thus the layers of abstraction above it.

As noted previously, there are those who advocate for this kind of technically grounded literacy to be a part of the instruction of video game and new media design and critique. This is called *procedural literacy*, and it typically entails a higher-level, architectural understanding of the logical operations of technical languages rather than in-depth, specialized fluency in any particular programming language itself. Procedural literacy entails "the ability to read and write processes, to engage procedural representation and aesthetics, to understand the interplay between the culturally-embedded practices of human meaning-making and technically-mediated processes" (Mateas, 2005, pp. 101, 102). It is a useful perspective in the study of video games and other new media objects because:

> without an understanding of how code operates as an expressive medium, new media scholars are forced to treat the operation of the media artifacts they study as a black box, losing the crucial relationship between authorship, code, and audience reception.
>
> *(p. 102)*

The medium of expression has influence over the types of stories and ideas artists are able to produce and the manner in which those stories and ideas are expressed. It is useful for the literate player to be able to distinguish authorial choices from the formal qualities of the digital medium and to be able to construct meaningful relationships with games (and other new media artifacts) using the language and logics of computation. For it is with the technical operation of the machine that players truly interact when playing games. The conceptual and representative layers of video games are translations of their fundamental, procedural processes.

This book balances both the experiential aesthetics of games and their procedural systemics in the formation of a holistic literacy model. For a more comprehensive, technical focus, Michael Mateas recommends the curated compilation *The New Media Reader*, edited by his UC Santa Cruz colleague Noah Wardrip-Fruin and Massachusetts Institute of Technology interactive fiction specialist Nick Montfort (2003).

Procedural Functions and Protostory

To review, game design begins as a function of abstract rule definition before being translated into its computational form as usable software. Unlike social games and sports, though, in which one could say that their "essential forms" can be adequately captured in their rule definition, the complexity and emergent nature of game systems resists such a reduction. This is partially because comparable elements of complexity and emergence are preconditions of social game and sport design. Physics and human cognition are the elements with which the rules of games such as baseball, tag, and Poker interact to create the interesting, unpredictable qualities that make those games exciting. But such preconditions are taken as a given in the definitions of those activities, so one does not describe the laws of gravity, inertia, and psychology when listing their rules. Thus, one can succinctly summarize and capture the essences of these games in a manner that feels true to their enacted expressions.

The same is not true of video games, though. All elements of the virtual are arbitrary, such that games that do rely upon simulated physics or AI will each manifest *their own* expressions of physics and AI that may or may not behave similarly to any others'. Whereas baseball is developed to interact with the existent physics of the Earth, *Super Mario Bros.* (1985) must define its own physics, its own Earth. The elements of greatest complexity and emergence are in the scope of design rather than the scope of presupposition.

As such, matters such as physics, the avatar's movement affordances, and the decision-making capabilities of non-player characters (NPCs) are expressive choices within the simulation. Elements are chosen for their abilities to create spontaneous and interesting reactions with one another, a property called *emergence*—the unpredictable but logical patterns that emerge from a large system as a result of the logical interactions between its individual components. Games scholar Janet Murray illustrates this property with the example of geese, flocking in a V shape as they fly. "Each goose [locates] itself with reference to its immediate neighbors but no goose [has] a goal of creating the emergent chevron shape of the group" (Murray, 2012, p. 418).

Game developers aim to create fascinating aesthetics and compelling structures of decision-making within the systems of emergence that the computer can produce. As such, the code that comprises the software structure of the game does not aim to represent a specific, deterministic vision as does the programming that constructs a 3D animated film or programmed lights display. Developers create stages for action potential; possibility spaces in which new dimensions of agency can be tested and explored.

That which developers program can be roughly divided into two categories: procedural content and protostory. Procedural content is that which is in service of the *emergent narrative*, the player-motivated experience of play. This includes opportunities for expressive player agency (real-time play or designated branching choices) and rule-based interactions that can produce emergent behaviors by the properties of their interrelationships.

Protostory, on the other hand, includes the prefabricated content or unalterable elements of narrative or experiential structure, such as dialogue, cutscenes, lore, sound effects, voice performances, scenarios, and more. Coined by Hartmut Koenitz, protostory "describes the concrete content, internal structure, and outward appearance of an IDN system as a space of potential narratives that is connected to any instantiated narrative through a participatory process" (Koenitz, 2023, p. 76). As Koenitz outlines, the protostory creates the structure and shape of the narrative space in which play unfolds. We can classify games with a *strong protostory* as those in which gameplay largely follows predefined routes or feature a large proportion of embedded narrative, while games in which activity and narrative are largely emergent would be classified as having a *weak protostory* (Grinblat et al., 2021).

While many disciplines of game development involve the construction of procedural systems with no *definite* shape before live instantiation enacts them, some disciplines craft *specific, static* materials that *do* have definite form and pre-exist their live, systemic enactment. For that reason, it is necessary to caveat the statement that video game narrative and art exist as procedural instruction that is instantiated in real time by the computer, because, obviously, vocal performances were recorded in advance, the text of a game's embedded narrative was written ahead of time, etc. But as a general differentiator from other mediums in which *all* of the material is fabricated prior to the audience experience (live theatre and music excepted), the procedural quality of game art is necessary to consider in its interpretation.

Computation

To review, the act of inscription performed by game developers involves the (literal) codification of a game experience into protostory (prefabricated content) and procedural content (parameters, variables, and contingencies that inform the behavior of the simulation and the player's affordances within it). The procedural content, which we can generalize as the *rules* of the system (nuances are addressed in a later section in this chapter), are both *absolute* within the context of the system (in that one cannot negotiate "house rules" with the computer in the same way that one can make on-the-fly modifications to rules of social games played with friends) but also *system-dependent*, meaning that the rules are executed within the specific system architecture of the host computer, and the proficiency and manner of execution might vary as a game is played across different types of systems.

The system architecture of early game computers and consoles was so distinct from one another that games would essentially have to be rebuilt entirely when "ported" to other systems, such as from the Super NES to the SEGA Genesis. Since then, as computational frameworks trend toward greater standardization, differences in processing power or specific hardware-grounded specialties drive differences between otherwise high-fidelity ports. For example, the PlayStation and its competitor, the Nintendo 64, relied upon, among other differences, different types of game storage media. PlayStation games were distributed on discs, which had a capacity of up to 650 MB, suitable for large assets like pre-rendered video, music, and textures, but they loaded slowly. Nintendo 64 games, on the other hand, were distributed on cartridges that had capacities of up to 64 MB but could be read by the system almost instantly. PlayStation games ported to Nintendo 64 typically had to reduce the number and quality of assets used, such that *Tony Hawk's Pro Skater* (1999) featured only about half as many songs in its licensed soundtrack on N64 as it did on PlayStation, while the N64 port of action game *Shadow Man* (1999) tended to be preferred to its PlayStation counterpart for its shorter load times.

In the modern age, game consoles and PCs have similar architectural structures such that porting from PlayStation 5 to Xbox Series to PC generally results in a high fidelity of experience between platforms, but peripheral design differences can result in game design changes evident between ports. For example, games ported from PlayStation 5 to Xbox Series must remove motion-sensing features and nuanced haptic feedback, as these features are not supported by the Xbox's controllers.

Even within the same platform category, games may execute differently on different machines. Gaming PCs are modular and highly configurable, such that gameplay experience on the platform is difficult to predict from a game developer's perspective. Some players have expensive PCs with cutting-edge technology that can run games at a level of visual performance beyond even what their developers expected, while other players may wish to run a game on a family laptop purchased primarily for spreadsheet and tax software purposes, without advanced graphics and sound technology. Some PCs may have unusual *bottlenecks*, such that one component may be cutting-edge and top-of-the-line while another component drags down performance. The more *scalable* a game is, the better able it is to adapt to different hardware environments, remaining adequately performant to support play.

This is all to say that game developers do not necessarily know the technological conditions in which their games will be played. Even when designing for a particular console, a game may be played with a nonstandard controller, emulated later (played within software that virtualizes the architecture of an older console, usually with additional features not available to players of the original console, such as the ability to save and reload the state of the game at any time or performance enhancements beyond that which the console was able to generate), or a particular computer may suffer component malfunctions or electrical issues that result in unintended game behavior.

As such, the *rules* of a game are not necessarily aligned with the rules as intended and designed by the game's developers. Play is constrained by the rules *as implemented by the specific system of play*. So not only are games open-ended, non-deterministic systems, but the rules that govern their play may be altered or disrupted depending on the hardware environment in which they are enacted.

The specific code written for a particular game is often built on top of a *game engine* (for example, Unreal, Unity, Frostbite, RE Engine, GameMaker), which is a prebuilt package of simulation parameters and runtime behaviors that manages foundational aspects of constructing the virtual space, such as managing physics, sound, animation, network communications, environmental stability, etc. Essentially, engines are tried-and-tested collections of the basic structures that *every* game requires, packaged by specialist studios so that developers do not need to reprogram these foundational aspects for *every* game that they produce. Engines have different specialities and may be better suited for particular genres or styles of games. Though engines are modified to suit the specific needs of each game programmed on top of them, most engine code is prewritten by teams outside of the individual game's development team.

Further, individual plugins and sub-engines may be added to a primary engine to support specialized functions. These *middleware* engines may specialize in general functions like physics (Havok, PhysX) or sound implementation (FMOD, Wwise), or they might support highly specific functions like facial animation (FaceWorks) or weather simulation (TrueSky).

Bespoke code, engine code, and middleware code execute within a host computer's operating system (OS), a runtime environment with its own set of architectural specificities. The OS communicates software functions into electrical and mechanical functions within the computer itself. The OS often serves an invisible communicative layer between the code and its representation, but the computer OS typically also has its own user interface (UI) that players navigate outside of the gameplay environment (such as Windows or Linux on PCs), and OS-level UI may even interact with aspects of games' runtime behaviors (such as Achievement tracking and popups on Xbox consoles or screenshot and video capture capabilities in many system environments).

OS activity translates runtime software execution to machine functions, managing processor behavior, data storage, and video and audio display, among other things. The sensory signals given to the player through audio, video, and haptic sensory systems are the result of this processing (as are many unseen processes), and it is at this stage in the chain of translation that players encounter the game as software.

Player Input and Feedback

Sensory representation is the only mode of insight and feedback that players have into the virtual simulation. Though the game *world* is ontologically fictional, the factors that comprise the simulation are marginally less so. Runtime behavior within the simulation follows a chain of translations that results in real, electrical, and mechanical behaviors within the host machine. These functions enable calculations and the memory of information that is then codified into the representational layer that comprises the game's fantasy.

From a design perspective, the representational layer comprises both prefabricated and player-configurable protostory assets, while the systems that drive emergence are primarily pre-representational, occurring within the procedural functions of the game's algorithmic layer with results being represented with assets from the protostory layer.

Player interactivity is confined within designated affordances. Unlike sports or immersive role-play situations like theme park storytelling, in which participants *can* perform all number of prohibited activities like fighting, virtual behaviors within a video game simulation are limited to explicitly (or unintentionally) afforded actions. The avatar cannot even move or look around unless the game has programmed movement and perspective systems. Within the bounds of those affordances, though, players often have a great amount of freedom to manipulate the simulation and personalize the experience of play.

Some games optimize for the greatest amount of player freedom possible (such as sandbox games like *Minecraft* [2011] and *Grand Theft Auto V* [2013]); some constrain players to narrow and predefined paths (such as games that wish to tell very specific stories, like *Life Is Strange* [2015] and *The Walking Dead* [2012]). Games that offer substantial freedom and react with appropriate systemic effect can be called *expressive*, a term I detail further in Chapter 12.

Players are the greatest, most unpredictable source of emergence within gameplay systems. Their choices and behaviors are highly personal, and many players engage in metagames directly contrary to the goals of designed play (for instance, the curiosity of how far off-course or in the opposite direction a game will allow a player to go before enforcing directional boundaries). As artifacts of artistic design, the shaping of gameplay into a meaningful form involves the design of all elements that comprise gameplay, including player agency and behavior. Game developers have techniques beyond the outright prohibition of particular behaviors whereby preferred behaviors may be elicited from players. These principles (elaborated upon later in this chapter) include piquing the player's curiosity and interest toward areas of greater design concentration or managing the availability of information (such as visual sight-lines) to direct players). From a design perspective, this is what Janet H. Murray (1997) terms *scripting the interactor* (p. 79). Without removing the player's active agency, this type of player direction makes preferred behaviors more likely, such that gameplay experiences can be paced and optimized around these expected but nondeterministic routes of activity.

As extensively detailed in Chapter 4, player input into the system of gameplay is mediated through "threshold objects" (Murray, 2012, p. 297) that translate the player's physical actions (themselves translations of mental impulses) into digital signals interpretable by the computer. In a sense, the receptive interaction affordances of games and the functions encoded into controller inputs represent a language of play. Particular thumb and finger movements represent certain diegetic actions in the same way that particular vocalizations represent specific ideas in spoken language. In well-designed play, this "language" quickly becomes intuitive and even transparent (see Chapter 4), and the player's attention and cognition instead turn toward the task of determining the language-like logic of diegetic and mechanical interplay. In other words, inhabiting the avatar or locus of mediated manipulation becomes second nature, and the player can take a fully embodied role in solving and participating in the systems of ludic challenge.

Players form agential relationships with game systems through the feedback that games provide to these inputs and to non-player-driven activity within the game world. Feedback, and particularly visual feedback, forms the link between controller inputs and avatar actions that makes control transparency and projective embodiment possible (see Chapter 4). The elucidation of cause-effect relationships (or *perceivable consequence* [Church, 1999]) is what enables players to internalize a "vocabulary" of action and participate in the "conversation" of play. Like any other language, patterns of control activity become conventional through repetitive use, amidst the full range of possible control inputs. As players form preferences for particular patterns of behavior, their individual play styles, like accents or dialects, become personal and identifiable, a factor of expressive play, detailed in Chapter 12.

In that sense, players, like game developers, utilize a kind of design language (though one that is less verbal and formalized than that of game design) in order to translate their motivated intentions for (diegetic) objective achievement into a technical language of symbolic gestures, "programming" their intended actions into controllers that, in turn, translate those inputs into the machine language executable by the computer. There is a kind of symmetry in the tasks of the developer and player, and each contributes to the form taken by the gameplay enactment.

RULES

The linguistic framing of the previous section is intentional. In the beginning of this book, I defined art as something that not only generates novel experiences but is also specifically *communicative*, allowing artists to inscribe and transmit feelings, aesthetics, and senses that are not directly translatable through direct, informational exchange. Video games are unique among the arts for not only including this kind of exchange of inscribed intangibility but also allowing *bidirectional* conversation between the work (by intentional extension, the artist) and the player.

Gameplay is commonly framed as being a "conversation". Action is met with response, and the appropriateness of that response is judged by paradigms of rules and conventions. The player queries the game; the game responds. The game tests the player; the player responds. The most engrossing moments of gameplay are the situations in which player actions do not terminate further conversation (with a totalizing solution to a singular problem) but open up new questions and possibilities, unearthing unforeseen complexities and nuances of the simulated situations.

Players are (apart from extremely rare examples) not actually conversing with the human developers of the games through play, but players converse with systems and mechanics specifically designed to anticipate and respond to a wide variety of player actions. The developer, in the design of the game's procedural systems, encodes a proxy representation of herself into the conversational structure of play. More than just a static representative of thematic interests, as with traditional arts, she encodes a logic by which the whole of the virtual world operates.

A game's rules establish the "grammar" by which the conversation between player and game takes place. They determine what a player can do, cannot do, and establish the context for why the player may or may not want to pursue particular objectives.

Defining Rules

Many have defined *rule* in the context of games. Miguel Sicart (2013) defines rules as "formal structures of the game, the boundaries within which play takes place and is freely accepted by players" (p. 26). Jesper Juul (2005) notes that rules "provide challenges that require ingenuity to overcome", emphasizing their role in providing direction and structure to the game (p. 55). Salen and Zimmerman (2003) call rules "'sets of instructions', and following those instructions means doing what the rules require and not doing something else instead", emphasizing their role in constraining player actions into the game's particular set of allowed actions. Steve Swink (2009) calls rules "arbitrary, designed [relationships] between parameters or objects in a game. Arbitrary because there is no higher order guiding the creation of such relationships and designed because it is a relationship intentionally created by a designer" (p. 179), insisting that the process of game design is in the formation of meaningful relationships between game components, described by rules. "[The] meaning of a coin, a star or any other such part of a game is given only by its relationship to other parts of the game" (Swink, 2009, p. 98).

Swink describes three types of rules. High-level rules (goals and incentives) orient play toward specific ends. A game has an objective and a conclusion, while free play does not. Rules **direct** play and **define incentives.** Mid-level rules assign special meanings to objects in the field of play, such that, during a game, possession and direction of a football become critically important, not as a property of the ball itself but as an assigned importance bestowed by the rules. After the game, the football returns to its original state of being fairly unimportant. Rules **designate value.** Low-level rules define the properties of game components. For example, the slipperiness of an ice floor in an action game is a low-level property of the environment (being an ice floor as opposed to a normal floor) and of the relationship between the avatar and environment (inertia). Rules **define relationships** (Swink, 2009, pp. 179, 180).

The previously quoted Katie Salen (Tekinbaş) and Eric Zimmerman provide one of the most robust definitions in their aptly-titled *Rules of Play* (2003). They identify several characteristics of rules that are useful to consider. Below are their categories as well as some exceptions and alternate perspectives as they are applied to video games.

Rules limit player action. Rules provide structure to game activities, constraining play action by prohibiting certain types of actions. This is what philosopher Bernard Suits calls adopting a *lusory attitude*; we intentionally take on inefficient means of pursuing our goals in order to create more interesting structures of challenge. In his famous example, he describes the absurdity of golf. "[If] my end were simply to get a ball into a number of holes in the ground, I would not be likely to use a golf club in order to achieve it, nor would I stand at a considerable distance from each hole" (Suits, 1978, p. 23); rather, it would be more efficient to carry the ball over to the hole and drop it in by hand. In order to create a more engrossing structure of challenge, though, we take on inefficient means for pursuing the (arbitrary) objectives in front of us. We limit ourselves from doing things most efficiently.

Jesper Juul (2005) notes that this definition is incomplete. "The rules of a game also *set up potential actions*, actions that are meaningful inside the game but meaningless outside. [...] Rules specify *limitations* and *affordances*" (p. 58). His criticism is particularly relevant in the context of video games. It is not a limitation that Donkey Kong cannot carry a golf ball and drop it into a hole in *Mario Golf* (1999), since Donkey Kong does not exist as an entity separate from his programmed instantiation. His actions are not *limited*, per se; he is only able to utilize the set of actions he has been afforded. In the context of *Mario Golf* as software rather than *Mario Golf* as fantasy, Donkey Kong is only able to hit balls with his club; he has no inclination or ability to cheat because that action is outside of his total available actions. Since *all* actions in video games are arbitrary and bestowed, it can be more useful to think of (at least low-level) rules as primarily describing affordances and *justifying* (or contextualizing) limitations.

In fact, the reason Donkey Kong cannot cheat in *Mario Golf* is *because it is impossible.* Were players to find a way to cheat, perhaps by pivoting the character back and forth in such a way that nudged the golf ball forward without counting as a stroke, the "game" (or, more accurately, the *metagame*) of *Mario Golf* would instead evolve to be which player could most successfully exploit this design oversight rather than who can play the best game of golf. Donkey Kong does not obey the rules of *golf*; he (and the player) are subject only to the rules of the *software*, and to the degree that the *software* can be exploited in a manner that is contrary to the rules of *golf*, the game does not punish or limit such exploitation in its non-conscious impartiality as referee of ludic action. Rather, we can say that the rules of golf provide semantic justification to the player for the software constraints that may or may not be evenly and accurately applied. This distinction will be pulled into greater focus in the Metagame section below.

Salen and Zimmerman (2003) note that rules limit *player* action, in particular. While this is true for the reason stated above (a Chess player limits herself to moving her knight pieces in an L-shaped pattern even when she wishes they could move elsewhere, though a Chess-playing computer is not *limited* because it does not consider movement beyond the knights' L-shaped pattern to be a possibility), if we consider rules in terms of both limitations *and* affordances, we can say that rules apply equally to players and other entities within the system of play. Computer-controlled opponents, for example, are constrained in a similar manner to human players. Sometimes these constraints are symmetrical, as when facing off against a computer-controlled opponent in a fighting game, and sometimes they are asymmetrical, such as the limited affordances of a Goomba compared to the player's Mario. Even in cases of asymmetry, though, computer-controlled entities follow rule-based patterns of behavior. To succeed against artificial opponents, such as the ghosts in *PAC-MAN* (1980), the player must read motivation into their patterned actions in order to anticipate what they will do. For the behavior of *PAC-MAN*'s ghosts to make sense, the player must understand them in terms of the rules that constrain, define, and give value to their activities: they aim to kill Pac-Man, they are limited to moving in the same channels of the maze as Pac-Man does, and they become vulnerable to counter-attack when Pac-Man consumes a Power Pellet. Rules direct their actions as individual actors and collectively in service of the system of gameplay. So rather than specifying that rules direct *player* action, it is useful to instead frame rules as directing the actions of *all agents* within the gameplay system (or all intelligent or artificially intelligent elements, if you are not comfortable anthropomorphizing NPCs for the sake of the metaphor).

Rules are explicit and unambiguous. Salen and Zimmerman (2003) note that rules must be discernible; otherwise, gameplay collapses as proceedings seem arbitrary and unfair. I believe that this characteristic is carried forward from traditional games and is not necessarily true of video games. Card and board games require that players maintain the structure of play through their internalized understanding of the game's rules during play, thus the requirement to read through the rule pamphlet when playing an unfamiliar game. If players do not provide this load-bearing integrity by way of rule-obedient play and active refereeing, the game has no other mechanisms for enforcing the rules itself; it becomes formless.

Video games, on the other hand, do not require this level of rule maintenance from players, since rules *are* enforced mechanistically and automatically by the software system. Playing Chess requires that players know the objective and movement patterns of each piece and understand the mechanics of play; otherwise, gameplay will degrade into formlessness. Playing a video game adaptation of Chess, though, is possible without a knowledge of the rules. An unfamiliar player may not make *good* choices with an absence of knowledge of the objective, but she cannot *but* move her pieces in the afforded movement patterns and abide by the basic structure of the game. She cannot cheat because the system does not afford such options, whereas I am sure everyone has been in a situation in which players of a card or board game discovered midway through play that they had all been "cheating" due to misunderstanding a rule upon reviewing the pamphlet.

Because video game rules are enforced automatically, many video games obscure rules from their players. Determining these rules may be the primary puzzle involved with these games. Sometimes this is a temporary obscurity with rules eventually becoming explicit and unambiguous over the course of play, as with games about mechanical deduction, such as *Outer Wilds* (2019), *Starseed Pilgrim* (2013), and *Riven* (1997). Some games maintain a "black box" model by which one can come to understand the general logic of the system but not its *precise* variables, common in city-builder and business tycoon-style games in which the player always aims to build a *better* system to suit the balance of needs as they evolve without ever achieving optimal equilibrium (see games like *SimCity* [1989] and *Planet Coaster* [2016]). Obscurity of the rules that guide NPC behavior and motivation can create more believable characters, such as in *Viva Piñata* (2006), in which the magical animals that live in the game's world may be attracted to or repelled from the player's garden based on a combination of known likes/dislikes and other emergent factors that give the impression of personality-driven decision-making. Other games use a lack of explicit clarity of rules to create a spontaneous and improvisational style of play, challenging players to think on their feet and adapt to changing circumstances with no time to prepare, such as *WarioWare, Inc.: Mega Microgames!* (2003) and *WHAT THE GOLF?* (2019).

Rules are shared by all players. This refers to a fair application that leads to the exciting unpredictability of games that anyone has the ability to win. Salen and Zimmerman do not make this explicit in their writing, but one can presume that they did not mean to imply that rules are *identical* among all players. Golf handicaps aim for equity rather than equality, orienting play toward a closeness of competition rather than absolute fairness in the challenge of skills. There are also several games constructed with an asymmetrical structure, such as tag, where one player ("it") opposes all others and has a different objective and set of affordances than those who she chases. In the video game realm, games like *Dead by Daylight* (2016) and *Predator: Hunting Grounds* (2020) cast one player as a dangerous monster or killer and all others as disempowered survivors that only stand a chance against the lone player through collective cooperation. Other games create interesting asymmetries through the unequal distribution of knowledge, such as *Among Us* (2018) or the *Luigi's Ghost Mansion* minigame in the *Nintendo Land* (2012) collection.

In those cases of asymmetry, though, the understanding that *there will be* asymmetry is shared by all players. In that sense, all players "share" the rule that play affordances are asymmetrically balanced. So then this might be a reflection of the fact that all game elements are in relationship with one another. If Mario has the property of being able to jump on Goombas' heads to destroy them, Goombas have the inverse property of being vulnerable to Mario's jump. In that sense, all rules are "shared" by extension of being properties of relationships.

Rules are fixed. Playing games with children often involves resisting their impulses to alter the rules at any moment in which different parameters may advantage them. Such is the comical observation of *Calvin & Hobbes*' (Watterson, 1985–1995) Calvinball, a "game" with rules in perpetual flux based on the whims of its creator. In order for play to be directed and sensible, rules are fixed and not up for renegotiation during the course of play. As Salen and Zimmerman (2003) call out, there are games that *do* allow for changing of rules over the course of play, but these games have rules that determine when and how such rule-changing can take place.

In video games, the "fixedness" of rules is subject to technical implementation. If "rules" are considered the *semantic* rules that developers designed in order to embed into the game systems (such as the rules of golf in *Mario Golf* [1999]), then those rules only apply insofar as they cannot be exploited within the superseding technical structure of the metagame. If "rules" are considered to be all technical affordances, such that the rules of *Mario Golf* are "whatever the player can make the simulation do" rather than aligning to the rules of real-world golf, then this level of rules is subject to the stability and predictability of said technical implementation. If a glitch prevents a golf ball appropriately hit into a hole from being recognized, the "rule" has changed. It is a common point of frustration for players to have progress halted by glitches. Unlike the types of routine glitches that players may reliably exploit in order to gain an advantage, some glitches occur intermittently, unpredictably, and destructively. Certainly these represent the kind of disruption that breaks the sanctity of a game to which Salen and Zimmerman refer.

Rules are binding. In other words, in order to maintain the structure of play, players should respect the authority of rules. Deliberate subversion makes one a spoilsport who degrades the integrity and stability of the game as a social experience.

Again, I hold this claim in contention with video games as self-enforcing systems. If a player *can* subvert a "rule", that subversion becomes a part of the metagame. In fact, deliberate subversion often makes gameplay more expressive and creative (see Chapters 12 and 13). The player does not have the responsibility to respect the authority of rules; the player is subject to the automatically enforced rules, and being able to topple this hierarchical relationship can be cathartic in itself.

Rules are repeatable. This refers to the "transportability" of rules, such that *anyone* with a deck of cards can play Solitaire or Poker as long as they have the knowledge of the rules that direct play. This can refer to the holistic transmission of rules, but one can also separate and transport individual rules from games and apply them to others. These transmutable rule-elements are called *ludemes* (Parlett, 2007). One can, for instance, extract the "three point line" ludeme from basketball, for instance, and apply it to hockey, whereby one can award additional points for goals that are made from a certain distance from the net. Or one can extract the "hidden game piece identity" ludeme from Stratego and apply it to Chess to alter the game experience. I go into greater depth on ludemes in Chapter 7.

The transportability of video game rules brings up some interesting considerations, some of which relate to that which was explored earlier in this chapter. If someone draws an 8×8 grid on the ground and improvises Checker pieces from acorns and leaves, it is reasonable to say that they can play a real game of Checkers because the "soul" of the game lies not in its physical board and game pieces but in the relationships it designates between arbitrary tokens and spaces. Conversely, even if one were able to distill and represent the mathematical logics, relationships, and spaces of *Pokémon* (1996), one could still not play *Pokémon* with acorns and leaves (except for in the loose sense in which one can imaginatively "play doctor"). As such, the ephemeral "rules" of video games are not "transportable" in whole in that manner.

Katamari Damacy (2004) was ported to the Unity engine from the custom engine on which it was originally built for its 2018 remake, and while experienced players can feel *some* difference between the versions, a dedication to high-fidelity equivalency of rules makes the experience seem approximately equivalent. So rule systems might not be able to necessarily break *out* of the digital medium, but there is a level of transportability within the medium.

Further, rules in isolation can be identified and followed between games as ludemes. In the same way that board game players can extract logics from those games and apply them to others, video games have a long history of reappropriating and iterating upon individual mechanics across games.

Rules and Forces

Many definitions of "games" utilize the structure provided by rules and objectives to differentiate them from free play. Whereas free play is spontaneous and imaginative, games are focused and constrained. The objective of golf is *very* specific, while an imaginary game of playing house may involve a dynamic, loose relationship with boundaries and roles. "Probably the most basic definition of a game is that it is organized play, that is to say rule-based. If you don't have rules you have free play, not a game" (Prensky, 2007, p. 119). Yet even free play has *some* rules. Free play ends when one participant injures or offends another. As play scholar Johan Huizinga remarks in the opening paragraph of his seminal *Homo Ludens* (1938), "[animals at play] keep to the rule that you shall not bite, or not bite hard, your brother's ear" (p. 1). There seems to be a requirement of maintaining the good nature of the play activity. Free play is also, obviously, confined by natural laws. When role-playing as an airplane, one cannot *actually* fly, and this natural restriction imposes a kind of "rule" around the type of imagining that is permitted.

This latter type of "rule" does not feel appropriate to classify as such, though. One does not *agree* to obey the laws of gravity when playing baseball, even though the laws of gravity are *necessary* for baseball to work (such that, if baseball were played on the moon, it would require a fundamental reassessment of the rules that bear relationships to Earthbound physics). Early play researcher Roger Caillois (1958) asserts that games must be "voluntary" (p. 6); that one enters into and can exit from the conditions of play, which implies that games would not include the forces that continue to apply outside of the context of play. As such, we might constrain the definition of rules to the social contracts of behavior alignment necessary for the maintenance of gameplay. Thus, the inverse of this statement finds that it should be possible to *choose* to break rules.

This challenges our paradigm when applied to video games, because players do not *voluntarily* obey video game rules. They cannot choose to disobey. Thus, even the most arbitrary parameters of play in video games are equivalent to the laws of physics in sports. "Videogames conflate the rules of a game with the mechanics of the equipment. [...] Players have no choice but to work within the limitations of these involuntary systems" (Boluk & LeMieux, 2017, p. 8). One can argue that code-level manipulation, or "modding", represents a voluntary disregard of a game's rules, but, in actuality, it is engagement with a *separate* metagame:

> Whereas rules can be broken at a moment's notice, mechanics cannot be turned off. There is no cheating in *Super Mario Bros.* [1985] Editing the code is like corking the bat—the deception occurs within the equipment and changes the game itself.
>
> *(Boluk & LeMieux, 2017, p. 9)*

Instead, we might consider these parameters to be *forces*, invariabilities necessary to play but involuntary in their implementation. "*Forces* compose a system of material-energetic tendencies which are fully actual and not abstract" (Kanaga, 2015). Some go so far as to say that video games *only* contain forces and *do not* support rules (Boluk & LeMieux, p. 8). I find this claim to be, though intellectually interesting, colloquially alienating. It runs contrary to the intuitive understanding that people have about games and complicates some of the useful framings we can implement in the meaning-making process (such as, for example, gameplay actions as comprising a grammar).

Jesper Juul (2005) notes that such forces in sports act as "*objets trouvés* or *found objects*" (p. 67). There is an assumption of something that pre-exists the game being appropriated within it. Though video game rules are involuntarily administered, they are not appropriated; they were designed specifically for the purpose of administering a particular type of play experience. They are elements of design rather than forces that *act upon* a game's design or to which the game's design *reacts*. The choice to play a particular game is a voluntary choice to engage with a set of play mechanics. Though they cannot be rejected individually without wholly rejecting play of the game, the manner of their design and inscription holds closer parallels to what we consider *rules* than *forces*.

I respect that there are reasonable arguments for not calling video game parameters "rules". For the purpose of colloquial clarity and alignment with the language and practices of the community, though, I will continue to refer to these parameters as rules for their role in the structuring and direction of motivated play.

Mechanics

The other term relevant to this definition of rules is *mechanic*. Among the community of video game players, the terms are used almost interchangeably. Among game researchers, there is a tremendous variance in the ways in which *mechanics* are defined and differentiated from *rules*.

With this lack of consensus among my peers in mind, the definition that I will use in this book addresses the issue with rule inscription noted earlier in this chapter. A *rule* is the abstract principle that defines a parameter of play (such as the turn order in a game of Poker), while a *mechanic* is the concrete automation of the allowance and/or enforcement of a rule. A rule is a matter of ephemeral design, whereas a mechanic is a systemic implementation. Rules are semantic, and mechanics are algorithmic.

Again, though, colloquial usages vary greatly within the community of players and researchers. Miguel Sicart (2008) grapples with the diversity of implications, noting that players refer to third-person shooter *Gears of War*'s (2006) "cover mechanic" to apply to a category of similar actions rather than referring to a specific and singular "cover" action. Further, he talks about outer space-based games that have a "mechanic" whereby players can "slingshot" their crafts around planets using their gravitational fields, referring to parameters of the system as mechanics rather than active affordances of individual agents.

Further, many definitions of *mechanic* specify that mechanics are exclusively *player* affordances (Järvinen, 2008, p. 39; Hunicke et al., 2004; Rouse, 2005, p. 310; Fullerton, 2004; Cook, 2006; Fernández-Vara, 2014, p. 122). While this distinction is likely to draw forth the importance of *agency*, mechanics being affordances for choice, it is unnecessary to distinguish human and computer-controlled agents within the game system in the way that this definition is applied. For the purpose of game legibility, computer-controlled agents (and even elements of the system itself) can be read as performing motivated actions and utilizing mechanics of the simulation in an ordered manner similar or identical to the manner in which human players perform such actions. Seeing games as an *interchange* between entities within the simulation makes such practical distinctions between players and other entities unhelpful.

My definition posited above avoids the ambiguity that arises from the diversity of communal applications. I offer a flexible application of the term, such that a mechanic may be actions invoked by an agent or a pattern of behavior invoked by the system itself.

Emergence

Games are wholly rule-based systems, and one of the primary joys of video game play is prodding at the elaborate systems of interlocking rules and seeing what behaviors result. There is a particular beauty in observing the operation of a complex machine.

Imagine sitting on the corner of a busy intersection in a large city. You watch the traffic lights turn from red to green as cars, buses, and bicyclists flow through in an orderly manner. As the light turns yellow and red, the perpendicular pathway motors and pedals through. Pedestrians cross in clumps at crosswalks, people from all walks of life sharing the sidewalks as they all go to their separate destinations. These passageways carry the flow of hundreds of people and vehicles every hour, like arteries connecting the city. The rhythms of stopping and going—north to south, then east to west—are like heartbeats. Each person traveling through the city has her own reason for commuting: work, exercise, school, shopping, romance… But pull far enough back from the individual, and all kinds of beautiful patterns emerge. This is the experience of a property called emergence.

Emergence is "movement from low-level rules to higher-level sophistication" (Johnson, 2001, p. 21). It is organization and "intelligence" that arise from the bottom up rather than the top down. It is the assemblage of individual active components into patterns at a higher level that they likely do not even understand that they are a part of, like the diversity of cells, each with their own "aims", unaware of each other, much less the complex human being that they constitute.

Emergence arises from rule-based systems. Any action that is *truly* random resists the patterning of emergence. But true randomness is almost impossible to produce, so systems trend toward pattern-making as they become larger in scale. Rules created with the intention of producing emergent effects should also be designed to perpetuate or ripple outwards to induce interactions with other rules. Rules that immediately terminate can preclude emergent possibilities.

Because emergence arises from rule-based systems, emergence is both logical at the scale of its individual units and unpredictable at the scale of the whole system. Or rather, unpredictable in a practical sense. Part of the beauty of emergence is that, if an observer has knowledge of all of the variables that mediate the relationships within a system, she could predict with certainty the state of the system at any point. Video games are the same way. Video games execute algorithmic code in a wholly logical, mathematically sound manner. Were one able to read the code of a game in any moment of play and understand all of its variables, she could calculate and chart the state of the system in the next moment, and so forth. For systems as complex as those modeled by video games, this is a practical impossibility, though—at least in real-time. The technical marvel of the computer is that it is able to perform these multitudinous calculations and keep in memory the states of thousands of elements many times per second.

Emergence is the result of rules in relationship with one another. *One* rule is not enough to produce emergent effects. For example, a rule of "add 8 and repeat" *does* result in a pattern (8, 16, 24, 32…), but not a very interesting one; not one that takes on emergent properties. Two rules that are *not in relationship with each other* are also not suitable. "Add 8 and repeat, but subtract 5 if the resulting number is odd" results in the same pattern, since +8 never results in an odd number (if the pattern begins with an even number).

But rules do not need to be complex to produce stunning emergent qualities. British mathematician John Conway produced a famous cellular automaton model called the Game of Life in 1970. It takes place in a grid of squares (infinitely scalable). Each square has two possible states, live or dead (1 or 0). Each cell makes "decisions" about whether it will remain as-is or change to the opposite state one per "step", "generation", or "tick" (point at which all cells within the system recalculate their state), based on the states of the eight cells immediately bordering them (in the cardinal directions and diagonally). The system follows four rules:

1. If a cell is live, die if bordered by fewer than two live cells.
2. If a cell is live, remain live if bordered by two to three live cells.
3. If a cell is live, die if bordered by more than three live cells.
4. If a cell is dead, become live if bordered by exactly three live cells.

The "player" enters a *seed* value into the system; simply, a determination of which cells begin the simulation live or dead. From there, the principles apply, requiring no further inputs. The patterns that emerge from the system have surprising qualities, even resembling simple life forms. Some patterns, such as the "gliders", maintain a relatively stable shape as they move across the grid. The "glider gun" is a stable pattern that generates gliders infinitely. "Puffer trains" are stable shapes that translate across the grid, leaving patterns in their wake.

The illusion of life and even intelligence or motivated intent that arises from these systems of pure mathematical functioning is an exhibition of how even simple rules can create aesthetic experiences when in relationship with one another. Again, it is not the result of any special "magic" or unique logic of computational systems. One can easily calculate each generation in Conway's Game of Life by hand with sheets of graph paper. But this kind of *procedural emergence* is well-suited to computers because of their ability to make these state-based calculations and display results much faster than humans can, so we can observe emergent effects in something like real-time.

There are many sources of emergence in video games. The two primary categories at play within the diegesis of the digital simulation are AI and physics (Mateas, 2003). AI refers to rule-based behaviors that represent (the illusion of) motivated or active intent. This is usually personified as NPC behavior. For example, the movement patterns of *PAC-MAN*'s (1980) ghosts are "motivated" by their "intent" to catch Pac-Man. Physics, on the other hand, are the rules into which "intelligence" cannot be read; reactions that lack intention (Mateas, 2005). For example, a boulder rolling down a hill or a simulated weather system.

The complexity, granularity/sensitivity, and freedom of these systems affect the degree of unpredictable emergence that will arise from their interactions. Freedom pertains to the degree to which "intelligent" actors are able to pursue motivated goals rather than following scripts of action and the degree to which physics objects are unconstrained in their movement. For example, the ghosts in *PAC-MAN* produce highly emergent patterns of behavior because they simply pursue their rule-based goal of catching Pac-Man, while the villager NPCs in *The Legend of Zelda: Link's Awakening* (1993) have minimal freedom, standing still or performing repetitive actions, dispensing one or two lines of text when spoken to but pursuing no motivated goals. They serve as set dressing or exposition deliverers rather than active agents in the world that are capable of producing unprompted behavior.

The richest source of emergence, though, is always human players. Emergence is not necessarily something that a program does in *response to* human input; emergence involves human activity because players are a part of the system that produces gameplay. Like *artificially* intelligent actors, human players have the greatest capacity for producing or contributing to emergent outcomes when they are given the greatest expressive freedom (see Chapter 12). The adoption of alternate forms of play (metagames, including speedrunning or self-imposed challenges, for instance) are highly emergent, systemic behaviors that result in players exercising their freedom within reactive systems.

As a matter of artistic expression, emergence allows developers to not only inscribe semiotic specificities (protostory) but also logics. Whereas traditional storytellers communicate narrative logics through implication by example, video games can instantiate reactive systems within which particular logics are ever-present and can be tested and observed through player action. This renders such variables both highly visible (in that one of the core challenges in most games involves deducing the way in which game logics operate so as to be able to predict and overcome them) and invisible (as "assumptions" of the world, they are often presented as natural course rather than specific decisions). For example, AI systems in the urban sandbox game *Grand Theft Auto V* (2013) are tuned to be highly aggressive and confrontational. Pedestrians will engage in fistfights if the player bumps into them or stands too close to them for too long. NPCs drive aggressively. Police immediately turn to deadly force instead of de-escalation when crimes occur. These systems create an aesthetic of hostility and conflict and contribute to emergent consequences of frequent cascading chaos, but they also make implicit implications about the nature of urban life. The fact that the system presents naturalistically rather than explicitly as a fable dissuades (in some ways) a reading of the design of its logics unless players specifically attune to their artificiality.

Affordances and Resistance

Players' inputs into the ludic activity of the game simulation (whether a game simulates a diegetic world or not) can never be direct. Interaction must pass through layers of mediation: first through the codified inputs of the controller (which translate physical impulses to digital signals, detected by button actuation, analog stick or trigger position, motion/orientation detection, or microphone activation), are translated to digital signals interpretable by the software, and are usually expressed within the game by an avatar or non-personified locus of manipulation that serves to concentrate and direct action. A further level of designed mediation occurs between the avatar and the element of the system toward which she directs action. See Chapter 4 for a full exploration of this process. The player can never interact with the virtual world directly; she always requires an intermediary that *belongs to* the virtual.

As a member of the virtual world, the avatar is designed and rule-bound like every other element of the gameplay system. Depending on the perspective by which the player imagines the flow of action, different terminology is utilized by different theoretical models. Considering the avatar as a mediating tool focusing the intent of the player into performed action in the virtual space, we may use the word *affordances* to describe the abilities that the avatar extends to the player. It is a design term (Gibson, 1979, pp. 128–143; Norman, 1988) that describes the "action possibilities" that a tool, object, or feature of the environment affords its user. For example, a screwdriver affords its user the ability to tighten screws past the point that an unassisted person would be able. Similarly, each action an avatar can perform affords particular virtual interactions that would be impossible otherwise.

Alternatively, from a perspective of projective, embodied play, we can simply call these actions *verbs* (Anthropy & Clark, 2014, p. 15) as an easy-to-understand translation into the linguistic/conversational metaphor of play. The terms have slight variance in their intonations. Whereas "verb" simply signals the outgoing action of an agent regardless of the purpose or effect of the action, "affordance" denotes both the action and the environment's ability to receive and reciprocate that action; it is not only *action*, it manipulates something or serves a purpose (Hirose, 2002).

The player's impulses are "programmed" into the system of gameplay via controller manipulation. This first step includes two layers of designed mediation: the physical design of the controller (the layout, capabilities, and ergonomics of the control affect what can be done comfortably and simultaneously) and the software-specific, designated associations of each input ("A" button = send signal to jump, for example).

The digital signals generated by these programmed inputs are interpreted by the game state and enacted in a designed, context-sensitive manner. Programmed inputs only enact action if the system is contextually ready to receive them. For example, pressing the "A" button to jump only triggers a jump if the avatar is touching the ground. Pressing the "A" button mid-air does not trigger a jump because the system has deemed that action not contextually appropriate.

Some of these contextual judgments are properties of the avatar, and some are properties of the environment or game state. For example, the comedic adventure game *Thank Goodness You're Here!* (2024) features three verbs: move, jump, and slap. The slap function is the primary means of interaction with the game world. The avatar can perform the slap function at almost every moment during gameplay. Whether or not the slap begins a conversation, has a physical effect on the world, or triggers a minigame is a function of environmental context. The slap is a *universal action.* The action is performable at all times, and the effect of the action is decided by what is targeted. On the other hand, the function of the "A" button in *The Legend of Zelda: The Wind Waker* (2002) is to perform a series of *contextual actions.* Normally, pressing "A" will cause Link to swing his sword (a universal action), but this function will change when he stands directly in front of an NPC or a special object like a treasure chest. When Link is positioned in front of an NPC, "A" will initiate a conversation. When Link stands in front of a treasure chest, "A" will open the chest. Link's universal action is exchanged with contextual actions based on his in-world position relative to other elements. Both methods result in similar design mediation but utilize different techniques. Though roughly equivalent in outcome, they communicate different semiotic characterization. If Link initiated conversation with a sword slash in the manner that the *Thank Goodness* protagonist engages every NPC with a slap, he would not appear as virtuous as he might if he addressed them politely.

As the player through the avatar acts upon the game world, the game world reciprocates or acts upon the avatar (and itself). *Resistance* is a function of design that designates specific boundaries (the avatar cannot walk through solid walls; the presence of walls resists the players impulse to navigate further in that direction) and creates elements of challenge (a powerful enemy stands in the way of a treasure chest, resisting the player's desire to open the chest and see what is inside).

Though these two forms of resistance appear quite different (natural, physical boundaries and designed challenges), they should really be thought of as points on a single continuum. An enemy of sufficient challenge may be an absolute boundary, not an indictment of lack of player skill (particularly in stat-based games like RPGs in which a player may simply not yet have the numerical strength to best an enemy early in the adventure). And a physical boundary may be able to be circumnavigated through clever play or employment of glitches (making its passage a metagame possibility). Both are simply aspects of designed resistance.

From a design perspective, resistance has a wide variety of meanings, and it can sometimes be difficult to determine its communicative purpose. The placement of a particularly challenging enemy, for instance, can sometimes signal, "you are not supposed to be here yet. Turn your attention elsewhere and come back once you have become more powerful", but the experience of challenge may be a result of not having figured out how to effectively manage that enemy.

The Witness (2016) is a puzzle game set on a freely-explorable, 3D island. Each of the game's puzzles—line puzzles that typically involve drawing a line from a designated starting point to an exit—are presented on computer screen-like panels all across the island. Different parts of the island will feature different clusters of panels, each of which introduces novel mechanics into the puzzles that need to be solved. Within each cluster, the puzzles are arranged such that players, following the most likely paths through the space, encounter them from most simple (to gently introduce new mechanics) to most challenging. Because the island is freely explorable, though, there is no guarantee that the player is going to approach each cluster from the expected direction. Therefore, the player may naturally encounter a difficult puzzle before she has had a chance to warm up to the novel mechanic in easier iterations.

When the player encounters a baffling puzzle, she is left with the question—did I find an out-of-sequence puzzle? Should I leave this puzzle and try to find an easier one in this cluster? Or do I simply not understand the mechanic at play? The ambiguity caused by the game's mode of resistance creates a unique aesthetic of challenge. Constraint (if we consider a sufficiently sophisticated puzzle effectively "unsolvable" without an understanding of the underlying mechanics) and resistance (the appropriate amount of challenge one can expect from being presented with a novel puzzle type) intermix to cause feelings of self-doubt, design mistrust, and eventually the heartened resolution to push past these inhibitions and bear with a puzzle.

Individually, elements of resistance create moments of choice—texture in a gameplay experience. Individual players may be invigorated by or balk at particular challenges. They may succeed or fail. At scale, though, resistance (in relationship with designed affordances) creates the designed "shape" of a game. In the way that a river carves a path through the land through a centuries-long process of erosion, producing natural propensities for water flow, even minor elements of resistance are likely to be seen as channels of challenge across the experiences of the hundreds or thousands of people who play a particular game. Consider how many people must have died to *Super Mario Bros.*' (1985) first Goomba since the game was released in 1985. It is at this scale that games' design becomes most apparent.

In fact, the 2D platformer *Super Meat Boy* (2010) features a replay function after completing each level, overlaying all of a player's attempts at beating a stage on top of one another, playing simultaneously. What begins as (potentially) a herd of Meat Boys eventually thins as unsuccessful attempts terminate, leaving the one successful attempt to reach the goal. Emergent patterns, driven by player behavior and shaped by resistance, form as preferred routes are chosen and particular challenges serve as roadblocks that terminate many attempts.

Objectives

Affordances and resistance are primarily meaningful in the context of directed objectives. If Mario has nowhere he needs to be, it does not matter that he can run and jump. The emergent "shape" observed in the *Super Meat Boy* (2010) example above only forms its river-like course because the player is motivated to pursue a particular goal. Objectives direct play, and the manner in which objectives are designed affects the way that all of the other aspects of game design are experienced.

Super Mario Bros. (1985) gives players singular, sequential objectives. The player must reach the end of each level—on the macro scale, the player must reach the end of the game, defeat King Koopa, and rescue Princess Toadstool. Once a level is completed, Mario is sent to the next level, and its completion becomes the primary objective (and represents a step forward toward the macro-level goal of game completion).

The 3D platformer *Banjo-Kazooie* (1998) presents a wider range of objectives at any given time. The game has a singular macro-objective (complete the game) and a somewhat stable sequence of objectives at the next level down—completing the game requires access to the witch Gruntilda's tower, and accessing that tower requires a certain number of accumulative collectables and character abilities earned throughout the adventure. To collect enough of these tokens and gain these necessary abilities, Banjo-Kazooie must visit and complete challenges within each (or most) of the game's nine levels, though these are not linear levels like *Super Mario Bros.*' unidirectional courses. Banjo-Kazooie needs only to complete *enough* challenges to open the next stage (gated by puzzles and doors that demand particular numbers of collectable tokens). For instance, a level might have ten main challenges, but only five might be required to progress toward the game's ultimate goal, allowing players freedom in which challenges they pursue. A heat map-style analysis of multiple playthroughs would certainly elucidate preferred pathways mediated by areas of resistance, but the multiple goals would make for a more diffuse scattering of routes than the singular, deterministic course of a *Super Mario Bros.* level.

Games like *The Sims* (2000) lack definitive, macro-scale objectives (that is to say, the game cannot be "beaten"), but it has a plethora of mid-level objectives (personality-dependent life aspirations that a player may choose to pursue or not to). More importantly, the game features a wealth of *incentives*; rewarded activities with which the player can optionally engage, rewarded with in-game resources that broaden the player's expressive agency (such as currency or deepened relationships with other Sims) and encourage the formation of intrinsically motivated objectives. *Minecraft* (2011) relies primarily upon intrinsic motivation. Though it *does* have an endgame, most players are driven by their creative urges. There is no formal reward for building an elaborate castle (that exceeds the basic necessity of a purely functional and perfunctory shelter), but the game's flexible creative engine and personal creative pride drive players to set their own goals. The game's structure of resistance creates interesting and emergent happenings regardless of what the player chooses to pursue. As a flexible system of interesting logics, *a singular goal* is not necessary to orient play; *any goal* slots nicely into the game's open-ended structure.

When playing games, consider how objectives—whether totalizing or incremental—structure and pace play. Do games involve the pursuit of singular goals with fairly narrow ranges of affordances for completing them, like *Super Mario Bros.* (1985), *Galaxian* (1979), or *Rock Band* (2007)? Do games let players choose their own sub-goals or routes in pursuit of singular totalizing goals, like *Banjo-Kazooie* (1998), *HITMAN* (2016), or *Sid Meier's Civilization VI* (2016)? Do games inspire the pursuit of intrinsic, self-directed goals rather than prescriptive objectives, like *The Sims* (2000), *Minecraft* (2011), and *Dwarf Fortress* (2022)? How does the objective and incentive structure affect the sequence and rate at which players encounter resistance and interesting emergent properties of the system?

PLAY AS CONVERSATION

Interaction with game systems is frequently framed as conversation, a back-and-forth exchange of ideas: challenges posed by developers by proxy in their design of objectives and constraints and responses posed by players by proxy in their avatars. Like linguistic conversation, players are only able to act and respond in structured, systematized manners. The verbs of play become grammars of action, and the challenges posed become questions in need of response. The following sections will explore how to productively frame and take part in the conversation of gameplay, treating developers as collaborative agents in the production of interesting conversation rather than adversaries in competitive sparring.

Instrumental Providence

Part of the appeal of wilderness hiking is the uncertainty of success. When hiking off-trail, there is no guarantee that a chosen direction will allow safe, unencumbered passage. The chosen direction may lead to a sheer cliff face, river, or an impassible cluster of vegetation.

Conversely, games—however difficult—are designed to be playable. When engaging with a video game, players should assume that it has been intelligently designed expressly for the purpose of furthering gameplay objectives. To take it one step further, players should assume that the game world has been *benevolently* designed (though exceptions exist, they are relatively few). When assured of benevolence and intentionality in design, players can use these axioms to their advantage. For example, games almost never let the player get irreversibly trapped, so a door locking behind the avatar is a sign of affirmation of progress, a communicative measure.

This is a principle I call *instrumental providence*. Game worlds are, in a real sense, presided over by "gods"—in as far as they have been created by intelligent creators for a purpose. The player's role within the game is guided by "providence". Though games are built to introduce challenge and resistance (one might intuit the position of the developers as being adversarial in that regard), developers actually take a cooperative orientation. The challenges are designed to be overcome, and all of the tools needed to achieve the game's goals are presented to the player within the game itself.

Not only is the player readily equipped with all of the resources she needs to overcome the game's challenges—the entire world is designed expressly to facilitate progression. Unlike the real world, where designed spaces are built around the immutable and sometimes inconvenient realities of our natural surroundings (many a city has been lost to landslides, unstable ground, and flooding), the artificial landscapes within video games are hand-designed to help the player (even if momentary inconveniences might present as a function of inscribed challenge). Important events will occur only when they come into the player's view; viewpoints are strategically positioned to draw players' eyes to important destinations. The world exists only for the purpose of leading the player toward her goals. Like *The Truman Show* (Weir, 1998), incredible power comes from being able to read and understand the artifice of the worlds within which players are immersed.

In this sense, the ultimate meta-goal of every game—that which leads to ultimate mastery of the game and its systems—is learning how to *see* the artifice and interpret the guiding hand of "god" (the developers). At that point, the game ceases to be a scramble for survival in a hostile and random world. It is, instead, a cooperative effort between the player and developers. Instrumentally, the world exists only to put on a show for the player.

Beyond basic narrative protostory, games are interlaced with a secret channel of communication between developers and players. The design decisions outlined in the previous section form not only a structure of *experience* but also a language to ground *expectations* and *objective formation*. Playing a game is, at its heart, a conversation between the player and the developer (through the proxy of a programmed set of systems and mechanics), and like real-life theists believe, great wisdom can come from searching for signs and signals from its creators. It is through the world and the design of the game's systems that those signs are sent by the developers to the players. In the following sections, I will highlight several ways that developers communicate to players.

Breadcrumbing

Breadcrumbing, named for the fable of Hansel and Gretel, who left behind a trail of breadcrumbs as they walked into the woods that they could follow out if they became lost, is the practice of using small rewards or aesthetic cues to guide players toward important points of interest, usually much larger rewards or additional challenges. This is one of the manners in which game developers communicate with players through the provision of design.

One game that exhibits breadcrumbing particularly well is *Donkey Kong Country* (1994), a 2D platformer in which titular gorilla Donkey Kong and his atelidae partner Diddy Kong trek across dangerous jungle and industrial environments to confront the leader of an invading reptilian species who stole the Kongs' prized banana stash. As is common for games in the platformer genre, several types of collectibles are placed throughout the game's many levels. The most common are floating bananas, found virtually everywhere in the game. Picking up 100 bananas grants the Kongs an extra life—a welcome resource as the game becomes more challenging in later worlds, but not enough to make any single banana immensely exciting to find. It is 1% of the needed total, an incremental reward. It could be argued that they serve a greater purpose as Pavlovian rewards (picking them up is accompanied by a satisfying "ding", and watching the banana total rise toward 100 feels like a productive increase) than providing a great instrumental utility. Gathering them becomes a routine part of the rhythm of the game. Occasionally, though, they are placed in unexpected locations, like floating dangerously above a bottomless pit. When viewed with a design-oriented mindset, this can be seen for what it is: a message from the developer. Using the established language of the game (bananas are lain intentionally along the path of play) in a way that breaks the established pattern (a lone banana is not only off the pathway but is in a location that would surely result in a death to reach), the developers are communicating one of two possible messages:

1. The "bananas line the pathway" pattern observed to this point is incorrect. Bananas are actually placed randomly without consideration for their retrievability. Or,
2. The dangerous-looking area is a viable pathway.

In these cases, pursuing the wayward banana leads the Kongs to invisible secrets and hidden rewards. The player is rewarded for recognizing the design language and solving a simple lateral thinking puzzle ("dropping into that pit would kill me, but the banana is highlighting that spot for a reason. I'll take a risk and investigate"). This is an example of breadcrumbing, because the developers leave clues (breadcrumbs) to indicate to players that something unseen awaits them, prompting curiosity.

Following breadcrumbs doesn't have to be as literal as noticing a straight line of floating collectibles. Following a game's design language means attuning oneself to all aspects of situational artifice. Players can notice clusters or lines of "dense design" amidst otherwise "sparse design". This principle is most applicable to 3D games, particularly those with open worlds.

Early 3D open-world games (or games with large, open levels) tended to be set in densely designed areas practically oriented toward facilitating the game's primary verbs of play, often to the point of being highly abstract spaces. *Super Mario 64* (1996), for example, features abstract playgrounds of colorful geometric platforming courses. Each ledge serves a purpose of helping Mario reach one of the game's many goals (or providing resistance to meeting those challenges). In future titles, though, 3D levels evolved in scale, and greater technology allowed developers to create more realistic and natural settings. With this increase in size and naturalism came the necessity for "empty" space, at least with regard to space expressly oriented toward goal progression. Suddenly, games set in cities required long drives between objectives through relatively non-interactable stretches of town. Games set in nature separated points of interest with long walks to put players in the mindset of the quiet peacefulness and grandeur of being in nature. It not only made for more realistic-feeling settings, but it also changed the pacing of the experience to comfortable ebbs and flows of activity rather than constant demand on players.

We can consider these "empty" spaces—spaces between points of interest—as areas of sparse design. They may include standard enemy encounters or materials to gather, but their primary purpose is to be passed through on the way to the next point of interest. To instill and reward exploratory impetus, though, clusters of designed experience (scripted encounters, rewards, optional challenges) are often dotted throughout these areas. These clusters of dense design can become noticeable if players attune to the design language of play.

Assassin's Creed IV: Black Flag (2013) is a swashbuckling stealth action game set on an enormous, sprawling map of tropical Caribbean islands. The player takes on the role of Edward Kenway, a Welsh, up-and-coming pirate-turned-assassin, as he sails his ship from island to island in pursuit of the secrets of the mysterious Brotherhood of Assassins (and treasure, naturally; he is still a pirate, after all). The game's immense map stretches to over 230 sq km (over 90 sq mi). Though much of that space consists of stretches of ocean between islands, explorable landmasses are plentiful as well. Though much of the jungle landscape on land is fairly unremarkable, the player can quickly become attuned to indications of designed pathways within the environment. Fallen trees are positioned at an exact angle to act as a ramp or bridge. Vines or ropes positioned near elevated edges can be swung from. Obvious handholds and footholds draw attention to climbable surfaces. When these or other design markers are found in sequence, the player can follow a designed "line" (a collection of verb-reactive objects in a game environment arranged to form a linear sequence). These lines either led to valuable treasure or were used within the mini-narrative of a later mission (nothing draws attention to the artifice of a frantic foot chase like it steering into a line the player had previously discovered as the realization dawns, "oh, that is why this was here").

Attuning to what is "natural" versus what is "designed" (in relative terms; no space within a game is truly natural, but certainly some spaces are designed with less intentionality toward embedded challenges than others) is a valuable skill in learning to notice the developers' hidden means of communication. Entire games are built on the back of this challenge altogether. *The Legend of Zelda: Breath of the Wild* (2017), for instance, is a story about a lone knight traveling throughout a callous but beautiful open world to save his kingdom from a great evil that has corrupted the land. Though the world is made to feel quiet, lonely, and serene (achieved through appropriately sparse design), the countryside is littered with curiosities. These points of interest are not marked on any map. They are to be observed visually, arousing players' curiosity at a glance. Visual landmarks (such as buildings, encampments, or smoke from fires) draw the player toward the pockets of dense design. Players intuitively notice breaks in the patterns of what is "natural" in that world. Densely designed spaces pique curiosity and prompt further exploration.

Macro-scale breadcrumbing is also a common method for keeping game progression moving forward at a steady pace. Like other artistic mediums, pacing is important in video games. Poor pacing can drag down a video game experience as much as it can a film or book. Developers face a unique challenge in designing games, though—*players* determine the pace at which the story progresses through their actions. If players are truly left to explore and play at their own leisure, how can developers ensure that the resulting experience is well-paced?

There are two predominant ways in which intended pacing can be interrupted in gameplay: the player chooses to ignore plot-progressing objectives, or the player intends to progress the plot but is unable. In cases of the former, players have knowledge of how to progress the story but choose to spend additional time on smaller side objectives or just wish to play within the space in its current state. This may present a poorly paced story if one were only to recount the events of the story that pertain to the primary story being told, but it does not necessarily represent a failure of experiential pacing. The player explores at her own whim, presumably, because she finds the act of exploring innately enjoyable. The ratio of activity related to the progression of the plot versus that which is irrelevant from a storytelling perspective may produce an overall narrative that is unsuitable for more traditional storytelling mediums but often still results in highly engaging video game experiences.

Alternatively, players can become stuck if they do not know how (or are unable) to progress, which can obviously present serious pacing problems. The repetition of failed levels is, itself, not an unforgivable pacing sin. Overcoming adversity often requires repeated attempts, and the additional time spent on a level can cement that portion of the game in the player's memory as a point of heightened drama and tension, and overcoming it can be all the sweeter on the other side. Repeated struggle can be forgiven from a storytelling perspective (though, like anything, it can become excessive after a certain point), but cluelessly wandering rarely increases the dramatic tension of a story in a way that is at all narratively satisfying. Knowing the path forward and finding it challenging can lead to either determination or frustration, while not understanding how to progress results in bewilderment, confusion, and apathy. This can seriously hurt the pacing of a game, for our memories of a game (or periods of our lives, more generally) are not determined predominantly by the amount of time (in minutes and hours) that it takes but rather by the number of novel events that occur in that time. A forty-hour game with constant novelty can feel like it flies by, while a two-hour game in which long stretches of time go by without much happening can feel interminable.

To ensure that players are equipped with the information that they need to continue forward progression (not that they must, but that they can if they choose), developers will often breadcrumb at the macro level, placing reminders of core objectives throughout the world and smaller incentives to guide players back toward the central storyline. For example, high-fantasy JRPG *DRAGON QUEST XI: Echoes of an Elusive Age* (2017) sees a destined Luminary, the bearer of a magical sigil prophesied to rid darkness from the kingdom, engage in a world-trekking quest across multiple cities and continents. The main storyline takes the form of smaller quests—micro-adventures—that act like chapters in a book. To ensure that the player never becomes lost and frustrated in the immense world, the game generously places specific NPCs in each quest zone that will give very specific direction as to where to go and what needs to be done (delivered with great charisma of writing and performance). These NPCs are marked with clearly noticeable pink speech bubbles hanging above their heads. These are not quest-givers, in the traditional sense; they do not assign quests. They are only reminders, often placed strategically so that approaching them already sets the Luminary in the correct direction to meet an actual quest-giver or to perform tasks necessary for the current objective. They are breadcrumbs to ensure that players always have full knowledge of where to go to progress the main storyline. The choice is put into the player's hands.

Soft-Gating

Another tool that developers use to communicate to players through a game's design, using in-fiction vocabulary, is *gating*. Gating is the restriction of an area, tool, or option until certain conditions are met. This can most commonly be seen as the progression or expansion of the explorable space as a game progresses. For example, an open-world game may begin on an island, and after completing a series of plot-progressing quests, another series of islands around the starting island may open up. Alternatively, in level-based games like *Super Mario World* (1990), beating a level opens up the pathway to the next. Imposing these binary restrictions (locked vs. unlocked) is called hard-gating. Hard-gating can be conceptualized as lock-and-key mechanisms applied to progression.

In contrast, soft-gating describes the practice of using resistance to *discourage* access to areas, tools, or options without outright *restricting* access until *softer* (more variable) conditions are met. For instance, instead of blocking off a late-game area with a literal drawbridge that is not lowered until the previous area's boss has been defeated, players can instead be softly discouraged from exploring that area if it is filled with enemies that vastly outmatch players early in their adventure. Players can still choose to explore the late-game area, but they run the risk of being swiftly killed by the region's monsters until they reach an appropriate power level. What power level that is may be different for different players, as those with more skill may be able to challenge those powerful monsters at a lower level, bridging the stat difference with their own play skill, while less skilled players may have to wait until they vastly outrank the monsters before they feel confident in advancing into this portion of the map.

A famous example of soft-gating is in the opening hours of the medieval fantasy action RPG *Dark Souls* (2011). After completing a short tutorial area, the player's avatar is carried off by a giant crow and dropped off in the game's central hub area: Firelink Shrine. *Dark Souls* is neither traditionally open-world nor level-based. Most of the game's world is interconnected and absent of hard, binary progress gates (apart from bosses at some of the game's key intersections), but each area has a very narrow explorable path (often castle corridors, village alleys, or forest paths), encouraging methodical, linear progression. Firelink, as a hub through which players pass many times as the densely interconnected path through the game circles back in upon itself, is directly connected to three areas: the Undead Burg, the New Londo Ruins, and the Catacombs. At the beginning of the adventure, the player is intended to venture into the Undead Burg, a trek through aqueducts and rooftops of a ruined city. Enemies and bosses in this area are appropriately leveled for early-game players, and the Burg leads to some valuable early-game resources, like a blacksmith who can enhance players' weapons and armor.

Though the Undead Burg is the intended next leg of the journey, nothing prevents players from venturing into the Catacombs or New Londo Ruins instead. In fact, the Catacombs may be a more obvious path forward from a layout perspective. The catacombs are located on the other side of a graveyard immediately connected to Firelink Shrine; a very short walk players are likely to naturally encounter while exploring the Shrine, as opposed to the Undead Burg that lies on the other side of a wall up a steep hill—relatively hidden from view. The Catacombs swarm with skeleton warriors, though, that are vastly overpowered for early-game players. With the low level and insufficient stats that players are likely to have at this point in the game, the skeletons take many hits to defeat but can kill the player character with ease. To make matters worse, any skeletons that the underpowered player is able to kill quickly come back to life unless particular conditions are met, making it difficult to make lasting progress.

The New Londo Ruins, the flooded remains of a ruined town found in a deep cave beneath Firelink Shrine, pose an even greater challenge. The city is infested with ghosts that emerge from the walls and floors in great numbers, aggressively attacking the avatar on sight with their ghastly, sickle-like hands. These ghosts cannot be fought without equipping a cursed weapon or using a particular item to self-inflict a curse. Without being able to repel enemies, New Londo Ruins can be extremely hostile for new players.

Through the use of high-leveled skeletons and (at this point) invincible ghosts, *Dark Souls* discourages exploration into the Catacombs and New Londo Ruins, respectively, but it does not outright close these areas off. Players possessing great skill can stand their own against the skeletons, and enemies in either location can be run past (though this is inadvisable if players do not already know where they are going. There is nothing worse than getting cornered by a dozen enemies at once). In fact, seasoned *Dark Souls* players often work this into their strategies by performing "loot runs", perilous sprints through these dangerous areas to pick up treasures that would be appropriate rewards for the point in the game at which players are supposed to enter those areas; truly game-changing for players to get their hands on these rewards so early.

This is why soft-gating can be so effective. It enforces a desired path of progression via increased resistance while still providing players choice, allowing players who have already mastered the game to have significantly different experiences in later playthroughs. In a sense, it allows players to choose their preferred difficulty using the in-fiction "vocabulary" of the world. Players who wish to take greater risks are given greater rewards or may be able to skip entire portions of a game altogether.

A form of soft-gating that has been successfully utilized recently is called *knowledge gating*. While the *Dark Souls* example above is still tied to the stats and mechanics of the game (over-leveled enemies and possession of uncommon items), knowledge gates restrict player progression only (or primarily) through the possession or lack of knowledge and understanding of game logic. In the most pure examples, players do not gain *any* new abilities or unlock any "hard" locks throughout the course of the entire game. Throughout the game, players only *learn* of options or actions that have always been available but did not occur to them. Theoretically, players could perform the actions necessary to finish the game immediately if they already possess the knowledge necessary to perform these actions.

Space-exploration adventure *Outer Wilds* (2019) epitomizes this approach. In *Outer Wilds*, players take on the role of an interplanetary explorer blessed (or cursed) by a mysterious, alien statue to begin the day anew if ever they die in their explorations, which is a certainty, for 22 minutes after the young Hearthian awakens, the galaxy's sun undergoes a supernova, destroying all life in the cluster of planets the Hearthians call home. Stuck in a *Groundhog Day* (Ramis, 1993)-like time loop, experiencing the events of the galaxy's final 22 minutes, the player must travel from planet to planet in search of the galaxy's greatest mysteries, in hopes that one of them may provide a way to circumvent the calamity of galactic destruction.

In *Outer Wilds*, players must fly to and explore five planets (and a handful of moons, space stations, and other such destinations in space). Each planet contains information about the physics of the simulated universe: the behavior of quantum objects that change position when they exit an observer's line of sight, the behavior of wormhole-like black holes, the effects of unusual weather patterns, etc. With the implementation of this knowledge, players can progress further into the galaxy's other planets to learn greater and more bizarre secrets. Equally, players can think like scientists themselves, performing experiments and finding these secrets organically without the game telling them outright. Equally, players with knowledge of the physics and geography of the game's galaxy can bypass this journey of self-education and solve the game's final puzzle from the outset.

To clarify, not all knowledge can be considered a soft-gate. Many puzzle games, such as the 1993 exploration puzzler *Myst* use knowledge in such a way that is more comparable to a hard-gate through the use of key-like riddles by way of numerical and symbolic passwords. Though these passwords can be entered at any time, allowing players on repeat playthroughs to skip the leg of the journey involved with finding these passwords, it is not reasonable to expect new players to be able to deduce these passwords through natural experimentation and curiosity. These passwords are not conclusions at which players can more naturally arrive. Finding those passwords is like finding keys to specific locks, as opposed to Outer Wilds' puzzles, which are mostly centered around logic pertaining to the physics and geography of the simulated universe.

Action RPG *TUNIC* (2022) makes use of both hard and soft gating. *TUNIC* is a sword-and-shield adventure set in a magical world deliberately evocative of the early *Legend of Zelda* games. Presented mostly context-free without an introductory backstory or explanation of what motivates the adventure, a tunic-wearing fox wakes up on a sun-drenched beach at the southern end of a peninsula. Throughout the adventure, the player makes use of a combination of combat and puzzle-solving, in traditional *Zelda* fashion, to gain new abilities and progress deeper into this mysterious land.

Hidden throughout the world are pages of an extradiegetic instruction manual, styled after the instruction manuals that used to be packaged in with games in the 1980s and 1990s, and more specifically making references in format and art style to the manual that was packed in with *The Legend of Zelda* in 1986. The manual is written almost entirely in a fictional language with an unreadable character set, but players can use deductive reasoning and the manual's illustrations to get a rough idea of what the manual says. The manual tutorializes the functions of gameplay (such as controls and item usage) and provides helpful maps and explanations for how to interact with elements of the game world. Beyond the basic controls, which the developers presume that players will be able to naturally infer by experimenting with the controller at the beginning of the game (aided by their familiarity with similar titles), the manual contains vital clues for mechanics in the game that are unlikely to occur to the player naturally. This is where the knowledge gating is utilized.

Many of *TUNIC*'s cryptic, vital actions are available to players from the beginning of the game, but they are not obvious. For example, one of the first areas that the player passes through at the outset of the game features a prominent yellow square on the ground. The player can interact with the square at this time, but the method of doing so uses somewhat unusual gameplay vocabulary (it involves holding down a button for a few seconds; something that does not provide any immediate visual feedback). It is not until players find a specific page of the in-game instruction manual later in their adventure that this method is explained outright, by which point players have passed several of these mysterious squares. Possessing this knowledge, players can revisit the earlier areas and properly interact with the yellow squares. This is knowledge-gated progression, since no new mechanics are formally "unlocked"; it is only the player's knowledge of the design language that gives her the impetus to engage with certain mechanics.

Like *Outer Wilds*, though, players can discover soft-gated elements sooner than "intended". In my playthrough of *TUNIC*, I learned how to interact with the yellow squares before I found the page of the instruction booklet that told me how to do so. I had previously found other instruction manual pages that taught me how to operate other mechanisms and how to engage other hidden mechanics in the game world, and I began to understand the logic of that particular game's design language. I understood that the game tended to use simple item interactions or button inputs in unexpected ways to hide the answers to its mechanics-driven riddles in plain sight. I performed a mental exercise that I often find helpful when solving video game puzzles. With the understanding that video game puzzles are intelligently designed, and knowing the outcome (even if incomplete) that I expect but not how to achieve it (in this case, I inferred from the obviousness of the squares' visual design that they were somehow interactable, but I did not know how they could be engaged), and utilizing the patterns I had observed within the design language so far (the developers like to hide mechanical capabilities in plain sight using unexpected yet simple inputs and interactions rather than locking vital functions behind hard gates such as acquired items), I asked, "If I were this game's developer, where would I hide the function that I currently seek?".

Asking that question is perhaps the most direct and useful way to engage with the design-oriented layer of games. Across genres, this question is consistently helpful. "If I were designing this room, where would I hide the key to the locked chest?". "If I created this dungeon, where would I have placed traps to punish unobservant players?". Puzzles in video games are designed not to perplex but to satisfy when solved. More often than not, I find that taking on this mindset attunes my perception to the correct details in the scene to help me solve the present puzzle. When asking myself where I would hide a hidden key, I think "somewhere obscured from view" and notice a bush in the corner that would be a perfect place to hide a key. When asking myself where I would hide traps in a trap-filled dungeon, I realize that I would place them in an area where players are likely to be distracted and let their guard down, and I notice a prominently-placed and alluring item off in the distance, seemingly unprotected and easy to approach. Surely, a hidden trap is waiting to punish my greed. I should be very careful when approaching the treasure by watching where I step and checking around blind corners.

By applying this design-oriented thought to *TUNIC*, I was able to correctly deduce the method of interaction with the game's mysterious yellow squares. The advantage of knowledge-gated obstacles rather than hard-gated obstacles is that players can take individually unique routes to arrive at a conclusion, and the game does not discriminate based on how the conclusion is reached. It is just as valid to be told a piece of information directly, witness an unexpected cause-effect relationship play out by chance, or conduct hypothesis-driven experiments to arrive at a conclusion. This can be contrasted with what is all too common in games: characters' knowledge is treated like an inventory in which certain pieces of knowledge wholly exist or are wholly absent. A character may read a book that teaches her how to cook scrambled eggs, but before reading that book, there is no way of cooking scrambled eggs, even if the player knows the recipe, and even if the desired action is something that one could reasonably presume that someone could discover on their own if the game was truly simulating a realistic scenario. Arriving at a conclusion but being unable to enact it until guiding the avatar through an arbitrary set of prerequisite steps has the feeling of correctly solving a math problem in elementary school but being marked down for not showing the work. These moments of friction and disallowance remind the player of the psychological distance between herself and her protagonist, something that most games aim to minimize for the sake of increasing immersion.

Knowledge can be very difficult to test in games. Consider an example as simple as determining whether one has learned someone else's name. In real life, they can ask directly, "What is my name?", and, based on the answer, they can tell whether or not the tested individual has internalized that information. In a game, though, it is not as simple. If a character asks, "Do you remember my name?", the player may be prompted to type in the name on a keyboard. Depending on how many spelling variations developers accounted for, a character named Caroline may or may not accept "Karoline" or "caroline", or "Carolyn", or any other possible number of spellings. Consider how much more complex the task becomes when ascertaining the retention of information that would take multiple sentences to explain, such as who performed a murder and for what reason. Free text entry can also be cumbersome when utilizing a controller, and the entry of any more than one or two words can feel daunting. For that reason, games often default to multiple-choice responses in tests of knowledge. Being asked a character's name and being presented with four options—"Margery", "Caroline", "Mina", or "Valerie"—is only a test of recognition, not truly internalized knowledge. Even a blind guess has a 25% chance of returning a correct answer. Again, applying this kind of testing method to more complex questions, such as the motive for a murder, may inadvertently give the player parts of the answer that she has not yet deduced herself.

Most games employ tests of instrumental or associative knowledge. The player proves her understanding of how to light a room by using an item in her inventory (a matchstick) with an object in the environment (a candle), for instance. This can be a reasonably effective way of determining understanding of complex information without the game inadvertently giving away too much information that the player had not yet internalized, as it might in a multiple-choice scenario.

Phoenix Wright: Ace Attorney (2001) is a visual novel-style detective game in which players take on the role of a defense attorney. In tense courtroom scenes, the player must defend her clients, accused of severe crimes, by finding contradictions in the testimonies of witnesses. These contradictions can be exposed by presenting evidence of the lie, by way of indicating which piece of court evidence (of which each case has an extensive inventory) disproves a particular line of the witness' statement. The player, in selecting which piece of evidence to present in objection to which particular line of testimony, demonstrates an instrumental knowledge of the story. The player should be reasonably confident that she understands why or how that particular piece of evidence contradicts the testimony rather than just blindly throwing each piece of evidence at each line of the testimony in succession. The game enforces a careful approach by penalizing incorrect evidence presentation. It is still possible for the player to unintentionally stumble upon correct answers (perhaps by having an alternate "garden path" theory that ends up arriving at the correct answer but for incorrect reasons), but it does a reasonably good job of ensuring that the player has a solid cause/effect hypothesis in mind before providing an answer.

More often, games are driven forward through hard gating as a way of managing verbs (available actions), routing, and pacing. Routing and pacing are important for storytelling. Each story has a beginning, middle, and end, and it is important for moments of tension, conflict, and resolution to be appropriately placed throughout to give the story its shape. Entirely knowledge-gated games like *Outer Wilds* (2019) run the risk of losing control over this aspect of the storytelling. If all that stands in the way of progression is knowledge, and if players can obtain that knowledge through experimentation or chance observations, an entire leg of the adventure that was intended to lead players to a particular piece of knowledge may become unnecessary. Theoretically, if a new player somehow intuits all of *Outer Wilds*' key information from the beginning, she can immediately set in motion the events that conclude the game within minutes (though this is unlikely, as the completion of *Outer Wilds* also requires specific knowledge such as the locations of certain areas and the design of alien-language glyphs).

Hard gating is much easier to control from a storytelling perspective. If defeating the boss of one area opens the gate to the next, the developer can count on players being at a particular point in their journeys upon entering that latter area. Players have cleared a certain bar of challenge and have obtained the items necessary to reach and clear the boss. From that point forward, developers can set an appropriate level of challenge and require the use of the items (verbs) that they know the player now possesses.

THE BLACK BOX

Video games differ from social games and tabletop games, which require player or spectator arbitration to ensure that play conforms to the rules (and, thus, the intended shape) of the game. When playing tag in the schoolyard or *Dungeons & Dragons* (Gygax & Arneson, 1974) in a long-running tabletop campaign, rules of the game must be understood by those playing, those overseeing (referees, dungeon masters…), or both. Even in complex games, such as tabletop tactics games like Warhammer, the rules of engagement must be knowable, or at least knowable to an extent that can be supplemented by referencing back to the manual. Every action and interaction is knowable to the enforcing parties, as they hold the responsibility of enforcing the constructs of the game.

The same is not true of video games. Arbitrated by computers, the rules that govern the simulation need not be knowable to players. This allows video games to simulate mechanical complexities in every moment of play that would be impossible (or would take such a long time to calculate that doing so would draw gameplay to a crawl) in a tabletop or social setting. These calculations are no more *arbitrary* than the manual calculations of a tabletop game, though rather than being calculated slowly by players or enforcers, these parameters are determined in advance by game developers and enacted through the computer on which the game is being played. Since the player is not responsible for socially enforcing the rules, it is not always necessary for the player to know the rules and parameters.

There are certainly advantages to these calculations being withheld from players. Imagine how different an experience it would be to play a tabletop version of *Super Mario Bros.* (1985), with the momentum, inertia, trajectory, and angle of each jump painstakingly modeled against a set of formulas that represent the game's guiding physics system. Each movement, individually calculated by patient players, would need to incorporate all active factors that contribute to and act against the game's current state and transformation from the previous state. To maintain pace and urgency, it is likely that the game would be calculated as a series of representative probability and statistical analyses (for example, "a pit lies in front of you, a die roll must total four or higher to successfully clear the jump, otherwise, you fall into the pit and lose one life") rather than as a continuous physics simulation. In a video game setting, it is conceivable and preferable for the parameters of the simulation (in this case, the physics model that determines the manner in which Mario's jump executes) to be calculated instantly by the computer, without the specific numerical measures being known by the player. The player can "feel" the limiting factors of the simulation rather than knowing them outright.

This "invisible" information that can be inferred through play is known as *black box* information. The inaccessibility of the black box serves dual purposes: it serves the goal of embodiment by automating the task of *existing* within the virtual space (as in the example above, one can move and operate the avatar as an embodied presence within the world of the game, exposed to and affected by the physics of the game world), and the black box turns the deduction of guiding mechanics into one of the core puzzles of gameplay. To illustrate the latter point, consider simulation games like *SimCity* (1989), in which the player is tasked with building and managing a city. The simulation allows players not only to zone areas for residential, commercial, and industrial use as well as set individual buildings that serve public functions like sewage plants, fire stations, and airports, but it also allows players to set city policies, such as determining tax rates and investment in public health resources. The layout, resources, and policies applied to each city affect a number of factors: citizen health and happiness, crime rate, cleanliness, education... The way in which each factor affects the gestalt of the city is roughly explained and reasonably inferable in isolation, but the challenge and joy of *SimCity* come from determining the dynamics of how these guiding systemic factors interact. The fact that the specific dynamics of gameplay are hidden from the player prompts the player to prod and experiment within the game's systems.

The black box design of games represents not an objective unknowability; games are not *truly* random in their dynamics and constructions. These mechanical nuances are planned and known by developers. Thus, the prominence of black box design presents a slight problem for our purposes of video game literacy. By most definitions, literacy involves both the ability to read and write, to consume and create, and to decode and encode. For our purposes, I do not believe that a basic video game literacy *requires* the ability to program video games using the coding languages of modern computers, but it should include the ability to speak effectively about the systems and mechanics that a game employs and to be able to hypothesize about how different mechanical decisions may affect the dynamics and resulting play aesthetics of a game (following Huincke et al. [2004]'s model). Does black box design prevent us from understanding the specificities of design and decisions that contribute to the mechanical formation of the games we play? Does the obliqueness of computer arbitration prevent us from becoming effective producers, or at least slow the passage of design wisdom from developers to players? James Dunnigan calls this the Black Box Syndrome. He says:

> Another advantage of paper games is that you know why things are happening a certain way in the game. All the rules and probability tables are right there in front of you. Yes, it takes a lot of effort to wade through all of that detail, but you do end up with a good idea of how the inner workings of the game function. A popular benefit of this is the opportunity to change the [game's] rules and probability tables. Many players do this, and that's how gamers eventually turn into game designers. Computer [games] show you very little of how [they do their] thing. The computer program just does it.
>
> *(Dunnigan, 2000, pp. 74, 75)*

This lack of transparency can contribute to problems when modeling real-world systems. Since our understanding of most reasonably complex systems, particularly those involving the behavior of people, is incomplete (black boxes, themselves), their translations into executable mechanics will be built on an incomplete understanding. The black box of games serves as an anti-disclosure practice that enacts consequences without making known the root assumptions that underlie relationships. As Colleen Macklin says, "*SimCity* [1989] doesn't actually simulate a real city. It simulates the inside of [director] Will Wright's brain" (quoted in Soren Johnson's presentation, GDC [2023]).

Video games, though operating through the execution of computer code, cannot be dissected and formally understood as one can open a pocket watch and observe the operation and function of its gears. Once games are compiled into the executable programs that players' computers interpret, the underlying source code is not accessible. The exact operations of these games can only be inferred through extensive, systematic experimentation. As such, is there a degree to which video games do not adequately prepare players to become contributors to the creative community to the same degree that other art forms might?

I do not believe that obliqueness of mechanical specificities constitutes a crisis for literacy (though instances of loss of source code certainly present a crisis for game preservation, but that is a subject for a different book). Though a certain unknowability is a part of the essence of digital gameplay, players can be trained to intelligently observe and understand the resulting dynamics of gameplay and, with experience, make informed inferences of the mechanical decisions that underlie these dynamic out-workings. With proper observational training and experience, players can make educated inferences suitably specific for critical discourse. This is simpatico with critical practices surrounding other artistic mediums.

In a similar manner, black box design can obfuscate the ideologies that underlie the systemic interactions of game simulations. As we frame video games as an expressive, narrative medium, and particularly focus on the degree to which gameplay dynamics have the capacity to express meaning-laden narratives, we must conclude that systemic dynamics of gameplay can and will express some form of ideology. The shape of available verbs that constitute a player's agency within a game and the assumptions and "truths" that game systems are built with and built to represent unavoidably make implicit claims about how certain dynamics resolve and what tools and actions are appropriate for the resolution of certain conflicts or tensions. For example, even in the quite robust simulation of *Grand Theft Auto V* (2013), the only ways in which the player's avatar can interact with most of the simulation's citizens are violent (the avatar can punch, stab, and use firearms but cannot casually greet or hold productive conversations with the majority of NPCs throughout the simulated world—something that the developers, Rockstar Games, addressed to a degree in their follow-up game, *Red Dead Redemption 2* [2018]), and ambiguous interactions, such as walking too close to a standard NPC, tend to be interpreted as a suspicious or hostile action and responded to in kind. Through the limitations of the game's focused action affordances, the game endorses not necessarily a *generalizable* social rhetoric but rather a pattern of situational dynamics that are specific to the unique context of the game at the time of first observation but become more broadly generalizable heuristics as similar patterns are observed in multiple games and settings.

Better game literacy prepares us to regard these dynamics and the underlying ideologies within as decisions determined by games' development teams rather than natural "truths" as we may observe in the laws of physics that govern the real world. The relative invisibility of black box dynamics and underlying ideologies requires active attenuation to the language of game design dynamics. Reading ideologies from game mechanics is further discussed in Chapter 14.

REFERENCES

Anthropy, A. & Clark, N. (2014). *A game design vocabulary: Exploring the foundational principles behind good game design*. Addison-Wesley.

Boluk, S. & LeMieux, P. (2017). *Metagaming: Playing, competing, spectating, cheating, trading, making, and breaking videogames*. University of Minnesota Press.

Caillois, R. (1958). *Man, play, and games*. Librairie Gallimard.

Church, D. (1999). *Formal abstract design tools*. Game Developer. https://www.gamedeveloper.com/design/formal-abstract-design-tools

Cook, D. (2006). *What are game mechanics?* Lostgarden. https://lostgarden.com/2006/10/24/what-are-game-mechanics/comment-page-1/

Dunnigan, J. F. (2000). *Wargames handbook: How to play and design commercial and professional wargames*. Writers Club Press.

Fernández-Vara, C. (2014). *Introduction to game analysis*. Routledge. doi:10.4324/9781003355779

Fullerton, T. (2004). *Game design workshop: Designing, prototyping, & playtesting games*. CRC Press.

GDC (2023, September 6). *You have no idea how hard it is to run a sweatshop* [Video]. YouTube. https://youtu.be/YsCigLYxNYs

Gibson, J. J. (1979). *The ecological approach to visual perception*. Routledge.

Grinblat, J., Manning, C., & Kreminski, M. (2021). *Emergent narrative and reparative play*. Springer. doi:10.1007/978-3-030-92300-6_19

Gygax, G. & Arneson, D. (1974). *Dungeons & Dragons*. TSR, Inc.

Hirose, N. (2002). An ecological approach to embodiment and cognition. *Cognitive Systems Research, 3*(3), 289–299. doi:10.1016/S1389-0417(02)00044-X

Huizinga, J. (1938). *Homo ludens: A study of the play element in culture*. Beacon Press.

Hunicke, R., LeBlanc, M., & Zubek, R. (2004). MDA: A formal approach to game design and game research. *Proceedings of the AAAI Workshop on Challenges in Game AI, 4*(1), 1722.

Järvinen, A. (2008). *Games without frontiers*. Tampere University Press.

Johnson, S. (2001). *Emergence: The connected lives of ants, brains, cities, and software*. Scribner.

Juul, J. (2005). *Half-real: Video games between real rules and fictional worlds*. The MIT Press.

Kanaga, D. (2015). *Intro to ludic ecologonomy (pt. 1)*. https://wombflashforest.blogspot.com/2015/04/intro-to-ludic-ecologonomy-pt-1.html

Koenitz, H. (2023). *Understanding interactive digital narrative*. Routledge. doi:10.4324/9781003106425

Mateas, M. (2003). Expressive AI. *Proceedings of the 2003 DiGRA International Conference: Level Up, 2*.

Mateas, M. (2005). Procedural literacy: Educating the new media practitioner. *On the Horizon: The International Journal of Learning Futures, 13*(2), 101–111. doi:10.1108/10748120510608133

Murray, J. H. (1997). *Hamlet on the holodeck: The future of narrative in cyberspace*. The MIT Press.

Murray, J. H. (2012). *Inventing the medium: Principles of interaction design as cultural practice*. The MIT Press.

Norman, D. (1988). *The design of everyday things*. Basic Books.

Parlett, D. (2007). *What's a ludeme? And who really invented it?* Parlett Games. https://www.parlettgames.uk/gamester/whatsaludeme.html

Prensky, M. (2007). *Digital game-based learning*. Paragon House.

Ramis, H. (Director). (1993). *Groundhog day* [Film]. Columbia Pictures.

Rouse III, R. (2005). *Game design: Theory and practice*. Wordware.

Salen, K. & Zimmerman, E. (2003). *Rules of play: Game design fundamentals*. The MIT Press.

Sicart, M. (2008). Defining game mechanics. *Game Studies, 8*(2). https://gamestudies.org/0802/articles/sicart

Sicart, M. (2013). *Beyond choices: The design of ethical gameplay*. The MIT Press.

Suits, B. (1978). *The grasshopper: Games, life and Utopia*. Broadview Press.

Swink, S. (2009). *Game feel: A game designer's guide to virtual sensation*. Morgan Kaufmann Publishers.

Wardrip-Fruin, N. & Montfort, N. (2003). *The new media reader*. The MIT Press.

Watterson, B. (1985–1995). *Calvin and Hobbes*. Andrews McMeel Publishing.

Weir, P. (Director). (1998). *The Truman show* [Film]. Paramount Pictures.

Yang, R. (2025, in press). *The level design book*. The Level Design Book. https://book.leveldesignbook.com/

CHAPTER 4

Interfacing with Games

THE ACT OF PLAYING video games involves not only the mental tasks of decoding and interpretation shared with other artistic mediums but also a participatory act of utilizing a controller (hereafter used to describe any number of input devices, from game console controllers to mice and keyboards to less traditional control mechanisms like touchscreens, motion controls, and full-body cameras like the Xbox Kinect). As frequently referenced as one of the core arguments of this book, video game literacy is not only an examination of the semiotic details communicated through representation (that which occurs within the diegesis or symbolism of the on-screen fiction) but equally (or, I would argue, more importantly) we must consider the non-semiotic (procedural) narrative of player actions and systems dynamics. This is to say that the narrative of *Super Mario Bros.* (1985), for our purposes, does not primarily concern the fiction of a Brooklyn-born plumber entering the magical Mushroom Kingdom to save Princess Peach from the evil King Bowser. Rather, the primary narrative of *Super Mario Bros.* is the challenging journey of jumps and maneuvers and demands of mastery over increasingly complex systems experienced by the player, contextualized by the semiotic details. Enactment is the core of video game storytelling. Performance is the heart of the character. Within this framing, consideration of the participatory act of playing a game is fundamental to establishing an informed literacy of the medium.

This is not a radical departure from the theory guiding the study of other mediums. Though the interpretation of almost all other mediums privileges the semiotic details above the circumstances of audience experience, experiential details have always been of some concern, and increasingly so during and after the age of art and philosophy classified as postmodern. Of increasing frequency, books like Mark Z. Danielewski's *House of Leaves* (2000) will use nontraditional text and page formatting to affect the pacing and intensity of the semiotic story by directly altering how the book is physically read (a technique borrowed from and perfected by comic books and manga, a lineage that we could trace back to the illuminated manuscripts of the 5th–12th centuries, or even the Egyptian hieroglyphs originating thousands of years before the current era). Similarly, immersive theatrical productions like Punchdrunk's *Macbeth* adaptation *Sleep No More* (Barrett & Doyle, 2003–2025) require physical audience participation, as the audience is free to explore and follow their own curiosities as actors perform roles and move around an expansive physical space. Though we can trace this kind of consideration of form, context, and audience experience as far back as the earliest artistic creations, it has become a topic of increasing fascination within the last century, and video gaming is perhaps the foremost medium exploring this aspect of artistic communication.

In this chapter, we will explore the act of physically interfacing with a controller to direct virtual functions, describe the relationship between the player and their virtual representation/counterpart (the avatar), and reconcile the implications of acting as a distributed being in the physical and virtual spaces. Input and control are core to a non-semiotic understanding of video games, thus vital for the video game literacy we aim to develop.

DOI: 10.1201/9781003530961-4

GAMEPLAY AS SYSTEM

The play-performance of video games is a physical act. As previously discussed, this is true to varying degrees of many artistic mediums. For instance, a book requires nominal physical involvement from its readers, as its story will not continue until each page is physically turned. The degree to which the audience is physically involved in the conveyance of video game narrative is rare, though. Relatively few games would be considered strenuous physical exertion (to those of normative physical ability levels), but video games require a level of participatory enactment that sets them apart from other narrative mediums. While the act of turning a book's page may not be considered *central* to the process of becoming textually literate, physical and cognitive interfacing are key to the experience of playing video games. A literary examination of games is incomplete without consideration for the means of human–computer interface.

This is not to say that the only avenue in which one exercises video game literacy is when directly interfacing with games. As noted previously, a form of video game literacy is also utilized when watching someone else play video games. Even the second-hand enjoyment of a video game requires contending with the player's physical enactment of the game and the consideration of the alternative actions that could have been performed or opportunities that were achieved or missed due to abundance or lack of skillful enactment. It is similar to domain-specific sports literacy. An understanding of basketball limited to the abstract rules of play is incomplete without also considering the operation of the human bodies performing the game (or dog bodies, as not explicitly prohibited by the rule book). The game is designed to push athletically trained bodies to the limits of human physical achievement. To be literate in basketball, one must also have basic expectations of the limits and capabilities of human physiology. In the same way, means of physical and cognitive interface with computers must be considered to become functionally literate in video games.

Player, Computer, Context

The live-enacted video game should be thought of as a system consisting of three parts: *player*, *computer*, and *context*. Each of these elements (which can be further broken down; they are certainly not atomic units) affects and feeds back to one another. Each also contains physical and non-physical elements that are utilized within the live enactment of gameplay.

The player is a physical being in the real world with specific physical capabilities. Most video games require fine motor dexterity, and these relevant capabilities may be affected by a player's age, disabilities, or certain medical conditions such as arthritis. Similarly, the player is a cognitive being as well. Video game worlds are non-literal, virtual spaces, and the manner in which the player interacts with these spaces is through a mediated translation of impulse to enacted virtual action. While physical actions that players express are *representative* of "physical" actions that occur within the game world, mental processes undergo a more direct translation. To solve a puzzle in the virtual world, the player often has to *understand* the logic of the puzzle in the same manner that the diegetic avatar might. In that sense, mental processes involving the manipulation of information are qualitatively alike on both sides of the real/virtual divide. Differing levels of cognitive expediency relating to gameplay-relevant tasks affect the degree to which players' intentions can directly translate into the virtual world. Someone who fully understands their virtual affordances for action within the game world will be able to better effect their intentions within the game world than those who lack that familiarity, and this often extends to familiarity with genre conventions outside of a particular title. Additionally, cognitive disabilities may establish particular challenges for gameplay expression.

Regarding the *player* portion of the system of gameplay, we can note the co-location of the player between the real and virtual worlds. The physical player is situated in the real world, and her physical actions communicate purposeful intention to the computer, which manages the simulation. Mentally, though, the player "exists" in both the real and virtual worlds; her cognitive centers not only operate the physical, fine-motor actions that compel the above-noted communication but also interface within the game world at the non-representative level of thought through mediating forces that we will explore later in this chapter. To summarize points we will explore later, if we are to read the actions of non-player characters (NPCs) as (artificially) intelligent because their actions exhibit motivation, so too must we read the player-motivated actions of the avatar character as being intelligent in a diegetically relevant manner, making player intention and cognition directly relevant on the level of the diegesis. The process by which player cognition "extends" into the game world will be addressed shortly.

The computer is the second part of the system of gameplay enactment. Like the player, the computer contains elements that are both physical and virtual. Most obviously, the computer creates and maintains the gameplay simulation. Virtually, this involves the enactment and enforcement of pre-programmed *rules*; conditional mechanics that guide and constrain the behaviors of all objects within the game world, including the player's mediating avatar, as well as the procedural elements of the simulation itself. This is done through concurrent and often complicated calculations that the computer runs perpetually, calculating and recalculating the *game state* multiple times per second while also outputting relevant sensory information to communicate the present game state to the player through on-screen visuals, audio information, and oftentimes haptics (such as controller vibration) or other sensory elements. Methods of computer-to-player communication are further detailed in Chapter 3, in which we further explore *feedback*.

Game state can be understood as the confluence of rules. Each of a game's possible states expresses a *theoretically* knowable and predictable result of the game's constellation of rules, such that, *if the player had access to the game's entire set of rules and affordances*, she would be able to accurately predict the game state at any moment of play (discounting divergent systemic behaviors resulting from technical glitches). Even elements of (seemingly) random generation are *technically* knowable if the player were to know the "random" number generation algorithm and seed value, since computers are unable to produce *truly* random results. In this way, video games are not dissimilar from other systemically structured games, like Chess. With a knowledge of the rules and affordances that underlie the movement of each Chess piece, players can predict with absolute certainty every possible game state that can emerge from a current game state. The difference between video games and board games like Chess is that computers are capable of running far more calculations in significantly less time than any human could. These calculations, executing at an operational speed, allow for the real-time enactment of incredibly complex simulations. So while a player with a complete set of rules *could* calculate and chart a complete game of *PAC-MAN*, it is only with a computer that the game can operate in real time and provide that action-packed level of kinesthetic involvement.

Examined at multiple levels, virtual operations reduce to physical, real-world actions. As described above, operational behaviors are based on rules, conceptualized and designed by developers; units of thought that operate within systems of pure logic. These rules are operationalized within computer operations through the use of a programming language, a pidgin language that approximates natural, semiotic communication between human and computer by using a mixture of the linguistics of humans and the mathematical logics of computers. That programming language is translated into purely mathematical code and then into hexadecimal and binary, which, at its simplest level, directs the electrical flow between circuits within the computer processor that *physically* carries out the operations (computations) that maintain the gameplay simulation.

In this sense, the gameplay simulation is a physical occurrence, though it is only "readable" through its virtual expression. Even so, the fact that it is rooted in a basic physicality means that the virtual can be *affected* by physical occurrences in the real world (and not just the "allowed" expressions through designated input devices like we have already covered). A power surge or a loose connection between physical components within a computer may affect the simulation, most often breaking or crashing it altogether but sometimes producing visual/auditory glitches or even unexpected behaviors of virtual objects. The effects of unsanctioned physical actions on the virtual world tend to be too unpredictable or catastrophic to utilize as mechanisms for "cheating" in the way that physically tilting a pinball table exploits the inherent physicality of that game in predictable ways, but there are *some* codified methods for using physical interference to produce specific, favorable conditions in games, such as the practice of "cartridge tilting", in which games played on cartridge-based consoles like the Nintendo 64 can be partially removed (tilted) within the cartridge interface slot to break *some* but not *all* of the circuit connections between the console and the game cartridge, causing particular behaviors or even access to debug interfaces.

Other relevant physical elements of the *computer* portion of the gameplay system involve the mechanical operations of the computer itself. Internal fans manage the heat of computer components, and discs are spun at high speeds and read with lasers. Electricity is gleaned from a power source and efficiently circulated to necessary components. Computers are not just information systems; they are elegant *machines.* As they receive information in the form of input functions from player-operated controllers, they undergo a series of physical operations that ultimately result in noticeable change to the game state within the virtual world.

The third part of the gameplay system is *context.* This interfaces with and feeds back to both of the above elements. It is also the easiest to overlook in our gameplay readings. Context is a wide category that includes similarly physical and ephemeral layers. If gameplay can be conceptualized as being like a "conversation" between the player and the computer, context is what gives shape to that conversation and assists in the transmission of signals in both directions.

The element of context most relevant to this chapter is the controller through which the player translates her intents into virtual actions. This device is configured to "sense" a particular set of physical manipulations; to which manipulations it is sensitive varies with each type of controller. For example, a computer keyboard contains 50–120 binary switches (switches that only recognize "fully off" and "fully on" states). A PlayStation 5 controller contains 14 binary switches (D-pad, face buttons, "guide", "share", and PlayStation buttons, microphone mute button, and the R1/L1 shoulder buttons), 6 *analog* (allowing degrees of control more sensitive than the binary "off" and "on") inputs (thumbsticks that can be pressed in as additional binary switches, R2/L2 triggers, motion/tilt sensitivity, and a small touchpad that can also be pressed in as another binary switch), and a built-in microphone sensitive to soundwaves (which *is* a form of physical manipulation through vibration).

The controller translates physical manipulations from the player into electrical signals that convey information to the computer, which materializes those inputs as actions within the simulation. Unlike the player and computer, though, the controller is not co-located between the physical and the virtual. The controller is a wholly physical interface object *complemented* within the virtual space by a wholly *virtual* object that continues its function: the avatar, to which we will return in great detail later in this chapter. Together, the controller and avatar form what Janet Murray terms a *threshold object*: a communicative agent between the physical and game worlds that manifests an instrumental connection between the two worlds (2012, p. 297).

Another important element of context is the physical environment in which gameplay takes place. Is the player comfortably seated for a long gameplay session? What size is the screen from which visual feedback is being read, and where is it located relative to the player? Is the player distracted by other people, devices, or pets demanding her attention? Is the player multitasking during play? If gameplay is given its artistic identity through its live enactment, a reasonable argument could be made that the conditions under which the player experiences a game radically alter the expressive identity of the resulting gameplay enactment.

Like the player's physical environment, social environment also changes the expression of gameplay. If the expression of the game world is the enforcement of *rules*, as established previously, it is important to consider that the presence of other players within a play space creates a separate set of rules that will be socially enforced, rather than mechanically enforced, that similarly constitutes the "shape" of possible play. Other players may enforce specific "house rules" with explicit boundaries (such as not allowing anyone to pick the character Oddjob in competitive first-person shooter *GoldenEye 007* (1997), because his smaller stature gives an unfair competitive advantage) or through softer communal interpretations of honorable and shameful play (*Dark Souls* players have established a culture of sportsmanship in competitive duels, not ambushing a player with a surprise attack and taking the time to politely bow and allow both duelists to heal to full health before engaging in a fight; not formally enforced by gameplay systems but an expected grace within the community, such that players who do not honor these rituals are viewed as being dishonorable and are excluded from the benefits of communal play).

Player communication also contributes greatly to the tone and nature of shared, multiplayer game spaces. Multiplayer sessions in which other players behave rudely toward others and shout abuse throughout the match can create a very hostile environment, particularly when said abuse targets particular groups of players who abusers may view as being a part of an "out-group". By itself, this is not a novel observation; reading a book would also be a worse experience if an angry teenager was yelling profanities at you the entire time. We can consider, though, how patterns of community behavior emerge over time for particular games and series. Why does *League of Legends* (2009) have such a reputation for abusive player communications while *Monster Hunter* (2004–present) has developed such a supportive and generous community? Are there elements of their systemic construction that push players in one direction or another? Is it a matter of moderation and soft-rule enforcement by developers? Are there elements of the semiotic fiction that encourage or discourage player hostility? These types of questions are all relevant to the practice of literate gaming.

Furthermore, cultural context affects the ways in which gameplay operations are read by the player and mediates the actions players express within gameplay. This will be more explicitly detailed in Chapter 8, but in brief, certain semiotic symbols and signifiers hold particular meanings in particular cultural contexts that do not always translate to other cultural contexts in the exact same way. Invocations of particular mythologies may impart obvious meaning to a player raised in a particular culture but be entirely indecipherable to a player in another. Players in differing cultural contexts may also be predisposed to viewing particular interactions with inherently cooperative or competitive framings. Since gameplay actions are expressions of player intent, a player's knowledge, attitudes, and beliefs can often be directly relevant to enacted gameplay occurrences.

Together, these elements of gameplay enactment form an open system of feedback and interaction. The player, through the contextual threshold object of the controller, translates her intent into virtualized action in the computer-maintained simulation. The computer perpetually recalculates and tracks the current game state and feeds necessary information back to the player through visual, audio, and haptic signals through contextual threshold objects. This information is interpreted by the player through her social and cognitive frames, informing intent for further action.

Each of these three general categories can be broken down into any number of smaller subcategories, depending on the specific framework or areas of interest of a particular interpreter. For example, Steve Swink outlines a system composed of seven elements: (1) the human operator (the player's cognitive mechanisms), (2) muscles (the player's mechanisms of direct physical manipulation), (3) input devices (controllers), (4) the computer (the levels of electrical circuitry and digital operation), (5) the game world (the diegetic fiction), (6) output devices (screens, speakers, and haptics), and (7) the senses (sensory inputs of the human player) (2009). This closed-circuit design maps nicely onto the categorical framework that we have established and provides a quite sensible outline of the mechanisms of input and feedback engaged during gameplay.

AVATAR

Before further detailing means of interface, I need to briefly define two terms that sit at the center of this subject: the avatar and the pointer. Across the field of game studies and broader game (and adjacent) cultures, the terms are used to describe a number of related and semi-related aspects of digital interface, including and separate from games, art, and entertainment. Due to the disparate meanings that vary by discipline and situation, I want to be very precise with how I define and use the terms in this particular exploration.

For the purpose of this book, I define avatar as the diegetic, embodied locus of will-expression within the virtual game space. The avatar serves a mediating function through which the real, physical player can willfully and meaningfully interact with the virtual game world. An avatar is an embodied presence within the game world, meaning that not only can the player act through it, but it can be acted upon by the game world. In other words, an avatar is a part of a game world not only in its influence within the game world but also in its *exposure to* the game world. The avatar is typically engaged projectively, meaning that the player extends or projects an aspect of selfhood onto (or into) the avatar.

To highlight a point of crucial divergence, the pointer is, similarly, a centralized entity or point of focus within a game through which the player can express her will. It is, conversely, *not* exposed to the influence of the fictional game world. In other words, whereas the avatar is a part of the diegetic fiction, the pointer facilitates the expression of player will by maintaining a spatially located but non-diegetic relationship with the game world. The pointer does not invite a projective posture of play, but it may accompany a projective avatar, or it may implicitly represent an unseen projective figure (for example, the cursor in *SimCity* [1989] abstractly represents the attention of will of the city's government, or perhaps a god).

The difference between these two concepts can be clearly illustrated through the comparison of avatar- and non-avatar-based games. Avatar-based games typically center around a character, vehicle, or object that has a proprioceptive relationship with the virtual world. In other words, they occupy a definable (or roughly definable) space within the game world in a way that is facilitative to their relative influence over the world and their vulnerability to it. Avatars invite projective embodiment from the player by contextualizing their presence in the virtual space through familiarly bounded "physicality". By contrast, non-avatar-based games manifest the direct control function with a point of focus that does not share a proprioceptive relationship with the game world. Though the relationship is still spatial (interaction and feedback are primarily communicated visually, so the focused point-of-player-influence typically occupies space on the screen), it is not "physical", by the standard of physicality by which the rest of the game world diegetically operates.

Avatars typically manifest as controllable characters, vehicles, or objects. Avatars often provide characterization and further semiotic context. Pointers typically manifest as mouse cursors, crosshairs, or selection highlights. Pointers serve only to direct player manipulation and focus player attention.

Certain genres are typically avatar-based, such as action, platformers, sports, racing, and fighting. Others are more often non-avatar-based, such as puzzle and strategy. Some genres mix the two modalities in ways that split typical avatar functions between an avatar and a pointer. For example, many point-and-click adventure games and CRPGs feature on-screen characters who have expressive and proprioceptive relationships with the game world, but control is directed through a cursor; the player does not have direct control over the character.

The ways in which avatars and/or pointers behave and manifest vary between genres and between games, so to provide the greatest clarity and flexibility, I will outline a number of purposes that avatars typically fulfill in avatar-based games. Of the below list, avatars usually serve *all* of these purposes, but sometimes they manifest fewer or split those functions amongst multiple entities. In such cases, we may notice the dual presence of an avatar and pointer, a pointer in isolation, or an avatar with some functions supplemented by other in-game objects. In avatar-based games in which the avatar does not fulfill all of the below attributes, we should seek to designate one primary avatar and label supplementary loci of functions as such. I will provide several demonstrations toward the end of this section.

An avatar is identifiable as some or all of the following. A pointer typically only manifests the first two:

- Locus of direct control
- Locus of manipulation
- Locus of perspective
- Locus of consequence
- Locus of spatial position and proprioception
- Locus of identifiability or identity expression

The above list will be detailed after some preliminary context is set.

Etymology and Contemporary Use

The etymology of the word "avatar" is from Sanskrit roots (with the rough literal meaning "descent") and was first utilized in an English context in the late 18th century to describe the incarnate personified embodiment of Hindu deities in particular myths. The term was later generalized in the early 1800s to describe a tangible embodiment of an abstract force or being. Most relevantly, the term has been adopted to describe human representation in a digital world following the use of the term in Neal Stephenson's 1992 novel *Snow Crash*.

Perhaps the term's most common usage in modern culture (at least, outside of being used as a proper noun in Nickelodeon or James Cameron-adjacent contexts) is to describe self-representation in digital social spaces. On forums and message boards of the 1990s and 2000s, for instance, a user's avatar was the image that accompanied their posts, which (in the times before MySpace and Facebook normalized the practice of connecting with online friends using actual, real-world identities) was often a fictional character or piece of artwork that was identifiable and "ownable" as an identity within the community but not literally representative of the person behind the screen. In this vein, and in a manner that is poetically adjacent to the original meaning of the word, "avatar" became a common term to describe player-controlled characters in video games, particularly in multiplayer settings in which players have some control over the appearance and identity of this character, such as in MMORPGs or social simulations like *The Sims Online* (2002).

Within game studies, "avatar" is often used to describe a player-controlled character, though the boundaries around this definition differ between scholars. The best definition I have found in the game studies literature is Rune Klevjer's: "The avatar is that which extends our embodied self into game space in a direct and intuitive sense, beyond merely agency or perspective, in a way that makes us belong to and exposed to a gameworld" (2022, p. 11).

Every game requires virtual ambassadorship to translate the impulses of the player into actions recognized and enacted in the virtual space, since the real, physical player cannot directly interact with the virtual world of the game. Even VR games, often seen "through players' own eyes" and interacted "through players' natural hand movements", require a digital double, mapped onto the movements of the player, that uses game-recognized tools (virtual cameras, collision objects) to produce the illusion of direct interaction. In such cases, and even in the cases of the simplest games, the literate player should be thoughtful about the translation and mediation of commands and the centralized digital representations through which these commands are enacted within the virtual space.

Embodied Presence

I go into more detail on the mechanisms of embodiment in the next section of this chapter, as the point at which the player psychologically assimilates the avatar as an operational, instrumental component of an extended, networked "self" for the purposes of mediated expression and perception. In those sections, I use the example of a screwdriver; when held, "I" (an extended "self" now systemically inclusive of the screwdriver) have abilities afforded by the tool: to tighten or loosen screws, for which I have limited ability unassisted. Similarly, when I assimilate the tool of the game avatar, I am granted agential affordances within the virtual world, with which I would not be able to directly interact unaided by that mediating avatar. Klevjer's definition aligns with this networked instrumentality, as he notes that "the avatar [...] extends our embodied self into game space" (Klevjer, 2022). He correctly notes that the avatar is primarily a vector of instrumental self-extension, a mediation rather than a collaborative but separate agent.

The concept of "embodiment" can be defined using many of the same parameters as I used above to define the component functions of a virtual avatar. We "embody" our physical selves to the degree that we have direct control, manipulative ability, a perspective, and a sense of spatial presence defined by our singular physical bounds, we experience consequence through our physical body, and we self-identify with our physical form. In the course of life, some of us may temporarily or permanently lack in some of these categories, and we often experience that as disembodiment of some form. For example, certain drugs may give users an "out of body" experience, some physical or psychological injuries or disabilities may alienate individuals from the feeling of ownership and agency over parts of their own bodies, and, conversely, normal feelings of self-identity questioning often manifest in bodily dissatisfaction.

It can be challenging to formalize an airtight definition for embodiment to assist in avatar identifiability. For that reason, I use the term "avatar" when such a centralized embodiment is, as Klevjer says, "direct and intuitive", but I find accompanying terms useful in situations in which the relationship is not as direct. I will often identify when a function of the avatar is supplemented by an additional locus of perspective, locus of manipulation, locus of consequence, etc. It is useful in our communications and conceptualizations of video games to be able to identify when typical avatar component functions are atypically applied or spread across multiple virtual entities rather than simply identifying the avatar as if all avatars operate identically. For example, it is precise and useful to identify that "*The Secret of Monkey Island* (1990) supplements avatar Guybrush Threepwood with a separate locus of direct control and manipulation in the game's mouse cursor" or "stealth game *République* (2016) splits avatar functions between two characters: Hope, the embodied agent sneaking around the facility who acts as the locus of consequence, proprioception, and identifiability, and the remote hacker who remotely oversees her espionage through security cameras and computerized interventions, who serves as the locus of perspective, direct control, and manipulation".

Component Functions of the Avatar

As described previously, the avatar typically performs a series of functions that assist in the aims of performance of player-initiated actions, feedback, and spatial embodiment. The avatar most often fulfills all of these functions, but there are instances in which some of these functions are split between multiple on-screen entities, sometimes including a pointer and sometimes not. In most cases, a centralized avatar can be recognized and named as such. In cases in which individual functions are partitioned onto other entities, they can be named functionally, e.g., "the avatar is supported by a separate locus of perspective". In very rare cases, these functions may be so distributed that all should be evoked using "locus" language without spending the extra effort arguing the identity of one central avatar, but the intent should usually be to intuitively understand the elements of the game that have been designated and partitioned to facilitate the player's agential expression.

Locus of Direct Control

As will be elaborated upon in the next chapter, the first step in the process of "decoding" (in a manner analogous to reading) a video game as a player is the identification of the aspect(s) of the virtual world over which the player has controller-mediated direct influence. Typically, controller inputs will direct one on-screen entity while not affecting the rest of the world. Due to the intuitive relationship between control and embodiment (we perceive ourselves as embodied owners of our own bodies because our cognitive impulses compel their movement while not being able to, unaided, control anything or anyone else in the outside environment), the object or character under direct control is usually also the avatar.

Change is usually effected onto the virtual world through the object over which we have the most control. Video games are inherently spatially structured, and interaction usually requires some kind of traversal (literalized as movement across the fictional world in avatar-based games or the crossing of screen real estate in non-avatar-based games), so centering interactability around a moveable element is nearly universal. If a video game's puzzle involves lighting three torches, the player needs a character who can walk between the torches to light them, or the player needs a non-diegetic element with which she can spatially communicate her will to light the torches.

An archetypical example of this is Mario in *Super Mario Bros.* (1985). The player directly controls Mario with controller inputs, situating him as the player avatar. To cite an example of the locus of direct control being separated from the avatar's affordances, the aforementioned point-and-click adventure *The Secret of Monkey Island* (1990)'s avatar, Guybrush Threepwood, is identifiably the avatar due to his role as the locus of manipulation, locus of consequence, locus of spatial position and proprioception, and locus of identifiability. He is not under direct player control, though; instead, the player controls a cursor and issues movement and interaction commands indirectly.

Locus of Manipulation

As video games are interactive by nature, the player requires a means by which she can act and effect change within the game world. This is usually fulfilled by the avatar for the reason stated above: a participatory, spatially structured medium requires a force through which players can spatially indicate the subject of their intentions and command actions.

Consider the example of Kratos from the Greek mythology-inspired action game *God of War* (2005). Kratos performs all of the player's instrumental actions—fighting, defending, climbing, opening treasure chests, and demolishing destructible objects. As he is under direct player control, he performs the two major categories of instrumental function: "go" and "do".

Sometimes, though, the locus of manipulation is separate from the locus of direct control. Detective

CRPG *Disco Elysium* (2019) sees players directly controlling a pointer and indirectly controlling detective Harry du Bois in a click-to-move manner similar to the *Secret of Monkey Island* (1990) example above. Though the player clicks on objects to indicate her will to interact with them, the interaction does not initiate until Detective du Bois is in instrumental proximity to the object. Though Detective du Bois is indirectly controlled, actions are still being performed through him as the avatar.

Avatar-based games in which manipulation is separated from the avatar figure are rare. Most commonly, we can cite examples of games without an avatar (such as *Lemmings* [1991] or *FantaVision* [2000]) or games in which avatars are diegetic dramatizations of non-diegetic gameplay (*As Dusk Falls* [2022], *Elite Beat Agents* [2006]).

Locus of Perspective

Typically, the avatar directs the visual information shown to the player. The usual arrangement is that if the avatar can see something, so too can the player. This is at its most literal in first-person games in which the game's perspective is diegetically *through the eyes* of the avatar character. Some first-person games (like *GoldenEye 007* [1997] and *Perfect Dark* [2000]) literalize this conceit with the in-game camera flying through the back of the avatars' heads to resolve to their eyesight perspectives at the end of third-person, cinematic cutscenes.

Even third-person games are most often centered around avatars' perspectives. Though not as literal as first-person titles (third-person shooters, for example, feature the avatar character in-frame, obviously not mirroring their subjective experience), the additional, non-naturalistic visual affordances can be contextualized as a mechanical metaphor for the sensory information that the character would reasonably have in an embodied situation that cannot be communicated so directly to the player. Being able to see the immediate proximity around a character in an over-the-shoulder perspective, as can be seen in *Resident Evil 4* (2005), for example, communicates to the player the additional information that avatar Leon Kennedy would naturally receive through his peripheral vision, sense of hearing, and other natural aids of situational awareness. A third-person perspective gives players a sense of proprioceptive awareness that reasonably mirrors that of the character better than a first-person perspective. Post-apocalyptic parcel delivery game *Death Stranding* (2019), for example, which centers around the traversal of challenging terrain, provides a naturalistic experience in its depiction of avatar Sam Bridges' full body. Through his proprioceptive and tactile senses, he would have an innate sense of how his body is balanced and the type and evenness of terrain on which he steps without looking directly at it. In this and most other cases, the third-person view provides the player information in an honest, if not naturalistic, manner.

Some games that take heavily abstracted camera angles, like the extreme bird's-eye views of the chaotic gorilla action game *APE OUT* (2019) or action heist game *Monaco: What's Yours Is Mine* (2013), will hide and reveal details of the environment and enemy positions as they fall in and outside of the avatars' fields of vision. Similarly, many strategy games like *Age of Empires II: The Age of Kings* (2001) employ a "fog of war" mechanic by which explored but unoccupied parts of the terrain remain faintly visible (as the civilization would have a map/memory for the land that had been previously explored), but other civilizations' passage through those spaces or changes made to the spaces in the time since they were explored (trees cut down, new buildings erected) would not become visible until a friendly unit is again within visual range, giving lookout and scout units a premium importance in maintaining intelligence about the competing civilizations.

The locus of perspective is rarely decoupled from the avatar. Since most virtual interactions are performed through the avatar, it is sensible to ensure that the means of interaction and locus of consequence remain visible and present at all times. Games that do allow perspective control separate from the avatar tend to be strategy games (as noted above) and CRPGs in which the player directly controls a cursor rather than directly controlling the character. Affording free movement of the camera allows the player to plan with the knowledge and context of the surrounding area, queuing up actions in a location where the avatar is not (for example, taking the screen view back to the avatar's home and clicking on the bed will start the avatar on her journey back home). It is worth noting that most of the games in this category allow players to swap between multiple avatars (party members or army/civilization units) and are structured such that these multiple avatars can diverge and complete separate tasks simultaneously, perhaps suggesting that the subjective experience of a singular point-of-view character is not their priority.

Other points in which perspective breaks from character embodiment include moments of restricted or absent player control. Cinematic cutscenes, for example, can switch between locations and feature scenes in the absence of the player character since there is no expectation of agential expression. Likewise, some scripted scenes that limit player control can present non-naturalistic viewpoints. For example, the 3D platformer *Crash Bandicoot 2: Cortex Strikes Back* (1997) features a number of escape sequences in which Crash Bandicoot runs toward the screen, away from a dangerous beast or boulder that occupies most of the visual field. This gives players a view roughly opposite of what we could assume is Crash's subjective perspective. Players can see in great detail that which is pursuing him (sometimes a giant bear, sometimes a rolling boulder, as in the sequence that inspired these sections in *Raiders of the Lost Ark* [Spielberg, 1981]), but a very poor view of the obstacles in front of him. This limited perspective increases the terror of the chase (by consistently highlighting how close the pursuant danger is to Crash) and necessitates a reactive, improvisational style of play (as the player must react immediately to the obstacles that appear in Crash's path, not having a greater view of what lies in front of him).

Further exceptions can be argued on technicality. 3D platformer *Super Mario 64* (1996) features a third-person viewpoint that operates very similarly to genre kin. As argued above, that type of perspective can be viewed as not wholly naturalistic (as Mario would not appear within his own field of vision), but the abstraction translates information that Mario would have proprioceptively into information that the game can communicate visually. For all intents and purposes, the perspective is that of Mario. Except that, diegetically, players are introduced to Lakitu, a flying creature that follows Mario around holding a movie camera. Functionally, Mario (the avatar) is the locus of perspective, but within the canon of the story, the locus of perspective is actually a separate character.

Locus of Consequence

Borrowing terminology from Klevjer's aforementioned avatar definition, not only does the avatar (typically) act *within* the game world, the avatar *belongs* to and is *exposed to* the game world. This means that consequences of play are typically performed upon and affect the avatar. For example, in *Super Mario Bros.* (1985), the presence of enemies or other hazards does not affect gameplay feedback until they collide with Mario (the avatar), at which point a consequence is dealt. If the enemy collides with Mario from the side or above, Mario either loses a powerup or dies. If the enemy collides with Mario from below, the enemy is removed and Mario earns points. Similarly, power-ups are only obtained if Mario collides with them, granting him additional abilities or size in a way that directly affects the actions afforded to the player through the avatar Mario. Triggering the appearance of a fire flower, for instance, does not further empower Mario unless Mario touches the flower. All game consequences, positive and negative, are effected through actions Mario takes and are performed upon Mario.

The avatar is usually the locus of consequence, as this creates the most intuitively understandable cause-and-effect sequence, but this can sometimes be externalized. Games or quests that require the protection of another character or object can unpair consequences from the controlled avatar. The aforementioned *Lemmings* (1991) requires players to construct a safe pathway for perpetually forward-marching lemmings to walk, and consequences for failure are performed upon the lemmings (there is no proper avatar in Lemmings). The genres of tower defense and MOBAs require the protection of buildings or artifacts, and to the degree to which particular examples feature avatars, usually the self-preservation of the avatar is not the primary objective; the player must protect the assigned buildings. Escort quests, like the protection of Ashley in *Resident Evil 4* (2005), often feature multiple loci of consequence, with the (usually defenseless) escorted character requiring protection from danger, though also requiring that the player maintain the safety of her own avatar, not being recklessly cavalier in their acts of heroism.

Locus of Spatial Position and Proprioception

One of the primary tasks of the avatar is to centralize an embodied, spatial presence. This is related to each of the concepts above. For an avatar to be spatially controllable by the player, it must exist in one point and not all other points so that it can then move to other points. For the avatar to be an appropriate locus of consequence, there must be definable boundaries defining where the avatar is and is not, such that an attack against the avatar's body inflicts consequence, but an attack that does not connect is not consequential in the same way. A sense of definable "physicality" is important to embodied avatars, as it mirrors the subjective singularity by which we experience our own individual lives.

A sense of bodily presence is most commonly mechanically reflected in collision susceptibility. Most avatars cease forward momentum when they collide with a wall. Gunshots are only consequential when they collide with the body and are inconsequential when they miss. The avatar can typically only pick up objects within arms' reach. This does not mean, though, that unseen avatars lack spatially bounded presence, though. While first-person shooters like *GoldenEye 007* (1997) feature gameplay from the first-person perspective of the avatar (in which James Bond broadly cannot see himself, save for his arms), a proprioceptive sense is still very important. The player must be able to intuit the approximate shape of the avatar's body so that gunfire wounds feel fair (it would be frustrating if the avatar takes damage for a gunshot that clearly should have missed the unseen body) and so that navigation remains intuitive (games that require first-person avatars to duck or crawl to enter vents, require the avatar to jump over gaps, or require the avoidance of traps such as landmines must feature intuitive proprioceptive communication).

Even canonically incorporeal avatars still communicate a sense of spatial being. Exploration adventure game *Everybody's Gone to the Rapture* (2015) features an incorporeal avatar (represented toward the end of the game as a floating ball of light), but, while its shape is undefined and unimportant for the purpose of play, it maintains a consistent first-person perspective, hovers at a set distance from the ground, and maintains a consistent velocity in its ambulation around the world. Though it is not strictly "physical", it maintains a consistent "embodied" presence.

Games that truly separate the locus of spatial position from the avatar are extremely rare, apart from games that have no definable avatar. Perhaps the most common subversion involves proprioceptive properties being copied amongst multiple entities. Games like *Venineth* (2020) and *Binary Land* (1984) feature puzzles in which a copy of the avatar is made (in a separate room or in a mirror reflection), and controller inputs control both the original avatar and the doppelgänger. Each must be navigated through separate labyrinths or obstacles simultaneously, so the player must account for not only the spatial position of her original avatar but also the remote spatial position of the copy.

Locus of Identifiability or Identity Expression

Finally, the last function that an avatar typically fulfills is in aesthetic presentation. These are, mechanically, the least important of the aspects, but it can serve in the identification of avatars when all else fails.

Identifiability refers to the degree to which an object or character feels akin or familiar to the player. Most video game protagonists are either humans or creatures with humanoid body structures that display human-like emotions and mannerisms. We have an intuitive sense of how humanoid bodies operate, and when we see humanoid characters (even with some layers of cartoonish abstraction like Sonic the Hedgehog), we have not only an intuitive sense of how that character might move and behave, but we also have an innate empathetic intuition for what the character may feel or think in a situation. This is one reason why, in games with diverse casts of human and non-human characters, player avatars tend to be the "relatable everyman" (for example, Lucas in *Mother 3* (2006) or the human child protagonist in any *Pokémon* game). As avatars are intended as vehicles of projective embodiment, players have an easier time projecting into familiar characters that they imagine being similar to themselves than physically or behaviorally alien characters. Much of the challenge of playing games that feature distinctly non-human-like avatars is forming a new mental model for how such an avatar may move and act within its world. For example, *Mushroom 11* (2015) tasks players with controlling a culture of fungus by "erasing" part of the culture, which regrows on the culture's opposite side.

Identity expression refers to the expressive function of avatars. In games that allow for aesthetic customization of characters, typically the greatest expressive capabilities are placed on the avatar. This is not to say that there are no other avenues through which players can express themselves; the house furnishings in *The Sims* series and the coloring-book world that can be freely painted in *Chicory: A Colorful Tale* (2021) demonstrate that players can sometimes aesthetically alter elements other than their avatars to express elements of their identities. But avatars are the most commonly customizable. In multiplayer games, the customized avatar often serves a social function similar to that in which "avatars" (using the web forum and social media meaning of the word) assert the identity of the player represented.

The specific capabilities of each character creator, particularly in multiplayer settings, develop disparate community practices that contribute to the tone and tenor of gameplay. Games like *Black Desert Online* (2015) and *Monster Hunter: World* (2018) feature detailed, realistic character creation engines that give players the capability to create avatars that look remarkably like their real-world selves (or, at least, highly idealized versions of their real selves). *The Sims 4* (2014) takes this even further by allowing for a greater diversity of body shapes, prosthetic limbs, surgery scars, glucose monitors, and a wide array of indicators of non-binary gender expression, giving players even greater capability to depict themselves or friends and loved ones while still allowing for purely imaginative character development as well. This encourages role-playing and empathetic projection. *Street Fighter 6* (2023) allows avatar bodies to greatly deviate beyond the bounds of normal human physical appearance. It is extraordinarily easy to create characters with comically exaggerated proportions, leading to online lobbies being populated with intentionally silly looking avatars, often looking more Muppet than human. This produces a lighthearted, "just for fun" environment that may diffuse some of the tensions of online competition.

DISTRIBUTED COGNITION AND PROJECTIVE EMBODIMENT

Distributed Cognition

Though each of the above-listed component functions of video game avatars is important, the paramount functions of the avatar are sensing and acting. Through the avatar, the player forms a sensory model of the game world and translates intent into performed action. In its capacity as a sensory and instrumental tool, the avatar becomes a component of what we will call the player's *networked self*. The networked self is a concept describing the psychological assimilation of tools into the self while the tools are being used. We view our extended capabilities as originating from our extended self. For example, when I hold a screwdriver, I view the tool as an extension of the expression of my will, giving me the capabilities to tighten and loosen screws, a task for which I have limited capacity unassisted.

Many tools supplement and extend our natural abilities by allowing us to offload or share the load of cognitive and physical tasks. A pen and paper allows us to offload the task of memorizing the grocery list. The paper can use its capacity for "memory" (retaining imbued meaning) so that our brains are free to use that energy for something else. In doing this, the pen and paper enters our cognitive network, supplementing our memory just as glasses supplement poor eyesight. This principle is called *distributed cognition* or *material intelligence*. It is not only inanimate tools into which we extend our cognitive selves; we also network and extend into other people or beings. In *Inventing the Medium*, Janet Murray shares the example of bees: "Bees in a hive have distributed cognition of where to find nectar and how to make honey, with no single bee knowing the whole process" (2012, p. 417). Likewise, we can conceptualize the cultural schemas, traditions, and "coordinated rituals" as capacities that rest in our *collective unconscious* (to use Jungian terminology), extending outside of our individual minds.

The video game avatar (and surrounding systems representing her inventory, learned skills, etc.) is networked with the player through the offloading of some memorization, expressive, and executional tasks within the virtual space. Not only does the player *act* through the avatar; the player *senses* through the avatar. Steve Swink draws a parallel to a blind man's assistive cane.

> When the blind man first starts using a cane, it is unfamiliar and requires a lot of reflection. The tapping movements are unpracticed, abstract movements to him. As he gradually builds skill at perceiving the world through the cane, he is able to more accurately and effortlessly tap around, getting a clearer read on his surroundings. His intent begins to flow

> effortlessly from the cane, any barrier between himself and the cane is removed, and the cane becomes an integrated part of his perceptual field.
>
> *(Swink, 2009, p. 57)*

As Swink illustrates above, our experience of the elements that constitute *our own bodily space* is reflective of the potential actions that they can take; tools and augmentations may enter or leave our "perceptual selves" situationally. The video game avatar is used to *probe* an unfamiliar world and send *feedback* to the player in a manner very similar to the cane above.

If we view the avatar as a living being (which she is not, but indulge me this brief fantasy), she also offloads some of *her* essential functions onto the player, such as volition and thought. Bidirectionally, the avatar is a part of the player's networked self, and the player is a part of the avatar's networked self. I refer to this enmeshed duality as the *player-avatar extended being.*

The result of distributed cognition is *projective embodiment.* Projective embodiment is the experience in which the player ceases to view the avatar as external to the self and rather centers her cognitive being around the avatar. It is not quite as *mystical* as it sounds. The player does not dissociate and go into a trance; rather, the avatar becomes the primary point of focus, and the physical self fades into secondary focus.

When driving a car, the driver's sense of proprioception (sense of what space she occupies in relation to her surrounding environment) ceases to primarily center on her own body but rather extends to the boundaries of the car. She gains an intuitive "muscle memory" for accelerating, braking, and turning, one that must be adjusted and relearned when driving unfamiliar vehicles. Were it not for projective embodiment, parallel parking and changing lanes would be significantly more difficult. Notice how people describe fender-benders with phrases such as "she hit me!" rather than "she hit my car!".

Projective Embodiment

In the medium of video games, projective embodiment is the experience during gameplay in which the player ceases to view the on-screen avatar (if such an avatar exists) as a separate being to which she issues orders and rather as an extension of her own *self* into the virtual world. The component elements of this term are *projection*: "the mental process by which people attribute to others what is in their own minds" (Duignan, 2019), and *embodiment*: the "sense of 'phenomenological presence', the way that a variety of interactive phenomena arise from a direct and engaged participation in the world" (Dourish, 2001, p. 115). To combine the ideas, we project our mental experience outward and experience the on-screen avatar as an extension of our embodied perceptual "*selves*". Danger to the on-screen character is phenomenologically experienced as danger to the self (to a low-level degree; I do not mean to suggest that players mistake the fictional hazards for real dangers as if it is a 21st-century, interactive *L'Arrivée d'un train en gare de La Ciotat* [Lumière & Lumière, 1896]), and the player begins to think of the avatar's abilities as domain-specific abilities that *she* possesses, in the same way that one gains specific abilities when holding a screwdriver (such as loosening or tightening screws) that she would not otherwise have.

Jeffrey B. Holmes frames objects as having special kinds of "knowledge" that they introduce to the extended mind-body network. To use his example,

> I leverage the potential for action possible in a hammer (that [it] can be used to hit a nail), but it does some work in the system (it actually hits the nail). The hammer 'knows' how to do this work in a kind of way possible because of its shape and the laws of gravity and so on. But it also requires me—and my mind-body unit, which now includes the hammer [...] to activate this affordance.
>
> *(Holmes, 2010)*

As such, the hammer is a low-knowledge node in the extended mind-body network, as it is still primarily directed by the actor. To contrast, a computer, which we may direct to retrieve stored information by clicking on a file, operates beyond (most of) our understanding of code, electricity, mechanical processes involved in hard disk drives, networking protocols, etc. In that mind-body network, it is actually the actor that is the low-knowledge node.

Following this schema, avatars can act as either low-knowledge nodes (Mario has the "knowledge" of how to jump, but it is up to the player to determine when and to what end that action is performed) or high-knowledge nodes (my RPG character retains all of the magic spells that she has read in all of the books that I have found throughout the game, offloading the player's responsibility to memorize and perform specific incantations). These knowledge states are intuitively understood by players and lead to common rituals of player behavior. Players feel confident setting down their controller to grab a snack, knowing that Mario, even when standing within visual range of his goal, will not act on his own behalf; he will be waiting for player input just as she left him when she returns. Conversely, players often open and immediately close books, letters, and documents scattered throughout the game world, knowing that pertinent information will be assimilated into the avatar's "knowledge" as soon as the book is interacted with (the "document read" flag is triggered, to use design language), without requiring the player to *read* and *understand* the information herself.

In-game avatars being direct outlets for player agency, the mental task of projective embodiment is natural. Players will very quickly identify game characters as ego extensions. "I fell down the pit", "the monster was coming right for me", "I can't believe you found me while I was camouflaged". This is a somewhat more complicated relationship than using a hammer, though. Whereas a hammer can be held in the hand and operated directly, players and video game avatars are separated by several steps of mediation (the player interfaces with the physical controller; the controller sends and receives signals from the console or computer that maintains the simulation; the computer interprets the player's commands and drives appropriate action within the virtual world; the results of the player's actions are fed back to the player through an electronic screen). Those steps become invisible, though, and players quickly project. The player not only *controls* the on-screen avatar, but, in a loose manner of speaking, she *is* the avatar. The avatar ceases to simply be a character within the virtual world and is rather seen as an extension of the player's ego boundary.

INTERWORLD AMBASSADORSHIP

But why is the avatar *necessary*? There are other mediums that provide immersive, narrative experiences that do not require the mediation of an avatar character. Theme park visitors are often involved in elements of role-playing and fantasy that do not require the adoption of a separate character persona. Certainly, there are many *video games* that forego the need for avatars, allowing something *approximating* direct or disembodied control (using a touchscreen to control a tile-matching puzzle game like *Bejeweled* (2001), for instance, presents a naturalistic method of control that is not dissimilar from how one may presume such a game would be played if a tactile version was made in real life; it does not require taking on a fictional identity that exists separately within the game diegesis).

The *Bejeweled* example stumbles into a pattern of illusory thinking, though. The player is *not* dragging around actual, colorful jewels, though, in the manner that she physically picks up and places the marbles in a game of Chinese Checkers. The player simply interacts with a touchscreen that sends informational data to a processing unit that has been programmed to recognize particular types of input and feedback sensible outputs. The player and elements of the game world are separated by a layer of unreality that she cannot cross on her own.

To arrange the books on my bookshelf, I must either walk to my bookshelf and arrange the books myself or send someone in my stead. I could send a friend, a particularly well-trained pet, or even a machine to do it, but the bookshelf, grounded in physical reality, *demands* of its arranger a matching corporeality. My intent for the arrangement of the books does not begin as a corporeal reality, though. It begins as an ephemeral thought. "Maybe I should arrange my books alphabetically by title, or by author last name, or by color, or by size, or by genre". I, as a human, contain both ephemeral and physical capacities; as such, I can directly translate my thoughts into physical action. Or, I may transfer information on the level of ephemerality to someone or something else. I may tell a friend, "I wish for the books to be arranged alphabetically by title", and they may use their co-capacities to perform this second-hand action on my behalf.

Video game worlds are inherently ephemeral. Thus, interaction between elements of the ephemeral world must be performed by ephemeral entities. There is presently no method for interacting with a video game space *directly* as a corporeal, non-fictional being.

Video game simulations are *rooted* in a base-level physicality, though, as we have demonstrated above. The informational structure that constitutes the simulation is performed as a series of electrical transfers within the processor of the computer. This externalizes the ephemerality, requiring a method of communication between the player and the computer.

Social games played between friends are rooted in the ephemeral level of thought. Even if there are physical play activities layered on top that literalize the conceptual rules and contrivances, the shared fiction that maintains the game is informational; thus, a player may suggest additional elements at any time that translate directly into the construction of the shared fiction: "the floor is now lava". Artistic mediums like live theatre and literature share a complicated relationship with their ephemeral and physical aspects. Though each is manifested physically (in a stage performance or the written words in a book), audiences understand that the fiction is rooted in the ephemeral, such that a rogue audience member running on stage or a book's previous owner crossing out a paragraph and writing their own passage in the margins is not understood as *fundamentally canonical* to the story as it exists in its *truest* form. Were the rogue audience member to be greeted by the actors with a fictional identity in a moment of improvisation ("Oh, I wasn't expecting to see you today, Cousin Pearl"), that may be seen as an allowance of the physical disruption to alter the ephemeral fiction by way of ephemeral, diegetic acknowledgement.

Players are unable to transfer the ephemerality of their thoughts into the ephemerality of ludic fiction directly. If the computer could "think" with the degree of complexity of a friend group playing a social game, the layer of mediating physicality might not be necessary. Likewise, if the game could *operate* within the mind of the player, like a particularly vivid lucid dream, mediation would also be unnecessary. With our present technology, though, an intermediary between the reality of the player and the unreality of the game world is needed.

Through the controller, the player is able to translate her intent into representative, physical actions. The controller translates the physical manipulations into information, which the computer receives and manifests within the fiction. The journey from player intent to game world action involves three major transformations: intent (thought) to controller manipulation (physical action), controller "sensation" to information, and information to afforded, diegetic action. We can compare this journey to the communication of thoughts between people. The transmitter forms intent to transmit a thought; she physically manipulates her mouth, vocal cords, and tongue to form vibrations in the air. These vibrations are sensed by the ear bones of the receiver; these manipulations are interpreted by the brain as sound signals and decoded using familiarity schemas to ascertain the meaning of the message.

The engine literalizes controller inputs as avatar actions, and the avatar can perform the tasks within the game world that the player cannot. This involves two layers of mediation, though. The controller is designed to accept particular types of inputs and not others and for these inputs to be of varying degrees of sensitivity. The avatar is also designed to be able to perform particular types of actions in particular contexts and not others. Thus, the avatar is not a direct and unrestricted conduit of player expression within the world of the game; the player is highly constrained by the specific affordances of the controller and avatar. Different controllers will afford different types and sensitivities, and different avatars will afford different expressive and instrumental actions within game worlds.

Controllers and avatars that afford the greatest degree of sensitivity are often the most "invisible". VR games are typically controlled from the first-person perspective using highly sensitive motion- and position-tracked handheld controllers. This confluence of elements often creates an illusion of direct, physical interaction within the game world. A player can reach out and "grab" a virtual object in much the same way that she can reach out and grab a similar object in real life. This is still a mediated exchange, though, and does, indeed, involve an avatar. Controller positions and motion are gathered by the computer as informational inputs and translated into diegetic action of an invisible avatar overlaid onto the algorithmically determined bodily position of the player. When the computer loses track of one of the controllers, the player is not able to interact with virtual objects until the information stream is re-established and the computer "understands" the avatar's spatial position once again.

Similarly, circling back to the example that kicked off this section, touchscreen-controlled games like *Bejeweled* do not typically, diegetically, literalize an avatar character, but the functional translation of physical signals to information operates in a similar manner that "proxies" player physical behaviors into a simplified form of inputs that the computer can understand and operationalize.

Projection vs. Proxy

As noted above, ego extension can be thought of as being bidirectional. Though we would not typically say that an inanimate object has an "ego self", one could say that not only does the screwdriver extend her abilities to tighten and loosen screws, but she also extends the screwdriver's abilities to move within three-dimensional space and accomplish tasks. This may be a silly point to make, since we cannot attribute any kind of *motivational drive* to a screwdriver beyond the *abstract* sense of design motivation (a screwdriver manifests its *purpose* when utilized for the task for which it was designed. This is *embodied* in the potential of the tool but not *felt* or *experienced* by the tool, obviously; Buzz Lightyears not withstanding).

Ego boundaries extend outward from the user of a tool, but video game role adoption also involves *identity* adoption. When playing *The Witcher* (2007), it would be equally reasonable to say that I *become* Geralt of Rivia as saying that Geralt of Rivia *becomes* me. Though video game characters *are* inanimate tools and *not* thinking and feeling beings in their own right, we can consider the primacy of their identities and personhood conceits of the fiction. On the level of the game world, these characters are *people*, in the same way that Lady Macbeth is a *person* with ambitions, emotions, and decision-making capacities within the fiction of *Macbeth* (Shakespeare, 1623).

Honoring the fictionality for a purely theoretical exercise, we must acknowledge that the task of projective embodiment involves a more complicated exchange when assimilating the functions and fictions of an avatar rather than when simply using a screwdriver. Game designer Jonathan Blow terms this process *proxied embodiment*. Blow's position, summarized eloquently by a peer, asserts that "because a game world represents its own reality external to its avatar's bodily space in the same way that the physical world is external to our own bodily space, it seems much more like a substitution than an extension" (Swink, 2009, p. 59).

I disagree that *substitution* is the appropriate framing, but it is reasonable to conceptualize the meeting of two "minds" less as a wholly *assimilative* extension and more as a bidirectional symbiosis. Miguel Sicart frames avatars as "company players accept as they explore different worlds" (2013, p. 13). Sicart's interest is in the ethical conflict that emerges when the player and avatar character (as written) have differing motivations that may result in the expression of afforded actions that would seem contradictory to one of the two "halves" of the shared identity. Separately exploring this complexity, Sicart writes

> [the avatar's] company is more than just a guide. It determines, to a large extent, players' ethical presence in that world. The values of this [character] are important in the fictional creation of that world: players explore those values and live by them.
>
> *(2012)*

Engaging with a game world as diegetic fiction, we accept entering into a world in which meaning is "always-already present" (Bayliss, 2007). We adopt meaningful elements of the avatar's identity, reflected in the values and ideology of the game world, just as actors adopt the socio-cultural complexities of character identities that they temporarily inhabit during a play or movie. This subject will be revisited in greater detail in Chapter 6.

THE CASE OF THE DISAPPEARING CONTROLLER

Projective embodiment involves a degree of cognitive transportation. The player comes to feel that she, inhabiting the mediating avatar, is a member of the fictional world of the game. Beyond simply instrumental agency, the player experiences a sense of presence or, to use a word that has so many meanings within the gaming space that it has become almost entirely meaningless, *immersion*. The truest expression of projective embodiment facilitates a sense of seeing *through* the screen and *into* a game world. Reality fades as occurrent attention is paid to the fictional diegesis.

This is often framed as a kind of *gamer hypnosis*, a concerning detachment from reality, worryingly portrayed in the "video games cause violence" debates as a blurring between realities that can *only* result in utter desensitization to violence and uncritical adoption of whatever implicit ideology a game may endorse. I do not go this far; players do not enter an *uncritical fugue state* in which realities blur, dizzyingly together. Players do, though, *extend into* ludic sub-realities in a manner that feels engrossing and encapsulating. The manner by which this occurs *begins with* a fluency of expression, afforded by an avatar of great expressive capacity.

Transparency

The endpoint of projective embodiment is a sense of transparency of mediation between player impulse and diegetic action. Transparency is a phenomenological marker that an object has been incorporated into a user's extended being, utilized with *automaticity*, *lack of attention*, and *effortlessness*. With proficiency and familiarity, the use of a tool to sense or act upon the world falls out of occurrent attention and becomes natural and automatic; a *transparent medium*. When a cognitive artifact becomes transparent, the user can subjectively experience and act upon the external world through the networked object directly rather than as conscious mediation.

The classic example of this is the above-cited blind man with a cane; once he becomes familiar with its use, he experiences the sensation of spatial probing and feedback as occurring in the tip of his cane rather than in the interface between the cane and the nerves and musculature of his hands. The brain has assimilated the cane into his bodily schema, and he experiences touch-based sensation *as if* it were through the cane *directly*. Obviously, the cane does not contain nerve receptors; the blind man gains the sensory information from *dynamic touch*, a sense based on muscular effort and stimulation of mechanoreceptors embedded in muscles and tissue (Gibson, 1966, p. 109), but the brain interprets these sensory signals in the context of the self-referential bodily model, which, when holding an assistive cane, *includes* the tool. When this vicarious sensation has become fluent, it can be termed *transparent*.

Transparency is achieved through continuous or consistent feedback and familiarity. The blind man assimilates his cane into his perceptual self through learned fluency, and the typist learns the procedural mechanisms of typing to a great enough degree that the keyboard becomes a transparent tool, not requiring occurrent attention. Applying the concept of transparency to video game control becomes more complex, though, as there are multiple levels of mediation that need to pass from occurrent attention.

The first level is the most natural and hardly worth mentioning. We must acknowledge that our own bodies are tools, grounded in the physical world (at least partially) separable from our ephemeral centers of conscious cognition. Their transparency, effortlessness of control, and familiarity are typically self-evident, but this is not always the case. Our senses of bodily familiarity and transparency are socially and culturally mediated, as Iris Young reminds us, susceptible to change based on enculturation and socialization (2005). Effortlessness of control is a fragile condition, as anyone with experience of motor disability can attest. And certainly we can acknowledge that one *can* become separated from one's arm, witnessing a tool of effortless, embodied operation suddenly become a disembodied component of the external environment. While we do not typically classify our bodies as components that *extend* our networked selves (the division between the internal and external typically borders at the skin), it is worth acknowledging that the body performs the first translative mediation, transforming cognitive intent into physical action, and like all other points of translation and interchange in the system, this translation involves the introduction of *some level* of noise. I can attest that, when I go out dancing, my physical actions *rarely* match my cognitive intent one to one.

The second level of interchange occurs between the hand and the controller. This is classical tool use. The body physically manipulates the controller and receives sensory feedback from the controller (not only artificial haptics, such as a controller's "rumble" feature, but also the weight of the controller and the resistance and boundaries of buttons, triggers, and thumbsticks). The actualization of intent is communicated through the enactment of appropriate, virtual action. For example, moving the mouse corresponds with movement of the cursor on-screen, and eventually, the player does not consciously consider the action of moving the *mouse* as much as she considers the action of moving the *cursor directly.* Control mastery of non-avatar-based games culminates with transparency at this level. Once the player becomes adequately familiar with the inputs and sensitivity of the controller, she can actualize her intents with increasing precision and effortlessness. Just as a skillful typist does not have to think about the placement of each key on the keyboard, a game player who has achieved controller transparency can actualize her intentions without constant occurrent reference to the layout and operation of the controller.

In avatar-based games, though, as we have already noted, the avatar itself is a tool that has its own set of affordances and effectivities that we operate indirectly through the controller. This level is not entirely *separate* from the previous level; for avatar-based games, the feedback relevant to the expression of motivated action enacted through the controller is typically expressed *through* avatar action (becoming familiar with the task of pressing the "A" button to jump is assisted only through the visual feedback of the jumping action of the avatar; there is no way to become fluent in that input *apart* from avatar action and feedback), but, as noted above, games without avatars grant the experience of transparency of controllers without the avatar extension, making it useful to be able to consider the two separately in select circumstances.

The achievement of transparency of the avatar is successful projective embodiment. This does not mean that the player ceases to *see* or *consider* the avatar; rather, she incorporates it into her perceptual self, her extended bodily model. The blind man does not *forget* he is holding a cane, but he has cognitively assimilated the tool to such a degree that he is able to sense the world through it automatically and effortlessly. To transparently embody an avatar is to experience the virtual world through the avatar with a similar sense of automaticity. With an adequately fluent transparency, the player achieves what we may term *vicariosensation*, a sense of the "physicality" of the virtual world and the embodied experience of being within it.

One may object, though, that the player receives sensory feedback in a form dissimilar from how we would naturally gather tactile information. Video games primarily provide sensory feedback through visuals; how can we form a tactile understanding of the virtual world through visual feedback alone? Like-for-like sensory augmentation is not a requirement for distributed cognition and transparency, though. The blind man's cane performs a roughly opposite task: conveying visual information about the external world through tactile sensation. Similarly, our brains are adept at discerning patterns and properties through visual observation. There are several mechanisms by which this occurs:

Empathetic sensation. As noted above, one of the primary functions of the avatar is as the locus of identification. Most video game avatars are human because it is easy to identify with human characters. We intuitively understand the operation, capabilities, and vulnerability of the human body. When a character picks up a virtual object, we can glean clues about its weight from the avatar's performance. If the avatar carries it underhand, staggering with one pained footstep at a time, sweating and grimacing, we can infer that the object is quite heavy. If the avatar is able to carry the object above her head without slowing her stride or displaying any signs of visible exertion, we can presume the object is quite light. Even abstract symbolism can be effectively discerned as tactile feedback. For example, many games will put a throbbing red border around the screen and desaturate other colors when the avatar has sustained serious injury. Though this does not match the naturalistic experience of getting hurt, it is true to the subjective experience and has an affective clarity that we can immediately recognize and internalize.

Responsive sensation. As the player uses the avatar to probe the virtual world, she observes how it responds to differing types or levels of action. The player may notice that a virtual body of water ripples gently as the avatar walks through it, is more heavily churned and disturbed when the avatar runs through it, and splashes magnificently when the avatar jumps into it from a great height. This communicates potentially useful information about the fluid dynamics of the world and is observable through repeated experience and experimentation. While we can use familiarity heuristics to *presume* how an object in the game world *might* respond to input of different kinds (something that appears like glass *might* shatter when shot with a gun), it is not until we test through motivated action that this is confirmed and our understanding of the world transitions from hypothetical to sensational.

Translative sensation. Many physical properties are visually communicated using novel or secondary characteristics compared to how they would present in real life. Weight is often communicated through velocity and inertia, for example. Massive objects are given a sense of weightiness and enormity through slow movement, such as the lumbering giants from *Shadow of the Colossus* (2005). Were the colossi to be animated with the quick and reactive movements of the human-scale avatar, they would appear lighter, incongruous with our expectations for something of that magnitude. Tactile sensations are also translated to other forms: the auditory feedback of an avatar stepping on crunchy, dry leaves may be exaggerated to communicate the tactile sensation. Likewise, a sudden rumble of the controller's haptic engine does not *feel* like getting shot, but it may appropriately alert the player to that diegetic occurrence through the evocation of complimentary emotions, such as surprise.

Through these and other methods, we embody the avatar as a transparent extension of our sensory systems. Similarly, avatars are subsumed into our active motivational systems through fluency of control. When avatar control becomes truly transparent, the player does not need to consider each action as a button input; she experiences the affordances of the avatar directly and effortlessly. She internalizes the abilities and limitations of the avatar and operates in the world *as* and *through* the avatar. Just as the cane is the part of the blind man's extended body that senses the outside world, the avatar becomes the part of the player's extended body that senses and manipulates the virtual world.

Breaking Transparency

Transparency of control and mediation is not the intended experience of every game. Even games that present an otherwise transparent, embodied experience can interrupt their transparent embodiment for the purpose of modulating gameplay texture or fulfilling other experiential priorities. Games tend to both punish and reward players with interruptions to embodied continuity. Failure is typically punished with avatar "death", which temporarily expels player control and breaks the embodied experience. On the level of mechanical metaphor, this is appropriate, as death in the real world also involves the stark removal of agency and embodiment. Victories are also often accompanied by an "end of play" state; a cutscene may push the narrative forward at the end of a level, or a multiplayer match may conclude with a victory ceremony. In these cases, players are similarly expelled from avatar embodiment.

Transparency is typically achieved through continuous feedback and sustained engagement, so these occurrences may ultimately work against the depth of embodiment that players are able to achieve. Generally speaking, games have been generally trending toward greater sustained embodiment in recent decades. *Half-Life 2* (2004) was notable at the time of its launch in 2004 for not removing player control during story segments that would otherwise be non-interactive cutscenes in other games. Characters perform pre-staged actions and deliver dialogue in typical cutscene fashion, but these scenes are framed from the perspective of player avatar Gordon Freeman, and players are still able to freely ambulate around these scenes. Interactions with these scenes are minimal, so it could be argued that the player embodies the role of a cameraman rather than an active agent during these scenes, but the commitment to never expelling the player from the embodied perspective from beginning to end (apart from at-the-time technologically necessary loading screens) was felt in what is remembered as a particularly immersive game.

The transparency of the controller and the transparency of the avatar, though framed above as two sides of the same coin, are sometimes separated for effect that deepens the embodied experience. Games will sometimes require strenuous actions of the player to complement strenuous or dexterous activities performed by the avatar. For example, *Metal Gear Solid 4: Guns of the Patriots* (2008) features a harrowing scene in its final act that requires protagonist and avatar Solid Snake to crawl through a tunnel irradiated with microwaves that slowly kill him as he pulls himself painfully forward. The player is tasked with rapidly pressing a button on the controller, long after the point at which it becomes uncomfortable. The player expends strenuous effort in parallel with Snake. On the other side of the spectrum, many games feature lockpicking minigames that require the player to hold each thumbstick in particular positions (communicated through controller rumble) without losing those "sweet spots", representing the dexterous precision required in the lockpicking of a professional thief.

In these moments, the player becomes acutely aware of the controller and its specific physical properties, but these moments create compelling operational metaphors that cleverly benefit our engrossment in the diegetic action instead of pulling us out of the experience.

FORMIC DETERMINISM AND PLURALITY

As noted previously, player expression is mediated not only by avatar affordances but also by the engineered design, capabilities, and sensitivity of the controller. The choice of controller can make a *fundamental* difference to the gameplay experience, such that it would be reasonable to question whether two players running the same game software but using formally distinct types of controllers are even having comparable gameplay experiences. Someone at the arcade playing the full-body, kinesthetic rhythm game *Dance Dance Revolution* (1998; using the full-size dance pad that requires stomping on each symbol pad with her foot in time with the music) has a very different gameplay experience from someone playing identical software using the thumb-operated buttons of a handheld game controller. In this case, the physicality of play *is* a primary factor of its challenge.

Communities of players engage in metagame challenges, intentionally playing difficult games with the *least optimal* controller varieties. It has become a tradition of tongue-in-cheek community one-upmanship to play the challenging ARPG *Dark Souls* (2011) with increasingly absurd controller varieties; for example, the bongo drums developed for the rhythm game *Donkey Konga* (2003) or the motion-controlled steering wheel accessory developed for *Mario Kart Wii* (2008).

Though the experiential differences are obvious in the above examples, a game executes the same *code* and operates by the same *rules* regardless of the controller being used.[1] Surely the *game* itself is the same, regardless of how it is being played.

Returning to an earlier point, gameplay is a system inclusive of the player, the computer (including the software), and context (including the controller). Though the software executes in an identical manner for *Dark Souls* (2011) players using standard controllers or *Donkey Konga* (2003) bongos, the holistic *system* of gameplay enactment is altered in a manner that will affect the meaningful output of the gameplay. This is a point of greater importance in Chapter 11 when I argue that the game software does not constitute the artistic artifact that is "processed" by the audience into the resulting *artistic experience*; rather, specific, instantiated gameplay enactment is what I will term the *artistic potentiator*.

Returning to the point at hand, gameplay is a designed and directed experience. It is not *free* play comparable to an individual directing her own daydream. Gameplay is shepherded toward particular, desired expressions through lightly deterministic elements, shaped by *affordances* and *constraints/resistance* (see Chapter 3). Controllers constitute some of the designed elements that give shape to gameplay expression. Some games are designed to be experienced in a *very particular* way, while others factor the plurality of input interfaces into their experiential design. For example, the rhythm series *Guitar Hero* (2005–2015) aims to elicit a particular rockstar fantasy abetted by holding the custom-designed, guitar-shaped controller in hand, pressing fret-analog buttons while strumming a bar analogous to guitar strings. Earlier entries in the series *can* be played using standard gamepad controllers, but this is a suboptimal form of experiencing the desired fantasy.

Proficient video game literacy does not mean extensively researching the design intentions of each game and refusing to play any game using anything but its *optimal* configuration. Rather, it necessitates an awareness of this plurality and the language and context to hypothesize how *different* configurations may affect different enactments of gameplay. In their plurality, these different expressions of gameplay sum to the total expressive capacity of each game. As we experientially develop a better sense of how these control affordances translate to diegetic expression, we can better witness the *shape* of the game's design from multiple angles. Reading this type of holistic design formulation is a focus of Chapter 11.

Formic Plurality and Primacy

Video games are, definitionally, digital software. As such, the "game", as we would typically define it, does not self-contain all of the necessary components an audience needs to engage with it. This is not unique to video games. While a painting or sculpture contains the entirety of the described art in its definitionally irreducible core (though meaning can be enriched by curated context, a complimentary frame, etc.), the core artistic product of a cabaret performance, for example, is in its specific enactment, which is not able to be singularly and wholly preserved in its script, set dressing, or even a video recording. Similarly, musical concerts are often discussed in terms of individual performances, and a setlist or recording does not represent a platonic ideal version of that show but a separate, remediated artifact.

In a similar manner, the core artistic product of a video game is the enactment of play. What exists on-disc, on-cartridge, or within the digital download sold to players is compiled code, unremarkable and useless without a computer that can execute that code. Video games, as sold to customers, are essentially instructions that a computer can follow to enact the core artistic artifact (gameplay) in real time. To further complicate the matter, different computers often execute the same code differently. Sometimes fundamentally (early consoles with significantly different technical architectures had differing capabilities and required the production of similar but distinct versions of the same games when porting between consoles) and sometimes incrementally (the powerful Xbox Series X runs the same fundamental code as its lower-cost and less technically ambitious sibling console, the Xbox Series S, and the extra power allows for gameplay at higher resolution, higher frame rate, and with greater performance stability).

As such, how do we understand and contextualize games as works of intentionally communicative art? While I primarily recommend individual reflection and discussion of games to be grounded in the unique and personal enactments of play (as this not only contextualizes technically rooted differences but also play divergences due to player choices or execution), there are situations in which it is necessary to conceptualize individual games singularly. For example, when making claims about the lineage of mechanics or ideas, it may be necessary to consider progenitor games as they would have performed and would have been experienced by players at the time rather than how more powerful hardware and future revisions of the game may allow it to be experienced today. Similarly, when considering aspects of artist intent, we should consider the appropriateness of inferences given the lack of a knowable, singular platonic ideal version of the game.

It is tempting to label the most performant version of a game to be its platonic ideal. Surely, an experience of *Crysis* (2007) running at 144 frames per second is a more fundamentally *true-as-intended* version of *Crysis* than playing it on a computer that struggles to run it at a consistent 30 frames per second. But this is not always the case. Many games were programmed with the limitations of their target consoles in mind, such that more performant play is detrimental to the play experience.

Shmups, in that genre's golden age, pushed sprite count (number of on-screen objects) beyond what systems of the time could efficiently draw, causing slowdown during particularly busy sections. Though this started as a side effect of over-ambitious design, it was embraced by the shmup player and developer community as a natural and necessary change in play pace. As such, re-releases of classic shmup games on more powerful hardware often artificially emulate this slowdown despite the lack of technical constraint. In fact, the experiential arc of *Space Invaders* (1978), one of the earliest shmup games, relies upon what was, at the time of development, unintended consequences of technical over-ambition. *Space Invaders*, a game about shooting down a fleet of extraterrestrial attackers who approach the gunship avatar in formation, famously becomes faster and more frantic as the battle progresses. This arose accidentally from technical limitation: the computers of the time struggled to draw and track the number of sprites on screen at the beginning of the battle, and the pace of gameplay increased as sprites were cleared from the screen and freed from computer memory. Even modest modern computers are able to run *Space Invaders* at full speed without a hitch, but the speed escalation, at first unintentionally modulated by technical constraint, is additive to the game experience and is, thus, emulated in later re-releases.

This kind of experiential differentiation not only occurs due to the hardware on which a game runs but also separate components of technical enactment. The type of visual display often makes a significant difference in the interpretation of game graphics. There are many modern games that utilize "retro" stylization, emulating the sprite-based pixel artwork of the 8-, 16-, and 32-bit consoles of the 1980s and 1990s. Were our perspective on this art style only informed by these recent games (or re-releases and emulations of 1980s and 1990s titles), we may form an aesthetic expectation for the sharp edges of sprites and harsh borders between colors, creating beautiful mosaic abstractions. During the 1980s and 1990s, though, video games were primarily played on cathode ray tube (CRT) displays, which produced fuzzy, less-distinct imagery than modern monitors, often effectively blurring the sharp edges of this art into more naturalistic gradients and softer shapes. As such, we should consider whether the increased clarity of modern displays grants us additional perspective and a more "truthful" representation of game visuals as they exist in the code or whether we should consider the ways in which game visuals were specifically designed to incorporate the imperfections of then-utilized technology.

Though some elements of the intended experience may be lost when playing past titles on then-future technology, we can equally argue that technical improvements and later re-releases enhance a game's experience relative to contemporaneous expectations more than would playing it on original hardware. First-person espionage shooter classic *GoldenEye 007* (1997), originally released for the Nintendo 64, maintained a technical performance roughly equivalent to other 3D games of its day and had an innovative and functional control scheme before first-person shooter controls had been broadly standardized on consoles. Playing the Nintendo 64 version of the game today, though, is shocking by comparison to modern expectations, as modern players expect games to perform with much higher frame rates, and decades of first-person shooter standardization may leave modern players missing expected quality-of-life (QoL) features that have since become standard. Though *GoldenEye 007*'s original N64 release can be useful to revisit from an educational perspective, it could easily be argued that the Xbox One re-release from 2023 presents players with modern expectations of a version of the game experience closer to equivalence with that of players in 1997 relative to *their* contextual expectations.

Considering video games as artifacts of artistic expression, we must contend with whether game code has a singular identity as a set of rules, conditions, and mechanics, regardless of the hardware on which it is played, or whether ports and adaptations represent distinct instancing to be held in separate contention. There is precedent for the former perspective; considering game code as a script, it could be contextualized in a similar manner as we discuss theatrical dramas: *Hamlet* (Shakespeare, 1599) remains *Hamlet* even if performed by a roller-skating children's troupe. On the other hand, dramatic re-versioning or even re-contextualization of existing work can often make drastically different statements and is often considered separately, with respect to the deviation from the vision and form of the original piece.

Developers enter into game creation with knowledge that their works are technologically unbound. Though a game is most often developed and optimized for one or many contemporaneous platforms, the history of game development and community has proven an inclination toward preservation and technical remastering past the time of a game's original release. Just as building architects know that their work will be subject to natural degradation over time, they must build in such a way that functionally and aesthetically preserves the core vision and structural integrity; game developers enter into an inverse contract; they know that future technological advancements will almost always be able to run code more efficiently and effectively, without the necessity of further intentional development (through the normal course of computer advancement) or with their involvement (by updating their game through downloadable patches). Video games are formally nomadic, adaptable to new computational environments in ways that both improve and hurt the game experience. This is unavoidable but is a necessary reality, particularly as old hardware becomes less accessible to modern audiences, or as equivalent hardware (such as PCs that undergo regular incremental upgrades rather than generational "clean slate" changes like we witness with video game consoles) becomes architecturally distinct enough to alienate older software through gradual incompatibility of drivers and system tools.

From the player's perspective, convenient availability of older titles is beneficial, but we should also educate ourselves about the ways in which this technological resettlement on new hardware affects the experience of play, both internally (e.g., how may QoL features help or hinder the experiential aims of this game?) and externally (e.g., in what manner may my modern video display expose flaws that contemporaneous technology may have minimized?). Playing on original hardware is a valuable experience in calibrating time-relative expectations, but it is not a solution that can be easily recommended widely for all players, as original hardware, original game discs or cartridges, and compatible technical accompaniments (video displays, necessary cables, controllers, etc.) can be restrictively expensive and rare. To accommodate the widest possible audience of historically curious players, it is better to endorse a default position of prioritizing access (through official re-releases, ports, or emulation of arguable legality) and emphasize original hardware experience primarily for educational context as opportunity permits.

As such, proper video game literacy for modern players who wish to experience older titles requires familiarity with how technological recontextualization typically affects the experience of play relative to intended or contemporaneous experiences. It is also beneficial to be able to identify experts and records that may be able to explain these contextual details in a manner that may help players modulate their expectations. From a meaning-making perspective, taking an art history-like approach can be beneficial, as all games (like all other artworks) are created in progressive conversation with their contemporaries and the works that have come before them. Reading a work of the past with a modern context can illuminate the work's capacity to transcend its particular moment, but it is also always useful to keep in mind its contextual placement in that ongoing conversation. Artistic choices become evident when there is a clear expectation of what the statement is *deviating from*, and such statements may be *lost* on beholders who only experience works with knowledge of the modern, such that their *innovations* are recognizable only as the *conventions* that they inspired.

Types of Formic Differences

I strongly suggest thoughtfully playing games available on multiple platforms (whether historical or contemporary) with an interest in the ways in which platform migration/plurality may affect the experience. Without side-by-side comparisons, though, this can be difficult to achieve and verify individually. The interested player should familiarize herself with other resources that may provide helpful information in this regard. Contemporary reviews, even for older games, are often archived and readily accessible online and can explain how games met or fell short of contemporary expectations, sometimes even providing a useful perspective on how games have changed over time where original versions may no longer be accessible at all, such as pre-patch versions of digital-only games or online multiplayer games no longer playable after servers have been deactivated.

The field of *platform studies* can be a useful area of study for interested game players. This field collates and studies information about types of computers and consoles holistically and historically, identifying design trends, technical capabilities, and contemporary audience and marketplace considerations for particular computers embedded in a specific point in history. The Platform Studies series of books from The MIT Press and the publications of Bitmap Books can improve readers' historically grounded, contextual understandings of games played from particular points in time.

Finally, there exist a number of resources that specifically seek to historically contextualize games in an approachable and understandable manner, such as the series of biographical Boss Fight Books and the historically grounded *Cane and Rinse* podcast (Cox, 2011–present), to which I contribute. Additional resources that focus more on behind-the-scenes achievements of how games are produced can also provide useful contextual grounding for technical and design implementations; I recommend video game development documentarians *People Make Games* (Bratt & Sayers, 2018–present), *Noclip* (O'Dwyer, 2016–present), and *2PlayerProductions* (Owens et al., 2005).

To guide our education regarding the ways in which these contextual differences affect gameplay experiences, we should understand the avenues in which formic differences may present. Though not exhaustive, this section catalogues a number of the most common factors, internal and external to the software, that affect players' experience of gameplay across settings. This applies to both historical games being played in modern contexts and modern games being played on different platforms. This section provides some useful questions to consider when playing games with a contextual interest.

Console/Computer

The power and unique capabilities of a given platform can greatly affect the ways in which a game plays. All gaming-compatible hardware are complex, multi-faceted machines, so "power" is not a single metric by which machines can be cleanly ranked. Often, hardware can excel in some domains of computing and lack in others, relative to their contemporaries. For that reason, games may play differently in specific ways across multiple platforms rather than being cleanly *better* or *worse,* as different technical components provide different capabilities. For example, the Sony PlayStation and Nintendo 64 were contemporary competitors with significantly different internal architectures. The PlayStation read games from discs, and the N64 read games from cartridges, and the differences between these storage media produced some interesting differences. PlayStation discs had higher storage capacities than N64 cartridges, benefitting games like *FINAL FANTASY VII* (1997), which features extensive pre-rendered videos and backgrounds that would be prohibitively large for cartridge storage, and *Gex: Enter the Gecko* (1998), which features a large amount of voiced dialogue, which was scaled back significantly when the game was ported to N64. Though lower capacity, the N64 could read its cartridges more quickly than information can be read from a disc, though, reducing or often eliminating load times that could hurt the pacing of equivalent games on PlayStation.

When considering platform differences, think about the effects of storage media (read speed, writability, capacity), internal storage format (read/write speed, capacity), memory (amount of available partitioned RAM/ROM, read/write speed), VRAM/graphical load, sound capabilities (number of channels and available "instruments"/waveforms in older machines), graphical rendering limits/style (great insight can be gained by understanding the sprite layers, background capabilities, and graphical modes of older hardware), accessory compatibility, and peculiarities/uniformity of technical architecture (for example, the Xbox 360 was built in a manner complimentary to PC architecture, making the adaptation of games built for PC relatively straightforward, while its contemporary PlayStation 3 was built with a severely non-standard design architecture that made cross-platform adaptation challenging and led to some disastrous ports, particularly early in its lifespan).

Control Interface

Covered more thoroughly in the previous sections, the control interface is one of the primary details that affects the experience of playing a game. This can vary in layout (equivalently featured controllers may be more or less comfortable or suited for a particular type of game), capabilities (number of inputs, analog/digital inputs, sensitivity of inputs, non-standard inputs such as touch or motion controls), and integration (whether button prompts appear correctly in-game, whether features of non-standard controllers are supported; often a consideration with PC ports or emulation). Some games translate well between multiple controller formats, while others are almost impossible to effectively reproduce with hardware other than that of the original system (such as the puzzle-arcade game *Boom Blox* (2008), which used the Nintendo Wii's unique motion controllers in its number of Jenga-like stacking block games. Emulation with any controller other than an original Wii remote drastically affects the legibility and playability of the game).

Specificity of bespoke controllers (such as *Guitar Hero* [2005–2015]'s aforementioned guitars or *Steel Battalion* [2002]'s enormous control panel) may account for an intended format of play, even if alternate schemes are possible. The use of non-standard controllers is a form of metagame, as outlined previously, that can provide new "life" to an existing codebase. In the invocation of metagames, we can consider games not only as singular entities but as platforms, in and of themselves, in which alternate games of self- and community-administered challenge can be played.

Alternate control inputs are also an important consideration for video game accessibility. Players who may be unable to play a game with a particular controller because of motor or sensory disability might experience greater success of access with alternative options. The allowance of alternate control schemes and interfaces (including interfaces with completely different input affordances, like voice-commanded interfaces) lessens restrictions of access, particularly when afforded at the platform level. Particularly configurable *accessibility controllers* are becoming more widely available as retail products, and organizations like AbleGamers create bespoke control interfaces for players with highly restrictive disabilities.

Video Output

Different screen technologies have different capabilities and can affect the aesthetic and legibility of game assets.

We should consider screen type (CRTs have a fuzzy and imprecise image beneficial to the smoothing of the sprite art of the 1980s and 1990s, while the LCD, plasma, and OLED displays of the 2000s–2020s benefit the readability of the more text and detail-dense games of that era), resolution (generally speaking, higher resolution increases picture clarity in still or low-motion settings), frame rate (generally speaking, higher frame rate increases picture clarity while the view or objects in the scene are in motion), color range, number of displays (in the case of Nintendo's DS, 3DS, and Wii U families of systems, VR headsets, or a number of multi-screen arcade games), and even display-specific expected player behavior (for example, players are expected to sit very close to PC screens and far away from television screens, leading to design differences in games produced for PCs vs. consoles, including font size, UI scale, and density of visual information presented). There are several types of non-standard displays that are difficult or impossible to experientially reproduce with other types of displays, such as the clean and responsive vector displays seen in some early arcade games or the home Vectrex system, or the unique (or at least uniquely headache-inducing) system of mirror-refracted LED arrays of Nintendo's Virtual Boy.

Multi-System Connectivity

Particularly relevant to multiplayer games, form and method of multi-system connectivity affects the ways in which games are experienced. Most modern systems connect players to friends and wider communities through the internet. Handheld systems of previous generations often included methods of non-internet-dependent direct wireless connection (sometimes actively, like the Nintendo DS' multiplayer functionality, or sometimes asynchronously and discretely, like the Nintendo 3DS' whimsical StreetPass feature). Other systems would need to be connected by wire, whether directly (as with the Game Boy Link Cable) or through more complex wired network hubs (as with LAN-compatible games on PC and Xbox). Some systems, even in the absence of direct connection, allow the easy passage of files between systems, such as the easy sharing of save games using the external memory cards of the PlayStation, PlayStation 2, and GameCube. Some systems even allow connection with other platforms that are different in type entirely (for example, a handful of games make use of a special connectivity feature that links the GameCube and Game Boy Advance, and many modern games allow for cross-platform online multiplayer, connecting players on multiple types of consoles and computers in competition with each other).

Historical Context of Design Lineage

Beyond technical differences, playing games from years and decades past often benefits from contextual understanding of where they sit in the lineage of relevant design concepts. Games that may appear quite peculiar or cumbersome in our modern context might make more sense when contextualized amongst contemporary peers. Rather than being a result of how or through which technical arrangement the title is played, this is a difference in contextual knowledge and perspective.

INTENTIONALITY OF CONTROL

When thinking about player input, we should consider control and choice (or agency) as separate values. Control, in this case, means the capacity for the player to affect the happenings within the game, and choice means the ability for the player's intentions to be reflected within the simulation. In action-based games, players have a great amount of control over the avatar, but their ability to make meaningful choices is mediated by skillful execution. For example, in *Super Mario 64* (1996), Mario can perform a great many movement-based actions, modified by a great many factors (such as momentum, movement direction, suddenness of directional shifts…), but the player's meaningful choice to jump over or fall into a pit is mediated by her ability to control Mario effectively. In this sense, it can be argued that skillful players have more choices than less skillful players in action games, despite having equal access to the game's moment-to-moment control mechanisms.

Other games may offer an inverse relationship: they offer relatively few mechanisms of control but have reliable mechanisms for player choice. For example, puzzle, strategy, and text-heavy adventure games tend to feature simple control mechanisms not tied to executional thresholds. If the player intends to move a card from one stack to another in Solitaire, that action can be easily and reliably performed (as long as it is a legal move). The executional demands of the game do not interfere with the player's choice. Skillful and unskilled players have equal ability to control and choose (though the ability to successfully make a choice does not mean that the player has made the optimal or correct choice).

Exploration of these factors is important to video game literacy because it gives us better awareness of the asks and affordances games give players at various points. When considering control and choice, we must recognize the factors that mediate their expression and how this affects gameplay. Particularly when comparing experiences between players of different skill levels, we should recognize when and how control and choice affect players' individual experiences, and we may hypothesize about how those experiences would be different if control and choice were otherwise balanced. In this section, we will explore several configurations of control and choice to illustrate the relationship these factors have on the experience of players.

Mediated Intentionality

The distinction between the terms control and choice may be fuzzy at times. What is control but a series of small, moment-to-moment, incidental choices? In the first moments of any platformer game, for instance, I can make a choice to initiate avatar movement or let the avatar stand still, issued with a directional input (or lack of one) from the controller. For the sake of this argument, though, control will be defined as a value-neutral expression of a game's verb set, while choice will represent contextual, value-laden sequences of action that work toward measured or implicit goals. Control is solely concerned with the player-initiated actions of the avatar, while choices take into account the avatar in relation to the game world.

To illustrate the difference, we can say that causing Mario to jump is an expression of control, while causing Mario to jump over a pit is a choice. While the action of jumping is directly triggered by the player's controller input, jumping is a value-neutral expression of control. Whether Mario jumps or does not jump may be valued as good or bad depending on the context in which the action is performed. Jumping over a pit is an intention that may be successful or unsuccessful based on skillful application of control. Framing the action in this way not only recognizes the player-controlled jump, but it puts it in the context of a value-laden situation; clearing the pit will be a successful expression of the player's intention, while falling into the pit will be a failed expression of intention and may even be penalized by the game in some way.

One of the most common expressions of the relationship between control and choice is mediated intentionality. This is most clearly seen in action-based games such as fighting games, shooters, platformers, rhythm games, and other genres that require skillful control over moment-to-moment action. Games in these genres present an astronomical number of moment-to-moment control outcomes. In 3D action games, the avatar can move freely within the three-dimensional world as well as perform a number of universal actions (such as sprinting and jumping) and context-dependent actions (actions that require the use of particular items or may only be performed in particular settings, such as diving from a diving board). In free, 3D movement, there are nearly limitless possible combinations of actions that can be performed if we consider the analog nature of movement and timing (in which "moved at half speed in a 4 o'clock direction" is a different action than "moved at full speed in a 5 o'clock direction"). Meaningful choice, though, is heavily mediated by how skillfully the avatar is controlled. Even a basic choice, such as "strike the enemy with my sword", may or may not be successful, based on the avatar's relative positioning, orientation, momentum, attack timing, etc. The player's intentions may or may not be carried through, mediated by their skillful execution of gameplay actions.

Gameplay execution is not the only factor that can mediate the expression of player intention. CRPGs often mediate the success or failure of player choices with checks against random chance, often called "dice rolls", after the mechanic of tabletop RPGs like *Dungeons & Dragons* (Gygax & Arneson, 1974) from which this mechanic was borrowed. Sometimes literalized with on-screen dice (as in the detective noir CRPG *Disco Elysium* [2019]) or calculated invisibly (as are "critical hit" chances in many turn-based JRPG battle systems), these systems perform a similar mediatory function as the skillful execution of actions in the previous examples; whether or not the avatar's sword hits an enemy is not a matter of correct spatial judgment and timing; it is an expression of chance that skillful players can weight in their favor through systemic stat upgrades rather than executional aptitude.

"Dice rolls", in these types of games, are not completely random. Most often, they interact with systems into which players have input, such as character stats. In CRPGs, characters are often given an allotment of stat points at the beginning of the game and with each level-up. Players may spend these stat points to raise numerical representations of a number of attributes and skills that the character might have, such as strength, agility, persuasiveness, and luck. Games featuring dice roll mechanics will often augment these dice rolls with the stat points that players have invested into relevant skills, giving players the opportunity to weight these chance checks. Swinging a heavy sword may have a 1/30 chance of dealing additional damage, though players who have invested ten points into the character's strength stat may see that rise to an 11/30 chance, for example. In that sense, the outcomes of battles, skill checks, or conversations are still highly reactive to player decisions (and potentially expressive, as argued in Chapter 12), but successful outcomes are mediated by long-term planning and wise investment of resources rather than skillful execution of moment-to-moment actions.

Within both of the above archetypes, player intention is mediated by different factors—skillful execution or random/weighted chance. While the latter provides roughly equal opportunity to players of all performance skill levels (from a purely executional perspective, not including knowledge of how to wisely invest stat points), the former will wildly vary from one player to the next based on their comfort and familiarity with the game's control mechanisms. If we hypothetically depict player skill as a numerical percentage of encounter success, a skilled player, when presented with an early game combat encounter in a familiar action game, may have a 95% chance to successfully defeat an enemy, while a less skillful player may only achieve success in battle 20% of the time. More challenging enemies may see 75% and 5% chances of success, respectively. While both players technically have equal access to the game's mechanical affordances, functionally, the more skilled player has a greater range of effective choices, cumulatively, than the less skilled player. This disparity is what difficulty adjustments and accessibility settings are designed to overcome.

To cite an example of how this can play out, I will use the example of the sword-and-sorcery ARPG *Dark Souls* (2011). Early in the game, the player encounters a crossroads, out of which branch many directions that she may follow. The path of least resistance, guarded by a small handful of weak enemies, belies the intended path of forward progress. In the opposite direction, though, lies the graveyard, guarded by a horde of animated skeletons, enemies that, at the low level players are during this early section of the game, are quite challenging to defeat. The graveyard contains some very useful items, though, including one of the best early game weapons, the Zweihander, a two-handed sword of enormous proportions. Skilled players can brave the graveyard and retrieve this powerful weapon at this early point in the game (either by fighting or skillfully avoiding the ever-increasing army of skeleton warriors), though unskilled players are unlikely to survive long enough in the dangerous graveyard to reach the weapon. Functionally, this choice is unavailable to unskilled players. Considering that access to this powerful weapon may make future encounters easier, it further broadens the gulf of "available" choices between skilled and unskilled players by creating a feedback loop of difficulty, subtly making the game easier for skilled players and more challenging for unskilled players, the opposite of what most would consider ideal.

To say that a player is "unskilled" is not to frame her derisively. There are many factors that may lead to players not possessing the necessary skill to reliably overcome some of a game's challenges. Well-practiced players with disabilities may face increased challenges in games compared to equally practiced able-bodied players. Technology can inhibit playability; a television that introduces picture lag or an aging computer that has regular game performance stutters can put players at a disadvantage. Players inexperienced with similar games in the same genre may be slower to acclimatize to a new game than genre veterans, who can pick up quickly on conventions and generalize acquired knowledge. Any number of factors can mediate the comfort or ease of play a player may experience when playing a particular game. Players can have a great diversity of experiences with these types of games. We should consider how variable enactment of gameplay can lead to a diversity of meaningful interpretations. As we mentally summarize our own gameplay narratives, with peaks of dramatic challenge and moments of respite between them, differential experiences of challenge may cause players to assign differing narrative weight to a game's elements.

Unrestricted Intentionality

While action-based games mediate player choices through executional demand, non-action-based genres tend to allow a *relatively* unrestricted intentionality. Many puzzle and strategy games, for instance, have minimal executional demands, allowing each player equal, unmediated access to the game's strategic challenges. Strategy is a core component of most genres of games. In action-based genres like platformers or shooters, players must not only execute gameplay actions at an appropriate level; they must also have a plan to guide their action. In 3D platformers, such as *Banjo-Kazooie* (1998), the player may spot a goal or reward in the distance and strategize a plan to get the avatar to that difficult-to-reach spot. This is a navigational puzzle. In first-person shooters such as *Halo: Combat Evolved* (2001), the player must recognize how the varying enemy types and/or hazards of the environment may pose differing threats to the avatar and plan a strategy of eliminating all threats in a way that mitigates these risks. This is a puzzle of prioritization.[2] Most genres include some form of strategic challenge that may or may not be complicated by executional demand. Unrestricted intentionality refers to the types of games in which strategic demands are not mediated by executional demands.

Turn-based RPGs or strategy games are good examples of games that allow unrestricted enactment of player intentions and allow all players, regardless of executional ability, equal access to the demands of strategic decision-making. Turn-based battles queue player and enemy actions sequentially, usually allowing each side an unlimited amount of time to think about what next action should be taken. Series like *Pokémon* (1996–present) or *Persona* (1996–present) have low executional demand but high strategic demand. The player is given the time to consider appropriate actions, and the interface to choose those actions is usually a simple menu. Player intention is not always expressed perfectly; there are sometimes random-chance mediating factors that may cause intended actions to fail, and players can only enact actions allowed within the game's set of active affordances (a *Pokémon* battle cannot be concluded by reasoning with the opposing monster), but the level of access players have to the full suite of available affordances of the game is limited only by knowledge and investment.

Puzzle games and adventure games also tend to offer unrestricted intentional enactment. Games like *Bejeweled* (2001) and *The Secret of Monkey Island* (1990) offer gameplay at a pace determined by the player, making no demands of quick, reactive performance; letting players guide interactions through uncomplicated control interfaces, such as mouse cursors or direct touchscreen control. These types of games tend to not even punish errant actions; moving a gem in *Bejeweled* into a non-matching sequence or clicking on a noninteractable object in *The Secret of Monkey Island* will result in a gentle nothingness; the gems will animate and return to their previous positions, or Guybrush may walk to the clicked area and make a comment, acknowledging the reception of the command but not mechanically punishing the incorrect input. This encourages experimentation and curiosity-guided exploration as players form stronger strategic understandings of the mechanic sets. This can be contrasted against action-based games, in which executional errors or unmotivated actions can incur harsh penalties or even result in failing a gameplay sequence.

Unrestricted intentionality tends to result in slower-paced experiences, either in a stop-and-start pace of mechanical interaction (as in the above examples) or in uninterrupted mechanical interaction but a relaxed density of content pacing guided by player discovery, as in exploration adventure games like *Everybody's Gone to the Rapture* (2015) and *What Remains of Edith Finch* (2017). The latter style of game allows constant, real-time player control and expression of the games' full verb sets at any time but makes no action-based demands that require executional finesse. Narrative content (indicating progress) is doled out as discovered by players, leading to a stop-and-start pace, of sorts, of narrative novelty rather than a stop-and-start mechanical rhythm.

Mediated and unrestricted intentionality often map onto the differing forms of expressivity discussed in Chapter 12. Micro-expressivity, or the propensity for a game to meaningfully react to divergent moment-to-moment play, tends to be correlated with mediated intentionality, as the central locus of challenge and achievement is executional. Conversely, macro-expressiveness, or the propensity for a game to meaningfully react to large, overarching, systemic interaction such as story branch choice or strategic decision-making, tends to correlate with unrestricted intentionality, as the decisions that facilitate that type of variability tend to present in executionally non-demanding contexts.

Autonomic Control

Autonomic control is another form of gameplay interface methodology. This has been relatively rare through the first few decades of game design but has become more common in recent years. Unlike intentional physical interfaces, which are based on the intentional, appropriate application of fine and gross motor functions to control on-screen behaviors, autonomic control interfaces with games through automatic or unintentional physiological mechanisms. This is usually expressed as a challenge of physiological self-control. Games that make use of autonomic control build mechanics around the subconscious operation of players' bodies and, thus, may interface with measures such as heart rate, breathing, startle reaction, or blinking.

Autonomic video game control is made possible by advancements in more sensitive or specialized control inputs. Narrative adventure game *Before Your Eyes* (2021) tells a story that advances in time whenever the player blinks (as monitored by the computer's camera), whether or not the current scene has finished. Though the player can make an effort to not blink so that she may see more of a scene, the game is designed with the anticipation that players will naturally blink as a subconscious action when not expressly thinking about it. This gameplay mechanic serves the narrative function of demonstrating the ephemerality of the moments that constitute our lives. In the blink of an eye, they are past and can never be relived.

Horror games make occasional yet effective use of autonomic control. Horror narrative adventure game *Until Dawn* (2015) features several sections in which the player must hold still, usually representing a character hiding in the darkness, trying to stay quiet while a threat looms nearby. The game measures player movement through the motion control feature of the PlayStation 4 controller and noise detection from the console's optional camera peripheral. These moments are often punctuated with a jumpscare intended to startle players, and successful execution requires players to steady their nerves in these moments of panic. Similarly, indie horror game *Nevermind* (2015) uses a medical heart rate monitor to track players' levels of physiological control. The game becomes more challenging when the player has a higher heart rate, encouraging them to stay calm under pressure (and resulting in a feedback loop once that control is lost).

Autonomic control has an unusual relationship with player control and choice. With practice, players can become better at managing their autonomic reactions, but these challenges are built with their inherent unpredictability in mind. As such, autonomic reactions represent a step between choice and non-choice. They are more player-dependent than random chance checks, but they have a higher degree of unintentionality than typical controller interface actions.

In the future, autonomic control may become more common as more sensitive technologies proliferate. Modern VR headsets, for instance, often include foveal tracking, and sensitive motion controls are standard features of a greater number of input devices with each console generation. As more games become voice- or motion-controlled, there are greater opportunities to introduce more autonomic features into games' designs.

Practical Application of Interface Observation

To illustrate the above classifications, particularly mediated and unrestricted intentionality, I've outlined genres that typify each design philosophy, and while this is broadly true and useful for illustrative purposes, in reality, most games tend to feature moments of both mediated and unrestricted intentionality to varying degrees. Different sequences of gameplay will allow for more direct or more constrained player control and/or choice. In learning to recognize the signifiers of these shifts, we can better categorize gameplay chunks and speak more efficiently about the manner in which each modality is constructed and the effect that it has on the experiential narrative. Adjusting the gradients of freedom and demand affects the pacing of a holistic gameplay experience, and variability is key to not only creating engaging, sustained gameplay experiences but also more broadly to basic storytelling and myth-making.

One can practice the technique of identification by reflecting upon the relationship the player experiences between control and choice at multiple points during gameplay. To review, control can be simplified to mean a value-neutral expression of the game's verb set (avatar actions), while choice represents a value-laden enactment of intended actions. For example, performing a jump (control) vs. jumping over an obstacle to reach the other side (choice). This relationship certainly changes when games shift modalities to different types of actions; for instance, many grand adventure RPGs allow players to take part in mechanically distinct side activities such as fishing. There are certainly clear modal shifts between battling, exploring, and fishing.

Practiced observers can see the gradual and perpetual waxing and waning of these relationships through continuous gameplay segments of the same modality, as well, though. For example, in a platformer like the improvisational parkour game *Mirror's Edge* (2008), the player may find herself scrambling up a dense pattern of fire escapes to reach the top of a building, to crest the roof, and find a sparse plateau across which she must run to the next objective. The game has not shifted modalities—it has not transitioned into a cutscene or initiated a combat sequence—and the amount of control that the player has over the avatar remains the same, but she has fewer meaningful choices to make at the moment that she crests the roof than she did moments before. Though short-lived while she rushes to her next objective, this relatively low-choice gameplay segment provides a respite from the high-choice-density journey up the side of the building, creating an appropriate counterpoint to the moments of high tension before it.

Recognizing the rhythm of control and choice density from moment to moment can give players insight into and better language to describe the pacing of the experiential narrative. The identification of the elements of design (mechanics, environmental design, or even aesthetic differences) that contribute to these pacing shifts elucidates the design language and exposes the intentionality of design.

Though moment-to-moment differences in the relationship between control and choice are typically a shift in degrees rather than polar shifts, we often observe absolute transitions as well. Going from exploratory gameplay to an NPC conversation, for instance, represents a difference of type rather than degrees. Outlined below are generalized, non-comprehensive descriptions of the extremes of each polarity, against which we can compare and recognize differing expressions during gameplay:

- **High control, low choice**: This tends to be represented in tests of mastery (quintessential mediated intentionality). Tests of mastery are considered low-choice because they archetypically have binary outcomes: pass and fail. The most direct expression of this is rhythm games, which challenge players to (typically) hit a series of buttons in a proper sequence and with precise timing along with the music. Players have highly sensitive but narrow control (the game recognizes and registers button-press timing and punishes missing the exact timing by even fractions of a second), but low levels of meaningful choice: though the game recognizes any sequence of buttons that they hit, all sequences except for the correct sequence are equally incorrect. The degree to which players can choose to enter the correct sequence is mediated by their skill at playing the game. Though the test of mastery represents the furthest polarity of the high control, low choice paradigm, this combination can also express in moments of low-density traversal or periods of pacing respite. Open-world or open-zone games like *ELDEN RING* (2022) or *Monster Hunter: World* (2018) will separate the densely designed portions of their worlds with large, low-density expanses to not only create a more believably structured world but also to create natural high/low-tension rhythms in the gameplay experience. While players still have full control over their avatars, there are intentionally fewer choices to make in these spaces, producing the necessary variety of pace.

- **High control, high choice**: This most often represents unrestricted, dense, yet low-challenge exploration. As noted above, high challenge narrows the range of possible choices to or toward binaries of success and failure. A greater number of meaningful choices must reflect a looser structure. There may still be only one objective (reach the top of the mountain, for example), but there will be multiple viable ways to achieve that, or at least make incremental progress toward that goal. A high density of design is important in defining these high-choice areas, since choice is definitionally value-dependent. In low-density spaces in which players retain full control, they can perform a great number of actions, but those actions only become value-laden when working toward an intended goal (whether formalized by the game or not; the player may intend for the avatar to jump over a pit regardless of whether or not a formal reward exists on the other side. The intention of the player imbues the action with value that it would not have had if it were not accomplishing an intrinsic goal). By contrast, high-density areas naturally have more elements against which intention can be exercised. A good example of a gameplay space that gives players high levels of control and choice is the vibrant New Donk City from the 3D platformer *Super Mario Odyssey* (2017). The majority of the time spent in this city is engaged in unstructured, curiosity-driven, low-challenge (or rather, low-consequence) exploration. Being a dense city center, there are always dozens of places to go and objects with which to interact within Mario's immediate vicinity. Intention-driven engagement and traversal creates a high density of value-laden interactions, yet the loose structure of the zone's nebulous core objective allows players to pursue these multiple choices without punishing them for going "off-course".

- **Low control, low choice**: Moments of low control and low choice tend to center around moments in which the game most directly tells its authored, embedded narrative. Cutscenes take control away from players completely, and non-interactive dialogue encounters reduce control to a bare minimum: usually just a button press to advance to the next line of dialogue. These moments can provide necessary context to enrich the narrative stakes of the gameplay that surrounds it, but it is most often essentially a break from storytelling through mechanics and a reversion to engaging more traditional storytelling techniques. There are times when moments of low control and low choice can make compelling additions to experiential storytelling rhythms (for instance, becoming frozen or otherwise incapacitated in a tense battle can create moments of high tension while players anxiously wait for the effect to subside), but it is most commonly used in moments of semiotic narrative conveyance. This can also be expressed as gameplay segments that narrow to brief and simple tests of mastery. For example, the open-zone, action-packed platforming series *Ratchet & Clank* (2002–present) commonly features rails that connect areas of free exploration and combat. When engaged, Ratchet "grinds" (rides, as one would on a skateboard) the rail, locking him into a period of constant forward travel in which the only action that can be taken is the avoidance of obstacles. Compared to the normal pace of gameplay, control options are drastically reduced, and the consequentiality of failure to react to obstacles narrows the spectrum of choice. This is noticed in comparison to the normal pace of gameplay, as one could reasonably produce a game that is entirely comprised of similar grinding segments that, without a point of comparison, would not be easily classifiable as "low control", since it would not represent a culling of available gameplay actions.
- **Low control, high choice**: These are moments of high consequence that are enacted by limited means of control. Dialogue scenes with meaningful choices or menu-navigated encounters give players the opportunity to make strategic or narrative-consequential decisions without executional demand. This is quintessential unrestricted intentionality. The player is able to directly command consequential choices without fear of failing due to imperfect execution. This does not mean that her will is directly expressed as intended; strategies can be poorly considered, certain effects are given random chance checks, and dialogue choices can land with conversation partners in unintended ways (just like real conversations), but this represents the most direct means of empowerment of choice.

These four extremes, representing four quadrants in a control vs. choice intersection, can bring about different feelings of agency and responsibility for events. Recognition of the ways in which they are typically used empowers players to understand the intended emotional pacing of the gameplay experience and may reveal insights into why some sections feel wholly appropriate or tragically misplaced.

NOTES

1 Presuming the same version of the game is run on the same type of computer hardware. Fundamental code is necessarily adapted and can, itself, create quite divergent experiences when ported between different systems. This point will be explored in greater context shortly.

2 "Puzzle" here is used in a colloquial sense. By the strictest definitions, some may reserve "puzzle" only for challenges that involve the discernment of a single, unambiguous solution rather than the Banjo-Kazooie and Halo examples, which may have several viable approaches.

REFERENCES

Barrett, F. & Doyle, M. (Directors). (2003–2025). *Sleep no more* by Punchdrunk [Play]. London.

Bayliss, P. (2007). Beings in the game-world. *Proceedings of the 4th Australian Conference on Interactive Entertainment, 4*, 1–6.

Bratt, C. & Sayers, A. (2018-present). *People make games* [YouTube channel]. YouTube. Retrieved September 15, 2024, from https://www.youtube.com/@PeopleMakeGames.

Cox, L. (Host). (2011-present). *Cane and rinse* [Audio podcast]. Cane and Rinse. https://caneandrinse.com/

Danielewski, M. Z. (2000). *House of leaves*. Pantheon Books.

Dourish, P. (2001). *Where the action is*. The MIT Press.

Duignan, B. (2019). *Projection*. Britannica. https://www.britannica.com/science/projection-psychology

Gibson, J. J. (1966). *The senses considered as perceptual systems*. George Allen & Unwin Ltd.

Gygax, G. & Arneson, D. (1974). Dungeons & Dragons. TSR, Inc.

Holmes, J. B. (2010). *Blurring the boundaries: Projective embodiment in videogames and digital spaces*. Arizona State University.

Klevjer, R. (2022). *What is the avatar?*. Transcript.

Lumière, A. & Lumière, L. (Directors). (1896). *L'Arrivée d'un train en gare de La Ciotat* [Film]. Société Lumière.

Murray, J. H. (2012). *Inventing the medium: Principles of interaction design as cultural practice*. The MIT Press.

O'Dwyer, D. (2016-present). *Noclip – Video game documentaries* [YouTube channel]. YouTube. Retrieved September 15, 2024, from https://www.youtube.com/@NoclipDocs.

Owens, P., Levering, P., & Siddiky, A. (2005-present). *2PlayerProductions* [YouTube channel]. YouTube. Retrieved September 15, 2024, from https://www.youtube.com/@2PlayerProductions.

Shakespeare, W. (Playwright). (1599). *The Tragedy of Hamlet, Prince of Denmark* [Play]. London.

Shakespeare, W. (Playwright). (1623). *The Tragedie of Macbeth* [Play]. London.

Sicart, M. (2012). Digital games as ethical technologies. In J. R. Sageng, H. J. Fossheim, & T. M. Larsen (Eds.), *The philosophy of computer games* (pp. 101–124). Springer.

Sicart, M. (2013). *Beyond choices: The design of ethical gameplay*. The MIT Press.

Spielberg, S. (Director). (1981). *Raiders of the lost ark* [Film]. Paramount Pictures.

Stephenson, N. (1992). *Snow Crash*. Bantam Books.

Swink, S. (2009). *Game feel: A game designer's guide to virtual sensation*. Morgan Kaufmann Publishers.

Young, I. M. (2005). Throwing like a girl: A phenomenology of feminine body comportment, motility, and spatiality. In *On female body experience: "Throwing like a girl" and other essays* (pp. 27–45). Oxford University Press. doi:10.1093/0195161920.003.0003

CHAPTER 5

Other Models of Meaning-Making for Video Games

In the last chapter, we examined the methods by which players interface with games, primarily focusing on how the controller and avatar are used to translate and mediate player intention into virtual action. We now transition from practical operation to a greater focus on discerning meaning from game interactions.

This chapter begins by identifying the type of language we wish to use for the purpose of play-oriented meaning-making before outlining three existing frameworks for procedural meaning-making. I will overview the MDA model (Mechanics, Dynamics, Aesthetics) as developed by Robin Hunicke, Marc LeBlanc, and Robert Zubek, which serves as the broad framework from which most future models were derived. I will then detail the Proceduralist model authored by Mike Treanor, Bobby Schweizer, Ian Bogost, and Michael Mateas, which establishes a proof-like formula by which claims for meaning-laden procedural actions can be expressly and effectively communicated. Finally, I will share about the Ludic framework, currently being developed and refined by Frédéric Seraphine, which delineates a very useful grammar for making ontological claims about meaning-laden procedural actions.

In the next chapters, I will outline my own model for procedural sense-making and meaning-making, building on the strengths of the established models and oriented toward this book's guiding objective of analyzing games as cultural artifacts, expressive of developer and player, situated within cultural and physical contexts.

The models are presented in order from the oldest to the most recent, but this is not to imply that any of them are vestigial or surpassed by the others. All are useful in different contexts to answer different types of questions; they should be framed as expansions of perspective scope rather than linear evolutions.

NARROWING FOCUS

As discussed in the introductory chapter, it is necessary to focus our exploration on particular elements of the video game artifact in our exploration of the video game artifact. The video game is a medium that contains a multitude of other expressive forms. Video games often contain abundances of linear text, not dissimilar in form and function to that found in other literary mediums. Games will often break into non-interactive *cutscenes*, cinematic sequences that present with the visual storytelling techniques of films. Dialogue is often delivered by voice actors whose performances can be assessed in the same manner one would assess a performance in a drama. These and other borrowed forms are elements of video game expression, important in the constitution of the experiential whole, but they are peripheral in the framing of a video game *literacy*.

This is not to minimize the talent or effort that has gone into any of these aspects; in fact, the unpredictable and multilinear nature of video games often makes elements of borrowed art more difficult to adapt for games than they would be in more traditional forms. Rather, these borrowed elements are largely

DOI: 10.1201/9781003530961-5

excluded from our video game literacy exploration because it can be reasonably assumed that audiences are already familiar and comfortable with interpreting these forms. Though cutscene interpretation is necessary in video game literacy, the practice does not differ *greatly* from that of the interpretation of standard, linear film. As such, these models of video game interpretation focus on the expressive elements *unique* to video games and the ways in which *borrowed* elements are *uniquely affected* by their remediation into the video game form.

In the introduction, I identified a division between semiotic and non-semiotic content of games. If the semiotic content represents everything expressed with language, signs, and symbols, the non-semiotic dynamics are not linguistically or symbolically communicated. To use a real-life example, if you see a large object speeding toward you, you may identify semiotic features of the object to identify its type. Its familiar silhouette is that of a car, and its yellow color and checkerboard decal make it easily identifiable as a taxi. Regardless of the semiotic information that you were able to glean from its conventional form, there are more fundamental dynamics at play: a heavy object moving at high speeds toward you has the possibility of resulting in a dangerous collision. Before you are a pedestrian and a taxi cab, you are more essentially two bodies moving through space that can interact in consequential ways. The semiotic context may allow you to make inferences about the expected behavior of the other body-in-space ("taxis are financially incentivized to drive quickly and perhaps dangerously", or "my arm is positioned in a way so as to hail the cab; it is driving towards me to pick me up and will stop before colliding with me").

In video games, there are three primary categories of non-semiotic dynamics that constitute the essential elements of focus for our exploration of games literacy: spatial simulation, emergence, and agential affordance. In other words, these are the dynamics of the simulation of virtual spaces, mathematical logics, and user interaction. Each of these elements can be dynamic ends for ludic expression (much of the aesthetic experience of *SimCity* [1989], for example, is the appreciation of the beauty of complex mathematical and logical operations modeled at a large scale; an aesthetic distillation of pure complex procedure). The frameworks of video game literacy presented in this chapter and the next demonstrate how to explicate meaning from these elements of gameplay.

That meaning will, in the best cases, be greatly enhanced by semiotic detail, but I believe that it is useful to be able to separate the aesthetic components in our minds and understand how each component dynamic operates toward (or sometimes against) the aesthetic aims of the gestalt. For that reason, each analysis that we perform will favor the non-semiotic action to the semiotic context. Naturally, presented as written descriptions, these non-semiotic activities have to be translated *into* language so that they can be inscribed in this book, an unfortunate concession, but the forthcoming models are useful for focusing our language around action, operational logic, and emotion, such that we may preserve as much of the experiential factor of these elements in our communication about them.

CORE DYNAMICS OF GAMEPLAY

I briefly identified three primary dynamics of gameplay above: spatial simulation, procedural emergence, and agency. These constitute the core of the *medium* of gameplay expression, around which further semiotic storytelling is built. These dynamics serve dual purposes, as means of inscription and as means of generation. Inscription refers to these dynamics' capacity to serve as a medium of developer-embedded meaning in the game. Generation refers to the dynamics' capacity to generate novel meaning unique to each player's experience upon play enactment.

If a musician expresses herself through the patterning of sound, and the painter through the skillful manipulation of light, the game developer expresses herself through the structuring of spatial simulation, the expression of procedural logics, and the shaping of player agency. In turn, these dynamics are processed by players alongside the semiotic detail in pre-reflective and reflective capacities, respectively, to understand the meaning embedded into the system and to express meaning from the player herself.

The manner in which players process the non-semiotic aspects of gameplay is also subtly different than the manner in which the dynamics of other art forms are processed. While arts such as cinema and literature are almost wholly depictive and representational, avatar-based gameplay enacts a form of mediated *actual experience* brought about by the player's projective telepresence. When the player protectively embodies the avatar, extending her networked "self" into the virtual space through the adoption of the avatar "tool" (as established in the last chapter), aesthetic distance is minimized, and the dynamics identified above are experienced in an embodied fashion; reflexively, pre-reflectively, in a manner that approximates primary sensation. For if we consider the avatar to be an extension of the player's naturalized *self*, she relates to the virtual environment as a virtual actor, assuming a temporary identity and extended personhood that is not separated from the game diegesis by the fictive vs. natural division of the non-extended audience member.

This projective stance differs from the empathetic stance assumed by cinematic audiences, where the viewer, though emotionally involved, always observes the action from a position of safe distance, whereas, when extending an embodied presence into the virtual world, the player assumes a *part* of herself, however peripheral, that exists on the same plane as the virtual action. The player becomes a like actor within the diegesis.

As such, these dynamics have the capacity to drastically affect the player's play experience while being (in their pre-reflective nature) difficult for players to identify and discuss. Each of the meaning-making models shared in this chapter and the next will present different methods for identifying these core dynamics, making the non-semiotic layer of gameplay expression legible. Each model accounts for how meaning is inscribed and received from the perspective of the artist and audience, respectively. In other words, the models show how meaning is *embedded* into systems by developers and how meaning is *generated* through reparative reading and novel recombination at the point of gameplay enactment. As these dynamics will orient our further exploration, I will go into greater detail about each of the three.

Spatial Simulation

This is not simply the modeling of wondrous virtual worlds. The spatial simulation aesthetic concerns embodied telepresence within a virtual space, as discussed in the last chapter. This is the feeling of existing somewhere else. This goes beyond appreciation of sights and sounds, though these elements are important in creating a sense of atmosphere (or *stimmung*, a wonderfully evocative term used by early 20th-century film critic Lotte H. Eisner to evoke a "musical condition" describing the mood, atmosphere, and "metaphysical accord" of a cinematic image [Sinnerbrink, 2012]). Spatial simulation involves the sense of observing a game world from within and the movement of bodies in that space.

Spatial simulation includes elements that involve the player, such as navigational requirement: the sense of learning one's way around an unfamiliar space, as well as aspects that operate separately from player involvement, such as the shape of explorable space, simulated movements of NPCs, and the dynamic reactions of the game's physics engine (aspects that bleed into the procedural emergence dynamic as interactions become layered and complex).

Spatial simulation can be used as an inscriptive tool, primarily as a means of parameter-setting. The construction of a space and the behaviors of its constituent elements determine much about the aesthetic experiences that take place within it. A game set in a wide, open space creates a different navigational dynamic than a game that takes place within a constricting and confusing labyrinth. A game with unobstructed sightlines and a long draw distance (the ability to see objects in the far distance) will create a different feeling and allow the player to focus her attention on different aspects of the game world than a game with a shallow field of view. A world filled with dangers, enemies, and hazards will require navigational attention that may not be necessary in a world that is relatively safe.

In these ways, we can observe that spatial simulation is not only a matter of the geometric construction of the game world. It is also decided by the rules of the game and player affordances. For, certainly, a player's sense of presence within the game world is affected by her capacity to move and act within it. As such, the three dynamics are intrinsically linked to one another: the rules that constitute the simulated space blossom into unpredictable emergence in their interaction with one another, and the construction of the game world affords and limits the actions that the player is able to express within it.

Procedural Emergence

Procedural emergence describes the emergent, surprising behavior that arises from the interaction of game rules (or preconditions).[1] Rules, in this context, are not limited to the explicit objectives and limitations of the game; rather, "rules" broadly describes any logical function dictating how something behaves within the system of the game. In game design terms, these types of parameters are typically chunked into logical sequences referred to as mechanics. For example, a very common game mechanic is the action of jumping. To initiate a jump, the game checks and enacts multiple dependencies and logical operations. The game receives a command from the player's input device (controller) and recognizes that, in the current game state, that input translates to the initiation of a jump action. The game checks whether the avatar is able to initiate a jump (on solid ground, not in a cutscene, has room overhead...), calculates the initial trajectory of the jump (determined by current location, momentum, inertia, travel direction...), plays the jump animation and associated sound, and enacts the arc and journey of the jump (calculated against the game's gravity parameters, responding to further inputs if in-air control is allowed...). Holistically, this sequence of actions constitutes a "jump" mechanic, but we can observe that the computer performs several calculations and logical operations to enact that one mechanic. As such, a mechanic may be thought of as a foundational *design* unit, but it is, by no means, irreducible. The behavior of every object, whether attributable to artificial intelligence or physics, is determined by multiple mechanics, and each mechanic is determined by multiple logical parameters.

Some mechanics require only relatively simple logical sequences. For example, if the avatar collides with a coin, remove the coin from the game world and add +1 to the player's score. Often, though, even simple actions are the result of a dense collection of logical parameters. Consider the multiplicity of parameters that determine the behavior of fire in a game. Particular to the intended experience of the specific game, the developers decide which types of virtual objects are flammable (a pile of wood may be highly flammable while a bucket of water may be impossible to set alight), how they may become ignited (perhaps flammable objects catch on fire immediately upon contact with a flame, or perhaps it requires sustained contact over the course of many seconds), whether fire spreads to adjacent objects (the simulation may create an out-of-control inferno or keep fires relatively domesticated), whether fire damages the player's avatar or NPCs within the game world, whether fire produces smoke (which would require its own set of parameters regarding its capacity to spread and damage simulated actors, separate to those of the fire)... In fact, the non-semiotic behavior of fire supersedes its semiotic identifiability *as* fire. The chain of parameters above could equally be applied to modeling the spread of an infectious disease or even the spread of an idea amongst a population. This is why I advocate for recognizing the behavioral logics *separately* from their semiotic coding; for as much enriching context as semiotic coding may provide, it can be equally restricting, narrowing our understanding of a set of behaviors to a single representational concept rather than encouraging us to consider the ways in which behavioral expressions may relate to one another.

In the above examples, we would not expect collecting a coin, which adds +1 to the player's score, to produce a procedural or emergent behavior. Such a simple, logical chain produces what should be an entirely consistent and predictable behavior. Setting an object on fire within a virtual physics system with a robust flame simulation model, though, will likely produce emergent, procedural results. Lighting a campfire may ignite a nearby tree and cause an uncontrollable forest fire, perhaps causing forest animals to flee from the forest and stampede into a nearby village; a surprising yet logical result of the interaction of multiple mechanics. Emergence may also *underwhelm*. Perhaps the player ran a long fuse to ignite something dangerous from a safe distance but did not consider that the game's physics system had caused water to puddle somewhere along its path, extinguishing the fuse before the igniting spark was able to reach its intended target. Multiple mechanics intersected to produce a *surprising* (yet logical) result that resulted in greater *harmony* than was intended; emergence does not always describe a positive feedback cycle of chaos.

Emergence rides a careful balance between surprise and predictability. Crucially, emergence is not *randomness*; it is the logical result of deterministic operations. But emergence is *surprising*. In this case, *surprising* does not mean *unpredictable*. Functionally, a procedural action in a game world may *be* unpredictable to the player, but it does not express actual randomness. Were the player to have complete knowledge of all of the parameters from which an action is performed and the time to perform all of the calculations that the computer performs, the player should be able to perfectly anticipate subsequent actions. What makes this *functionally* impossible, though, is the volume and speed of information processing computers can accomplish in real time. As a result, game simulations are complex enough to give the illusion of spontaneity and to require improvisational thinking while being *ordered* enough to present an aesthetic experience of logical operation.

At its heart, emergence is the beauty of complex maths. Rather, (straightforwardly) emergence and the procedurality from which it is generated is the beauty of procedures, of which math is a prime (though not exclusive) example. Sometimes this is expressed very directly (the aesthetic appeal of the moreish card game *Balatro* (2024) comes from the logical yet surprising ways in which score multipliers and operational rule modifiers "stack" to skyrocket the score of played hands against increasingly demanding requirements), while other times the maths are abstracted into downstream representations (such as physics systems). This mathematical beauty is comparable to the aesthetic appeal of fractal designs or the hypnotizing beauty of the movements of a flame (seemingly *alive* in its unpredictable dance, yet ultimately following a deterministic course, guided by its fuel, chemistry, and environment).

Whereas mechanics are constituted of cause → effect relationships, emergence is the sequence of cause → effect → effect → effect, and so on. As with spatial simulation before it, emergence is closely related to the other two core dynamics. The rules that constitute the simulation can easily become procedural emergence when they combine beyond what the player can keep immediate track of (thus, the inducing of surprise). Emergence combines with agency to create a dynamically-evolving "shape" of possible actions, requiring the player to think dynamically and improvisationally rather than with the detached ambivalence of uninterrupted, functional action and reaction as one would take toward a word processor.

It is easy to mistakenly presume that procedural emergence is always the result of digitally computed actions. Emergence *is* the result of the intersection of *rules*, but rules are functions of the *system* that enacts gameplay, and that holistic system includes non-digital elements. Human players and environments can certainly contribute to emergence (to the degree that their properties and actions can be anticipated and incorporated into rule sets). Sports and board games enact emergence despite having minimal digital elements. The party game Telephone is a game *about* emergence, in which a message is whispered to be repeated down a long line of players, inevitably becoming distorted through an accumulation of slight misunderstandings along the way. The final message serves as the punchline of the experience as every player recognizes their role in imperfect information transfer. The game's emergence is based on the precondition of human aural perception and cognitive processing. It is only amusing in intersection with average humans' specific balance of information loss and retention. Should our hearing and transmission methods be better, the message would not distort, erasing the comedy of error. Were our hearing or transmission significantly impaired, the message would be *too* distorted to be a recognizable derivative, and there would not be the necessary expectation of proper transference. It is only compared against this expectation ("whispering a short message to a friend is easy; surely we will not lose track of the message in the way a group of children might") that the comedic surprise emerges. It is a strike against our hubris that amuses us so.

There are several factors outside of the computer that can act as anticipated constants and variables in the planning of procedural dynamics. As cited in the previous chapter, developers can create gameplay segments that require rapidly pressing a button over a long stretch of time to create an exhaustion in the player that mirrors a strenuous effort undergone by the game character (such as struggling to lift something heavy), creating an aesthetic parallel between player and avatar. Of course, since variables outside of the simulation cannot be *controlled* to the same degree than those within the simulation can, there exists the risk of improper tuning for particular players, including those with motor disabilities. Multiplayer games are also structured to produce procedural occurrences using player psychology and motivation as procedural variables. The existence of a taunt command in many fighting games serves no purpose but to elicit a psychological response during moments of heated competition, which, like the mind games played during a game of Poker, *does* have an effect on the play of the game.

An element that introduces surprise into the game world but seems to resist elements of our definition of emergence is the presence of other human players. Certainly, the actions that other players take in multiplayer games are routinely surprising, but do they fulfill a demonstration of *procedural* beauty? If we're including human actions to be a part of the expressive capacity of games, it means that we must consider them to be inscriptive; a variable of *design* rather than only a product of *use*. The actions of other players do not necessarily follow logically from preceding conditions because human players are not wholly logical actors, meaning that, even when directed, they may not carry the same capacity for meaning-bearing as would the programmed facilities of the game. A philosophically inclined reader may argue that whereas we can *theoretically* predict the reaction of any virtual action with sufficient knowledge of preconditions and operational parameters, one may argue that we too can predict the behavior of *humans* if we had access to the parameters by which their individual brains operate and every possible precondition that precedes that present moment. Presuming the absence of omniscient deities from this book's audience, we can *functionally* term human players as *transiently logical*.

So do the actions of other players contribute to the procedural dynamic? Yes, but not deterministically. While other players may not be *logical operators* within the deterministic sequences of engine-level emergence, they act expressively (and, yes, express agency) utilizing the designed affordances of the game's mechanics. Their ability to interact within the game system is *not* unlimited and is, thus, another (less predictable) factor constituting the interrelationships of rules. Late in a game of Chess, another player may only have five possible actions available to her. There may be an "optimal" move of the five that she may or may not recognize and may or may not take, but her actions are not free, unrestrained, or chaotic. *Truly* chaotic action outside of the ruleset of the game, such as frustratedly flipping the game board, signals an end of the game. Thus, player psychology becomes another, looser aspect of the design of a multiplayer game. The player knows that other players' capabilities will fall within a narrow range of action affordances, and she will seek to anticipate the most likely behaviors that they will perform, knowing that the other player anticipates *that* anticipation and may act unexpectedly to disrupt the response. Reasonably, one may say that other players' actions do not manifest the procedural dynamic because players are, themselves, not *procedures*, but conversely we can observe other players' actions are limited, directed, and incentivized in order to generate particular emergent dynamics and not others. Thus, though an imperfect analogy, we can reasonably consider player behaviors to be designed (or quasi-designed) expressions of the intersections between game mechanics. Their expressive "shape" is drawn through the design of their individual agencies, which leads us to our final dynamic.

Agency

Colloquially, we may reduce *agency* to the player's ability to interact within the game software, and many definitions of agency focus on the specific affordances that allow players to take motivated action and receive legible feedback. More accurately, though, agency is a function of the entire *system* of gameplay, including not only the bidirectional input/output cycles of player interaction and computer response but also its situation in the context of the play environment. It is most useful to consider agency in terms of the entire system of play enactment, as design in any aspect of the system can alter agential capacities.

Agency is sometimes misunderstood as the player's ability to *resist* design. While the rest of the game simulation operates under mathematical operation, the player's capacity to *choose* and *act* introduces the only non-deterministic element within an otherwise determined system. The player is the bull in the China shop, the only actor with free will amongst a legion of automatons. This is aesthetically reinforced. Much of the pleasure of single-player games is the feeling of overcoming odds; the player is the one that overcomes, and *the rest of the simulation* is the odds.

This is not accurate, though. As discussed in the previous section, the player is not afforded unlimited freedom. Agency is designed through the constrained affordances made available to the player in each particular game. This serves not only an operational function (defining the flow of the game by determining what actions may be taken within the system) but also an aesthetic function. Whereas the spatial simulation dynamic includes the aesthetic experience of *being* within another world, the agency dynamic includes the aesthetic pleasure of *acting* within another world.

Evidencing the fact that agency is designed requires only recognizing the obvious active-aesthetic differences between games. Though similar in genre and presentation, we can compare the aesthetic experiences of first-person shooters *Halo: Combat Evolved* (2001) and *Time Crisis 4* (2006). *Halo* is a shooter that primarily takes place in open, geographically diverse environments that require intelligent and improvisational use of the explorable space to the player's advantage during dynamic and unpredictable firefights against alien enemies. *Time Crisis* is an "on-rails" shooter, named as such because the avatar is advanced automatically through a series of environments, stopping periodically to engage in a series of staged shooting-gallery-style encounters. The player is not able to move freely through the environment, only able to change course at predetermined branch points. *Halo* requires creative thinking, finding ways to exploit the shape of the environment and the behavior of enemies to create situations that are advantageous to the player. *Time Crisis* incentivizes memorization, building habitual efficiencies to more effectively overcome familiar challenges over the course of repeated playthroughs. *Halo*'s incentive structure propels players through a linear narrative, rewarding survival with progress toward a determined end, while *Time Crisis* places a greater emphasis on its arcade-like score system, incentivizing masterful execution as the ultimate expression of gameplay action. Ultimately, the feeling of playing each of these two games differs greatly for a number of reasons, but one of those crucial divergences lies in this one agential dissimilarity between the games, encouraging different play priorities and radically different gameplay aesthetics.

Crucially, we must understand that agency is not only a mode of operation; it is also a mode of expressive inscription. Just as the potter expresses aesthetic ends through the shaping of clay, the game developer expresses ideas through the shaping of agency. Agency does not *rebel against* the medium; agency *is* the medium. As philosopher C. Thi Nguyen beautifully describes it,

> [Games] are a unique social technology. They are a method for inscribing forms of agency into artifactual vessels: for recording them, preserving them, and passing them around. [...] Just as novels let us [experience] lives we have not lived, games let us experience forms of agency we might not have discovered on our own.
>
> *(2020, p. 1)*

Just as our philosophical horizon may be expanded with the introduction of a new idea, the art of game design posits that there is something worthwhile in the embodied enactment of novel capacities for action.

While spatial simulation and emergence are constitutionally expressive of games' developers, agency has the capacity to be expressive of both developer and player. Agency represents the aspects of the artistic artifact that players help compose. Some elements of indeterminacy resolve in the recombination of existing elements (when the player chooses a story branch resulting in the display of one of three pre-scripted cutscenes, for instance), and some are truly generative (behavior of the player avatar during free gameplay). Though the freest of these modes feel most obviously expressive of the player, a crucial task of video game literacy is distinguishing intentional developer design from these player-afforded capacities. As such, when observing free gameplay, a familiar viewer would be able to identify both the expressive voices of the developer and player.

Semiotic Detail

As is reasserted throughout the exploration, the above dynamics are enacted in parallel with the semiotic level of expression. The simulated space, though fundamentally operating as a physic-bounded space occupied by moving bodies, is navigated as a semiotic space as well. NPCs are not simply viewed as moving bodies; they are identified by their visual coding. One does not need to wait to see how a figure behaves to identify her as a member of an allied or opposing army in a shooter game, for instance; one instead gleans that information from their uniform decoration from a safe distance. While the models that will serve as the focus of these chapters are models for discerning meaning primarily from the non-semiotic layer, it does not mean that the semiotic detail is unimportant; only semiotic and non-semiotic elements have different capacities for communicating meaning. As my model outlines in the next chapter, I find it most useful to examine the layers separately and again together as an enmeshed gestalt. For our purposes, though, non-semiotic "reading" is given instructional priority, as semiotic interpretation is a familiar skill, so instruction will focus on the specific ways in which it differs from its familiar form in the medium of games.

MEANING

To properly contextualize the models that I will overview in these chapters, it is important to also specify the type of meaning that we aim to find and create in our literate readings of video game artifacts. The particular type of meaning privileged in an encounter with any kind of text or artifact depends upon the way in which the artifact is framed and the context in which it is read. As established in this book's introduction, our primary interest in video games in our current exploration is as artistic artifacts. They act as cultural ciphers, giving us insight into the cultures from which they emerge and are accepted. They are vessels of inscribed meaning through which developers can express particular philosophies, emotions, or mental realities. They are generative artifacts, finding new, richer meaning in the interpretations of audiences.

Second-Order States

This first type of meaning is the most general. The definition of art proposed in this book's introductory chapter expressed that art involves a transformative process by which an artifact is observed and processed through the specific cognitive and emotional predispositions of each individual audience member, resulting in the evocation of a second-order mental reality unique to that particular beholder. Art is created to share these second-order realities that would be uncommunicable otherwise. Harriet Wadeson writes, "The artist has created an illusion, a separate 'reality', a personal vision that through transformation into an art object may be shared with others" (1987, p. 4). It is through this peculiar method of inscription that these otherwise uncommunicable mental states can be shared, though imprecisely. No audience member will conjure the *exact* mental state that the artist wished to share, but successful artistic communication will transport each beholder into one of a range of states. The most interesting artwork accounts for the diversity of reactions.

Second-order states is a way of grouping a number of ephemeral mental states that can be evoked by artworks. This category is named as such in relation to Harriet Wadeson's quote above; there is something of a novel "reality" that is greater than the sum of information conveyed. This can include emotional response, evoking feelings and eventual catharsis that can feel as deep and rich as those brought about by our natural experiences. It can also manifest as a sense of "being" somewhere else, as if, in staring at a painting of ships at a dock, one can *almost* smell the saltwater and hear the cries of gulls. Art can create an overwhelming sense of "history", drawing forth a curious nostalgia for a life never lived in an evocative space only ever visited vicariously. Generally speaking, these are longings of the heart and feelings of the gut.

These are typically referred to as (or conceptualized as the direct result of) artistic *aesthetics*. The emotion that a piece of art evokes may be called its aesthetic experience, as can the "mood" or "vibe" of a piece. Deeply felt but often difficult to articulate outright, the arts are particularly suited for the transmission of these cognitive states. They cannot be directly conveyed through purely informational transference; they can only be evoked through the inscription of poignant potentiation, which the artist hopes blossoms within the audience as something greater.

Ludomotifs

Where the previous category of meaning communicated novel senses and methods of *being* and *acting* within a separate world, this category represents the "stickiness" of that experience across games. Inter-domain transference is obvious with semiotic information: if we learn in one context that amphibians live both in water and on land, we can obviously invoke that information in a separate context. However, if we consider that artistic artifacts "package" non-semiotic experience, we must expect a resonance between artistic experiences as well.

Gilles Deleuze wrote about the *movement-image* and *time-image*; methods by which films consolidate *change* and *subjective time* into "images" that can be transmitted and unpacked into more complex ideas than the literal information that they contain. The techniques by which this "packaging" occurs can be, themselves, resonant concepts invoked in future works. Through aesthetic parallel, a film can call upon the time-image of a previous film, utilizing it not only as a technique that serves an immediate purpose but also as a resonant motif that carries with it the *meaning* associated with its previous usages. Like sampling in music, the repurposing of a recognizable bassline not only serves a rhythmic purpose in the *new* song, but it also draws into the "conversation" the legacy and associations of the original.

Thus, if video games create transmittable "images" of agency, the resonances associated with those "images" become a part of the "language" with which developers can tell future stories. This is a category of meaning that may not be *immediately actionable* to the *player*, but it is important to recognize it as a distinct form of meaning subconsciously created that lies dormant until awoken by a future experience.

Ultimately, the cross-applicability of agential action between games is necessary at a very basic level. Once a player learns how a particular type of game is played, she is likely to instinctively draw upon that knowledge when playing similar games in the future. Playing the car-racing game *Need for Speed: Most Wanted* (2005) primes a principle of action, such that, when picking up *Forza Horizon 5* (2021), the player instinctively squeezes the controller's right trigger to accelerate and steers with the left thumbstick. Perhaps the player bristles at surprising discontinuities, such as *Mario Kart 8* (2014) mapping its accelerator function to the A face button instead of the expected right trigger.

This category of meaning is deeper than control conventions, though. Specific resonances create unquantifiable "feelings" of play unique to particular games. There is something about how certain actions that the avatar protagonist of 3D platformer *A Hat in Time* (2017) performs that *feels* remarkably similar to Mario's movement in *Super Mario 64* (1996). Despite the *hundreds* of 3D platformers released between *A Hat in Time* and *Super Mario 64*, one cannot help but draw that *specific* link. Hat Kid has not just a genre-appropriate jump; she has *Mario's* jump!

I call this form of meaning *ludomotif*. In music, the term *leitmotif* describes a short musical phrase that is repeated in different contexts throughout a piece or series of pieces to represent an idea or a narrative subject. For example, the musical score of the *Star Wars* films (1977-present) features several short musical phrases that represent key characters (such as Darth Vader and Princess Leia) and non-human subjects (such as the mystical Force). These themes are subtly interwoven into the soundtrack not only to cue characters' or concepts' active presence within a scene (reinforcing the connection of the leitmotif and its subject) but also to signal an unspoken relevance of the subject to what is happening (signaling a character may be thinking or indirectly invoking a subject, even in its absence). This allows storytellers to communicate aspects of their fiction on otherwise difficult-to-access levels of thought, emotion, and spirit.

There are differing forms of motifs in storycraft (and reality): colors, fonts, symbols, animals. Many things can form associations with particular elements of a story. In the same way, ludomotifs can be used as shorthand to invoke meanings associated with other ways of acting and of choosing. The controls of *A Hat in Time* mirror those of *Super Mario 64*, not because piggybacking on an established scheme of successfully employed action affordances is easier than creating a novel set from scratch; rather, the ludic parallel is intended to specifically put players in mind of Mario and encourage interaction with its world in the manner players previously interacted with the world of *Super Mario 64*. It cues attitudes of Mario-like improvisation when navigating the environment. It signals a "leap before looking" strategy of excited, forward movement typical of Mario's 3D adventures. It also carries with it the memories, emotions, and nostalgic resonances the player carries forward from any past experiences with *Super Mario 64*. In establishing that connection, *A Hat in Time* is not only an extension of the legacy of 3D platformers in general; it is an extension of the player's personal history with Mario (despite Mario being absent from and formally unrelated to *A Hat in Time* altogether).

As "readers" of game texts, our literacy models will not identify the inception of new ludomotifs, but we will be sensitive and conscious of the traces of ludomotifs from our past gameplay experiences that we detect in the new. At the beginning of one's video game experience, these motifs will be very general ("pressing a button to jump in *Donkey Kong Country* [1994] reminds me of pressing a button to jump in *Super Mario World* [1990]"), but as a greater quantity of experiences accumulates, more granular resonances will become apparent ("jumping in *Kaze and the*

Wild Masks [2021] reminds me *very specifically* of the jumping mechanics from the *Donkey Kong Country* series and *not* of similar genre kin). Ludomotifs are necessarily retrospectively oriented.

Perspective Transformation

Whereas ludomotifs represent a resonance of gameplay logics that carry across games, perspective transformation details how resonances carry outside of games. Exposure to artworks has the capacity to fundamentally alter one's perspective on the rest of the world even after the artistic encounter has concluded. Perhaps the empathetic experience of an artwork (the visceral sensation of living another's life and aligning with another's feelings within the context of a story, for instance) results in a lasting empathy and greater understanding of other perspectives and experiences. Perhaps the aesthetic experience of another artwork inspires previously unconsidered avenues of communication and expression, broadening the scope of a beholder's expressive capacity. It can result in lingering associations, pulling the aesthetic associated with one experience into related artworks encountered later (such is the power of sampling in music; artists shape the aesthetic takeaway of their songs by drawing upon the richness of meaning and context embedded in existing works).

This realignment of perspectives serves the purpose of defamiliarization. Viktor Shklovsky wrote of defamiliarization (or, in more literal translations, "making strange") as the making strange and, thus, conscious of that which is common and non-occurrent. Writes Shklovsky,

> The purpose of art is to impart the sensation of things as they are perceived and not as they are known. The technique of art is to make objects 'unfamiliar', to make forms difficult, to increase the difficulty and length of perception because the process of perception is an aesthetic end in itself and must be prolonged.
>
> *(1919/2015)*

In other words, art should allow audiences to practice perceiving in novel and difficult ways in order that our perception of *all things* may be improved. Art challenges the "over-automatization" of our perceptive and reflective capacities.

Video games are particularly adept at perspective transformation, as almost all video games involve the adoption of a new way of seeing or operating within the simulation that can be surprisingly "sticky" outside of the simulation as well. The third-person perspective adopted by most driving and sports games gives players a novel way of envisioning their spatial presence in associated activities. I improved at playing tennis, for instance, after playing *Mario Tennis* (2000) because it gave me a greater holistic perspective on the spatial management of the course and my options for optimally moving within it. Players often report that this effect can be so strong that it becomes intrusive. *Tetris* (1985) players often report "seeing" shape matches in their environment, and *Tony Hawk's Pro Skater* (1999) players often cannot help but see the world around them in terms of objects that a skateboarder could grind upon and jump between.

Ultimately, this can powerfully manifest not only as a language of visual and aural associations but also as a deepening pool of functional reference points. Because games are engaged as procedural systems, we can form patterned recognition of not only aesthetic components but also of the operational logics that underlie games' systems. This leads nicely into our final category of meaning.

Procedural Rhetoric

Procedural rhetoric is a term coined by games researcher Ian Bogost for his 2007 book, *Persuasive Games*. In it, he defines it as "the art of persuasion through rule-based representations and interactions rather than the spoken word, writing, images, or moving pictures" (2007, p. ix). The purpose of Bogost's specific exploration was the identification of ideological conveyance and political frameworks in games. He later describes procedural rhetorics as "[making] a claim about how something works" (2009); norm-setting ideological statements. His definition is structured around an intentional "persuasion" and framed as a *rhetorical* device. He argues that the most elegant way to make an argument or posit a normative statement about processes is through "the process-native environment of the computer" (Bogost, 2009).

Procedural rhetoric is unidirectional communication. Whereas the other categories of meaning have the capacity for facilitating the inscription of meaning from the authorial developer and expressing ideas of the player, procedural rhetoric is concerned with arguments latent within the design itself and the propensities of systems it produces. Bogost writes, "Procedural representation explains processes with other processes. Procedural representation is a form of symbolic expression that uses process rather than language [...] *Procedural representation itself* requires inscription in a medium that actually enacts processes rather than merely describes them" (Bogost, 2007, p. 9). Players may offer novel (or even contradictory) readings of particular procedural dynamics, but each is posited as a hypothesis regarding what is inherent to the ludic systems rather than being a truly *creative* expression of the players themselves.

This does not mean that the description of procedural rhetorics specifically means identifying authorial intent, though. Many of the most interesting examples Bogost provides identify instances in which systemic logics work *against* the intended messages of their games. The *intent* of a developer to endorse a particular point of view can be undercut by the design of gameplay systems that more readily play out the opposite perspective. Bogost argues that unintended arguments can be made in the procedural layer of a game that undermine stated or implicit goals of their semiotic layer. Bogost identifies procedural emergence as a form of rhetoric for the purpose of forming a discipline by which dissonant framings can be identified and resolved. In the same way that the verbal presentation of an argument can complement or interfere with the informational content of the message (using nervous and avoidant body language can make a message seem less reliable even when the speaker genuinely believes it), Bogost considers how game mechanics and systems model and, thus, make implicit arguments about the operations of the real world.

Procedural rhetorics can be difficult to identify because they feel inherent to the operations of their games. They are posited as *simply the way the simulated world works* rather than being pitched straightforwardly *as* arguments. In *SimCity* (1989), it is a normative argument that placing a police station in a city reduces crime in its immediate vicinity. In the game, this functions as an uncomplicated mediator to criminal occurrences, which unavoidably makes *an argument* (whether accurate or not) about the purpose and effect of police in real cities. In the real world, there are reasonable political positions that may support or oppose this particular argument, and certainly one can identify mediating factors that can complement or complicate this relationship in the real world. Within the context of the simulation, though, the systemic effect of police presence is abstracted, simplified, and objectified. The game positions an objective, systemic property within the system and *implicitly* argues that a similar relationship exists in real-world contexts as well.

In fact, the transparency of normative rhetoric is well-recognized in other forms of media as well, and identifying connotative arguments is one of the important goals of most forms of literacy. Roland Barthes (1972) writes about the manner in which cultural myths posit arguments as if they were natural, typically as a way of maintaining an artificial status quo advantageous to the dominant group within a society. He writes

> Myth does not deny things. On the contrary, its function is to talk about them; simply, it purifies them, it makes them innocent, it gives them a natural and eternal justification, it gives them a clarity which is not that of explanation but that of a statement of fact. If I state the fact of French imperiality without explaining it, I am very near to finding that it is natural and goes without saying.
>
> *(p. 143)*

That is, by presenting something as being inherent within an instance of communication, the communicator frames it as being separate from arguable subjectivity. If it is not straightforwardly presented *as* an argument, it does not *invite* counterargument. Thus, highly artificial relationships and structures, such as national borders and racial hierarchies, are implicitly posited and maintained *as if* they were properties of the world as natural as gravity and inertia (until they are recognized and explicitly called out). The truly literate reader must learn to make these distinctions and identify illusory normality.

Crucially, *no* property of a game world is *inherent*. Every element is designed. The parameters that define the physics of a game world are designed and, thus, open to design interrogation. Not every arbitrary property *makes an argument*, but each possesses a positional propensity.

Procedural rhetoric is ultimately examined reflectively and semiotically, as opposed to the reflexive and non-semiotic processing of some other forms of meaning. The systemic interactions procedural rhetoric *describes* are *encountered* reflexively, but engaging with them *as* rhetoric requires a reflective and semiotic posture of examination, and one that is positioned in reference to the real world.

Besides Bogost's specific ideological and political interest, his theory posits a general grammar of procedurality that is useful even outside of the identification of rhetorical arguments. The privileging of systemic relationships in tasks of meaning-making forms a general practice of reading games for their *operational logics* (Wardrip-Fruin, 2020) separately from their semiotic coding. He names *procedural figures*, individual expressive figures comparable to the literary metaphor or synecdoche (Bogost, 2007, pp. 12–15), around which we can begin to observe *genres* of procedure separate (or complimentary) to the aesthetically relevant genre of any particular work.

This is the most sophisticated form of meaning that will be examined in this exploration of video game literacy, and not every model introduced will engage at this level. The topic of procedural rhetoric will be further explored during our examination of systemic ideology and ethics in Chapter 14.

MDA MODEL: MECHANICS, DYNAMICS, AESTHETICS

The first analytical model I wish to highlight is foundational to the development of most others. Originally developed and proposed in a series of workshops and lectures at the Game Developers Conference from 2001–2004, its most commonly cited source is its formal operationalization, published by Robin Hunicke, Marc LeBlanc, and Robert Zubek in 2004. It was developed as a bidirectional model that can be used equally well from the perspective of the game designer (creating the hard mechanics that blossom into experiential qualities upon enactment of play) or of the player (who directly experiences the aesthetics of gameplay and can work backwards toward discerning the designed conditions that brought about that experience). The model is flexible, simple, and broadly useful. It is no wonder that even models that are critical of its particularities use this framework as a basis.

The model outlines a relationship between a game's *mechanics*, *dynamics*, and aesthetics. **Mechanics**, as outlined previously, refer to sequentially-chunked rule clusters that form the basic actions, boundaries, and operations of gameplay. **Dynamics** in this model are more specific than the general dynamics discussed in the previous section. Dynamics in the MDA model are the interactions between behavioral mechanics, the intersection of rules that produce buds of procedural emergence. Finally, **aesthetics** differ from colloquial usage, in which they are often a shorthand for visual design ("this dining room has a midcentury-modern aesthetic"); rather, *aesthetic* in MDA refers to the emotional, philosophical, or generally *second-order* (in reference to the definition of *art* established in this book's introductory chapter) experience of the player. I will go into greater detail regarding each of these components in the following sections.

The model posits a linear relationship between these elements. Developers program mechanics into game code that define the operations of elements within the game world and the manners in which players can interact with these elements. Dynamics are runtime behavior; they do not instantiate until the live enactment of gameplay. They are *anticipated* by design but not programmed *outright*. If mechanics are roads, dynamics are the traffic patterns that fulfill their structural affordances. Developers have only indirect control over the enactment of dynamics. Finally, dynamics are experienced by players during enacted play and create experiential aesthetics. Going back to the traffic example, bottlenecks of high congestion are likely to result in aesthetics like frustration and rage.

Ultimately, the developer is designing *for* the desired aesthetic but is only able to alter the game at the level of the mechanics. The model posits that changing underlying mechanics will produce different dynamics, which lead to different aesthetics. The audience, on the other hand, experiences aesthetics pre-critically. The reflective and literate player observes their emotional aesthetic response and forms hypotheses about the dynamics that induce that aesthetic. From there, they can identify the particular mechanics at work that enact those dynamics, and they may even hypothesize about how those mechanics may be changed to alter the resulting aesthetic. For example,

> I am so frustrated by this level. I always die at the point where twenty zombies rush me. The zombies move too quickly, take too much damage to kill, and do so much damage to my avatar that I do not have enough time to destroy them all before they overwhelm me. If the zombies were easier to kill, or if my weapon had more ammunition, or if they took a bit longer to reach my defensive position, I expect that it would be a less frustrating level.

Mechanics

Mechanics are defined in the MDA paper as "the particular components of the game, at the level of data representation and algorithms" (Hunicke et al., 2004). This particular definition leaves more ambiguity than I prefer. "Data representation", in particular, could be extrapolated to refer to *just about anything* within a game system. The music and sound effects of a Game Boy game is a *representation of data*, for example, in that it translates the raw code into an aesthetically perceivable form (sound), but it would be errant to refer to the background music of (most) games as *mechanics*.

I have already defined *mechanics* in the manner in which I use the term in Chapter 2, where I contrasted *mechanics* and *rules*, where *rules* represent the abstract conventions describing how a game *should* be played, whereas *mechanics* are the concrete, computational translations of those elements of design into computer-executed code. Crucially, rules form a *social contract*, such that one can *break* or *negotiate to modify* the rules of a particular game, whereas mechanics are impersonally enforced, so one cannot choose to *break* or *negotiate* their enforcement.

That definition aligns with my personal reading and set of priorities. It is a commonly used word with a multitude of connotations. Definitions from other researchers and professionals exhibit a high degree of variability. They often center around player-initiated actions. Miguel Sicart (2012) describes mechanics as "methods for interaction by the agent with the game system". "Agent" carries some ambiguity in that definition, as some researchers restrict the term "agent" to conscious (human) actors, while some conceptualizations include computers as "agents" within the system of human-computer interaction ("interaction" implying a bidirectional exchange between two participants). Sicart (2013) clarifies his position in a book published the following year, in which he defines mechanics as "the actions afforded by the system to the players so that they can interact with the game state and with other players" (p. 26). This clarifies his interest in mechanics as specifically player-afforded actions.

"Game feel" researcher Steve Swink (2009) takes a slightly softer stance. "A 'game mechanic' is one complete loop of interaction, such as a single mouse twitch, button press, or foot stomp that can be traced through the game's programmed response and back to the player over and over again" (p. 70). Swink implies that mechanics originate with an instigating action of the player but leaves the definitional clause (before the "such as") directionally ambiguous. Considering games as holistic systems inclusive of player, computer, and context, this leaves open the possibility of computer-initiated actions "processed" through the player and responded to by the player to the computer.

Treanor et al. (2010) argue that mechanics "determine the results of interactions between game entities". This definition includes, but is not limited to, player-involved actions. Similarly, Janet H. Murray (2012) describes mechanics as "the rule-based, abstract processes and rituals by which games are structured" (p. 421); "rituals" imply conscious observance, but "processes" is a distinctly systemic term that evokes computers more than (individual) human actions. Though I take exception to the "abstract" adjective in Murray's definition, I am aligned to the perspective that mechanics may be invoked to describe systemic behaviors that do not originate with or involve the human player.

Particularly within the context of the MDA framework, it is important to recognize that the enactment of parameters that cause interesting dynamic interactions often occurs without direct player involvement. The interactions between NPCs' complex behavioral systems create mesmerizing procedural occurrences regularly within games like *The Sims* (2000) and *Grand Theft Auto V* (2013). There is a beauty to the surprising interactions between self-motivated computer agents in complex simulations. Restricting "mechanics" to describe only player affordances seems like it creates an incomplete grammar of simulation.

Mechanics are not only behavioral, comprising game action; they may instead contribute to game logic. A "scoring mechanic" does not represent an affordance of the actors within a virtual diegesis; it represents a logical, totalizing reaction to gamic action. If a game offers higher and higher scores for enemies defeated in quick succession, this does not affect the action affordances of either the player-avatar or NPC actors, but it does represent an important parameter of the game logic that may impact player motivation and procedural occurrences.

Dynamics

Dynamics are interactions between mechanics and/or player behavior. This includes both the systemic consequences of mechanical intersections ("feedback systems within gameplay to determine how particular states or changes affect the overall state of gameplay"; Hunicke et al., 2004) and also player response to mechanics-driven situations. Hunicke, LeBlanc, and Zubek define dynamics as "the run-time behavior of the mechanics acting on player inputs and each other's outputs over time", and there are several interesting things going on in that definition.

The authors mention "time" twice in the definition, first to note that dynamics are "run-time behavior[s]" and again to note that dynamics are expressed "over time". The former usage reminds us of the increasing abstraction and separation from formal design that each layer of the MDA model presents. A dynamic is not a formal property of a game. It may be planned, and it may even be dependably predictable, but dynamics are not programmed into code outright. Interactions that are programmed directly into the code of the game are mechanics. Dynamics occur as the logical consequences of the programmed parameters (or the intermittently logical behaviors of players) intersect, and this is only expressed during run-time execution. As such, the expression of dynamics will vary, to small or large degrees, each time a game is played. As such, a defining line can be drawn between mechanics, behaviors, and properties one can say that a game possesses, and dynamics, procedural occurrences that an individual playthrough enacts, amidst many other possible expressions of the same mechanical intersections.

The second mention of "time" in the authors' definition reminds us that procedural occurrences are not immediate, one-step transformations. Again, such simple transformations are better conceived of as mechanics. Pressing a button to alphabetize a list in a spreadsheet program invokes mechanics of that software; it performs a single function immediately. Dynamics are better conceived of as chain reactions of logical occurrences, initiated by single conditions but rippling outward into emergent chains of consequence.

As has been frequently reinforced throughout this chapter, we should conceive of gameplay not as a closed system that executes and occurs wholly within the computer but as an open system inclusive of computer, player, and context. The authors' definition accounts for this, for dynamics take place not only in the surprising procedural emergences that arise from the interaction of coded elements but also within the psychology of players and even aspects of the environment of play. In fact, player psychology is a greater focus than simulation dynamics in the original paper, due to the authors' focus on designing toward intended player experience. The framework challenges us to consider how small mechanical changes manifest in the experience of play and how that experience blossoms into differing play aesthetics. Because gameplay is framed as a broader system than *only* what occurs within the computer, differing player behaviors can be counted as a form of emergence as well.

For example, the bomb-defusing party game *Keep Talking and Nobody Explodes* (2015) tasks groups of players to work together to neutralize a series of bombs. One player, looking through either a screen or a VR helmet, is presented with a semi-randomized bomb with an array of wires, buttons, keypads, and lights but, crucially, no instructions pertaining to how to safely defuse the device. Other players have an instruction booklet (preferably printed on paper) but cannot see the bomb. The player with the screen must communicate the properties of the bomb in front of them, and the paper players must interpret this information and cross-reference the player's imprecise descriptions with the bomb defusing manual to relay instructions for how to safely dispose of the bomb. As a cooperative task, it has some of the engaging elements of the children's game Telephone, in which information is transmitted and inevitably distorted in its transfer. Keypad symbols that the player must describe are rarely familiar shapes; most require a level of semantic reconstruction in their description.

On its own, though, the task would be eminently achievable were it not for the additional mechanic that makes the game much more interesting: the time limit. Not only do the players have to find and exchange often complicated information as precisely as possible, but they also have to do so under the pressure of time. Skipping ahead in the model, the aesthetic result of this mechanical addition is obvious: it instills a feeling of urgency and panic and often results in a lot of (playful) yelling as players try to clarify crucial details in the valuable moments that they have. Strictly from the perspective of MDA dynamics, though, consider how that inclusion interfaces with player psychology to result in different gameplay outcomes. Knowing that time is limited, the player viewing the bomb may not be able to describe *every* detail of the symbols on the bomb; ambiguity is introduced, crucial to the game's aesthetic as a frantic party game. Paper players may choose to skim valuable paragraphs in the instruction manual instead of reading and retaining every word in detail, perhaps leading to hilarious, unintended consequences of incomplete information. The need to communicate quickly often causes players to speak *over* each other, injecting additional noise into the information transfer, increasing the risk of crucial information getting lost. These procedural, player-based occurrences are just as much a part of the identity of the game as anything programmed into the software or written in the paper manual.

Further, we can consider how altering the mechanical parameter (the amount of time allotted to each round) alters the resulting dynamics. We might hypothesize that drastically decreasing the amount of time allotted may increase the tension, but perhaps players quickly learn that our new, minimal time limit does not give them enough time to exchange crucial information even when communicating efficiently. This may lead to resignation, the feeling that victory is not achievable. Alternatively, we might hypothesize that increasing the time limit may lead to a more relaxed pace of the transfer of more accurate and useful information. Again, though, we might find that the lessened time demand causes players to share *too much* detail, causing the most crucial elements to get lost amidst unimportant information. Of course, because dynamics are procedural interactions, their expressions may vary between play sessions or groups of players.

Ultimately, dynamics comprise the dramatic structure of games. In fact, dramatics proves to be a useful lens for understanding MDA dynamics. Consider an example of a family drama; each family member has specific mechanics/dispositions that define their behavior and temperament in the family unit. Leon wanted to be a dancer but recently broke his leg and is feeling sensitive about his unsure future, but he hasn't told his siblings. Cecilia stole one of Leon's prized poodles, and she doesn't think he's on to her. Val has been having a secret affair with Cecilia's husband. Marty was bullied by Cecilia and Leon while growing up and is still afraid to be alone with them. Buster knows all of their secrets and enjoys subtly playing them against each other. Whenever these characters enter into scenes with one another, their underlying "mechanics" underscore the ways in which they interact and prime particular dramatic situations to occur. Any expression of dissonance or even harmony between these characters is an expression of the dynamics at play in that scene, and such dynamics would be altered by adding or changing mechanics to any of the characters ("…is deathly afraid of spiders", "…recently dropped out of medical school", "…is tutoring a student she increasingly believes may be a ghost from the 14th century"…).

Aesthetics

"Aesthetic" is a term with a wide variety of meanings. It can be used as a substitute for *art* holistically (Frank Lantz [2023] uses "aesthetic form" to describe the endeavors we pursue "for their own sake, in search of beauty, pleasure, and meaning"; p. 17). It can describe the *aesthetic theory* of the arts, as developed by Immanuel Kant, Friedrich von Schiller, Suzanne Langer, and Theodor W. Adorno, which delineates a unifying philosophy of underpinning our experiences of beauty and the formation of aesthetic taste. Within that framework, an artwork's "aesthetic" is its transcendent and sometimes non-specific quality that allows the beholder to experience an encounter with beauty. As such, it is applied broadly in colloquial parlance. "The painting has a creepy aesthetic", "the song communicates a working-class aesthetic", etc.

Amongst particular subcultures, particularly those surrounding the internet-based *vaporwave* musical genre, which remediates nostalgic jazz, lounge, and commercial music from the 1980s and 1990s into dreamlike, lo-fi remixes, the term "aesthetic" is often used on its own (often stylized as A E S T H E T I C) to describe a holistic irreducibility of an experience of beauty. A work does not contain *aesthetic properties*; rather, the work *is* aesthetic. It is contrary to the specificity that the study of aesthetics intends to engender, but it is remarkably honest to the experience of aesthetics as an audience, as if it is a wave that overcomes the beholder completely, no longer experienced as a set of artistic *choices* but rather as a transformative state of mind.

The *aesthetics* described in the MDA framework are narrower than the total *aesthetics of games* outlined in Chapter 2. The original paper defines this particular aesthetic measure as "the desirable emotional responses evoked in the player when she interacts with the game system" (Hunicke et al., 2004). Essentially, it is the pre-reflective, pre-critical experience of gameplay enjoyed by the player. For the purpose of orienting systemic design choices toward desired player experiences, as was the practical purpose of this original paper, this serves as a reasonable position. For the purpose of the theory of literacy outlined in this book, though, I have a few disagreements that will require slight restructuring and reframing of this definition.

The definition begins with "the desirable emotional responses". "Desirable" is not a necessary qualifier. Surely, undesirable responses would be classified as aesthetics as well. If, for example, the introduction of a companion character in an exploration game was intended to relieve player loneliness and increase fellowship within the game world but instead only aggravated players and made them feel anxious, those undesired responses are experienced as aesthetics of that system and will be affected by changes to the preceding mechanics and dynamics.[2] The point that this example illustrates is the implication that "desirable" gives authorial intent. Even if a player experienced an unintended emotion, that was her aesthetic experience, regardless of the design intention.

Secondly, "emotional responses" is a narrower framing of the experience of play than I prefer to use. There are many types of reactions that play evokes, even on the primal, "gut" level, that I would not describe as being "emotional"; the intellectual stimulation of a puzzle, for instance, or the way that a game *feels* to control (*game feel*, see Chapter 4), or of *flow* (Csíkszentmihályi, 1975). One can reasonably argue that these states of mind are reflective descriptions of experiences encountered as emotions in their moments of inception, but I believe that framing them as "emotions" in the theoretical model orients us toward a more restrictive framing than is necessary.

Finally, the definition concludes with "...evoked in the player when she interacts with the game system". This is a small but fundamental difference in the ways in which the authors and I frame gameplay as a system. Hunicke, LeBlanc, and Zubek, writing from a design perspective, frame the system of gameplay as taking place within the software. Changes to the mechanics of the software affect the resulting systemic dynamics. As explained throughout this book, my understanding of the system of gameplay *includes* the player (and context of play) in vital interchange with the computer and its software. As such, the player does not "interact with" the game system; the player *is a part of* the game system, interacting with*in* it.

Hunicke, LeBlanc, and Zubek outline an aesthetic taxonomy in which the (emotional) responses of players can be categorized:

Sensation: *Game as sense-pleasure*

Fantasy: *Game as make-believe*

Narrative: *Game as drama*

Challenge: *Game as obstacle course*

Fellowship: *Game as social framework*

Discovery: *Game as uncharted territory*

Expression: *Game as self-discovery*

Submission: *Game as pastime*

(Hunicke et al., 2004)[3]

Games are then understood in terms of the particular aesthetics that they produce. Hunicke et al. (2004) give the example of the party game Charades, which evokes the aesthetics of fellowship, expression, and challenge. Adjustments of game mechanics are likely to affect the game along those dimensions. They give a second example of a life simulation video game, *The Sims* (2000), which expresses aesthetics of discovery, fantasy, expression, and narrative. This gives players a more useful, nuanced experiential grammar than uncomplicated assessments of *fun* or *flow*.

A *Sims* player can reflect upon the aesthetic of *narrative* in isolation;

> what dynamics of play brought about the narrative drama in my last play session with *The Sims*? The most dramatically-compelling moment was when a character went into a jealous fit after walking in on an unfaithful romantic partner with their neighbor. This moment of drama was enriched by the non-specificity of the gibberish dialogue (allowing me to fill in the semantic gaps with my imagination), the semi-autonomy of Sim actions, and the system by which relationships and emotions are managed and simulated. I hypothesize that the dramatic intrigue of the situation would be lessened if the dialogue was written in discernible text, as the prescripted lines would not feel as specific and nuanced as what I imagined the characters saying in my interpretation of their gibberish performances.

For the purpose of our exploration, we will treat the aesthetics described in the MDA framework more broadly than the authors describe them. Aesthetics describe not only the emotions of play but more broadly the "abstract sensations" (Treanor et al., 2010), informed by the player's context and culture. Game feel, associative significance, physiological response, and more can be considered as byproducts (or are at least affected by) the chain of mechanics → dynamics enacted within game systems.

Metagames

The MDA framework is a broad model, serving as a directional description of aesthetic formation more than a detailed description of particular ludic elements. For this reason, it serves as a useful grammatical *structure* to describe and prompt examination of almost every gameplay event sequence, but a particular weakness of the model is that it does not account for metagamic elements. This is not necessarily a deficiency of the model, nor do I wish to imply that its authors were lax in their theoretical formation; the model was intended as a frame for game developers, in particular, and metagame elements cannot be *directly* designed; thus they fall outside of this model's scope of focus. This book's interest in literacy from the player's perspective, though, makes this model insufficient in isolation.

Metagame elements *certainly* create unique dynamics and aesthetics of their own. The behavior of other players in multiplayer games, for instance, can create unique dynamics and aesthetics that one would never encounter in a purely single-player exploration of game systems. Metagame interactions create a second layer of *rules* (socially-enforced) that cannot be accurately termed *mechanics* outright. For instance, *Dark Souls* (2011) players' observance of custom to not engage in PvP combat until both combatants have healed and bowed to one another creates a specific dynamic of multiplayer encounters, but this is a matter of communal etiquette, not a programmed, deterministic mechanic. It affects the dynamics and aesthetics of the mechanics with which it intersects, but it would not, itself, be termed a "mechanic". It is like a "house rule" of play; a social convention.

To the credit of the model's authors, metagame behaviors are expressed within the bounds of mechanical affordances. Developers cannot design player behavior outright, but they can choose the particular affordances with which players can express themselves. From a design perspective, player behavior expresses as a dynamic of the mechanics that they have set. From a player's perspective, though, the choices and behavior of other players set the specific structural bounds of the play experience, as *essential* to the play experience as the physics and logical structures.

Were I to rewrite the MDA model to better suit the perspective of the player rather than the design-oriented developer, I might suggest restructuring the model as *Mechanics* → *(Dynamics* ⇆ *Metagame)* → *Aesthetics*, as even single-player games produce metagame elements through the intersection of diegetic principle and real-world knowledge (this is more thoroughly explained in Chapter 13). In this case, "metagame" and "dynamics" sit on a roughly equivalent level; mechanics feed into metagame and dynamics equally, dynamics feed into metagame, and metagame feeds into dynamics. But, of course, calling it the "MDMA model" invites a *whole host* of other questions, so perhaps it is best that I make no further rebranding recommendations.

PROCEDURALISM

While the MDA model presents a well-reasoned structure by which mechanical interactions can be identified for their aesthetic potential, it is a rather broad framework, lacking in the specificity necessary for building an operational grammar of design. The next model I would like to introduce is called Proceduralism, developed by Mike Treanor in collaboration with his academic mentor, Michael Mateas, and writer/researcher Ian Bogost. Like many concepts in game studies, Proceduralism, as a term, is used for multiple purposes (and often by the same people), riddling its usages of a frustrating inconsistency. For instance, Proceduralism as I use it in this chapter, refers to an analytical framework, whereas the before-cited Ian Bogost also uses the term to describe a particular movement of games developed in and around the late 2000s that utilized *procedural rhetorics* (detailed above) in service of gameplay experiences that utilized introspection, abstraction of instantial assets, subjective representation, and singularity of authorial voice (Bogost, 2009). Certainly, the Proceduralist analytical methodology can be used to name and assess the qualities emphasized in the Proceduralist design movement, but equally, the Proceduralist methodology can be used to analyze games outside of that particular movement.

The Proceduralist model is not a *radical* departure from MDA before it; rather, it adds detail and standardizes notation of systemic interrelationships while following a broadly similar analytical trajectory. In fact, *mechanics*, *dynamics*, and *aesthetics* are all present within the Proceduralist model, but their relationships and interactions are further contextualized in pursuit of different ends. Whereas the MDA model culminates in the identification of *aesthetic*, the ephemeral *experience* and *emotions* of play, Proceduralism instead works toward the identification of *meaning*, following on from Bogost's conceptualization of *procedural rhetoric*, which models and characterizes a position about how something works (or fails to work) or how something *should* work through operational procedurality of game systems rather than via semiotic means (Bogost, 2007). Whereas the MDA framework gives us structure to identify and justify the experiential quality of gameplay beyond simple descriptors like "fun" or "frustrating", Proceduralism aims to empower players with a methodology for uncovering and discussing the persuasive arguments implicit in games' operational systems.

The Proceduralist model was developed in response to unsatisfying procedurally oriented readings of popular games from other authors. Mike Treanor et al. cite Janet H. Murray (1997)'s reading of *Tetris* (1985) as "the perfect enactment of the overtasked lives of Americans" (p. 143) and Steven Poole's reading of *PAC-MAN* (1980) as a metaphor for American consumerism are cited as examples of contentious interpretations, poorly supported by the game texts (Bogost, 2007). "The interpretations hold only as long as the interpreter omits much of the experience of playing the game and selectively considers only the abstract experience of playing or interpretations of the game's theme" (Treanor et al., 2010).

These concerns are addressed by the two pillars of Proceduralist interpretations: internal comprehensiveness and unidirectionality (Zhou et al., 2022). For a Proceduralist reading to be internally comprehensive, it must include as many details informed by the game's mechanics as possible. Individual systems should not be discussed in isolation when they can be brought into greater context with the other load-bearing systems at play within a game. This is framed as "evidence"; a poorly evidenced reading cannot make a strong claim to validity.

Secondly, the Proceduralist model of meaning-making proceeds unidirectionally from evidence to meaning. This is evident in the framework's graphic model. "One can see that the node labeled Meaning is a sink – all arrows [point] towards it without itself having any arrows pointing outwards" (Zhou et al., 2022). Evidence should justify meaning; meaning interpretation should not be "reverse-engineered" to produce (potentially illusory or misleading) evidence.

Personally, I am caught between agreement and disagreement with the objections Proceduralists make toward their cited "poorly-evidenced" readings. Certainly, the readings to which the authors object are *undisciplined*, and it would strain credulity to insist that either describes what *Tetris* or *PAC-MAN* are *about* as artistic works if we temporarily adopt the assumption that artistic works are *about* singular themes altogether. Certainly, positing such a *meaning* would require more comprehensive "textual" (in this case, systemic) support than either interpretation has offered. On the other hand, if one assumes (as I do) that artistic works do not *contain* meaning that must be uncovered but rather *prompt* the *creation* of meaning in dynamic interchange with their beholders, these could be justified as "successful" artistic experiences. Even if *PAC-MAN* is not "about" consumerism, it is significant that it is played (and designed) in a consumerist cultural context. The game's practical objective (eating all of the Pac-dots within the maze) will unavoidably interact with our experiences of and feelings toward consumption, scarcity, and obstacles to acquisition that we draw from all other avenues of life. A criticism of such readings may say that they "say more about the reader than the text", but within our framing of artistic creation, the reader (player) *is a part of the system* of textual (gameplay) production.

Miguel Sicart (2011) expresses a similar line of criticism, arguing that the Proceduralist model frames ludic meaning as existing "exclusively in the formal system of the game". This undermines the player's role as an agent of collaborative meaning production within the system of play. Further, Zhou et al. frame this objection in the context of Gilles Deleuze's Philosophy of Differences:

> Meaning production, in the context of play, is the production of identity as a symbolic understanding of the play process – an idea about the game, a theme extracted from the experience, or a representation summarizing the play session.
>
> *(Zhou et al., 2022)*

This Deleuzean framing counters the Proceduralist assumptions of comprehensiveness and unidirectionality, proposing instead a necessary polydirectionality in the construction and maintenance of meaning (Zhou et al., 2022).

Further, while the unidirectionality of the model provides an appropriate discipline for structuring rhetorical arguments, as a more broadly *interpretive* framework, such that we might require for a more comprehensive literacy framework, we must consider that the interpretation of meaning feeds back into the production of the artistic *content* of play. Meaning, as interpreted and held in the mind of the player, influences the following decisions that she will make as an agential actor within the game fiction, which determines the shape of the artistic product in its enactment. In Proceduralist terms, evidence produces meaning, *and* meaning shapes the gameplay that then becomes evidence. To the model's credit, it is primarily used as a tool for identifying meaning within the *mechanics* of designed systems *specifically* rather than being a model for analyzing run-time *play* behaviors. It is worth noting these differences in objectives as we compare and build upon different models of meaning-making.

Despite these minor reservations, I find this methodology to be quite fascinating and useful as a step toward a descriptive ludic literacy. The disciplined comprehensiveness of the model materializes as a very useful grammar for delineating procedural rhetorics in a form echoing equation-like philosophical proof statements.

The Proceduralist model builds upon the MDA model before it with unidirectional abstraction from *code* (*mechanics* and their semiotic *definitions*; rightly suggesting consideration of rule-based design parameters *with* and *without* semiotic interpretation) to *dynamics* and *theme* to *aesthetics*. Dynamics, aesthetics, theme, and *cultural context* sum to *meaning*.

Unlike the MDA framework, this model is designed specifically for "*reading*" games rather than designing games. While the MDA model provides useful structure to guide game interpretations, its focus on guiding design decisions brought about some of the limitations listed previously. Conversely, this model, structured from the perspective of players, may not be *as* useful for guiding design iteration.

Definitions

The *code* level of the Proceduralist model contains two distinct aspects: definitions and mechanics. Each arises from a different form of "code": mechanics are defined by the operational programming code that structures and maintains the simulation, and definitions emerge from our semiotic code by which we interpret the game world. Analysis begins with definitions; an attempt to identify and index (as comprehensively as possible) the game's entities, meters, goals, and mechanisms of control.

An *entity* is "any element that can be described by a game mechanic" (Treanor et al., 2010) that contributes to the behavior of a system. Avatars and NPCs are entities; power-ups are entities; enemies are entities; physics objects are entities in as far as they contribute to the dynamics of play. Further, entities "can be themed to produce meaning" (Treanor et al., 2010). This requirement of semantic value differentiates entities from structural (and even mechanical) but unthemed elements of the game's architecture, such as invisible lines (termed "flags" or "triggers") that initiate cutscenes, for instance. Though that invisible line serves a mechanical purpose (transitioning gameplay from active play to non-interactive cutscene), there is no semantically definable unit within the simulation that performs this function. In short, an entity can be said to be *themed* if its visual or textual coding contextualizes and sets expectations for its mechanical function. For instance, a set of unthemed polygons may not arouse particular behavioral expectations, but if those polygons are themed to resemble a chicken, one may form behavioral expectations (sentient, has limited capacity of flight, skittish when approached, may excite the attention of foxes and other predators…).

Meters refer to mechanisms of tracking meaningful changes in the game state, typically tracking players' progress or resource allotment. These can be visible (such as the persistent score indicators perpetually on-screen in many arcade games) or invisible (the semi-random intervals between random encounters in JRPGs). On the level of their programming code, video games contain *many* parameters and dynamic variables that are never brought to players' attention; for the sake of Proceduralist definitions, though, focus is narrowed to the meters that are inferable through play and potentially hold rhetorical meaning.

Goals give player-directed actions direction. In the Proceduralist framing, goals are better characterized as motivational trajectories rather than destinations. The goal is not necessarily the game's "victory condition" or the point of completion of any task (though these elements are certainly *included* within that definition). Rather, a goal may be perpetual and unresolvable (such as up-leveling and empowerment in RPGs, which is a general player ambition but does not contain a discrete endpoint) or impossible goals that exist to prompt the player to "attempt the designated task for as long as it takes to realize the task is overwhelmingly difficult" (Treanor et al., 2010) which serves a rhetorical strategy. Whether it represents ultimate resolution or simply the next step in the journey, it is important to take note of the goals that guide players throughout play.

Finally, players should note and define their loci of control and agential expression throughout analyzed games. From a rhetorical perspective, it is important to recognize that avatar-based narrative games place players in the perspective of characters in pursuit of particular goals. Those goals or the means available to the avatar characters to pursue those goals may not align with the goals or ethical principles of the player. Video games are encountered as moments of enacted play rather than as holistic texts, and players' involvement in goal-motivated problem solving creates a series of micro-choices that are more occurrent or present in the mind of the player than the large-scale narrative. The player may disagree with the narrative actions at the macro scale (building a globe-spanning empire in *Sid Meier's Civilization VI* [2016] or performing assassinations for profit in *HITMAN* [2016]), but the player *is* aligned to the goals at the micro, moment-to-moment level (winning the competitive match or evading pursuers within the simulation). As such, players may not be conscious of the rhetorical function of perspective alignment. Identifying and defining the loci of control and expression explicitly and objectively provides the necessary distance required to observe this rhetoric in action.

In summary, the *definitions* step of the Proceduralist model seeks to elucidate the relevant details of the simulation required to unpack its rhetorical arguments. The objective is to be thorough. Not *every* entity or goal will contribute to *every* rhetoric of a game, but seeking comprehensiveness in the definitional stage prevents selective readings that are contradicted by other elements within the game.

An example definition list of the game *PAC-MAN* (1980) may identify the following:

Entities:

- Pac-Man (avatar; yellow circle with gaping mouth)
- Ghosts (because the ghosts exhibit different behavioral patterns, it is better to list each

as separate entities: Inky, Pinky, Blinky, and Clyde; blue, pink, red, and orange semi-circles, respectively)

- Pac-dots (small, white circles) Power pellets (larger, white circles positioned near the corners of the mazes)
- Fruits (a variety of shapes and colors that appear toward the center of the maze)
- Walls

Meters:

- Score
- Lives
- Level
- Duration of Power Pellet power-up

Goals:

- Clear the maze of Pac-dots
- Avoid ghosts, or eat ghosts during the Power Pellet power-up
- Maximize score
- *(For advanced players)* reach killscreen at level 256

Control:

- Player is Pac-Man, the yellow circle controlled with directional inputs from the arcade joystick
- Pac-Man has no discernible narrative goal other than the consumption of maximal fruits and Pac-dots

Mechanics

Mechanics, in this framework, can be viewed as "individual units of meaning that possess rhetorical possibilities" (Treanor et al., 2010), meaning that each mechanic (semantically-whole sequence of rule-guided actions) has the potential to make a statement—a value expression.

Crucially, the separation of mechanics and definitions suggests that we should maintain a parallel awareness of rule-guided actions as representative/semiotically-describable sequences and, separately, as non-semiotic/matter-of-fact occurrences viewed *without* semiotic interpretation. As discussed in Chapter 4, avatar-based simulation differs from purely representational media (such as film and literature) in nature in that gameplay occurrences operate on both sides of the line dividing reality and non-reality. As Jesper Juul (2005) identifies in his influential book Half-Real, the diegetic context of a game world is fictional, but the rules that structure the actions that take place within a game space operate in reality and are performed by real agents. It is fictional that my virtual team of athletes plays football on my television, but it is *true* and *actual* that, if I operate the control interface in such a way that they score a goal, the outcome of the game will change in accordance to the rules. Diegetic decisions are made in the space of the real world, and the actions (or interferences) of the real world directly affect diegetic action.

The separate consideration of mechanics and definitions encourages these rule-based actions to be understood not only for what they semiotically represent but also purely for their effects within the ludic space. This preserves specificity and ambiguity that may be lost (or "smoothed-over") when interpreted through their representational visual or textual coding. For instance, at the mechanical level, the Pac-dots that line the mazes in *PAC-MAN* (1980) are removed from the play space when the Pac-Man avatar collides with them. We semiotically understand this as representing Pac-Man *eating* the dots, suggested by the rhythmic opening-and-closing animation of the character's giant mouth with which he leads as he moves throughout the maze. When reading *PAC-MAN* from a Proceduralist perspective, removal-upon-collision is the *mechanic,* and "eating" is the *definition.* Reasonably, one could interpret the Pac-dots as coins that Pac-Man greedily stuffs into his pockets, or we could even imagine that the Pac-dots are prickly burs that stick to Pac-Man's socks as he walks around the maze.

This is important when considering the rhetorical value of mechanics. The visual coding of an action might *suggest* a particular reading, but considered at the literal level of pre-interpretive action, we may find that the rhetorical position is undermined. If someone made a version of *PAC-MAN* (1980) in which he was freeing prisoners of war from an enemy fortress, it might not make sense for the dots (now representing allied prisoners) to disappear upon collision, as this may not suggest *freedom* from captivity as much as it suggests death or subsumption. Flattening mechanics and descriptions may also cause important distinctions to get lost. *DOOM Eternal* (2020) includes guns that utilize a rayscan model of bullet trajectory (essentially, the game calculates where the gun is pointing and inflicts bullet damage on anything in its calculated vector trajectory instantly when the trigger is pulled) and some that launch projectiles as modeled objects within the game world (which move slower and can be avoided). Both could be described as "shooting a gun", but each enacts within the game world differently and will lead to distinct dynamics. Naturally, when writing or talking about mechanics, it is unavoidable that we refer to them by their semiotic label, but we should hold within our minds (or even make explicit) the dual layers at play in this description.

Some Proceduralist reports list mechanics as plain-language descriptions; others number mechanics and/or use programming-like language to describe their effects (for example, "mechanic[1]: driving LeftToRight[Car], mechanic[2]: flyingBackAndForth[Plane], mechanic[3]: dropFrom[CEO,Plane]…"; Treanor et al., 2010). The chosen methodology depends upon the purpose and audience of the description. The mechanics are numbered so that they can be easily referenced in the construction of dynamic arguments.

Continuing the example reading of *PAC-MAN* (1980) from the previous section, a rules and mechanics section (written in the plain-language method) may look like this:

Rules and Mechanics:

- **mechanic(1)**: The maze is populated with Pac-dots at the beginning of each stage.
- **mechanic(2)**: Pac-Man moves in cardinal directions when not obstructed by walls.
- **mechanic(3)**: When Pac-Man collides with a Pac-dot or fruit, the Pac-dot or fruit is cleared and the score meter increases in value.
- **mechanic(4)**: When Pac-Man collides with a Power Pellet, the game state shifts and the relationships between Pac-Man and ghosts are inverted.
- **mechanic(5)**: Ghosts pursue Pac-Man (each with different behavioral patterns) throughout the maze.
    - **mechanic(5a)**: The above is true unless a Power Pellet power-up is active, in which case, the ghosts flee from Pac-Man.
- **mechanic(6)**: When Pac-Man and a ghost collide, Pac-Man is killed, causing his position within the maze to reset and the lives meter to decrease.
    - **mechanic(6a)**: The above is true unless a Power Pellet power-up is active, in which case the ghost is "eaten": reset to the center of the maze, and incrementally large additions are made to the score meter.
- **mechanic(7)**: Upon clearing all Pac-dots, the maze is reset, the level increases, the speed of gameplay increases, and the duration of the Power Pellet power-up decreases

Culture

Culture is very important to Proceduralist readings but also resistant to Proceduralist methodology. Culture cannot be comprehensively defined in the "all cards out on the table", transparent strategy of other elements within the model, but cultural context will absolutely affect the manner in which ludic elements are interpreted and even *noticed*.

Rather than being exhaustively defined in each Proceduralist reading, cultural context should be interjected into relevant interpretations. Assumptions based on cultural convention must be explicitly stated (for example, a game that uses a check mark to signify "yes" is a cultural convention that may not be universal). Players should try to be occurrently aware of the cultural associations and assumptions that they are bringing into their interpretation of gameplay, as well as the influence the cultural context of the team who designed the game might have over the meaning and assumptions inscribed into it.

Culture does not entail all sources of interpretive subjectivity. The authors of the model state that culturally dependent interpretations should be relatively stable across all members of a culture (or subculture, as it may be; Treanor et al., 2010).

Dynamics

Like in the MDA model, dynamics describe the interactions between mechanics. This is where emergent behaviors arise. This is considered an interpretive element, but unlike other interpretive elements within the model, dynamics are the result of code-based interactions and are, thus, not affected by culture. The model's authors note, though, that culture may prime players to attend to particular dynamics and fail to notice others (Treanor et al., 2010).

In Proceduralist arguments, dynamics are numbered, and the mechanics that contribute to their expression are clearly stated with an emphasis on elucidating the cause-and- effect interaction that constitutes each. Like the mechanics above, some methodologies favor plain-language descriptions of dynamics, while others present formula-like sequences in the style of philosophical proofs.

Continuing our *PAC-MAN* (1980) example, each of the below methods is an appropriate way of describing the same dynamic:

dynamic(1): Because ghosts pursue Pac-Man when not in the Power Pellet phase, and because consuming multiple ghosts during a single Power Pellet phase awards significantly more points, and because the Power Pellet phase has a limited duration, the most optimal time to activate a Power Pellet is when the ghosts are close to Pac-Man. Because ghosts pursue Pac-Man in difficult-to-predict patterns, and because a collision with a ghost outside of the Power Pellet phase results in the loss of a life, delaying the Power Pellet acquisition until all ghosts are close to Pac-Man creates additional risk.

Alternatively:

- mechanic(5) ^ mechanic(4) ^ mechanic(5a) ^ controls(player, Pac-Man) ^ goal(survive) ^ goal(maximize(score)) → **dynamic(1)**: The optimal time to activate a Power Pellet is when ghosts are grouped close to Pac-Man, but it is also the time of highest risk

Theme

Theme represents what we refer to throughout this book as the semiotic layer of representation. If dynamics represent the interplay of mechanics rooted purely in code, theme represents the aspects of associative communication rooted purely in culture. The model's authors introduce theme as "visual representation or textual explanation, clarifies assumptions being made about a game and shapes the interpretation of mechanics" (Treanor et al., 2010). The authors later add auditory representation to this list; further, I would add some kinds of haptic representation as well. Essentially, theme encompasses aspects of the digital simulation (outward from the computer to the player) that rely upon associations with knowledge external to the simulation.

For example, a game entity may present as a sports car. It is recognizable because we have associations from the real world and other fictions that constitute our mental model of what a sports car looks like (four wheels, sleek body, windows, headlights, possibly a convertible top, bright colors…). These associations guide our expectations for how the entity will behave in-game (can achieve speeds of over 100mph, not confined to tracks like a train, cannot fly like an airplane, can make relatively precise turns on surfaces visually coded to represent asphalt but will likely lose traction and become difficult to control on surfaces visually coded as sand, mud, or stones). Our associations also inform aspects of its cultural/social value (a typically expensive car that signifies wealth and frivolous spending, associated with thrill-seekers who want to drive fast, often associated with mid-life crises), and these associations have a "stickiness" that carries with them the emotions, memories, and context from other uses of similar symbols (even in another game, and even when not positioned as a deliberate homage, driving a red convertible in a beachside town brings back memories of playing *Out Run* (1986), and the visual echo recalls within my mind the music, the arcade competitions, and the feeling of first seeing *Out Run*'s bright colors).

Further, theme guides our interpretation of cause/effect and the relationship between entities, mechanics, and dynamics. Treanor et al. give the example of two entities (A and B); if they collide, B disappears. This abstract relationship can have many different interpretations. If A is visually represented as a man with an open mouth and B is visually represented as a hamburger, it is reasonable to assume that B has been *eaten* (Treanor et al., 2010); however, if A is a bug zapper and B is a mosquito, it would be more reasonable to read the relationship as the mosquito having been electrocuted.

This immiscible relationship between mechanics and theme is what allows ludomotifs to diversify and subvert expectations. A game can trace a mechanical echo of a previous game (or established genre conventions), *re-themed* (or "reskinned") with a different set of representational specifics to communicate different types of meaning and fundamentally separate messages. For example, *Disco Elysium* (2019) uses the stats-heavy mechanics of RPG battle encounters to inform the logic of its conversation system, representing the exchange of information and shifts of status within a conversation as "attacks" that can cause of sustain psychic damage. Similarly, *HuniePop* (2015) uses the conventions of match-three tile-arranging puzzle games (like *Bejeweled* [2001]) to represent the dance of emotions and relating to one another that occurs during dates. Several games that have satirical or persuasive goals capitalize upon the familiarity audiences have with classic game archetypes to frame and structure their ludic arguments, making them common subjects of the study of procedural rhetorics in the writings of Ian Bogost and his contemporaries.

The model's authors state that "purely abstract mechanics cannot reliably carry meaning" (Treanor et al., 2010), arguing that theme is a necessary component of all meaning inscriptions. This holds true for the objectives outlined in the papers that established this model, with a primary interest in discerning procedural rhetorics, specific arguments made through procedural simulation, but this is not necessarily true in the context of the wider variety of meanings identified earlier in this chapter that guide this book's exploration. Considering the inducement of second-order mental or emotional states to be a category of artistic meaning within this exploration, pre-reflective fear, arousal, excitement, etc., can exist on a non-semiotic level.

In fact, one of the most powerful and persistent perspective transformations (identified above as one of our primary categories of meaning) involves the player learning to see *past* theme; to be able to hold the game world separately and concurrently as both a representational and abstract space. As described above, the experience of playing the *Tony Hawk's Pro Skater* series (1999-present) is being placed in semi-naturalistic, familiar settings (like a school, shopping mall, or cruise ship) and being able to abstract their architectural features purely in terms of movement and mechanical affordances. Edges with hard angles become grindable surfaces; angled surfaces become ramps… The ability to abstract the game space translates into real-world perception. The "message" of *Tony Hawk's Pro Skater* is the rebellious notion that the social restrictions polite society places on the movement through spaces is artificial; there is an innate pleasure and an inalienable moral goodness to the irreducible movement of bodies through space. The *Tony Hawk's Pro Skater* games *do* use theme to convey aspects of this message, but to arrive at this conclusion, one has to approach the game with a perspective that meaning (of such that can sum to a greater meaning) can be conveyed cogently and essentially through purely abstract mechanics without theme. Even if it were presented in a purely abstract manner, *Tony Hawk's Pro Skater* would still contain most of the components of its philosophy of movement.

Theme is not only used to inform but also to subvert expectations. The juxtaposition of conflicting themes can create memorable moments of surprise, comedy, or estrangement. Sega Saturn fighting game *Fighters Megamix* (1996) featured a playable car, which would "stand" on its rear bumper and throw "punches and kicks" with its wheels. It contained the visual coding of both a car (in its shape and texture) *and* a human (in its posture and animation) that created a humorous mismatch.

Before moving on from theme, it is important to note that theme, relying so heavily upon cultural context and "sticky" associations, is the level of analysis that will present the widest divisions between different players' interpretations of ludic meaning. Basic associations are highly relative based on cultural context (whether monkeys signify humor, mischief, wisdom, sacredness, or nuisance depends upon the culture of the player), and interpretations may depend upon the sensibilities and even the present mood of the player (are the exaggerated, gory deaths of enemies in games such as *Unreal Tournament* [1999] or *I Am Your Beast* [2024] comedic slapstick or appalling body horror?).

Rather than positing any contextually-specific thematic interpretation to be "correct", I believe that works of art gain strength from the diversity of thematic readings. Great artworks are written *for* this ambiguity, not pitched with "skeleton key" interpretations that *consolidate* the ambiguity. For this reason, it is important to be aware of the contextual factors that inform one's readings. In compiling Proceduralist readings, culture and even locally contextual factors that inform our thematic definitions should be named.

An example thematic assessment of *PAC-MAN* (1980) in the Proceduralist style may look like the following:

Themes:

- **theme(1)**: The large eyes and bright (culturally regarded as happy, "spring" colors) of the ghosts give them a cute, non-threatening appearance.
  - **theme(1a)**: When gameplay is in a Power Pellet phase, the ghosts become dark blue and appear to grimace.
- **theme(2)**: Pac-Man is bright yellow (a color with no *dominant* association in my culture) and lacks eyes or any facial features other than his shark-like mouth.
- **theme(3)**: Clearing Pac-dots from the maze creates a compulsive pleasure associated with cleanliness and order. It presents a clear visual indication of how proportionally "clear" the maze is at every point during gameplay.
- **theme(4)**: The predominant blackness of the game background evokes associations with dark, threatening labyrinths, such as Daedalus' labyrinth from Greek mythology.

Aesthetics

In the Proceduralist model, aesthetics are the abstract sensations of play. They are positioned as being influenced by dynamics (like in the MDA model), theme, and (implicitly) culture. This measure includes the emotions of play (frustration, excitement, fear, tension…) as well as what is commonly called *game feel* (the sense of "being" a character in a space, the "viscerality" of play; see Chapter 4).

The inclusion of theme and culture in this model gives interpretations a greater degree of specificity than those of the MDA model. Someone with a phobia of spiders may experience a gut-churning fear while playing tarantula-starring games *Deadly Creatures* (2009) or *Webbed* (2021) that would be difficult to justify within the purely dynamics-oriented MDA model. Proceduralism gives us a better framework with which to examine the various factors that comprise the *experience* of gameplay as artistic communication.

In Proceduralist reports, aesthetics should be evidenced by the dynamics and themes that constitute them. If an aesthetic is influenced by a personal or cultural factor that has not been previously referenced as a theme, that should be named as well.

An example aesthetics report for *PAC-MAN* (1980) features below:

- dynamic(1) ∧ theme(1a) ∧ mechanic(4) ∧ goal(maximize(score)) ∧ mechanic(6a) ∧ goal(survive) → **aesthetic(1)**: Because of the risk involved in delaying Power Pellet acquisition until the ghosts are close to Pac-Man, the sudden inversion of the predator/prey relationship is exciting and satisfying.

Meanings

Finally, dynamics, aesthetics, theme, and culture sum to produce meaning. This is the most important differentiator from the MDA model, which culminates in the recognition/design of aesthetics and does not purport to formalize a method for the inscription of meaning in procedural systems. Indeed, the authors of the Proceduralist model argue that "it is impossible for game designers to *embed* any meaning at all inside of a game, as they have no power over how players choose to narrate the operation of the game as machine" (Treanor & Mateas, 2011). This claim, based on Brian Cantwell Smith's claim about the source of computational meaning (Cantwell Smith, 2010), presumes that "meaning arises from the dialectical interplay between the game as mechanism and the meaning ascribed to it by the player" (Treanor & Mateas, 2011). Again, this claim, privileging procedural rhetorics as semantically specific arguments made within the operations of the gameplay system, arises from a definition of meaning narrower than the definition that guides this exploration. For our purposes, I hold that it is possible for game designers to create forms of pre-reflective meaning through the shaping of systemic affordances and consequences.

As noted earlier, meaning derivation within the Proceduralist model is traditionally unidirectional. Meaning arises from the elements of the gameplay system and can, thus, be evidenced in the form of Proceduralist proofs. Some within Proceduralist circles are critical of this assumption, though, suggesting poly-directionality instead, noting that some gameplay evidence *can* be justified retroactively (Zhou et al., 2022). For the purpose of our exploration, I agree with this particular criticism. Within the visual model of the framework, "one can see that the node labeled Meaning is a sink-- all arrows are pointing towards it without itself having any arrow pointing outwards" (Zhou et al., 2022). If player-directed gameplay choices constitute the evidence from which meaning is ultimately derived, it is useful to remember that the post-reflective meaning players derive from *ongoing* gameplay affects their decisions, shaping further evidence. Indeed, meaning feeds back into gameplay at the very base level of the model. This is not currently accounted for in the Proceduralist model and is one of the most significant points of division between that model and my own.

Meanings, like dynamics and aesthetics before, should be properly evidenced in reports. Meanings are quite subjective, though, so the proof-like formula should not be mistaken for representing a claim to objectivity. It is a framework for structuring an argument: not proving a universal truth. Meanings can also reference and feed into other meaning claims. With the model's focus on identifying procedural rhetorics, Proceduralist meanings should be generalizable outside of gameplay as making a claim about the human experience.

An example meaning derived from our exploration of *PAC-MAN* (1980) below:

- goal(increase(score)) ^ mechanic(3) ^ theme(3) & goal(survive) ^ mechanic(4) ^ mechanic(5) ^ mechanic(6a) ^ theme(1a) ^ theme(2) ^ theme(4) ^ aesthetic(1) → **meaning(1)**: Those on the back foot, pursuing necessary goals only to survive, can quickly become hyper-consumers themselves when placed in a system of unbounded resource reward.

I admit I played a bit of a mean trick, working toward "evidencing" one of the "poor" readings of a game that the Proceduralist authors cite as an inciting motivation to formalize their model. My point in doing so was not necessarily to vindicate Steven Poole's original reading; it was only to demonstrate that the model, though structured in an equation-like manner, is surprisingly flexible, celebrating the subjectivity of its multiple readings, even permitting a type of reading that we *know* its authors would find unsatisfying. Rather than a framework that enshrines and embeds a particular personal "taste" within its systemic structure, the Proceduralist model can be used to explore and argue a great variety and diversity of concepts, providing structure for arguing points rather than narrowing the conversational field to only allow positions that its authors may find agreeable from the outset. Reasonable arguments can be made *against* the above *PAC-MAN* (1980) reading (I, for one, would find that particular message more compellingly conveyed in a system in which Pac-Man and the ghosts were competing for resources, providing a Tragedy of the Commons allegory); the Proceduralist framework has provided a structure by which it *can* be argued (for and against) and met with alternative readings in a consistent form. Providing the structure for positing artistic arguments is more valuable than providing an equation for finding "correct" answers.

LUDIC FRAMEWORK

The most recently developed framework I wish to introduce is still in active development by French scholar Frédéric Seraphine. The Ludic framework is an ontology of video game interactivity. Seraphine identifies *ludics* as the most basic units of interactivity, organizing and categorizing them in a structure adapted from Peircean semiotics (Seraphine, 2016a). Ludics are smaller, more molecular units than the mechanics encountered in MDA and even smaller than *rules* in many cases, often constituting individual actions independent of their reactions.

The ludic model positions the computer and virtual actors (such as NPCs) to be reactive agents within the system of gameplay, observing and reacting to the player, just like the player observes and reacts to the game's systems. This is not to anthropomorphize non-conscious elements of the gameplay system, only to structure a logic of symmetrical interaction from which a structural grammar can be built. Anthropomorphized language is employed in ludic descriptions (for instance, one might remark about how the simulation changes behavior when it "interprets" player behavior as friendly or aggressive), but this is intended only as shorthand for the interpretive capabilities of the developers anticipating and designing contingencies for specific types of afforded player behaviors pre-hoc. A computer's capacity to "react" and "interpret" is only an extension of the programmed parameters that enact the intended situational logics of their creators.[4] Framing gameplay as a "conversation" between players and developers (as discussed in Chapter 3), the Ludics framework provides a vocabulary to chart the "conversational" exchanges.

Whereas MDA positions the bidirectionality of its model between the player (experiencing the aesthetics and working inwards to deduce mechanics) and the developer (programming mechanics in an effort to elicit particular aesthetics), the Ludic framework plots the relationships between players and the simulation itself. As the player interacts with the game, so too does the game interact with the player. Every term describing an interaction performed by the player upon the game world has an equal opposite in the interactions the game world can perform toward the game player (through the avatar).

Whereas the Proceduralist framework contends with the elements of culture that *produce* meaning in game dynamics, the Ludic Framework instead creates a grammar by which systemic interactions can be classified and taxonomized. In that sense, it may not be wholly *complete* as an analytical lens, but it allows us to talk about intre-system interactions with remarkable clarity and precision.

Peircean Semiotics

Seraphine's framework is a direct adaptation of Charles Sanders Peirce's semiotics. Implicit to Seraphine's work is the assumption that actions (and interactions) within video game worlds serve not only the practical purpose of operational manipulation within the simulation but are also communicative. The player, using the limited affordances of the controller inputs, signals intent to the computer, and the computer signals changes in game state to the player. To present the Ludics structure, we must first review Peirce's theory of signs.

Peirce identifies three trichotomies of signs: monadic "signs" (essence of the object, at a primary level Peirce calls *firstness*), dyadic signs (objects that stand for something else, at a representative level he calls *secondness*), and signs/transformations of signs of the interpretant (at a level he calls *thirdness*). In essence, *firstness* is the truth or concept that a transmitter wishes to communicate; *secondness* is the abstracted language and conventions that the transmitter uses in order to transform the truth or concept into an idea that can be verbally communicated; and *thirdness* is the process by which the receiver understands and interprets the message, de-abstracting the message into a concept that may or may not match that which was intended to be communicated in the first place.

Seraphine cites Douglas R. Anderson's interpretation of Peirce pertaining to the creation and interpretation of art:

> the goal of creativity is to make monadic concepts belonging to the firstness (such as emotions) intelligible through reasoning at the level of the thirdness. To simplify, the goal of an artist or a designer is to lead a user to a certain monadic emotional state. The artist will do so by creating semiotic systems that will guide the user to this emotional state.
>
> *(Seraphine, 2016a)*

Peirce's Theory of Signs (as interpreted and outlined in Seraphine [2016a] and Seraphine [2016b])

- **Firstness**: The essence of the object. Evidence or attributes rather than *signs*, as these essences precede their communicative functions. Monadic: "referring" only to itself.
  - **Qualisign**: A quality or property of something that can serve as a sign or an element of one. For example, the *greenness* of a bush is an abstract quality before it is applied to the "bush" object. Green itself can be a property of many things or may refer only to itself (*greenness* as a concept). It comes to refer to something *specific* in combination with other qualities.
  - **Sinsign**: An object or idea as defined by its sum of qualities (qualisigns). The bush from which greenness was abstracted above is

an existent object with properties beyond and including its greenness. It is the combination of these qualities that makes it identifiable as a bush.

- **Legisign**: Conventions or laws that structure the logic of sign/message formation. For example, musical notations and Morse code point to particular meanings by way of conventions.

- **Secondness**: A sign that refers to (signifies) something else. Dyadic: positioned in reference to an object or concept.
  - **Icon**: An abstracted sign that signifies a sinsign by the nature of shared qualisigns. A restroom sign denotes the concept of "woman" through its silhouette (understood in context of a conventional dress legisign). This icon shares little beyond its heavily abstracted silhouette with real women. Even less abstract representations care icons: a realistic wax sculpture of Nicolas Cage is an *icon* of Nicolas Cage by the nature of a great deal of similarities it shares with the real actor, but it is *not* actually Cage, evidenced by the greater number of qualitative dissimilarities (not made of actual organic material, not alive, did not grow up in Long Beach, California, did not star in *Vampire's Kiss* [Bierman, 1989]…).
  - **Index**: Denotes an object by immediate relation. The reflection of an object in a mirror is both an icon of that object (it shares some qualities with its object, such as silhouette and visual appearance, while lacking others, such as tactile texture and mass) and an index (as it indicates the immediate presence of the object in the space reflected).
  - **Symbol**: Denotes an object or idea through legisign. A red traffic light communicates "stop" by cultural convention.

- **Thirdness**: The sign, received and interpreted by a receiver. Triadic: involving an object/concept, sign/message, and interpretant.
  - **Rheme**: Possible interpretations of a sign, not yet selected or made more or less likely by context. The utterance "for/fore/four" as a decontextualized sound has a great number of meanings; the evidence of context will make clear which of its possible meanings is an appropriate interpretation.
  - **Dicisign**: A propositional sign that posits a concept that may be deemed true or false. A weather report is a dicisign; it points beyond itself and makes an assertion that can be independently verified.
  - **Argument**: An argument combines other forms of signs to provide reasoning or evidence for an assertion. It makes a logical case for a statement.

Actum, Tactum, and Factum

Frédéric Seraphine (2016b) applies the above Peircean model to the signs involved in video game interactions. Each Peircean sign is given an indication of origin/directionality by the terms *actum*, *tactum*, and *factum*. Because of the vicariousness of avatar-mediated actions within the simulation, Peirce's monadic/dyadic structure does not translate to this model, since the ideas of the player are expressed through the avatar, including by nature *at least* two "parties" in sign expression.

Actum *(reaction)* refers to an action directed by player input. Direct control of an avatar is the most obvious example; the player leverages a mechanical affordance of the controller to directly effect a specific result within the simulation.

Tactum *(interaction)* is an interaction between the player-avatar and in-game objects. If we consider the avatar as a direct (though mediated) vector of player expression, the avatar → game world (and game world → avatar) interactions are not solely digital actions but rather interactions of the without and within. For example, when Pac-Man eats a ghost, this is an interaction between the player-controlled vector of expression (the avatar; Pac-Man) and an object of the simulation (the ghost); thus, a tactum. Similarly, the ghost attacking Pac-Man is the interaction of a game object acting upon the player vector.

Factum *(fact)* refers to the action of objects within the simulation. NPC actions or the spontaneous occurrences of simulated physics systems (such as weather occurrences) are prime examples.

Factums may or may not affect the avatar *indirectly* (territorial clashes between the enormous monsters in the *Monster Hunter* (2004-present) series are often dangerous to bystander avatars, even if they are not *directly* involved in the fight), and may or may not have been indirectly caused by avatar action (in the aforementioned example, a monster may have been "lured" into another's territory in pursuit of the player, but the fight between the monsters is an interaction of their individual AI systems). Considering actums as vectors of player expression, factums are the opposite: vectors of simulation "choices" (including diegetic NPCs, non-diegetic systemic elements, and even other human players opposite one's own perspective).

Actums and factums are directional opposites. In multiplayer games, one player's actums (choices expressed through avatar action within the simulation) are witnessed as another player's factums (objective occurrences operating separate from the player's own actions). Actum/factum is not a division of human/machine; it is merely a directional designation of transmission/reception from the privileged perspective of the interpreter-player.

Actums, tactums, and factums are presented alongside (as directional modifiers to) Peirce's categories of signs. Every gamic action can be conceived of in some combination of Seraphenic prefix and Peircean category. Presented below are non-exhaustive examples of Seraphine's terms presented in **bold** alongside Peirce's referents in *italics*, summarizing an example of a "jump" action presented in Seraphine (2016a).

- **Actum**-*qualisign*: The possibility of a jump controlled by the player. The monadic idea of an avatar's jump. Purely abstract; height nor direction are specified.
- **Actum**-sinsign: An executed jump with a given distance, direction, and height.
- **Tactum**-legisign: A rule or convention associated with the concept of jumping.

OTHER USEFUL RESOURCES

While the above represent the most significant influences on the model I will develop in the next few chapters, I would like to call out a few other works that I found very helpful. I highly recommend the below-referenced texts if you have a greater interest in exploring this subject matter.

Curating Simulated Storyworlds, a 2018 dissertation by James Ryan. Ryan studied at UC Santa Cruz, where Michael Mateas and Noah Wardrip-Fruin work (both of whom served on Ryan's dissertation board) and Mike Treanor studied—all of whom have been cited in the Proceduralism section previously. Ryan, adapting Hayden White's *Metahistory* (1973), puts forward a theory of narrativization of gameplay, arguing that meaning-making is an act of curation. Ryan presents a useful insight that games are experienced like non-fiction rather than fiction—the emergent events that occur do so as a result of logical operations performing for and with the player. That which the player witnesses is unlikely to play out exactly the same for anyone else. Gameplay is akin to lived experience, and as Hayden White (1973) says, "the difference between 'history' and 'fiction' resides in the fact that the historian 'finds' his stories, whereas the fiction writer 'invents' his" (p. 6). Ryan proposes a framework by which meaning is curated from gameplay experience and hypothesizes about ways in which a similar curationist approach could be implemented into game systems themselves.

Games without Frontiers, a 2008 dissertation by Aki Järvinen. Järvinen's dissertation, written for Tampere University in Finland, asserts that "any known game in the universe can be deconstructed into parts with a single, unified set of theoretical concepts" (p. 29). Järvinen takes a thoughtful approach to breaking down the elements that comprise gameplay and noting how they interface with one another. Using Proceduralism as a starting point, he details more granular relationships without overburdening the model with complexity. He produces a very successful systemic model that traces the transfer of influence and information in the production of gameplay. His dissertation is billed as "applied ludology" and is written to be of equal use to game players and developers.

Introduction to Game Analysis by Clara Fernández-Vara (2014). I only discovered this book late in the process of writing my own, so I was unfortunately not able to consider her framings in the construction of my own text, but I was pleased to find significant areas of agreement between our models of meaning-making. Fernández-Vara gives a very thorough breakdown of the building blocks of meaning in video games, starting from context to the properties of the game itself to the formal elements of its design. Her design is very approachable for game players of all levels of experience.

Game Feel: A Game Designer's Guide to Virtual Sensation by Steve Swink (2009). Though aimed at developers more than players, Swink's book puts forward a well-researched, phenomenologically grounded model of the system of gameplay. He correctly places computers, players, and context in the model of gameplay construction and gives very detailed examples of how elements across these categories interface with one another. Like any system, all elements are in relationship, and Swink is perhaps the most thorough in exploring these complexities.

Labanotation by Ann Hutchinson Guest (2005). I am interested in future research based on the movement notation system developed by Rudolf von Laban, an Austro-Hungarian dancer and choreographer who created a system for inscribing human movement. Laban Movement Analysis recognizes and measures aspects of Body, Effort, Shape, and Space in movements (particularly within dance), and Labanotation is a notation system that can record these qualities in a manner that reads like sheet music. In video game studies, very little is written about the dynamic degrees of physical effort of different types of controller inputs or how players vicariously experience the movement of the avatar within the virtual realm. A thoughtful gameplay effort and movement notation system—plotted against axes of time or space, depending on genre—could give us a better framework for understanding the experience of virtual play, and I argue that Laban's studies are a great place to start in that direction.

NOTES

1 *Preconditions* are structural elements of the gameplay system with which the rules necessarily interact but are not decided upon or specifically designed during development. Gravity is a precondition for the game of Basketball, and a great many of the game's rules would no longer function if gravity were not present. The rules of Basketball do not specify that the game must be played in a gravity-rich environment, but the interaction of the chosen rules with the unchosen *precondition* of gravity creates the exciting, emergent possibilities of Basketball.

In video games, the limits of the operating computer hardware or elements of the player's physical interaction with the controller are preconditions. For example, vertically-oriented spaceship shmup *Space Invaders* (1978) famously increases in pace as enemies are destroyed, making the final few invaders difficult to shoot and increasing the dramatic tension of each level as it approaches its conclusion. This was not originally programmed purposefully, though. Rather, the program featured more "sprites" (game world objects) than early computers could efficiently track and draw, causing it to run slower than intended. As enemies were destroyed (and sprites cleared), it freed up some of that encumbered processing power, causing the game to run progressively faster. The game speed modification was not a *rule*, defined in code as such, it was an emergent interaction of the game's rules with an existent precondition (at least in the earliest version of the game; it has since become a core part of *Space Invaders* play on all subsequent versions, artificially replicated on more powerful hardware).

2 This is not to say that aggravation and anxiety are *always* undesired emotional responses. The dramatic tension of many genres is built on the back of the skillful modulation of anxiety.

3 There has been some criticism of this model for lack of adherence to its own "emotional" framing of aesthetics. Frédéric Seraphine (2016a) argues that some of the MDA framework's aesthetics, including challenge and fantasy, are *not* primary aesthetics but are rather higher dynamics that enact primary aesthetics. "Challenge could make us feel frustrated, proud, or entertained".

4 However, while this bidirectional model positions both human and computer as intelligent agents only in abstract as a lens to frame its conversational metaphor, Seraphine considers that, with increases in the complexity and capabilities of artificial intelligence (AI) and quantum computing, it is not unreasonable to consider a future in which the computer *can* act as an interpretive agent (Seraphine, 2016a).

REFERENCES

Barthes, R. (1972). *Mythologies* (A. Lavers, Ed. & Trans.). Farrar, Straus and Giroux. (Original work published 1957)

Bierman, R. (Director). (1989). *Vampire's kiss* [Film]. Hemdale Film Corporation.

Bogost, I. (2007). *Persuasive games: The expressive power of videogames*. The MIT Press.

Bogost, I. (2009). *Persuasive games: The proceduralist style*. Game Developer. https://www.gamedeveloper.com/design/persuasive-games-the-proceduralist-style

Cantwell Smith, B. (2010). *Age of significance*. Self-published.

Csíkszentmihályi, M. (1975). *Beyond boredom and anxiety: Experiencing flow in work and play*. Jossey-Bass.

Fernández-Vara, C. (2014). *Introduction to game analysis*. Routledge. doi:10.4324/9781003355779

Hunicke, R., LeBlanc, M., & Zubek, R. (2004). MDA: A formal approach to game design and game research. *Proceedings of the AAAI Workshop on Challenges in Game AI, 4*(1).

Hutchinson Guest, A. (2005). *Labanotation: The system of analyzing and recording movement*. Routledge.

Järvinen, A. (2008). *Games without frontiers*. Tampere University Press.

Juul, J. (2005). *Half-real: Video games between real rules and fictional worlds*. The MIT Press.

Lantz, F. (2023). *The beauty of games*. The MIT Press.

Murray, J. H. (1997). *Hamlet on the holodeck: The future of narrative in cyberspace*. The MIT Press.

Murray, J. H. (2012). *Inventing the medium: Principles of interaction design as cultural practice*. The MIT Press.

Nguyen, C. T. (2020). *Games: Agency as art*. Oxford University Press.

Ryan, J. (2018). *Curating simulated storyworlds* [Doctoral dissertation, UC Santa Cruz]. UC Santa Cruz Electronic Theses and Dissertations. https://escholarship.org/uc/item/1340j5h2#main

Seraphine, F. (2016a). The ludic framework. *Digital Game Research Association Japan Proceedings of the Annual Conference*. Shibaura Institute of Technology.

Seraphine, F. (2016b). *Ludophrases*. Self-published. doi:10.13140/RG.2.2.34313.85603/2

Shklovsky, V. (2015). Art, as device (A. Berlina, Ed. & Trans.). *Poetics Today, 36*(3). (Original work published 1919). doi:10.1215/03335372-3160709

Sicart, M. (2011). Against procedurality. *Game Studies, 11*(3).

Sicart, M. (2012). Digital games as ethical technologies. In J. R. Sageng, H. J. Fossheim, & T. M. Larsen (Eds.), *The philosophy of computer games* (pp. 101–124). Springer.

Sicart, M. (2013). *Beyond choices: The design of ethical gameplay*. The MIT Press.

Sinnerbrink, R. (2012). Stimmung: Exploring the aesthetics of mood. *Screen, 53*(2), 148–163. doi:10.1093/screen/hjs007

Swink, S. (2009). *Game feel: A game designer's guide to virtual sensation*. Morgan Kaufmann Publishers.

Treanor, M. & Mateas, M. (2011). An account of proceduralist meaning. *Proceedings of DiGRA 2011 Conference: Think Design Play*.

Treanor, M., Schweizer, B., Bogost, I., & Mateas, M. (2010). Proceduralist readings: How to find meaning in games with graphical logics. *FDG '11: Proceedings of the 6th International Conference on Foundations of Digital Games*, New York. doi:10.1145/2159365.2159381

Wadeson, H. (1987). *Art psychotherapy*. John Wiley & Sons, Inc.

Wardrip-Fruin, N. (2020). *How Pac-Man eats*. The MIT Press.

White, H. (1973). *Metahistory: The historical imagination in nineteenth-century Europe*. Johns Hopkins University Press.

Zhou, H., Gonzalez, K., Altice, N., Wardrip-Fruin, N., & Forbes, A. G. (2022). On the maintenance of meaning: A Deleuziana view on proceduralism. *Proceedings of DiGRA 2022*, Krakow.

CHAPTER 6

Layered Literacy, Part 1

Diegesis, Mimesis, and Methexis

THE MODELS OF SENSE-MAKING and meaning-making shared in the previous chapter involve movement through multiple levels or types of expression. The MDA model frames its mechanics and dynamics in terms of systemic operation but resolves with aesthetics, a measure of emotional appeal that the player experiences. The Proceduralist model frames aesthetics as an intersection between the non-semiotic elements of procedural operation and "theme", a layer of cultural, semiotic context. That model resolves into meaning primarily framed as procedural rhetorics; arguments about the behavior of systems generalizable outside of the simulated space. The Ludic model downplays systemic interrelation for the tracing of ideas throughout the levels of gameplay, framing each step as primarily communicative and lessening a traditional mechanical focus.

The model that I will introduce in this chapter aims to maintain the heterogeneity between the layers of ludic expression. Rather than translating mechanics into aesthetics, I opt for a framing that maintains an active focus on three tasks (or positions) of player involvement simultaneously and perpetually. To varying degrees throughout the play experience, the player performs three roles: as an operator of discrete systems, as an actor in a directed narrative, and as immersed being in fantasy world.

These postures of play map cleanly onto two narrative perspectives used commonly throughout the history of narrative study: diegesis and mimesis; and the third player position, that of the player as a systemic operator, necessitates a new narrative perspective to compliment the others: methexis.

Before outlining the model of video game literacy at the heart of this exploration, it is important to establish the framing of these core terms, as the model will be presented in terms of how these positions interrelate.

GENERATIVE FICTION

The exploration of any representational text is rooted in its ability to invoke a generative fiction, a "world" separate from the audience's own in which the established fiction independently "exists" (not in an ontologically "true" manner, but only in as much as its formic constitution establishes a set of "rules" and suppositions that generate "truth", or more accurately "fiction", in a manner that bounds and guides the viewer beyond her imaginative whims). That is to say, a painting of a ship in a storm invites the viewer into a generative, imagined "reality" in which the viewer witnesses that dramatic sight. It generates truths beyond what the form can portray (for example, we can presume that the waves are in violent motion despite a still painting being unable to depict such motion) and implies further indeterminant truths, which may generate equally valid but mutually exclusive imagined realities (for example, the ship painting may imply an unseen frightened crew aboard, desperately fighting for their lives against the elements. Equally, one could imagine the possibility that the crew is unpainted because the ship is empty, pulled out to sea from the docks

DOI: 10.1201/9781003530961-6

by the violent storm, or floating unmanned after the crew met a mysterious fate on the seas). The representational art, by nature, invokes some kind of fiction beyond the literal truth of its material substance. If someone's only takeaway from viewing that painting is "there are colorful oils atop that canvas", they have not fundamentally engaged with the artistic product.

This generative, representational engagement not only invites viewers into the "world" of the art, it also reaches into our own world. For example, a statue of someone riding a horse not only draws viewers into its fiction ("who is she, and where is she riding?") but also generates fiction in its real-world context (the fact that the statue is positioned in a particular space implies that the rider is fictionally in that space in a manner perhaps not literal within the fiction but important to the formation of the generative fiction).

This conceptualization of representational art, as outlined by Kendall L. Walton in his 1990 book *Mimesis as Make-Believe*, is fundamentally interactive; it requires active, imaginative generation by the viewer, even in engaging with static art forms that we would deem "non-interactive" (contrasted against the reactive, procedural "interactivity" of video games). In fact, Walton frames engagement with all representational art as imaginative play. Representational art requires the active involvement of viewers to imagine fuller fictions than it can depict on its own. In this process-based representation of art, one could argue that the interactivity of video games and the interactivity of generative mimesis is a difference of degree of complexity rather than a difference of type. Walton proposes a systemic framing complimentary to my own framing, even in the consideration of static artifacts.

In Walton's theory, this gamic fiction has an external grounding relative to both the work and to the viewer. Throughout his book, he uses the example of an imaginative game that might be played in the forest: players might agree that tree stumps represent bears in a game of make-believe. When encountering a tree stump, one should behave as one would if she had encountered a bear. The stumps are generative props in this game of make-believe. They generate fictional "truths" within the construct of the game, separate from the decisions and observations of the players. Reasonably, we could assume that a small stump represents a baby bear, while a very large stump represents an enormous and terrifying bear. Equally so, the fictional "truth" does not rely upon conscious interpretation. If a stump is hidden behind some bushes, unnoticed by the players, it is "true" within the fiction of the game that a bear hid in the bushes, quiet and unseen. It does not need to be noticed or acknowledged to become a prop in the game. If the players had noticed the stump on the return journey, they might remark "what a close call! It could have ambushed us earlier!". As such, we can observe that the fiction evoked by a game of make-believe is external to the conscious recognition of the viewer. We may view this gamic conceit as "a 'world' in which tree stumps are actually bears". This commonly used "world" framing establishes the gist of the exercise; in playing the game, the players enter into a set of diegetic conceits capable of generating truths independent of observation or participation. The players enact the fiction, but in establishing rules, they tacitly agree that elements of the fiction become "true" of the imagined "world" *before* they are enacted.

This "world" framing is comparable to cultural historian Johan Huizinga's magic circle, a conceptualization put forth in his 1938 book *Homo Ludens*. *Homo Ludens* (roughly, "man, the player") is an early sociological and philosophical exploration of play behaviors in humankind, previously referenced in this book while defining terms like "play" and "game". The magic circle, only briefly referenced in Huizinga's original text, refers to the concept of a social "space" in which gamic rules are adopted and normal rules of the real world are suspended. It is the social contract by which participants in imaginative games collaboratively maintain the shared fiction that bounds the game; what philosopher Bernard Suits (1978) would call the *lusory attitude*: the adoption of rules, conceits, and inefficiencies for the maintenance of the shared space of play (pp. 38, 39).

The social contract of the magic circle and the bounds of internal consistency within fictive "worlds" protect continuity and order of experience within otherwise imaginary practices. This continuity and order allow these exercises to become legible narratives (discernible continuity is what separates progressive narratives from collections of unrelated moments) and are required for the expression of agential interaction (perceiving one's actions to be meaningful requires some degree of predictability of result, such that intentionality can be guided by hypotheses and discernibility of results; at least a partial understanding of how and why a chosen action led to the eventual outcome). As such, the legibility and interactivity of any representational art requires the maintenance of boundaries and expectations in a manner not dissimilar to our relationship with the real world; a probing and incomplete knowledge of what we can posture as "existing" externally to the observer.

This is not to say that the primary or "correct" manner to engage with art requires slavish adherence to the canon of a text, with further interpretations being a kind of ahistorical heresy; rather, it is the acknowledgment that for differential interpretations and conclusions to be reachable at all requires structural legibility grounded in the maintenance of load-bearing rules that define the shape and suppositions of a distinct fiction. Core to Walton's argument is the idea that engaging with representational art is a form of game. Just as the maintenance of the playability of a game of tag requires all players to honor a set of rules that give shape to the tag experience (one player deemed "it" must chase and tag all other players who wish to avoid being transferred the "it" role through touch. Once a player is tagged and the role is transferred, the previous "it" becomes one of the chasees and the new "it" adopts the objective of passing on the role to someone else), so too do different art forms suggest rules of engagement with their works in order to construct meaningful artistic encounters amongst audiences. Artworks generate fictions by means of their construction, context, or representational content, serving as props within the imaginative game of interpretation and meaning-making.

DIEGESIS AND MIMESIS

The above framing of collaboratively maintained games of social play draws out evidence of the simultaneous maintenance of multiple roles during play. In an imaginative game that evokes a shared fiction, such as children play-acting doctor and patient roles, the players adopt split perspectives: as the characters within the imagined fiction and as participants in a (semi-)structured game. To role-play as a doctor, one imaginatively projects into the headspace of a character for whom her occupation and identity are self-evident. She acts, reacts, and thinks *as* the doctor, as does the player portraying the patient. If the patient presents with an imagined broken leg, she has established a diegetic "truth" of the character and situation. The player then must choose to playact the role by utilizing the diegetic conceit as a structural rule, maintaining the fiction. Once the player decides, "my broken leg has turned into a mild cough", the diegetic fiction is broken.

These tasks are related but separate. To imagine a "world" of the scenario is to construct a fiction in which these "truths" are self-evident; the patient cannot but have a broken leg; it is inalienably true of her circumstance by the established "lore" of the fictional world. But to *enact* that world into literalized play, the player adopts the role of an actor who actively *chooses* to maintain the fiction, translated from the imagined diegesis into the performance of the game as "rules".

This is the first distinction I would like to establish: *diegesis* and *mimesis*. These are ancient words, established in Plato's *The Republic* (375 BCE), and have undergone a complicated series of reappropriations throughout the centuries of narrative and artistic discourse that have (unfortunately) diversified their meanings so broadly that some usages in different contexts can appear *contradictory*. This introduces some ambiguity that I must clarify before freely utilizing these terms.

Diegesis and mimesis describe manners by which narratives can be conveyed. By Plato's original definitions, *diegesis* ("speaking", sharing a root with "dialogue") refers to the act of narration, and *mimesis* ("imitation", sharing a root with "mimic") refers to the act of portraying or acting out. To (overly) simplify, classical diegetic narrative elements refer to narration, and classical mimetic narrative elements refer to portrayal. Later narratologists realigned these terms to roughly correspond with the narrative authoritativeness of storytelling techniques per medium, such that diegesis refers to the authoritative (or "independently 'true'") details of the world of a story. In the classical poetics of Plato's time, that which the poet decreed represented the truth of the story being told, whereas in cinema, for instance, we can imagine a "world" of the fiction internal to the story, in which the events of the narrative play out, like the historical events in our own world. This corresponds *closely* with what is shown (the actions of the actors—classical mimesis—typically represent the truth of the story world, as if we were observing the events first-hand). Though on-screen portrayal (mimesis) even supersedes diegetic truth in cases of subjective photography, which may portray hallucinations or literalize metaphorical elements in accordance with characters' thoughts and subjective experiences, not claiming those elements are "of the diegetic story world".

To use an example that illustrates the confusion these terms can create, Plato would define the narration of a story as its diegesis, but in modern, cinematic terms, a disembodied narrator would be considered a non-diegetic element of the narrative world, illustrated by the fact that the characters in the world of the story cannot hear or see the narrator. They do not exist on the same storytelling level.

A Crisis of Definition?

It is with this context that I must turn on the emergency sirens and get out in front of some very reasonable criticism that I can anticipate with the ways that I end up defining the terms in my own model. As I will detail in the coming paragraphs, I end up suggesting that video game players hold three separate perspectives when playing digital games: the diegetic perspective (concerned with the sense of embodied presence in the game world), the mimetic perspective (concerned with role-playing as a character in a determined narrative), and the methectic perspective (concerned with using the full affordances of the game as an artificial construct to overcome its challenges). Setting aside methexis for now, I would like to address my diegetic and mimetic perspectives.

Following on from the strictest interpretations of the classical definitions, one could reasonably argue that the naming of those perspectives should be *reversed*. Mimesis is to imitate reality (not necessarily the *reality* of the real world, but *a* reality of some *hypothetical* world). The sense of embodied presence as the avatar within the digital space typifies this kind of imitation. On the other hand, *diegesis*, aligned with classical narration, describes the way that the story is told—given or bestowed, even. One may reasonably argue that role-playing along a designated narrative path is an alignment with what we may consider video games' form of *narration*; the degree to which guided actions are deterministically *done* rather than *told*. To focus on advancing the story rather than the more toylike "free play" of embodied telepresence is to enact "narration". And conversely, free play of the avatar in space is a mimetic imitation of what it's like to move and act in our own world, of-kind.

I justify my chosen alignments of terms thusly. In modern study, the *diegesis* of a fiction is understood to represent the internal story world. Whether a bastardization of the original meaning or a logical (if complicated) throughline, this is the manner in which it is used and understood by the current generation. Aligning with the example of diegetic music, for example, being music played within the fiction, versus non-diegetic music being the soundtrack that would not be audible to the characters, I think it will be most intuitive for readers to imagine a diegetic perspective being one that privileges "being of and within the story world".

This leaves the question of mimesis, seemingly being used against purpose. In fact, an early and influential essay by Roger Giner-Sorolla (1996) labeled the obviousness of the guiding hand of the designer as constituting Crimes against *mimesis*, arguing that game design should portray naturalistic or internally consistent game worlds rather than those that are clearly built to house riddles and puzzles or push forward the development of the story.

My use of the term aligns with the theatrical tradition of mimetic performance. To perform a role is not to be convinced of its reality but to portray a fiction in such a way that the dissonance of the audience is resolved—they are made to suspend their disbelief. This is a *disciplined* portrayal in which consistency is favored over the improvisational whims of the actors. Thus, to play *mimetically* is to be presented with fiction and to acquiesce to our role in portraying it consistently, with motivations that align with the role being played. Conversely, to play *diegetically* is to prioritize the pleasures of *being* within the sub-reality without concern for the game's theatre-like portrayal of the behaviors and cadences of a consistent reality. In simpler terms, I believe that playing (diegetically) as a knight and experiencing the toylike pleasures of swinging a sword to cut down trees provides a less internally consistent imitation of the story world than the player who role-plays through the story and performs heroically and chivalrously. Considering that games are an art of *doing* rather than *beholding*, I believe this justifies my position on the diegetic/mimetic division, which, from the perspective of other arts, may appear misapplied.

METHEXIS

In the diegetic position, the player (through the avatar) acts within the game world as a member of its ontological "reality". In the mimetic position, the player role-plays to participate in a guided fiction, maintaining her identity as an ontological opposite to the story world. These two positions are insufficient for a comprehensive analysis of player actions and motivations, though.

While the player plays *within* and *to* the fiction, the player also balances a perspective separate from and superior to the fiction. If the mimetic position requires the player to recognize the artifice and acquiesce to her designed role within it, the player holds in balance a position that recognizes the artifice and rejects the call to role-play as a member of that world, instead manipulating the systems of the game in complete ontological detachment.

To describe this position, I use the word **methexis**, a term similarly borrowed from ancient Greek theatre. Translating to "participation", *methexis* typically describes audience involvement in the actions of drama and ritual at the theatre. The fourth wall is not maintained; the audience is invited to participate in the construction of the fiction through an implicit acknowledgment of its artificiality or, from another perspective, a reckoning with the *reality* of its mimetic rituals. Following the metaphor of the theatre, video game players are *both* performers (taking on roles to enact the fiction) *and* audience (the fiction is *being* enacted for the player's benefit and entertainment, after all).

The methectic position involves playing the game as a *software system* that is ultimately subservient to the machine operations of its code rather than its story logics or diegetic conceits.

Players have an intuitive knowledge that all operations within video games are the result of chains of computer logic and mathematical calculation. The player looks past the diegetic fiction and "plays the code". Not in a technical sense; the player does not typically *hack* the game, but the player seeks to discern the mathematical and logical principles that guide the diegetic action. For example, players have studied the behaviors of the four enemy ghosts in *PAC-MAN* (1980), discerning the exact algorithmic patterns that "motivate" their behaviors (one pursues Pac-Man's current position, one pursues a point four "tiles" [standardized units of space in the maze] in front of Pac-Man, etc.). Patient players find that even the most complex of problems is ultimately a puzzle with a logical solution if the game is treated as a software rather than as a fiction.

Methectic strategies may align well with mimetic performance. Understanding that the game world is an artificial space designed specifically to produce interesting player experiences, the player can confidently send the avatar down any path when given a choice without fearing irreparable harm or becoming irreversibly stuck (a concept I introduce as *instrumental providence* in Chapter 3). Other situations require a suspension of diegetic belief. Leveling up in RPGs is a highly artificial action; the player may defer treating the wounds of an ally on the verge of leveling up if she knows that a level-up is rewarded with the character's health being fully replenished. The methectic position may also be used *in opposition to* the intended design and diegetic/mimetic continuity, such as the deliberate use of glitches or exploits to gain an advantage (see Chapter 13). If a game's design is pointing a player to take an intended route through a space but the player knows that she can "glitch" through an unintended gap in the wall to bypass a large portion of the level, she has foregone the diegetic and mimetic strategies and has employed a methectic strategy instead.

Some games bury their methectic operation beneath layers of diegetic artifice. The life simulation series *The Sims* (2000–present) is ultimately guided by a series of mathematical logics and contingencies, but the behavioral possibilities of each Sim's artificial intelligence (AI) are so dense that they *appear* to act and think *more* like people than like algorithmically determinant machines (most of the time, anyway). Other games present their methexis on the surface. Strategy games like *Sid Meier's Civilization* (1991) encourages players to think of their cities and armies as units of abstract value that primarily serve practical purposes in a game of conquest rather than as population centers and people. They are like the pieces of a board game rather than fictional locations one is intended to imagine herself living in.

In fact, some games are *so* abstractly systemic that it can be quite challenging to determine the diegetic world that they posit. The non-digital board game Chess, for instance, insists upon its own interpretability through its pieces, evocatively named after the knights, bishops, and rooks of medieval feudal hierarchies, but its central metaphor is so ambiguous that no single interpretation is deemed authoritatively correct.

While the diegesis of a board game like Chess may be its mechanical metaphor, implying that non-digital games *without* metaphor (such as Jacks) *lack* a diegesis, the same is not necessarily true of video games. Almost all digital games have a diegesis, the representational level of a game's presentation. Even a game like digital Solitaire posits a diegetic spatial relationship between its elements; cards are stacked and moved around a surface that does not actually exist. The card game's translation into digital ephemerality is a layer of metaphor.[1] The only type of video game that has no diegetic conceit is the non-spatially oriented word or number puzzle, such as cryptogram-solving games or Wordle (2021). In these rare exception cases, the experience of playing these games digitally is remarkably similar to how they would be played with pen and paper or even mentally.

Again, my model of video game literacy posits that the player, at all times when playing most types of video games, simultaneously holds three framing positions: as a diegetic agent, as a mimetic performer, and as a methectic strategist. These correspond with three different types of play: to be *playful* (as a child would play with a toy or climb upon an inviting structure), to *play* a role (in a *play*; a dramatic performance), and to *play* (exploit) the systems ("she *played* me and took me for $100"). The primacy and proportion of attention given to each perspective varies between different types of games and moment to moment within a game. My model will interrogate, throughout the phenomenological sense-making process, the player's motivations and cognitive tasks from each of these perspectives and, in its meaning-making phase, will determine what kinds of meaning emerge from each play perspective.

EXCEPTIONAL DIEGESIS

The medium of video games presents some challenges to formalizing consistent diegetic boundaries. Author and professor Alexander R. Galloway (2006) defines gamic diegesis as "the game's total world of narrative action" (p. 7), though therein lies the factor of games that complicates the diegetic relationship: narrative action. The narrative actions within other mediums are internally executed and motivated; that is, the formic elements that constitute the narrative artifact compel all narrative actions. For example, the narrative actions that take place within a stage play are communicated (or inferred) wholly by the elements internal to the stage production (actors, sets, props). Non-diegetic elements support the construction of the story; in reality, the actors have memorized their dialogue from written scripts, but within the diegesis of the story, it is fictional (true of the story) that the characters speak spontaneously instead. Since narrative action in video games is compelled by both the machine and the player in collaboration, elements of questionable diegesis are introduced and sometimes integrated into the fictional world of the game. Just as an actor's lavalier microphone is considered non-diegetic to a stage play (it does not "exist" within the diegetic fiction), so too may be elements of the gamic experience used exclusively to amplify or communicate information to the player. There are many edge cases that present difficulties when drawing definitive lines between diegetic and non-diegetic elements.

As described in Chapter 4, in which we define the properties of the avatar within video games, several games use non-naturalistic graphical displays to visually represent senses that games would otherwise be unable to present to players. The *Tony Hawk's Pro Skater* series (1999–present) of extreme skateboarding games features a graphical overlay when the avatar engages in a balance-dependent task, such as a skateboard manual, grind, or lip trick. The player is tasked with keeping an arrow from reaching either terminus of a gauge representative of the avatar's balance; the avatar will fall ("bail", to use the skateboarding colloquialism) if either pole is reached. The graphical gauge, though non-naturalistic in its presentation, communicates proprioceptive information that would be available to the avatar skater's natural senses.

The Witcher 3: Wild Hunt (2015), which tells the story of a supernaturally skilled monster hunter, allows the player to shift into a mode of heightened senses, visually depicting monsters' scent trails that linger in the air (which Geralt would, in fiction, be able to perceive through his olfactory senses) and highlighting visual details that would be too subtle to notice on-screen but would be apparent to an experienced hunter, such as drops of blood on the ground or footprints necessary for tracking a wounded beast. In placing players (presumably not experienced hunters) into the role of a seasoned, supernatural monster hunter, the game crosses sensory boundaries (by translating olfactory information into visual cues) or heightens the presentation of visual detail in order to more closely align the player's experience of inhabiting the character with what it would actually be like to *be* that character, including the sensory experiences that games, in their limited means of communication, would be otherwise ill-equipped to represent.

Such elements of these games' user interfaces (UI) represent sensory information but (presumably) not in the manner that the characters would experience them. Speaking to him about these types of exception cases, Alexander R. Galloway told me that he considers these elements non-diegetic, comparing them to film scores, which is strictly considered non-diegetic in most cases yet can reflect and give insights into the emotions of characters. I agree in principle but offer additional nuances to consider; most importantly, there exists a difference in authoritative perspective between video games and film that makes this an imperfect analogy.

When watching a film, one takes the perspective of an observer witnessing a scene from afar. As Kendall L. Walton argues in *Mimesis as Make-Believe* (1990), representational arts prescribe *de se* imaginings. That is to say, "to imagine seeing a rhinoceros is to imagine *oneself* seeing a rhinoceros" (p. 31). More to the point, to participate in the fiction of a film (or painting, play, sculpture, etc.) is to imagine oneself observing the events depicted from a first-hand perspective, present to but separate from the depicted action. The film camera serves a point of view that is representative of a singular perspective position external to any of the depicted characters. As such, the types of sensory information to which we could expect access are largely accounted for through the depictive capabilities of the film: visual and auditory information.

The perspective positions of (most) video games differ. Rather than being external observers of characters and action as the audience is in the cinematic realm, players of avatar-based video games inhabit these character roles and perspectives directly. While visuals and sound provide all *expected* sensory information from the cinematic perspective, they are not sufficient for communicating all sensory information necessary to represent the experience of *physicalized presence* within the game world.

Proprioception, somatosensation, olfaction, and other related senses are expected in the diegetic experience in avatar projection. Visual elements like *Tony Hawk's Pro Skater*'s (1999) balance gauges or *The Witcher 3: Wild Hunt*'s (2015) scent representations fulfill these expected sensory roles, utilizing the limited representational vocabulary available to video games. While a non-diegetic score may communicate insights about the emotional states of characters in the film, this is extra information delivered from an omniscient perspective outside of the diegesis, beyond that which the detached perspective insinuated by the camera's perspective implies *should* be available. Conversely, non-naturalistic displays of diegetically *expected* information provide information analogous to the inhabited perspective within the fiction. The film score originates from outside of the fiction, while *Tony Hawk* balance gauges originate from within.

Perhaps the closest analog between these elements and cinematic counterparts is cinema's use of nonliteral, subjective imagery, such as character-grounded hallucinations (as seen in films like *A Beautiful Mind* [Howard, 2001], *Fight Club* [Fincher, 1999], or *Fear and Loathing in Las Vegas* [Gilliam, 1998]). In such cases, the film depicts literally that which a character experiences subjectively. These elements would still be considered non-diegetic (as they do not represent the *objective* reality of the story worlds), but they represent the experiential truth of the character (many a great ghost story, such as *The Innocents* [Clayton, 1961], trade *precisely* in the ambiguity between subjective and objective imagery).

This does not mean that every element that would be classified as non-diegetic in film necessarily becomes diegetic in video games. Musical accompaniment, for instance, can play a similar role in games as Galloway notes it does in cinema: giving insight into characters' emotional states. Even though players inhabit characters in avatar-based games and would expect access to their emotional states, this information is not, strictly speaking, *missing* in the same way that somatosensation is from audio/visual display. As players agentially motivate the actions of avatar characters, they act as the cognitive, motivational cores of these avatar beings. When a player solves a puzzle in a video game, this represents the avatar character achieving the insight diegetically.

During play, the player fulfills many of the roles of avatar interiority (though not all; for example, the computer assists with memory tasks, such that the avatar will address known characters by their correct names without requiring that the player also recalls each character name at all times). As such, the avatar character's diegetic emotional state is (ideally, in a well-told gamic story) represented by the player's emotional state. Thus, the musical accompaniment does not necessarily represent an internally motivated reflection of avatar emotions (as the emotional core of the avatar is instead situated within the player), rather, it serves as an externally motivated cue seeking to influence the player's emotional state toward the emotional state desired by the developers in accordance with the semiotic story being told.

This, as further discussed in Chapter 4, is a result of the dual nature (or "shared custody") of many video game avatars that serve separate (and often divergent) purposes in the semiotic and non-semiotic layers of game narrative. Within the semiotic narrative, the character may grieve the loss of her husband, while the player (representing the emotional truth of the avatar during gameplay) holds no special connection to the late husband and feels no such grief. Non-diegetic cues (such as music) may be used to persuade players' feelings to align with that of the avatar character's, from both diegetic and mimetic perspectives.

Ultimately, these elements of liminal, translative diegesis necessitate a more nuanced understanding of the diegesis of game fiction. Rather than rooting our understanding of fictional diegesis within the confines of traditional narrative structures like literature and cinema, in which mimetic stories are unilaterally told to an outside audience, it will be more fruitful to, instead, consider game diegesis in the context of immersive theatre or theme park story worlds. Theme parks and immersive theatre are multi-dimensional narrative spaces that differ from cinema and traditional theatre in their involvement of audience presence. While a painting or movie prescribes a point of view through which the fictional world can be imagined, that point of view is separate from diegetic presence, such that diegetic acknowledgment of that point of view (such as instances of "mugging to camera" in Bugs Bunny cartoons) is viewed as a break of convention, a shattering of the "fourth wall", and a sudden reminder of the artifice of the art, and an acknowledgement of the voyeuristic audience perspective. Conversely, theme parks are designed to facilitate immersive experiences for guests physically in attendance, mimetically participating in role-playing dramas. Thus, costumed characters may directly acknowledge and interact with guests, and guests may interact in allowed ways with the diegetic space.

That which is true of the theme park attendee's experience is true of the story crafted in that space. Since analogous direct presence within video game spaces is deferred to the liminal avatar figure (into whom the player projects and extends), it is necessary to extend affordances of presence in a manner that supersedes the naturalism of presentation. I call this diegetic extension **interdiegesis**, and it is the first of our diegetic positions I will detail below.

TYPES OF DIEGESIS

The last section detailed a subtype of diegesis employed commonly in video games, interdiegesis. **Interdiegesis** describes the elements and mechanisms of translation between the fictional game world of the simulation and the real world of the player that literalize as diegetic action. As described above, a common way in which interdiegetic details manifest is by depicting details necessary for avatar embodiment by translating unavailable sensory forms into forms that can be depicted by the simulation. The aforementioned balance meters from the *Tony Hawk's Pro Skater* series (1999–present) translate the character's proprioceptive sense into a form that the game can communicate back to the player: visuals. Another example common to first-person shooters is the display of a throbbing, red vignette when the avatar has been injured; some implementations even feature an indicator specifying the direction from which the pain had been experienced (so that we may identify from what direction the avatar had been shot). This is information that would be naturalistically available to someone in the simulated circumstance but requires reframing in order to demonstrate it through the video, audio, or haptic outputs of the computer.

We can also frame certain types of information moving from the external world *into* the simulation as being interdiegetic. Player inhabitation of the avatar role is a diegetic position that motivates diegetic action, but it would not be entirely fair to classify player psychology *holistically* as being diegetic. The adoption of the diegetic avatar role is balanced with the mimetic and methectic roles in parallel, and the motivated action of the avatar would not be fictionally understood as also comprising the mimetic and methectic knowledge of her own artificiality. Player psychology *cannot* be contextualized as being wholly *non-diegetic*, though, in the same way, we might say that the score of a film is non-diegetic. Player cognition and psychology animates and motivates the avatar, a fact that is abundantly evidenced during gameplay. If a player does not understand a puzzle, the avatar also will not solve that puzzle, diegetically, until the player has worked out the solution. The moment of player epiphany *is* the moment of avatar epiphany. Similarly, a player's emotional panic affects the performance of the avatar (translating to, perhaps, fumbled movements or impulsiveness in high-pressure situations) such that we can conclude that the emotional state of the player directly informs the emotional state of the avatar. In the symbiotic relationship described in Chapter 4, the avatar's ontological instrumentality and the player's motivational cognition both construct a collective, shared being.

As such, player psychology directly manifests as diegetic action but can be understood as undergoing translation of type and content, such that we may understand the motivating functions of player cognition as being constitutive of the avatar's being without also having to posit that every avatar I play, within the fiction, knows my home address and social security number. Just as the *Tony Hawk* balance meter presents diegetic information in a form it would not naturalistically appear, player cognition is translated *into* the diegesis in a form *it* would not naturalistically manifest.

This can be contrasted with **extradiegesis**, elements, and mechanisms that directly or indirectly affect diegetic action but which are *external* to the fictional game world. This is distinct from interdiegesis because extradiegetic elements are not understood to be existent or present, in whole or in part, to the fictional world (as player cognition is, because it constitutes the avatar's diegetic cognition). It is distinct from *non-diegetic* elements as well, though, because it still affects diegetic action, whereas non-diegetic elements remain comfortably separate from diegetic effect, reflective rather than active.

Glitches are prime examples of this form of diegesis. Glitches impact the diegetic behavior of the avatar but are not *communicative* of the fictional world. They are not (representationally) "recognized" by the fiction, as they are counter-intentional to the game's design. But they undeniably affect diegetic action in a manner more significant than that which we may cleanly classify as being non-diegetic. For example, impossible intersections between physics objects in 3D games is a commonly encountered glitch. Trying to resolve the physical impossibility of two objects occupying the same space causes erratic behavior, such as objects spontaneously flopping and bouncing around the space as the computer processes the impossible intersection as being a perpetual collision applied to both objects from multiple contradictory directions. The resulting chaos of physics interplay affects the diegetic world (as the impossible object interacts with other physics objects in its vicinity, knocking items off of shelves, and potentially even injuring the avatar or NPCs). It is true to say of this event that it undeniably *happened* within the enacted fiction but also that it is not *true* of the game world's designed operation. The glitch originated from *within* the game engine as a software instance but from *without* the fiction, yet its manifestation was *within* the fiction.

We may also consider the operation of the controller to be an extradiegetic element of play. As an object, it is not understood to "exist" within the fiction of the diegesis, but it is nevertheless a designed element of feedback that constructs the player-avatar-embodied telepresence. Not necessarily because it is the mechanism by which inputs are passed from the player to the simulation but because the controller's *resistance* manifests an element of the *effort* quality of embodied play. Some games use repeated, rapid tapping of buttons to effect exhaustion in players, mirroring a strenuous activity performed by the avatar. This is a designed element of the embodied experience of *being* the fictional avatar. Similarly, most thumbsticks, buttons, and triggers are designed to revert to their neutral positions once pressure is no longer applied to them; this means that, to a small degree, the controller pushes back on the player when the player operates the controller. This resistance, though perhaps incidental to the design of any *particular* game optimized to utilize prefabricated, standard controllers, is important to the sense of virtual embodiment holistically.

Examples of games that utilize *bespoke* controllers intended to evoke *particular* embodied experiences with their physicality demonstrate this principle most clearly. Consider the evocatively mimetic *Guitar Hero* (2005) and *Rock Band* (2007) instruments, the full-body "dance mats" of *Dance Dance Revolution* (1998), and the immersive, mechanical pedals, steering wheels, and gear shifts of many arcade racing cabinets.

Some elements of play can constitute either interdiegetic or extradiegetic actions. Social functions, such as voice chat, for instance, are often extradiegetic (the game engine serves as a medium for having casual conversations with friends, often unrelated to the activity, as one would have while fishing or eating together, originating from and concerning only the real world external to the simulation, though still diegetically *framed* as conversational interactions between agents within the virtual world). But there are other instances in which chat can be interdiegetic (trash-talking an opponent to provoke a diegetic reaction, strategically coordinating with teammates, and mimetic role-playing all translate to a direct diegetic effect). Playing with or against other human players involves different kinds of metagames than playing in games populated only with NPCs, implying a diegetic effect of sociality even when players *cannot* linguistically interact.

Contextually, transformations of time-flow or spatial representation common in games, such as the ability to pause action, can be seen as either interdiegetic or extradiegetic. The player's ability to pause gameplay at any time with a controller input (traditionally, the Start button) is an extradiegetic function. It is not recognized to actually *occur* within the fiction posited by the game world, but it is experienced by the player and, thus, affects the diegetic performance of the avatar, particularly in moments in which the paused game world is still explorable, such as games that include a "photo mode", in which the player may navigate the free-floating camera with assured safety to peek around corners and scout out upcoming dangers. Conversely, the stop-start time-flow cadence of turn-based battles common in RPGs can be justified as an interdiegetic element. We may say that these pauses represent moments of thought and preparation during battles that would be *diegetically* experienced as being instantaneous but require additional time affordance when translated to the video game format. For example, RPG battles typically involve menu navigation from which the player may choose any number of offensive, defensive, magical, or practical actions. The character, in a natural context, would be able to perform any of these actions instantly, but the fact that they must be selected from sometimes complicated menus introduces a level of friction to the process that is presumably not "true" of the metaphor of these mechanics. The time-flow *pauses* so that the player may cue a variety of actions as naturally as the character may diegetically perform them.

Further, we can consider elements external to the "space" of play that still inform diegetically fulfilled motivations and actions to be extradiegetic. Elements like OS-level achievements (such as Xbox Achievements or PlayStation Trophies) are extradiegetic. They react to and motivate diegetic action but are not posited as being present within the fiction of the game world. The rules and mechanics of the game, understood in the abstract, can also be called extradiegetic in that the player's knowledge of them motivates her methectic and mimetic actions, but it is not "true" of the fictional game world that the characters are actually governed by these "divinely ordained" behavioral parameters. The rules of the game originate from and exist abstractly *outside* of the game world, but they directly compel diegetic action within it.

Many of the categories of actions that I have classified into interdiegetic and extradiegetic categories would be called *non-diegetic operator acts* or *non-diegetic machine acts* in Galloway (2006). As discussed earlier in this chapter, I find Alexander Galloway's framing to be very useful and insightful, but based on the presuppositions of this literacy theory, I find it necessary to have additional degrees of nuance between the wholly diegetic and the wholly non-diegetic. It is hard to classify any action that results in a direct, story-level, diegetic effect as cleanly *non-diegetic*, so I think the intermediary degrees provide adequate context for framing a greater variety of gameplay actions. The four categories (diegetic, interdiegetic, extradiegetic, and non-diegetic) can be correlated with each of the three components of the player-computer-context system of gameplay. Illustrated below is a non-exhaustive list of the categories as they manifest in each of the systemic positions.

NOTE

1. Similarly, one could argue that non-digital Solitaire played with a physical deck of cards is, itself, a metaphor for the purest form of the game consisting only of its logical structures, played within the mind of the player without props. The cards serve the purpose of externalizing the task of remembering the game's current state. Were one able to randomize and remember the positions of each number, face, and suit without the physicalized mnemonics, one could play an entire game of Solitaire mentally. Thus, one could argue that playing cards are diegetic props.

REFERENCES

Clayton, J. (Director). (1961). *The innocents* [Film]. 20th Century Fox.

Fincher, D. (Director). (1999). *Fight club* [Film]. 20th Century Fox.

Galloway, A. R. (2006). *Gaming: Essays on algorithmic culture*. University of Minnesota Press.

Gilliam, T. (Director). (1998). *Fear and loathing in Las Vegas* [Film]. Universal Pictures.

Giner-Sorolla, R. (1996). *Crimes against mimesis*. Aetus Kane. https://web.archive.org/web/20050619081931/https://www.geocities.com/aetus_kane/writing/cam.html

Howard, R. (Director). (2001). *A beautiful mind* [Film]. Universal Pictures, DreamWorks Pictures.

Huizinga, J. (1938). *Homo ludens: A study of the play element in culture*. Beacon Press.

Plato (375 BCE). *The republic*.

Suits, B. (1978). *The grasshopper: Games, life and utopia*. Broadview Press.

Walton, K. L. (1990). *Mimesis as make-believe: On the foundations of the representational arts*. Harvard Press.

CHAPTER 7

Layered Literacy, Part 2

Sense-Making

WITH THE CONTEXT OF the previous chapters established, I can now build out my model for sense-making and meaning-making. It is divided as such, as I see these as different tasks with different objectives; each culminates in insights that are independently useful; thus, each can be performed independently, though each also feeds back into the other in an unusual recursiveness appropriate to a medium that eschews traditional narrative uni-linearity.

Though this model is developed specifically around the formic affordances of video games (particularly systemic structure and procedural emergence), the model can be utilized (with careful adaptations) to suit other procedural arts (such as immersive theatre, theme park interactive narrative, and formally indeterminant abstract art). As I argue in the introductory chapter, *all* art can be considered in a process-oriented manner in which meaning is *generated* through novel interpretation of the beholder rather than *extracted* from the work, surgically, so elements of this model and the type of interpretive practice that it endorses will be useful in the general study of the arts as well.

The objectives of this model set it apart from past models of meaning-making in games, like those outlined in the previous chapter. This model is, first and foremost, oriented to the perspective of the player (analogous to the *reader* of other literacy models) rather than the designer. As such, greater emphasis is given to the discernment (and generation) of multiple, personal meanings through literate interpretation rather than the inscription of *specific* meaning *into* the artifact.

This model is oriented toward procedural emergence, projective embodiment, the holistic system of player-computer context, and the triune simultaneity of play perspectives (in diegetic, mimetic, and methectic orientations). This model does not consolidate these perspectives but rather preserves their plurality, as I believe players hold all in their minds during play, and the interplay between these perspectives creates the unique and exciting dynamics of play.

This model is primarily developed to explore games in which players control a diegetic avatar. This model *also* suits non-avatar-based games, and I will specifically call out any adaptations of approach that must be made to suit this separate condition, but the language that I will use, primarily, in my description of the model assumes that there is an avatar involved.

This first section, labeled *sense-making*, can also be conceived of as the process of decoding—making sense of what happens in any moment of play. At its simplest, it involves forming an understanding of the cause-and-effect relationships of systemic interactions, from the basic relationship between inputs and on-screen action to the strategic implications of a game's most complex systemic procedurality. As defined above, I am interested in framing the process of sense-making and its eventual culmination from the player perspectives of diegesis, mimesis, and methexis, resolving in the triune positions of projective embodiment, narrative agency, and strategic initiative, respectively; the positions from which the proceeding meaning-making study will begin.

DOI: 10.1201/9781003530961-7

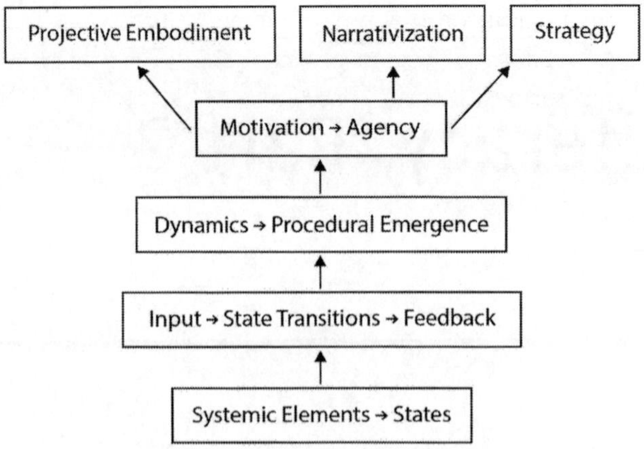

FIGURE 7.1 The sense-making chart that constitutes the lower (first) half of the total model being demonstrated in these chapters.

IDENTIFYING SYSTEMIC ELEMENTS → STATES

The first step of sense-making in novel video game experiences grounds the player in a systemic orientation. Games are *systems* of production and transformation. As Salen and Zimmerman define it in *Rules of Play* (2003), "a **system** is a set of things that affect one another within an environment to form a larger pattern that is different from any of the individual parts". In other words, a system is a collection of components that organize into a larger pattern from which unique behavior can be observed holistically. The individual components may or may not have knowledge or intention of contributing to the larger, patterned whole, but the components of the system have behavioral relationships between one another that increase or decrease holistic harmony.

For example, economies can be understood as systems. The actions of individual actors within the system (some of greater magnitude than others) contribute to patterns of supply and demand, inflation and recession, etc. that affect the balance and resources with which the other components of the system may act. Our bodies are also systems held in fragile harmony by the actions and interactions of different types of cells and microorganisms. They each perform singular roles that enable dependent components to perform *their* roles; from a distant enough perspective, the individual relationships between components disappear, and we instead see the holistic pattern: the human being. If the harmony between the systemic components is disrupted, say by illness or injury, not only are the immediate relationships between components affected, but we can witness changes to the behavior of the holistic system as well.

Systems require change or the possibility of change. Even when a system is held in stable harmony, it possesses the potential for disruption. Like a perfectly balanced stack of stones, the components are in harmony with one another, counterbalancing the forces that would lead to systemic chaos, but all of the systemic elements are still being acted upon by gravity, and all hold within them the potential energy that *would* drive the system toward chaos were it not for their current, supportive arrangements. Were one rock to be removed from the base of the pile, each of the inter-component relationships would change, and the system as a whole would either result in chaos (the at-once unleashing of all potential energies held within each component) or a new harmony (as the stones settle into a new harmonious arrangement).

Games, video and otherwise, are specifically *information systems*. Though energy *is* exchanged at multiple intersections of game systems (players exert force to press buttons or move game pieces, computers draw electricity, etc.), the organizing principles of game systems are primarily oriented around producing and transforming particular configurations of information. Rather than, say, the types of systems that are built to transform solar energy into usable electricity or wood pulp into paper, all relationships between game components are in service of producing configurations of information, made meaningful by their closeness to implicit or explicit goals.

The configuration of pieces on a Chessboard is just a concrete display/mnemonic representing informational, rule-based relationships in service of arbitrary goals. Even games in which primary mechanics are constructed around the exchange of kinetic energy, such as sumo wrestling, ultimately sublimate this energy exchange to an information-based goal. In the sumo wrestling example, this is the pursuit of an arbitrary goal: pushing the opponent over a boundary that separates an arbitrarily valorized victory from loss. The task is physical, but the configuration of systemic components is only meaningful and valorized in the context of the artificial rule that designates the agreed-upon victory condition.[1] What is valuable in a sumo wrestling match is not necessarily how much energy has been exchanged between the wrestlers but what their positions are relative to each other and relative to the boundaries of the allotted play space. One can abstractly consider the wrestlers to be like game tokens, like the pieces in Chess. Each possesses information meaningful to the holistic system (position) and properties of self that they seek to utilize to achieve rule-based goals.

Systemic Elements

Systems either self-organize or are externally organized around sets of rules that direct individually motivated agents into patterns observable at a larger scale. Urban traffic systems are intentionally organized to increase the productive flow of their systemic components (primarily: vehicles and pedestrians) and minimize chaotic disharmony through the implementation of mediating rules: affordances and restrictions of various components that seek to organize into the greatest holistic harmony. Some of these rules are conveyed informationally, using semiotic symbols (speed limit signs, stoplights, crosswalks…) to communicate the rules of operation to each systemic component. Other systemic capacities and limitations are held within the components themselves. Vehicles possess a physical property that prevents them from occupying the same space as other vehicles, limiting their movement affordances. In bumper-to-bumper traffic, a vehicle is prevented from accessing a lane without an open space, but the vehicle may communicate its intent to move into an occupied space with the use of the semiotic turn signal in hope that another agent within the system may open a space for it to move into.

Knowledge of a system requires knowledge of its elements. The elements of a system include its components, environment, information, and rules. Some elements, like the vehicles and pedestrians of an urban traffic system, are singularly distinguishable. A car, bus, or pedestrian is a singular component of the system.[2] Other elements, such as the general rules of right of way, are better conceived as "belonging to" the holistic system itself. Games are similar; a Chess piece is a singular component, but the victory condition that motivates play can be thought of as a property of the game state itself.

Since games are information systems, the primary functions of their elements are to hold, transform, and communicate information (about their individual states and relationships to other pieces and the rest of the system, holistically). The principle that guides our definition of game elements is isolating where information is held, how information moves between elements, and how information is transformed in that transfer. In board, card, and social games, information generally flows from the player into the game state or to another player, though there are also instances of information from the game state transferring to players (such as the value of each drawn card in Blackjack; the game state "knows" the value of all cards at all times, but the players each have imperfect information and make choices that either prove advantageous or disadvantageous when information is revealed). Games generally have perfect "knowledge" of systemic information *except* for player intent. When the player acts, that introduces new information into the game state that results in specific transformations of information.

As explained in Chapter 5, the Proceduralist model of game rhetoric discernment implores players to define the systemic elements of the simulated diegesis, particularly three types: *entities* ("any element that can be described by a game mechanic, is involved in the dynamics of the system, and can be themed to produce meaning"; Treanor et al., 2010), *meters* ("a special kind of entity which can appear on screen but may also exist behind the scenes. They can keep track of a player's progress or count the number of times an event has occurred. Meters track events in the system and have a descriptive word that precedes their number or graphical representation to note what they are keeping track of"; Treanor et al., 2010), and *goals*. This is a clean ontology, but it does not serve every needed purpose of the current model. This definitional structure does not distinguish "ownership" of each element; thus player entities, opponent entities, simulated "intelligent" entities, and even aspects of the game environment are not distinguished at this definitional level.

The Ludic Framework, also introduced in Chapter 5, does not explicate a method for defining game elements like the Proceduralists do, but Seraphine's model *does* separate its various types of interactions based on whether the interaction originated with player action (*actum*), game state action (*factum*), or mechanics-mediated, procedural interaction between simulated objects (*tactum*; Seraphine, 2016). This is a useful perspective realignment, but does not provide enough structure in conceptualizing the elements of the system beyond its active dynamics.

The most useful model for guiding our recognition and categorization of game elements comes from Aki Järvinen's dissertation study, *Games without Frontiers* (2008). In this study, all elements are classified as being either *elements-of-self* (that which "belongs to" the player or avatar), *elements-of-other* (that which "belongs to" other players), or *elements-of-system* (that which "belongs to" the ruleset or environment of the game itself). For the purpose of the present literacy model, I will implement a few small changes to Järvinen's categories. In Dr. Järvinen's model, *elements-of-other* specifically refer to elements that belong to other human players, with elements that belong to computer-controlled NPCs being classified as *elements-of-system*. I would like to reverse this decision, using *elements-of-other* to refer to elements that belong to any other *competing or cooperating agent*, human or not. The "competing or cooperating" caveat distinguishes NPCs with whom the player will have direct conflict or of-kind cooperation. This excludes NPCs that *truly* do not factor into the competitive or consequential balance of the gameplay, such as "decorative" townsfolk who may just speak a line or two of flavor text but have no other direct impact upon game dynamics. In such cases, they are mostly "unimportant" as systemic actors, instead serving an aesthetic purpose in aggregate, resources of the system, holistically.

One could argue that computer-controlled opponents do not have an individual stake in winning an encounter like a human opponent does, meaning that they *too* operate in aggregate in service to the holistic system (an especially convincing argument when considering situations in which such enemies are presented by the hundreds and are a threat only in culmination, such as the enemies in the zombie outbreak survival game *Dead Rising* [2006] or the armies slain *en masse* in *Dynasty Warriors 8* [2013]). But even human opponents are "designed" to operate in service of intended gameplay rhythms and actions through the specific affordances and restrictions given to their means of interaction. Just as computer-controlled opponents have limited action sets from which behaviors are chosen to create competitive challenges, other players are similarly constrained in service of the designed agencies the game elicits. From the perspective of the player, there is not a great degree of experiential difference between opponents controlled by humans and opponents controlled by sufficiently sophisticated algorithms. With regard to the types of actions such opponents can employ, it is useful to analyze them with similar interpretive schemas.

Secondly, rather than using *elements-of-system* to refer to elements that "belong to" the game in a general sense, I prefer *elements-of-game-state*. These elements include environments, physics systems, props, and NPCs that populate the game world that are not in possession of an opposing or allying agent. I dislike "system" in this context, since *all* of gameplay is framed as a system, including non-diegetic elements such as the player herself and the context of play. This leads to ambiguity when using a term as broad as "system" at this level.[3]

Ownership, as specified by the *-self*, *-other*, and *-game-state* above, is a property that can change during gameplay. When the player's avatar picks up an item, for instance, that item transitions from being a *component-of-game-state* to a *component-of-self*. Elements can also hold multiple degrees of ownership at once. In a team-based multiplayer game, your opponents and allies are both *others*, but your allies are closer to the *self* position than your opponents, since you can reliably count on your allies to serve as resources in strategy crafting as you work toward your *goals-of-self*. There are situations when it makes more sense to consider teammates for their separateness and individual agencies, and there are times in which it is useful to consider the entire team as collective resources, extending them into the goal-oriented "*-self*" perspective.

Following Järvinen's classification model, we can identify several types of elements:

Components include the tools for action-taking within the game, including "possessions, resources, and/or representatives (characters/pieces)" (Järvinen, 2008, p. 65). Components represent the actions that can be taken, "remember" the actions that are taken, and communicate information about the game state back and pertinent inter-component relationships to the player. In card games and board games, *components* would be the majority of the items that are not the board/play environment itself—cards, tokens, game pieces, etc. In video games, the avatar is the most important *component-of-self*, and we can *generally* consider components to be the literalized game elements that afford action potential (weapons, items, NPCs, opponents, vehicles, power-ups, cards, etc.). A component does not necessarily need to be diegetic (in non-avatar-based games, the cursor is a component-of-self as the player's locus of manipulation, even though it is not "embedded" into the game world environment in a manner of simulated physicality). Additionally, non-diegetic components of the holistic gameplay system affect the expression and operation of play. The player's controller is a *component-of-self*, as is her physical body, as the type of controller being used and her physical ability level constrain and change the manner of play and are relevant to the considerations of game design.

Environment includes the space allocated to play and the properties of that space. In Chess, the board is the *environment-of-game-state* on which the action takes place. In games that confer or exchange ownership over parts of the playfield, such as King of the Hill or Capture the Flag, we can consider the respective allocations to be *environment-of-self* or *environment-of-other*. There is sometimes overlap between environments and components. Consider an environmentally embedded "bounce pad" in the 3D platformer *Sonic Adventure* (1998) or a ramp in *Tony Hawk's Pro Skater* (1999); these objects give the avatars specific action affordances (jumping higher than would otherwise be possible), but they are static features of the environmental design. In such cases, it is worth calling out their split identities as both components and environmental features. We might consider the bounce pad or ramp *components-of-environment-of-game-state*. Or perhaps, in a shooter game, a static turret currently occupied by the player could be considered a *component-of-environment-of-self*. Environments need not simulate naturalistic space; *PAC-MAN*'s (1980) board is abstract and topologically minimalist while still presenting constraints that make for interesting spatial problem-solving opportunities. Even the rare non-spatially dependent games like Poker present *setups* that require relative arrangements of game components (cards in hand versus cards in the common area) to preserve its hidden information mechanic.

Ruleset includes the rules that afford and constrain game action. Rules are abstract elements of design. When a game developer designs a game in an abstract capacity, she designs rules that dictate what players can and cannot do and for what reasons. So long as games remain in an abstract form, rules are appropriate to guide their actions. Enacted, rules become matters of social convention, dictating the manner in which a game *ought* to be played. If I sneak some additional dollar notes from the bank in Monopoly or discreetly remove a Chess piece from the board, I have broken the rules. I have violated the social convention of sporting play.

While social play maintained by humans in social contracts with one another has a capacity for abstraction, computers do not. As such, the abstract rules must be translated into concrete computations called **mechanics**. Mechanics are not social contracts; they are impersonally and objectively enforced, in the same way that the laws of physics are enacted impersonally upon a game of football. Unlike board, card, and tabletop games, which require players or designated referees to hold rules in mind and enforce them throughout play, video game mechanics are enforced by the computer, so they do not need to be fully known and understood by players to affect the course of play (just as one does not have to understand gravity to be affected by it). For that reason, while game components typically *represent* rules in board, card, and tabletop games (the knight in Chess represents its abstract, L-shaped movement affordance), video game components and environments typically *embody* their mechanics (Järvinen, 2008, p. 66). For instance, the impassibility of a wall in the board game Clue is a property of the rules, enforced by players (whose game pieces are only allowed, through social contract, to enter and leave rooms through designated passageways), whereas the impassibility of a wall in *Super Mario 64* (1996) is a property of the wall itself. The player *discovers* the mechanics of the game through her embodied interaction with the components and environments of the game rather than being required to read and internalize the rules of the game ahead of time.

Theme, as an element of play, includes the semiotic details applied to the mechanics and elements of play that contextualize them in terms of something other than their literal, algorithmic operations (Järvinen, 2008, p. 77). Theme, an element that Järvinen's model shares with Proceduralism, serves the role of abetting understandability of systems through associative context. For instance, a moving object within a game may be *themed* to represent a car, which gives the player an idea of what to expect from that component's behavior. Rather than every game object being a gray box that must be studied to discover the rules and mechanics it embodies, theme allows game scenes to be *roughly* readable with appropriate context before interaction and "testing" begins. Of course, theme serves not only a role in decoding a scene but also a vital component of meaning-making. Since theme is a layer of aesthetic detail applied to the procedural, algorithmic operations of the simulation, theme *can* be replaced or repurposed. Theoretically, one could replace all of the textures and sound effects of *Super Mario 64* to present the *same gameplay action* in a bleak, futuristic landscape that would invoke a significantly different mood and experiential aesthetic. For that reason, when we reach the meaning-making portion of this literacy model, theme and operation are considered as co-supportive but separate elements. We will ask: how does the theme interact with the mechanics of play, and how might these same mechanics express if they were re-themed? Retheming is a common practice in modding/user-generated content (UGC) communities, and that subject will be explored in Chapter 13.

Interface includes the elements of interdiegetic and extradiegetic communication between player and game state. Interface is not a form of direct informational transference; it is translative (in both directions between player-compatible cognitive representation and virtually compatible computational operation) and an agent of storytelling. Steven Johnson comes to this conclusion in *Interface Culture* (1997), writing, "our interfaces are stories we tell ourselves to ward off senselessness". Highly influential book *Computers as Theatre* by Brenda Laurel (2014) suggests a theatrical metaphor for the role of the computer interface, suggesting that the human-computer interface threshold is primarily dramatic; the highly representative actions and outputs of engaging with a graphic interface to a purely data-driven information stream are one of dramatic mimesis.

Information is a crucial element created, transformed, and exchanged during play. Since games are information systems, a great portion of gameplay dynamics can be understood by following the transformation of information. As expressed earlier, information ownership is a key consideration. Imperfect information games like Poker built their entire dynamic tension around the fact that some information is known to the player (*information-of-self*), some information is known only to opponents (*information-of-others*), and some information is not known by any players (which we consider "known" by the mechanics-bound systems, as the *information-of-game-state*). In video games, information can be obscured (many RTS games feature a "fog of war" mechanic that hides activity outside of the immediate line of sight of the player's units) or even misleading—"information" does not mean *correct* information. For example, in the team-based, multiplayer first-person shooter *Team Fortress 2* (2007), the Spy class can disguise himself as a random member of the opposite team. To members of that team, *incorrect* information is being transmitted. The *information-of-self* and *information-of-others* refer to the same subject, but the content of that information is different for different observers.

These elements together comprise the totality of gameplay. Throughout the rest of the model, we will consider how these elements interact, transform, combine, and create to produce meaningful gameplay experiences. Crucially, as touched upon in the ruleset and mechanics section, these play elements have the capacity to embody properties and behaviors of their own. These properties and behaviors manifest as and transform the *states* of each element and of the gameplay system as a whole.

States

The sense-making model begins with a systemic orientation. Gameplay is the structured animation of a system inclusive of player, computer, and context. To study gameplay, one must expand her scope of analysis beyond the diegesis of the simulation. Though it is tempting to draw strict, ontological distinctions between the digital and the physical context of play, games *require* elements of the non-digital to enact. Without a player, a video game would be uniquely dormant in a manner not true of most other art forms. Though all *art* requires a conscious interpreter to transform the raw, representational *artifact* into a meaningful *artistic experience*, video games are amongst a minority in which the *artifact* (gameplay) does not exist until beheld. Whereas a painting exists as-is without an audience, a video game without a player is only a set of computational *instructions* until gameplay is produced during live enactment.

This is similar to live theatre from a certain perspective. A play's script is a set of instructions by which the artistic artifact (dramatic performance) is produced upon live enactment. Dramatic enactment requires only its actors, though. A performance can proceed without an audience. Video games complicate this relationship, though, as the player holds *three* roles appropriate to this particular metaphor: the player is *audience*, *actor*, and *co-playwright*. So a video game without a player is not like a dramatic performance without an audience; it is like a dramatic performance without audience, actor, or co-playwright. Fundamentally, the game's artistic form does not exist without player involvement. For that reason, to understand gameplay as an art form, we must understand gameplay as a system consisting of separate elements in dynamic relationships of tension and harmony with one another. It is a system that connects the diegetic, non-diegetic, and all layers in between.

Fundamentally, computers are state machines—systems that specialize in the transition between and memory of states. A **state** is the set of values or variables held by a system or a component within a system. Computers are such useful devices because they can hold an incredible magnitude of states in memory and storage at once (saving a document stores it for near-instant recall even years later), and the computer can perform many state transitions and transformations every second.

There are many ways of looking at states. We could snapshot a computer's state, examining in any moment each of the values held in memory and the transformations it is potentiated to enact upon them. We can also conceive of the dynamics of a system's state, noting whether the system as a whole is in a state of ambient harmony or activity and whether it is trending toward resolving or amplifying activity. For example, a snapshot of a broom's state might tell us that its body is angled at 65°, but a dynamics-oriented examination can tell us that the system is trending toward activity (falling over) as it is being acted upon by a greater system that contains it (the world's physics).

Games as State Machines

Games are fundamentally state-based systems as well, and most of the props involved in playing games serve the purpose of "remembering" or transforming the game state. A Chess board, for example, visualizes and "remembers" the game state (the position of each game piece in relation to one another). A board is not *necessary* to play Chess, as players can play chess by mail or even through unaided conversation by speaking their moves to one another, but the concreteness of the board relieves the need to keep the position of each piece in mind and resolves any disagreements about which piece is where, in the case that one or the other player forgets.

Similarly, a Nintendo GameCube is not *necessary* to play *Luigi's Mansion* (2001), should the player somehow internalize *all* of the variables, inputs, and state transformations that can possibly occur. With a deep enough knowledge of the game's code and enough time, the player *could* calculate every possible game state in every moment, but it would take *ages* to run the calculations and visualize the feedback that the computer is able to feed back to the player 30 times per second with even the rather meager power of the GameCube (and the player would miss out on the game's catchy music, besides).

While even the most fluent programmer and mathematician cannot hope to keep up with the speed or complexity of computers when it comes to state transformations, it still benefits us to think about game states, generally. Dynamically, is the game state in a state of harmony or chaos? Do the current positions of game pieces (objects) in relation to one another create or require opportunities for action? Are there particular game states that are desirable (high score) or undesirable (game over)? How are the components of the gameplay system relating to one another to produce or resolve change in the system holistically?

Crucially, because gameplay is a system that involves player, computer, and context, the game state includes not only values and variables within the simulation but those in the non-diegetic world of the player as well. The player herself contributes to the game state. Consider an extreme example: full-body rhythm game *Dance Dance Revolution* (1998) is comprised of fairly simple, discrete states *within* the simulation: the animation of directional arrows, a measure of how close to the rhythmically determined "activation zone" a directional input is triggered, and a score tally determined by said accuracy. The interesting variables in the game are primarily physical: the player's mental acuity (ability to "read" the demands of the song) and physical balance (ability to execute the dance-like patterns of leg movements necessary to step on the directional pads in time with the music). Thus, a player's balance in any given moment is a component of the dynamic game state.

Similarly, the player's mind is a part of the game state. Since the player is the motivating and activating force that drives avatar actions, her motivations, expectations, and understanding of the game world directly drive diegetic action. Should the player become distracted or intoxicated, the operation of the entire system will reflect this change, as its primary motivating force exhibits different behavioral patterns. Thus, we can consider cognitive measures throughout gameplay; a puzzle may be "solved" cognitively before the solution is enacted within the diegesis.

Finally, the context of play contributes to the game state. Environmental distractions alter the "positions" of other elements of the systems by pulling the attention of the player. Environmental factors, such as the glare of the sun against a screen, can interfere with the readability of crucial feedback, in essence severing or inhibiting the connection between the avatar being and the avatar's "brain" (the player). Other players may impose "house rules" or develop metagame around which the player must strategize, changing the shape of permissible or advisable strategies.

Continuous and Discrete States

As observed above, some states (such as the current score in a game of *PAC-MAN* [1980]) can be observed moment to moment, while others (such as the position of the waves on a simulated ocean) are better observed from a dynamic perspective, understood as the continuous action of a system in motion. Computers make stark, binary state changes (such as answering a math problem; after the process completes, the answer is drawn on-screen where there was not an answer before) and perpetual, subtle changes in state (the constantly refreshing position of the mouse cursor on-screen, for instance). As such, we can conceive of computers (and similar systems) transitioning between **discrete states** (those of recognizable value and practical purpose, such as answering a math problem) or maintaining **continuous** (or **perpetual**) **states.**

Continuous states may involve the maintenance of ongoing (and background) processes but do not *necessarily* change in a manner that represents a fundamental value change. This is a subjective categorization based on what the user's intentions and desires are when using the device, as the maintenance of background processes can still require a significant amount of systemic "effort" to achieve. Consider, for example, the harmony of the systems that are our bodies. Cells are constantly being replaced, energy metabolized, resources circulated... In most cases, cell replacement may be thought of as a continuous (or idle) state; a maintenance of systemic harmony. But in the case of a lesion healing over, the replacement of cells represents a value change of particular interest—not to mention that any of these continuous functions would *quickly become a subject of urgent attention* if they were to cease their perpetual, almost unnoticeable function.

Dynamic and Ambient States

The states of gameplay-involved systems (both the intre-simulational system and the relationships between player, computer, and context) can be organized into *dynamic* and *ambient* states. **Dynamic states** are those of activity. Even if the player *does not act* upon this state, change will inevitably transpire. In game, we can consider multiplayer matches of competitive action games like *VALORANT* (2020). Should the player put down the controller and step away during an active match, the avatar is likely to be killed quickly, and the team's score will be disadvantaged by the player's inactivity.

Conversely, **ambient states** (named for the *ambient act* described in Galloway [2006]) represent moments of systemic harmony. The system may still undergo *change* (such as the perpetual replacement of cells in the human body), but the system will not change the states of its most sensitive, "valuable" states, nor will it engage in feedback loops that *amplify* small changes into more titanic dynamics. Galloway gives the example of the RPG *Shenmue* (1999), which simulates (very impressively, for its time) the life and routines of the citizens of a small town in 1980s Yokosuka, Japan. Within the peaceful town, the game maintains its rhythms of urban life, creating a comfortable hum of activity that the player can passively observe for as long as she likes. "The game is slowly walking in place, shifting from side to side and back again to the center. It is running, playing itself, perhaps" (Galloway, 2006, p. 10). Most games begin in an ambient state, and it is typically regarded as best practice to resolve cutscenes or non-interactive story scenes into an ambient state instead of dropping players *immediately* into danger when they may have put their controllers down or relaxed their focused attention during the period of non-interactivity.

The player herself transfers between dynamic states and ambient states; physically (depending on the type of controller input that is necessary at any time), cognitively (responding to novelty vs. favoring automatic reactions; solving logic puzzles vs. engaging in action), and strategically (adjusting behavior vs. maintaining course of present technique; redefining micro/macro objectives vs. maintaining present motivations).

General States

Game states can be considered *generally* (the state of holistic systems of gameplay) or on an object-to-object basis. A **general state** describes the values and variables of a whole system, but it does not necessarily have to be the largest, most inclusive system. The interrelationships between player, computer, and context comprise a general game state, but similarly, so do the purely diegetic relationships between in-game objects. The score counter can be considered a general game state, as it is a reflection of the actions and relationships between game objects.

In fact, we can categorize the various types of general game states in terms of our levels of diegesis. The *diegetic general game state* includes the interrelationships between all diegetic game objects—their properties, propensities, positions, and paths. The *interdiegetic general game state* describes measures that condense or reveal information about diegetic action to the player, like the score total. The *extradiegetic general game state* includes the state of the elements that structure the play experience, such as the computer's operating system and the state of operation of the game engine. Similarly, we can consider the interrelationships between the player and diegetic elements to fit within this category, or even the communication between players in a multiplayer game. The *non-diegetic general game state* includes the interrelationships between objects in the context of play.

Object States

General game states can be contrasted with **object states**, which are the values, variables, and behaviors of individual objects within the system of gameplay. Every NPC, every enemy, and every physics object has an object state: a current position and behavior. The actions performed by each game object ladder up to affect the holistic game state and have the ability to alter the object states of other objects, for an object state is not only a reflection of the internal values of the individual object but also reflects the game state within them.

Consider again a game of Chess. When a piece places a king in "check", it is not only the active piece that has altered its object state (position on the board), but the king's object state has been altered as well ("in check") in a way that will affect and limit its movement affordances in the next turn (it *must* move out of check).

Object states, like general states, are often able to be divided into points of finer granularity. We can conceive of the object state of an individual enemy in a first-person shooter. The enemy possesses certain attributes (30 bullets with 6 bullets per clip before a reload is required; 100 points of health; 50 points of armor; movement speed of 10); however (depending on the way that the game is programmed), we may break that down. We can conceive of the enemy and the gun she is holding as separate objects. The *gun* possesses the ammo count, such that if the enemy is killed and drops the gun, that which remains can be picked up by the player (an object state that outlives the "enemy" object), or the enemy can pick up a different gun to change ammo-related metrics altogether. We might consider each body part of the enemy to possess individual object states (the enemy might possess 100 health points overall, but maybe each leg has 10 health points, allowing the careful marksman to limit the enemy's movement capacities without flipping the holistic alive/dead binary).

It is impossible for the general game state to change without affecting the object states of the objects within it. Similarly, all object state changes reflect upon the total game state for the system(s) they exist within. The relationships *between* object states *form* general states. Consider a game of catch. Every time the ball is thrown between players, several relationships are dynamically altered, and the states of each object within those relationships are changed. Spatial relationships between the ball and thrower, ball and receiver, ball and Earth, ball and gravitational pull, thrower and thrower's hand, thrower and receiver, etc. Behavioral relationships between thrower and receiver, ball and receiver, etc.

To use a video game example, consider the arrangement of enemy aliens in arcade shmup *Space Invaders* (1978). Each alien possesses describable object states (position, movement direction, velocity, alive/dead), but defeating each alien alters the general state of the "enemy horde" (how many aliens are left) and the general state of "score" (defeating an enemy adds to the score).

Behavior

As described above, object behaviors alter both object states and game states. As such, it is tempting to consider behavior as being primarily active manipulation—being for the purpose of altering states. But behavior can be, itself, a state of an object (or a general state, to an abstract degree). The ghosts in *PAC-MAN* (1980) transition from a *patrol* state to an *escape* state when Pac-Man collects a Power Pellet. To exhibit a general behavioral state, stealth games like *Metal Gear Solid* (1998) involve avoiding detection by groups of patrolling enemies. Once the avatar enters the sightline of an enemy, all enemies in the immediate area are alerted and change their behavioral pattern, actively pursuing the avatar instead of passively patrolling. After a set amount of time evading pursuit, the guards *collectively* return to their passive patrol behavior.

Behavioral state changes can occur rapidly—sometimes too fast to be considered *as* "states" in the moment. Fighting game players engage in several behavioral states based on the general state of the positioning of the two fighters on-screen. When both fighters are outside of the other's immediate attack range, players enter a behavioral phase called "footsies" within the fighting game community. This involves trying to sneak into attack range without drawing punishment from the other player or feigning movement to draw out disadvantageous behavior from the opponent. It's a behavioral state of mind games, daring each other to enter the zone in which the avatars are the most vulnerable. When the zone has been entered, players shift into a state of more aggressive and improvisational combat, sometimes seeking to "reset" to the footsies state, sometimes seeking to push the opponent into a more exploitable position, like against a wall.

Systemic Elements → States Summary

What to look for

- Throughout the process of gameplay analysis, consider each element in-game (avatars, NPCs, physics objects, items, rules, score counters, locations, etc.) as being independently able to possess its own state.

   - Consider whether each element of focus is in harmony (can maintain its present state) or disharmony (naturally trending toward state change).
   - Notice what prompts state changes for each element of focus.

- Consider also that the *game itself* exhibits a state and state-change behavior. This can be observed at multiple levels: as a virtual environment (diegesis), as a story with interpersonal or political tensions (mimesis), and as a battlefield of strategic considerations (methexis).
   - Notice whether the system as a whole exhibits an *ambient state* or *dynamic state* at any given moment and what prompts shifts between them.
- Finally, extend this state-focused approach outside of the software and consider player, computer, and context in relation with one another, each moving between states of their own and contributing to state change in the *total system.*
   - What resonances and tensions interplay *between* the levels of systems—diegetic and real? Does a particular diegetic action, item, or actor cause interesting state changes in the system grounded in reality? For instance, a particular weapon or activity might require simultaneous, unusual button combinations that necessitate holding the controller with a grip other than what is most common and comfortable, as can be observed in the play of *Monster Hunter* (2004–present) or *Mario Party* (1998–present) games.

Questions to ask

- What kinds of information are given to the player at the beginning of the play session? How is this information embodied or likely to be embodied in the elements of the game system?
- Based on the theming of the game system, what types of relationships can we infer or anticipate between elements? For example, game elements themed as wolves and sheep have relationships that we can anticipate before mechanics are tested.
   - What inferences about relationships, rules, and objectives can I infer from the game's genre presentation or relation to other media?
- Are elements of the system in ambient harmony with one another, or do they trend toward conflict and disharmony naturally, even separate from input?
- How is information "chunked" in the game system? Are spaces presented as discrete levels or continuous space? How do spaces relate to one another, in terms of literal configuration, metaphorical importance to the narrative, and strategic affordance?
- Are mechanics embodied in characters or held abstractly by the game state?
- Can the player infer a goal or objective prior to interaction? Is the player's attention or view naturally guided in a particular direction or toward an element prior to interaction?
   - What importance is this objective given? Is it important from a mechanical perspective or a narrative perspective?

Key terms

- A **state** is a snapshot of the current values of the variables that make up a game or an object within that game. Contains information about an element's relationship to all other elements in the system.
- **Rules** abstractly determine how objects ought to transition from one state to another. These are abstract concepts determined during the design process, which transform into *mechanics* when implemented into concrete, computational code.
- **Mechanics** are computational parameters that concretely (and approximately) embody the *rules* of a game's design. Unlike *rules*, which are abstract and maintained through social contract, mechanics are impersonally applied and cannot

be negotiated or cheated (unless an external tool is used to interfere with or change the operation of game code).

{RULES > MECHANICS < INPUTS}

This layer of the model is not based around a task or orientation that the player adopts but is, rather, an acknowledgment of a layer that exists below conscious observation and an orientation that the player will adopt throughout the rest of the model. Consider this a necessary digression in between steps rather than a *proper* "step two" of the process.

Inherent in our description of game states and object states is the framing that states possess parameters by which they may transition into other states. Webs of relationships dictate how each element and game state can affect one another. These parameters are the game's *mechanics*, the enacted, enforced manifestations of the abstract *rules*. As Stephanie Boluk and Patrick LeMieux (2017) note, "rules are voluntary constraints and social contracts" (p. 8). Sports, board games, and social games possess rules: the acceptable manners of play as accepted and enforced by players and referees. Rules are adopted by players and are, crucially, negotiable; thus an instance of a game may adopt non-standard "house rules".

Mechanics, on the other hand, are the non-negotiable parameters of play imposed objectively and impartially upon play. Boluk and LeMieux (2017) give the example that "nowhere in the official rulebook of Major League Baseball [...] are the laws of physics defined" (p. 8). Baseball's rules shape a game that is played *within* the non-negotiable parameters of Newtonian physics. In fact, baseball could be conceived of as a *metagame* played with the forces of physics, a way to find expressive fun in those natural laws.

Video games are *designed* with rules, abstract prescriptions of how the game ought to be played ("Mario can jump whenever his feet are on a solid surface"), but video games *enact* mechanics—algorithmic expressions of concrete parameters. Whereas one could *conceivably* persuade an opponent in a particular game of Chess to change the rules, "I think knights should move in a pattern of *three* forward and one across this time", one cannot argue a case to the computer, which enforces all mechanics—even rules that still *appear* quite abstract like turn-order—as "facts" of the system. One cannot argue that "Mario should be able to jump higher this one time" without the assistance of an external tool that alters the game at the level of code, such as a mod or cheat tool such as a Game Genie or GameShark.

As such, this creates a division between the game's rules as designed and its mechanics in execution. The computer does not *understand* the rules of the game on the same abstract level as the players of Tag understand theirs. The computer only processes numbers and runs calculations. The mechanics of turn-taking *might as well be* natural laws.

But this also means that the mechanics of a game represent that which *can be done* rather than that which *ought to be done*. If players can find a circumstance in which Mario *can* jump higher than typically allowed (by exploiting a glitch in the game's programming, perhaps), the computer does not recognize this as an illegal or improper action in the way that a Poker player might recognize the illegitimacy of a player sneaking an extra ace into her hand. This is a level of *metagame* consideration: playing the game as it *allows* rather than as its design *intends*.

To "play the metagame" is to recognize the unique position of the player as one that pushes *against* mechanics rather than one who is tasked with *maintaining* rules. In competitive settings, players compete on the level of affordances rather than on the level of sportsmanlike adherence to the spirit of the law. Thus, when an exploit or imbalanced parameter is discovered, it is said to "change the metagame" (or "the meta", for short), and players must compete around *that* contingency.

As such, we can view and discuss games on differing levels of abstraction. We can discuss its designed "rules", we can discuss its computationally enforced mechanics, and we can discuss its unintended mechanical metagame (total affordances). With respect to the rest of game studies literature, which tends to be written from the perspective of the developer rather than the player, this division is recognized (code implements mechanics and not rules), but "mechanics" still typically refers to *intended* mechanics rather than unintentional exploits. In the conventions of design-centric writing, it would come across as disrespectful to say, "*Pokémon* (1996) has a mechanic by which a glitched Pokémon named Missingno can be encountered and can duplicate the item held in the second slot of the player's inventory". To say it like this is to imply that the mechanic was *designed* and *intended*. Mechanics are treated similarly to abstract rules; thus, it comes across as a bad faith interpretation of the game's design intention.

For that reason, I wish to be clear about my use of three words to represent the three levels of abstraction: a rule is the *abstract, semantic description of a parameter's intended purpose and process*; a mechanic is an *abstract description of a computer's concrete runtime behavior that intends to express a rule*; and language-like input, parameter, and feedback express *the concrete, runtime behavior of the gameplay system during live enactment, whether in accordance with intended rules or not*. In cases in which behavior is identifiably contrary to intended design, I try to use language like *exploit* and *glitch*, but please understand that doing so does not imply judgment or call out *cheating*; my perspective is that players *ultimately* play the metagame rather than the abstractly intended game, and the use of unintended affordances is an exciting frontier of player improvisation and creative expression (see Chapter 13 for a more thorough discussion of metagame-level exploits).

INPUT → STATE TRANSITIONS → FEEDBACK

The State → Transition conceit of sense-making frames the interpretation of games at its most basic level as a recognition of changes in state—of the game state as a whole, of its component objects, and of any combination of components therewithin. This step focuses our attention on the manners in which object inputs translate into state changes.

We have discussed how mechanics (runtime expressions of the abstract rules of design) are embedded into the parameters as held within general and object states. The game, in a particular state, mandates how particular objects within it behave and transform over time or as a result of specific inputs, but these parameters may not be true when the game is in a different state. For example, when *Grand Theft Auto V* (2013) is in an ambient state, the avatar may run and drive through the game world without being pursued or aggressed against, though when the game state shifts into the "wanted" state, caused when the avatar commits certain types of crimes, certain objects (police, police cars, police helicopters) will pursue, shoot at, and attempt to arrest or kill the avatar (these games are set in the United States, after all). Because the game state has transitioned, the object behaviors of anything in the "police" class change, creating a different dynamic of play.

In this section, I identify an *input* as anything that originates from an object or system that results in an altered general or object state. In the above *Grand Theft Auto* example, the avatar performed an input upon an object that was the subject of his crime (the avatar may have stolen a car, for example, changing its state from ambient to player-operated). That action was an input on any police that may have been near enough to witness the crime (changing the police's state from ambient to "witnessed crime"). That police object sent an input to the game state (changing it from ambient to "wanted"). The game state sent an input to all objects in the police class (changing their behaviors from ambient to "patrol"). When the avatar enters the line of sight of a patrolling police object during the "wanted" game state, that police object instance changes its state from "patrol" to "pursuit". All the while, the game state is feeding a background "input" into itself: a timer that counts down to the end of the "wanted" phase that counts down when the player remains out of sight of objects of the police class.

Input

Inputs activate mechanics, which express as state changes. As mentioned before, every general state change represents a (sometimes subtle) shift in the relationships between objects, and every object state change represents a shift in the general game state. This input → state transition framing includes but does not exclusively apply to player → controller inputs. The multidirectionality of this framing is important. Inputs (and, thus, mechanics) are available to all objects and agents within a simulation. Though NPCs and objects controlled by game systems do not exhibit conscious intelligence, they still invoke mechanics to perform state changes. That is to say, if the specific affordances that constrain and empower the human player's avatar within the simulation constitute a layer of mechanics, so too can we frame the specific affordances and properties of computer-controlled objects as mechanics (and "inputs", more generally).

This invokes the Ludic Framework exhibited in Chapter 5. Frédéric Seraphine's (2016) model differentiated between the *actum*, *factum*, and *tactum* to name interactions that were a result of player input, interactions that were a result of computer input, and interactions that result from the intersection of simulated objects, respectively. While the core focus of the literacy model is to make gameplay sensible to the perspective of the player, it does not mean that the player's actions are the only actions worth considering. Player choices (and, thus, player agency) are performed in the context of the dynamic interrelationships of simulated objects with ongoing behavioral relationships with each other and with the game state. The layering of these interrelationships eventually blossoms into procedural emergence, as we will explore shortly.

As I say often throughout this explanation, our gameplay model extends outside of the diegesis of the simulation to include the player, computer, and context. These elements exist in dynamic interrelationship with one another *and* with the objects within the simulation. For when a diegetic enemy attacks the avatar, it is the physical player that must alter her behavioral patterns (changing *her* object state) to change the way that she operates the game controller and her avatar. Similarly, environmental distraction, in pulling the attention of the player, has the diegetic effect of "distracting" the avatar, since the player's cognitions motivate and animate diegetic avatar action. In conceiving of the relationships between objects and the inputs that alter these states, always consider how player and environment states (as well as extradiegetic general states such as the operation of the computer's operating system) input into one another.

Feedback

Not all general or object states, and thus not all state transitions, are visible to the player. Background processes track crucial variables that need not be persistently occurrent within the mind of the player. Those that do inform the player's decision-making, though, rely upon understandable and consistent feedback from the system. If the player avatar attacks an enemy boss but the boss does not exhibit any visual feedback to avatar attacks (such as flashing red or triggering a "hurt" animation), it can be difficult to discern whether the attacks are having any effect and whether they are worth performing.

With our model of gameplay input and effect being multidirectional, we can also consider the ways in which the player provides feedback to the other objects in the gameplay system. Though the game state and other diegetic objects do not need "feedback" in as such, from the avatar (being a diegetic object, itself, the game's systems have direct access to all metrics and properties that govern its state; thus, an NPC does not need to see a "hurt" animation to know that the avatar has been damaged), game systems are programmed to elicit and react to player feedback. If we consider a diegetic action (an attack from an enemy NPC, let's say) to alter the relationship not only between the NPC and the avatar but also between the NPC and the *player*, the player's physical response (literalized as muscular action → controller input → avatar action) provides the system feedback as to whether said attack was successful, not on a *mechanical* level, but on a *design* level. As a designed challenge, did the player overcome or fail? If the player failed it, the game may ask her to repeat it (via death → retry mechanic) or will allow her to proceed past it if her response was successful. This can be thought of as a form of "feedback" in an abstract design sense. In the way that an incorrect school quiz question is feedback to the teacher that a student does not understand a particular aspect of the course material, player success or failure feeds back understanding or mastery to the "developer" represented, by proxy, by the pre-programmed set of conditional contingencies embedded within the game's systems.

Avatar Identification

As noted previously, operation within virtual systems crosses an ontological border. The real and the virtual cannot directly interact, so an agent of mediated translation is needed between the levels. Controllers are threshold objects (Murray, 1997) that translate the physical actions of the player into digital signals interpretable by the computer (*itself* a second degree of translation *already*, with mental impulses *first* being translated to muscular movement). Rather than commanding the virtual system *holistically*, diegetic actions require a singular object that focuses manipulative intention. Just like our bodies ground our manipulative capacities to that which we reach out and touch (when I press a key on a keyboard, my fingers focus my will to specific action rather than pressing downwards *generally* on the whole of the universe), the avatar (or pointer) distinguishes a small portion of the total game or screen space as the subject of manipulative influence. Rare moments of *general* control typically involve pre-directed interface control, such as "press A to continue" prompts that may advance dialogue or transition scenes. For everything else, a point of focused attention is required.

Identification of the avatar is discussed in great depth in Chapter 4, but to summarize the phenomenological task of forming that agential connection, avatar (or pointer) identification is a task of simple cause-and-effect linking. In the seminal *Game Feel* (2009), Steve Swink outlines a set of cognitive processing tasks (and parameters that determine their effectiveness) that allows the brain to make the connection between controller inputs and real-time control of the avatar. Swink finds that the game must respond to controller inputs within 240 ms for the player to feel that she has real-time control. That accounts for 100 ms of perceptual processing (the travel from the sensory organs to the brain and the cognitive schematic appraisal), 70 ms of cognitive processing (comparing the current state against the ideal intended state), and 70 ms of motor processing (sending the following motivated action or adjustment to the muscles that can execute that action). To maintain the cognitive link between inputs and on-screen action, the entire cycle of input → feedback must take no more than 240 ms (Swink, 2009, pp. 36, 37).

Games *can* feature avatars that fall outside of this 240 ms window, but characters of this type tend not to elicit projective embodiment. Control does not become "transparent"; these characters are viewed as being separate from the player, watched but not inhabited (such as the protagonists of *Dragon's Lair* [1983] or *The Secret of Monkey Island* [1990]). Real-time control is not prioritized, and these characters function to a greater degree as loci of consequence and identifiability rather than loci of direct control or vessels for projective embodiment.

Under typical conditions, identification of the avatar is relatively straightforward. Often games begin (in their ambient state) with little else on screen *but* the avatar (see the opening screens of *Donkey Kong Country* [1994] and *Bloodborne* [2015]), and games that open with cinematic cutscenes will typically introduce the avatar protagonist during that scene (as in *Super Mario 64* [1996] and *God of War* [2018]). In games in which the avatar is not immediately obvious (such as *Thomas Was Alone* [2012], in which none of the on-screen shapes in its minimalist first screen resembles a typical game protagonist), real-time control as described above makes a cognitive link surprisingly quickly and effectively.

Testing State Changes

The period of learning input and feedback relationships is the point at which the game is most toy-like. Guided by curiosity and desire to learn rather than pursuing specific objectives, the player can ascertain a *basic* understanding of the operational fundamentals even without any explicit tutorialization. In many cases, giving players a pressure-free opportunity to experiment is preferable to tutorializing, as players new to a game may not have the experientially grounded context necessary to understand or internalize tutorial messages that precede hands-on experimentation. Board games require rule instruction upfront, since it is up to the players to maintain the operational structure of gameplay. This responsibility is placed on the computer when playing video games, though, alleviating the necessity for player understanding of rules before gameplay begins.

Game designer and educator Mark Brown noted how effectively *Super Mario 3D World* (2013) teaches its mechanical twists (each stage has at least one novel "gimmick" that the player must learn) by introducing novel mechanics in safe areas absent from punishment, so players can "play" with the novel mechanics before the game subjects them to an executional challenge that penalizes failure (Game Maker's Toolkit, 2015). Allowing the player to experiment with the state change capabilities of the avatar or experiment with the state change of other objects *while the game is in an ambient state* gives players the chance to form their own working understandings of these relationships in a manner more interactive and memorable than written tutorials.

At this basic stage of diegetic attuning, the player gains an understanding of how the avatar can act within and upon the game world and how the game world can act upon the avatar and upon itself. Through the vicariosensation of the avatar (see Chapter 4), the unique visual language of the game becomes interpretable by the player, such that the player develops a sense of *presence* in the game space. The player learns which details are important, requiring attention, and which details are merely peripheral or decorative. The player interprets the game world on two levels:

as a series of non-semiotic action affordances and obstacles and as a semiotically contextualized space of symbolic, representational communication. This mirrors the method by which we perceive the real world. Semiotic details inform our understanding of spaces and cue the choices we make within them, but the objects that prompt these semiotic understandings have underlying physical properties separate from and ambivalent to their semiotic purposes. We recognize a dinner table for the socially contextualized purpose it performs, and we primarily use it for that purpose, but it has underlying physical properties that give it additional affordances separate from its intended purpose. One *can* stand on it to reach and change out a lightbulb, or one *could* turn it upside down and sled down a snow-covered hill on its face.

Forming an embodied understanding of the virtual game world is explored in Chapter 4. Unlike our embodied experience in *our own* world, grounded in our somatosensation, primarily visual and audio cues are used to provide the basic feedback necessary to enable the projective embodiment within the game world. Reactivity and animation communicate the physical properties of objects within the game world. A virtual hammer that the avatar picks up slowly, takes a long time to accelerate when swinging, and carries a great amount of inertia in its follow-through looks heavier than one that the avatar can swing quickly with minimal inertial effect. Elements of **polish** also contribute to the readability of vicariosensation. Polish refers to peripheral details of the presentation that do not affect the *operation* of the game but enhance the embodied representation of the effects of interaction. For example, *particle effects* (a term used to describe visual effects consisting of aggregate movement of smaller "particles" to represent complex, often difficult-to-predict physical phenomena like smoke, fire, and sparks) may be employed to emit clouds of dust and scattered sparks wherever a virtual hammer strikes. The hammer strike may be accompanied by a resounding "clang", and the screen perspective may shake when it strikes, contributing to its "feeling" of heft. These elements of polish do not *affect* gameplay at the level of its operational rules (if the dust, sparks, sound, and screen shake were removed, the hammer strike would be unchanged in its diegetic operation), but they contribute to the perceived physical properties of the object that inform the vicariosensation of the game world.

Mimesis and Methexis

The vicariosensorial grounding of embodied presence in the game world informs the player's diegetic perspective as an agent within a virtual space. On an even more practical level, input and feedback inform the goal-directed behaviors players express in the mimetic and methectic perspectives as well.

The mimetic perspective concerns the player's role as actor and participant within a guided and directed narrative. As such, the type of feedback sought within this perspective is not as much that which emerges from purely mechanical interactions but that which expresses the intent of the developers. To use the common metaphor described in Chapter 3, this is *entering into conversation* with the developers through the discernment of explicitly communicative elements of design.

Feedback elucidates not only the dispassionate "physics" of the game world but also directs and tailors the player's experience. While the methods for discerning these kinds of communicative design elements are discussed in greater detail in Chapter 3, to briefly summarize, the player attunes to the forms of feedback that direct attention, prompt motivation, and reveal information. For example, the player may notice that, when crossing an invisible threshold in the game world, the camera pulls back to frame the avatar in relation to a particular object of interest. Or perhaps an NPC calls out to the avatar once the avatar enters a building. This directs players' attention toward a designed interaction. Conversely, exploration of a particular part of the game world being met with an overabundance of dangers and enemies (elements of resistance; see Chapter 3) directs players' attention *away* from particular areas until they become skillful or diegetically empowered to an extent that those resistances are no longer a deterrence.

Some feedback prompts motivation. Collecting a particular token that is rewarded with empowerment or story advancement prompts the player to find similar tokens. The direction of attention toward an area or object of interest prompts the player to reach that spot. The state change triggered by the consumption of a Power Pellet in *PAC-MAN* (1980), consisting of a change in sound effects and the ghosts taking on a distressed appearance and behavior, prompts the player to reorient her current motivation from eating all of the maze's Pac-dots to instead pursuing the ghosts.

Other feedback reveals information crucial to pursuing mimetic goals. Speaking to particular NPCs may reveal important information, such as the location of a treasure or an enemy's weak points. Acting upon a game object may reveal information about its purpose or function that can inform when and how to utilize (or avoid) it in the future. Sometimes pressing a button may pull up an arrow that points toward a particular objective or gives the player a hint as to what to do next. This is informational feedback intended to keep the player on track in their designed mimetic role within the game's story.

Finally, feedback plays a crucial role in the player's methectic decision-making. Understanding the operational functions of the game's components allows the player to utilize them in methectic strategy. As discussed in the diegetic section, methectic strategy is *metagame* strategy, so the feedback that informs it is not limited to that of intentional design. In a racing game, if the player finds that driving into fire hydrants causes the physics to glitch and send the car flying in a predictable direction at high speed, she may use this as a form of unintentional shortcut. The systemic feedback prompts strategic reconsideration, as any action not explicitly *disallowed* by the system is a potentially useful tool to be used by the player.

Input → Feedback Summary

What to look for

- Tracking state changes of the game system as a whole or elements within the game system should be approached with a curiosity for cause-and-effect relationships.
- Games are fundamentally communicative systems with great care put into the legibility of these cause-and-effect relationships. Though many of these relationships can be ascertained through impersonal observation alone (such as watching interpersonal interactions between NPCs from afar), embodied presence that informs practical expression within the game world is informed by prodding the system through the directed action of the avatar and observation of the feedback provided.
- Correspondence of controller input and localized diegetic reaction allows the player to distinguish the avatar (or other locus of agential manipulation), either as a diegetic actor, an interdiegetic attention-focusing shape on-screen (such as a mouse cursor), or as a diegetic but unseen locus of perspective (as in first-person games).
- With an identified avatar or locus of manipulation, the player forms a working, operational understanding of the game world on three levels:
  - **Diegesis**: The action affordances and vicariosensation grounded in embodied presence within the virtual game world.
  - **Mimesis**: "Entering into conversation" with intentional design by observing the feedback that motivates directed action as a participant in the narrative or intended course of a game.
  - **Methexis**: Observing feedback at a purely systemic level, looking for ways in which systemic interaction informs metagame strategy.

Questions to ask

- What element(s) of the game world change in correspondence with controller inputs? Is control substantiated into a singular *avatar* figure (see Chapter 4) or distributed more generally in a non-personified manner?
- Through whatever locus of manipulation the game system affords, what elements of the game world can the player affect? What kind of relationship does the locus of manipulation have with the rest of the game world?
- How do the states of each object within the game contribute to and transform the state of the game holistically?
- How do the mechanics of interaction correspond with the intended (abstract) rules of the game? How might concrete mechanics and abstract rules *differ*? What ways can the player find to bend or break the "rules" within the boundaries of the mechanics?

{INTERACTION → LUDEMES → SCHEMAS}

This section, interactions and ludemes, does not constitute a separate step in the sense-making process. Rather, it is a link between the previous and next steps and a co-occurrence that schematizes and eases the decoding process.

A complete expression of input and feedback forms an interaction; an actor within the system performs an action and receives a meaningful result. Interactions can occur between any and all systemic actors, directly or indirectly within, into, and out from the diegetic simulation.

Whereas in the previous step, we expressed inputs and their results in terms of individual actions performed by individual actors and the specific state transformations that result from those actions, this inter-step link reframes each cause-and-effect relationship as a unit that can be assessed not only in an internally descriptive manner but also in conjunction with separate and contemporary interactions to form *configurations*; essentially, contextualized interactions.

Configurations, which I sometimes illustratively call *constellations*, form the bases of *choice*, a pre-motivational expression of agency, to which we will return later in this section. Configurations explain the variance in instances of feedback that respond to otherwise similar inputs. To use golf as an example, swinging a club to hit the ball is an action—an input—that changes the state of multiple systemic elements (the ball, the club, the athlete, the holistic game state with regard to score [number of strokes] and distance/orientation of the ball in relation to the pin, and any course obstacles). A "swing" is not a singular thing, though, like a Platonic ideal. One does not simply *swing*; one *swings in some way, against some condition*. The use of a driver, wedge, or putter constitutes a different type of swing. Hitting the ball off of the fairway, rough, or a sand trap changes the technique and expected trajectory of the hit. Even conditions such as the fatigue or muscular injury of the golfer affect the manner in which the swing performs.

So whereas our previous step may have examined each of these "inputs" and their respective results in parallel with one another (the choice of club acting upon the golfer and ball, the terrain acting upon the ball, the muscles acting upon the golfer and subsequently upon the ball…), we must reframe now to consider the entire configuration of relevant conditions, for it is between *configurations*, not *inputs*, that systemic agents choose when acting.

Again, *choice*, at this stage in the process, is pre-motivational. That is to say, these are not necessarily choices aiming toward optimal execution of desired goals or outcomes; we are simply seeking to understand the actions that *can* be taken at a given moment in a given game state.

These contextualized interactions form **ludemes** (a term that yet has a loose definition, not yet having been properly formalized). A ludeme, similar to other structuralist terms such as *phoneme* and lexeme, describes an "atomic unit of gameplay" (Koster, 2005), or, more specifically, a primary unit of choice in gameplay. The term is useful in describing how choice affordances are (non-semiotically) recognized and transferable between games, in a manner similar to Richard Dawkins' (1976) more generalized meme; the "unit of cultural transmission, or a unit of imitation". So while, definitionally, "ludeme" may seem duplicative of less-pretentious terms we already use, like "rule" and "mechanic", it is separately useful in framing how we cognitively contextualize, transmit, and transfer these rules and mechanics across a lifetime of gaming. In that sense, a ludeme is not functionally equivalent to the rule, mechanic, or interaction that it describes but is instead descriptive of the schema that we form to understand it.[4]

Schemas help us form functional "shortcuts" in our processing of novel information. For example, one may never have encountered an iguana, but she can make assumptions about iguanas from her previous knowledge and experience of the "reptile" schema. She may be quite familiar with skinks, snakes, and chameleons and may assume iguanas share similar attributes that tend to be true of the entire schematic group (cold-blooded, scaly skin, have tails) and may be curious about whether or not it shares attributes found infrequently amongst the schematic group (changes colors, no limbs, eats birds). Schemas help us cognitively group and parse information to inform novel encounters. There is no reason why, for instance, a novel encounter with a Honda Civic should require from-scratch analysis of its behavior, appearance, operation, and construction. Instead, the brain goes through a hierarchical series of associative recognitions (machines → automobiles → cars → sedans → Japanese cars → Hondas), by which point only a small number of focused, particular curiosities need to be satisfied to form a fairly comprehensive functional knowledge.

In that context, we can consider how particular configurations of interactions inform meaningful schemas that aid in the choices that a player makes during gameplay. This "sense memory" of action or rules carries forward throughout a game's play (one comes to recognize particular configurations and the actions they afford) and also carries *between* games (a player familiar with a first-person shooter will carry forward the intuitive knowledge and recognition of elements of visual and procedural communication into other first-person shooter games, allowing them to "skip" past stages in the learning process). This is where the concept of ludemes is useful.

A ludeme can be a rule (in many card games, aces can be scored as either low or high cards), an input/control mechanic ("mouse look": using the mouse to pivot the field of view), a motivation/objective (finding "towers" or viewpoints in open-world games to gain a wider perspective of the game space), or semiotic/cultural context. Ludemes can be general and broadly applied (using the left thumbstick to control avatar movement, for instance), applicable across most games, or a ludeme can be incredibly specific (for instance, the *specific* way that Mario controls in his 3D adventures, with his specific speed, turning radius, and set of acrobatic jumping affordances). In such cases, one can sense echoes of specific games in others (Hat Kid from *A Hat in Time* [2017] controls not only in an intuitively familiar manner for the genre of 3D platformers, but she specifically controls *like Mario* in certain ways, and one familiar with 3D Mario games will experience a muscle memory and sense recognition more specific than the general 3D platforming familiarity).

Ludemes can be surprisingly versatile as well, carrying across genres and contexts. Becoming familiar with first-person movement and camera control in an action-packed shooter will also translate into intuitive control knowledge in a peaceful first-person exploration adventure game. Our ludic schemas are sensitive to differences in specific instantiations, becoming more versatile and discerning as a greater number of games are played. It is worth calling out explicitly: ludemes are not *strictly* abstract. While the abstract rules of a game *can be* ludemes, so too can rules' concrete expressions. Ludemes can also express non-diegetic elements of the system of gameplay. The particular muscle memory for performing a Dragon Punch in *Street Fighter II* (1991) is a ludeme, as are metagame elements involving the real-world culture of players surrounding a game (for example, politely bowing before a duel in *Dark Souls* [2011] is a community expectation but is not rewarded or punished by the mechanics of the game; its memetic expression and propagation is a metagame ludeme).

I will return to ludemes in the meaning-making portion of the literacy model, as I consider ludemes to be a primary form of meaning that games can convey. I wished to introduce it here because, during play and the observation of input → feedback relationships, players intuitively internalize configuration schemas in the form of ludemes that guide and contextualize further play. Additionally, players pull from their experiences of ludemes from other games. This familiarization and schematizing occurs in parallel with the feedback-oriented sense-making process, eventually proportionally overtaking it altogether. Whereas at the beginning of a player's relationship with a game, she has to carefully consider, test, and learn from each interaction, she soon grows to recognize familiar configurations and will start to act upon them intuitively.

This is why I like defining ludemes in terms of player *choice*. For if we consider interactions to be contextualized within configurations of elements, we can consider ludemes to *be* elements within those configurations, since they are contextually relevant factors that inform the choices available and preferable in any configuration. When a player encounters a particular configuration, let's say that she has 15 meaningful choices she can make in that moment. If she is inexperienced with the game, each of those 15 choices may seem equally preferable, and she might actually be overwhelmed by the number of choices available to her. As she becomes more experienced, though, forming strong ludemes and honing her ludic schemas, she may recognize three of those choices as being tested and effective, essentially eliminating 12 choices from her choice pool. The amount of cognitive processing necessary for making these experience-informed choices decreases as her fluency with the game's systems (the language of ludemes the game employs) deepens.

DYNAMICS → PROCEDURAL EMERGENCE

So far in the sense-making model, we have found that gameplay systems (and the subsystems and elements within them) exist in differing rhythms of state change. By observing the behavior of systems and elements, we can gain a limited understanding of the processes that govern the system. By acting upon the system and receiving feedback for inputs specifically initiated by the player, we can gain a greater understanding of the ways in which the system operates and the ways in which those operational behaviors can be used to our strategic advantage.

A model that culminates with a simple cause-and-effect, input-and-output relationship would not tell the whole story, though. The "magic" of video games—the factor that makes them the most compelling as artistic artifacts—is their *procedural emergence*, the ability for causal chains to ripple and intersect to create unpredictable but ultimately logical, unique outcomes. It is this tension between unpredictability and logical consistency that makes video games so interesting and engaging.

Like balancing a ball on the tip of a cone, there are dozens of factors that influence the way in which it might roll. It appears random but is the result of forces that *are* absolutely consistent, if unpredictable in their influence, given every factor in balance with one another. Theoretically, one *can* predict every outcome in a video game with *complete* knowledge of every system and mechanic at play (though even the most brilliant player could not perform the necessary calculations to accurately envision every progressive game state at the speed of a computer), just like one *can* predict the roll of the ball off of the cone with complete knowledge of every physical phenomenon at play in that interaction.

Dynamics

The outcome of procedural emergence is enabled by the principle of *dynamics*, as described in the MDA and Proceduralist models overviewed in Chapter 5. To review, the authors of the MDA model define dynamics as "the run-time behavior of the mechanics acting on player inputs and each others' outputs over time" (Hunicke et al., 2004). The Proceduralist authors highlight the logical extension of this definition: dynamics are not just the result of run-time mechanical outputs; outputs of dynamic interactions create further dynamic interactions themselves (Treanor et al., 2010). This recursive cycle of dynamics either intensifies (as a positive feedback loop) or resolves toward harmony (as a negative feedback loop).

Dynamics keep gameplay interesting; they require the player to be adaptable to changing (dynamic) conditions. Dynamics are what separate video games from traditional, operational software. A calculator has only one "mechanic" that operates at any time; it adds *or* subtracts *or* divides *or* squares, etc., and its input-output relationship is uncomplicated and wholly predictable. Were the calculator to introduce a *second* active mechanic that intersected with the first, it would produce a dynamic and become inherently more game-like. Say, for instance, it *only* divides on the 3rd, 13th, 23rd, 33rd, 43rd, or 53rd second of every minute. Then, all of a sudden, the operator has to juggle precise timing with the arithmetic tasks she wishes to perform, and it becomes, if not a game, more game-like. It creates a dynamic between the two mechanics that makes the pursuit of the objective perhaps not more *interesting*, but certainly more *active*.

Procedural Emergence

The above example of the intermittent calculator demonstrates a dynamic but not emergence. Dynamics satisfy the requirement of a multistep process, but emergence requires complexity. Salen and Zimmerman (2003) define *emergence* as "unplanned patterns" appearing from within the complexity of a system. They quote writer Steven Johnson (2001), who calls emergence, "the movement from low-level rules to higher-level sophistication". In that quote, Johnson isn't specifically referring to the rules of a game; rather, his interest is in studying systems such as ant colonies and urban centers. In his definition, rules include the organizing principles and parameters that mediate the intersection of elements of the systems; they are analogous and applicable to the rules of games, certainly, but wider than that domain in its totality.

Parallel to the above definition, we can observe emergence amongst systems of multiple individual agents, making decisions individually. The degree to which this fits the definition of "following rules" is a matter of philosophical perspective. The individual choices of a great enough population of individual agents over a great enough period of time frequently create patterns that can be observed from a removed perspective, which can be interpreted as logical propensities that make such patterns more *likely* or as a kind of "collective agency" of the system as a whole, as we might ascribe to ant colonies. Traffic congestion, for example, can be attributed to patterns arising from a number of factors that create strong propensities; in particular cultural contexts, the rhythms of eating and sleeping roughly match across a population, meaning that the dinner custom falls at a roughly consistent time of day for most, necessitating similar work and travel hours; urban and suburban zoning means that a great number of people take similar routes to work from home and vice versa at these similar times of day; etc. Those of a particular philosophical persuasion may argue that the decisions of individual agents all boil down to rule-based outcomes; that the differences in personality and preference are emergent systems of predispositions and environmental factors. Whether you align with a determinist or propensity-patterned principle, the framing of procedurality as an outcome of multiple-agent interactions will be necessary context for the consideration of multiplayer emergence.

As described at the beginning of this section, procedural emergence occupies an interesting intersection between unpredictability and logical consistency. The cascade of effects leads to unpredictable ends, but the effects of each *individual* interaction should be easy to understand, clearly adhering to the rules that the system has established. Especially in the domain of video games, parameters that influence procedural emergence are typically *designed* to be legible. Were they complex enough to appear random, the perceived "fairness" of the game would be in question. Ultimately, procedural emergence in video games serves three purposes: to prompt player reactivity and improvisation (it is the difference between solving the same maze over and over again vs. undergoing challenges that call upon the application of the same problem-solving *principles* in differing contexts and instantiations), to model (simulate) claims or perspectives about the complex systems of other domains (see the section about *procedural rhetoric* in Chapter 5), and as an aesthetic end upon itself (the beauty of patterns arising from the apparent chaos of complex systems is an inherent joy, and one that computers are especially well-suited to exhibit).

Non-diegetic Dynamics and Procedural Emergence

Applying the principles of dynamics and procedural emergence to the other components of our system of literacy, we can consider how game mechanics interact with the "mechanics" of the player and the context of play. Considering the physicality of the player to comprise component mechanics of the overall system of play, the design affordances of the controller and the physical limitations of the player *absolutely* produce unique dynamics.

For example, the medieval dark fantasy ARPG *Demon's Souls* (2009) differed from genre contemporaries by assigning its sword and magic attack inputs to the PlayStation 3's shoulder buttons (operated with the pointer and sometimes middle fingers of each hand) rather than the conventional face buttons (operated with the thumb of the right hand). This was done to free the right thumb from constant face button responsibilities, allowing the thumb to primarily rest upon the right thumbstick, which orientates the game's camera perspective. Because the game eases the competing responsibilities of the right thumb, the game is able to assign tasks that require simultaneous attack and camera control, as is sometimes necessary when fighting large enemies or fighting within tight spaces. Were the game to use the conventional face buttons as attack inputs, any camera movement (of the right thumbstick) would require temporarily sacrificing the ability to attack (with the face buttons). Each of these control setups produces different diegetic-to-extradiegetic dynamics.

To cite another similar example, rhythm series *Guitar Hero* (2005–2015) and *Rock Band* (2007–2015) feature handheld, guitar-shaped controllers. To activate a temporary score multiplier (earned by playing specific sequences of notes without any mistakes), the player must tilt the neck of the guitar controller upwards (emulating the kind of expressive showmanship a rock star might deploy during a stage show). Because the score multiplier is temporary, the player is incentivized to activate it during a period of the song in which a great number of notes will be played (so that the modifier will multiply the scores of the greatest number of notes). There is also a penalty for *missing* notes, such that a base multiplier will be reset upon an error. The physical action of tilting the guitar controller makes notes slightly more difficult to play. The changed posture requires mental adjustment, as the player must compensate for the different relative orientation of the fret buttons compared to the standard play posture for which the player has developed muscle memory. The full-body gesture is also distracting, breaking the flow and "transparency" of controller operation achieved to that point. It is *safest* to tilt the guitar during periods of relative ease in the song, so as to not disrupt portions that require intense concentration, but this burns valuable multiplier time in a portion of the song that is relatively sparse. It is *optimal* to activate the multiplier during the most note-dense portion of the song, though these portions are when the player needs the greatest sustained attention, and missing a note at the beginning of the multiplier's time period because of broken concentration basically nullifies its benefit. This is a specific dynamic that leads to interesting improvisational choices that emerge as a result of the interaction between the game's scoring mechanics and the physical and cognitive "mechanics" of the player.

In this perspective, video games are designed around the (presumed) physical and cognitive "mechanics" of the player. It is incorrect to separate the player's abilities and affordances from the conceptualization of game design. We would never alienate the specific human physicality of play from the party game Twister, and we would never judge the operation of a computer keyboard separate from the physical capabilities of the human hands that are its intended operators. Yet some resist this kind of use-oriented design consideration for video games, particularly as it applies to players with physical or cognitive disabilities. Diegetic action (the most apparent layer of play) is sometimes seen as equalizing, and it is *to an extent*, in that it affords the weak and strong, short and tall the same diegetic abilities to slay dragons or conquer kingdoms, but considering non-diegetic affordances as fundamental to systemic enactment, players with one hand or dyslexia or partial paralysis are being given a *very different game* than those with the normative ability parameters around which the game is typically designed. For the empowering equalization of video games' diegetic affordances, relatively little care is sometimes given to the systemic components that sit outside of the simulation.

From a sense-making perspective, consider not only the dynamics within the diegesis of the simulation and the interesting emergent proceduralities that they produce but also consider how those mechanics interact with the body of the player, the mind of the player, the cultural context of the player, the physical context of play, and the ways in which it structures the interactions *between* players, as applicable. Consider also how these elements of the gameplay system produce not only procedural emergence *within* the simulation but also how the simulation *incorporates* these extradiegetic and non-diegetic elements *into* procedural expressions or even *enacts* particular proceduralities *within* or *upon* these components. For example, the full-body dancing game *Dance Dance Revolution* (1998) requires strenuous physical exertion to play at higher difficulties; thus, the experience of play of any song becomes a dynamic affected heavily by the physical exhaustion of the player, ultimately resolving in the player's body to a greater degree than the game's software. Likewise, some games, like *The Sims* (2000; in its conversation system) and *Her Story* (2015; in its mystery narrative), use ambiguity and lack of specifically detailed revelation to resolve their semiotic implications in the interpretive mind of the player rather than in the explicit text of the game. Differing interpretations, all equally systemically privileged, are ultimately procedural outcomes that resolve in the mind of the player alone.

Mimetic and Methectic Dynamics and Procedural Emergence

At the moment-to-moment level, an understanding of a game's dynamic and emergent capabilities influences the mimetic and methectic play in a similar manner as the attenuation to input and feedback: in the development of agential and problem-solving capabilities, the player must account for the logical yet unpredictable nature of emergent enactment. Some games, like Solitaire, feature minimal emergence beyond patterning, but some games, like physics puzzlers *Poly Bridge* (2016) and *Tricky Towers* (2016), feature highly emergent elements injected into puzzles with binary (or linearly progressive) objectives. In such cases, creating an optimal methectic strategy (or enacting an optimal mimetic performance) requires understanding the *range* of what *might* occur and making risk-reward decisions to either prepare for the greatest range of possibilities or gamble heavily on particular expected eventualities.

This strategic quandary is at the heart of most games that feature procedural generation, particularly Roguelikes and Roguelites. For example, Roguelike card game *Balatro* (2024) prompts the player to seek high scores (and surpass increasingly challenging score thresholds) by forming Poker hands from cards drawn from a standard 52-card deck. Between each round, though, the player visits a shop from which cards that act as modifiers to score accumulation can be purchased with in-game money awarded for clearing challenges. The most interesting variety of modifiers is the Joker card. There are 150 unique Joker cards in the game; two to four are available in each shop, and the player can hold five at a time (under normal circumstances). Jokers have a range of effects. For example, one Joker may incrementally multiply each played hand for every consecutive hand played without a scoring face card. Another Joker may cause hearts and diamonds to count as the same suit (same for clubs and spades), making it easier to play flushes or royal flushes. Because the player can hold five Jokers at a time, she may find interesting synergies between these Joker effects. But the player never knows *which* and *when* particular Jokers will become available during the course of a game. Some Jokers are quite useless on their own (for example, the Pareidolia Joker causes all cards to count as face cards when scored) but can become quite useful when paired with the Smiley Face Joker, which adds a +5 score multiplier for every scored face card, which now includes *every* card. The risk-reward of Roguelikes involves building toward synergies when future affordances are unknown and adapting during play if intended "builds" do not actualize. Forming a strategy involves either planning for all possible eventualities and narrowing the strategy as possible outcomes become determined or taking risks on narrow probabilities with potentially favorable outcomes.

Many practices of methectic metagaming involve either the production of specific states or conditions through the manipulation of particular dynamics or proceduralities or the mitigation of emergent qualities. For instance, a shmup player may bait computerized enemies into firing a number of bullets at once sufficient to overpopulate the computational capacities of the computer and cause slowdown, making difficult sections easier to navigate. Metagame proceduralities extend outside of the simulation as well. Playing "mind games" with human opponents by tricking them with feints or prompting destabilizing emotions is essentially prompting an emergent outcome using extradiegetic and non-diegetic elements of the system of gameplay.

Dynamics → Procedural Emergence Summary
What to look for

- **Dynamics** emerge from the intersection of mechanics. When the effects of one rule mediate or modify the outcome or development of another, the resulting state will be more novel and unpredictable than single-mechanic happenings.
- **Procedural emergence** arises from systemic complexity, either through the intersection of *many* dynamics, long chains of dynamic outcomes, or the interaction of multiple agents.
    - Procedural emergence is both **unpredictable** (due to the complexity of the factors that bear it) *and* **logically consistent** (due to the deterministic outplaying of each component mechanic and dynamic).
    - Procedural emergence is useful and engaging in video games because it requires players to be reactive and improvisational, due to the balance of novelty/unpredictability of occurrences and operational reliability of its enactment.
- Because gameplay is an expression of the triune interaction between player, computer, and context, dynamics and procedurality may emerge *not only* through the intersection of diegetic mechanics but also through interaction with or resolution in the extradiegetic and non-diegetic elements of the gameplay system.
- Strategy is, at its heart, preparation for the emergent expression of play. Whereas problem-solving involves the resolution of a particular obstacle, *strategy* (ultimate outcome of the methectic element of sense-making) involves the preparation of optimal decision routes through indeterminate problems.

- Metagame consideration of procedural emergence involves not only diegetic strategizing but also consideration of games as imperfect and potentially manipulatable *software* and opponents as humans with potential psychological vulnerabilities that may procedurally alter the flow of the game.

Questions to ask

- How do the properties or mechanics of game elements interact to produce emergent happenings? Are relationships so abstract as to be mystifying, or are the steps logical enough to be legible?
- How may the player enact procedural emergence to extend the breadth of available actions and strategies beyond that which is directly afforded to the avatar?
- Do emergent actions confound player agency, or do they extend the creative expressivity that the player is able to enact?

MOTIVATION → AGENCY

While the prior steps in the sense-making process *primarily* involve discernment of what takes place within the diegesis of the simulation (through extended to include extradiegetic and non-diegetic elements of play as well), this step is primarily player-oriented. As the player develops a working knowledge of the possible states and the direct or emergent means by which the game and the total gameplay system transition between them, she develops objectives and, thus, motivation to perform certain actions and achieve certain ends.

This is important to the understanding of gameplay as an expressive medium because motivated player action is ultimately what animates and individualizes each gameplay enactment. Without player input, gameplay is a dead system (if not static, certainly directionless); without player *motivation*, gameplay is absentminded, lacking in enacted narrative. Gameplay requires more than the changing of states or input into a controller—a computer script could be generated that *triggers random inputs*, but that would not produce *gameplay*. Gameplay requires direction just like a book requires authorship and a film requires intent. Games are designed to *elicit* and *require* motivation.

In turn, motivation is required to express agency. Without investment in the outcome of actions, the player's inputs are not but uncontextualized actions. It is the formation of desire—of motivation—that turns player inputs into relevant *expressions of will.* Agency is a core aesthetic of video games, and it is only through the intersection of desire and feedback that it is able to emerge.

Motivation

Motivation, though necessary for the play of a game, is not sufficient for making something intrinsically more game-like in isolation. Whether I am aimlessly mopping or motivated to mop the entire floor for a particular purpose, this is a work activity. I may add other conditions to make it more game-like, such as the inclusion of a time limit or a competitive element, but motivation by itself does not *necessarily* propel an activity toward game-ness. That said, many "gamification" initiatives (the layering of game-like elements onto traditionally unengaging rituals of work, commerce, or education in order to increase engagement) include little more than incentive structuring and feedback cycles in order to *produce* motivation.

Motivation is the adoption or development of objectives. While games typically outline macro-level objectives very clearly through the structure and presentation of gameplay systems (high score, princesses to rescue, victory conditions…), these are not the only contributors to player motivation. Motivation, like system dynamics, can be broken down into smaller and smaller micro-objectives. *Super Mario 64* (1996) may provide me the explicit objective of collecting the star at the top of the mountain, but upon entering the level, I must form motivated actions to help me reach that goal. To reach the star at the top of the mountain, I may set a more general goal of "ascend"—any upwards movement is positive progress in the right direction. Further, I may set a goal of "find something I can climb or jump on to get higher", "explore over there for something to jump on", "jump on that rock", etc.

The most bite-sized expressions of motivation are guided by player curiosity. Here we see the intersection with the previous steps of the model. "Find out what controller input corresponds with the jump action"; "figure out how to change the state of an obstacle"… Even if the player is not working toward the explicit victory condition of a level, she can still be motivated by her curiosity, her desire to explore, or her desire to be playful. Exploring in a direction opposite the explicit objective indulges a curiosity and potentially arouses an intrinsic joy. While the explicit objectives provide a course of action for mimetic play, the joys of telepresence and immersion are vital diegetic aesthetics.

Agency

Agency is one of the core aesthetics of video games and, as Janet H. Murray argues, the whole of the digital medium. "When the behavior of the computer is coherent and the results of participation are clear and well motivated, the interactor experiences the pleasure of agency, of making something happen in a dynamically responsive world" (Murray, 2012). As such, agency is the culmination of all previous levels of the model.

Agency requires the ability to effect changes; player input is reflected in state transitions in which the player's impact is reflected with clear feedback that elucidates cause-and-effect relationships. Players' impact on the game world is amplified and diversified through intersecting dynamics that produce procedural emergence. The unpredictability and diversity of procedural ends necessitate the adoption of personal motivations, more nuanced than the type of motivation required for the uncomplicated operation of a non-dynamics-oriented system (such as deriving a sum from a calculator). This means that, while our example calculator is a tool that can satisfy a particular desired action of the operator, a video game player expresses a greater, more textured *agency* in her more complex interactions with a reactive and dynamic digital simulation.

Agency is both something that is *in-and-of-itself* true of a particular simulation (in offering more dynamic interaction with more nuanced and amplified reactivity, *DOOM* [1993] offers a greater degree of agency than *Chip's Challenge* [1989]) and something that is subjectively felt or experienced (someone with a greater mastery of *DOOM*'s controls may feel a greater sense of agency within the game than someone who struggles with basic operation). In the former example, the game offers a greater degree of expressive affordances, and in the latter example, the more experienced player has *functional access* to the game's full suite of affordances. In that sense, agency is a function of the *entire system* of gameplay. To possess expressive agency within the game, the player must have the knowledge and ability to interface with the game's specific affordances, the game must afford useful and expressive actions, and the context of play must not interfere with the adoption of motivation or the coherence of feedback.

One may reasonably question the appropriateness of including motivation and agency within the sense-making model. The MDA and Proceduralist models examined in Chapter 5 did not include agency in their model constructions, nor do traditional models of literacy include such implicit steps as "maintaining the desire to continue reading" (though as anyone who has struggled with this can attest, it *is* necessary to the discernment of meaning from the page). Instead, the MDA and Proceduralist models treat the video game artifact in a similar manner to more traditional media: the meaning-laden content of the artifact is that which is expressed on-screen, is "read" by the beholder, and from which meaning is *derived*. Thus, while both models feature nodes of subjectivity (aesthetics, theme, meaning), these are *reflective* nodes that *evaluate* the *constructive* elements of the game. Mechanics constitute gameplay, and aesthetics are a reflective result of gameplay.

I disagree with this implicit framing, instead positioning the motivation and agency of the player as central *constructive* elements of gameplay meaning formation. To use an analogy of textual literacy, mechanics are not analogous to the words and sentences that comprise a text; mechanics are the grammars of action that give shape to the *actual* message of the text: the player's personal, expressive agency. Thus, in my model's framing, video games are not *primarily* artifacts with implicit "text" accessed and enacted by the player; video games are structures in which the meaningful expression of player agency is shaped and experienced. In other words, while the *art* of literature is in the meaning of its text, and its artistic experience is in the reflection upon its text, the *art* of video games is in the shape and expression of the player's agency, and its artistic experience is in the embodied performance of play. The player's experience of agency *is* the "text" of the game artifact.

Thus, while we may examine how a game's systems and mechanics carry implicit propensities toward meaning (and it is useful to do so in the comparison between different games and the study of design), a holistic model of game literacy *must* be rooted in the active, embodied agency of the player. Video games are like architecture in that way; we can admire their ornamentation from a detached perspective, but their truest expression involves the experience of movement through them. Otherwise beautiful architecture unfit for human traversal, with one-foot-tall doorways and stairs too steep to be climbed, would forfeit a crucial and core component of its value.

Further, my model's framing displaces the locus of artistic, procedural enactment from the *simulation* to the holistic gameplay *system*. If the art of games is truly the shaping of player agency, then a game's expressive "canvas" includes not only the structural simulation but also the player's representation of the game world in her own mind. For the actions of the player, as both co-author and diegetic agent, feed back into the manifest construction of gameplay enactment. As such, the player's interpretation of diegetic actions grounds not only a *reflective* subjectivity but also *informs further action*. As game designers and studio Tale of Tales founders Michaël Samyn and Auriea Harvey said in an interview with Mark Newheiser:

> We are not story-tellers in the traditional sense of the word. In the sense that we know a story and we want to share it with you. Our work is more about exploring the narrative potential of a situation. We create only the situation. And the actual story emerges from playing, partially in the game, partially in the player's mind.
>
> *(Newheiser, 2009)*

With this in mind, we can reframe our perspective on games as artistic artifacts. One does not *play Super Mario 64* (1996) in the same way that one *reads Moby-Dick* (Melville, 1851), such that another reader may have different interpretations but is still reading the same text. Rather, *Super Mario 64* forms an instantiated experience of player agency that cannot be experienced in-kind again. The individual expression of agency instantiated in gameplay is the artistic artifact that prompts reflection and contextualization. This is to say, one does not play *Super Mario 64*; one experiences individually instantiated gameplay shaped by the structural forces of *Super Mario 64*. This concept is explored in greater depth in Chapter 11.

Obviously, video games *do* contain inscriptive meaning as well. Stories such as *Steins;Gate* (2009) and *The Last of Us* (2013) contain relatively self-contained embedded narratives, minimally impacted by the specific agencies of their players. They can be adapted to unilinear media while preserving the identifiable hearts of their respective embedded narratives (both have been adapted for television). My framing is not intended to imply that such inscribed meanings and embedded narratives (referred to as the semiotic elements throughout this book) are not valuable; only that they are not *specific* to video games as a medium. As reiterated throughout this book, this model of sense-making and meaning-making is not intended to *exhaustively* elucidate *all* sources of meaning from games; it is only intended to provide structure to understand and enrich the forms of meaning for which other models of literacy have not already accounted, that which is novel and specific to video games. As such, we can affirm the value of the semiotic content and embedded narrative of games while focusing our study specifically on the ways in which the dynamism of agency interfaces with these embedded elements.

Diegetic Locus of Motivation and Agency

While the elements of the previous stages in the sense-making model have been expressed differently by the various diegetic and non-diegetic components of the holistic gameplay system, motivation and agency are each largely singular. To consider gameplay agency is to focus on the player's capacity for expression and action-taking within the simulation. This primarily unidirectional relationship is inherently interdiegetic, though, and is acted upon by all of the systemic components.

Motivation and agency are interdiegetic because they form communicative links between the diegetic fiction of the game world and the practical reality of the player's world. In both "worlds", they are internally justified while crossing the border between real and unreal, the player's world and the fictional diegesis. In the player's world (and mind), the player forms motivations and experiences agency toward the game as an external object, from all three outlined perspectives (diegetically, as a "toylike" object with which the player may playfully engage; mimetically, as a designed narrative in which the player assumes a role to push the action forward; and methectically, as a puzzle-like object that challenges the player to find strategic solutions to mechanical challenges). Within the game world, though, the avatar is most often contextualized as an intelligent being, and the motivating agency of the player *fulfills the role of* the agency *of the character*. As explored in Chapter 4, the epiphanies and motivated actions of the player are diegetically justified as arising from the avatar. When the player is stumped by a diegetic puzzle, the avatar also cannot proceed with her journey. The moment that the player figures out the puzzle is the moment that the avatar can (in a manner of speaking) put that solution into action. The player's intelligence is the intelligence of the avatar. The player's fear or love or bravery is expressed as the fear or love or bravery of the avatar. This is because the player and the avatar form two components of a projectively linked whole; an intrinsically interdiegetic agent that extends into and out from the screen.

While the active agential relationship extends from player to computer, an implicit agential relationship exists between the game's developers (represented by their active proxy in the design of the software). Recalling the "games are a conversation between the player and developers" metaphor from Chapter 3, we can experience a *kind of* agency extending outward from the game toward the player. Motivation is informed by the developers' intent (the type of gameplay experience that they want the player to have) and is conditioned into the game through the design of its systems. Because the developers are not present during play, this is not a *true* agency, as they cannot *actively* react to the players' choices, apart from programming contingencies ahead of time. Despite the fact that the developers (*thinking agents*) are absent from the final system, the programmed dynamics of the game's procedural systems can create a stunning illusion of multi-agent interaction. This relationship is often literalized within the diegesis through the presence of "agents" that express simulated motivations and simulated agency through their behavioral AI. It is a misnomer to wholly distill this semi-agency of the developers into the behavioral AI of NPC actors, though, for even the mechanics we classify as unintelligent (physics, parameters, and constitutive rules) are tools that the developer uses to funnel gameplay toward desired forms of enactment. Thus, they are equally tools by which the developer takes a vicarious, deferred role in expressing motivated will within the gameplay system.

So while we might think of developers as deferred agents within the system of gameplay, and we might contextualize AI NPCs as proxy actors from which we may discern anthropomorphized motivations, the truest expression of agency arising from outside of the player within the system of gameplay is in the motivated actions of *other players* during multiplayer games. Other human players *are* active, thinking agents, responding to and affected by the actions of the POV player. To complicate this relationship, in the sense that *my* in-game motivations are guided and shaped by the incentives, affordances, and restrictions of play, all *other* players express not only *their* agential wills but their wills *as mediated by* the game's design. Thus, their behaviors express both *their* wills *and* the *developers'* wills to various degrees. In other words, if the developers' vicarious "agency" is injected into the system through expressive design that shapes the procedural dynamics of the gameplay experience through its programmed AI and non-intelligent components, the developers' vicarious "agency" is *also* expressed in the intelligent behaviors of *other human players* because their affordances for activity and expression are *mediated* by the same elements of design that constrain play from *my* perspective.

To illustrate this with an example, multiplayer-focused first-person shooter *Quake III Arena* (1999) is designed to deliver fast-paced, action-packed gameplay, and it consistently achieves this despite being primarily populated by players who could, at any time, choose not to play it in that way. Its fast, twitchy controls; incentive structure; arsenal of offensive weaponry and limited defensive options; and design of its maps make particular metagame strategies *inevitable*, ensuring that, regardless of the players with and against whom it is played, *Quake III Arena* retains an identifiably unique pace and aesthetic of play.

Motivation → Agency Summary

What to look for

- Upon forming a working knowledge of the procedural expression of a game world, grounded in its operational cause-and-effect relationships, the player **motivations**.

- Macro-level motivations may be directed by a game's explicit objectives or win conditions, but micro-level motivations are player-determined goals and curiosities that either satisfy the next step toward a macro-level goal or indulge a separate player desire.
- Motivation is intrinsically interdiegetic, for the same desire that the player feels to accomplish goals and indulge curiosities is diegetically expressed as the avatar character's animating motivity. In this way, the player acts simultaneously as author, actor, and character within the game's enacted narrative.
- **Agency** is the feeling of performing motivated action in a manner that feels impactful, informed by coherent feedback.
- Agency is both an objective property of a game (a game with highly expressive and reactive control affords a greater systemic agency than a game with limited choice affordance) *and* a subjective property of player integration (even in a game that *affords* a high degree of agency, a player may experience low active agency if she cannot operate or understand its systems).
- Ultimately, the shape and experience of mediated agency is the heart of video games' unique expressive artistry. The mechanics and semiotic ornamentation of games serve the purpose of instantiating a unique experience of contextualized agency.
- Motivation and agency each express as singular, primarily unidirectional, and interdiegetic relationships from the player toward the game, but these singular relationships are acted upon and mediated by all of the components of the gameplay system.
- We can infer an artificial "agency" from NPC actors that populate a game world. This creates a dynamic of play acting with and against other intelligent entities.
- The behavioral parameters of NPC AI and the parameters of the simulation from which actor motivations cannot be discerned (such as its physics system) can be thought of as a means by which developers express a deferred, by-proxy "agency". Though they are not able to *actively* respond to the changing conditions of play (as they are not, themselves, *present* within the system as intelligent agents), we can still read motivated will through the design parameters that constrain and afford play actions.
- Other players in multiplayer games express active, intelligent agency. Beyond expressing their own wills, though, they can also be thought of as proxies for the limited, vicarious "agency" of developers, as, though players choose what actions they perform, developers shape the actions that *can be* performed and which actions are *desirable* to perform at any moment.

Questions to ask

- How does the game orient player attention toward particular objectives? How does the player create individually motivated sub-objectives in order to reach the game's designated goals?
- Does the player develop goals *separate* from those designated by the game system? Do these personal goals form a metagame structure?
- What goals and motivations can the player read into (or project onto) NPCs? How do these relate to the player's objectives (designated or personal)?
- Can the player read different behavioral patterns from the different types or classes of NPCs encountered? How does visual theming cue behavioral expectations?

PROJECTIVE EMBODIMENT/NARRATIVIZATION/STRATEGY

The sense-making model has, so far, encompassed the active steps in the "reading" or decoding of the non-semiotic layer of gameplay: the recognition of states and a formation of hypotheses regarding what causes the game as a whole or its component elements to change states, the adoption of an active role through input into the system and a deepening understanding of cause-effect relationships with attention to feedback, the observance and understanding of dynamics and the unpredictable but logical proceduralities they produce, and finally the adoption of active motivations and the experience of agency within the digital space. Concerning the tasks that the player performs in the decoding of gameplay, the sense-making portion of the model could resolve here.

While the decoding steps are perpetual, though, ongoing throughout gameplay, achieving and maintaining them gives players access to three particular modalities of play that separate casual, uninvolved play from active, deeply involving play. Some writers invoke Mihály Csíkszentmihályi's concept of *flow* (Csíkszentmihályi, 1975; 1990), a mental state in which an appropriately challenging activity is sustained with a state of absorbing focus resulting in a pleasurable feeling of optimal processing. It is intuitively recognized as the feeling of being "in the zone" when performing an activity for which the participant is well-suited. It is said to be brought about by activities that offer challenges that push us to the edge of our capabilities but do not exceed them; it balances upon the border between boredom (mastery exceeds challenge) and frustration (challenge exceeds mastery). As such, it is often invoked by game studies literature, as video games are designed *specifically* to provide appropriately scaling challenges and (ideally) keep players in this kind of highly involved state.

Flow, though well-established in the psychological literature, is not without its controversies. Braxton Soderman reminds us in *Against Flow: Video Games and the Flowing Subject* (2021) that Csíkszentmihályi introduced flow not only as a phenomenological principle but also as a critical theory—an alternative to the warning of Marxist philosopher György Lukács, who feared that play and art may *distract* the subjected classes from recognizing the alienation brought upon by their work and marketplace exploitation—a recognition necessary to achieve a unifying class consciousness that can drive political affiliation to improve conditions of life. Instead, Csíkszentmihályi's concept of flow provided an alternate "solution" to the problem of alienation. Instead of being alienated from their labor, they can find the play and the optimal experience *within* their labor, satisfying the dissonance without cause for collective action (Soderman, 2021, pp. 24, 25). Soderman notes, "the theory of flow promotes ideologies that privilege the individual over the social, intentional agents over fragmented subjects, growth over homeostasis, and action over critical evaluation" (p. 22).

Primarily, though, I find flow to be both too limiting and too non-specific to be a satisfying culmination of the sense-making model. Flow is experienced by students, athletes, musicians, religious devotees, and by wide ranges of other populations in the performance of a great number of activities. That it is evoked by and experienced during video game play is neither surprising nor illuminating; it describes a natural cognitive reaction to any activity of adequately stimulating challenge rather than elucidating something specific about video games in particular. Furthermore, flow is not an *inevitable* or *necessary* response to video game play. Some games are not intended to be played with sustained attention and perpetual challenge. Many games, such as simulations like *Animal Crossing* (2001) and *The Sims* (2000) or RPGs like *Pokémon* (1996) and *FINAL FANTASY* (1987), are intended to be played slowly, with infrequent peaks of challenge spread across hours of incremental progress and embedded narrative content. One may experience moments of flow during these games, but a lack of that *particular* experience does not mean that one was *unsuccessful* in achieving optimally literate play.

Rather, the sense-making portion of my model resolves with three types of experiences. Each can *evoke* flow, but none *require* it. I think they are natural extensions of the process outlined so far. These three experiences also provide the starting point for the meaning-making half of the model. They also align with the three perspectives held in concurrent attention during play. From the diegetic position, the player experiences *projective embodiment*; from the mimetic position, the player experiences *narrative involvement;* and from the methectic position, the player develops *strategy.* It is not necessary to maximize the feeling of each of these, as they are held to varying degrees in different types of games and in different postures of play, but recognizing the purpose and presence of each will unlock useful insights about the unique expressive capacity of video games.

Projective Embodiment

Projective embodiment is described in great detail in Chapter 4. To summarize, projective embodiment is a feeling of direct, embodied presence and control of the avatar character within the simulation. It evolves from the learned control proficiency and increased feedback sensitivity, evolving into a fluency of control and eventually a "transparency" of the layers of mediation between the player and the avatar. The fine motor control of the controller's buttons and their inexact translation into avatar-performed diegetic action fade from occurrent attention. With sustained concentration, the player stops seeing the avatar as a separate being; rather, she assimilates the avatar into an extended "self" as a new networked facet of her own mind/body that allows her the ability to perform afforded actions and extend her sensory perception within the virtual diegesis. In the same way that the car becomes an extension of our mobility capabilities when driving, and in the same way that a cane becomes an extension of a blind person's perceptual capabilities, the avatar becomes a direct link into the "other world" *through* and *as* which the player can act. Optimally, the player does not even think about her hands and the controller any longer. She knows the types of actions that the avatar can perform, and she enacts them as naturally as the brain commands the body.

Projective embodiment is an aesthetic pleasure in and of itself. It involves the joys of controlling a responsive and capable body (consider the joy of performing backflips and long jumps as Mario in *Super Mario Odyssey* (2017), even when not working toward a particular goal), as well as the joy of *telepresence*, of *being* in an imaginative space (an experience of "virtual tourism" is often described by players; the intrinsic pleasure of being somewhere new and compelling).

Projective embodiment is an ultimate expression of the trajectory of the diegetic track of literacy. A first-hand experience of the manipulability of the game world is rooted in an understanding of the input-feedback relationship initiated by avatar action. Motivation and agency can be achieved separately from projective embodiment, but the kind of direct agency that asserts, "*I* can express my will in the game world", creates a stronger sense of connection to the play experience than the still active but consciously vicarious "I can *command my avatar* to express my will in the game world". The degree to which avatar identification can be assimilated into self-identification, the player will gain a greater sense of direct autonomy in the diegetic actions performed.

Obviously, projective embodiment is not an experience afforded by *all* types of games. The terminology is most appropriate when applied to avatar-based games, and even within that category, games with real-time control tend to create a greater sense of active connection between player and avatar than games with indirect or stop-and-start, turn-based control schemes. While it is not my intention to exhaustively chronicle how different genres of games achieve similar experiences of direct diegetic telepresence, it is useful for players to consider, when playing games not obviously avatar-based or not utilizing responsive, real-time control schemes, how the game extends and embeds the player's conscious attention into the game world or why it may resist doing so. Some games, like the match-three puzzle game *Bejeweled* (2001), trade avatar presence for other types of involving tactility that give the "world" of the game a sense of involving immediacy, implying a thin barrier between player and diegesis even though its visuals are fairly abstract. Other games, like *Disco Elysium* (2019), *have* avatar protagonists that are controlled indirectly to emphasize the player's sense of detachment—creating a distance that encourages role-playing and acting against instincts rather than enmeshing the player's own sense of self and, with it, her ethical and ideological attitudes.

Narrativization

From the mimetic perspective, the player seeks to fulfill and express agency within the designed narrative structure of the game by performing the role of the avatar character within the fiction and completing the objectives outlined by the game's structure of challenges. Though this perspective aims to draw out from the game that which has been inscribed and intended in its design, it does not mean that the player takes a passive, consuming role. Rather, she privileges the fantasy and expresses agency in terms of the fictional layer of the experience. This is done through goal-oriented (motivated) play, performance of the avatar as a character within the storyworld, and steering the course of the in-game narrative.

This can best be understood in contrast to the diegetic perspective, which is primarily (though not exclusively) semiotically ambivalent. In other words, the aesthetic pleasures of being and moving within a space by way of projective embodiment are, at their core, inherent to the "physical" relationship between the avatar and the space. If, for instance, a space in a 3D platformer is made into a challenging and satisfying obstacle course, one could expect that it would remain as thrilling to explore and jump around within regardless of its thematic skin. A space could be re-themed to look like a shopping mall, a haunted house, or a carnival, and it would not affect the spatial relationships between its objects and the avatar's affordances within them.

On the other hand, the mimetic perspective takes a greater interest in "entering into conversation" with the game's design and narrative. For the player in the mimetic state of mind, there is joy not only in *being* within a space but in overcoming designed challenges within that space. There is joy not only in *movement* but in *progression* toward a goal. Ultimately, the mimetic perspective can be boiled down to the task of role playing, of performing a character. It is important not only that the avatar moves through a virtual space; it is important that *this character* with a *specific history, personality, and goals* moves through *a narratively contextualized space with a history of its own.* The player adopts that which is important to the avatar character as her own goals and considers her role not only as a projective agent but as an actor performing a role in a story.

The diegetic and mimetic perspectives hold some tension between one another, but they are not opposites. Mimetic performance involves the surrender of some of the freedom of diegetic, embodied play. In focusing on reaching a particular objective or performing the avatar role in a manner adherent with characterization, the player limits the scope of desirable actions from near-infinite to a select few that advance the chosen paths of progression or narrative. But mimetic performance also amplifies diegetic pleasures by giving free play greater context and stakes. Ideally, designed objectives lead players to and through opportunities for inherently pleasurable diegetic play. In elegant examples, the mimetic structure anticipates follows that which the diegetically immersed player is, herself, motivated to do already, giving the illusion that the embedded narrative animates around player actions rather than the player deferring her unconstrained freedom for the purpose of narrative progress.

In this description of mimetic play, it may seem counterintuitive to group the acts of narrative role-playing and following gameplay objectives as both being acts of *narrativization*. Semiotic storytelling and non-semiotic play are often held separately, and it is often noticeable when one "interrupts" the momentum of the other, implying some kind of inherent opposition (the "narrative paradox" as discussed by Aylett [2000]). Actually, though, goals and the rules that limit and structure play are also structural narrative and characterization elements. To pursue a designated objective is to partake in the story of the character's motivation and action. Like an actor hitting a mark, objectives give character performances direction. It is important to the characterization of Mario that he is driven to save the princess from Bowser, and gameplay pursuit of the designated objective works toward the narrative goal of framing Mario as a "princess-rescuer".

This culminating mimetic task is one of *narrativization*, which can be defined as the act of spinning narrative patterns from events or data. It is an act of *reparative interpretation*. Narrativization involves the translation of information into a narrative. It is an approach of curation; data that contributes to or supports a specific narrative thread is pulled together and separated from that which we deem irrelevant, based on the specific story being told.[5] As opposed to fiction, in which each word or image is designed to suit the story, narrativization of events in real life requires this intentional reparation: the selection of pertinent information, the erasure of irrelevant information, and the inference of linking elements for which direct experience is not available. For example, a story like "my wife snapped at me twice today, she must be having a bad day" involves drawing a narrative line through multiple pieces of information (two episodes of a short temper) held in context (this is unusual behavior), the erasure of irrelevant information (the storyteller went to the store and pet a dog that day, but those details are irrelevant to the story being told), and a bit of inference that holds the story together (hypothesizing about the storyteller's wife's mood).

Audiences narrativize most arts, and the process of forming narratives and inferences to resolve artistic ambiguity is an appealing way to participate with art. It exercises one of the most primary and useful evolutionary traits of the human species: the ability to recognize patterns and draw speculative (or fanciful) links and trends. This is closely related to Eve Kosofsky Sedgwick's conceptualization of *reparative reading*, an "additive and accretive" form of reading that "wants to assemble and confer plenitude on an object" (Sedgwick,

2003). From a reparative perspective, narratives are presented with indeterminate meaning. The reader utilizes the "part-objects"—narrative fragments—of a text and constructs a subjective, personal "whole" meaning from these part-objects' relations to one another and knowledge and beliefs from the reader's life. Sedgewick positions her reparative reading in opposition to the stance that was more common in critical analysis at the time, which she terms *paranoid reading*, a revelatory perspective in which the reader interrogates the text for embedded meaning with the presumption that a singular, discernible "truth" can and will be expressed by the narrative.

In the context of video games, all narrative artifacts that arise from gameplay require differing levels of repair and narrativization. This includes both levels of embedded and emergent narratives. The emergent narrative, characterized by the events that emerge from the dynamic interplay of systemic elements and variables, requires the most obvious reparative and narrativistic reconciliation. Linking emergent events not only in terms of cause-effect chains but, further, into meaningful narratives is one of the primary aesthetic pleasures of playing heavily systemic games. Embedded narratives, though, characterized by the prefabricated, semiotic stories written by the game's developers, intuitively seem to instead involve a process of discovery, inviting a paranoid style of reading. Despite the prefabricated nature of embedded narrative elements, though, taking part in these stories is still a widely variable process that requires elements of reparative play (Grinblat et al., 2021).

The level of repair involved in embedded narrative interpretation depends upon the degree of narrative configurability afforded by the system as well as the reactivity to role-playing variation. In games that afford high levels of narrative configurability (what Jason Grinblat [2017] would call *open* story volumes), stories may present players with frequent opportunities for branching storylines, the ability to alter or disrupt the sequence in which prefabricated narrative events take place, or narrative ambiguity that requires interpretation rather than insisting upon rigid structure and answers. From a character performance perspective, some games allow for highly variable expressions, even during moments of scripted storytelling (such as *Baldur's Gate 3* [2023], in which players are presented with a large array of dialogue options during each social encounter that allow for nuanced and variable characterization), while others wrestle back character expression during dialogue and cutscene moments without regard for the variable expressions enacted during play (such as *OCTOPATH TRAVELER II* [2023], in which members of the party are strongly characterized with voiced performances primarily during non-interactive, prefabricated cutscenes).

Narrativization, though primarily a meaning-making process, concludes the mimetic perspective of the sense-making process because discerning narrative logic and forming a mental sequence of privileged events that transpire during play inform the choices made *during* play, constructive of the enacted gameplay artifact. In the sense that players are not only *audience* of games but also co-authors and performers within the experience, the task of narrativization takes on not only an *interpretive* dimension but also a highly practical dimension of informing motivation, agency, and further action. Role-playing as a character within the fiction and configuring the sequence and manner of narrative events define important variables in the way in which the fictional proceedings will be later interpreted; it defines the *manifest content* (see Chapter 11).

As such, while the projective embodiment aim of the diegetic perspective tunes the player into the aesthetic pleasures of interacting with and within a system (privileging the toyetic aspects of video games), the mimetic task of narrativization coheres enacted play into structured texts as narratives (of developer-embedded texts and player-directed actions) and sets the stage for methectic coherence as *games*. For further elaboration into the process of narrativization, see Chapters 9 and 11.

Strategy

Finally, the sense-making model resolves the player's methectic perspective through strategic consideration. Methexis spotlights player involvement in the game as a *software system* without respect to the mimetic functions of its diegetic elements. The game is a puzzle to be solved and a challenge to be overcome, and it is not important whether that is done in a way that respects or runs contrary to the fiction.

In a war game, it is the methectic portion of a player's perspective that weighs the strategic advantage of sacrificing a character in battle, while it's the mimetic perspective that becomes emotional when considering the loss. Considered from the methectic perspective, the game can be reduced to a series of numbers and functions.

We can call this perspective *metagaming*; the consideration of the game as a series of rules and parameters that can be optimized, reconfigured, or even exploited. Stephanie Boluk and Patrick LeMieux (2017) say, "the metagame emerges as the material trace of the discontinuity between the phenomenal experience of play and the mechanics of digital games" (p. 9). Metagaming considers the context of play, including the community and culture surrounding it, in conversation and contention with its design. The methectic perspective encourages the player to recognize the artifice of the game and retains an apprehension toward playing the directed role. Not (necessarily) in a spirit of rebelliousness, though; it is necessary to play "beyond the screen" and invoke the detached perspective of real-world knowledge of the player in order to overcome the challenges set out in front of us.

The formation of agency is not a sufficient resolution of the methectic perspective. Agency is motivated by objectives and prompts the player to *recognize* her capabilities to achieve those objectives, but strategic planning is ultimately what structures and animates her agency from a perspective of empowerment to the fulfillment of her motivations. To be able to "read" that which occurs on-screen without being able to form strategic hypotheses for their exploitation would be an incomplete understanding of the game. If (an element of) the *art* of gameplay can be boiled down to the shaping and structure of the aesthetic pleasure of agency, strategy is how that agency is focused, directed, and utilized to fulfill the player's specific motivations.

Though I position methexis in *somewhat of an* opposition to mimesis with regard to the acceptance or rejection of the call to acquiesce to playing a designed role in the narrative (mimesis prompts investment in narrative through the following of direction in the form of incentives, while methexis seeks to overcome challenges through pushing against and circumventing direction in the form of challenges), methexis *recognizes* and *utilizes* diegesis and mimesis in strategic consideration. The diegetic conceit of the game world as a space of "natural" (or unprivileged) ontology may grant unconventional strategic insights. For example, players of the first-person shooter *Quake* (1996) recognized that one of the properties of the game's *explosion* mechanic is to propel objects (including characters) away from it with great force, so players developed an unexpected strategy of firing explosives at their feet while jumping to propel them higher into the air than an unassisted jump would naturally carry them. This metagame technique, termed *rocket jumping*, has become a strategic consideration in competitive play because it increases mobility affordances. Similarly, methexis values mimetic direction for its strategic possibilities. If the game seems to be incentivizing a particular type of action, there is a good chance that it is directing players toward a planned (and advantageous) contingency. If the camera or dialogue highlights an unexplored part of the map, for instance, perhaps something strategically valuable can be found there. The methectic perspective skeptically scrutinizes but is not ambivalent to the other perspectives.

During play, the player should consider what types of strategies seem to be effective in achieving particular goals. Does it appear that those strategies align with the "intended" style of play, or has the player uncovered a clever exploit that is perhaps not in the spirit of the intended experience (see Chapter 13 for further review of glitches and exploits)? As the model veers into meaning-making consideration, do the employed strategies reflect or invoke an ideological perspective? If so, is it an expression of the developers, evident in design, or of the player, emerging from self-determined play?

NOTES

1. Rare edge-case games in which victory and loss conditions are of primary significance and do not need to be informationally valorized (such as Russian Roulette) present challenges to classification.
2. "Singular" is not to imply irreducibility. A "car" component is, itself, a system, and its systemic components have relationships with the components at *its* level *and* at the holistic level. For example, a car's braking mechanism is a component of the singular car subsystem, but failure of the car's brakes will result in a change in behavior of the car as a system that will escalate to change in the traffic system above it, particularly if it leads to a collision.

3. I recognize that this term does not completely resolve the issue of ambiguity. A more precise term might be *elements-of-processor*, but I think "game state" strikes the best balance between the non-specificity of "system" and a colloquial understandability.
4. Ludemes represent specific sequences of action that follow from choices made during gameplay. The specific pattern of movement of a Chess piece or the specific reaction a systemic actor has to a form of input represents a ludeme, which may be quoted and repurposed. This term is similar but distinct to a (maddeningly similar) term to which we will return in the meaning-making section of the model: ludic. I will go into greater detail later, but for now, we can distinguish the two because a ludeme represents an image of action in a game whereas a ludic represents an image of agency.
5. Additional exploration of this curation-like approach is performed in Chapter 5, citing James Ryan's dissertation which outlines a robust "Curationist" methodology for video game interpretation.

REFERENCES

Aylett, R. (2000). Emergent narrative, social immersion and "storification". *The 1st International Workshop on Narrative Interaction for Learning Environments*, Edinburgh.

Boluk, S. & LeMieux, P. (2017). *Metagaming: Playing, competing, spectating, cheating, trading, making, and breaking videogames.* University of Minnesota Press.

Csíkszentmihályi, M. (1975). *Beyond boredom and anxiety: Experiencing flow in work and play.* Jossey-Bass.

Csíkszentmihályi, M. (1990). *Flow: The psychology of optimal experience.* Harper Perennial.

Dawkins, R. (1976). *The selfish gene.* Oxford University Press.

Game Maker's Toolkit (2015, March 16). *Super Mario 3D World's 4 step level design* [Video]. YouTube. https://youtu.be/dBmIkEvEBtA

Grinblat, J. (2017). Emergent narratives and story volumes. In T. S. Short & T. Adams (Eds.), *Procedural generation in game design* (pp. 199–207). CRC Press.

Grinblat, J., Manning, C., & Kreminski, M. (2021). *Emergent narrative and reparative play.* Springer. doi:10.1007/978-3-030-92300-6_19

Hunicke, R., LeBlanc, M., & Zubek, R. (2004). MDA: A formal approach to game design and game research. *Proceedings of the AAAI Workshop on Challenges in Game AI,* 4(1).

Järvinen, A. (2008). *Games without frontiers.* Tampere University Press.

Johnson, S. (1997). *Interface culture: How new technology transforms the way we create & communicate.* Basic Books.

Johnson, S. (2001). *Emergence: The connected lives of ants, brains, cities, and software.* Scribner.

Koster, R. (2005). A grammar of gameplay: Game design atoms, can games be diagrammed? *Proceedings of the Game Developers Conference 2005.*

Laurel, B. (2014). *Computers as theatre,* 2nd ed. Addison-Wesley.

Melville, H. (1851). *Moby-Dick; or, the whale.* Richard Bentley.

Murray, J. H. (1997). *Hamlet on the holodeck: The future of narrative in cyberspace.* The MIT Press.

Murray, J. H. (2012). *Inventing the medium: Principles of interaction design as cultural practice.* The MIT Press.

Newheiser, M. (2009). *Michaël Samyn, Auriea Harvey, Tale of Tales.* Adventure Classic Gaming. https://www.adventureclassicgaming.com/index.php/site/interviews/473/

Salen, K. & Zimmerman, E. (2003). *Rules of play: Game design fundamentals.* The MIT Press.

Sedgwick, E. K. (2003). *Touching feeling: Affect, pedagogy, performativity.* Duke University Press.

Seraphine, F. (2016). The ludic framework. *Digital Game Research Association Japan Proceedings of the Annual Conference.*

Soderman, B. (2021). *Against flow: Video games and the flowing subject.* The MIT Press.

Swink, S. (2009). *Game feel: A game designer's guide to virtual sensation.* Morgan Kaufmann Publishers.

Treanor, M., Schweizer, B., Bogost, I., & Mateas, M. (2010). Proceduralist readings: How to find meaning in games with graphical logics. *FDG '11: Proceedings of the 6th International Conference on Foundations of Digital Games.* doi:10.1145/2159365.2159381

CHAPTER 8

Layered Literacy, Part 3

Meaning-Making

AS I INTRODUCED AT the beginning of this model explanation, this literacy model is divided into two parts: sense-making and meaning-making. The first portion, sense-making (which we have already covered), entails the methods by which players "decode" the information involved in gameplay—distinguishing systemic actors, forming an understanding of the system's operations, and finding how they may interact with the system. It culminates in three distinct but concurrent participatory activities: projective embodiment (from the diegetic perspective), narrative agency (from the mimetic perspective), and strategy (from the methectic perspective). The sense-making model is *largely* non-semiotic (pre-reflective), meaning that the types of decoding performed and perspectives reached are not predominantly dependent upon the game's linguistic, symbolic, or representational content. Those elements inform and contextualize, but the types of perspectives reached would be equally valid and achievable were the game to be "reskinned", that is, given a completely different semiotic coding and context.

Whereas the sense-making process informs the player's practical understanding and interaction with the system, the meaning-making process is where interpretations of greater significance and value are formed. Rather than practical operation, the search for meaning is the engagement with the *art* of games: the elements that point *beyond* themselves, that communicate something about the human experience, and that aim toward personal, cultural, and universal insights. For, as defined in the introductory chapter of this book, the purpose of art is to communicate second-order meaning: that which cannot be expressed directly and informationally. Whereas I can tell you directly what time it is or how to drive to the store, I must communicate separate states of mind (such as emotions or empathetic perspectives) through inference. Feelings and perspectives must be stirred from within, using evocative "raw materials", shaped and molded through an individual's own centers of cognitive and emotional processing. I cannot make you feel sadness as directly as I can transfer to you the image of a horse riding a bicycle (which I was able to do with those few words); I must instead tell you a story, or show you a picture, or perform for you a song, or, indeed, create an interactive digital scenario that *makes* you sad; an inexact science that results in different effects for every beholder.

Moving into the meaning-making part of the model, I seek to explain how this deeper meaning is achieved and how we, as literate players, may further deepen the meanings that we can pull from gameplay. The division of the model *does not* represent a split between the play activity and post-play reflection. Rather, video games have the rare complication of audience meaning-making directly *affecting* the construction of the artistic product (gameplay). That is to say, whereas deriving meaning from a painting involves interpretation of a largely static work, determined in its content, deriving meaning from video games affects the choices that the player will make as she continues to enact the systemic story.

DOI: 10.1201/9781003530961-8

Remember, in the process of artistic engagement, there exists the artistic *potentiator*—the artifact, or "raw material", that is fed into the beholder's individual, subjective processing—and the artistic *experience*—the processed, reflective meanings and insights derived from the artwork. For video games, the packaged good that we may call the "game" (the code or its abstract rules) is *not* the artistic potentiator; it is the *structural parameter from which* the artistic potentiator is constructed. The actual artistic potentiator is live gameplay—created and consumed simultaneously and in real time by the player. Thus, the meanings derived from video games are expressive of *both* developer (in the shaping of gameplay action) and player (in the enactment of gameplay action).

A wide variety of types of meaning will be explored in this latter half of the model, ranging from the pre-reflective evocation of lived (virtual) experience to complexly expressed ideology. Further, the model will explore the implications of different types of meaning feeding back into gameplay enactment. Additionally, this latter half of the model maintains the structural conceit of its previous half: the simultaneous occurrence of diegetic, mimetic, and methectic perspectives. Further, this portion of the model continues to frame the system by which gameplay is produced as inclusive of player, computer, and context holistically rather than only framing the narrow relationship between player impulse and diegetic action.

PRE-REFLECTIVE AESTHETICS

Before formal meaning is derived, gameplay is experienced as pre-reflective aesthetics. This contributes to what I call the *lived experience principle* of games (which I will detail shortly). *Aesthetics* as a category derives from the MDA model and the models that were based on it. MDA defines aesthetics as an "emotional reaction" that players have in response to the dynamics of gameplay (Hunicke et al., 2004), but I believe a greater variety of pre-reflective responses exist within this categorical designation. I broaden the term to refer not only to *emotional* evocation but also to all forms of pre-reflective reaction (many of which *are* emotional, but some, including a sense of *presence*, I would not feel comfortable labeling as "emotional").

Aesthetics, more thoroughly explored in Chapter 2, is most often defined in terms of the core pleasures of a work of art—the elements of the artwork that are abstractly appreciated (Kirkpatrick, 2011). The elements that contribute to the wordless, *felt* experience of each artwork vary from medium to medium, making it difficult to craft a concrete definition. Ultimately, the theory of aesthetics seeks to describe *why* people like or connect with certain artworks and not others. One can argue that the theory of aesthetics doesn't describe artworks but instead describes the human mind, observed through its interactions with artworks in a similar manner to how one "observes" a black hole by analyzing the effects it has on the celestial objects around it.

Despite ambiguity in its definition, aesthetics are typically considered to be *primary* to the experiential relationship between art and beholder. One *experiences* a reaction to an artwork before one processes its meaning or context. One may be disgusted by an artwork and grow to appreciate it with greater contextual knowledge, but the aesthetic elements that contributed to that initial disgust hold an experiential primacy and are held in mind separately from the reflective re-evaluation.

My specification of *pre-reflective* breaks from the MDA model's definition. Hunicke et al. define a taxonomy of gameplay aesthetics, producing a list of both pre-reflective and processed reactions: Sensation (game as sense-pleasure), Fantasy (game as make-believe), Narrative (game as drama), Challenge (game as obstacle course), Fellowship (game as social framework), Competition (game as expression of dominance), Discovery (game as uncharted territory), Expression (game as self-discovery), and Submission (game as pastime) (Hunicke et al., 2004). Of this set, I list Sensation, Challenge, Expression, and Submission as pre-reflective (along with my own additions: Vertigo, Presence, Progress, Ontological Upset, and Compulsion; this would leave Fantasy, Narrative, Fellowship, Competition, and Discovery as being primarily thoughtfully engaged (as well as Expression and Progress, which cross both categories). This division distinguishes between the feelings that are experienced automatically in the moment and those that are experienced in the context of semiotic, meaning-based assessment. The latter group will be revisited shortly as *critical aesthetics* and is highly relevant to the meaning-making process, but I wish to first call attention to the ways in which pre-reflective aesthetics contribute to the latter category.

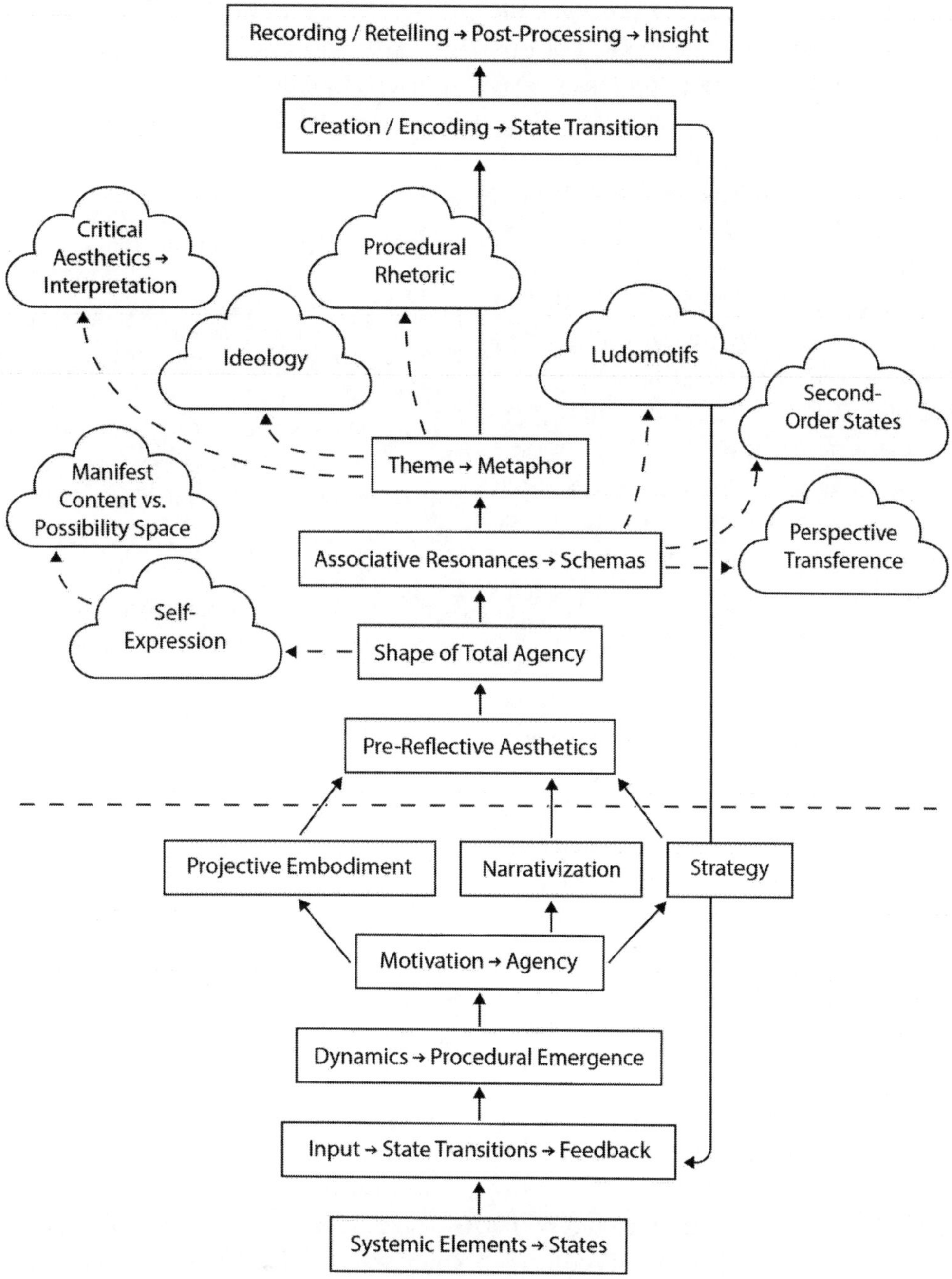

FIGURE 8.1 The complete sense-making and meaning-making model. The upper half represents the meaning-making process explored in this chapter. The cloud-shaped bubbles represent forms of meaning that the player extracts from gameplay.

Another manner in which I differ from Hunicke et al.'s definition, as well as some general definitions of aesthetics outside of the video game sphere, is more a matter of explicitness of definition than actual definitional difference, I believe. Many definitions of *aesthetics* put emphasis on sense-*pleasures* and seek to examine why audiences find certain works *beautiful* or *pleasing*. Hunicke et al.'s section on aesthetics seeks to answer "what makes a game 'fun'?" (2004). When asked, I expect that most would admit that examining *displeasures* and *negative* reactions to artworks is just as useful, as many (if not most) arts are constructed to elicit *some degree* of dissonance in beholders in addition to sense-pleasure. The artistic elicitation of emotions we typically label with a negative valence can be just as core to the experience of a work as its pleasures. I feel that this is *implicit* in other definitions, but I want to be explicit in the context of this model. Aesthetic reactions can be of positive, negative, or mixed valences. Many of the core aesthetics of play involve feelings of struggle and deferred reward, typically resolving into the positive feeling of striving but certainly peppered with moments of defeat, frustration, boredom, and strenuousness.

Each of the aesthetics listed above is detailed in Chapter 2 and will not be reviewed again in detail here, but generally, they describe the elements of dynamics and interactions that *grip* or *compel* players. For example, the aesthetic of Discovery compels players' curiosity, and the aesthetic of Competition engages players' instinct to triumph over opponents. If dynamics are interactions between parts of a system that affect the operation or outputs of the system, aesthetics are the *felt, experiential* results of player involvement with the system. Aesthetics of play are specifically aesthetics *of* interaction, agency, presence, and procedurality. Other aesthetic reactions, such as reactions to visual arts, music, or sound effects, provide context and can amplify or diminish these aesthetics of play, but they will not be detailed extensively in this book because the process by which they are judged does not differ greatly from how these aesthetics are appreciated in other art forms, save a greater need and priority for practical legibility.

Lived Experience Principle

The aesthetics of most narrative artworks involve a degree of empathetic vicariousness. We may be terrified by a horror novel on behalf of the peril of the characters that we have come to care about. While elements of video game narratives are encountered empathetically as well, the agential identity extension involved in projective embodiment (see Chapter 4) causes elements of games' moment-to-moment enactment to be experienced as primary, lived experience. Not in the sense that players become confused about reality and fiction (as some critical of the hobby suggest), but that play occurrences are experienced as unique and personal circumstances.

Game designer Jason Grinblat (2017) writes:

> emergent narratives are also authentic. In resulting from the collision of systems rather than the script of an author, they mirror the experiences we have in our everyday lives, the stories we hear from our family and friends, and the tales we read about in history books.
>
> *(p. 201)*

Because the emergent events that occur as the result of systemic interaction are not authorially determined, players can sense their spontaneity, and this affects the manner in which these experiences are regarded and remembered.

To participate in a world modeled by the interaction of mechanics is different from hearing tales set within worlds of story alone. The world being modeled does not require fidelity to the real world—the laws of virtual physics do not need to model the physics of Earth to be convincingly "worldish"; they only need to be internally consistent. This is bottom-up simulation as opposed to top-down narrative (Ryan, 2018, p. 67).

James Ryan lists several aesthetics (as the word is used in Chapter 2) associated with emergent narratives, and many of them relate back to the core experience of video games as "lived" and personal. He names the *aesthetics of the actual*: "when a story recounts (ostensibly) actual events, it will likely be more interesting than a fictional, but otherwise identical, counterpart" (p. 92). Though the *game world* is artificial, the processes that enact its events do not fabricate events in the way a storyteller imagines events; they occur as a result of impersonal procedures, thus, any happening within them has the chance to be unique and surprising.

Ryan also lists the *aesthetics of the personal*: "when a story recounts events to which a recipient is personally connected, it will likely be more interesting to her (with all other things being equal)" (p. 93) and the *aesthetics of a larger context*: "a special intrigue is attached to stories that transpire against the backdrop of a larger storyworld. While all narrative works imply (and at times concretely model) a storyworld, world simulation is the organizing [principle] in emergent narrative" (p. 93). Several additional aesthetics in his list point back to the catalyzing uniqueness of the video game as artform: *aesthetics of the unauthored* (which he borrows from Jason Grinblat [2018]), *aesthetics of the uncovered*, *aesthetics of the improbable*, and the *aesthetics of the ephemeral* (Ryan, 2018, pp. 94–98).

The lived experience principle is explored in greater depth in Chapter 11.

Aesthetics toward Meaning

Aesthetics form an experiential lens through which gameplay is viewed. While the remaining steps in the meaning-making model engage, to a greater degree, with thoughtful reflection and inspection, they must be understood in the context of the layer of aesthetics that mediates the relationship between pure systemic expression and players' experience of it.

The role of aesthetics in meaning-making is well-illustrated in the Proceduralist model detailed in Chapter 5, in which aesthetics are one of three elements that contribute to meaning, the others being dynamics (which pose direct procedural arguments) and theme (which decorates the interactive layer but is not, itself, interactive). To use an example from a foundational Proceduralist paper, Treanor et al. describe one instance of *meaning* in *The Free Culture Game* (2008) with the following argument:

> dynamic(1) ^ aesthetic(1) ^ theme(1) → **meaning**(1): New ideas are hard to control but, with careful attention, they will benefit everybody

Expanding the operators in the argument:

> {**dynamic**(1): Because producers create new ideas, the player's goal is to turn everybody green[. As] the player exerts force on new ideas, *the player will push ideas toward green people to keep them from turning grey*} ^ {**aesthetic**(1): the lack of control over the indirect force that determines how the player's cursor acts on the ideas is frustrating} ^ {**theme**(1): Green people are made to look happier than grey through color and animation} → **meaning**(1): New ideas are hard to control but, with careful attention, they will benefit everybody.
>
> *(Treanor et al., 2010)*

Regarding the above argument, a hypothetical "objective" reading of the mechanical rhetoric (one that includes **dynamic**(1) and **theme**(1) but excludes the player's subjective experience of frustration with the controls in **aesthetic**(1)) may reach a *similar* conclusion. Perhaps something like: "New ideas should be intentionally distributed to make people happier". This is *an* adequate meaning, but it misses out on a crucial component of the game's argument: that ideas can be difficult to control. To ignore the aesthetic layer, perhaps in pursuit of an "unbiased objectivity", fails to recognize that the subjective experience is a vital medium of design. Developers plan dynamic proceduralities in order to communicate desired elements of their procedural arguments through our aesthetic facilities. Not every aesthetic reaction may match that which is desired or intended by the developers (for example, a colorblind player may experience great frustration with a color-matching puzzle intended to be a relaxing palate-cleanser), but aesthetics (even "atypical" aesthetic experiences) express the total capabilities of the designed system, and the system *is* the argument.

As such, aesthetic reaction is not something to be recognized for the purpose of *minimizing* its effect on our ludic interpretations. Aesthetics are intentional and constructive to the total meaning of gameplay. It is a rhetorical tool in the creation of meaning. It should be recognized and made explicit when forming summaries or arguments about the meaning of gameplay experiences (to improve the legibility of our summaries and arguments to those who had differing aesthetic reactions), but it should not be treated as a "lesser" element of systemic meaning-making just because it *seems to* express more about the player than the meaning inscribed *into* the system by the developers. As I say frequently, gameplay is unavoidably expressive of both player and developer; both are co-authors. To privilege one at the detriment of the other is to form an incomplete picture of the game.

Aesthetics from the Three Perspectives

Largely being automatic reactions to gameplay, the *formation* of aesthetic reactions does not require a large amount of theoretical justification, but it is useful to be able to recognize which aesthetics are primed by each of our sense-making endpoints. Each endpoint stems from one of the three simultaneously held gameplay perspectives (diegetic, mimetic, methectic), allowing us to carry these three simultaneous perspectives into the meaning-making portion of the model.

Projective embodiment (of the diegetic perspective) evokes the aesthetics of Sensation, Vertigo, Presence, Discovery, Ontological Upset, and Expression.

Narrative agency (of the mimetic perspective) evokes the aesthetics of Sensation, Vertigo, Fantasy, Narrative, Fellowship, Competition, Discovery, Progress, Ontological Upset, Expression, and Compulsion.

Strategy (of the methectic perspective) evokes the aesthetics of Challenge, Fellowship, Competition, Progress, Discovery, Ontological Upset, Expression, Submission, and Compulsion.

SHAPE OF TOTAL AGENCY

During play, the player unavoidably undergoes a pre-critical aesthetic experience. She will notice highs and lows, frustrations and catharsis, that form natural experiential texture during play. Unpacking these variances and understanding what underscores the rhythm of play is a matter of examining changes in the "shape" of total afforded actions that correspond with changing game states.

As states change, the number and types of choices available to players change with it, broadening toward infinity, narrowing toward a binary, or sometimes skewing toward particular possibility clusters and away from others. Were each possible choice in every moment of gameplay to be plotted onto a decision tree chart, we would be able to see patterns of expansion and narrowing. This visual metaphor informs what is called the "shape of the possibility space", or the shape of agency.

C. Thi Nguyen describes the centrality of agency to the medium of games:

> Games, then, are a unique social technology. They are a method for inscribing forms of agency into artifactual vessels: for recording them, preserving them, and passing them around. And we possess a special ability: we can be fluid with our agency; we can submerge ourselves in alternate agencies designed by another. In other words, we can use games to communicate forms of agency. Games turn out to be part of the human practices of inscription. Painting lets us record sights, music lets us record sounds, stories let us record narratives, and games let us record agencies.
>
> *(Nguyen, 2020, p. 1)*

To Nguyen's point, the experience of differing agencies carries inherent meaning and is a primary construct behind most other forms of meaning that games produce. Understanding the changing shape of agency throughout the experience of play is crucial to literate play.

Designed Agency

Agency is the primary medium through which non-semiotic video game narratives are conveyed. The shape of agency, varying over time and/or spatial/semiotic context, forms the primary dramatic structure of the game altogether. As explained before, agency consists of three primary variables: motivation, ability to effect change, and understandability of results of performed action. To experience a feeling of agency, the player must wish to do something, have the ability to act, and be able to discern the effects of their action. If any one of these is limited, the player will experience a narrowing or even an inversion of total agency.

Motivation

Games regularly alter all three of these variables in order to create textured experiences. Motivation, as discussed in the sense-making portion of the model, is altered through manipulation of incentives and punishments. Consider the example of the open-world ARPG *The Legend of Zelda: Breath of the Wild* (2017). When engaging in unstructured exploration, the player's incentive structure is in constant flux, primarily swayed by dynamic informational conveyance and threat urgency. The game's reward system tends to be gentle and low-level. Rewards typically grant small, incremental upgrades for deferred, long-term advantage or more significant *temporary* benefits with little long-term effect. The former rewards are typically granted for the completion of shrines: standalone, enclosed puzzles scattered throughout the world. Each grants a Spirit Orb, four of which can be exchanged for either a small expansion of Link's total health (amount of damage that he can take from enemies before experiencing a game over) or stamina (amount of time Link can perform strenuous actions, such as climbing or sprinting, before tiring). Temporary rewards include weapons, which break after a number of uses, and consumables such as arrows for Link's bow and foods that can refill Link's health when depleted.

Because the incremental upgrades are small (and only granted for every four Spirit Orbs) and other rewards are temporary, incentives are not given immediate urgency; the dedicated pursuit of these incentives does not overwhelm the player's curiosity-driven exploration. Rewards are *just* useful enough to make self-guided exploration beneficial but are not of such overwhelming importance that they demand attention *instead of* or *before* self-guided exploration. The player is also not made overtly aware of the locations of these rewards; shrines and other points of interest tend not to be marked on the map. The player must find these locations in the course of their curiosity-driven exploration of the game world. The game's world is also designed to present a limited amount of information uncovered in this naturalistic, exploration-guided way: the land of Hyrule is hilly and mountainous, so the player is given micro-incentives to summit these viewpoints to gain a less obstructed view of the surrounding world and find out what she could not see before. At any position in the game world, there are always *one or two* interesting things that warrant the player's investigation: smoke rising above a hill that signals the presence of a campfire, the distinctive glow of a shrine in the distance, the activity of enemies or wild animals in the distance...

In this case, we can attribute the shaping of incentives to the spatial construction of the game world. If there was a point in the world from which the player could spy twelve different points of interest, that might overwhelm her feeling of self-guided curiosity with the compulsion to clear all of them. She has found an "optimal" vantage point, so pressing further into the wilderness is not necessary until she earns all of the rewards available to her in her immediate proximity. It is like she has discovered a full-course menu of options available in one space. Say, instead, that the space was designed so that ten of those options were obscured by hills, forests, and mountains. She still has knowledge of three rewards in her immediate vicinity and can choose which to prioritize and pursue, but these rewards will quickly exhaust; she must continue to explore, taking risks by venturing further into the unknown, to learn of the location of others. Continued curiosity and exploration are incentivized. The persistent incentive is the need for more spatial information, fostering an exploratory spirit.

Consider the opposite perspective. The quickest way to narrow the player's incentive shape is to introduce the threat of punishment. In *Breath of the Wild*, if the player sees enemies scurrying about in the distance, they may have relatively small influence on her incentive structure. The enemies may *signal* the presence of something worthwhile (what are they guarding?), but the player may choose to indulge other curiosities instead. When an enemy engages the player in active combat, though, the incentive space narrows. Surviving the encounter becomes the most urgent motivation. If the avatar does not survive, all other choices become unavailable. *During* a combat encounter, the motivational space changes shape constantly. The primary motivation is to defeat or escape the enemy, but when the enemy lunges at Link with their weapon, Link must dodge or defend. When an enemy swings a sword, starts a fire, or triggers an explosion, those spaces of immediate danger become impassable. Movement affordances narrow.

This is perhaps best demonstrated by "bullet-hell" shmup games, like *Radiant Silvergun* (1998) or *Crimzon Clover* (2011). Enemy vessels fire patterned arrays of bullets that can destroy the avatar vessel upon impact. In low-bullet-density scenarios, the player's incentive is to position the avatar optimally so that her projectile attacks destroy priority targets, but in high-bullet-density scenarios, the player's primary incentive shifts to survivability: navigating the maze, even if her attack position becomes suboptimal. The push-and-pull, risk-and-reward relationship is in dynamic variance. Each game state (attack vs. defend phase, remaining health of boss enemy, number of avatar lives remaining) shapes incentives and agency in a way that becomes like a vocabulary of action itself.

Action Affordance

Obviously, the shape of agency changes as the number or types of affordances change. This can be on the macro, long-term scale (in a strategy game like *Sid Meier's Civilization VI* (2016), the payer may earn the ability to construct new types of buildings or units by reaching research or resource milestones, expanding her strategic affordances) or at the micro, moment-to-moment scale (immediately after throwing a heavy punch in a fighting game such as *Street Fighter 6* (2023), the player is unable to issue subsequent commands until the animation completes, leaving her open to counter-attack if her punch missed).

Afforded actions are in constant fluctuation alongside changes in the game state. There are 20 actions afforded to the player in the first turn of a Chess match. As the game state changes, this number can grow (as pieces are unblocked after pawns disperse) or shrink (as pieces are removed from the game state or the king is put into check). The most stark and consistent rhythm follows the turn structure. A player has zero (on-board) actions afforded to her when it is her opponent's turn.

Throughout a game, afforded actions constantly change. In *Super Mario 64* (1996), Mario cannot ground slam when standing on the ground (he must be airborne) and cannot jump while already airborne. In *PAC-MAN* (1980), Pac-Man cannot move forward if he is pressed up against the maze's wall. The parameters that outline the game's operational logic give shape to contextually afforded actions and, thus, a game state's total player agency.

Feedback

While a sense of "fairness" requires a certain level of consistency of feedback legibility, small variances are enough to give the shape of agency some interesting texture. The density of activity can obscure feedback, or the urgency of attentional focus can distract from the mechanisms of feedback. For instance, if an enemy takes three hits from a sword to defeat, it is fairly easy to keep track of one's progress through a fight in a one-on-one encounter, but this task becomes much more challenging when fighting ten enemies at once. How many enemies did one sword swipe hit? Which enemies have been hit once or twice already? Or say that the avatar's health is displayed in an upper corner of the screen, providing constant feedback about the avatar's state vis-à-vis her survivability. An intense fight that requires unbroken attention toward the center of the screen may cause the player to be unable to check the health metric, else she would break her concentration. The player then views that feedback metric as a risk, balanced between the reward of perhaps necessary game state knowledge vs. the punishment of broken attention.

Determining and Tracking the Shape of Agency

Each of the above mechanisms of agential shaping map onto variables of interest in the sense-making portion of the model. The player should have already taken an active interest in her afforded capacities to change the game state and the mechanisms of feedback that narrate her effectiveness in doing so. What remains is congealing these observations into a meaningful structure from which we can observe the artistic and rhetorical moves that the system makes through this manipulation of agency.

To do so, we must consider how the shape of agency changes across three variables: time, space, and dramatic context. That is to say, how does my agency change over a course of time (for instance, an exhausted gun clip in a first-person shooter eliminates my ability to shoot until the *amount of time* associated with the "reload" function transpires), based on where the avatar is positioned in the game world (Mario cannot jump while airborne; he must have ground under his feet), and based on dramatic contingency (typically measured in terms of risk vs. reward; for instance, missing an attack in a fighting game and leaving myself temporarily vulnerable to a "punish" counterattack creates a strategic consideration that is constructed to produce dramatic moments of triumph and turnabout throughout each match).

Ultimately, these variables form an elastic view of gameplay's dramatic structure. We can use it to observe the *dramatic potential* present in any given game state (the total weight of available actions' possible rewards vs. possible risks; high-risk, high-reward produces moments of high dramatic potential, while low-risk, low-reward produces moments of low dramatic potential) *or* the *dramatic purpose* of actors, actions, or objects within the game space (how do the behavioral parameters of any single element within the system affect the scene's total dramatic shape?).

Further, as is reinforced throughout this literacy model, these measures are not limited to the diegetic realm. The gameplay system includes player, computer, and context, and the design of agency involves the structural manipulation of each. Consider how motivation, available actions, and feedback affect the player's physical interface with a controller. Particular diegetic actions may be disincentivized because certain controller manipulations are uncomfortable or unreliable (consider the difficulty of performing demanding button sequences to trigger special moves in fighting games, creating dramatic risk vs. reward considerations throughout the match). Feedback is particularly important when considering the physical act of play. Controller "transparency" and, thus, projective embodiment can be difficult to achieve when the controller does not provide adequate feedback to fade from active attention. For example, using "virtual buttons" on touchscreens (as are sometimes applied when porting console games to phone interfaces) often engenders an uncertainty of input due to the ambiguity of physical feedback. Physical buttons on controllers have definite boundaries. The player can feel their edges with her thumb and feel them depress and spring back to their neutral state with each activation. Virtual buttons on touchscreens offer no such feedback. Their region is communicated only visually, and they have no physical travel in their activation. They are still usable, but it requires more active attention to ensure that virtual buttons are being triggered as intended than physical buttons.

Chosen Action vs. Total Possibility Space

The shape of agency is not the same as the shape of the total possibility space. The shape of agency *includes* the affordances and restrictions that comprise the space of total possible actions, but ultimately, agency is a *feeling* that exists within the player rather than an objective measure of systemic potential; it is a sense of ownership and impact of one's actions. Remember, agency requires motivation and an understanding of feedback. If the player is offered a wide variety of options but has no particular motivation to perform any of them or cannot discern how the results follow from her inputs, she is experiencing *low agency.*

Considering agency as a medium of artistic expression, as C. Thi Nguyen does in the previously quoted passage, we must remember that what is being shaped is player affect and perception rather than objective systemic action. The artistic experience stems from the active interaction; thus, the structural elements of the artifact all work toward making that core experience of choosing and acting as impactful and significant as possible. As such, each choice is held in the context of the choices that were not made. Agency requires choices to be consequential, and that means not only that the effects of those choices must feel significant but the alternate choices (even if only presumed) must be significant as well. If a game presents the player with a button that starts a nuclear war, destroying the entire world in which the game is set, that is a significant action, but if the game hangs in suspended animation *until* it is pressed, the nuclear winter ceases to be an impactful expression of agency and is instead an inevitability of the narrative, the way that the story *must* unfold. The player is not making a choice; her actions are predetermined.

Though actions with no alternatives (such as the above example) do not take appropriate advantage of the ludic form, I do not wish to imply that choices that offer *many* alternatives are necessarily "better" than those that offer binary choice. The total number of choices that lead to non-terminal outcomes (in action-oriented games, those that do not "kill" the avatar) most often naturally narrows when sequences become greater tests of mastery. If, for example, a spaceship can fly in eight directions in any given moment, the player makes, at every moment, one of eight possible decisions. If the spaceship flies into a hazardous asteroid belt, though, requiring the player to navigate through the flying rocks like a dynamic labyrinth, the player may only have two or three of the eight directions in any given moment that will not cause the ship to collide with an asteroid. The possibility space has narrowed, and the risk and severity of punishment for inopportune navigation have increased. Though the player has fewer choices, the choices she has left have greater impact due to the significance of their alternatives (crashing the spaceship resulting in game over). Thus, the possibility space has narrowed, but she has not experienced a loss of agency. She may even feel *greater* agency during these moments because her actions feel more consequential.

Every game features different relationships between agency and possibility space. In Chapter 11, we explore the significance of the chosen or enacted path through a game in relation to the possibility space as we compare the *manifest content* and the *potential content* of a particular playthrough. In Chapter 12, we explore how the system's reactivity to individualized choice results in a game's *expressivity*, the degree to which it expresses the creativity and humanity of its player. Finally, in Chapter 13, we explore how the possibility space extends beyond intentional affordances with an examination of metagame practices of exploiting glitches and design oversights.

Agency from the Three Perspectives

The sense-making model concluded with three primary player dynamics based on the three perspectives of play: projective embodiment (diegetic), narrative agency (mimetic), and strategy (methectic). Agential design and the shape of agency interplay with each of these perspectives differently, contributing to the pacing and rhythms of play over the course of each game.

Projective embodiment and narrative agency tend to share a relationship of mixed valence. Projective embodiment is characterized by of-kind action within the game world; a high level of expressive agency with regard to the actions of the avatar. The mimetic perspective, on the other hand, often involves a deferment or narrowing of agency, such that one is working toward *bestowed* objectives instead of one's own self-determined objectives, or one is role-playing as a character like an actor performing a role, not truly experiencing "what do I wish to do in any given moment?" but "what action would the character perform here?". The diegetic perspective naturally plays to the degree to which the player *is* the avatar, and the mimetic perspective plays to the degree to which the player *is not* the avatar. By one framing, one could argue that an increase in one results in a deferment of the other.

Yet, diegetic agency is increased when those inward-out decisions are made in pursuit of outward-in pressures. They are given significance by the pursuit of extrinsically rewarding goals and in achievement over obstacles. That is to say, the joy of controlling Mario has an intrinsic pleasure, but one experiences greater projective agency in using his action affordances to overcome difficult challenges. Likewise, mimetic pleasure is greater in the context of narrative agency than narrative obedience. Even in the performance of an assigned role against scripted challenges, the expressive potential of games lies in the ways in which the game reflects the nuances of the player's performance in the unfolding of its story. Narrative agency needs not be radical shifts in narrative outcome; there is an unavoidable imbuement of self into the narrative as it is enacted.

As such, we can consider the personal agency of projective embodiment and narrative agency to both contribute, in their tension *and* harmony, to the aesthetics of Fantasy and Expression. Video game mimesis is most powerful when being viewed from within, with personal investment as a projective member of the diegesis. Likewise, diegetic involvement is at its most immediate in moments of dramatic significance, in struggle and catharsis afforded by the mimetic layer.

Similarly, the methectic perspective holds fraught ambivalence toward the other perspectives. By the measure of metagame prioritization, it aligns well with the diegetic perspective and can be counter to the mimetic. In the prioritization of overcoming challenges *by any means necessary*, the player strategizes with the game as software; systems that can be exploited, even if doing so breaks the conventional expectations of the fantasy. Metagame perspective is, in a sense, an absolute embrace of the diegetic (the player prioritizes the full range of action affordances; inward-out expression) and also an absolute rejection of the diegetic (metagame rejects the fantasy; the player is powerful because of her detachment from the game world. In seeing the patterns, algorithms, and systems that govern the fantasy, she can overcome it).

But on the other hand, the methectic perspective aligns with the mimetic conceit of the player as separate, a performer (of tasks rather than of fantasy). Methectic agency is at its strongest when oriented toward a goal. Whether the player develops a strategy complimentary or contrary to the mimetic fantasy, both agencies thrive on the impact of actions (toward assigned goals and in avoidance of designed obstacles) and similar forms of systemic feedback.

From the *diegetic perspective*, consider how the game's systems are designed to make self-directed action feel responsive, consequential, and contextualized within the diegesis as a space of designed harmonies and tensions with the avatar. Consider when, throughout the game, you feel the most projectively connected to the avatar and when you feel the most ontologically alienated. Note when mimetic direction works toward deepening your immersion into the projective perspective and when your separation is the most pronounced.

From the *mimetic perspective*, consider how your agency is being directed toward the game's designated objectives. In the most successful moments, the games' objectives (literal mission goals or narrative aims) and your internal desires align, and in the least successful moments, these goals feel arbitrary, intrusive, or alienating. Consider how the adoption of a narrative "persona" contextually embeds you into the dramatic stakes of the fantasy or how it fails to do so.

From the *methectic perspective*, consider how your strategic, metagame choices align or break with your projective agency within the diegesis or your embedded role within the mimetic narrative. Under what conditions do you feel the most strategic agency: when the possibility space is wide and expressive or when it is narrow and consequential?

Ludics

In order to examine the meaning of an element of agential design, we need a word with which we can congeal the essence of agency. For this, I turn to Frédéric Seraphine's *ludic*. Gilles Deleuze hypothesized that the *movement-image* and *time-image* represent the means by which individual *ideas* are outlined and communicated in filmmaking, and Seraphine seeks to define a similar term for communicating an *idea* in video game design (Seraphine, 2016). If it holds true that the medium of game design is the shaping of agency, the appropriately Deleuzean term might be an *agency-image*—not an image in the visual sense but an assemblage: a way to communicate the relationships within a system; "to make perceptible, to make visible, relationships of time which cannot be seen in the represented object" (Deleuze, 1985, p. xii).

As alluded to in a footnote within the sense-making model, I do recognize and apologize for the potential for confusion when using both *ludeme* and *ludic* in similar capacities at different points in the model. The terms are related, but there are subtle differences in what they describe. A *ludeme* is a conceptual element of play; a specific rule, affordance, or restriction that could be transposed to another game. The rate of fire of a particular gun in *DOOM* (1993) is a ludeme of that game, and that parameter could be applied to a gun in *DOOM 64* (1997) to give it an echo of that particular gameplay element from the original. Similarly, a Chess piece could be transposed into a game of Checkers and retain its particular movement affordances.

A *ludic*, on the other hand, is specifically an image of agency, in the sense that C. Thi Nguyen describes: not the *parameters* around deciding and doing but the *act* of deciding and doing. If Nguyen hypothesizes that games are a vessel for "recording […], preserving […], and passing" (Nguyen, 2020, p. 1) unique expressions of agency, the ludic is that which is developed. An example of a ludic in *DOOM* that might be passed along to *DOOM 64* would involve how the design of enemy types requires a certain prioritization in offensive and defensive options. Even with different enemies entirely, a game that preserves this ludic could be said to require a similar manner of approach to reading the scene and decision-making to *DOOM*. An aspect of *player involvement* can remain recognizable even apart from the specific ludemes.

A ludic can refer to any parts of the construction of an identifiable agency: motivation, action consideration, or legibility of consequence, to the degree that the game is identifiable in their expressions. Strategic considerations, the shape of the metagame, motivation adoption, and consequence contextualization are not as easily *transferable* between games as a single ludeme describing a rule-based affordance, but we can subjectively. The transfer of ludemes and ludics will become a focus of the *ludomotif* form of meaning discussed later in this chapter.

ASSOCIATIVE RESONANCES → SCHEMAS

Now that we have some context and vocabulary with which to understand the different types of agency at play in games, we can start to draw in connections from outside of the immediate system of play to make these agential relationships more meaningful. The variables, contingencies, and agencies expressed during play are not *inherently* meaningful; they become meaningful when thoughtfully contextualized through interpretive association. The striving, struggle, and catharsis of play express perspectives on the human condition, but only when interpreted by human subjects (and the greater context the subject has, the more significant meaning they can derive).

I described art in the introductory chapter and earlier in this chapter as a process that behaves like a machine. It takes the "raw material" of an artifact (the artistic potentiator) and processes it through the cognitive and emotional reactions of the beholder until what results is no longer the concrete form of the artifact but, instead, the abstract form of the artistic experience, specific to each beholder based on their particular constellations of thoughts, associations, memories, emotions, cultural context, etc.

This step of the meaning-making process describes the essence of that process. It is the acknowledgment that, besides certain types of innate aesthetic reactions, artistic meaning is formed from the *reconfiguration* of information and the formation of novel *connections* between points rather than in the introduction of novel information. Each artistic experience involves the conveyance of *some* level of novelty, but I argue that this new information is primarily processed in terms of its connection to what is already known and what is already within our experiential memories.

That is to say, the utility of informational conveyance is the communication of new or non-occurrent information, but the purpose of art is to communicate second-order experience or emotion, and this is achieved by strumming existing resonances. Pure information cannot produce catharsis or resonance apart from its interaction with existing structures of feeling. One who has never known loss of any kind cannot be made to feel the sorrow of loss through fiction. That said, this evocation of feeling is surprisingly robust; one does not need to have experienced the death of a father to sympathize with Hamlet (Shakespeare, 1599). The story cues emotional associations one might retain from a friend moving away or losing a pet. But the second-order feelings produced by art are not like the first-order feelings caused by hallucinogens, for example, which can interact directly with the structures of the ingesting party's brain and body to produce a primary effect; art produces its experience by "hijacking" the existing primary experiences of the beholder and reconfiguring them into novel experiences.

This novel reconfiguration then *becomes* a primary experience with which future artistic experiences can build. Perhaps my sorrow at Hamlet's plight recalls the emotions I experienced watching *Titanic* (Cameron, 1997). And perhaps *that* experience was colored by the resonance of a breakup. I will not go so far as to say that *all experience* is reducible to the shock of the infant first having her favorite toy taken away, but I believe it is useful to think of our experiential vocabulary in terms of compounding resonances. As such, those with a great depth and diversity of experiences (in life or the arts) exponentially increase their capacities to derive powerful and unique feelings and meanings from the arts. Colloquially, we can call this the formation of *taste*: not the cultivation of more "high-class" artistic sensibilities (whatever that may represent in any given cultural context), but the nurturance of *greater context* by which experiences of a kind may be understood. As such, I would argue that someone who has seen thousands of "popcorn films" (films that are not conventionally seen as being artistically ambitious) is likely to have better *taste* (capacity for rich and nuanced contextualization of novel experiences of kind) than someone who has only ever seen the ten most-acclaimed art films of all time. Art is a construction of *differences*; each new encounter is distinguished by the ways in which it *is not* all others.

Associative resonances can be affective (we can "feel" the pain of someone being punched in a movie because our brain recalls injuries that we have sustained in our own lives), but they can also be quite complex, semiotic structures. Allegory and allusion can recall ideological or philosophical resonances (consider how often the myth of Icarus is directly or inferentially invoked in fiction). An associative cue may trigger an entire chain of resonances with all kinds of meaning stuck to it (as is the intention and power of sampling in hip-hop and electronic music, which carries forward not only the explicit themes of the song being recontextualized but also all of the cultural and personal associations *with* that song).

When discerning how associations made during gameplay lead to the construction of meaning, it is useful to examine this from the "perspectives" of each element of the system of gameplay: what personal associations affect the player's interpretation, what personal and conventional associations influenced the design and imbued meaning by the developers (represented by proxy by the computer and its software), and what cultural associations contextualize the production, reception, and current play environment of the game?

Associative Resonance

Being the primary conduit through which meaning is developed, associative resonances ring through all layers of gameplay. Thematic resonance is the most obvious, functioning in much the same way that it does when making meaning from linear media. Allusions and references are common, as is the appropriation of common story structures, used as shorthand to instill discernible motivational structure without interrupting players from gameplay for too long; thus, the common trend of games that involve saving princesses from variants of dragons or wizards. Likewise, visual semiotics borrow heavily from genre tropes established in film, fantasy novels, and comic books.

Beyond theming, though, associative resonance is crucial for diegetic projective embodiment. Truly embodied play involves a vicariosensory connection to the game world (vicariously sensory, expanded upon in Chapter 4). In other words, the player should develop a *proprioceptive*, *tactile* sense of presence within the diegetic space. The game, though, has to communicate the tactility of its diegetic space primarily in terms of visual and audio feedback. This is an indirect pathway to a vicariously "physicalized" embodiment; tactility by inference. Physical interactions are observed from a removed perspective but must feel accurate to a lived experience. In other words, designers tend not to prioritize a sense of scientific realism in their construction of game physics but an experiential "realism" reflecting the heightened "reality" of subjective experience. If the player is to embody the character, the priority is not in depicting the world as it appears when we watch other people within it; game physics (and logic) should reflect the experience of what it's like to subjectively experience it[1] (if realism is the goal; heightening of feedback amplification should be even *greater* when aiming for an unrealistic, cartoon-y aesthetic).

But the above primarily describes the process of decoding—sense-making. It describes how we gain a practical working knowledge of the avatar's operational presence within the game world. Game physics (used here in the manner in which it is used by designer, educator, and researcher Michael Mateas, to include any operational logics of the simulation that are not attributable to motivated intent/artificial intelligence) can form *meaningful* relationships when they coalesce into *ludomotifs* (which will be detailed in the next section): resonances of rules, affordances, and agencies "quoted" across a variety of titles. For a game to call forward an operational association from another is a form of making a meaningful allusion, comparable to the semiotic allusions made so often in literature.

Considering how agency can be packaged and recontextualized or even recognized in games separate from the resonance's origin, we can conceive of each agential ludic as being a unit of experiential meaning. These agency images can not only resonate between games but outside of games as well. The images of time, space, and movement that film distills ultimately represent (and make philosophical inferences about) the experiences of those forces in life, and we can recognize or feel moments when the experience of time, space, and movement reminds us greatly of how they were expressed in particular films. Similarly, the unique experiences of agency produced by particular games can resonate in the agencies we express in real life as well. This kind of transferability, a hallmark of a particular kind of primary meaning, will be discussed in the section *Perspective Transference* below.

Circumstantial Resonance

With associative resonance being the primary conduit of meaning in artistic interpretation, it is useful to reflect upon the sources of primary meaning that are pulled into relationship with the gameplay artifact in order to produce new, second-order meanings. In addition to critically examining our own associative dispositions, it is also worth considering the associative dispositions of the game's developers, not to uncover the game's deterministic "true meaning" (we live in a post-The Death of the Author [Barthes, 1967] world), but to discover how the propensities *toward* certain types of meanings may have been embedded in the game and how those resonances of the developers may influence or persuade one's own reading.

Finally, it is separately useful to consider the associative dispositions of the culture into which the game was released or was later rediscovered. Whether the community accepted or rejected the game, and for what hypothesized reasons, can provide a useful cipher into the understanding of a particular people group at a particular point in history. We should not underestimate the potential usefulness of artworks as subjects by which the culture as a whole can be examined.

The most volatile form of associative meaning is circumstantial. This can include the beholder's mood at the time, any recent experiences that might prime particular resonances, and the context in which a work is viewed. We all have experiences of shutting out an artistic experience because we have been in a bad mood. Or sometimes coincidental synchronicities can lend works greater meaning (I first saw the films *Oppenheimer* [Nolan, 2023] and *The Wind Rises* [Miyazaki, 2013] in short succession, and parallels between the films' themes and structure became apparent that might not have been, were these experiences not so temporally proximal). Just because the priming factor is temporary, it does not mean that the resonant association will not linger. My first experience with the *Yogi Bear* cartoon (Hanna & Barbera, 1961–1962) was in an all-day marathon while I was home sick from school. Bored, over-snacking, and sick to my stomach while forming that first experience, I still become queasy when I see reference to Jellystone Park. How many songs can we recall from our own lives that are forever colored by associations with happy memories or heartbreaks?

Context is perhaps the most constructive form of circumstantial association. Museums carefully curate displays of multiple artworks to build associative narratives and instill greater meaning into the works than if they were presented on their own. Is the same type of contextual curation productive with video games? Whereas paintings can be viewed in quick succession to one another, video games prompt ontological immersion. One becomes engrossed in a game during embodied play, perhaps diminishing peripheral awareness of surrounding works. For their immersiveness, video games are *somewhat* context-obscuring.

If we recall that the core artistic "message" of games is presenting novel and meaningful forms of agency and presence, these aspects can certainly benefit from contextual curation. If we consider a gameplay experience to pose an "argument" about a particular form of agency, other games that present complementary or alternative "arguments" about similar agencies create a more complete and sophisticated picture of the agencies being explored. When curating these kinds of inter-game resonances, we can consider "arguments" posed through control methods (for example, different takes on the "twin engine" tank control scheme: *Battlezone* [1980], *Katamari Damacy* [2004], and *STAR WARS Episode I: Racer* [1999]), presence in virtual space (for example, co-existence in multiple, overlapping worlds: *Legacy of Kain: Soul Reaver* [1999], *Titanfall 2* [2016], *Quantum Break* [2016], and *tapestry* [2024]), perspectives (for example, games that let perspective dictate reality: *Superliminal* [2019], *Viewfinder* [2023], and *FEZ* [2012]), player bodily activity (for example, games that evoke the muscle memory of certain physical tasks in how they are played: *Rock Band* [2007], *The Climb* [2016], and *Donkey Kong Jungle Beat* [2004]), etc. There are endless possibilities, but it requires thinking in a non-semiotic orientation to find these agential resonances. Consider shared ludics, or even trace the lineage and legacy of a ludic of interest.

Personal Resonance

Personal associations are those that are more lastingly true of an individual than the circumstantial associations of the last few paragraphs. These include an individual's memories, beliefs, temperament, ideologies, and knowledge. These associations will produce the most telling person-to-person differences in interpretation.

Despite their personal nature, though, they are not completely out of the control of the author of a work. We make these associations not only based on our own *personal* experience but also experiences of an imagined or external source. That is to say that referential schemas can be implicated; through the language or semiotic framing that a game uses, specific associative schemas may be primed that would differ from our natural set. This is an essential property of empathy. The semiotic material of a game primes the player for the type of meaning she will seek and the perspective from which her personal associations will arise.

When a game presents the player with a hospital setting and casts her avatar as a surgeon, she will not only approach the material through the lens of her personal associations, but she will naturally assume the perspective of a surgeon, or what she imagines a surgeon might know, believe, and feel in a particular circumstance based on either her personal experience with surgeons or vicarious observations about surgeons from life, art, or imagination. This is an expression of *situated cognition*, the idea that thought is never "general" but is always situated in a "material, social, and cultural world" (Gee, 2003, p. 6). Just as I contextualize that which I observe and experience in the material, social, and cultural contexts by which I live, I can adopt temporary perspectives that may be more suitable to a particular situation.

James Paul Gee (2003) argues that those who learn well in a classroom setting are often those who can self-convincingly take on a relevant, imagined identity, a concept called *projective identity*. To excel in biology class, he argues, the student must leave her own identity as someone who will likely rarely encounter a practical need for Punnett squares and allelomorphs and instead adopt a projective identity as an imagined scientist, for whom she has aspirations of scientific excellence around which she can build operational values (p. 64). The student can "tap into" the presumed skills and motivations of the imagined scientist to make a task that previously had no bearing on her *own* personality and motivations personally relevant to her adopted identity.

Similarly, detective novels spend so much time detailing the often eccentric thought patterns of their point-of-view protagonists not only to outline how that particular protagonist reaches her conclusions but also to encourage a certain modality of thought in the reader. The reader becomes a detective alongside the protagonist, playing the "game" of the novel as she reads. Thus, projective embodiment (as described in Chapter 4) is not only a means of immersing the player within the ludic fiction, but it is also a means of immersing the ludic fiction within the player.

As such, meaningful associations are called forth not only from the player's own thoughts, beliefs, and experiences but also from proximity to the identity that she adopts during play. An identity that she may or may not have experience inhabiting in life. To cite an effective example of this at work, consider 2019's comedic, mischievous puzzle-adventure game, *Untitled Goose Game* (2019). The player controls a realistically animated goose avatar that makes its way through a quiet English countryside town and its residents' gardens. After a short, minimalist tutorial explaining the basic action affordances, the avatar encounters the game's first human NPC: a gardener tending to his vegetables. Though the gardener immediately has more in common with the human player than does the goose avatar, he immediately reads as "alien" and slightly threatening. The objectives that the player adopts, though more sophisticated than would be naturally attributable to a goose, align with the motivations and limitations of the imagined goose identity. In moments of metacognitive reflection, it is startling how quickly and naturally the game impresses upon the player the feeling of being a goose, wanting what a goose wants, and seeing the world as a goose would see it.

Cultural Resonance

As noted previously, many of the frames through which we construct meaning from the world around us are through the perspectives of the cultural groups to which we belong. Like the other associative perspectives, these are not *deterministic* perspectives (there is not a singular "Canadian reading" of a work), but affiliation with broader cultural contexts will make certain types of information and associations more apparent and accessible. This can be most easily illustrated with the example of allusion: good allusion has inalienable meaning apart from its metaphoric quality, but the degree to which one is familiar with the story to which the metaphor alludes will determine how much the deeper, more substantive parallels inform the reading.

In this sense, it is worth remaining aware of one's own contextual framings while appreciating a work and considering the limitations of one's own cultural knowledge and experience. For example, in a story about vampires, it is worth keeping in mind the author's cultural framing and whether a mismatch might produce unintended perspectives on the metaphor at play. If one's experience of vampire fiction lies in the European tradition of Ossenfelder and Stoker, one is likely to make certain types of associations that may differ from a reader whose cultural context follows the Chinese tradition of the jiāngshī. This is not to say that a European reading of a Chinese vampire novel is *destructive* to its meaning; differing cultures are split evolutionary paths stemming from the common, primal experiences of being human. It is often quite *productive* to approach texts from novel perspectives (see the tradition of "a feminist reading of…" or any cultural/ideological perspective by which novel truths and nuances of a work can be explicated). It is necessary, though, to recognize one's cultural frames and present one's readings appropriately.

Ultimately, no single reading is a reaction to the work itself in isolation. Every reading is an introduction of the text into a novel context. The same is true of gameplay. Though the non-semiotic operation of systems seems to exist at a level of cognition "beneath" our cultural consciousness (perhaps closer to that purely *behavioral* humanity at the root of the evolutionary divergences of culture alluded to above), calling into attention the unavoidably cultural (and, yes, ideological, political, and ethical) manners of play illuminates for us how other behavioral acts *in life* are similarly culturally prescribed.

With behaviors as simple as setting micro-objectives or moving through a space, can I recognize the manners in which she "sets micro-objectives consistent with her American-influenced ideology", "moves through the space in a punk rock manner", or "observes and decodes a space as a Hindu, as opposed to how she might observe and decode the space as a Catholic"?

In recognizing the manners in which *our* agential behaviors reflect (or situate within) our cultural contexts, we can also consider whether games' systems are designed to elicit particular cultural perspectives, a step toward discerning embedded ideologies. Does the pace of play and shape of total agency express or reward a particular cultural approach? May I gain greater or more congruous agency by modulating my natural perspective and perhaps empathetically adopting a cultural perspective during play that elucidates differing motivations?

This is not to encourage behaviors of tokenizing reductionism that may be associated with a performative imitation of a separate cultural perspective (a "digital blackface", so to speak); the point is not to modulate *expression* as much as it is to modulate *perspective*. Works originating from or cueing a cultural context separate from the player's own require a knowledge of the boundaries of one's own contextual knowledge (lived experience) and a receptive attitude to the differing forms of thought and agency that the game evokes. Additional research outside of the game systems can also enrich the experience, such that one can gain greater contextual knowledge of the mythologies, customs, and ideologies that inform particular systemic expressions.

Encountering friction with the "assumptions" made by the logic of a simulation is a natural experience of being culturally alienated from a game, but the player does not need to feel *excluded* from it. Resolving this alienation with curiosity and greater learned knowledge about the unexpected logics of a system can broaden one's cultural literacy even *outside* of games. Cultural adaptability requires sensitivity to customs and modes of thought more subtle and ingrained than linguistic paradigms and codifications of etiquette. Games, if played thoughtfully, can be a great place to practice this form of behavioral plasticity.

Furthermore, beyond elucidating the effects of culture within behavioral expression, thoughtful game players can become aware of the ways in which behavioral expression is used to *prescribe cultural attitudes*. We might be aware of the effect by which a capitalistic ideology might inform a player's reading of an in-game reward system, and we may be able to detect the ways in which capitalistic assumptions are built into said reward system; from this, we can also consider how particular structures of incentivization *reinforce* capitalistic ideology in their participants (capitalism here is only an example; any ideology can be systemically integrated). With greater fluency for how culture expresses itself within systems and mediates the expression of participants with those systems, we can gain greater insight into the ways in which similar systemic patterns manifest in the real world.

More and more spaces are becoming "gamified" in the real world; some in service of increasing participation in pro-social systems (such as education), and some as means of increasing the compulsory "stickiness" of modes of capital extraction or ideological conversion. Becoming sensitive to how games express and prescribe particular cultural and ideological rhetorics through their systems better prepares us to be *informed consumers* (and *producers*) of systemic rhetorics in life that may otherwise go unnoticed (felt, but not contextually qualifiable). The identification of ideological and ethical rhetorics in procedural systems and players' participation with them is the subject of Chapter 14.

This assumption ran throughout this section, but I would like to state it explicitly: one does not belong to a single cultural group in isolation; cultural perspectives stack, additively, on top of one another. One can be a Millennial immigrant Buddhist salsa dancer who skis and writes free verse poetry; each descriptor describes a different cultural group, each of which carries with it mythology, attitudes, and elements of shared experience that can inform an interpretation of a game. In that way, each player's cultural associations can be as unique as the associations and resonances that stem from her personal experience. Cultural context is also something that anyone can choose to expand; greater knowledge of differing cultural perspectives and greater experience and empathy with those in other cultural groups can increase our context and, thus, our literacy. One forms more sophisticated and rich readings with more diversified constellations of cultural frames through which meaning can be glimpsed.

Authorial Perspective

As games are expressive of both player *and* developers, it is not only the associations of the player that are worth considering in the meaning-making process. Though I happily endorse the postmodern perspective that a work's meaning *should not* be dictated by the author's intended meaning as the "be all and end all" consideration, a recognition of the perspectives embedded within a game's systems will provide a useful point of reference for the counterpoint of players' individual perspectives and expressions.

Being able to *identify* the aspects of gameplay that express the player versus those that express the embedded design of the developers is a vital skill. Even *as* the player, these expressive capacities can be difficult to disentangle. "Am I approaching this game impatiently because *I* am impatient (temperamentally or situationally), or are the systems designed to incentivize an 'act without thinking' approach through their reward and punishment structures?".

The most reliable method for making this determination is with greater knowledge of the self. As one plays more games (particularly within the same genre), she will notice patterns of behavior that emerge between them. Not just surface-level patterns like "poor reaction time", but behavioral patterns. For example, I notice that I, when entering new rooms in exploration-based games, tend to explore the perimeter/walls thoroughly and work my way inwards rather than starting from the centerpoint (where I am most often directed toward, as the location where a room's scripted events are most likely to play out) and working outwards from there. This is, by itself, a mundane observation, but it is a pattern I have recognized about myself, so when I notice myself consistently doing the opposite in a particular game, I can then ask, "what about this game's design caused me to deviate from my typical pattern of behavior?", and upon recognizing those elements, I can further explore whether or not that difference expresses something of ideological interest about that particular game.

If video games make an art of the expression of agency, the ways in which they guide and incentivize *particular* expressions of agency ultimately underlie their rhetorical cores. Gameplay is about the player *doing* and *acting*, so, to express a procedural argument, the game has to invoke methods to galvanize particular actions from players.

This kind of prescriptive orientation might become more apparent with knowledge of the context in which the game was designed. Understanding key creative personnel (particularly for games with small development teams or individual creators) can cue the player to recognize patterns of agential expression with their root within the systems themselves. Cultural origins make for useful points of reference, not only for the specifics of tradition or mythology that may manifest within the game's semiotic layer but also as an extension of the *community* of design from which a game emerged. Games from Japanese studios, for example, may manifest similarities that have nothing to do with cultural mythologies and traditions, simply due to the fact that the developers that constructed them are more likely to know each other and perhaps have worked together in the past. Regional trade and social meetings allow for the exchange of ideas, best practices, reactions, and even the exchange of personnel between teams. It is reductive to think of a game as being *deterministically* Japanese, but it can be useful to think about how a particular work fits into the exchange of ideas of Tokyo-based studios in the 1990s, for example.

Furthermore, studying the lineage and legacy of a game can reveal a lot about what a particular iteration is doing "under the hood". The ideology and associations of a particular creator or team might be difficult to explicate while playing a single game, but patterns of design and philosophy may emerge when multiple games of theirs are viewed in the context of one another (for a *beautiful* realization of this exploration into a creator's personal history and style, see Digital Eclipse's 2024 arcade collection/digital documentary *Llamasoft: The Jeff Minter Story* (2024), which collects over 40 games developed by eccentric designer Jeff Minter, narrativizing the trajectory of his design practices and sharing useful context about the environments in which they were made). Being contextually curious improves our recognition of forms of meaning tremendously.

Simulated Referents

In the sense-making portion of the model, we explored how (semiotic) themes make game operations more immediately understandable than pairing the same actions with abstract or irrelevant aesthetic cues. When a game object *looks* like a sword, it gives a clue to its possible action affordances. Theme, meaning the visual, auditory, or descriptive detail given to elements of the game in order to give context to their purpose or behavior, is a useful tool for games' simulative capacity. Games do not *need* to simulate systems outside of themselves, but most do, to some extent.

Games like *Grand Theft Auto V* (2013) and *The Sims* (2000) extensively simulate multiple systems that govern our lives (social interaction, occupational systems, urban systems of transportation, etc.); games do not need to depict life with such fidelity to simulate existent systems. Subway route-planning puzzle game *Mini Metro* (2015) features highly abstract representations of the subway lines its players build, theming its visuals in reference to the style of subway maps rather than lifelike visual depiction, and *Animal Crossing* (2001) simulates a simplified version of stock trading through the purchase and sale of turnips rather than company stock. In these cases, what is being modeled is the *behavior* of systems, and not necessarily their outward appearances.

The implications of simulation will be the subject of the next section of this model, but for now, it is relevant to note the details that cue *what* is being simulated. All ludic simulation is an abstraction; therefore, all ludic simulation makes some kind of claim or statement about the system it simulates. This claim or statement may not carry *ideological weight* (though it often does), but every simulation includes choices and incomplete fidelity. In their abstraction, developers choose which elements of the referent system to model and which to exclude. For example, city-builder games like *SimCity* (1989) and *Cities: Skylines* (2015) simulate many of the processes of building and managing cities, such as managing population happiness, traffic systems, resource exhaustion, taxation, pollution, etc., but they do not tend to simulate the bureaucratic processes involved in administrative governance. For the sake of the type of experience that these games were designed to create, it was deemed a higher priority to give players (situated in roles of urban planning and/or mayoral governance) rather unrestricted agency rather than requiring they wade through the challenges that politicians and urban planners in those positions might in real life. Though the games do not make claims to absolute fidelity, the prioritization of some aspects over others does imply relative importance in the vision of the systems that these simulations were built to depict.

Determining the referent systems that a game's systems are modeled to simulate provides a useful piece of contextual information that will become very important through the rest of the meaning-making process. At the recognition stage, the identification of referent systems is largely associative and is subject to similar diversions and expansion of meaning as all other forms of referent associations detailed throughout this section. Even when not presented with complete thematic fidelity, associative details can still give clues to the systems to which simulations refer.

THEME → METAPHOR

As we identify the systems that games simulate, we recognize two implicit statements that the simulation makes:

1. The relationships being simulated are *appropriate* to conceptualize as a system.
2. The behavior of the simulation demonstrates something about the behavior of the referent system.

The first implicit statement contains an ideological quality. For a behavior to be modeled by a system, it has to have a systemic quality—the patterns of behavior of its constituent parts have to sum to a greater pattern with behaviors recognizable in their repetition. To simulate traffic systems, one recognizes that the system as a whole exhibits behavioral trends influenced by but greater than the sum of its constituent parts, and the choices made in the construction of the system's components are reflected in the behavioral dynamics of the whole. While positing traffic patterns from a systemic perspective should be relatively uncontroversial, ideological considerations become more charged when simulations model the development and spread of religions, political radicalization, or the history of colonialism, to name a few issues that some are viscerally resistant to framing systemically. In framing something in the context of a system—as behaviors that can be convincingly or compellingly performed by a procedural algorithm—developers frame not only the simulation but also the *referent* as systems.

The aforementioned abstraction necessary in simulative adaptation leads to the second implicit statement: the behavior of the simulation demonstrates *something* about the behavior of the referent system. Even the most studied simulations do not have one-to-one fidelity to their referents (a parable of this impossibility can be read in the satirical On Exactitude in Science by Jorge Luis Borges [1946]). Simulations and games all involve degrees of consolidation. Cars in video games do not *actually* model the explosions that occur within a piston engine to animate its parts. The aural roar of the car is added as an aesthetic detail (theme), but in operation, no such explosions are actually modeled. In this small way (invisible to the player), the game makes an implicit statement that cars are more fundamentally *movement machines* than *explosion machines*. In pursuit of the type of experience developers want players to have, modeling cars' movement affordances was given priority over operational fidelity. This simulation demonstrates *something* about cars but not *everything*. The things that it *does* model are privileged and framed as central to the aesthetic and rhetoric of that particular simulation.

Case Study: *HITMAN*

To consider a more complex example, we can look at the behavioral simulation of the NPCs in 2016's *HITMAN* (2016), a third-person stealth-action game about being an assassin. Each of *HITMAN*'s levels are complex, clockwork-like settings teeming with people—a lavish Paris mansion hosting a fashion show and secret black market auction, an armed militia compound in rural Colorado, a bustling seaside town on the coast of Italy that houses a secret lab where a deadly virus is being cultivated, etc. The game involves navigating avatar Agent 47 into secure locations to find his designated targets of assassination, doing his job, and fleeing the scene without being spotted by the security forces that patrol each environment. He can do so by staying out of sight—moving between unseen pockets of the environment when guards are not watching—or by disguising himself as someone who can reasonably blend in to the areas he needs to infiltrate without arousing suspicion. To pass through a dining room, he might have to don the disguise of a waiter.

Players who watch the behaviors of NPCs within *HITMAN*'s environments will notice that NPCs (even Agent 47's targets) tend to perform "loops" of behaviors, either planted in one space, performing the same action forever, or moving from space to space, repeating the same series of tasks before returning to their starting positions and beginning their cycle anew. This quirk of the NPCs' behavioral patterns may strike players as glaringly artificial for a game with such realistically rendered visuals—a mismatch in simulative fidelities. Players who probe deeper into the system can find ever more "robotic" and artificial behaviors that result from the interactions Agent 47 can have with NPCs. Guards take a precise and predictable amount of time to detect Agent 47 if he is within their sightline, depending on how far away he is, and ducking out of sight right before detection draws the guard to investigate. NPCs will always take the same amount of time to "investigate" distractions, and all NPCs of particular classes have the same escalation patterns when suspicion is aroused. The predictability of NPC behaviors is so reliable, it becomes a strategic affordance—methectically, the player recognizes the artificiality and uses it as a metagame affordance.

The clockwork, predictable behaviors of each environment's NPCs do not reflect a *shortcoming* of the game's simulative fidelity—it is an intentional framing device to make the behavior of the system more board-game-like. In terms of procedural rhetoric, the game is *not* implying that "people are ultimately destined to mindlessly repeat one activity for as long as another cares to observe them". Rather, the rhetorical statement made by the game is one about Agent 47's honed, cold perception. In pursuit of his objectives, he subdivides the unpredictable world of human interactions into classes of obstacles and opportunities. His sense of patience and observational prediction are systemically literalized as a clockwork repetition in which *he* is the only agent with *true* expressive choice, *not* because it represents the reality in which the game is set but because it serves as a *ludic metaphor* for the experience of *being* a professional assassin and seeing the world through his eyes. Agent 47 sees others as tools that he may utilize to accomplish his objectives. In this sense, *infidelity* to the simulated referent *draws attention toward* a separate systemic rhetoric. In order to communicate the experience (agency) of *being* Agent 47, the system's behaviors skew into the *unrealistic* but *metaphorically appropriate.*

Metaphor

Not all simulative abstraction is in service to rhetorical metaphor. Metaphor is a rhetorical device by which two things are compared or co-presented in order to reveal a truth or perspective about one or both. In linguistics, one might say "time is a river" in order to communicate a perspective about the way in which time *flows.* Since video games are an art form of constructed and transformed agency, we are primarily interested in the metaphor of agential or procedural construction. In other words, while the most common linguistic metaphors are structured "*[noun]* as *[noun]*", ludic metaphors most often present as "*[verb]* as *[verb]*".

In the *HITMAN* example above, the ludic metaphor involves the behavior of a system. We can summarize its rhetorical position as: "*the group behavior of people* is *like clockwork* to the *patient professional who thinks only of opportunity and risk*". It depicts a version of a system's behavior not because it is *how it really is,* but because it amplifies the player's agency in a manner that allows the average player—who has not been cloned and trained for years specifically to become a master assassin—to experience the world in the way that someone that *has* would experience it. Not only is this the kind of amplification of *skill* that most games require (playing *NBA Jam* [1993] does not require the athleticism of a trained basketball player), but *HITMAN*'s behavioral abstraction also presents an amplification of *perspective* that presents a knowingly unrealistic systemic behavior in order to say something about its protagonist.

This is a rather complex metaphor, but it is common to use simpler mechanics to stand for a form of agency that cannot be directly accessed through the medium. Sometimes the metaphors translate fairly directly and do not convey a deeper layer of meaning (the "three point" precision minigame played to determine the strength and accuracy of a swing in *Everybody's Golf* [1997] substitutes the finesse required to swing a golf club with a quick micro-challenge that requires precision), and sometimes these substitutions make more profound statements (such as the use of a JRPG-standard battle mechanic used in *Thirsty Suitors* [2023] to represent the rhythms and hazards of conversing with ex-lovers after messy breakups).

The intent of ludic metaphors is often communicated through the theming layer applied to games' systems, but another way to determine mechanical metaphors (or even posit metaphors in the system beyond what is intended) is to consider observed ludemes. To review, ludemes are rules or groups of rules that form recognizable, singular units, which could (theoretically) be utilized of-kind in different games. Recognizing ludemes (particularly at a pre-semiotic level) allows us to compare a game's utilization and compare it against other games' usages, expanding our "vocabulary" of what a particular ludeme can mean in different contexts. It is in contrast to a "mean" (average) expression that artistic choices and the meaning they contain are made evident. In the above *Thirsty Suitors* example, the metaphor of "conversing with ex-lovers is like strategic battle" is only meaningful if one recognizes the ludeme, prepared with the contextual knowledge to be able to recognize JRPG battle conventions. Now that I am prepared with *Thirsty Suitors*' argument that conversations can be like tactical battles, I can compare that expression to future occurrences of turn-based battle ludemes and determine whether a conversational metaphor would also be appropriate in those contexts.

Secondly, ludemes can be compared against experiences in real life. Particular rhythms of action can cue associations and resonances of lived experience. Those who are attuned to the non-semiotic level of the experiences will be rewarded with the most novel and unexpected of connections. Again, game-specific storytelling involves the creation and novel recontextualization of forms of agency; drawing connections between the non-semiotic behaviors of systems and consequences of actions speaks to the specific artistic capacities of the medium.

Physical Metaphor

The forms of metaphor described above involve diegetic theme and embodied action, enacting forms of representational correspondence within a game. Embodied action extends beyond the digital realm, though, and it is also beneficial to consider how the player's embodied actions are shaped and guided to contribute to ludic metaphor as well.

The most obvious form of physical metaphor involves the use of specialty controllers that require the player to emulate diegetic action with her own body. The instrument-shaped controllers of the *Rock Band* (2007–2015) and *Guitar Hero* (2005–2015) series provide simplified approximations of playing such instruments in a live performance setting, and skillful players can often be observed throwing the kinds of flourishes into their performances that rock stars might incorporate into their shows. The games also intelligently push players to "peacock" during performances through the design of particular in-game mechanics. The previously described Star Power/Overdrive mechanics that add a multiplier to players' scores are activated by tilting the neck of the guitar upwards, emulating the kind of flourish a live guitarist might use to excite the crowd. Additionally, "Big Rock Endings" in the final moments of particular songs award points for hitting as many of the fret buttons as possible within the allotted time. Since the second set of frets high on the neck of the guitar (closest to the guitar body) are closer together than the frets farthest on the neck, it is easier to press these in rapid succession, causing players to emulate the physical expression of performing rapid hammer-ons during the dramatic climax of the song.

Other prominent examples of highly emulative specialty controllers include the elaborate control panel of *Steel Battalion* (2002), which mirrors the buttons, knobs, and levers of the cockpits of the fictional mech vehicles the player is tasked with piloting. Especially committed players of more realistically grounded vehicle simulation games, such as *Assetto Corsa* (2014) and *Microsoft Flight Simulator* (2020), choose to buy steering wheels or flight sticks specialty controllers that emulate the controls real operators utilize to manage such vehicles. Some fishing games utilize specialty controllers to emulate the actions of casting and reeling a realistic fishing rod. These more literal adaptations create highly *embodied* play experiences, but they do not necessarily present meaningful *metaphors*, in that actions are not used to *stand-in for* or *represent* other actions or agencies; they are not used to further rhetorical points. The *Rock Band/Guitar Hero* example makes a stronger case for metaphorical representation, as the actions the specialty controllers push players toward are representative of the mindset and performative bravado of rock stars.

Even without a specialty controller, though, physical metaphor can be fruitfully employed. The physicality of controller inputs does not need to "represent" in-game action to form strong rhetorical statements. Developers can use elements of physical performance such as exertion, precision, coordination, timing, and restraint to emulate the required mindset embodied in particular actions, even if their literal expressions are quite different.

An interesting exercise can be to identify a ludeme associated with a particular physical action and observe how that action is expressed in terms of controller inputs through multiple games. A fascinating exploration has been compiled by Dim Bulb Games, who, in 2022, released *Museum of Mechanics: Lockpicking* (2022), a game that compiles and recreates the minigames associated with the action of lockpicking in several games over the decades. These expressions are surprisingly diverse, but most hold some similarities: typically, an emphasis on precision, the need to move slowly and carefully (sometimes against a time limit, which adds dramatic tension to the activity), holding "pins" in place for sustained amounts of time, and often operating multiple controls at once (such as rotating two wheels to find their "sweet spots" simultaneously). Commonalities and differences in the ways in which various games express the lockpicking action reveal the non-literal elements of the activity that are experientially central, as opposed to those that are expendable and optional. Seeing them all in one place, as compiled into the *Museum of Mechanics* software, presents a fascinating history of ludic adaptation.

As opposed to lockpicking, which tends to be expressed in terms of small, careful movements, certain actions are often expressed in such a way that is intended to be physically taxing on the player. *The Last of Us* (2013) features several sequences in which avatar Joel has to lift something heavy, and this is represented in the game's control scheme as a demand to hit a button rapidly for an amount of time. Though a "smaller" fine motor action than the gross motor activity that Joel expresses diegetically, the rapid repetition exhausts the muscles of the player; she longs for relief from the demand of performing the physical activity just as Joel longs to release the heavy object.

Games can also present non-metaphorical control activities early in play and make metaphorical turns in their later modification. Puzzle adventure game *Brothers: A Tale of Two Sons* (2013) features two controllable characters—an older brother and a younger brother—each controllable with the left and right halves of the controller, respectively. The older brother is controlled with the left half of the controller and the younger brother, the right. The control scheme is simple and largely non-metaphorical: each brother is moved using either the left or right thumbstick, and contextual actions are performed by pressing or holding their respective forefinger triggers. The brothers each have different abilities: the older brother can swim and carry heavy objects, for instance, while the younger brother can fit in small places. The challenge of the game comes from splitting one's attention between the simultaneous, separate demands and performing increasingly complex, coordinated but separate actions with each hand (an interesting demand, but not particularly metaphorical—there is no indication that either brother feels this distracting "mind-splitting" demand).

Late in the game, though, the brothers become separated, and the younger brother, now alone, finds that the path forward requires the use of one of the older brother's abilities. In order to progress, the player has to press the contextual action trigger on the *left* side of the controller, metaphorically representing the younger brother drawing from within himself the influence of his brother to overcome an obstacle that he, himself, would have been unable to pass. The metaphor, in this case, makes a powerful statement about the ways in which we learn from others and invoke the "spiritual presence" of those who we love to push ourselves to do what we would otherwise find impossible. At no point during the game does the physical performance of control inputs more closely resemble their diegetic counterparts, but the recontextualization of a control scheme established earlier (establishing it as a component of the game's experiential "language") creates a metaphorical "turn" that contains one of the game's core messages.

Physical metaphor tends to temporarily negate the controller's "transparency" (see Chapter 4) by drawing occurrent attention back to the physical activity of the interface. In such cases, the *projective embodiment* of the avatar is replaced (or supplemented) with the *embodied* presence of the player—at worst, breaking "flow", but at best, drawing a deeper and more lasting experiential connection between the two embodied positions. Used intelligently, the physical interface of the player becomes an experiential link into the diegesis.

MEANING: SECOND-ORDER STATES

At the beginning of the book, I identified *second-order states* as being the primary product of artistic experiences. The transfer of information from transmitter to receiver does not require artistic expression, and if the intended product of an artistic work was simply informational transference, the arts would be a poor conduit for that message (consider the difficulty potentially introduced if someone were to write their shopping list as a metaphor-heavy poem instead of a straightforwardly presented list of items). The arts are useful for communicating emotions and states of mind that are not *directly* accessible through informational communication. I can easily tell you my wife's name, but if I want to communicate how I feel when I hear her name, I must veer into the realm of indirect communication—the evocation of emotion through poetry or metaphor.

I call art indirect because the artistic artifact (the *artistic potentiator*) does not transfer this second-order state directly; it activates meaning-making processes in the mind of the beholder. An idea or an image is received and processed by the beholder, shaped and molded by the beholder's mind—memories, knowledge, beliefs, temperament, mood...—*becoming* a form of *primary experience* rather than received information. The artist can *intend* for certain triggers to be processed in certain ways, but she can never be sure that the beholder will approach the piece with a constellation of preconditions that will lead to the desired outcome. As such, the arts are prepared in such a way that a variety of experiences can be evoked—each feeling (and actually) true to each beholder. This is why our experiences and interpretations of art can feel so personal. This multitude of expressions is not the result of *noise* in the system causing meaning to be lost or distorted—the variation is the point, and it is what makes art powerful and able to live beyond its specific originating context. While an artwork will evoke a different second-order state in each beholder, the aspects that unite (or provide interesting tension between) all beholders reveal our unifying, underlying shared humanity.

Like any other art form, video games evoke second-order states in their players. The simple emotions like frustration, flow, or the sense of having fun are first-order reactions—these can be reliably invoked by pulling certain evolutionary/cognitive "triggers" in the mind. If someone is obstructed from reaching a goal that is important to them, they will reliably become frustrated. This does not require processing through the aesthetic and meaning-oriented centers of the mind. This is as unsophisticated as using a feather to evoke a ticklish reaction. The second-order states of interest are those that result from the aesthetic and associative processes of meaning-making that we have already covered.

From the diegetic perspective, the player can experience a sense of embodied presence in a virtual space, and the properties and affordances of that space can evoke aspects of one's embodied presence elsewhere, or it can serve as a primary source of embodied spatial experience on which a future spatial exploration can riff. The properties of spaces can be recontextualized and alternative affordances can be proposed, which causes the total meaning of the experience of space to be broadened. For example, the *Tony Hawk's Pro Skater* series (1999–present) presents spaces evocative of the mundane, "non-game" spaces that we encounter throughout our lives, but the spaces, mundane in their appearance, have been packed, full-to-bursting, with novel movement affordances, as everyday objects are transformed into ramps, rails, ledges, and flats on which the skateboarding avatar can grind, lip, or propel herself into the air. The presentation of mundane spaces that invoke the "known", coupled with the embodied affordances and goal incentives to perform expressive actions within these spaces, pair to create second-order states—a feeling of *freedom*, embodied *rebelliousness*, a desire to rediscover the inherent joy of embodied movement afresh.

From a mimetic perspective, participation in a designed narrative and the interaction with a cast of characters and imaginative locations gives the sense of fulfillment of ambitions and fantasies. Overcoming a narrative challenge may be reducible to pressing the correct series of buttons, but its evocative, thematic representation gives the player context in which these achievements become meaningful. Well-written characters become trusted partners, on whom we can rely on our difficult journey. The events that transpire through and alongside player action become the *history* of an imagined world, imbued with weight and significance through the player's lived experience of witnessing it. The narrative experiences of love, loss, and triumph are made "real" by way of the evocative power of cognitive contextualization, and these experiences contribute to the basis by which future experiences are contextualized. Having spent tens of hours in a world, struggling alongside characters, these connections and experiences contain an element of "reality" unmatched by other art forms because their enactment contained a "reality"—the effort expended was real effort; the problem solving was real mental challenge; the victories were due to the player's own decisive actions. It is no wonder fans of *FINAL FANTASY VII* (1997) or *Psychonauts* (2005) grow so attached to the characters—in performing a mimetic role in the story, players invest a part of themselves into the fantasy. To the degree that Cloud or Razputin are "real" (they are vessels for the motivating consciousness of the player within the virtual realm), the relationships between avatars and cast and avatars and setting have a flavor of "reality" that enriches these experiences.

Finally, from a methectic perspective, the player is challenged and rewarded for skill and manners of thought not often elsewhere valued in life. Tactical thinking, risk-taking, and outside-of-the-box strategizing are so often counter-balanced by the need to be reasonably measured in our daringness in life. For the sake of maintaining an acceptable level of risk in life, we rarely push ourselves to our true limits or actively tempt fate. As we wonder about our unrealized potential, games give relatively low-impact (but narratively high-stakes) sandboxes in which our strategic minds can play, shoot for the sky, and taste deserved victory or loss. The mind delights in overcoming challenges and being tested to its limit. Games give players an opportunity to sublimate the unrealized aspects of our own cleverness and intelligence into a form of playful experimentation. In presenting a puzzle or a systemic challenge to a player, meaning is brought into it through the efforts and agencies the player utilizes to overcome it.

MEANING: LUDOMOTIFS

Earlier in the sense-making model, we identified *ludemes*, individual "ideas" expressed by the rules and affordances of a game, such as the specific movement patterns of each Chess piece (Parlett, 2007) or each player competing to put herself in a losing position as opposed to the game's typical victory state. Any of these ideas can be recognized in isolation and "exported" to other games. How would Checkers change if each player were given a rook from Chess with its movement and offensive capabilities, for example?

Later, in the meaning-making model, we identified *ludics*, individual expressions of *agency* that could be similarly "exported" to other games. For instance, the objectives and affordances of golf games require a different attention to the topology of a space than a less physics-dependent activity, so if a space designed for one type of game was recontextualized *into* a golf game, it would require thinking about the familiar space in a different lens (as has been evocatively proven in the adaptation of the island from exploration puzzle game *Myst* [1993] into the VR mini-golf simulation *Walkabout Mini Golf* [2020]). In this case, the *ludic* involves the way of "reading" the topological space, based on the player's contextual objective. That manner of perspective prioritization can be "exported" to other pre-existing virtual spaces by way of objective and affordance realignment.

When a ludeme or ludic has been identified, we can recognize reappropriation or adaptation of that ludeme or ludic in other games, or even within the same game. Such repetition of an idea is *ludomotif*. Like a *leitmotif* that represents an idea or characteristic in a piece of music that can be modified or invoked in its repetition, ludomotifs make meaningful statements in their reutilization either by establishing contextual links to other actions or works or by calling attention to meaningful differences in their variations (like in the *Brothers: A Tale of Two Sons* example above).

Ludomotif is a useful tool for grounding the exploration of the lineage and legacy of an idea. The active nature of gameplay allows developers to make specific invocations of other games without calling them out explicitly in the semiotic layer of the experience. In invoking a past title, a game is drawn "into conversation" with the quoted work. Like sampling in hip-hop or electronic music, the new game pulls forward not only the "sampled" aesthetic but also elements of the context surrounding the original work. Breakfast cereal promotional pack-in game *Chex Quest* (1996) ran on the engine and employed the gameplay rhythms and structure of the controversial first-person shooter *DOOM* (1993). In doing so, it not only borrowed a proven, effective gameplay loop from a genre titan, but it also brought *Chex Quest*, a child-friendly game advertising a cereal brand, into conversation with *DOOM*'s counter-cultural reputation. It became notable not only that *Chex Quest* was a *compelling* first-person shooter (rare for free, advertisement games) but that it also "sanitized" a game built around gore, Satanic imagery, and heavy metal music. General Mills positioned the brand of Chex (a rather bland cereal) as being a part of the counterculture, as being youthful and quietly rebellious.

Other times, ludomotif allows developers to "cite their sources" and claim a place (or argue for another work's inclusion) in the legacy of mechanical and genre development. 2D platformer *Donkey Kong Country: Tropical Freeze* (2014) made fan-favorite character Cranky Kong playable for the first time in the series' history, giving him the character-specific ability to "pogo" bounce on his walking cane. This mechanic was a ludomotif echoing back to 1989 platformer *DuckTales* (1989), in which avatar Scrooge McDuck could bounce around the stage on *his* cane. The physics of Cranky Kong's cane bounce mirrored Scrooge's closely; it was clearly an intentional callback. It was not done because there is any connection in the lore between the two games or shared personnel between them—it is simply a desire to re-explore a ludeme from 25 years prior. It positions *Tropical Freeze* as being an extension of a longer design trajectory, and it asserts the continued relevance of a game with which younger players of the time might not have been familiar.

Similarly, but to opposite effect, ludemes or ludics can be invoked to draw attention to a particular *dissimilarity*, a variation on a theme. Fighting game *Street Fighter Alpha* (1995) introduced "joke character" Dan Hibiki, whose action affordances mirrored those of "shoto"-style characters Ryu and Ken but tuned to be comically ineffective. He was designed as an aesthetic riff on character designs typical of rival fighting game franchise *Art of Fighting* (1992–1996); he was a good-natured ribbing of that series, a mechanical "accusation" of *Art of Fighting*'s design team "copying" *Street Fighter* design archetypes, presenting a character in their aesthetic style as an impotent variation of the series' signature fighters. Dan's "joke" only reads if the player is familiar with the ludemes associated with the shoto fighter archetype and the ludics involved with active decision-making when controlling such fighters.

In summary, ludomotifs situate a game or a mechanic in a greater context, emphasizing similarities where they might not otherwise be obvious and drawing out characteristic differences. For ludomotif to be an effective category of meaning-making, we have to recognize that ludemes and ludics form a primary *proto-meaning* as elements of the "grammar" of gameplay. As the player is able to separate individual ludics and ludemes from the gestalt of gameplay, these evocative echoes become meaningful in their positioning and usages.

MEANING: PERSPECTIVE TRANSFERENCE

If ludomotifs create meaning by pulling forward "sticky" context alongside the repetition of ludemes or ludics, perspective transference is an inversion: the unintentional "stickiness" of ludemes and ludics when transferring contexts. In other words, this form of meaning involves the translation of experiences of particular ludic agencies *outside* of games.

My favorite example is the above-cited *Tony Hawk's Pro Skater* (1999). The recontextualization of mundane spaces as playgrounds for skateboard-enabled interaction affordances causes players to view spaces differently than they had before. As seasoned *Tony Hawk* players will attest, frequent play is often associated with (sometimes intrusive) imaginings of grinding along power lines and roadside barriers or kickflipping between tables and benches. In the game's radical reinterpretation of what it means to *actively exist within a space*, those ideas become not only diegetically relevant within the simulation, they broaden players' perspective in life as well. Once we become attuned to the "rules" of a simulation, it is natural that our minds search for similar patterns outside of it.

This is recognized by researchers as the Tetris Effect (Goldsmith, 1994), a recognized phenomenon by which people, primed with play of the falling-block puzzle game *Tetris* (1985), become temporarily more efficient and effective at performing spatial-organizational tasks, such as packing luggage or organizing storage drawers. This effect was a driving experiential metaphor (or, some may argue, "punchline") of the exploration-puzzle game *The Witness* (2016), a game that presents players with a series of line puzzles until, eventually, the player starts noticing line puzzles built into the diegetic environment *outside* of the regular puzzle context.

Perspective transference is a form of primary meaning. It is the result of a gameplay "idea" settling into the mind, expanding the capacities for thought and action beyond what existed before. Just as the semiotic level of artistic communication can increase our capacity for novel perspective from a linguistically contextualized angle, the non-semiotic actions in games expand our abilities to approach novel situations from differing active perspectives.

Of course, if useful and generally prosocial perspectives can transfer outside of games, we must be vigilant about the transferability of antisocial perspectives. While research has concluded that video games do not *cause* real-world violence (Anderson & Bushman, 2001; Anderson & Dill, 2000; Bushman & Huesman, 2000; Endresen & Olweus, 2005; Funk et al., 2004; McCormick, 2001) in the manner in which 1990s parents feared they might, one should be aware of the cause-and-effect links that gameplay posits to the mind of the player. If a game positions every conflict as being resolvable through violence, this may not *cause* a player to become more violent, but it at least increases the availability of this response as a problem-solving strategy for the period following play. Consider the effects of spending a great amount of time in a world in which the player is the only being of "value", with all other NPCs being expendable and ultimately subservient to the purpose of acting as characters in the player's singular story. This does not deterministically drive antisocial perspective, but the literate player will be aware of factors of games that suggest antisocial conclusions and will recognize her cognitive susceptibility to such influences. Attention to meaning in the arts means attention to the self and how works are internalized.

MEANING: CRITICAL AESTHETICS → INTERPRETATION

Procedural rhetoric is a property of the game's design to a greater degree than it is a property of its enactment. Though some of its constitutive elements (such as aesthetic and theme) are subjective and rely upon player observation and interpretation, the arguments advanced by procedural rhetorics can be considered to be "baked in" to the designed systems, such that they *should* convey similar meanings to anyone who analyzes the system using the specific Proceduralist methodology. Procedural rhetoric conveys a message, and the purpose of identifying procedural rhetorics in play is to be aware of the messages being transmitted through the structure of the designed systems.

Procedural rhetoric is interpreted with the *implied player* satisfying the "player position" in the system of gameplay, rather than a specific player and the *actual* choices she makes. A term borrowed from Aki Järvinen (2008):

> implied player is the one who embodies the 'player position' that a game system invites its supposed players into – in similar fashion as texts like film and literature posit their audiences into reading and viewing positions. In terms of design, implied players are the players who the game designer imagines will be playing the game, yet they are an idealisation.
>
> *(p. 104)*

Järvinen adapted that term from Wayne C. Booth (1961), Wolf Schmid (1973), and Wolfgang Iser (1974) *implied reader*, from literary theory.

As such, analyses of procedural rhetoric are conceived in manners similar to accounts of rhetoric in other mediums. Like the rhetorics of wartime propaganda films are conceived as embedded messages within those films, procedural rhetorics are posited as designed expressions of gameplay systems. The player's role in enacting the narratives is impersonal, such that the construction of a rhetorical analysis would not be subverted by a player deliberately choosing to play *against* its design. The *implied player* provides a somewhat impartial, hypothetically idealized fulfillment of the player's role in gameplay enactment.

The separate form of meaning that I label with the more general term "interpretation" relies upon reaction to *enacted play* rather than systemic potential. The meanings players draw from this form of interpretation will have greater variance based on the specific choices and actions that shape their experience of play. For this reason, it follows *critical aesthetics*, which is a relatively "immediate" reaction to the aspects of meaning-making that we have thus far covered.

Critical Aesthetics

Earlier in the meaning-making model, before agency, associations, themes, or metaphors were explored, we recognized a set of pre-reflective aesthetics—the elements of artistic representation that elicit "gut-level" reactions from the player. Defined by Hunicke et al. to evoke "emotional" reactions (Hunicke et al., 2004), I posited that the types of reactions that aesthetics elicit extend beyond that which would typically be termed "emotional", but the term appropriately cues the "baseness" of the experience of aesthetics. Aesthetics can be considered the "core pleasures" (and displeasures), which art is able to elicit from its audiences—the "tools" with which artists work to produce *felt* or *lived* experiences through the art. Each art form has a different set of "core aesthetics", the aspects of the form that, for some reason, strum the chords of the human soul.

In classifying the core aesthetics and their evocative potentials, I divided the list conceived by Hunicke et al. (*ibid*), with some additions from myself, into two categories, experienced on different planes of attention and thought. Pre-reflective aesthetics, as detailed previously, include Sensation, Vertigo, Presence, Challenge, Progress, Ontological Upset, Expression, Compulsion, and Submission. Once agency, theme, and the associative resonances that draw forth more specific, semiotically contextualized meaning are considered, a similar series of aesthetic reactions are naturally experienced by the player. Oriented around semiotic meaning, these are reflective aesthetics, or what I call *critical aesthetics*, and these natural reactions to the game's meaning-based content cue the player's interpretive capacities and inform the type of interpretation the game will undergo.

The critical aesthetics are Progress, Fantasy, Narrative, Fellowship, Competition, Discovery, and Expression. There are a couple of overlaps between the pre-reflective and critical sets, which express the relevance of particular considerations in both pre- and post-reflective capacities. These aesthetics have been thoroughly defined in Chapter 2, so I will not repeat the definitions here. Most of these critical aesthetics result from the mimetic and methectic perspectives of play, for they tend to have greater interface with the semiotics of game fantasy and thoughtful consideration of systems, as opposed to the diegetic perspective, which is experienced primarily from a (vicario)sensory orientation.

Critical aesthetics feed back into motivation, informing that which the player believes and wants in gameplay. This means that meaning-based evaluations shape the enactment of gameplay, which is further evaluated starting from a non-semiotic/pre-reflective perspective. In other words, the meaning of the artwork (gameplay) is not only diversified in its *interpretation* by the beholder (player) but said interpretation feeds back into changing the "shape" and content of the artwork itself.

Interpretation

The experience of critical aesthetics prompts interpretation. As the examination of procedural rhetorics drew into focus the potential of designed systems to contain persuasive messages, this exploration privileges the narrative-like expression of enacted gameplay. We do still consider how meaning is shaped by systems and mechanics, but this layer of meaning "de-idealizes" the player, calling into focus how systemic design produces a specific and unique series of events, expressive of the systemic design *and* the player as an agent within the system.

This interpretive task asks how the design of the gameplay system (holistically, including diegetic and nondiegetic elements) interacts to produce the experienced critical aesthetics. What elements within the simulation, in the physical interaction with the controller, or in the context of play create meaningful dynamics in their inter-relationships with one another? This exploration elucidates capacities for meaning generation from the gameplay system, and, like a narrative analysis, the most significant crux points of the player's experiential journey with the game are made apparent. If the identification of procedural rhetorics illuminated the areas in which the systems and mechanics of a game generated meaning, this exploration highlights the areas with the greatest potential for meaning in the intersection between the systems and mechanics of the *software* and the specific aesthetic preferences and triggers of the *player*. A particular systemic affordance might create meaningful and memorable gameplay experiences for another player but not for me, because viewing gameplay as a holistic system involving computer, player, and context, it should be obvious that a game would have different systemic capacities if player and context are changed.

So this formulation represents one form of a holistic summation of systemic analysis. The method by which meaning is derived and argued follows the structural model of the discernment of procedural rhetorics, but the interpreter can draw into the "argument" aspects of the personal. For example, if we were writing a formal analysis using the Proceduralist methodology described in Chapter 5, in addition to the typical elements of the argument (entities, goals, mechanics, dynamics, themes, aesthetics, and meanings), we can add elements that describe player and contextual elements of the system of gameplay (playerDesire, playerMood, contextDistraction, gameGlitch, etc.). This allows us to identify and articulate forms of meaning that express capabilities of the system without being so stiflingly objective as to remove core components of the system by which gameplay is brought to life.

On the metagame level, we can consider each individual expression of gameplay to be one of many possible expressions. One positions and argues her own experience with knowledge that it is no more "true" of an expression of a particular game's artistic capabilities than any other player's gameplay. Theoretically, we can consider a "model" in which all players' choices and experiences are held and compared against each other to create what we might understand as not the *total* affordances of the system, but something like a *weighted* average, acknowledging that player decisions will have been pulled and persuaded toward particular clusters and away from the extremities of what is *possible* within a system by its incentive structure, semiotic context, or aspects of human nature and psychology. This exercise of summing *all* player expressions is purely hypothetical and impossible to actually achieve, but it provides an important theoretical context in which players may evaluate their own experiences, which we will return to in the section Manifest Content vs. Possibility Space.

MEANING: PROCEDURAL RHETORIC

Theme and metaphor complement the systemic and emergent properties of game design to lead into the creation of procedural rhetorics. This term and its history are more thoroughly explained in Chapter 5, but in short: procedural rhetorics are persuasive or declarative models of the way a process works through rule-based systems or simulations. For example, as opposed to describing and advocating for a particular form of government structure, one can construct a simulation in which the interactor makes governing decisions, but the values and variables that manage the simulation reward or push the player toward desired political philosophies. Alternatively, procedural rhetorics do not need to be "disguised" as impartial systemic operations—they can be obvious and imaginative. A hypothetical game about being a landlord, tasked with "shooting" eviction notices at apartments once rent is past due but before tenants make late payments in order to replace them with units that gain greater passive income over time, makes a procedural statement, though it is not one that is presented as representationally naturalistic, but it still communicates a message about a subject—landlords and the tension between their financial incentive structures and the ethics of their role in the market.

Though examinations of implicit ideologies are among the most common among published procedural rhetoric explorations, it is not necessary for the underlying rhetoric to be advocating a specific ideological or ethical point—it only classifies a manner of communicating ideas. Researcher and writer Ian Bogost, who coined the term procedural rhetoric, advocates for Janet H. Murray's (1997) positioning of electronic media systems design as *procedural authorship*, "writing the rules by which the texts appear as well as writing the texts themselves" (p. 152). Bogost (2007) positions procedural rhetoric as a subdomain of procedural authorship (p. 29), emphasizing that it describes utilizing the design of an interactive system or simulation to effect a rhetorical affordance—in other words, to seek to change opinion or action.

As such, the identification of procedural rhetoric involves the identification of *embedded* meaning—determination of the intended meaning of a system that seeks to persuade. Separate meaningful interpretation will be advocated in a separate step in the model that explores (potentially) *unintended* positions advanced through the system's procedures. Though most of this literacy model de-emphasizes embedded meaning in favor of the meaning that is co-constructed through systemic interaction and player interpretation, it is an important task of any formal literacy to be able to identify rhetorical persuasion.

The creation of art is a means of cultural myth-making, and myths are often told to advance ideological causes by authoring scenarios of self-justifying "naturalness". As is explained by Roland Barthes (1972):

> Myth does not deny things. On the contrary, its function is to talk about them; simply, it purifies them, it makes them innocent, it gives them a natural and eternal justification, it gives them a clarity which is not that of explanation but that of a statement of fact. If I state the fact of French imperiality without explaining it, I am very near to finding that it is natural and goes without saying.
>
> *(p. 143)*

This is not to presuppose that all messages of cultural mythology are ignoble; the creative practice of the arts tends to attract those with curious and open minds, and many advance quite positive messages. But it is important for the reader of any text to recognize when they are being "sold" a message—when they are being asked to believe or implicitly agree with something that presents innocently but seeks to persuade. Outright propaganda is often easy to spot, but more subtle forms of truth assertions can slip by the inattentive beholder, particularly in interactive systems design where cause and effect relationships take center stage. That which occurs as a result of player action can feel as "natural" within the system as the reactions of physics in our universe.

Just because a procedural rhetoric is intentional does not mean it is *successful*. Some of Bogost's most interesting explorations of procedural rhetorics are examples of games that, through poorly considered systemic design, undercut the messages that the semiotic layer of the simulation ostensibly advances. Treanor et al. (2010) give the example of *Mayor Munch* (2010), a *PAC-MAN* (1980) clone reskinned to represent the Toronto mayoral elections. The candidate stands in for Pac-Man, Pac-dots represent ballots, and the ghosts have been replaced with political opponents. Its most obvious reading might be that the candidate is destroying or stealing ballots while powerful opponents can defeat him with a touch. This game attempts to make a persuasive political argument, but the procedural metaphors within its systems are misjudged.

For this reason, procedural rhetoric necessarily interfaces with theme (which is sometimes called *skin*, both as a noun and a verb, in Proceduralist analyses). Theme, the semiotic details that provide representational context for that which occurs within gameplay, points toward the procedural rhetorics (or at least situates those rhetorics within an appropriate domain). Unprompted metaphorical interpretations can still be valuable, but it belongs to a different form of meaning.

From the starting point of theme, procedural rhetorics can be identified within each of the three perspectives of play. From the diegetic perspective, consider how the avatar's embodied action affordances interface with the semiotic theme. With the understanding that actions are not "natural" but afforded by intentional design, consider which actions are allowed, which are unavailable, and how the specific affordances construct a hypothetical reality. What types of actions are presented as being effective, valorized, or important? How does this advance or counteract a persuasive argument about the thematic domain? What within the game world is presented as safe or advantageous, and what is presented as dangerous or evil? Do these designations thematically map onto elements of the real world?

From a mimetic perspective, consider the structure of goals and myth-making within the ludic fiction. Is the player directed toward advancing one character or faction's goals and positioned against another? Does the audience implicitly "agree" with the actions of the avatar or protagonist because she is operationalized as the point of view or locus of identification within the game world? Do the game's objectives or steps toward their achievement advocate a message or myth?

From a methectic perspective, do the strategic or tactical affordances of the gameplay system suggest or reward a particular way of thinking or approaching problems? Do metagame strategies or exploits exist that reinforce or undercut the game's thematic position, in so far as it can be determined? What non-semiotic behaviors of the system imply a "natural" result of particular interactions? Is there an ideology or worldview embedded in those assumptions, and how does that position interface with the game's theme?

MEANING: IDEOLOGY

The discernment of ideological or ethical positions explicitly or implicitly encoded into gameplay systems was an area of interest in the examination of procedural rhetorics earlier in this model. Following on from the player- and context-inclusive reframing of our more general critical interpretation above, we can also extend our sensitivity to ideological positions "held" by the system of gameplay. If procedural rhetorics are identified as properties of the embedded mechanics, context-independent and conceived against the hypothetical "ideal player", a broader ideological inquiry will explore not only the game's rhetorical affordances but also its ideological expressions in the context of the specific choices of an individual player and the ideological implications of its presentation in a particular context.

Several ideological contexts can be considered in the examination of a video game. One can consider the context of the game's production: do the systemic relationships expressed in-game hold particular relevance when considered alongside the game's culture of origin? For example, how do the themes and political ideologies expressed within the post-apocalyptic first-person shooter *S.T.A.L.K.E.R. 2: Heart of Chornobyl* (2024) reflect the real-world conditions under which it was made by Ukrainian developers during Russia's 2022 invasion of Ukraine? How might those positions be read differently were the game instead developed *in* Russia or by a team elsewhere in the world uninvolved with the conflict? How might a game's scale or mode of production impose particular ethical considerations? For example, might we read anti-capitalist or anti-establishment theming of games produced independently (like *Disco Elysium* [2019], *Night in the Woods* [2017], and *The Red Strings Club* [2018]) differently than we might read games produced by massive publishers that put on similar anti-capitalist affectations (like *Watch_Dogs 2* [2016], *Fallout 2* [1998], and *Cyberpunk* 2077 [2020])? Should it affect our interpretation and reading of a game if we find out it was made in an exploitative or abusive work environment?

We can consider games in the context of the market into which they launch. How might a game's marketing, price, or method of distribution express an ideological position? Can we read a game's marketplace success or indifference as reflecting an ideological match or mismatch with the culture? Considering the long development period games undergo, how might the ideological positions of a game be at tension with a shift in the culture's perception that grew during the period of its prolonged gestation (we can look at examples of games with particularly long development periods like *Duke Nukem Forever* (2011) to see how market expectations might shift over time)?

As living texts, we can compare video games' ideological expressions with the context in which the game is presently played. Unavoidably, elements of games released years or decades earlier will seem jarring when played from a modern context. What insights does this enable about our present culture and its evolution in the time since the game was produced? Do expectations based on play experience with modern games color the way in which elements of historical games' design are read?

Finally, we can consider the hyper-specific context of play instantiation. Are elements of gameplay at ideological tension with aspects of the play environment? For example, the pay-per-play monetization model of the arcade setting may be at ideological tension when a game is recontextualized to a home or museum setting. Are there relevant ideological considerations at play based on who is playing that might not be relevant with other configurations of players (age groups, sensitivities to ethnic representation, accessibility for particular disabilities…)? In what context is a game presented? Does it form ideological through-lines or discontinuities with other games played recently? Is it curated amongst other games, paratext, or media?

MEANING: SELF-EXPRESSION

One of the primary outputs of value and meaning in games is self-expression of the player. The arts are unique in their expressive capacity, but typically the expression evident in the artistic artifact is the expression of the artist rather than of the audience. The audience is certainly reflected in the meaning ascribed to the artistic *experience* in an interpretive manner, and the comparison of differing interpretations is a vital dimension by which an artistic work "lives on" through different times and contexts, but these audience interpretations affect context to a greater degree than they affect the content or form of the work itself. A radical reframing may change the way audiences view a particular work, but it does not change the work itself—all future audiences react to fundamentally the same work on the level of sensory stimuli.

The interactive nature of games, however, reforms this relationship between audience and creator. Because games are formally indeterminant until enacted play is individually instantiated, an individual expression of play—the *manifest content* of a particular play session, as I call it in Chapter 11—is expressive of both the player (in the individual choices made and actions performed) and the developers (in shaping the total possibility space and incentivizing or mechanically structuring particular expressions into greater likelihood than others).

While much of the formal analytical process covered thus far takes interest in determining the shape or propensities for action toward which a game is designed to push players (the procedural influence of developer expression), it is useful to consider the capacities a game permits players to express and learn about themselves through play. Games are structured around tasks of learning, primarily about specific systems and reactions against which the mechanical challenges of the game test the player, but games also have the capacity to give players opportunities to learn about themselves. Every piece of art facilitates self-discovery, pushing audiences to consider their reactions to novel situations and settings, but since player expression enacts into the instantiated manifest content of gameplay, this self-discovery becomes not only interpretive but also constructive, observable by other participants and onlookers.

Much of this self-discovery manifests through the semiotic content of a game (answering the question, "what would I do in this scenario?", perhaps), but literate players can glean self-insights from non-semiotic play as well. Behavioral patterns exhibit qualities such as risk tolerance, curiosity, and patience. Through play, qualities of the self exhibit in such a way that the player can become identifiable through gameplay alone. Decontextualized recordings of gameplay can be reviewed, and signatures of a particular player's expressive play style can become apparent to those who know what to look for. Members of the fighting game community can identify top players through their expressions of technique and strategy, for instance. Even those unfamiliar with a particular player's play patterns can identify qualities of play: skittishness, carelessness, apprehension, sense of humor, bravery...

These player expressions, though originating with and expressive of the player herself, are still dependent upon properties of design and are worth exploring in any formal analysis of a game, even one that aims for a more "objective" perspective that depersonalizes one's own individual experience. The type and amount of self-expression that a game affords a player is limited and specific to the designed vision for the game in question. Games that afford players a large degree of expressive freedom create a particular behavioral aesthetic in this affordance. In this sense, exploration of player expression is also an exploration of systems design.

Player expression as a property of a game's systems and mechanics is called *expressivity*, and it is further explored in Chapter 12. This includes not only affordances for enacting highly individualized performance of play but also the degree to which the game's systems *react* to individualized play with meaningful changes in the flow of action. If a game gives its player 300 options for action in a particular moment but every action results in an identical resolution, we might conclude that this is actually a rather shallow expressivity (though one that might still have rhetorical value in its "stubbornness").

In Chapter 12, I identify two types of expressivity: micro-expressivity (reactivity to highly individualized moment-to-moment play) and macro-expressivity (long-term reactivity to highly individualized systems operation). These elements are independent of one another, and their intersection describes different forms or demands of play. For instance, a game with high micro-expressivity but low macro-expressivity may describe a game that allows multiple approaches for solving a single, concrete challenge.

Micro- and macro-expressivity denote types of gameplay; they are not judgments of quality on their own. A game is not "worse" for having low expressivity in one or both categories; it only expresses a particular *type* of affordance or challenge. The balance between micro- and macro-expressivity also changes throughout the course of play, so these categories are to be regarded as dynamic variables rather than static values *essentially* true of a particular game. As such, it is useful to keep track of when and how these categories change along with changes in game state or state change of game elements. It is also useful to keep track of the particular *types* of choices that a game affords its players and what these might indicate about its design purpose or ideological goals.

The three perspectives of play tend to have affinities for the different types of expressivity. Diegetic play, expressed with projective embodiment, tends to correlate with micro-expressivity—choice made in the embodied, moment-to-moment operation of the avatar within the game space. Mimetic play, expressed in role-playing and narrative agency, tends to split between micro- and macro-expressivity, in that the structure of long- and medium-term objectives may be more or less freeform (a function of macro-expressivity), while narrative-relevant role-playing performance choices can straddle both levels of expressivity. Methectic play, expressed in strategic and metagame play, tends toward macro-expressivity (in long-term strategic consideration), but micro-expressivity factors into reactivity toward *enacting* certain types of strategies or taking advantage of exploits or glitches.

MEANING: MANIFEST CONTENT VS. POSSIBILITY SPACE

Determining the expressivity of a game system indicates values built into its structure. In this context, we can view the expression of each individual instantiation of play situated within the "shape" of the game's (or an element within the game's) total possibility space. As defined in Chapter 11, enacted play actions constitute the *manifest content* of that play session. Manifest content is a term borrowed from psychoanalytic theory, used to describe the specific events that occur within a dream. For instance, the manifest content of one play session of *The Legend of Zelda: Breath of the Wild* (2017) may instantiate the exploration of a plains region, the taming of a wild horse, riding to a mountain, exploring a cave, and finding a treasure chest that contains a rare weapon. From a narrative perspective, these events occurred during that particular play session, though it would not be wholly accurate to argue that this particular sequence of events is descriptive of *Breath of the Wild* as *every* player experiences it.

As such, the *manifest content* framing is useful for contextualizing types of game analysis. For instance, an argument about the procedural rhetoric of a game system is an argument about the system's propensity to funnel play into particular types or expressions of action, but an account of what transpires during a particular instantiation of play describes individual player choices rather than generalizing assertions of the "intent" of the game's design. Though analysis of manifest content is made valuable by an instantiated expression's relative placement to the total or intended design affordances, contextually.

As such, we can consider particular expressions of play (manifest content) to be more or less congruent with a hypothesized "intended" or "median" expression of play. If a player enacts a particular series of events, it is relevant to consider whether this expression is likely to be a common or design-congruent expression or whether the player is playing "against" the direction of design or the ways in which most players might approach it. This is not to identify the "correct" or "incorrect" form of play; rather, it is useful context with which the expressivity of a player can be understood.

Design-incongruent manifest content can often be a positive expression of player creativity, as she finds solutions to problems that were not intended or made obvious by the game's design. Highly incongruent play can also suggest alternative, entertaining ways of exploring a game system—metagame play in its finest form. For instance, players of the *Pokémon* series (1996–present) of monster-battling JRPGs have invented a novel metagame called the "Nuzlocke" form of play, in which, as a role-playing exercise, particular restrictions are self-enforced to make the game more challenging and interesting. Nuzlocke players only permit the capture of the first Pokémon encountered in each new area, and if a Pokémon ever "faints" (loses all of its health) during battle, the player releases it into the wild (as if it had been permanently "killed", while fainted Pokémon can typically be revived with items or at a checkpoint "PokéCenter"). These additional conditions of play are not enforced by the software, and there is nothing in the design of the game that "pushes" players toward this form of play (nor mechanically rewards it), but the mechanical structure "allows" this form of design-incongruent play. Thus, we can consider it an expression of the game's total possibility space, but we must also acknowledge that it exists toward the "edge" of this "space". It is a road less traveled, but it is still a valid exploration of the total affordances of the system and its interesting relationships. In fact, this form of play is valuable *because* it is unusual and "against" design.

Some forms of "unusual" play are explicitly accounted for in a game's design (such as a low-intelligence playthrough of post-apocalyptic ARPG *Fallout: New Vegas* (2010), which rewards players with comical dialogue options available only to avatars with low intelligence stats). Some are expected but not directly acknowledged or incentivized (such as "soul level one" runs of *Dark Souls* [2011], in which players challenge themselves to complete the game without ever "leveling up" [increasing] the skill stats of their avatars). Others are implicitly *contrary* to design or intent (such as speedruns that exploit glitches to circumvent portions of the game). In all of these forms (even the last), these unusual forms of play are still expressive of the total affordances of the system. Their peripherality to "intended" courses of play does not delegitimize them as meaningful expressions of ludic agency within the total possibility space of the game.

When forming an analytical perspective or making an argument about a game, be aware of whether what is being described is the system and its particular, directed affordances or a unique expression of manifest content of gameplay. Neither framing is inherently more "valuable" than the other from a critical perspective. I do not want to give the impression that the latter is only useful for self-reflection. Rather, highly expressive, individualized, and unusual play contributes a great deal to the total "shape" of a game's expressive potential. An account of play on the "fringes" of a system's "shape" not only gains value from its *difference* from more conventional play, it also makes conventional play more meaningful in its difference from the newly established fringe frontier. From a metagame perspective, a choice is only valuable in the context of what the chooser believes is possible to choose. With knowledge of fringe gameplay tactics, the choice to *remain* conventional is done *in context* and *with knowledge of* this wider shape.

Greater attention is given to expressivity in Chapter 12, and manifest content vs. the total possibility space is the focus of Chapter 11.

CREATION/ENCODING → STATE TRANSITION

If interpretation of gameplay is a *decoding* of game state information, play (input) is an act of *encoding*:

putting additional information into the system in order to change the states of its components. Play is not a *deconstruction* of the artistic artifact, as we may call audience viewership a deconstruction of a film or book in that each moment watched or word read is one fewer moment or word left in the static artifact. Instead, play is *constructive* of the instantiated product. Though the player is similarly working toward an end (either sanctioned or arbitrary), the artifact does not *reduce* the amount of total remaining information; information is in a perpetual state of transition from non-existence to existence. The player is consuming and creating in parallel.

As such, this step in the model represents the player's capacity to create. This is a necessary step in every literacy model, but it is structured differently in this model compared to those of other mediums. Textual literacy involves decoding (reading) and encoding (writing) the production of additional material of-kind with what was decoded. With that in mind, one might expect the equivalent of literate decoding (sense-making in gameplay) to be the ability to program a game. This is certainly *a* valuable form of encoding (and one that is beneficial to literate play—understanding the logics and limitations of code helps players grasp the operational logics of gameplay as a software-driven system). Enacting active play is a more immediate form of encoding, though. Relevant to this exercise because this model is fundamentally oriented around the understanding and interpretation of *gameplay*, not games as code-based structures. The model *involves* discerning logical operations embedded into the structures of code, but this is in service of making *live play* more readable and meaningful. Remember, the framing of this book asserts that games themselves are not the artistic artifacts of focus in our exploration; games (and their mechanical systems) are only instructions by which the actual artistic artifact, live play, is brought about. Therefore, encoding (by this model's framework) means not the production of *games* but the production of *gameplay*.

As expressed throughout the model, several of the avenues of meaning discernment result in perspective and motivational shifts with regard to gameplay operations. The player makes decisions based not on the *objective/true* operational values of the variables of the gameplay system but on her interpretation and understanding of the variables of gameplay. For this reason, the model of game interpretation folds back upon itself in a manner unlike the interpretive models of most other art forms. Interpretation becomes relevant not only to the *reflective analysis* of meaning but also to the *construction* of the gameplay artifact.

To illustrate this, consider the highly macro-expressive fantasy CRPG *Baldur's Gate 3* (2023). Throughout the game, the player has to make several weighty decisions about what actions to perform in contentious situations, whom to trust or distrust, and who she adventures alongside. Several of the game's main characters, recruitable into the player's adventuring party, present in threatening or chaotic ways. If a player interprets one of these characters as being an enemy instead of a potential ally, she may choose to do battle with them and forgo their accompaniment as a party member. This is not necessarily a "mistake"; she only receives a *different* story in which transpires a *different* series of events than she would have had if she had allied with that particular character, but it inevitably changes the shape of that playthrough's manifest content.

Or consider ambiguous visual design. Science-fiction ARPG *NieR:Automata* (2017) features a mechanic in which avatar deaths are represented in the worlds of other players, connected via the internet, as doll-like robot bodies lying on the ground in the spot where the player's avatar fell. Players can interact with these bodies to gain useful resources or even revive them as temporary, computer-controlled assistants in battle. Their visual appearance does not signal these helpful affordances, though, and players may, at first, interpret these figures as enemies or traps. This interpretation, though unsupported by the actual mechanics of the game, will affect the way that the player chooses to play. She may avoid these robot bodies altogether, taking circuitous routes to avoid the spaces in which they lie. This goes on to affect the expression of manifest content and directs the action that takes place during play. The player's interpretation feeds back into the sense-making process, which informs the expression of gameplay that alters the manifest content to which the meaning-making process reacts.

So whereas the reflective analysis of a painting alters only an individual's interpretation of the otherwise static work, the interpretation of gameplay fundamentally alters its form. This is the most radical aspect of games' interactive nature. The player does not only perform a role in an authored experience, like an actor performing the script of a play, but the player is also a performer *and* co-author, choosing and constructing the narrative that the game expresses (within the soft and hard boundaries set by the game's systemic design).

Ultimately, interpretation resolves to the base of our model: state transition. This is true in the sense that subjective interpretations *inform* the state transitions that players enact (the choices that they make to take particular actions over others) *and* in the sense that interpretation *is* a state change in an element of play: the player's mind. Since the player's mind is diegetically contextualized as the avatar's mind (in its role as the motivating force that embodies and animates the conscious action of the figure within the game world), that which alters player knowledge also alters avatar knowledge (in the practical sense of diegetic operation and in the figurative sense of the personified character within the narrative), thus altering the total "knowledge" contained by not only the system of play enactment but also the representational fantasy.

To illustrate the significance of this distinction, we can compare video game avatar performance and theatrical performance. A dramatic actor and her character are not contextualized as "sharing" a store of knowledge. Lady Macbeth does not "know" the consequences of King Duncan's murder, even though the actor plays the role with knowledge of the entire script. The actor performs the actions of the character as if they were matters of history; reflections of a series of events enacted by individuals experiencing the events linearly. On the other hand, a video game avatar must be understood to possess a *partially shared* "knowledge" with the player. In moments of play, the avatar can only enact solutions to puzzles when the player has solved them. If the player has knowledge that, for instance, a particular character will betray the avatar or a series of events will be futile, the avatar can act upon this knowledge directly. In fact, if we consider the gradual improvement of player skill and strategy as being a component of the character arc of the avatar, starting the game again from scratch after completing it dramatically affects the knowledge-based component of this journey of growth. It would be like the titular character retaining his athletic training when watching *Rocky* (Avildsen, 1976) for a second time.

This is the root of the reason why this model of ludic literacy is framed as a layered model. The player's three perspectives, diegetic, mimetic, and methectic, affect the expression of gameplay at all levels in the sense-making and meaning-making processes. The player is a member of the diegetic world (by the property of projective embodiment, viewing the fiction from the inside out), a performer of the fiction (role-playing from the outside in), and a strategist manipulating the game as a construct of software (employing full real-world knowledge to overcome challenges, from the outside-in). Each of these roles and perspectives are held in parallel balance with one another and all exist in dynamic balances of harmony and tension with one another. All work together to construct the gameplay artifact, extract *and* produce meaning within the system of gameplay, and perpetuate the cycle of construction and interpretation.

RECORDING/RETELLING → POST-PROCESSING → INSIGHT

The instantiation of gameplay is perpetual during play, but the exploration that we have thus far completed pertains only to that *live* enactment. Like the crest of a wave in motion, play is only live in an instant. Gameplay is always present tense. In fact, as soon as gameplay *is* enacted, it changes in form to something else with very different properties: a second artistic artifact is produced. One that is interpreted in a different manner.

Gameplay is a product of a system in motion. The player, as a vital component of that system, observes, reacts, and predicts in order to steer the operation of that system. The beauty of live gameplay and the central challenge of the literacy of that system is grappling with this conscious force that perpetually reshapes the system's expression and the shape of further expression yet to come. So whereas live gameplay is centrally configured around the player's agency, structured to produce interesting scenarios of choice-making and expression, the record of instantiated play is configured as a now-static, linear narrative and can be interpreted as such.

Once gameplay occurs, it undergoes a process called *recording*. This is, essentially, the transmutation of systemic potential into manifest content: it becomes a record of *history*. In this context, "recording" does not necessarily refer to capturing gameplay on video (though this remediation is a form of recording). Once gameplay occurs, any audiovisual evidence of it *as well as* the player's memory of play is a "recording" of events that retain their sequential linearity but lose their characteristic configurability (having already transpired).

Recordings (sometimes also called *playtraces* [Kreminski et al., 2019]) refer to the objective series of events as instantiated during play, while *retellings* are subjective accounts of gameplay sequences that may be shared with others as stories (Koenitz, 2023). Retellings extend the "data" of the recording with inferences about the portrayed fiction, elaborating upon character motivations, environmental context, and the lives of characters beyond that which is explicitly modeled or portrayed. For example, players often create extrapolative characterizations of their characters in *The Sims* (2000) by inferring the "juicy details" of their relationships and inner lives for the purpose of producing dramatic stories, even though details modeled within the simulation itself are largely ambiguous when it comes to Sims' particular thoughts and opinions.

Mirjam Palosaari Eladhari (2018) has argued that retellings constitute a fourth layer of game text (beyond the architectural layer of code, narrated content, and narrative discourse), re-conceived by Hartmut Koenitz (2023) as the roughly equivalent layers of system, process, and product in the SPP model. This is sometimes literalized beyond player interpretation within the text of the game itself in instances when games recap specifically instantiated events, such as in the diary entries of *Shenmue II* (2001; Eladhari, 2018) or the Nemesis System of *Middle-earth: Shadow of Mordor* (2014). These kinds of automated retellings may become a powerful tool for amplifying the power of emergent storytelling in games, as hypothesized by James Ryan (2018) in his insightful ludic reframing of Hayden White's (1973) theory of rhetorical curation. Following Hayden's terminology, Ryan frames recording as the *chronicle* of events from which the *story sifter* (human or machine element that extracts the "raw narrative material" from which a story can be narrativized) selects *material* (chosen narrative data) for the *narrativizer* (element that reconstructs the sifted material into a sensible story) to interpret into a *story*, which can be mounted as a *media experience* (a narrative artifact that can be witnessed or experienced by an experiencer; Ryan, 2018). Ryan's theory is further elaborated upon in Chapter 11.

Recordings and narrativized retellings offer split trajectories in this literacy model, looping back to inform elements of the sense-making process (informing the player's understanding of systemic interrelationships and contributing to the formation of player motivation) as well as producing an exit from the loop: post-processing.

Post-processing is the player's reflection on transpired gameplay. From the diegetic perspective, this can include memorable instances of instantiated action; from the mimetic perspective, this can be reflection upon the embedded and enacted narratives; and from the methectic perspective, this can be reflection upon game strategy and metagame structure. Post-processing gives the player further opportunity to put the experience of play into relevant contexts. Reflective post-processing crystallizes into insights as players resolve narrative and experiential meanings, drawing personal takeaways. Insights can change the way a player thinks and what she believes about the world, potentially altering the configuration of elements with which she will process all future artistic experiences.

NOTE

1. This is similar to the method espoused by actor Nicolas Cage, who is equally criticized and praised for his eccentric, over-the-top performances that eschew naturalism in favor of what Cage calls "emotional reality" (Bierman, 1989). His performances reflect not the outward expression of a person in his characters' situations but rather embody the sense of what it is like to feel those emotions. It is the performance of the internal experience rather than the outward expression.

REFERENCES

Anderson, C. A. & Bushman, B. J. (2001). Effects of violent video games on aggressive behavior, aggressive cognition, aggressive affect, psychological arousal, and prosocial behavior: A meta-analytic review of the scientific literature. *Psychological Science, 12*(5), 353–359.

Anderson, C. A. & Dill, K. E. (2000). Video games and aggressive thoughts, feelings and behavior in the laboratory and in life. *Journal of Personality and Social Psychology,* 78(4), 772–790.

Avildsen, J. G. (Director). (1976). *Rocky* [Film]. United Artists.

Barthes, R. (1967). The death of the author. *Aspen, 5*.

Barthes, R. (1972). *Mythologies* (A. Lavers, Ed. & Trans.). Farrar, Straus and Giroux. (Original work published 1957)

Bierman, R. (Director). (1989). *Vampire's kiss* [Film]. Hemdale Film Corporation.

Bogost, I. (2007). *Persuasive games: The expressive power of videogames*. The MIT Press.

Booth, W. C. (1961). *The rhetoric of fiction*. University of Chicago Press.

Borges, J. L. (1946). On exactitude in science. *Los Anales de Buenos Aires*.

Bushman, B. J. & Huesman, L. R. (2000). Effects of televised violence on aggression. In D. G. Singer & J. L. Singer (Eds.) *Handbook of children and the media*. Sage.

Cameron, J. (Director). (1997). *Titanic* [Film]. Paramount Pictures, 20th Century Fox.

Deleuze, G. (1985). *Cinema 2: The time-image*. Les Editions de Minuit.

Eladhari, M. P. (2018). Re-tellings: The fourth layer of narrative as an instrument for critique. *International Conference on Interactive Digital Storytelling*, 65–78. doi:10.1007/978-3-030-04028-4_5

Endresen, I. M. & Olweus, D. (2005). Participation in power sports and antisocial involvement in preadolescent and adolescent boys. *Journal of Child Psychology and Psychiatry*, 46(5), 468–478.

Funk, J. B., Baldacci, H. B., Pasold, T., & Baumgardner, J. (2004). Violence exposure in real-life, video games, television, movies, and the internet: Is there desensitization? *Journal of Adolescence, 27*, 23–49.

Gee, J. P. (2003). *What games have to teach us about learning and literacy*. St. Martin's Press.

Goldsmith, J. (1994). *This is your brain on Tetris*. Wired. https://www.wired.com/1994/05/tetris-2/

Grinblat, J. (2017). Emergent narratives and story volumes. In T. S. Short & T. Adams (Eds.), *Procedural generation in game design* (pp. 199–207). CRC Press.

Grinblat, J. [@ptychomancer] (2018, April 2). *I love maps & their promise of fractal discovery. I love procedural generation and the aesthetics of the unauthored. Where do these two loves intersect? Generated maps. I am the procgen map admirer. These are my favorite map generators and the folks who create them. 👇THREAD👇* [Images attached] [Post]. X. https://x.com/ptychomancer/status/980968298002006016

Hanna, W. & Barbera, J. (1961–1962). *The Yogi Bear show* [TV series]. Hanna-Barbera Productions.

Hunicke, R., LeBlanc, M., & Zubek, R. (2004). MDA: A formal approach to game design and game research. *Proceedings of the AAAI Workshop on Challenges in Game AI, 4*(1).

Iser, W. (1974). *The implied reader: Patterns of communication in prose from Bunyan to Beckett*. Johns Hopkins University Press.

Järvinen, A. (2008). *Games without frontiers*. Tampere University Press.

Koenitz, H. (2023). *Understanding interactive digital narrative*. Routledge. doi:10.4324/9781003106425

Kirkpatrick, G. (2011). *Aesthetic theory and the video game*. Manchester University Press.

Kreminski, M., Samuel, B., Melcer, E., & Wardrip-Fruin, N. (2019). Evaluating AI-based games through retellings. *Fifteenth AAAI Conference on Artificial Intelligence and Interactive Digital Entertainment, 15*(1), 45–51. doi:10.1609/aiide.v15i1.5223

McCormick, M. (2001). Is it wrong to play violent video games? *Ethics and Information Technology, 3*, 277–287.

Miyazaki, H. (2013). *The wind rises* [Film]. Toho.

Murray, J. H. (1997). *Hamlet on the holodeck: The future of narrative in cyberspace*. The MIT Press.

Nguyen, C. T. (2020). *Games: Agency as art*. Oxford University Press.

Nolan, C. (Director). (2023). *Oppenheimer* [Film]. Universal Pictures.

Parlett, D. (2007). *What's a ludeme? And who really invented it?* Parlett Games. https://www.parlettgames.uk/gamester/whatsaludeme.html

Ryan, J. (2018). *Curating simulated storyworlds* [Doctoral dissertation, UC Santa Cruz]. UC Santa Cruz Electronic Theses and Dissertations. https://escholarship.org/uc/item/1340j5h2#main

Schmid, W. (1973). *Der textaufbau in den erzählungen dostoevskijs*. Grüner.

Seraphine, F. (2016). The ludic framework. In *Digital Game Research Association Japan Proceedings of the Annual Conference*.

Shakespeare, W. (Playwright). (1599). *The Tragedy of Hamlet, Prince of Denmark* [Play]. London.

Treanor, M., Schweizer, B., Bogost, I., & Mateas, M. (2010). Proceduralist readings: How to find meaning in games with graphical logics. *FDG '11: Proceedings of the 6th International Conference on Foundations of Digital Games*. doi:10.1145/2159365.2159381

White, H. (1973). *Metahistory: The historical imagination in nineteenth-century Europe*. Johns Hopkins University Press.

CHAPTER 9

Narrative

OUR STUDY OF VIDEO games as expressive artistic artifacts has, thus far, acknowledged the role that formal narrative plays in games' formal apparatus, but outright narrative study has taken a peripheral focus to what I term the non-semiotic elements of the game's construction. Though games share many elements with more traditional narrative mediums, such as long passages of written text that perform the same function as the written text of books, or cinematically presented cutscenes, which are, essentially, short films, our primary interest has been in exploring the manner in which games diverge from typically linear media and introduce their own expressive dynamics. Our greatest attention has been paid toward exploring how to make sense and derive meaning from aspects of interaction, play, vicarious being, spatial construction, etc. With well-established interpretive traditions already extensively practiced for the literary, visual, and cinematic forms, re-establishing the tenets of those very familiar literacies would not be a good use of the limited space of this book.

The manners in which narrative has been discussed in this book have, instead, either centered around the experiential "narrative" arc that the player undergoes in the instantiation of gameplay, using narrative metaphor to ground elements of the study of interactivity, or framing *protostory* elements (Koenitz, 2023, pp. 76, 77; see Chapter 3) as contextual cues that guide, provide stakes for, and shape our interpretation of the non-semiotic interactive and emergent elements of gameplay. There are some points of narrative construction in video games that bear specific exploration, though. This chapter is a brief digression into the semiotic.

Relevant to this subject is context pertaining to the contentiousness of the study of narrative in video game studies. While, undoubtedly, fairly traditional narratives *are often presented* in video games through protostory representation, video games' unique structure does not cleanly align with the typical linear, uni-sequential structures of traditional narrative forms. As such, the application of traditional narrative frameworks as *primary schemas* guiding the interpretation of games would lead to a field of study that undercuts the unique elements of the ludic form and may prevent video games from exploring the true reaches of their formic potential due to schematic determinism—we cannot design more innovative works if the only language we have to conceptualize and discuss the medium is rooted in ill-fitting parallels to dissimilar media.

Those are some of the objections raised by some early video game scholars who came to become known as ludologists. Much writing in the games studies discipline has framed a confrontational "debate" between ludologists and their "adversaries", the narratologists (those who use narrative-centric framing as a starting point for understanding and contextualizing games as expressive artifacts). In fact, calling the exchange between these groups a "debate" or even particularly "adversarial" is an inaccurate yet common mythologizing of the very limited exchanges on this subject that actually occurred.

Ludologists are functionalists, while narratologists are formalists, generally speaking. The former approaches the exploration of games from the inside-out, framing games primarily as sets of rules from which interesting proceduralities emerge.

DOI: 10.1201/9781003530961-9

The latter approaches games from the outside-in, observing their narrative aesthetics and mapping these two rules and systems, to which they can assign roles in the constructive dramatic structure. Both disciplines pursue similar ends from differing perspectives. As Ian Bogost (2009) writes, the difference of approach only appears like a division when framed as a question of "'*is a game a system of rules, or is a game a kind of narrative?*', but the disjunction disappears when reframed as '*is a game a system of rules, like a story is a system of narration?*'".

Though the conflict is often overstated, whatever dissonance between approaches has been addressed by a number of theorists. Henry Jenkins (2004) proposed a now widely accepted framing of games as spaces ripe with many possible narrative expressions (p. 119). David Herman (2002) and Noah Wardrip-Fruin (2020) frame ludic structure in terms of logic, applying what more closely resembles a *cognitive* framework in their analysis. Janet H. Murray (2012) follows Brenda Laurel (2014)'s theatrical metaphor for computer interface, positioning the dynamics of the cyberdrama as the narrative basis for ludic interpretation. Nearly all models that followed Hunicke et al. (2004)'s framework of mechanics → dynamics → aesthetics (including the Proceduralist model discussed in Chapter 5) inherit the functional perspective of dynamics-based inquiry along with the formalist, grammar-like structure of preceding mechanics. This is all to say, the distance between the ludological and narratological approaches has been bridged, so engaging with more traditionally narratological terms, like we are about to do with this chapter, does not position this exploration as being peripheral or opposed to the primarily functionalist exploration of the rest of this book.

NARRATIVE

Video games tell and generate stories in a number of ways, some familiar recycling of the forms of other narrative media and some unique. Video games can tell stories by temporarily becoming films (as in-game cutscenes) or literature (via written text). Beyond these relatively static elements of narrative protostory, games are narrative engines through which players construct their own complex and layered narratives in acts of collaborative storytelling. To speak with precision about these types of narratives, we must have language to distinguish between the modalities of storytelling games utilize.

There are five storytelling layers with which our explorations will contend: authored/embedded narrative, emergent narrative, experiential narrative, lore, and meta-narrative. Being able to discern how design choices affect these layers separately and how elements of these layers affect one another will allow us to be more precise in our explorations and discussions of storytelling within games. Additionally, knowledge of these conceptual differences helps us resolve seemingly contradictory details once we examine how player interactivity interfaces with games' written stories in the process of meaning-making, and how multilinear narrative systems instantiate into linear narratives during the process of recording (see Chapter 11).

In short, experiential narrative is the player's narrativized experience of playing the game. Embedded narrative accounts for the happenings of a game's plot within the fiction of the game. Lore represents the authored elements of a game that set the necessary context for the player-involved action but are separate from the happenings of the game's performed plot. Emergent narrative describes the stories that occur as the natural outworking of interacting mechanics or system dynamics, not specifically planned and penned by the developers. Meta-narrative describes how the manner of play at-large changes over time. To further abbreviate, lore is the canonical-unexperienced, embedded narrative is the canonical-experienced, emergent narrative is the individually canonical-experienced, and experiential narrative is the non-canonical-experienced ("canonical" from the perspective of the fiction). Meta-narrative is non-canonical with distributed experience, usually across a large number of people or over an expanse of time.

Embedded Narrative

Embedded narrative, also called authored narrative, describes the planned and authored elements of the scenario enacted within a game. This is mostly composed of *protostory* elements (Koenitz, 2023; see Chapter 3). While separate players' experiences will be unavoidably divergent due to differences in play, a game's embedded narrative will remain more or less consistent across playthroughs, deviating at pre-planned points of divergence. The heaviest proportion of expositional content tends to be delivered through protostory elements, while active plot-forwarding action tends to be expressed during gameplay. The actions of the avatar propel this active layer of the plot. While moment-to-moment gameplay tends to constitute the emergent and experiential narrative layers, the broader progression, such as "the avatar defeated the first boss and moved into the haunted forest", constitutes a forwarding of the embedded scenario. The embedded narrative, insofar as it loosely aligns with *all* players' experience of a game, reflects *that* these plot-necessary progressions take place, but not necessarily *in what manner* they transpire, such that it is plot-relevant that Mario moves from level 1-1 to level 1-2 but not necessarily that Mario died four times in level 1-1.

The terms *embedded* and *emergent narratives* were proposed by game designer Marc LeBlanc (2000) in a lecture at the Game Developers Conference. Because of the relative consistency of protostory elements between playthroughs, we can roughly consider the embedded narrative to be the identifiable "what" that a game is "about". Despite this primacy, though, embedded narrative is ultimately subservient to the emergent and experiential narratives. Marie-Laure Ryan (2001) calls the use of embedded protostory elements in games "not an end in itself, but a means toward the goal of luring the player into the game-world". Richard Dansky (2007) says that embedded narrative serves primarily to provide "a justification, a reason, or an excuse for the gameplay encounters" (p. 6). Jesper Juul (2005) argues that the role of embedded narrative in games is primarily to provide context for the actions that take place at the level of gameplay. Markku Eskelinen (2001) framed the position quite provocatively (as he is wont to do), "stories are just uninteresting ornaments or gift-wrappings to games, and laying any emphasis on studying these kinds of marketing tools is just a waste of time and energy".

The dismissiveness of embedded narrative in these early perspectives does not account for the player as a component of the generative system of gameplay. Just as programming code makes the abstract *rules* of a game interpretable and proceduralizable by the computer, the semiotic context of the protostory and embedded narrative makes the procedural content of gameplay interpretable by the player. The player, as the primary catalyzing agent of the system of gameplay production, actions upon her understanding of the ludic simulation in order to bring about the motivated changes she desires from the system. As player agency is one of the primary sources of divergent emergence during play, embedded narrative is—far from being purely ornamental—a necessary component of systemic feedback.

Embedded narratives allow limited alterability. Video game plots are typically singular until they branch at developer-designated points, either due to player choice or systemically weighted factors of chance. The more of these branching intersection points that are built into a game, the more (ultimately linear) outcome "courses" are possible, but, despite their apparent diversity, these are all still planned, designed digressions. Some games, like *The Stanley Parable* (2013), are built to showcase a rapidly widening diversity of branches, intended to be explored in successive replays, while more singularly focused games, like *Alan Wake* (2010), tell one unalterable story that advances with successful achievement of skill-based action challenges, with player-galvanized diversification coming primarily from difference in moment-to-moment avatar performance.

Embedded narratives are usually either identical or at least recognizable between players and playthroughs. Though players' individual experiences may greatly differ, elements of the authored plot should align or branch predictably. As such, embedded narrative details can serve as anchor points around which more obviously divergent experiential discussions can revolve. Recaps of *God of War II* (2007), for instance, always begin with the battle against the Colossus of Rhodes and the betrayal by Zeus, but gameplay-dependent details of that battle vary from player to player. This is similar, though not fully analogous, to the way in which different readers will read different motivations and emotions into the characters in a book, though the on-page details remain the same. In games, though, the division is not between objective textual details and subjective interpretations but rather between static textual details (embedded and protostory elements), textual details reflective of play diversity, and subjective interpretation. In other words, it is not a division between story "truth" and subjective inference; both authored textual details and play-dependent textual details are equally "true" of the text as enacted (see Chapter 11). But embedded narrative details are structurally similar across all instantiations, while experiential narrative details are true and necessary for each unique instantiation. Both are meaningful, but they must be treated differently in comparative analyses. It is similar to multiple theatrical troupes performing the same scripted play with different actors; the details within the script unify the performances, but the details that the script leaves open to variation or interpretation, such as the performance choices of the actors, can still be a fertile ground for diversity of interpretive meaning.

Not all games feature embedded narratives. Some games, like the RC car-operated football game *Rocket League* (2015), are played in individual matches not connected by any linking continuity beside player stats and rewards. Long-term players will experience a story, of sorts, as they accrue wins and losses, improve at the game, and unlock exciting cosmetic rewards, but this journey is not "authored" as much as it is structured. Such a journey of triumphs and failures is intended through the systemic structure of the game, but it is not embedded or necessarily true of all playthroughs. Similarly, games like *Street Fighter 6* (2023) or *Sid Meier's Civilization VI* (2016) include story content, but their player communities so heavily prefer player-against-player matchups that framing discussion around plot details when comparing experiences of play is not likely to be the most productive way to frame such analyses. In these cases, the embedded narrative behaves more like *lore*: introducing characters and factions to set optionally relevant context for the "real game" as experienced in player vs. player matchups, a function of experiential narrative.

Whether the embedded narrative is proportionally dense, as in *Metal Gear Solid 4: Guns of the Patriots* (2008) and its solid *hours* of cutscenes that break up player-enacted play sections, or thinly applied, such as *Super Mario Bros.*' (1985) story that can be comprehensively explained in a single sentence, the embedded narrative is never absent of an experiential counterpoint. A game that is entirely *cutscene* is a movie, and a game that is only *non-interactive text* is an eBook. Elements of interaction introduce the inevitability of divergent experiences in ways that other mediums typically do not match. If a story is told in the form of a game, the experiential narrative should be preferentially considered, as this possibility of divergence of enactments should alter our reading and process of meaning-making of the text, but it is incorrect to dismiss the role of embedded narrative on systemic instantiation outright.

Emergent Narrative

Auteur game designers Auriea Harvey and Michaël Samyn write in their Realtime Art Manifesto (2006), "Embrace non-linearity. Let go of the idea of plot. Realtime is non-linear. […] let go of plot! Plot is not compatible with realtime. Think 'poetry', not 'prose'". Whereas the embedded narrative serves a similar purpose to the static, linear stories of other media, the emergent and experiential narratives express the dynamism of a generative system in motion. Emergent narrative arises from procedural simulation. These narrative elements are not as prescriptively planned as embedded narrative protostories, but there are mechanics and structures that guide the emergent narrative's instantiation.

Embedded elements *can* be presented in an emergent fashion. For example, the order and nature of the written and voice-acted character encounters in the Greek mythology action roguelike *Hades* (2020) varies depending not only on player choices but also on procedural, semi-random generation. In such cases, it should be recognized that the written text itself, as authored and acted, is an embedded, protostory element of the game, but the manner in which it is systemically deployed is emergent. This differs from, for example, the written and voice-acted story cutscenes of *Conker's Bad Fur Day* (2001). Though there is player-dependent variability in the length of time between these embedded story moments (and the player has occasional control over the sequence in which they are presented), there are no mechanical factors that drive this variability. Though the experiential narrative of *Conker's Bad Fur Day* may diverge, they do not exhibit emergent variability on the scale of the macro-story.

Emergent narratives are most often observable as the unpredictable outworking of multi-mechanic interactions, responsive to or separate from player interactions. Considering that video games are primarily coded as complex webs of conditional variables, the degree to which emergent behavior appears unpredictable, novel, and "intelligent" increases as the number of conditional, mechanical "decisions" the simulation makes. For example, traffic simulation systems in city-building simulators such as *Cities: Skylines* (2015) use instanced decision-making procedures to generate complex, emergent traffic patterns in a manner that (ideally) reflects driving behaviors in real life. Each car is assigned a destination, and each car "decides" how to reach its destination based on a number of factors, generally boiling down to finding the most efficient route (there may be other factors determining what kind of efficiency is preferred—time efficiency, fuel efficiency, etc.—influenced by external factors like gas prices, pollution levels, and more). Cars obey traffic laws along the way, stopping at stop signs and traffic signals, going in the correct direction around roundabouts, and obeying speed limits. For this reason, a poorly placed traffic light may slow down traffic on a busy road, causing other cars to reroute and overpopulate alternate routes, leading to significant traffic jams across the city. A specific traffic jam is not an authored occurrence; it is a procedural result of the game's multiple layers of interacting mechanical instructions.

In most cases, emergent narrative is subjectively observed rather than crucial and reflected within the game's embedded narrative. As the number and diversity of interacting mechanics increases, so too does the number of possible outcomes of any action. As such, the embedded narrative of a game is generally not programmed in such a way that it can recognize and react to each of these possible iterations. Embedded narrative may be reactive to simple emergent variations (for example, characters in CRPGs like *Disco Elysium* (2019) react to the success or failure of actions executed with "dice roll" semi-randomized mediation), but more extensive emergent chains will usually not be narratively integrated.

One way in which emergent details are sometimes honored by the embedded narrative is in downstream checks. A game may check whether or not a plot-relevant character is still alive or the degree to which a vehicle is damaged, for example, and issue embedded narrative-layer acknowledgement. Regardless of how the character died or the vehicle sustained damage (often the result of emergent chains of events), a character can react appropriately ("you weren't able to save Major Zhang" or "I told you to be careful with my car! This is going to cost a fortune to fix") without "understanding" how this outcome was reached.

Emergent narratives result from simulation. This includes character simulation (agents that act semi-autonomously in pursuit of instanced motivations; Ryan, 2018, pp. 20, 21) and physics simulation (Mateas, 2005, p. 107). The interactions between agents and with the system's physics simulation produce procedural dynamics, and dynamics are the component building blocks of emergent narrative. "It is the result of a different mode of human authorship: rather than crafting a narrative artifact, a human crafts a system out of which narrative artifacts may emerge" (Ryan, 2018, p. 19).

In this sense, the narrative form with which emergent narrative has the most in common is improvisational theatre. In the improv comedy game called Party Guests, for example, actors are assigned characters with specific motivations and personality quirks ("he is only comfortable conversing while using car metaphors", "she believes that she is a ghost of a Victorian-era countess trying to find forgiveness so that she can rest in peace", "he wants to make a marriage proposal but is too nervous to do so until he has had an adequate number of drinks"), and the dynamics of the scene result from these autonomous characters trying to fulfill their motivations and, naturally, interfering with and playing off of one another's quirks. The "authorship" of the scenario comes from creating interesting sets of rules and variables that hold a great amount of narrative potential. As such, we can classify emergent storytelling as a "simulationist" (bottom-up) approach, in contrast with embedded storytelling's "interventionist" (top-down) method (Ryan, 2018, pp. 22, 23, 220, 221).

Again, in early interpretive game studies, simulation-driven emergence was seen as somewhat antithetical to narrative structure. Greg Costikyan (2007) said, "To the degree that you make a game more like a story – a controlled, predetermined experience, with events occurring as the author wishes, you make it a less effective game. To the degree that you make a story more like a game – with alternative paths and outcomes – you make it a less effective story", or, as Jonathan Blow (2008) more succinctly put it, "Interactivity sabotages delivery. [...] Interactivity sabotages structure". More recent explorations, though, have identified methods for proceduralizing drama management from the bottom-up. James Ryan identifies *Façade* (2005) as a system that simulates drama management from the bottom up; a marriage of interventionalist methods using simulationist technique.

Experiential Narrative

The before-quoted Michaël Samyn and Auriea Harvey write,

> We are not story-tellers in the traditional sense of the word. In the sense that we know a story and we want to share it with you. Our work is more about exploring the narrative potential of a situation. We create only the situation. And the actual story emerges from playing, partially in the game, partially in the player's mind.
>
> *(Newheiser, 2009)*

As is the case with any representational art form, the experience of narrative and meaning pushes beyond the form of the work. Indeed, the "emergent narrative" label of the previous section is a bit of a misnomer; a series of events does not become a "narrative" or "story" until it is recognized by a conscious agent. Emergence does not become *narrative* until it is experienced. And while many definitions of *emergent narrative* include player experience and interpretation within the same categorical label (Anthropy & Clark, 2014), I find it useful to differentiate between *emergent narrative* (the dynamic simulation of systemic elements that interact in ways weighted for dramatic potential in order to produce narratively constructive emergent happenings) and *experiential narrative* (the player's personal mental representation of simulated happenings, as well as her own arc of progress and improvement with a game, rooted in the simulated diegesis but extending to the metagame and sensitive to context of play). So whereas specific instantiations of emergent narrative feel *unique*, instantiated experiential narratives feel *my own*.

Emergent narratives can become experiential narratives by either deepening or lessening player projection. Taking a projectively embodied perspective of play (see Chapter 4) makes the simulated happenings of the game world feel individual, like lived experiences (Ryan, 2018, pp. 75, 76; Brown, 2018). These stories are experienced from the inside-out, from the perspective of the *self* through the embodied avatar. Ambiguity fosters imagination and cognitive *closure* (McCloud, 1993, pp. 62–64), adding (player-generated) richness into the game world that is even richer than a computer can simulate. The degree to which a game world can be perceived as a cohesive whole, or even as a portion of a larger world outside of that which is simulated, is the result of the subjective interpretation and imagination of the player fulfilling a necessary role within the system of gameplay production.

Highly personal experiential narratives can also be produced when the player is most cognitively separate from the game world—that is, when she is not projecting into an avatar and when the threshold of interface between her and the simulation is at its least transparent. The experience of playing the game and the context in which the game is played form a narrative more relevant to the video game than to non-interactive media. Certainly, the context in which a film is watched will have an effect upon the viewer's interpretation of the film, but the context of play not only affects *interpretation* but also feeds back into the *manner* of play, which has diegetically and dramatically relevant ramifications. For instance, playing alone versus playing while being watched by someone else has the potential to affect the types of actions a player will choose (perhaps the player minimizes unethical behaviors when they feel that they may be judged by someone else) or the way in which the avatar character is performed (with the consideration of "putting on a show" for the spectator).

A player's experiential narrative experience of a game describes her personal journey through it. The experiential narrative is unique to each player, including not only the player-motivated events that occur within the simulation but also the player's experience of those events. The experiential narrative layer includes events that may be considered non-canonical within the fiction of the story, such as the avatar character dying and reverting to a checkpoint several times. As dramatic elements, these deaths and resets present resistance and conflict, which the player must overcome.

The player's experience of resistance, reward, and flow contributes to the experiential narrative. The player's multiple deaths (failures) in a challenging level of an action game may not be canonical on the story layer of the game (as in, the avatar character may be illustrated "in-universe" as an average, mortal being, thus "deaths" could be attributed to purely hypothetical failures, with only successful attempts being canonically acknowledged), but these peaks of difficulty and the experience of ultimately overcoming these hurdles form the basis for the narrative arc as understood in other storytelling mediums (escalating tension, climax, resolution, etc.). In the experiential narrative of a game, the *player* is the protagonist. Narrative resolution is achieved when she (the networked self-inclusive of the embodied avatar's instrumental, projective extension) overcomes the game's challenges.

I referred to experiential narrative previously as the "non-canonical-experienced" aspect of a game's storytelling capacities. By this, I mean that the player's experience includes extra-canonical and extradiegetic happenings, such as the multiplicity of deaths mentioned above, or the experience and exploitation of glitches. Though it is difficult to justify simulation glitches within a game's story (it is immersion-breaking when a character's body fails to load properly, leaving just a floating set of eyeballs and teeth where her face would normally be), these experiences form important and memorable (though unintended) moments within the experiential narrative. Similarly, if the player exploits a glitch to achieve victory over a challenge (such as a glitch that allows her to skip content or "cheese" a difficult fight [exploit a repetitive or low-skill strategy to overcome a challenge]), she *does* overcome the challenge, but not in a way that the story is programmed to be able to acknowledge.

The intentional utilization of glitches and exploits can be tremendously difficult and often requires the experimentation and collective knowledge of an entire community of enthusiastic players (as demonstrated by the creative techniques of the speedrunning community). Hearing accounts of the development of these glitch-reliant tricks is often more fascinating than the authored stories written for the games in which they are performed in the first place. Considering games as storytelling engines that are systemically structured to bring about narratively compelling experiences (beyond the authored stories present in the embedded content), the demonstration of skill and creative problem-solving exhibited in the exploitation of glitches or design oversights comprises a satisfying trajectory of meta-story. Further consideration of glitches and exploits can be found in Chapter 13.

As discussed above, games are engines through which narratively compelling situations may occur, even beyond authored segments. Systems and mechanics are tuned to bring about rich, procedural stories even without strict, intentional direction by developers. To demonstrate this, we can look at the example of police behavior in *Grand Theft Auto V* (2013), an open-world criminal action game. During free, player-motivated exploration, *Grand Theft Auto* simulates dense, activity rich cities that players can traverse and explore. Distributed throughout the cities are police cars, harmless when non-aggravated. Performance of illegal actions within line of sight or (even slight) vehicular collision with these police cruisers, though, will activate a hostile behavior condition and set them into pursuit and violent retaliation. To return to peaceful free exploration, the player must escape the police and remain out of sight for a set duration.

This mechanical structure of resistance (police pursue and shoot at the avatar, which can easily result in avatar "death" penalized by the loss of in-game money as the avatar "respawns" at a hospital or police station) and incentive (negative reinforcement; the cessation of pursuit and danger) galvanizes an exciting and intense car chase throughout the city. As the pursuit extends and more illegal actions are taken (which becomes difficult to avoid during a high-speed chase), additional police reinforcements are called in, including additional cars with more deadly weaponry and police helicopters. This intensification of conflict increases the desperation of the chase and necessitates taking bigger risks and making more creative, improvisational use of the city environment.

The player may jump their car off the side of a freeway, speed down tight alleyways in hopes of losing their tail, and switch cars when the line of sight is broken to confuse their pursuing enemies. The behavioral programming of these police units and the resistance/reward structure brings about a more compelling and dynamic narrative experience than would a segment of unstructured play. This emergent narrative is not wholly disconnected from the semiotic details of the game (this example is legible because we understand the semiotics of police from the real world and other fiction), but it exists primarily within the non-semiotic space, with the semiotic detail serving primarily as context for the narrative work accomplished in the pre-semiotic experience.

As such, rather than a film, which is textually whole and complete before an audience watches it, a game only becomes whole in its live systemic enactment. A game is essentially a set of instructions through which narrative is developed in real time. It contains authored elements (protostory) that are whole and complete in miniature (cutscenes, voice performances, dialogue text, etc.), but the whole of a game as a text fundamentally does not exist until it is enacted, and the resulting text inevitably and significantly varies between playthroughs. The player's individual experience with the game is both essential for the game to be enacted and fundamentally inseparable from the unique enactment that results.

Thus, narrative analysis requires contending with the experiential element. A film can be critically understood in semiotic terms, as audiences who react to it with different interpretations and emotional resonances ultimately still react to the same fundamental "text". The primary storytelling elements (plot, performances, visuals, music, etc.) are static. Video games, though they contain static, traditionally authored elements, tell their stories primarily through dynamic, systemic, procedural elements, so critical analysis must contend with the systems that produce experiential narrative divergence. This is not to say that fruitful analysis cannot be made from the consideration of static, semiotic storytelling elements alone (there have been plenty of stirring articles and essays written about the authored stories in games), but these are to be understood as analyses of elements of the whole rather than holistic explorations. It is the equivalent of elemental analyses of other mediums, like an essay about the use of color in *Amélie* (Jeunet, 2001); fruitful and enriching to our understanding of the whole but not a contention with the holistic text in its primary storytelling capability. To holistically analyze a game, we must ground our perspective in the experiential narrative, the systemic engine by which stories are procedurally produced during live gameplay.

To review, experiential narrative describes the medium-unique language by which video games produce stories enacted by and experienced by players, who are projectively linked to their avatars. The player is simultaneously audience, participant, and performer in the collaborative storytelling experience as structured by the systems and mechanics of the game. The embedded narrative, the static (or predictably alterable) authored, semiotic narrative elements of the game, surrounds the experiential narrative, giving context to the procedural action. Though an embedded narrative may tell a narratively complete story itself, within the context of a video game, it should be seen as a supporting element to the experiential narrative, which is the primary and unique means by which stories are told within the medium of games. The embedded narrative provides context, giving procedural actions additional stakes, providing characterization beyond what can be expressed systemically, and utilizing associative semiotics through which audience experience is enriched and semiotic themes can be explored.

Lore

If embedded narrative describes the authored content that provides context around the gameplay actions of the experiential narrative, lore describes the authored, semiotic fiction that is not directly enacted during gameplay. This consists of world-building and table-setting that either presents in non-interactive protostory (such as cutscenes) or paratexts. Embedded narrative (roughly) includes a game's plot, insofar as it pertains to the player's active involvement, while lore establishes setting and history. While the enactment of the central embedded narrative is typically mandatory to reach the conclusion of many types of games (even when story cutscenes are skipped, the game proceeds as if the scenes had canonically occurred), lore elements are more likely to be optionally encountered or inferential.

To illustrate this distinction with an example, JRPG *Persona 5* (2016) features involved and complex embedded narrative and lore. In the game, a player-named protagonist moves to modern-day Tokyo to live with a court-appointed caretaker. As he adjusts to the new community and matriculates at a new high school, he becomes mysteriously entangled with supernatural occurrences, allowing him and a growing group of friends to travel to a Jungian alternate dimension formed by the emotions and vices of people in the game's "real" world. In this new setting, he and his friends utilize the supernatural ability to command warrior spirits called Personas to infiltrate literalized psychological fortresses of evil, abusive people in order to steal the core psychological drives that lead these individuals to the exploitative pursuit of their selfish, destructive ambitions.

The authored and enacted events that play out during the game are *Persona 5*'s embedded narrative. The dense plot is supported by structural elements of lore. The history and rules of the alternate dimension and the magic that surrounds it are lore. The characters' backstories that primed them for the events of the story are lore elements. The fact that the game is set in a fictionalized version of a real-world setting implies that, to some degree, the real-world history of Tokyo is relevant lore, as too are versions of the real-world myths and traditions that define the game's cast of Persona spirits, most of which are named after characters from various real-world mythologies. To the degree to which contextual information is shared between games in the *Persona* series, previous *Persona* and *Shin Megami Tensei* games can be seen as metatextual lore.

Crucially, while most elements of embedded narrative should be communicated through the game itself (apart from events that occur off-screen or separate from the involvement or presence of the avatar), lore more often expands beyond the software. Besides that which can be found in-game, lore is often expanded upon through game instruction manuals, books, audio dramas, websites, separate games, novelizations, film or television adaptations, etc. Lore often pushes the stories of games into a multimedia space and encourages exploration outside of the realm of the simulation. These elements are forms of *paratexts, "texts that surround the main text being analyzed, which transform and condition how the audience interprets that main text" (Fernández-Vara, 2014, p. 7, summarizing Genette, 1987).

Lore, as optionally engaged content, is often used as intrinsically motivating rewards. As games' reward cycles primarily center around the interactive gameplay loop, rewards that feed back into the loop of play often do so by increasing instrumental affordances. For example, in a combat-oriented game, a more powerful sword may be a compelling reward for overcoming a challenge, as it extends the player's instrumental affordances, allowing her to more effectively and efficiently combat increasingly dangerous foes. A sword less powerful than the one already possessed by the avatar is seen as a less compelling or even useless (non-) reward, as it does not grant additional affordance or increase survivability. Thus, the breadcrumb incentivization of players with play-relevant rewards necessitates, to some extent, continually pushing the metrics of instrumental affordances higher and higher.

To prevent "power creep" from getting out of hand or leveling off into an emotionally flat treadmill of just keeping up with steadily rising enemy stats (creating an experientially flat gameplay challenge curve as player ability and challenge increase in parallel with each other), it can be useful to design other types of rewards within embedded narrative and lore domains. Embedded narrative rewards can present as story progress or the enactment of sub-stories, as the furthering of a game's story can be a valuable reward for overcoming a challenge even without play-loop empowerment. Similarly, lore can be a valuable reward for play achievement separate from play-relevant empowerment.

This is used effectively in *Dark Souls* (2011), in which the majority of play challenges are rewarded with weapons, armor, or items that, as previously described, become less intrinsically rewarding once the player has an adequately powerful weapon and armor pairing and a satisfactory allotment of gameplay items. To increase the value of a pool of rewards with limited instrumental use for each player, the developers gave each weapon, armor, and item a unique description that details an element of the game's lore, often referring to long-past events and characters from the fictional world's history. Considering the sparseness of semiotic detail given throughout the course of normal play, these item descriptions are the primary means by which semiotic narrative detail and context are given. To those interested in the world of the game, these item descriptions, in aggregate, form a compelling interpretive puzzle. Finding additional details and speculating about how they interrelate create a compelling loop of narrative discovery, not unlike being a real archaeologist or researcher of myths.

Meta-Narrative

While emergent and embedded narratives describe and are informed by the events of gameplay enactment, and while lore provides further context in often multi-medium formats, meta-narrative can develop from the longitudinal, "extra-narrative" changes in systems (or understanding of systems) initiated from outside of either the game or the individual player. Like the experiential narrative, meta-narrative includes elements of diegetic, extradiegetic, and non-diegetic (contextual) activity. To describe it with a metaphor, meta-narrative is like the story of how a river changes course after a geologic event. This is the longitudinal story of the *metagame* (see Chapter 13); the pattern of player engagement with a game on the community level, reactive to a constant state of re-optimization corresponding with developer-initiated, post-release changes (such as gameplay adjustment patches) or the discovery of new strategies.

Competitive games, such as fighting games and strategy card games, foster extensive communal metagames over their course of active popularity. Fighting game rosters are regularly "re-balanced" in the months and years following their launches, as developers empower ("buff") or weaken ("nerf") characters and strategies in reaction to observations of longitudinal player behavior and lopsided results (for example, if a particular character is so uniquely overly powerful or universally practical compared to the rest of the character roster, the developers may adjust elements of how the character performs to regress toward mean effectiveness to prevent a single strategy or character from becoming competitively ubiquitous). Likewise, even separate from developer meddling, competitive communities will, over time, discover new, effective strategies and counter-strategies that become widely dominant until countered by a later discovery. These changes in viable and dominant strategies are the metagame, or colloquially "the meta", and "following the meta" means being engaged with the community, discovering, and reacting to these changes. Metagames are covered in greater depth in Chapter 13.

Meta-narrative describes the longitudinal shift in metagame. This is often a communal story, reflecting the changing relationship that the community has with a game. This can often be a good reflection of post-launch support development, chronicling gameplay changes made in patches and expansions. Balance and technical adjustments made in patches and evolving community knowledge are usually not reflected in game canon (though they are sometimes disguised/justified as canonical events in live-service type games such as MMORPGs). As such, the story of the evolution of the meta-game is valuable as a separate layer of narrative from which meaning and insight can be derived separate from insights gained from the other forms of narrative.

Meta-narrative has analogues in other artistic mediums. We can longitudinally track the degradation and restoration of paintings, for example, or we can compare how the differences in subsequent cuts of a film or editions of a book affect the meaning of the story and reflect the evolution of thought and culture around it. With games, we must consider games not only as evolving cultural artifacts but also as practical artifacts. Meta-game changes reflect not only a change in attitude or intent but fundamentally also a shift in practical usefulness as players engage with the artifact differently.

Narrativization

We have examined the different forms of narrative content that can be drawn from games, but drawing narrative meaning from them may still be an unfamiliar task compared to reading other forms of media. Game narratives in all of the above detailed categories arrive in a state of disrepair and require active participation to configure into contiguous stories. This involves the process of narrativization. Simply put, narrativization is the process by which causal links are drawn between events so that they can be understood as stories. This should not be a wholly unfamiliar task, as all narrative interpretation and analysis requires some level of repair, but the manner by and extent to which video games require and permit narrative repair necessitates the practice of some medium-specific techniques. The topic of narrativization is revisited in Chapter 11, but I will briefly give relevant detail here as well.

(Systemically) internal narrativization describes an account of gameplay actions using the terminology, logic, and/or mechanics of the game about which the story is told. For example, a story from an RPG might state that "my character had dangerously low health toward the midway point of the boss battle, but she managed to kill one of the boss' minion enemies and get just enough experience to level up, instantly refilling her health and turning the tables of the fight".

Extrapolative narrativization describes gameplay accounts that extrapolate beyond systemic and/or mechanics-driven simulation to enrich the enacted story with additional, inferred detail. To return to the above RPG example, one may say

> she had been badly injured during the boss fight and her prospects looked grim. Defeating the boss' meddlesome minion, though, reinvigorated her, solidifying the lessons she had learned on her journey and giving her the internal strength she needed to overcome the boss.

The emotional expressions of the character are inferences; the game does not *simulate* the character drawing upon past lessons to reinvigorate her fighting spirit. The player reads between the lines to draw forth more human and, ultimately, compelling stories from the aspects that remain ambiguous.

Internal narrativization may be more common when game systems or mechanics are overdetermined or unrelatably abstract. Conversely, games may prompt extrapolative narrativization by presenting systems that are underdetermined or metaphorically identifiable. An overdetermined representation leaves little room to read between the lines, whereas underdetermined characters or systems necessitate reparative reading, an imaginative accounting for the ambiguity.

Kreminski et al. (2019) found a difference in the richness and types of stories told by players of two 4X strategy games: *Sid Meier's Civilization VI* (2016) and *Stellaris* (2016). They found that AAR (after-action reports; retellings of in-game events, in other words) shared by *Civilization* players tended to be direct retellings of events as they occurred and in terms of the game systems, while *Stellaris* stories were more likely to contain extrapolative elements and player imagination. About this difference, Kreminski et al. said,

> Due to their procedurally generated nature, *Stellaris* characters and factions are underdetermined, providing sketchy outlines of people and civilizations that players aren't familiar with from elsewhere. Randomly assigned character traits, species traits and portraits, civics, and other aspects of government structure provide lots of evocative details from which players are free to hang story bits, without worrying that they may [contradict] actual history as is sometimes the case in *Civilization VI*.
>
> *(Kreminski et al., 2019)*

An internal "completeness" leaves little room or need for extrapolation, whereas a shallowness or incompleteness of detail prompts the implication that the mechanical representation of elements of the game are impressionistic representations of a "fuller" internal truth.

This can be illustrated by examining systems of character status ailments in RPGs. Poison is a common RPG ailment. Straightforwardly, for the duration of time that a character is poisoned, she takes a set (or gradually increasing) amount of damage from the poison with every turn or set interval of time. To contrast, status effects that enrage characters tend to be less mechanically straightforward. The *Pokémon* series' (1996–present) Swagger attack greatly increases the afflicted character's attack power but also confuses her (gives her a random probability of either performing the commanded attack or damaging herself), or *FINAL FANTASY VII* (1997)'s Fury ailment (which decreases accuracy of attacks but increases the rate at which the character builds her Limit gauge, which, when full, enables her to perform a Limit Break signature attack). The clear mechanical give and take of Poison encourages an internal narrativization; that is, the Poison effect being applied to a character during a battle is likely to be considered and recounted in terms of the game's systems ("I knew that I was going to take 12 Poison damage per turn until I could clear the Poisoned status"), whereas an Enraged status invites an extrapolative reading ("the opponent taunted my Charizard and it started seeing red. It came out swinging and hurt itself in the process").

Overdetermination can manifest mechanically (as above) or semiotically. We can contrast the degree to which games encourage extrapolative player storytelling amongst games with overdetermined semiotic depictions as opposed to those that create semiotic ambiguity in key areas. Dollhouse-like life simulation game *The Sims* (2000) mechanically walks a line between characters being player-controlled and autonomous, with players able to take direct control of members of their simulated families at any time but allowing the Sims (simulated characters) to operate autonomously when the player has not issued them direct commands. As opposed to typical avatars over which players take direct, uncontested control, the relative semi-autonomy of the Sims gives play more of a feeling of collaborative storytelling rather than a completely player-determined expression of will.

For example, if a player commands a Sim to play games on the computer but the Sim is in desperate need of a toilet or is dying of hunger, the Sim will disobey the command of the player and seek a bathroom or the nearest refrigerator, respectively. This gives the sense of other-mindedness, that the Sim has thoughts and feelings separate from those of the player. With that context, the game makes excellent use of semiotic ambiguity to achieve its aim as an engine for creating procedural stories that encourage extrapolative interpretation. Conversations between Sims are conducted in "Simlish" (a made-up language) and illustrated through comic book-like speech bubbles with iconographic representations of the topics of conversation rather than detailed transcripts. A conversation with the pictorially represented subjects of a UFO and the face of a mutual neighbor could mean a number of different things: maybe the speaking Sim believes her neighbor is an alien. Perhaps she is relaying the story of the neighbor's alien encounter. Maybe the speaking Sim and her neighbor both read the same science fiction book. More importantly, the ambiguity allows players to extrapolate Sims' motives in encounters. Maybe the speaking Sim is spreading gossip about her neighbor out of jealousy. Perhaps she finds her neighbor's imagination infectiously inspirational. The game presents a litany of extrapolative threads as a storytelling engine in the absence of specific detail.

In addition, relatability or identifiability of mechanical metaphor can encourage extrapolative narrativization. For example, several shmup games feature floating power-ups that, if brought into collision with the avatar spaceship, grant additional weapon power or point bonuses. This has no identifiable analogue in real life. It is what is often pejoratively called "video game-y"—an abstract action that can only be understood in terms of the game mechanic that it supplements. We can compare this against mechanics in other shmups that are mechanically similar but differently contextualized from a representational perspective (what we call *ludemes* in Chapter 7). *PixelJunk Shooter* (2009) and *Resogun* (2013) feature stranded humans that the player ship must reach to rescue. Players are granted points for rescuing them or depositing them in a safe location elsewhere. Mechanically, this is identical to picking up a floating point cluster, but the identifiability of the mechanical representation encourages narrativization beyond the layer of mechanical abstractness. Whereas the first example can only be internally narrativized as "I picked up some bonus points", the latter encourages extrapolative narrativization, "I flew past the lava on a rescue mission and saved the two scientists".

This can be applied to more sophisticated mechanical metaphors as well. Horror ARPG *Bloodborne* (2015) features a system dubbed Insight; a persistent point total that increases throughout the game. Insight is gained by witnessing horrific or supernatural sights. For instance, encountering a new enemy boss or venturing to a new world location adds one Insight point. Among other effects, higher levels of Insight grant the ability to see horrors in the environment that were hidden to the player before, such as giant monsters perched on the side of buildings. Higher Insight levels also make the avatar more prone to Frenzy damage, essentially damage inflicted by enemies who can break the avatar's threshold of sanity; horrors so great that they "break" the avatar's mind. The mechanical metaphor, though sophisticated, is sound and well supported by the game's semiotic themes; the game starts in the realm of Gothic horror, in which the pursuit of knowledge of the truth of the universe could be terrifying but is ultimately empowering, and the game resolves within a tradition of Lovecraftian horror, in which certain truths of the universe are too great for the bounds of the human mind, and even glancing upon certain eldritch sights can irrevocably ruin the conscious brain. This mechanic begets rich extrapolative storytelling due to its identifiability and humanity.

Narrativization often determines the distinction between sense-making and meaning-making in the process of interpreting gameplay. Internal narrativization is a deductive practice, while extrapolative narrativization engages players creatively as collaborative storytellers. Games are rarely wholly one or the other, though. There are often moments of extrapolation intermixed in otherwise internally oriented stories, and sometimes central points or mechanical centerpieces are driven home with additional clarity to ensure central messages are not misinterpreted. When playing games, we can consider how these interpretive orientations are applied to the various layers of storytelling material: lore, embedded narrative, experiential narrative, and even the meta-narrative. Understanding how each of these storytelling elements is employed in the enactment of video game experiences gives us greater insight into the storytelling intentions of developers and the capabilities of the medium altogether.

STORY BRANCHES

Rolling a die and observing it land on three is not a rare occurrence, but rolling a five, then a three, then a one, then a two, then a one, and then another one is unlikely to be easily replicated. In fact, any combination of six rolls of a six-sided die has a 1 in 7,776 chance of occurring. Any one of these 7,776 combinations might not be inherently meaningful without further context (unless one happens to roll the same number six times or chance upon another sequence that can be interpreted as a pattern), but it goes to show how rapidly the number of possible outcomes grows across multiple throws.

In Chapter 11, the structure of video games was called *multilinear*, meaning that there are many possible routes by which the manifest content (see Chapter 11) of games can reach a conclusion. Ultimately, because video games are played in linear time, gameplay ends up resolving to a linear instantiation of the many multitudinous possible expressions. Thus, rather than the structure being *non-linear*, it is instead *multilinear*—instantiated play takes one of many (sometimes near-infinite) possible "routes" through the dense possibility space.

In interactive storytelling, stories are often conceptualized like trees. Each story theoretically begins at a singular point (though even this can vary, as many games allow players to choose different starting conditions that can alter the early-game experience in subtle or substantial ways). As the player is presented with scripted choices, the story "branches" into multiple possible conditions. From each of those branches, the story can branch again; so on and so forth.

Following this model, if a player is presented at three points with decisions that each feature three possible choices (branches), there are already 27 possible "storylines" that she may have experienced. Due to the cost and heft of generating new assets, recording new voice lines, and programming new gameplay interactions, her story will likely lead her through many of the same locations with some of the same dialogue and story beats as players who went down one of the 26 other paths. This is where the practicality of game-making can interfere with the illusion of uniqueness. We can conceptualize the "weight" of a choice as how consequential it is to the story, with heavy choices resulting in complete diversion or permanent alterations to the game world and light choices manifesting near-imperceptible differences. Not every choice can (or should) be heavy. Even extremely lightweight choices can still leave a tremendous impact.

The hauntingly beautiful point-and-click adventure game *Kentucky Route Zero* (2020) is full of meaningful but lightweight choices. During conversational scenes, players are often presented with dialogue choices that have no mechanical impact upon the game but alter how players conceptualize the characters they control. The very first choice players are presented in the game is at the enigmatic Equis Oils petrol station. Conway, the primary protagonist and avatar, drives a rickety truck up to the station while the sun sets over the hills. Conway and his old dog climb out of the truck and approach the station attendant, who lounges on a chair outside. After remarking upon the news of a recent automobile accident, the attendant asks Conway, "Did I hear a dog? What's your dog's name?", to which Conway can reply, "His name is Homer", "Her name is Blue", or "Just some dog; I don't know his name". This choice has no mechanical impact upon the rest of the game (besides setting the name and sex of the canine companion—variables that the game will remember and correctly reference throughout the game but not in a way that affects the course of gameplay). The game does not systemically change, but this choice is still meaningful in the mind of the player. If Conway says that the dog's name is Homer, perhaps we can infer that he is well-read and literary, having chosen the author of the *Iliad* (Homer, n.d.) and *Odyssey* (Homer, n.d.) as the namesake of his companion (or he could just be a *Simpsons* [Brooks et al., 1989–present] fan). If the dog is named Blue, it could indicate that Conway has simple and unpretentious tastes, having chosen a very common and somewhat melancholic name for his dog. To indicate that Conway has not named his dog may indicate that he is unsentimental, or perhaps he has respect for the autonomy of the dog to the point at which he doesn't feel like he should bestow a name that the dog had no part in choosing or understanding. This simple choice serves to characterize Conway rather than drive ludic action.

In some ways, these types of lightweight choices can be more meaningful than heavier choices. Each unexpectedly prompted memory referenced in a character's dialogue in *Kentucky Route Zero* builds a more nuanced picture of the character's life before the events of the story and reframes how the unfolding events are conceptualized by the player. Consequential choices that drastically alter the behavior of a character can quickly become incongruous. If a *Mass Effect* (2007) player repeatedly picks pacifist dialogue options and prioritizes conflict de-escalation, a choice later in the story that (intentionally or unintentionally) results in Commander Shepard punching another character in a fit of rage may conflict with the trajectory and characterization of the character to that point. There can be value in this (perhaps it illustrates that Shepard has a breaking point and a temper beneath her peaceful exterior), but it can just as often alienate players from their avatars. *The Sims* (2000) designer Matt Brown (2018) remarked in a GDC talk that the strategic use of ambiguity allows players' minds to fill in connective tissue in a consistent manner. A high degree of specificity risks interfering with players' own interpretations and characterizations—or even the concrete details of the story, which can be difficult to track as choices compound.

Types of Branching Structures

Referring to branching narratives specifically pertains to games that include discrete choice points. This refers to the structure of designated and designed choices. Real-time control can be thought of as affording many micro-decisions in every moment of play. Charting real-time control "decisions" within a branching tree structure would be unproductive because every moment of gameplay would radiate into each of the dozens of these micro-choices, which would each, themselves, radiate to the same degree. Branches are a better metaphor for considering the macro-level decision-making involved with determining the ultimate "shape" of a game's narrative expression.

Within those parameters, there are several recurring patterns that we can recognize. Anthropy and Clark (2014) identify the most common forms of branching narrative structures. The *shrub* is the story that branches outward at every decision point, never or rarely converging, leading to a great diversity of linear paths through the story. Every branching choice point expands the total story volume. This form gives the greatest amount of control to the player but is the most challenging to develop, as it requires the greatest amount of bespoke writing and design. The *reconverging branches* model takes a more linear structure while still providing choices. Choice points do still branch into a number of differing outcomes, but these divergent paths converge to ensure that *all* players witness specific narrative events along the way. Each branch is a digression along an ultimately linear pathway. It offers less freedom of self-determination, but it ensures that gameplay sticks to a determined narrative trajectory. This structure can be described as "do whatever you would like in the early afternoon, but make sure you catch the 4 o'clock train". The third structure they name is *choices at ending*, a structure that takes a fairly linear structure but offers a greater diversity of choices in the game's final moments. This allows the game to establish a context in which the player can make one particularly meaningful choice to decide the game's conclusion. It has the least mechanical impact upon the unfolding of gameplay, being at or near the very end of the game, but it leaves the game with a sense of consequence pertaining to the aspect of the story that will weigh heaviest upon the player's memory (*Anthropy & Clark, 2014*, pp. 168, 169).

In producing branching stories, developers have to consider design efficiency. Given the cost of production and time involved in the development, implementation, and testing of new, bespoke content, it can quickly become infeasible to manage wildly divergent branching stories. As such, limiting diversity with regular points of reconvergence can be a way of reining in the scope of the project. Alternatively, games regularly provide *illusory choices*. Unlike the lightweight, primarily aesthetic choices listed in the *Kentucky Route Zero* (2020) example above, illusory choices seem to imply that a choice will result in a greater digression than it actually does. Multiple dialogue options might prompt identical responses; choices of actions might be interrupted by factors outside of player control; in the least elegant examples, the avatar or other characters might just say "no" and proceed as if the developer-intended choice was chosen. When well-disguised, illusory choices can feel natural and can still give players the sense of impactful agency. It may only be upon replay or conversation with other players that she realizes that the consequences of the choice were shallower than they appeared.

We will continue our exploration of narrative structure and instantiation of specific events and storylines within the total narrative volume of a multilinear ludic structure in Chapter 11.

REFERENCES

Anthropy, A. & Clark, N. (2014). *A game design vocabulary: Exploring the foundational principles behind good game design*. Addison-Wesley.

Blow, J. (2008). Fundamental conflicts in contemporary game design. *Proceedings of Montreal International Game Summit 2008.*

Bogost, I. (2009). *Videogames are a mess*. Ian Bogost. https://bogost.com/writing/videogames_are_a_mess/

Brooks, J. L., Groening, M., Jean, A., Selman, M., Frink, J., Simon, S., Reiss, M., Mirkin, D., Oakley, B., Weinstein, J., Scully, M., Cohen, D. X., Meyer, G., Omine, C., Long, T., & Maxtone-Graham, I. (1989-present). *The Simpsons* [TV series]. Gracie Films; 20th Television; 20th Television Animation.

Brown, M. (2018). Emergent storytelling techniques in The Sims. *Proceedings of the Game Developers Conference 2018.*

Costikyan, G. (2007). *Games, storytelling, and breaking the string*. Electronic Book Review. https://electronicbookreview.com/essay/games-storytelling-and-breaking-the-string/

Dansky, R. (2007). What is the purpose of game narrative? In C. Bateman (Ed.), *Game writing: Narrative skills for videogames*. Bloomsbury Academic.

Eskelinen, M. (2001). The gaming situation. *Game Studies, 1*(1).

Fernández-Vara, C. (2014). *Introduction to game analysis*. Routledge. doi:10.4324/9781003355779

Genette, G. (1987). *Paratexts: Thresholds of interpretation*. Cambridge University Press.

Harvey, A. & Samyn, M. (2006). Realtime art manifesto. *Gaming Realities: The Challenge of Digital Culture*. https://tale-of-tales.com/tales/RAM.html

Herman, D. (2002). Story logic: Problems and possibilities of narrative. University of Nebraska Press.

Homer (n.d.). *Iliad*.

Homer (n.d.). *Odyssey*.

Hunicke, R., LeBlanc, M., & Zubek, R. (2004). MDA: A formal approach to game design and game research. *Proceedings of the AAAI Workshop on Challenges in Game AI, 4*(1), 1722.

Jenkins, H. (2004). Game design as narrative architecture. In N. Wardrip-Fruin & P. Harrington (Eds.), *First person: New media as story, performance, and game* (pp. 118–130). The MIT Press.

Jeunet, J. (Director). (2001). *Le Fabuleux Destin d'Amélie Poulain* [Film]. Claudie Ossard Productions; UGC; Victoires Productions; Tapioca Films; Frances 3 Cinéma; MMC Independent; Sofica Sofinergie 5; Filmstiftung; Canal+

Juul, J. (2005). Half-real: Video games between real rules and fictional worlds. The MIT Press.

Koenitz, H. (2023). *Understanding interactive digital narrative*. Routledge. doi:10.4324/9781003106425

Kreminski, M., Samuel, B., Melcer, E., & Wardrip-Fruin, N. (2019). Evaluating AI-based games through retellings. *Fifteenth AAAI Conference on Artificial Intelligence and Interactive Digital Entertainment, 15*(1), 45–51. doi:10.1609/aiide.v15i1.5223

Laurel, B. (2014). *Computers as theatre* (2nd ed.). Addison-Wesley.

LeBlanc, M. (2000). Formal design tools: Emergent complexity, emergent narrative. *Proceedings of the Game Developers Conference 2000.*

Mateas, M. (2005). Procedural literacy: Educating the new media practitioner. *On the Horizon: The International Journal of Learning Futures, 13*(2), 101–111. doi:10.1108/10748120510608133

McCloud, S. (1993). *Understanding comics: The invisible art*. Kitchen Sink Press.

Murray, J. H. (2012). Inventing the medium: Principles of interaction design as cultural practice. The MIT Press.

Newheiser, M. (2009). *Michaël Samyn, Auriea Harvey, Tale of Tales*. Adventure Classic Gaming. https://www.adventureclassicgaming.com/index.php/site/interviews/473/

Ryan, J. (2018). *Curating simulated storyworlds* [Doctoral dissertation, UC Santa Cruz]. UC Santa Cruz Electronic Theses and Dissertations. https://escholarship.org/uc/item/1340j5h2#main

Ryan, M. (2001). Beyond myth and metaphor: The case of narrative in digital media. *Game Studies, 1*(1).

Wardrip-Fruin, N. (2020). *How Pac-Man eats*. The MIT Press.

CHAPTER 10

Perspective-Taking

Chapter 4 discussed how, cognitively and instrumentally, players project onto game avatars and assimilate those avatars into their extended, networked selves. This is a practical assimilation, though, incorporating the functional affordances of the avatar into the player's expressive capabilities. The avatar is a means by which the player can express her will within the virtual world, similar to how one who operates a car may project onto the car and assimilate it into the instrumental capacities of her own networked self. While some game avatars are similarly function-oriented, like a tractor in a farming game, often avatars are presented as expressive characters. The projection is not only functional but also dramatic. Players not only assimilate a set of practical affordances, but they are also asked to play a role within a fiction. This can result in several empathetic postures during play. There are two axes along which these different projective postures may present: internal/external *personification*, and internal/external *identification*.

Whereas Chapter 4 primarily concerns the manner in which projection onto the avatar serves the purpose of strengthening the *diegetic perspective* (as identified in Chapter 6), this chapter and the next look further into the ways in which avatar projection is used in tasks of role-playing, corresponding to what this book labels the *mimetic perspective of play.*

DRAMATIC PROJECTION

Personification

Personification refers to the degree to which players dramatically situate themselves as members of a game's storyworld. If a game facilitates an internal personification, it encourages the player to operate as a member of the simulated world. Conversely, an external personification describes being psychologically separate from the simulated world, controlling actions from either a depersonalized position or as a god-like entity. Though players can choose to assume either of these dramatic postures while playing most types of games, certain genres, design elements, or camera perspectives have greater tendencies to encourage players to adopt one method or the other. For instance, games with a first-person perspective tend to encourage an internal personification. In first-person games, players view the world through the eyes (or sensors, windshield, navigational camera, etc., as appropriate) of a member of the game world, usually with equal perceptive capabilities as other members of the game world (be they other players or non-player characters [NPCs]).

In some first-person games, like the fantasy ARPG *The Elder Scrolls V: Skyrim* (2011) or the science-fiction shooter *Halo: Combat Evolved* (2001), NPCs make eye contact while speaking with the avatar (and player) and regard the avatar as a member of the fictional world (even if treated as a rather exceptional member of the game world). The protagonists of either game are held, to a degree, to the laws and social mores of their respective worlds. *Halo* punishes players for firing upon their own squadmates, and the *Skyrim* avatar encounters legal consequences, such as paying a fine or even capital punishment, if caught stealing another's belongings. As such, there are mechanical benefits for observing the world's laws and expectations that encourage this type of projective behavior from players.

DOI: 10.1201/9781003530961-10

Strategy and puzzle games tend to encourage external personification. Players see themselves as separate from the in-game action, either god-like in their influence on the game (as one would be commanding the armies of *Rome: Total War* [2004] or in their de-personified movement of gems in the tile-matching game *Bejeweled* [2001]), or navigating a database (like in the sports management simulator *Football Manager 2024 [2024]* or narrative-building puzzle game *Storyteller* [2023]). In such cases, there is not a concerted effort to "separate" the player from her own reality during gameplay through projection into the virtual world. The player is always presently aware of herself playing the game, as opposed to more "immersive" types of games that encourage projection and a "becoming" of the avatar.

While some players may experience this external personification as encouraging a psychological separateness from the game world, others may see this as a postural alignment between physical and simulated worlds. If one presumes that the god-like or database-style interfaces are being operated by an in-world being, the presumed "experience" of this in-universe "avatar" will be closely aligned to that of the players. Take, for example, *Her Story* (2015), a game that tasks players with searching and reviewing a database of disorganized video recordings of a murder suspect undergoing police interrogation. The act of playing the game is one of clicking around a database stylized like a mid-1990s computer operating system; the experience is not terribly dissimilar from watching videos on one's own desktop. Unlike *Skyrim*, the player does not navigate a fully realized 3D world and integrate into a simulated society. Yet, the player does embody a character, a fact that only becomes evident later in the game. The player can briefly catch glimpses of the reflection of a young woman sitting in front of the virtual computer screen. Canonically, it is this woman who reviews the interview footage, and it is not until the end of the game that the player learns the reason she is doing so. In *Her Story*, the player and the avatar character are performing the same actions in the same way. From a certain point of view, this aligns the player's experience with that of the character's to a greater degree than more conventionally immersive games like Skyrim, in which the player performs acts of great exertion with near-effortless button presses. This is not to imply that either perspective is better than the other, only that players may reasonably take internal or external perspectives on games, which one may presume would typically elicit the other. It is a matter of player psychology rather than artistic mandate.

Other design decisions can also push players in one direction or the other. While a first-person perspective typically encourages an internal personification, a third-person perspective can be as often interpreted in either direction. Direct or indirect control may be a better predictor in that case. Avatars players control directly, such as Mario in *Super Mario Odyssey* (2017), are typically personified internally, whereas indirect control, such as the click-to-move navigation of the virtual townspeople of *The Sims* (2000), may be more easily personified externally. Researchers are currently pursuing lines of inquiry regarding whether demographic or identity matching between player and avatar foster more or less immersed perspectives of play. While results within the literature are far from conclusive at the time of writing, we can hypothesize about the effects of what Lisa Nakamura (2000) terms *identity tourism*, the act of assuming an identity different from one's own in an electronic setting, such as assuming a gender or ethnic identity with which one does not identify in real life.

To review, an internal personification describes the player acting as if she is a member of the simulated world, while an external personification describes a posture of being external to the action taking place within a simulation, as one would be as a god, commander of an army, or in navigating a database. An external personification preserves a self-awareness of the player issuing commands to the game, while internal personification extends the player's capacity of will-expression to the avatar, encouraging a feeling of conscious continuity between player and avatar through which the player "inhabits" the avatar and performs actions fluently, as one does through one's own body. This maps closely onto Marie-Laure Ryan's definition of internal/external interactivity (Ryan, 2001) and roughly onto Espen J. Aarseth (1997)'s personal/impersonal perspectives.

Identification

Similarly, players may adopt internal or external stances of identification. This identification typically extends to the player-controlled character(s), but that may or may not cleanly align with the element that has the avatar function, depending on the game genre. For example, in computer role-playing games or point-and-click adventure games, the player typically assumes indirect control and interfaces with the game world through a mouse cursor. An avatar (or party of avatar characters) may still be identifiable, but they are controlled indirectly. Though indirect control doesn't encourage the same level of action-oriented projection as direct control, these non-avatar player-directed characters fulfill the dramatic role of protagonist characters. Identification refers to the degree to which the player emotionally aligns with the player-controlled character. Internal identification describes an empathetic posture in which the player deeply feels emotions in alignment with the character, and an external identification describes situations in which the player maintains an emotional distance from the lead character(s).

This distinction is not a mark of successful or failed storytelling. Assuming an external identification does not mean that a game has failed to make its lead character sympathetic. This can be an intentional design decision based on the type of story that the game is constructed to produce. When the protagonist experiences the events of the story, does the player feel (emotionally) like they happen to her, or does she watch with curious, differentiated interest? Do the player's motivations, goals, and reactions align with the character's, or is she like an actor playing a role "innerly distanciated from her character and simulating emotions she does not really have" (Ryan, 2001)?

Many, or perhaps even most, games are not designed to consistently elicit internal identification. Considering that most engage with art primarily for pleasure, consistent internal identification with protagonists limits the kinds of stories that can or should be told. If we truly internally identified with the protagonists of each story we encounter, we would never want to engage with tragedies like *Cyrano de Bergerac* (Rostand, 1897) or partake in narratives featuring morally repugnant leads, like *American History X* (Kaye, 1998) or *Fight Club* (Fincher, 1999). Reading or watching those works requires a balanced empathetic identification but also the maintenance of an emotional distance; otherwise, we will be pulled into artistically induced despair far too often.

Comparisons, in this regard, between games and other media are not symmetrical, though. When reading a book or watching a movie, we may be empathetic toward the agony or ecstasy of the characters, but they are always comfortably external and viewed from afar, not experienced as presently and significantly as *our own* emotions. Video game protagonists, on the other hand, are consciously enmeshed with the player. The player animates the character with volition and cognitive reasoning, without which the story would not progress, and the avatar serves as a conduit through which the player may express her will within the simulated world. It is often the player's choices or actions that lead to the story's dramatic consequences and moments of emotional climax. As such, there is a strange disconnect unique to the medium of games: the actions and choices of players directly contribute to the dramatic consequences game characters undergo, but the stakes of these dramatic consequences are non-real to the player. That is to say, a player's mistake may lead to the dramatic consequence of a character sustaining an injury during a battle, but the player knows that she will not sustain an actual injury as a result, despite this projectively embodied avatar being a networked extension of her own "self".

It is not true to say that players never experience actual consequences for in-game actions, but they are most often heavily asymmetrical. Failure in platformer games (missing a jump or running into an enemy) is typically punished with a character death, which, though the player thankfully does not experience of-kind punishment, penalizes players by resetting some of their progress. This halts forward momentum and "wastes" the player's time as she repeats a portion of the game that she had already played. Similarly, multiplayer shooters most often penalize deaths with a time penalty before players can return to the match. Though a time penalty is less severe than experiencing actual death, the player feels negative emotions such as frustration or disappointment. These serve as emotional nadirs that contribute to the dramatic rhythm of the game, necessary to punctuate the moments of victory and elation. Games played in arcades take this a step further by penalizing player failures not only with time and progress penalties but also by requiring additional money to be put into the machine to continue playing, a financial penalty for ludic action.

Further, these real-world stakes can be appended onto otherwise unreal stakes within the simulation to make the fictional stakes feel consequential and relevant to the player. In the open-world criminal action game *Grand Theft Auto V* (2013), being arrested or being killed not only punishes the player with a loss of time and momentum (as the character, outside of story missions, is sent to a hospital or police station, losing progress toward whatever the player was trying to accomplish at the time at which the death or arrest occurred), but the character also loses a portion of her in-game money, and her accumulated weapons may be confiscated. The acquisition of this money and these weapons requires time and effort from the player, so the loss of these resources represents a retroactive loss of the time and energy put into acquiring them. It also results in lessened agency, as the character has lesser (in-simulation) purchasing power and fewer combat options. The time and effort put into acquiring these fictional elements, and the fact that their ownership increases the agency that the player can express within the simulation, and often the joy that she can receive out of it, instills these elements with value, even if it is just a personal, non-transferrable value.

This externalization of fictional consequences is common across artistic mediums. Audiences of horror movies may be aware that they are in no physical danger from the film's antagonists, but they are at risk of being shown a gruesome and disturbing image or having their startle response triggered by a loud noise. These elicit real psychological or bodily reactions, instilling some actual consequence for the on-screen action. Similarly, a romance novel may be arousing in such a way that the reader physiologically longs for the story's romantic reconciliation in a manner similar to the protagonist. What these consequences lack is the sense of permanence and weight that may accompany them in real life, as well as the sense of causal attribution being laid at the feet of the audience. Through the projective extension that is the avatar, the player becomes an acting agent within the simulated world, altering the relationship between the audience and the dramatic stakes of the narrative.

Tying this back to the subject of identification, we can see how the unique consequentiality and player agency of gameplay may naturally push players toward an emotional experience in alignment with the character "experience", but while this is a component of identification, it is not the key differentiator between internal and external identification. Semiotic details should be taken into account as well, and we should notice whether or not a particular game is intended to elicit dramatic empathy. The elements that we have already examined are practical rewards and punishments: player success provides access to more of the game, and player failure obstructs or resets progress. This is not a dramatic stake, as it is the bestowal or revocation of something that the player intrinsically values, separate from the storytelling conceits of the game in question. In these instances, the player's motivation is selfish, not dramatically empathetic. The player wishes (for the avatar) to succeed in-game to maximize her own pleasure and minimize her own displeasure, not because she genuinely cares about Mario rescuing the princess or whatever the semiotic stakes of the story might be. But these intrinsic motivations may also be used to amplify the player's investment into the dramatic stakes of a story.

Affective Matching

In this sense, games operate differently to encourage internal or external identification responses. *God of War* (2005), the first of a series of violent character action games about a Spartan warrior who is betrayed by the Greek gods, begins with the tragic deaths of lead character Kratos' family, but the game never encourages or elicits a mournful response from the player. The player is encouraged to view Kratos as a character within a Greek tragedy, and she is encouraged to identify only with his motivating anger. He is wildly expressive of his fury, emoting early and consistently through the game. In fact, he is angry in the first moments of play before the player has had time to absorb and become truly empathetic to the dramatic stakes of his story. The player has no genuine anger or feeling of betrayal of her own. From the beginning, the character and player do not match emotionally, cueing the player to view Kratos as an external character, separate from the player's psychological space.

Throughout the game, the "camera" (the player's point of view) is dynamic during battles or set-piece encounters, often pulling out to depict the epic majesty of the surroundings or attacking monsters, letting Kratos become quite small on the screen. The camera operates cinematically, prioritizing the holistic scene even over optimal playability. Kratos' control scheme even encourages psychological distance. Though Kratos is controlled directly (as opposed to click-to-move characters), his attacks are sweeping and large rather than precise and dexterous, as he swings flaming chains in wide arcs around his body. Controlling Kratos feels more like issuing orders to a bull in a china shop rather than exhibiting player will directly and specifically.

This can be contrasted with more recent entries in the same series, such as the (annoyingly identically titled) *God of War* (2018), which seeks to draw pathos from the narrative by placing more dramatic weight on the relationship between Kratos and his new son Atreus, both mechanically (by making the pair dependent upon each other in both combat and cooperative exploration) and dramatically (by anchoring the development of both characters to their relationship with each other). To contrast the original *God of War, 2018* opens with Kratos in a solemn, inscrutable mood. While a strong vocal performance by actor Christopher Judge still conveys interiority, he does not overwhelm the scene with extreme reactions like he did in the original game until key dramatic peaks much later in the story.

At the beginning of the game, the player and Kratos exhibit a similar mood, inviting identification. The points of emotional turmoil come after the story has laid adequate groundwork to walk the player to those emotional peaks and valleys along with the character, keeping the player locked in to Kratos' psychological experience. The camera also follows Kratos much more closely. Though not first person, literally looking through Kratos' eyes and embodying his perspective in that sense, a tight over-the-shoulder perspective gives players a close approximation of his viewpoint while still adequately representing proprioceptive information necessary for navigation and combat. The camera prioritizes Kratos' perspective rather than sweeping, cinematic vistas, putting the player in mind of existing within a space as a physical being rather than watching a movie from a disembodied perspective.

Finally, Kratos' combat abilities have been reworked to require precision and intention, a change from the powerful, screen-filling attacks of the earlier *God of War* games. This also encourages the player to consider the physicality and arc of each attack, further grounding her within the physical space and with the body of Kratos, specifically. In these ways, the original *God of War* was made to feel impersonal, like watching an exciting action movie, whereas *2018* evokes a more personal experience and encourages internal identification with the character.

This affective matching can be an effective tool for making productive use of internal identification when used correctly. This is one of the reasons why many games that encourage identification with the main character(s) begin in a state of relative calm or neutrality and build to emotionally dramatic moments once stakes have been established. For example, the first full chapter of the eclectic JRPG *Mother 3* (2006) puts players in control of a stoic ranch owner (named by the player but canonically called Flint). Though the game introduces increasingly eccentric characters and circumstances throughout the game, it is notable that the opening chapter centers on an affectively neutral character who only exhibits strong emotions upon suffering a great personal loss about an hour into the game (long enough for players to internalize the weight of Flint's loss). This gently guides players toward the intended emotional reactions by seeing the change in a character that had previously mirrored their affective state.

Alternatively, there are some playable characters who begin the game in a state of affective neutrality but never progress beyond that neutral state. These blank slates are easy to project onto, as they never exhibit behavior discordant with the will of the player, but they underserve the dramatic capability of affective guiding. Blank slate and silent protagonists will be more fully examined in Chapter 11, but a couple of points are relevant to the idea of affective matching.

Silent protagonist Gordon Freeman from the science-fiction shooter *Half-Life 2* (2004) is a neutral, non-expressive presence throughout the game, allowing players to easily imagine themselves in the role, but Freeman's non-expressive performance does not ever escalate and lead players toward emotional heightening. Instead, the weight of emotional manipulation falls to sources external to the character, such as Freeman's far more expressive companion, Alyx, who accompanies Freeman through most of the game, or to atmospheric tone and world-building details. It can be argued in either direction whether *Half-Life 2* encourages internal or external identification with Gordon Freeman. On one hand, Gordon's lack of affective expression implies that the player's emotional reactions, cognitions, and curiosities fulfill that role (as the player fully inhabits the interior being of the character). On the other hand, because Gordon's affective expression never elevates to match that of the player during moments of dramatic tension or exertion, players may see that as the character diverging from their own experiences, viewing the neutrality as a specific character choice to depict someone who remains calm and coldly professional in all circumstances to an almost sociopathic degree.

Gordon Freeman's lack of affective matching is not a limitation of the first-person shooter genre or even of his role as a silent protagonist. To contrast, the silent protagonist in the action-packed science-fiction shooter *DOOM* (2016) is very expressive despite never speaking. Through his animations (all viewed from a first-person perspective), players witness him becoming impatient with exposition and the routine slowdowns that are common in games through his disrespectful destruction of exposition-delivery mechanisms and disinterested gestural performance, details that are likely to match the "been there, done that" attitude of some experienced players.

Again, external identification is not better or worse than internal identification. It is not a failed attempt at internal identification. There are many situations in which external identification is preferable. The horror game *Until Dawn* (2015) plays out like a 1980s American horror movie, following a harrowing night of deadly surprises for eight archetypal bratty, lusty, dishonest, and questionably intelligent teenagers stuck in a remote mountain cabin. The characters are intentionally abrasive and immature, keeping audiences from fully identifying with them, and player control often switches between protagonists, again reinforcing the idea that the player is an outside influence rather than fully embodying any of them.

The player, external to the emotional conditions of the characters, may soon see herself as a director of the action rather than an embodied entity within the drama. It can quickly become more enjoyable to play the game in such a way that results in a compelling horror story rather than an embodied mission to survive the night. As director, the player may gain greater enjoyment by guiding characters toward poetically just and dramatically exciting deaths rather than achieving optimal survivability. Far from punishing this autonomy, the game counts on players exhibiting their creative judgment, bending and branching the story to account for any number of eventualities. This new metagame, creating a thrilling 1980s slasher film-style narrative experience, is only possible because the player takes a stance of external identification.

Interplay between Personification and Identification

To conclude this section, let us review the differences between personification and identification and explore how the two can be used in concert with one another to achieve different storytelling aims and may affect audiences' dramatic experiences differently.

Personification describes how players imagine their roles in relation to the virtual world of the game. Internal personification describes the player processing her participatory role as if she (extending through her virtual avatar) is a member within the virtual world. External personification describes the player being cognitively separate from the virtual world, issuing orders while not directly "inhabiting" the space. Separately, identification pertains to the degree to which the player emotionally or dramatically inhabits the character(s) under her control. Internal identification describes a posture of emotional continuity between player and character, as the player feels, wants, and is driven by the same elements that affect the character(s). External identification describes a stance of emotional separateness from characters, responding empathetically but relating to characters as dramatic figures rather than as extensions of the players' interior selves. To contrast, personification is primarily practical, while identification is essentially emotional.

If we examine personification and identification as a four-quadrant chart, we can identify some key differences in the ways in which each interrelates with the other and produces different audience experiences.

Internal personification and internal identification creates optimally immersive gameplay experiences. The player operates as a part of the virtual world, mentally and emotionally inhabiting the lead character as an extension of herself. Examples of this type of game are *Halo: Combat Evolved* (2001), *What Remains of Edith Finch* (2017), and *Façade* (2005).

Internal personification and external identification results in a feeling of playing a dramatic role. The player comfortably immerses within the virtual world but feels mental separateness from the character. Though the avatar is an instrumental extension of the player's capacity for will-expression within the virtual space, the character is, dramatically, a fully realized, external being; a role for the player to perform as an actor would portray a character on stage or screen. Examples of this kind of game include *The Witcher 3: Wild Hunt* (2015), *UNCHARTED 4: A Thief's End* (2016), and *Duke Nukem 3D* (1996).

External personification and internal identification describes games in which the player feels separate from the actions of a game from a spatial, experiential perspective but still emotionally projects onto the controllable characters. Common in text- or interface-based story games, players feel deeply aligned with lead characters but do not "forget" or look past their real, physical selves as beings separate from the simulation. Outside of video games, we may look to the experience of playing *Dungeons & Dragons* (Gygax & Arneson, 1974) as players become dramatically enmeshed with their chosen characters but make no serious attempt to literalize their involvement from a physical perspective, always aware of the dice, character sheets, and mechanics that operationalize the story. Video games that exemplify this posture include *Baldur's Gate 3* (2023), *The Walking Dead* (2012), *Fire Emblem Awakening* (2012), *The Sims 4* (2014), and *Fallout 2: A Post Nuclear Role Playing Game* (1998).

External personification and external identification is perhaps the most similar to the manner in which other forms of media are consumed. The player does not operate as a member of the virtual world, issuing orders or arranging circumstances from outside of the game's diegesis, both positionally and emotionally separate from the game's world and dramatic occurrences. This does not mean that the story is not engrossing or emotionally effective—only that the player feels separate and external to the world and characters. The player either does not directly inhabit a role (such as in non-contextualized, purely interface-based games like *Mario Paint* [1992]) or she externally controls a character who is otherwise dramatically realized rather than being written to be reflective of her emotional state (like the protagonists in *PaRappa the Rapper* [1996] and *Asura's Wrath* [2012]). Games that follow this model include *Rhythm Heaven Fever* (2011), *League of Legends* (2009), and *Sam & Max Hit the Road* (1993).

PERSPECTIVE

As early as Chapter 2 and throughout the following chapters, I have identified a number of perspectives by which the visual information of gameplay is presented. This short section elaborates on the ways in which the perspective of the gameplay presentation serves dramatic and experiential purposes.

Most styles of gameplay presentation can be broken down into three categories: first-person perspective (the game world is viewed from the point of view of the avatar figure), a third-person perspective (the game world is viewed from an objective perspective outside of the embodied sensation of the avatar character), or non-spatial/non-representational (the information of gameplay is presented in a manner that is not spatially or representationally grounded, such as purely through text or iconographically / pictorially, such as how many visual novels present, with backgrounds establishing locations *generally* (such as "school hallway" or "sports field") and "billboard" character artwork representing who is speaking, but presenting neither in context of one another that a way that meaningfully simulates or represents the spatial relationships between elements and the environment.

Within these broad categorizations, subcategorizations are conventional. Third-person games may take over-the-shoulder, side-on, isometric, etc., perspectives. First-person perspectives exhibit less diversity of conventions since they are more closely imitative of physically grounded human perception, but we can still recognize examples as being more objective or subjective, with subjective perspectives more closely emulating the sensory experience of the observer (head bob, lens flare, motion of breathing, water or dirt on the simulated camera lens…) whereas objective perspectives maintain the spatial relationship of the point-of-view character and the environment but do not simulate the "imperfections" that may result from physical presence (smooth motion, clean perception, wider-than-natural field of view…). Even though third-person cameras are detached from the spatial presence of the avatar, games still often present similar subjective perspective effects from the third person, such as the swaying and blurred camera effects that are employed when avatar characters get drunk in *Grand Theft Auto IV* (2008) and *Conker's Bad Fur Day* (2001), or the hallucinations experienced by avatars in *Kane & Lynch: Dead Men* (2007) and *INDIKA* (2024).

Categorization of perspective is not solely based on visual representation. Certain audio-only games, previously mentioned in Chapter 2, that present spatial information to allow players to imagine a spatially grounded, sonically informed presence in the game world may still be thought of as first person, even though they do not present any visual information. They are observed from "inside" a presence in the simulated game world—only through the ears instead of through the eyes.

Edge cases abound. Games like *République* (2016) and *Manhunt* (2003) present gameplay action from outside of the point of view of the protagonist avatar, but this visual information is contextualized as being viewed through security cameras observing the action. Similarly, the third-person perspective of *Super Mario 64* (1996) is actually revealed to be operated by a flying Lakitu character, grounding the perspective as being third-person relative to the avatar Mario but actually first-person relative to Lakitu. Conversely, the purely navigational perspectives in games that do not feature avatar figures, such as *Myst* (1993) and *Viva Piñata* (2006), utilize first-person navigational conventions (simply because points of view *must* be singular) but do not meaningfully ground this perspective within the game world from a physical perspective.

Perspective and Drama

Just as affect matching can be used to draw players into emotional resonance with dramatic avatars, so too can perspective be used to create or minimize distance between players and their projective avatars. It is not as simple as concluding that games viewed from a first-person perspective create internal personification and identification, while a third-person perspective encourages external personification and identification, though. In many cases, the opposite is true. Instead, I will list a few techniques by which affective goals are achieved through perspective stylization.

Academic Kendall L. Walton (1990) proposes a concept called *perceptual empathy*. He notes that empathetic formation is a result of the naturalism of perspective, with highly *objective* perspectives feeling more coldly impersonal, prompting a detached perspective, while *subjective* views (even when representing non-realistic elements such as the hallucinations and perceptual discontinuities of protagonist Renton in *Trainspotting* [Boyle, 1996]) encourage greater experiential and emotional consonance between audience and character.

As discussed above, *avatar-detached, first-person perspective* is relatively rare in video games. The aforementioned examples of *République* (2016) and *Manhunt* (2003) observe their respective avatars from third-person perspectives, relative to the avatar, but spatially contextualized as being from the perspective of security cameras within the game's world. *République* takes it a step further—since the control of its avatar is indirect, issued through commands spoken to her from someone observing her activity from afar, it might be better to contextualize it as a first-person perspective from the point of view of the remote hacker, with the ostensible on-screen protagonist being a locus of consequence but not the direct figure of player identification.

The relative rarity of *inhabiting* an embodied figure in an environment and *controlling* another is surely a concession to control complexity or perceptual clarity. In rare instances, it has been successfully employed, such as in the VR platformer *Moss* (2018), in which the player is embodied, overlooking and lightly interacting with miniature environments as a masked spirit (one can look into pools to see the embodied avatar's reflection), but gameplay action involves controlling a small mouse within the dioramic world. The complexity of the split-projective task was mitigated by mapping the actions of either to different forms of control. The mouse is controlled entirely with the conventional buttons, triggers, and thumbsticks of VR controllers, while the large spirit is controlled (and inhabited) with VR's motion control capacities. Apart from such rare examples, one must wonder at the poetic possibilities of taking a more fluid approach to the presentation of embodied perspectives within the gameplay environment.

A final perspective technique that I would like to discuss here is *anamorphism*. The naturalistic means of representing perceptual perspective into simulated game worlds may be regarded as unremarkable. We may think, "*of course* the player moves through the space from a singular perspective reminiscent of her perceptual experience of three-dimensional space in real-life". But we have to remember that this is a choice; computer programs do not *necessitate* this grounded, spatial view. In fact, computers can process a great deal of information concurrently and can move between nodes of data in ways that are not bound by the spatial relationships that they may visually represent or imply. This kind of biologically grounded "naturalism" is actually a deviation from the ways in which computer systems manage data. Anamorphism represents a critical perspective *of* perspective; they "intentionally disrupt or distort the immediate experience of space [... and] experiment with digital-born forms of vision as a means of investigating the disconnect between the phenomenology of play and the alien topologies of computational space" (Boluk & LeMieux, 2017, p. 84).

Anamorphism in spatial representation can manifest as exploration of the arbitrariness of naturalistic spatial connectivity in the virtual setting (*Portal* [2007], *Antichamber* [2013]). It can pick apart the representational discontinuities of depicting 3D space on 2D apparatuses by intermixing perceptual logics with perspective puzzles (*Superliminal* [2019], *The Bridge* [2013], *Viewfinder* [2023], *echochrome II* [2010]). It can even comment upon conventional, abstracted, and iconic representations of space and how conventional visual representation can be recontextualized with different meanings when viewed from different perspectives (*Toodee and Topdee* [2021], *FEZ* [2012], *Starseed Pilgrim* [2013]). Anamorphic games have even explored theoretical spatial logics of fourth-dimensional spatiality, bringing to life conceptually difficult mathematical and scientific principles (*4D Toys* [2017], *Miegakure* [n.d.]) and the fascinating aesthetics of perceptually incongruent spatial representation (*Hyperbolica* [2022], which features a contiguous 3D world presented with an absurdly high FOV [field of view], such that the world appears to curve and bend back on itself in fascinating, disorienting, and hypnotic ways).

IMMERSION

The term "immersion" is used to describe (honestly, too great of a) diversity of semi-related concepts pertaining to video game play. The fluidity of definitions makes it somewhat dangerous to use in an academic respect, as, without contextualization, it resists the necessary specificity of meaning. It is used so commonly, though, within the culture surrounding video games that a basic understanding of its colloquial meanings should be established. In the exploration of this term, I can offer more academically useful words to better describe the separate elements of the gameplay experience to which immersion typically refers.

As Janet H. Murray (1997) describes,

> Immersion is a metaphorical term derived from the physical experience of being submerged in water. We seek the same feeling from a psychologically immersive experience that we do from a plunge in the ocean or swimming pool: the sensation of being surrounded by a completely other reality, as different from water is from air, that takes over all our attention, our whole perceptual apparatus.
>
> *(p. 98)*

Present in her definition, we can see the seeds of different ideas that would grow into such divergent meanings. Immersion is like a "physical experience"; games can be "psychologically immersive"; we can be "surrounded by a completely other reality"; it "takes over all our attention"; it overtakes our "whole perceptual apparatus". We can detect themes of place and spatial presence, of all-encompassing perceptual experience, and a sense of psychological purchase. Before exploring each of these themes further, we may also notice that Murray's definition can be applied equally well to many, if not most, other representational arts. Certainly, the magnificence of a film on a large theater screen in a dark room is intended to fully overtake the perceptual senses of the audience, and I am certain that every reader has experienced feeling wholly psychologically absorbed in the pages of a book. It is not necessary that *every* term we use to describe video games applies only to video games, but I believe most players will intuitively recognize a difference in the manner in which they are immersed in video games as opposed to how they become immersed in works of other mediums. It is worth refining our analytical language in order to be able to discern and communicate this difference.

Immersion as Spatial Presence

One common meaning of "immersion" as it pertains to video games is to describe a sense of presence in a virtual space. This may be deemed a transportive principle. This may manifest in a number of different ways. A virtual world rich in detail may be deemed more immersive than a world sparse in detail. For example, the excessively detailed heightened reality of the fictional Kamurochō district of Tokyo (modeled intricately after the real Kabukichō district) in SEGA's *Yakuza 6: The Song of Life* [2016] feels like a space modeled with consideration for the operations and necessities of a real urban space. Building interiors are designed individually rather than being templated and duplicated across the district, and consideration is paid to the advertisements, branding, construction, and wear of each location. This extends to the smallest detail, such that walking through Kamurochō feels like engaging in digital tourism. It is a stunning encapsulation of walking down the streets of Tokyo (and further, at the various points in history from the 1980s through the present, as the *Yakuza* series spans decades) in which the series takes place. It is such a richly detailed space that one can almost smell the takoyaki and feel the humidity of the Tokyo summers or the chill of the snowy winters against the skin while exploring within it. To be within a richly detailed virtual space is often to feel present within its world.

Similarly, the sense of presence within a virtual space can be increased through graphical fidelity. The hypothesis is that the more a world looks real, the more the mind will subconsciously believe it is real. In a realistically rendered world, there are potentially fewer perceptual reminders of the artificiality (and arbitrariness) of the space. Playing Asobo Studio's stunning *Microsoft Flight Simulator* (2020), there are brief moments in which the fact that it is a virtual simulation fades from memory entirely. At certain angles, the sight of an obsessively modeled plane soaring over the game's 1:1 map of the world as the sun peeks out from behind the clouds is indistinguishable from real aircraft photography.[1] While the visual convincingness of a space can certainly invite one to feel present within it, I am skeptical that it alone drives "immersion". Obviously, as photorealistic as video games become, they can never match or exceed the visual realism of sister mediums like photography and film. Were this the primary driver of "immersion", it would not only fall short of describing what sets video games apart from other mediums, but it would also consistently highlight the shortcomings of video games as a representational medium in comparison to sister mediums. This is not to say that it does not contribute to the feeling of becoming "immersed" in a world, but it cannot account for it alone.

Graphical realism is a risky metric against which to measure immersion due to the uncanny valley phenomenon, which hypothesizes that highly realistic representations (specifically of humans in the original literature but generalized elsewhere) can potentiate observers to psychologically counterreact when hints of unreality are present. More plainly, the more realistic something presents, the more fragile the illusion becomes. Audiences have a high degree of tolerance for abnormality in facial animation, for instance, in highly stylized animated characters, such as the stylized *Wallace and Gromit* (Park, 1989-present), but as figures more closely emulate the appearance of real humans or animals, the more sensitive beholders become to even slight abnormalities, as Masahiro Mori found when observing human-like robots being prototyped in the 1970s (Mori, 1970). Just as the slight "deadness in the eyes" of an otherwise human-like robot may create a sense of uneasiness or revulsion in observers, so too can the illusion of a realistic virtual space be broken by slight imperfections. Sudden and unexpected imperfections, such as those caused by visual glitches, can propel a player from their immersed state with startling ferocity, turning a scene immediately into a farce or a horror (a phenomenon I call *ontological upset* in Chapter 2). Additionally, the realism of video game graphics is a metric that is highly sensitive to intermedium comparison over time, such that looking at video games that were once considered marvels of photorealism, such as *Myst* (1993), *UNCHARTED 2: Among Thieves* (2009), and *Gran Turismo 3: A-Spec* (2001), is less convincingly "realistic" by modern standards as technological progress continues to drive expectations higher.

The sense of spatial presence can also be increased by a high degree of interactivity or reactivity within a virtual space (something that I argue in Chapter 12 also increases the game's expressivity). Shallow incidental interactivity within a space can lessen the sense of "being" in the space (as an agential actor) and give a game a rather "museum-like" quality: look but do not touch. This can be especially apparent in VR, in which the player shares a very close perceptual link to the virtual avatar such that the simulation sets the expectation that the player "is" a physical presence within the fictional world. Reaching out one's hand and knocking over the items on a desk can ground this sense of presence, but watching one's virtual hand pass, like a ghost, through other objects that were not designated to be interactive can dampen this immersion. Games like *Red Faction: Guerilla* (2009) and *Teardown* (2022) were lauded in their respective times for their high degree of interactivity in the form of environmental destruction that grounded their spaces in a sense of ontological nondiscrimination; *every* environmental object is destructible. It is not contextual. If an explosive is thrown at a wall, it should impact that wall in a manner consistent with the physics established within that virtual world.

Conversely, the sense of physical presence can be induced through a high degree of control (expressivity) of the playable avatar. This contributes to the sense of projective embodiment (see Chapter 4), the degree to which the player feels that she psychologically "inhabits" the playable character from a perceptive and proprioceptive perspective. If one feels like she inhabits the physicality of an avatar, surely she will feel more "immersed" within the space in which the avatar exists. Even in nominally manipulatable environments, like those of *Orbo's Odyssey* (2023) or *Super Meat Boy* (2010), feeling psychologically and physiologically "one" with a highly expressive and responsive avatar can drastically increase one's sense of connection to and presence within a virtual space.

All of these factors contribute to the colloquial "immersion", but they do not describe every occurrence of its usage. This category of experiential factors can be more usefully and accurately termed *presence*, the sense of *being* within a virtual space. Whether this is as a result of highly reactive avatars who can carry out players' agential acts or convincingly realized spaces, the sense of presence within a space is a major factor that sets video games apart from other mediums. It shares these qualities with closely related mediums of immersive theatre, immersive art exhibitions, and theme park storytelling/role play.

Immersion as All-Encompassing Perceptual Overtake

A common usage of "immersion" in other artistic mediums describes art exhibits that wholly overtake the senses. Closely related to the aforementioned sense of physical presence, immersive art exhibits are typically entered into and interactive. Meow Wolf's *House of Eternal Return* (Meow Wolf, 2016) is a 1,900 m^2 indoor facility. The exhibit includes several room-scale environments that range from an abandoned but naturalistic suburban home to a kitchen designed to evoke the illusion of being a two-dimensional 1920s "rubber hose" cartoon drawing. Each of its unique spaces, often paired with glimmering lights, unearthly sounds, and a backstory describing the supernatural context of the space, makes use of broken sight lines and perceptual illusions to make observers feel like they are stepping into a separate reality that may go on as such forever. In its most psychedelic spaces, audiences may experience a sense of transcendental disembodiment, forgetting the physicality of their own beings as they are wholly absorbed in the perceptual experience of the space.

Similarly, it is sometimes argued that games that more holistically encapsulate the perceptual space of the player present more "immersive" illusions. This is most obvious in VR games. Enclosed within a headset, players are blind to the physical world around them, and as the field of view represented by the headsets' twin screens (one for each eye to present the brain with the convincing illusion of natural sight) changes to match the natural head movements of the player, it can become immediately convincing that the player has entered a wholly separate reality. The perceptual illusion is so strong that even games that depict highly stylized spaces that do not strive toward replicating realistic visuals (such as *Walkabout Mini Golf* [2020] and *Accounting* [2016]) can evoke a powerful sense of presence, reinforced by the relatively naturalistic, motion-controlled "reach out and touch" control methods that most VR games employ.

Even games that do not imply a sense of physical presence within a definable space benefit from the "immersiveness" of VR. *Tetris Effect* (2018), *Rez* (2001), and *Thumper* (2016) all present fairly abstract, non-naturalistic experiences that are quite engrossing when played on standard screens but become transfixing when played in VR. In these cases, the VR headset acts like a sensory deprivation tank, blocking out all distractions from the outside world and solely, wholly focusing the player's attention on the game in front of her. For a short time, Tetris is all that exists within the void of blackness. The meditative singularity of focus is analogous to an ideal movie theater experience; the large screen and darkened space present the illusion that the world of the movie is all that exists for the duration of the film.

Though this is a factor that contributes to the colloquialism of "immersion", it is not immensely useful in distinguishing gamic "immersion" from that of other arts. To the degree that overtaking the audience's senses and isolating the audience from reminders of the "separateness" of the artistic unreality from their greater reality produces an immersive gameplay experience, it also creates an immersive filmic, theatrical, or architectural experience. For the sake of developing precise language, this factor can be called *sensory exclusivity*, the perceptual overtaking singularity of an artistic experience.

Immersion as Psychological Discontinuity

The other manner in which players describe video game experiences as "immersive" refers to the effect by which games can induce different psychological states that can temporarily reconfigure players' cognitive and emotional processing. Many players have the experience of "being sucked into" ("immersed within") a game and being surprised to look at the clock to find that hours have slipped by. This effect, known as "time loss", has been empirically studied (for instance, Wood et al., 2007; Sanders & Cairns, 2010) and found to possess both positive and negative effects; players often enjoy the sense of escape from the real world that games can grant, but others note that, taken to extremes, time loss can be associated with the compulsive patterns of behavioral addiction analogous to the sense of time loss experienced by problem gamblers. From the seminal *Addiction by Design* (2012), Natasha Dow Schüll describes how "gambling addicts may remain for seventeen hours or even whole weekends at machines, the 'clock time' (as they call it) by which those long stretches are measured 'stops mattering,' 'sits still,' is 'gone' or 'lost'"(p. 203).

This temporal distortion is also often associated with Mihály Csíkszentmihályi's theory of *flow* (which has been introduced in Chapter 7). Flow describes a state of peak psychological engagement with an activity. When a task challenges a subject such that full attention is required but not so much that the subject experiences significant failure or setback, the perpetual cognitive reward of achieving peak performance relative to the challenge at hand creates a self-sustaining feedback loop characterized by absorbing, energizing focus, often coupled with an experience of time distortion or a loss of attention to anything outside of the problem-solving feedback loop. As Csíkszentmihályi (1990) describes:

> The objective, external duration we measure with reference to outside events like night and day, or the orderly progression of clocks, is rendered irrelevant by the rhythms dictated by the activity. Often hours seem to pass by in minutes; in general, most people report that time seems to pass much faster. But occasionally the reverse occurs: Ballet dancers describe how a difficult turn that takes less than a second in real time stretches out for what seems like minutes.
>
> *(p. 66)*

This immersive productivity can seemingly adjust cognitive functioning in a positive manner, as demonstrated by the "Tetris effect" (later generalized to Game Transfer Phenomena; Oritz de Gortari et al., 2011). This widely reported and well-studied phenomenon posits that, after playing the falling-block arcade game *Tetris* (1985), players exhibit optimal performance in spatial organizational tasks in real life, outside of the game. These are sometimes accompanied by illusory imaginings (such as imagining the shape of blocks it would take to fill the negative space surrounding the skyscrapers of a city's downtown skyline) and sometimes productive (players often make more productive decisions in real-world spatial organizational tasks such as packing suitcases or stocking grocery store shelves after playing *Tetris*). It seems that the cognitive tasks invoked by certain types of games generalize to extraludic tasks, a phenomenon that I call *perspective transference* in Chapter 8. In this sense, immersion not only refers to the player becoming immersed in the space of the game but, in turn, the game also being "immersed" within the player and altering the lens through which she views and processes the world.

These related forms of immersion may be more usefully termed *cognitive molding*, a value-neutral term that can be used to describe the positive effects of exclusive escapism, the sense of flow, and the experience of the Tetris effect/Game Transfer Phenomena, as well as the negative effects of time loss, compulsive conditioning, and behavioral addiction.

NOTE

1 This is a sentiment that I am sure will become hilariously outdated, as all "this game looks *real*" sentiments end up being, with the passage of time and advancement of technology.

REFERENCES

Aarseth, E. J. (1997). *Cybertext: Perspectives on ergodic literature*. The Johns Hopkins University Press.

Boluk, S. & LeMieux, P. (2017). *Metagaming: Playing, competing, spectating, cheating, trading, making, and breaking videogames*. University of Minnesota Press.

Boyle, D. (Director). (1996). *Trainspotting* [Film]. Channel Four Films; Figment Films; Noel Gay Motion Picture Company.

Csíkszentmihályi, M. (1990). *Flow: The psychology of optimal experience*. Harper Perennial.

Fincher, D. (Director). (1999). *Fight club* [Film]. 20th Century Fox.

Gygax, G. & Arneson, D. (1974). *Dungeons & Dragons*. TSR, Inc.

Kaye, T. (Director). (1998). *American history x* [Film]. New Line Cinema; The Turman-Morrissey Company.

Meow Wolf (2016). *House of eternal return* [Exhibition]. Meow Wolf, Santa Fe, United States of America. https://meowwolf.com/visit/santa-fe

Mori, M. (1970). The uncanny valley. *IEEE Robotics and Automation, 19*(2), 98–100. doi:10.1109/MRA.2012.2192811

Murray, J. H. (1997). *Hamlet on the holodeck: The future of narrative in cyberspace*. The MIT Press.

Nakamura, L. (2000). Race in/for cyberspace: Identity tourism and racial passing on the internet. Massachusetts Institute of Technology. https://smg.media.mit.edu/library/nakamura1995.html

Oritz de Gortari, A. B., Aronsson, K., & Griffiths, M. (2011). Game transfer phenomena in video game playing: A qualitative interview study. *International Journal of Cyber Behavior, Psychology and Learning, 1*(3). doi:10.4018/ijcbpl.2011070102

Park, N. (Creator). (1989-present). *Wallace & Gromit* [Short film series]. National Film and Television School; Aardman Animations.

Rostand, E. (1897). *Cyrano de Bergerac* [Play]. Paris.

Ryan, M. (2001). Beyond myth and metaphor: The case of narrative in digital media. *Game Studies, 1*(1).

Sanders, T. & Cairns, P. (2010). Time perception, immersion and music in videogames. *Proceedings of HCI 2010*. doi:10.14236/ewic/HCI2010.21

Schüll, N. D. (2012). *Addiction by design: Machine gambling in Las Vegas*. Princeton University Press.

Walton, K. L. (1990). *Mimesis as make-believe: On the foundations of the representational arts*. Harvard Press.

Wood, R. T. A., Griffiths, M. D., & Parke, A. (2007). Experiences of time loss among videogame players: An empirical study. *CyberPsychology & Behavior*, 10(1). doi:10.1089/cpb.2006.9994

CHAPTER 11

Instantiation and Characterization

LINEARITY AND TEMPORALITY

The need for a specific *video game literacy* requiring different disciplines of attention and study than the literacies we apply to other narrative arts is due, in part, to the structural differences that the video game holds when compared to other narrative artifacts. As noted in Chapter 9, video games require reparative narrativization. That is to say, video games (describing the software that developers produce and players purchase) are not complete artworks; they are instructions that computers (in systemic relationship with player and context) instantiate into artwork in the form of gameplay in real time. As narrative works, the video game contains within its systems endless potential to manifest different narrative sequences, entailing dramatic shifts in macro-level story and potentially incidental shifts in moment-to-moment play. Through the course of play, though, the multitude of possible directions a game can go in coalesce into a single, linear set of events that *did* transpire. This chapter concerns the process of *recording*; the transformation that gameplay undergoes when transitioning from a multilinear system bursting with potential divergences to a single record of instantiated events.

Linearity

When video games are contrasted with traditional narrative media, particularly films and literature, the concept of *linearity* is often invoked. Conventionally, it is said that traditional narrative forms are linear while video games are *non-linear*, a problematic comparison that will be the focus of these early paragraphs. The intent of the comparison is to contrast strategies of structural configuration. Books and films have a set series of events inscribed in their pages and frames that prescribe an order of events, and as long as the beholder does not deliberately consume the narratives in a severely unconventional fashion, these predetermined series of events *will* be recalled as they were inscribed. With video games, on the other hand, sequences can often be reconfigured, resequenced, or may even procedurally emerge during the process of instantiation. There is not necessarily a pre-set order in which events must occur. Events may repeat. Different players may experience entirely different occurrences from the same game. There is an intuitive difference between the way that traditional narrative is conveyed and the way in which game narratives are instantiated.

First of all, calling traditional narratives wholly *linear* is not entirely accurate. If we frame literary narrative as a recounting of fictional sequences of events in which temporal linearity can be presumed, non-linear storytelling techniques have been employed since ancient times. *Iliad* (Homer, n.d.), *Mahabharata* (Vyasa, n.d.), and *One Thousand and One Nights* all feature stories that begin *in medias res* and include flashbacks that break the sequentiality of events in their telling. Further, texts like *Story of Your Life* (Chiang, 1998) and *Tenet* (Nolan, 2020), as well as time travel stories like *The Time Machine* (Wells, 1895) and *Back to the Future* (Zemeckis, 1985), disturb the expected sequence of cause and effect in a manner that makes reconciling a narrative timeline difficult. One can argue, though, that these non-sequential stories resolve to a sequential narration in their telling.

DOI: 10.1201/9781003530961-11

Works like *I Ching* and *The Naked Lunch* (Burroughs, 1959) destabilize this argument. *I Ching*, an ancient Chinese divination text, is made of 64 "hexagrams", each containing texts that combine according to randomizing rituals. As Espen J. Aarseth (1997) describes, "[by] manipulating three coins or forty-nine yarrow stalks according to a randomizing principle, the texts of two hexagrams are combined, producing one out of 4,096 possible texts" (p. 10). Similarly, William S. Burroughs' *The Naked Lunch* is written such that readers can read the book's chapters (or "routines", as Burroughs called them) in any order. These examples, both ancient and modern, imply that a strict linearity of formal sequentiality can also not be presumed.

The previous examples substantiate separate temporalities: a linearity of narrative events and a sequentiality of narrative presentation. The former represents the most common uses of "nonlinear" in reference to traditional narrative structure. Video games may or may not be appropriate examples of that kind of non-linearity. Apart from video games' tendency to repeat narrative sequences upon failure or replay (and allow different sequences of events to unfold), video game stories most often resolve to a *more coherent linearity* than most media in their enactment. Because players experience game action from the inside—often as characters or disembodied actors expressing agency within the world of the story—games tend to present the sections of greatest consequence in strict, coherent order, if not in absolute real time. Insofar as the player is projectively embodied in the role of the avatar character, the experience of the player should *roughly* match the presumed in-narrative experience of the character (during gameplay sequences).

Games, in their linear enactment, may still employ traditional techniques of "nonlinear" storytelling. Games can employ flashbacks, but these moments represent a shift in the audience position of the player relative to the game. In traditional narratives, a flashback exists wholly on the level of discourse (what structuralists would call *syuzhet*: the manner in which story events are presented to the audience). A flashback may be relevant to the events "presently" transpiring within the story, but we can presume that the characters *within* the flashback are operating with the knowledge that they *would have had* at that point in the linear flow of time posited by the story sequence. If Charles Foster Kane (Welles, 1941) flashes back to himself playing with his sled as a boy, the audience does not presume that young Kane *knows* that this is the happiest he will ever be. Young Kane does not *know* that he will grow up to become a newspaper magnate. The same cannot be said about narrative non-linearity in video games. Since the player inhabits the role of the avatar, choices made in flashbacks are done with "future" knowledge. The flashback is not only a discontinuity of discourse/*syuzhet* but also a discontinuity of story/*fabula*.

Narrative adventure game *As Dusk Falls* (2022) plays with this specifically. The player is presented with flashbacks establishing the history between characters *after* the player has already spent enough time with them in the "present" to form perspectives and hopes for their relationships. Even the most dedicated role-player cannot approach these moments without the knowledge of what follows. The sequence of events that occurs (chronologically) *after* the flashback *affects* the perspective of the player, who is not only the *audience* but also the *diegetic agent* and *animating motivation* of the characters. Insofar as the player can make decisions on behalf of the avatar characters, they functionally operate with a practical knowledge of the "future". Pointing out this "messy temporality" is not a criticism of the game; it is fascinating to explore the possibilities unlocked by telling stories in such a manner.

The same can be said for replaying a section of gameplay or an entire game. When a player carries with her a knowledge of a game's story, mechanics, or world from a previous playthrough, this has to be recognized at the level of story, not just discourse. For in so far as the player animates and motivates the avatar as an agent within the diegesis, the *player-avatar extended being* can act upon this knowledge. Sometimes this is implicitly dismissed. Monochromatic platformer *LIMBO* (2010) is sometimes called a "trial-and-error platformer". As the player progresses in the game, most of its hazards are easy to overcome but difficult to notice (traps may be visually obscured) or require a specific sequence of actions that may not be easily discernible upon initial encounter. For most players, the repeating loop of gameplay is dying unexpectedly (which, to be fair, is *barely* punished) in order to learn where a hazard lies and to gain information about how to overcome it. The avatar resets shortly before the hazard for the player to try another approach.

Implicitly, the game frames only *successful* passages through hazards as being "true" events in the story. Evidence of failure is wiped from the diegetic world; failures are framed as "what could have been but are not". As such, the game implicitly frames knowledge of the "future" as a necessary tool for advancing in the "present". To a degree, most games that feature a death/reset loop operate on similar presumptions.

Space-exploration puzzle-adventure game *Outer Wilds* (2019) intelligently frames such accumulation of future knowledge explicitly within its story. The game involves the exploration of a miniature galaxy featuring many distinctive planets. Ventures into the cosmos are cut short, though, by a calamitous solar event—the sun explodes 22 minutes after the adventure begins, annihilating all life within the galaxy. Luckily, the avatar protagonist encountered a mysterious statue that appears to let them re-experience these final 22 minutes endlessly, transmitting the knowledge of each adventure back in time to the protagonist at the beginning of the 22-minute cycle. Experientially, the avatar appears to live the same day again and again, like an interstellar *Groundhog Day* (Ramis, 1993). Narratively, though, there is *one* 22-minute sequence, and all experiential repetition is justified as a transmission of future "memories"; premembering, one could say. As the player explores the galaxy in 22-minute increments, she discovers that it may be possible to avert solar destruction and must scour the planets for the knowledge necessary to enact her plan. Formal "progression" does not persist between loops, only knowledge.

What is most interesting, though, is that *if the player already possesses the knowledge necessary to solve the game's final "puzzles"*, she can act upon this knowledge immediately and end the game shortly after it begins. This knowledge might come from a past playthrough or just reading the solutions online. Because of the narrative justification of the time loop, though, even this extradiegetic "foreknowledge" is in alignment with the game's themes. It is a justified and *actual* non-linearity of story (in, it can be noted, a game with a thoroughly linear discourse-level presentation. Player and avatar experience are roughly 1:1 from the beginning of the game up to its conclusion).

If "nonlinearity" is a better descriptor of story/fabula than discourse/syuzhet, then other than the non-linearity of knowledge and experience of the diegetic avatar/player, games have *similar* affordances for enacting narrative non-linearity as other narrative mediums. What tends to be more interesting to consider is the *structural* discontinuity of games rather than their *narrative* discontinuity. In the dynamic and unprescribed multidirectionality of game narratives, games express a multitude of possibilities that ultimately resolve to a single sequence of experienced events. "Nonlinear" is not a good description of *this* structural affordance, because it inevitably produces linear "texts".

Reparative Play

So what is a more appropriate framing? At the heart of what the "nonlinear" invocation usually alludes to is the exciting emergence and configurability of video game storytelling. It is the promise that no two narrative expressions of a game will ever be *truly identical*, and the player has a level of agency in the co-authorship of this bespoke adventure. Grinblat et al. connect this affordance of digital games to Eve Kosofsky Sedgwick's notion of *reparative reading* (Grinblat et al., 2021).

Though Sedgwick's theory is closer to a totalizing theory for the treatment of *all* information, application of its tenets in service of artistic analysis provides a useful framing for the process-oriented approach to artistic meaning-making outlined in Chapter 1. It describes approaching artworks not in an inquisitional manner, seeking to extract a singular and complete "true" meaning (what Paul Ricœur [1970] had previously identified as the "hermeneutics of suspicion", which Sedgwick [1997] calls "paranoid reading"), but rather to approach works additively, constructing meaning that is "flexible, mutable, and capable of being rearranged" (Grinblat et al., 2021). The "text" of a work is approached as a series of "part-objects" that are arranged in order to construct new, personal meaning for the beholder. This results in the construction of "something like a whole—though, I would emphasize, *not necessarily like any preexisting whole*" (Sedgwick, 1997).

This constructive process is framed as a form of "repair". With regard to meaning, text does not present "in disguise" as the paranoid perspective may posit; it arrives "in disrepair", presenting instead as a series of useful tools from which meaning—personal to and healing for the reader—can be instantiated.

As Grinblat et al. (2021) argue, this perspective is particularly applicable to the process of video game interpretation since games *literally* present as disordered narrative fragments that invite reconfiguration from players.

As such, the framing of gameplay narrative construction as the configuration of part-objects gives us a useful perspective from which we can approach the question of linearity. A reconfigurative, constructive approach does not frame the player's perspective of gameplay narrative as being *nonlinear*, since it does not accept a "hidden" (paranoid) *linearity* that underlies these potential instantiations. In other words, video game players are not "slicing up" a linear narrative and rearranging its pieces; the configurable fragments do not have a fundamental order from which any reconfiguration deviates. Players are not reading the chapters of a book out of order—they are constructing part-whole divinations of the *I Ching*. Therefore, the counter to the ill-fitting "linearity" is not its opposite; we must expose its multitudinous structure instead.

Multilinearity and Multisequentiality

Several alternative and more useful terms have been proposed. From a design-oriented perspective, Janet H. Murray proposes two terms: **multiform**, meaning "having more than one configuration based on the same general components or framework" (Murray, 2012, p. 430; 1997, p. 29), and **multisequential**, describing stories in which there is "more than one valid, coherent path through a set of segments" (Murray, 2012, pp. 430, 431). In narrative terms, a multiform narrative is one from which several valid instantiations can arise; Murray particularly highlights procedurality as an engine driving this diversity of possibilities. Multisequentiality puts greater attention on a player's journey through a multiform text. Her language in this latter definition favors a resequencing of prefabricated narrative content rather than the generative emergence of her first definition. She contrasts this latter term to **unisequentiality**, a term she prefers to "linear" to describe "media artifacts that are read, listened to, or viewed in a single authorized sequence" (p. 443).

Espen J. Aarseth offers terminology borrowed from Penelope Reed Doob's description of the classical labyrinth; **unicursal** and **multicursal**, describing singular paths (ostensibly through a labyrinth) with no decision points and paths with decision branches, respectively. These terms have the advantage of being oriented in an inherently game-like activity, and subjectively, I find the terms quite beautiful, but they seem resistant to colloquial use, so I prefer to use terms that are more immediately approachable.

While we're exploring the esoteric, Souvik Mukherjee adapts Aristotle's "telos", describing the end or objective of a story, to offer **multitelic**. This definition is interesting in that it incorporates an element of motivation, of working toward a goal. This frames the narrative not in terms of its multitudinous *structure* but in terms of motivated striving, appropriate for games.

I prefer the term **multilinear**. As Hartmut Koenitz (2023) notes, "all our experiences […] are time-forward and hence linear. Therefore, the term 'non-linear' creates a disconnect between presentation and experience—we can have a non-linear representation, but no non-linear experience" (p. 20). This touches upon an issue I raised above: since the player is both audience *and* member of the story world via embodied play of the avatar, non-linear representation will *always* be framed as a linear experience: by the nature of the fact that it takes (sequential) time to play games, they ultimately resolve to linear (experiential) narratives. Multilinear allows us to hold both the configurability and experiential linearity of game narratives in mind. Rather than framing games as being inherently non-linear (*resistant* to linearity), we can instead frame them as having the capacity to generate a multiplicity of linear narrative threads.

Time

Hand in hand with linearity and sequentiality, we must consider the manners in which time is represented in games. In film, the passage of time is presented relatively in its own terms. Because the role of film audience is one of witnessing that which appears real, the passage of *audience time* correlates closely with the time elapsed in the scene (or the subjective experience of it). Obviously, films do not typically present in *real-time*; time-skips are common, but these moments typically occur between scenes, when the audience has been expelled from the *witness* role. Time-skips that occur in breach of this contract (keeping the audience grounded in a physical space despite their temporal unmooring) tend to represent a subjective experience of time slipping by (such as in *A.I. Artificial Intelligence* [Spielberg, 2001] and *Requiem for a Dream* [2000]) or to unsettle and disorient the audience (as in *The Green Knight* [Lowery, 2021]). Not to mention the use of montage to abbreviate time into sequenced images (as in *The Godfather* [Coppola, 1972] or *Up* [Docter, 2009]) or to condense multiple images into abbreviated time (as in *Man with a Movie Camera* [Vertov, 1929]).

Subjective time is grounded in the perspective of a character (or something abstractly characterizable). *The Worst Person in the World* (Trier, 2021) features a memorable sequence in which the world around main character, Julie, experiences the world frozen around her, a manifestation of her indecision. Variations in the pacing of comic books are typically oriented around subjective time; multiple frames are dedicated to the fine details in a scene in moments of calm meditation or tense focus. The variable time-flow of comics can be framed as flowing spatially instead of temporally, as it does in film. Books similarly manage the flow of time spatially. Subjective time can be managed with the number of words dedicated to particular descriptions, corresponding to space on the page and the amount of time it takes the reader to read passages. Moments of slow concentration may be drawn out with lengthy descriptions, while moments of action keep the flow of words quick and breezy.

Games have a multimodal relationship with time. Given the commonness of embodied play (the player taking on an embodied role within the diegetic game world), it might seem reasonable to presume that real-time and fictional-time would predominantly match, but this is often not the case. While embodied action tends to progress at a pace approximating reality, the flow of time outside of the area of immediate influence tends to be non-literal. Time will either progress extremely quickly (in games with day/night cycles, time tends to progress very quickly; a complete cycle of day and night in *Red Dead Redemption 2* (2018) is approximately 48 minutes) or at a stop-start rhythm by which simulated time progresses in accordance with player-initiated action only (for example, time-sensitive events in *Yakuza 0* (2015) will hold indefinitely while the player spends time wandering the streets of Kamurochō and will immediately initiate once the avatar gets close enough to particular "trigger" points, and day/night transitions only progress in accordance with story progress. Avatar Kazuya Kiryu can wander the streets for a full 24 hours in real-time and not witness time meaningfully progress, despite the world bustling with activity around him).

Beyond the literal flow of time, we might measure time in terms of the dynamic propensity of "things happening". As such, we might consider the left-to-right spatial progression in *Super Mario Bros.* (1985) to be an expression of narrative time. As long as Mario stands still (outside of immediate danger), the game tends not to present the player with the new challenges that keep the game "narratively" interesting. The game is paced such that challenges are presented at an appropriate pace as the player moves through the course, and halting forward progress gives the player the opportunity to interrupt this intentional pacing (until the stage timer counts down, anyways). From a narrative perspective, this is not an insightful observation (the character stood still and nothing happened to him is not an interesting story), but for the purpose of "reading" game design, it is useful to understand the "axis" on which challenges progress. Spatial progress through a *Super Mario Bros.* level progresses through the sequence of designed gameplay events (similar to making spatial progress through the measures of sheet music), while games like *Galaxian* (1979) are wholly time-oriented; the avatar's limited movement does not push the game forward, and the pace of action is associated with the passage of time. Other factors that result in the progression of narrative time (such as progress through *key events*, as noted in the *Yakuza 0* example above) exist, and it can be a good exercise of budding game literacy to identify the rules by which narrative time progresses and when it cycles in and out of synchronization with real-time. The *progression axis* is useful to consider if one has a desire to design gameplay notation or take notes on the experience of play. Does it make more sense to anchor the exercise around the progression of time or space?

Beyond external temporality, subjective time is also very common in modern video games. Shooters *Max Payne* (2001) and *Vanquish* (2010) feature the ability to slow down time to focus on aim, representing the subjective experience of advanced combatants who gain the edge on their opponents by staying "cool under pressure", perhaps representing the extra acuity of their sharpened senses. Players can justify the pauses in the stop-and-start rhythm of turn-based combat (as seen in JRPGs and turn-based strategy games) as stretching out the instances in a battle when a combatant strategizes and considers her options. Particularly in situations in which menu navigation is necessary, the pauses in the pacing make up for the extra effort required of the player compared to the instantaneous impulse that the character would be able to command.

On a final note about time, Alexander R. Galloway (2006) makes an interesting note that gameplay makes relatively little use of the technique of montage. Due to the importance of retaining embodied perspective during play, the abbreviations of time and space inherent in montage would be disorienting in most gameplay situations. The rare instances in which it *is* used tend to be *because* of its disorientation effect (*WarioWare, Inc.: Mega Microgames!* [2003] and the humorous musical segment at the end of *Thank Goodness You're Here!* [2024]) or may present temporal or spatial abbreviations *as if* they took place in continuous temporality (the heavily condensed map of the continental United States in *The Crew 2* [2018] can be driven, from Pacific to Atlantic, in about 50 minutes, presenting a type of diegetic montage).

INSTANTIATION

Game design Sid Meier famously defined a game as "a series of interesting choices" (Rollings & Morris, 2000, p. 61). If we frame a game in terms of its potential choices or actions, we can envision a hypothetical chart that forks at every decision point. Considering that each branch will, itself, branch out at the next decision point, we can see how even a simple branching narrative can quickly produce a staggering number of possible routes from beginning to end. Such a graph would almost *immediately* become overwhelming for a game that operates with real-time control, such as *PAC-MAN* (1980) or *Super Mario Bros.* (1985), as the player makes incidental "choices" about avatar action in nearly every moment of play.

In the previous section, I called this branched structure with its many (or infinite) possible routes *multilinearity*, because each path that can be traced through it, from the beginning of a playthrough to its conclusion, is experienced as a linear series of events. Structurally, it may not be perpetual, forward, linear progress (a player may have to replay sections after failures or reload earlier saves), but these instances of repetition are experienced as sequential events in the player's experience with the game. Even from a narrative perspective, if we consider the primary narrative product of a game to be the player's lived experience of overcoming challenges and gaining agential mastery of the system, replaying content represents further progress in that narrative. In that sense, it is like watching two similar scenes in a movie rather than rewinding to watch the same scene play twice. Because the player takes on an embodied role within the narrative, the sequence in which gameplay "scenes" are experienced is *internally* recognized within the system, *because the player is a part of the system of the production of gameplay.*

Recording

Gameplay is a present-tense experience. Gameplay involves not only the variable changes within the virtual space but also the experience of player agency, of forming motivated intention in relation to the multilinear possibility space of the game. Once the moment passes and a particular action is enacted, the multiple possibilities of *what could be* congealed into the singular, linear experience of *what happened.* As discussed in the meaning-making model in Chapter 8, this transformation is called **recording.**

Recording does not refer to the production of a video or audio recording of a gameplay session; it is simply the process of a set of events passing into the record of history. There may remain no *evidence* of a recorded event, just as I do not remember what I ate for lunch last Sunday, but as a matter of historical record, I *did* eat *something*; there is an objectively correct answer to that inquiry, even if I have no way of recalling it.

Once gameplay has undergone recording (an enacted instantiation of its multiple possibilities), its linear transformation can be remediated into other narrative or media experiences. A **retelling** is a subjective account of events that have transpired in a game, such as it might be told to someone else (Eladhari, 2018). A **playtrace** is an objective account, such as that which a researcher or QA specialist might capture to objectively study gameplay behavior (which may be captured as a video recording or using other forms of telemetry; Kreminski et al., 2019). Video recordings become linear media that can be enjoyed by audiences as narrative artifacts rather than game artifacts, as they do not grant the audience the experience of agency that is central to games as an artistic form.

Retelling

Retellings involve extrapolative narrativization (further detailed in Chapter 9), which means that players reach beyond that which is explicitly modeled within the simulation when telling stories about their experiences. A close battle in a strategy game like *Sid Meier's Civilization VI* (2016) might be recounted, "the remaining, brave troops, outnumbered, planted their feet, breathed in the crisp, morning air, and with a swell of national pride, defended the city to the last man, as attackers came from every angle", though concepts like bravery, breathing, and national pride are not modeled within the system. This is a feature of all representative arts; they insist upon a world, history, and life beyond their literal form, filled in by the beholder's imagination. These extrapolative details contextualize and remediate the drama of play and make for richer narratives.

Retellings can, themselves, be remediated into standalone media experiences. Eladhari (2018) cites the story of *Alice and Kev*, a narrative written by Robin Burkinshaw about her experience of playing *The Sims 3* (2009) as a pair of unhoused Sims. She writes, "I created two Sims, moved them in to a place made to look like an abandoned park, removed all of their remaining money, and then attempted to help them survive without taking any of the game's unrealistically easy cash routes" (Burkinshaw, 2009). Others have created comics, prose, and even films based on their experiences within games. These media objects serve as **paratexts** (secondary texts that surround and reconfigure the context by which audiences interpret the main text; Genette, 1987), which can change the total experience of a piece of work as it is embedded within its surrounding media and fan culture.

Retellings are accounts of personal experiences with games, so games that feature a high degree of emergence tend to spawn the most personal and unique retellings. Recounting the authored events of the embedded narrative *does* involve an amount of narrativization, as does the interpretation of any media object, but retellings should always involve one's personal experience of play rather than being a depersonalized plot recap.

As further detailed in Chapter 5, James Ryan (2018) details a framework that describes the curatorial process of translating the raw data instantiated in the recording process of gameplay into emergent narratives. He notes that the process of narrativization inherent in the retelling of simulated stories inherently involves curation: the sifting of the *chronicle* (the record of what happened in the *simulated storyworld*) elucidates *material* that the *narrativizer* deems relevant to the *story* that she intends to tell. According to Ryan, for the process of curation to culminate, the story "must be mounted in a media experience" (p. 239). While players can and do produce these retellings, Ryan's primary interest is hypothesizing ways in which curatorial processes can be performed automatically and interjected back into the simulated storyworld as a way of enriching the *first-order media experience* of the game (a *feedback* approach, as opposed to the *feedforward* approach of mounting external, or *second-order*, media experiences [p. 233]). He argues for an "overgenerate and curate" approach by which the patterns and surprising outcomes of multitudinous and intersecting systems of procedural emergence are given meaning through narrativization greater than could have been authored through a game's embedded narrative.

Ryan notes the effectiveness of games that reliably generate *feedforward* patterns of narrative significance, curated and told by players, such as *Dwarf Fortress* (2022) and *The Sims* (2000). He also notes examples of games that have made advancements in *feedback* curation, in which "a generated narrative artifact is mounted back into the simulated storyworld itself" (Ryan, 2018, p. 241), such as *Middle-earth: Shadow of War* (2017)'s Nemesis System, which remembers details of encounters with particular orcs within the *Lord of the Rings* (1954)-derived armies of Mordor and carries those details into future encounters or recounts them as bard-like stories told within the game. For example, if a player mortally wounds but does not kill an orc enemy, that enemy may re-emerge with a grudge to settle and embodied evidence of the previous encounter (such as a prosthetic arm to replace the one that was lost in battle), and orcs throughout the land may tell tales of that encounter, "You are the one who humiliated Mormog the Poisoner!".

Non-automated feedback systems exist within games' metagame layer. Since players are a part of the system of gameplay, metagame player behavior *is* a system of emergence in gameplay capable of what scholar Marcus Carter (2015) calls **emitext**, "a form of paratext that emerges from within the game as a part of play, rather than a peripheral industry that surrounds it" (p. 311). Carter cites the example of factional propaganda designed by *EVE Online* (2003) players and mounted within the game, aimed to influence player behavior. This propaganda, developed from retellings of emergent narrative events, is fed back into the system of play by players as a metagame practice.

Playtrace

Whereas retellings are subjectively narrativized accounts of gameplay action, playtraces are objective data about instantiated systemic action. Like retellings, playtraces can be fed forward into new media experiences; video recordings of gameplay, such as in streams or "Longplay" records, can be counted as playtraces in so far as they provide objective accounts of action, though one can argue that edited playthroughs (in which sections of "unimportant" gameplay are removed) may be closer to a curated retelling. Such recordings, particularly when they include player commentary or for-audience diegetic staging or mimetic role-playing, may still be considered products of narrativization despite providing an objective account of gameplay activity.

Other feedforward playtraces include tools used for research or QA in which studying player behavior, such as routing through a virtual world, is important. Tools like Playtracer can create a heatmap of a game's environment, showing how much time players spend in any particular area (Liu et al., n.d.). More impressively, projects like *Foldit* (2008) gamify the variables and properties of real-world mathematical and biological processes that have been difficult to study due to their complexity. These tools, released as game-like experiences for the general public, benefit from the collective iteration of thousands of players worldwide, turning data from their collective playtraces into useful information for solving these challenging problems.

Games sometimes contain playtrace feedback information, usually as a record of the player's journey through a game to that point. *The Legend of Zelda: Breath of the Wild* (2017) introduced in an update the Adventure Log, a line that traces a player's journey through the world of Hyrule, which players can watch animate as an overlay on the game's map. This data, an objective account of instantiated activity, can easily be narrativized as a reminder of players' individual adventures. Other games, including many competitive titles in the sports, fighting, and shooter genres, can capture replays of action. In some cases, these replays (captured as systemic inputs rather than "flat" video and re-mounted in-engine) can even be examined from perspectives other than that of the perspective of the players during play, giving players an opportunity to glean additional insights from their past performance.

The Lived Experience Principle

Once a specific instance of gameplay action occurs, it is recorded from the multitudinous possibility space into the singular historical record. As has been noted previously, the open-ended, multilinear, expressive agency that defines live gameplay is recorded into a linear experience of instantiated events that can be analyzed more like a traditional, linear narrative. The record of that which has occurred in a particular playthrough is like a lived experience. Like a lived experience, analysis of this linear sequence must be held alongside a consideration of the choices of involved agents. Though a single occurrence *actually* transpired, it is still relevant to consider the possibilities of what could have been instantiated in its place. For example, if someone tells a story about going to the amusement park, it would be relevant to consider his chosen action as a choice agent if we learned that his wife was giving birth at the hospital at the same time. Unlike a fictional story, in which all contextual details are fabricated to suit the chosen narrative, stories of lived experiences (and stories of the simulated happenings of game storyworlds) are framed by objective context within which the agent acts.

To that point James Ryan (2018) explains:

> This points to a fundamental difference between a fictional world and a simulated world, which is that the latter emerges from a system of laws (the mechanics of the

> simulation), whereas the former obtains through a kind of human artifice.
>
> (p. 66)

Whereas fictional narrative is driven by the top-down needs of the narrative, simulated narrative is generated from bottom-up enactment of processes, themselves ambivalent to their narrative context (Ryan, 2018, p. 67).

The lived experience principle, derived from this observation, describes a crucial aspect of the experience of play within simulations. Because the occurrences within an emergent simulation are (or can be) unique to a particular instantiation of play, driven by the rules of the simulation rather than the whims of a storyteller, those occurrences are experienced as if they were first-hand experiences. Players inherently know that what they experience is unique, perhaps unreplicatable. It makes the emergent narratives generated by simulated systems feel personal, more interesting than a comparable story that had been prescribed. Ryan cites Roger C. Schank (1979)'s concept of *personal relatedness* (p. 15) as a factor that increases personal investment in stories that have these factors of personal, lived experiences.

As covered in Chapter 4, game avatars can be (under the correct circumstances and with the immersive intention of the player) experienced as a projective extension of the player's distributed consciousness. In such conditions, the player operates the embodied avatar, the layers of mediation that separate the player from the diegesis become transparent, and the player experiences the game world from the inside. The projective perspective begets the illusion of unmediated agency within the virtual world, and the player attunes a *vicariosensation*: a sense of proprioceptive space and even touch, translated from the visual, aural, and haptic feedback from the computer. Vicariosensation (a portmanteau of "vicarious sensation") does not mean that the player feels excruciating pain when the avatar is shot (though this is not a *terribly* outlandish notion; even in film, it is clear that the viewer experiences something *like* pain when watching the ankle-breaking scene in *Misery* [Reiner, 1990]), only that the player attunes to the spatial orientation of the avatar and the environmental features in the same manner as one can anticipate, with visual information alone, the physical displacement that an upcoming pothole will cause the car when driving.

The player maintains a stronger link to the video game avatar than to protagonists of other media, because it is through this avatar that the player can act, react, and express. As an extension of her will and, ultimately, herself within the virtual space, it is reasonable to conclude that video games possess a special property by which they may be interpreted as lived experiences. Other media does not subsume the individual self, so one may have a lived experience, remembering where one was when reading a book or with whom she watched a movie, but the projective properties of the video game produce memories of the lived experience variety for events and actions that take place within the simulation.

Going back to the trio of perspectives outlined in Chapter 6, the lived experience principle is more closely associated with the diegetic perspective than the mimetic. James Ryan shares an example from his experience playing *Grand Theft Auto: Vice City* (2002):

> In a mission called 'Psycho Killer', [...] the player is tasked with apprehending an unhinged character who seeks to kill the members of a band, Love Fist, with whom the player character is associated. The mission is designed to play out in a short car chase that culminates in the killing of the character being chased, but in my playthrough things went off the rails.
>
> Over the course of the car chase, both of our vehicles became damaged to the point of starting on fire—in the *Grand Theft Auto* series, this indicates that the vehicle is about to explode, which means that its passengers must promptly exit or else die in the explosion. As such, both the killer and I were forced to leave our vehicles, but because this occurred in a relatively empty neighborhood near the edge of the island city, there were no nearby vehicles for either of us to hijack. Having no other choice, the killer proceeded to run from me on foot, and I chased after by the same means. This is where the situation took on an almost magical quality. After a few blocks, the killer took a turn toward the water, walked out onto a marina, and hopped into

> a boat that was docked there. I followed after and commandeered another boat, and from here the chase transpired on water, through the beautiful ocean passages of Vice City. By this point, I was mesmerized and had become more interested in prolonging the chase than in executing the stipulated task of killing the killer. […] At this point I began debating whether it would be more poetic for the killer to get away—after taking such creative means, this seemed to perhaps be the just outcome—or to succumb finally to the mission's tragic design. I chose the latter, and this culmination terminated an emergent experience that I recall lasting upward of an hour.
>
> *(Ryan, 2018, pp. 76–78)*

Here Ryan demonstrates that the mission was memorable and interesting precisely *because* it veered off of its intended course. What the game presented instead was bespoke, unique, and personal. Ryan concludes:

> When the authored story of the mission (a brief car chase) veered off the rails into an emergent sequence that perhaps no other player ever experienced, something more akin to nonfiction obtained. This strange chase by car and foot and boat actually *happened*, and this makes it inherently more interesting—if the designers of the game had scripted a mission designed to transpire like my emergent experience did, the experience of that mission would not be as interesting.
>
> *(Ryan, 2018, p. 78)*

Ryan's experience in Vice City became akin to lived experience once it broke from the destined trajectory of its design, suggesting that it is the emergent qualities of game systems that produce these feelings of lived experience and personal relatedness. Emergence thrives because of the properties of unlikeliness and uniqueness. It was special to Ryan in the example above that the car, foot, and boat chase he experienced was unique. No one else has or ever will experience the series of events that he experienced in the way that he experienced them. They emerged from the intersection of mechanics, so they followed a logical, narratively cogent structure, rather than being truly, incoherently random.

This is not to say that designed encounters that play out with complete fidelity to their design are incapable of creating experiences that feel lived and memorable—audaciously designed "set-pieces" can be quite personally involving—but these sections lose some of their peculiarity and novelty with repetition, and they do not make for the kinds of "you HAVE to hear this" story that must be repeated outside of the game space, because every player will have experienced in roughly the same way. These scenarios are still experienced from within (when an avatar is present) and benefit from whatever level of agency and emergence are afforded, but an experienced player grows to recognize when she is experiencing something truly emergent and when she is operating within the expectations and bounds of the game's designed course.

Even within these prescriptively designed sections of play, though, the player does not need to *wait* for emergence to *just happen* through sheer happenstance. The chase from Ryan's example became memorable because both the pursuer and the pursuant's cars broke down in a neighborhood in which procuring another car would not have been easy—a narratively unlucky/experientially lucky place for the cars to break. Players, as elements within the system of gameplay, can become their own systems of emergence by playing in ways contrary or peripheral to the intended design. This can become a kind of metagame (see Chapter 13). How much will the game systems let the player get away with? How long will the game world suspend itself within an ambient state while the player chooses not to engage with the task at hand? Are there creative and unconventional means or routes that the player can take to accomplish a specific goal while avoiding or circumventing the path that is clearly prescribed? This is a way to achieve *expressive* play, as detailed in Chapter 12. Expressive play is emergence that utilizes the player as the vector of differentiation. Thus, even a narrowly prescriptive game, "incorrectly" played, can produce lived experience memories.

Possibility Space

Systemic emergence and emergence arising from the expressive and individualized play of the player create a wide variance in possible directions gameplay can take. As detailed previously, recording is the process by which one "path" through the sprawling jungle of possibilities is instantiated. In judging a "recorded" instantiation as a narrative artifact, it *does* coalesce into a singular, linear form, but it is always held in the context of its multilinear foundation. More than other narrative forms, an instantiated game narrative is as much a record of what it *is not* as what it *is*.

As referenced in Chapter 8, all possible actions that can be taken in a game constitute its *possibility space*. This is a frequently referenced concept, though it is almost always spoken of as a hypothetical measure. As noted earlier in this chapter, plotting all possible routes that gameplay can take results in an impossibly large map of action. Jesper Juul proves the implausibility of mapping the *whole* possibility space of a game by demonstrating on an extremely simple game: Tic-Tac-Toe (or Noughts and Crosses). He developed an algorithm that plotted all of the possible (legal) games of Tic-Tac-Toe and found that there are 255,168 unique games possible within its simple ruleset (Juul, 2003). Performing a similar exercise on even something as simple as *Pong* (1972) or *Breakout* (1976) would create near-infinite possibilities. As such, the possibility space is not something that is ever objectively measured, but it is a useful hypothetical construct when analyzing games. We can intuit a broad possibility space in moments of free play and a narrow possibility space in moments of prescriptive, mastery-oriented play. Plotting the general oscillations of possibility space gives us insight into the flow, pacing, dramatic structure, and arc of a game as a narrative artifact, holistically.

The above narrative properties reveal the challenging nature of the "possibility space" concept. Flow and pacing are time-oriented measures. The pacing of a song or film is affected by the rate at which elements of experiential significance occur in the temporal sequence of the linear work. "Possibility space" is a spatially oriented term, suggesting a metaphorical topology of action instead of a chronology of action, driven by the exploratory agency of the player. If the player determines her own journey through the possibility space, how can we discuss that in terms of pace? How can we reconcile pacing and spacing?

The metaphor of the possibility space is predicated on choice. Simply, a large number of choices will produce a large possibility space, and a small number of choices will produce a narrow possibility space. Consider the metaphor of a flowchart of possible actions; a greater number of branches would take a great amount of space when drawn. But this "objective" measure is unsatisfying; it gives preferential measure to games with real-time control over turn-based games without regard to strategic or agential expressivity. By this objective measure, we might say that a game in which a character runs around aimlessly in an empty field has a greater possibility space than Chess, if we consider that the "field runner" is offered 360 choices in every moment of gameplay while a Chess player has 20 choices in her first move (and increasingly more and then fewer throughout the course of the game).

Subjectively, we might remove or combine "meaningless" actions. Since the "running in a field" game has no objective, every movement is equally meaningful (and meaningless), so perhaps the number of choices reduces to one: "run". Perhaps the player sets her own goals and ascribes meaning in that way, such as running in a perfect circle. Though not a mandated objective, it does increase the number of actions that we might categorize as being meaningful. Meanwhile, because Chess has an objective, every possible action represents a step toward or away from its fulfillment, imbuing a greater sense of purpose and meaning onto the choices available. As the "perfect circle" player proves, though, objectives do not need to be sanctioned to provide structure and shape to the possibility space. The "perfect circle" player has developed her own metagame within the rules and affordances of the "running in a field" system. As such, she might subjectively categorize the space of meaningful possibility as being quite expansive (for her expressive ends), while someone uninterested in that metagame might subjectively view the possibility space as being quite narrow (when duplicative, inconsequential choices are reduced from her mapping).

Insofar as the total possibility space reflects the game's emergent capacities, a possibility space is not *authored* as much as it is *shaped*. As Salen and Zimmerman (2003) write, "as a game designer you can never directly craft the possible space of your game. You can only indirectly construct the space of possibility, through the rules you design" (p. 67). This is not *universally* true; the possibility space in games of minimal emergence, such as hypertext-like visual novels in which the only choices given to players are between pre-written story branches at known points of divergence, can be fully known by their developers in advance. But Salen and Zimmerman's statement holds true in the vast majority of situations. As a volume of emergent possibilities, we should consider the possibility space to be a matter of second-order design. The consequences for every action and occurrence are authored by the systems, and the systems are designed by the developers. The developers shape the possibility space and explicitly determine *some* but not *all* of its boundaries.

As such, the possibility space is a combination of three categorical vectors: the specific affordances and restrictions designated by the developers, emergence that arises from the game systems, and emergence that arises from the player (as an unpredictable agent within the gameplay system). The possibility space extends beyond what may be considered "intended" design. If a player can exploit a glitch or design oversight, that is included in the possibility space. In that sense, "possibility space" is a measure of the metagame rather than the game as designed. This means that we might consider the possibility space to be somewhat dynamic in its shape based on the evolution of a game's metagame amongst its play community. Once reliable glitches or exploits are *discovered*, they factor into metagame consideration, effectively broadening the effective possibility space, even though the technical possibility for said action was always *possible* within the game's code.

Though indirectly designed and dynamic in its effective range, we can consider a possibility space to possess a hypothetical shape. It is inexact, but it is theoretically "definite", such that certain actions are understood to be closer to the possibility space's "edge". This is a subjective measure of either uniqueness or deviance from what one assumes is the intended design path, such that the average player action or design-intended action sits at the center of the space, and abnormal or counter-design strategies sit at the fringes.

To read pacing and dramatic structure into a game's possibility space, this metric of "total meaningful, metagame affordances" must be measured against another variable, and depending on the genre of game being played, this variable will either be time, space, or sequence. For example, the possibility space of a fighting game match is best measured against time as the players' choices broaden and constrain over the course of a match. The possibility shape of a *Super Mario Bros.* (1985) course can be effectively measured spatially. The player has a broader or narrower set of available choices depending on where she is in the course, regardless of how quickly or slowly she arrived there. The shape of Chess possibilities is best understood sequentially, as each player is given an entirely new set of moves from which they must choose at the beginning of each turn, regardless of time spent.

As the possibility space (relative to itself within the game) expands, play becomes more expressive, giving the player additional freedom for creative self-expression, and as it narrows, play becomes more prescriptive, demanding greater fidelity to intended or ideal play. "The wider the possibility space of player choices e.g. regarding alternative game mechanics, the more individual strategies will be adopted, and there will be room for players to hone their skills and develop strategies" (Järvinen, 2008, p. 84). It is in near-constant fluctuation, and its rhythm of fluctuation contributes to the emotional drama of play. It is not deterministic in its directionality, though. The possibility space narrows as a situation becomes more desperate, as when the avatar has very little remaining health in a fight, but it also narrows in times of relief, such as when one closes in on an assured victory—placing the final few pieces in a jigsaw puzzle leaves very little room for choice; it represents a relaxation of the demand on complex problem-solving.

The property of the relative breadth of a moment's possibility space is not only relevant in informing the player's current feelings of agency in a moment of play. It also colors the way in which a sequence of play is remembered and contextualized. If all gameplay action reflects and expresses both the player and the developer, gameplay with a wide possibility space favors the expression of the player, and moments of narrow possibility space favor the developers' embedded design. As such, it is relevant to note the shape of the possibility space and track its dynamic changes when recounting the narrative of play. As we analyze a game as an expressive cultural artifact, the moments of narrow possibility space are relatively assured between all play experiences, while the situations that emerge during points at which the possibility space are the largest reflect the expressive capacities of the system but are least likely to be experienced as such by other players. Depending on the type of analysis being performed, one or the other may be more appropriate to report. If the beholder is writing an analysis of the embedded narrative, it is reasonable to show preference to what might be considered "archetypal" play: favoring moments of narrow possibility as the consistent "choke-points" of narrative and seeking the relative "center" of the possibility space in moments of greater total possible divergence. But when exploring the total expressive capacities of a game as a cultural artifact, its mode of expression is in the shaping and presentation of novel forms of agency, so presenting explorations of the "periphery" of the possibility space is the most useful in proving the total expressive capacity of a work, held alongside others' explorations of unconventional play within a game's systems.

This is not to say that the only way to effectively convey a game's nature is to "break" it or play it belligerently. Rather, as Souvik Mukherjee (2015) eloquently describes it:

> Every instance of gameplay is after all part of a gamesystem. It follows the game rules, is represented by the game graphics and mechanics and also has the same basic narrative environment. So it can be pointed out that the game consists of a multiplicity of gameplay that corresponds to the singularities of the game-environment, the basic framework that permits certain kinds of progress and not certain others, and the designated beginning(s) and ending(s), while at the same time also following differential tracks of progress depending upon the interaction between the game and the player.
>
> *(p. 138)*

Divergent Play and Story Volumes

As a narrative artifact, enacted gameplay holds not only its internal properties as a linear text but also the properties of the paths not chosen that contextualize it. Mukherjee (2015) continues:

> So it is not only the actualized state that should be studied to understand the state of a particular object, but the whole set of trajectories including the possible and non-actualized trajectories. [...] In the instances of gameplay in video games, too, any particular instance is influenced by the possible others.
>
> *(p. 139)*

Though games have multitudinous possible expressions, and no specific instantiation represents a *definitively* "true", totalizing expression of its narrative potential, this does not mean that any singular instantiation, even a *highly unconventional* instantiation, is to be attributed less narrative value. A novel is authored with a single narrative thread. We can speculate about "what would have happened if Romeo and Juliet never met?", but this hypothesization is insolvent to the play as written; it constitutes a separate narrative work. There is a temptation to treat video games similarly: as singular narrative threads from which players may choose to deviate, reconverge, or ignore completely. But this is not the case. Unconventional play does not *deviate* from a singular "true" narrative course. Games are developed as systems of narrative generation. The implicit social contract of game design is that the performance of its story *will* diverge. This is the intended and inevitable outcome.

As game designer Jason Grinblat (2017) explains, linear media have storylines, whereas multilinear media like video games have *story volumes*. "Whereas the author crafts a storyline that traverses narrative space, the procedural designer crafts a story volume that contains numerous adjacent stories exploring similar themes or invoking a similar mood" (p. 202). It describes the range of stories that a system is capable of telling rather than constraining a system to a single story from which divergences become "false" or "alternate". The building blocks of this plentitude of stories are, in Hartmut Koenitz's SPP (System, Process, Product) model, called *protostories*, "the concrete content, internal structure, and outward appearance of an IDN system as a space of potential narratives that is connected to any instantiated narrative through a participatory process" (Koenitz, 2023, p. 76).

We can categorize games with relatively inflexible guiding narratives or games about deducing specific narrative beats as having a strong protostory, while sandbox games in which semiotic detail serve primarily as context for emergent, play-driven narratives have a weak protostory (Grinblat et al., 2021). While a strong protostory constrains the types of stories that will emerge from a game system to a greater degree than does a weak protostory, both formulations are still best thought of as volumes containing equally valid "storylines", differentiated and driven through divergent play.

Each individual storyline—each series of events that a player instantiates within the story volume of all possible expressions within the system—is a valid, linear artifact that emerges from the system. It is the implicit social contract into which the game developer enters when designing an open-ended system of artistic production. This is true even in bases of belligerent, counter-design play, such as the deliberate exploitation of glitches and ethically repugnant play.

The latter point exposes the danger of creating such open-ended artistic artifacts. Terrible stories have emerged about players in the competitive survival horror game *Dead by Daylight* (2016) forming a communal metagame when utilizing one of the game's costumes for *The Texas Chain Saw Massacre* (Hooper, 1974)'s Leatherface character, specifically targeting Black players or players playing as Black characters (Parrish, 2022) or *Red Dead Online* (2019) players exploiting a glitch to spawn or disguise themselves as NPC members of the Ku Klux Klan hate group in order to target Black players and NPCs (Pettit, 2020). In both of the aforementioned situations, the developers patched out the costumes or glitches that were incentivizing this behavior, but these types of situations do leave unfortunate stains on games' legacies. Worse still, it contributes to the ongoing marginalization and symbolic violence against Black (and other unprotected groups) people in the cultural realm in ways that serve racist ideals of cultural hegemony and exclusion that transcend the digital stage within which they are performed.

Kishonna L. Gray (2020) writes:

> Any practice in cultural production can become a symbolic site of struggle over the power to enforce the dominant definition from a hegemonic standpoint; these practices delimit and restrict access to certain places for particular populations, outlining who is entitled to take part in defining, shaping, and innovating in the digital realm.
>
> *(summarizing Patricia Ewick & Susan S. Silbey, 1995)*

Greater attention will be paid to this subject in Chapter 14, but I highly recommend reading Gray's introductory chapter of *Intersectional Tech*, in which the theory and philosophy of technology and culture as sites of racial formation and exclusion are detailed thoroughly, with wide-ranging references to foundational and contemporary texts in the area of study.

With this context, we must consider the dark side of the story volume. In a system of emergent narrative generation, and accepting players as vectors of emergence within the system of play, we have to accept that ethically reprehensible play is included in the possible narrative outputs within the story volume. This, in fact, puts a greater responsibility on game developers to anticipate such experiences by interrogating the presumptions (of whiteness, maleness) that may be inbuilt within their systems (Noble, 2018; Everett, 2009; Kolko, 2000; all cited in Gray, 2020) or to respond swiftly and appropriately to the metagame emergence of communal tropes that perpetuate exclusionary and hateful behavior. Unfortunately, with games being sites of artistic generation rather than simply being products for interpretation alone, all play within the system *is* ultimately attributable to the meaningful capacities of that system.

Through play enactment, each player instantiates a single narrative thread from the total possibility space of a game's story volume. As a linear narrative, this instantiation is a narrative product of the game's systems. The resulting storyline can be examined as linear media. Assuming a player plays through a game only once, her resulting linear instantiation should be the experience on which narrative and artistic interpretation is primarily based. I encourage this practice. It is useful to compare one's own experience against the experience of others and to seek other writing and conversation around a game, but some players, when engaging in analytical writing about games, have a tendency to minimize their own experiences in favor of what they expect a hypothetical "average" or "ideal" playthrough might entail. When writing consumer reviews, perhaps there are situations in which it is useful to consider the experience an average player might have with a game rather than describing what might be a highly divergent experience. For critical and meaning-oriented analysis, though, writers must engage with the narrative experience that was generated, because the game *is* an engine of narrative generation, not a script from which the player may choose to deviate. In this context, there is no *incorrect* play (apart from, again, what we may argue is morally reprehensible); there are only outputs from a system designed to produce divergent outputs.

Each time a game is played, a fundamentally different set of actions will have taken place on-screen. Whereas three readers may read differing motivations into the character of Oliver Twist (Dickens, 1838), they are all reacting to the same basic set of facts and stimuli written in the book. Even the most linear, non-divergent story told in games varies in its delivery and, often, content from player to player.

To illustrate this, we can look at the example of *The Legend of Zelda: Ocarina of Time* (1998). Nintendo's ARPG, set in a world of swords and sorcery, tells the story of Link, a young boy hailing from the remote, magical woodlands, who is destined by the will of the goddesses to save the kingdom of Hyrule from the evil sorcerer Ganondorf. His adventures take him through mountains, towns, deserts, and even through the digestive tract of a particularly large fish. All the while, he (guided by the player) solves complex puzzles, bests his foes in intense combat encounters, and acquires increasingly powerful weapons and magical relics as he works toward his fated encounter with Ganondorf and the restoration of the blighted kingdom.

On its surface, *Ocarina of Time* has no trajectory-altering story branches. The game has one ending: Link emerges victorious in his confrontation against Ganondorf, and the kingdom is restored. Apart from engagements with optional side-content, players' journeys to this ending will hit all of the same major beats along the way. The variability in content as presented, though, is high. In one player's playthrough, Link is an adept warrior, courageously and single-mindedly overcoming every obstacle in his way without faltering from his primary objective. In another player's playthrough, Link struggles with combat but excels at solving the adventure's devious puzzles. In another playthrough, Link may spend his time primarily engaging in leisure activities, riding his horse through the fields and admiring the beauty of the land of Hyrule without considering the urgency of his fateful calling. In yet another playthrough, Link may abdicate his heroic title altogether, instead spending his time throwing pots and rocks at villagers and attacking chickens throughout the kingdom. This is all to say nothing of the playthrough in which Link executes a very specific series of precisely aligned jumps and item uses to "glitch" through the walls and floors of an early level to miraculously "load" into a late-game level, outside of the ordainment of the game's developers.

Should players let these differences affect their understanding and reactions to the presented story, or should players remove themselves and their influence from the story and try to read and understand it "objectively" (or as intended)? Is it fair to say "Link is crazy or malevolent" after experiencing the throwing-pots-at-villagers playthrough? The player was the one exercising her will in those moments, after all—not Link (if such a division can be drawn). If that's true, it would be equally impossible to claim that Link is a courageous and talented swordsman in the proficient playthrough, even though this interpretation of the character likely runs closest to his developer-intended destiny. Perhaps the most "honest" reading is to observe how Link behaves apart from the player's will. Without controller input, he stands still in his bedroom at the beginning of the game, never moving from that spot. But, surely, that cannot be the optimal way to read the story either. This is quite a conundrum.

In passively consumed mediums, we are often trained to separate our act of engaging with the art from our ultimate interpretation of that art. If we have difficulty finding Waldo on a particular page of a *Where's Waldo?* (Handford, 1987) book whereas another reader does not, we do not credit Waldo with finding a better hiding place in our reading of the book when compared with our friend's reading. If we pause a movie, we do not interpret that as the characters helpfully standing still while waiting for the viewer to take a bathroom break (though perhaps the interplay between fiction and metatext would be more thinly strained in a similar situation in which a stage play must briefly pause as a result of an audience member having a medical emergency).

There are many sources of gameplay variability. A great degree of player control (or, more precisely, player input responsiveness) will increase variability; though high randomness (outside of player control) will also lead to high variability. Expressive games (games that respond to creative, individualized play; see Chapter 12) will unavoidably feature a great degree of variability while games in more prescriptive genres, such as single-solution puzzle games, hidden object games, and visual novels, will feature relatively low amounts of variability, or variability that follows predictable, prescribed branches.

A Structural Digression

This distinction may appear similar to Viktor Shklovsky's structuralist approach to narrative: the dichotomy of the fabula (story; the internal order of events and spatial configurations) and syuzhet (discourse; the way a story is told, whether in temporal-spatial order, either consistent with the story world or in a state of narrative discontinuity; Shklovsky, 2015/1919), but these levels are not wholly parallel.

As these concepts are applied to video games, they typically align as fabula representing the previously referenced *prototext* of a game (its prefabricated narrative elements that live play reconfigures) and syuzhet representing play (discourse with the prototext). Syuzhet is typically understood as presentational flourish or discontinuity, primarily informing meaningful interpretation. A story told out of order implies that there is a true order in which the events it describes take place, from which the telling deviates. Discursive play, though, is not simply a difference in representational discontinuity. Play determines the order and manner in which the prefabricated protostory narrative fragments occur *at the story level.* If a player chooses to follow a forked pathway into its eastern branch before doubling back to its western branch, *this is the order in which those actions occurred within the story world of that particular instantiation.*

Separately, a game's protostory may utilize classically discursive techniques separate from player control. Games like *Beyond: Two Souls* (2013) and *The Last of Us Part II* (2020) feature numerous flashbacks and presentational discontinuities in a traditional manner.

So whereas Shklovsky conceptualized stories as being internally ordered with tellings (syuzhet) that obscure spatial-temporal details, video game stories are in internal narrative disrepair until enactment, subject to structural transformation by both developer and player. So there exist, theoretically, three structural layers in perpetual conversation: a fictional series of events that may or may not have an *a priori* order. This order can be rearranged by the developer in the telling of the story and again by the player as co-storyteller (syuzhet). Finally, the diegetic "truth" is determined in real-time during gameplay enactment by the player (as an agential performer in the mimetic drama) in a way that may be influenced by the (classical) syuzhet. More simply put: traditional narratives contain two layers of artifice: the fiction of the story and the structure of the telling. Video games contain three: the fiction of the story, the structure of its telling, and the performance of the player that is both internal to the diegetic fiction (as a character within the world) and aware of the structure (thus, the avatar character's internal performance may be influenced by the player's external, structural awareness).

To demonstrate how this differs from other forms of dramatic narrative, we can examine how a story in heavy structural disrepair may differ if presented in traditional narrative forms and video games. In linear media like film, stories that make heavy use of structural discontinuity (like the films *The Tree of Life* [Malick, 2011] or *Mulholland Drive* [Lynch, 2001]) may disorient and confuse the viewer, but the viewer can generally have faith that the characters ("existent" within the diegetic world of the film) can follow the events as they experience them linearly. Games presented in heavy structural disrepair (like *Before Your Eyes* [2021] or *Zero Escape: Virtue's Last Reward* [2012]) may disorient the player as the audience, but the player also operates as a performer within the dramatic space. The character within the fiction does not "know" what the player has not been presented (or may not yet understand) because the player serves as the avatar character's animating and cognitive force. A player's knowledge (or lack of knowledge) not only affects the viewing/reading of the story from the outside in but also affects the avatar character's performance as a dramatic agent from the inside out. Thus, a game can structurally hide information that would be diegetically obvious to the character (as in a particularly frustrating twist in the visual novel *Zero Time Dilemma* [2016]) or reveal things to the player that the character diegetically could not know (as in the

Columbo-like pre-mystery demonstrations of a crime taking place in the courtroom mystery visual novel *Phoenix Wright: Ace Attorney* [2001]), and the performance of the character is affected by this non-diegetic knowledge in a way that shapes the diegesis differently than it would have "naturally" unfolded.

This dramatic peculiarity arises (in avatar-based games) from the avatar's split function as expressive conduit of player will and character within the diegetic fiction. I examine the mental and dramatic link between the player and the avatar more fully in Chapter 4. As we try to make structural and narrative sense of games, particularly in a cooperative and comparative fashion with others in the game's player base, we must understand the forms of representation at play in games—the enacted "truth" of a single playthrough in the context of all other possible "truths" that equally well could have been enacted instead. This distinction between an instantiated storyline and a game's holistic story volume is the subject of the next section, in which I delineate between a playthrough's *manifest content* and its *potential content.*

Manifest Content

Manifest content refers to the specific series of events that occur within instantiated play. It is a term borrowed from Freudian dream analysis. In Freud's conceptualization, dreams are understood through the parallel interpretation of *manifest content* (that which occurs in a dream, such as standing up to give a presentation in front of your homeroom class) and *latent content* (the underlying, sub-conscious "meaning" that underwrites the manifest content). Freud may interpret the example dream as representing someone's fear of professional inadequacy, subconsciously correlated with their anxieties surrounding sexual inadequacy. He may make further conclusions about the dreamer's relationship with her parents and prescribe a truly 1890s volume of cocaine, but we need not get sidetracked.

Despite millennia of interest in the subject, modern psychologists still do not have a holistic understanding of dreams, but what we can confidently assert is that, despite dream analysts' conceptualizations of common themes and motifs that provide some level of sensible legibility to the bizarre happenings within the dream space, no two dreams are exactly the same. One does not have "the" homeroom presentation dream that plays identically to other dreamers' homeroom presentation dreams. The dream is constructed by the sleeping brain, or it may be more accurate to say *reconstructed* from the fragments of memory and thought that the brain sorts and processes while sleeping.

In a similar manner, the observable output enacted by video game play is highly individualized and bound to differ from player to player or even between playthroughs performed by the same player. Video games are specifically designed for diverse instantiation in a way that other artistic mediums are not. A film, in conjunction with the context in which it is watched, may result in a highly individualized experience while watching (if, for instance, one has to pause it several times to take restroom breaks or if one watches a film with a rowdy audience), but there is nothing in the design of the film object that provokes an instantiating process by which individualized experience is to be *expected.* While we may develop language to describe the context in which a film was watched, the instantiation of video game play primarily occurs within the digital artifact, and, thus, we must have language to discuss and understand individualized instancing of the product output itself. Despite differing contextual experiences, the content of a film is singular, static, and describable, whereas the content and happenings of a video game are unique to each playthrough (and may be further affected by contextual details in the same manner a film-watching experience may be). So while the events of a film are uncontroversially its singular "text", that which transpires in a video game is instanced, and bold assertions like "Mario defeated Bowser on his first attempt" may be true of an individual instanced playthrough but may not be true of all instanced playthroughs. Thus, the new term manifest content is necessary to describe that which is "manifested" in an individual instance of play.

Unlike the fixed content of a film, the manifest content of an instantiated play is ephemeral unless transformed into another media object. That is to say, though the consequences of a gameplay action may persist within the game, gameplay occurrences pass and cease to "exist" after they occur. Whereas a scene in a film can be rewound and watched again or a paragraph in a book read once more, the manifest content of a game requires transformation to extend beyond its specific moment in time. As discussed in a previous section, instantiated gameplay can be transformed into linear media (such as a video recording or a move-by-move transcription of a Chess match) or retold in a narrativized fashion.

In live gameplay, manifest content feeds back into the system of live instantiation (such that, if the avatar sustains an enemy's attack, the consequence of lowered health or lost life will be "remembered" as a systemic variable and state change). As live gameplay is recorded, either as memory, video record, transcript, or narrativized retelling, the manifest content represents the narrative "text" of the playthrough.

Interpretation and Characterization

How should the manifested "text" of a playthrough inform our subjective interpretations? If any instantiation of manifest content that emerges from a gameplay system's story volume produces an interpretively valid "text", can we perform the same textual interpretations on this instantiation that we might on a linear text? This question lies at the heart of the literacy model described in Chapters 6–8. Ultimately, I believe so. If we wish to position video games as engines of artistic and narrative generation, we have to be prepared to treat their generated outputs as fully featured narrative objects.

Again, there is a temptation to position video games as containing a *particular* (embedded) story, with the diversity of play experiences represented as being greater or lesser fidelity to that singular, narrative truth. This is often internally reinforced within games. Sometimes sequels will follow a "canonical" ending of the previous game, privileging one set of actions over all possible others. Sometimes characters will act in ways during cutscenes that do not honor the characterization choices players imbue during free play. This implies a strict division between *truth* and *play*. That which the developer embeds or decides is *true* of the story, and that which the player does is incidental, ancillary, or interpretive. I believe that this formulation of ludic storytelling is unsatisfactory, a result of immature design as the medium develops through its adolescence. I *do* grant developers a greater balance of narrative control than the player, in that they set the boundaries of expression and choose all systemic affordances, but, as I have said before, developers implicitly surrender narrative authority when designing within the medium of games. If they wish to express a singular vision, they have fundamentally chosen the wrong medium in which to present that story.

Is it fair to read characterization from manifested play? In our previous *Ocarina of Time* (1998) example, is it fair to read Link as a sadistic prankster in the "throw pots at my neighbors" playthrough? Yes. That which occurs on-screen is the "truth" of the story as it was manifested. Due to the implicit contract between video game developers and players, developers' intentions do not dictate the performance of video game narratives; they can only create a possibility space in which a range of actions can occur. We have to assume that any of those possibilities are narratively coherent and acceptable, as allowed by a game's systemic processes.

This is similar (though even less prescriptive) to the relationship between a playwright and an actor. A playwright may ostensibly create the "shape" of a character, but the actor (in coordination with the show's director) determines the specifics of her characterization in her performance. An actor can play the same role gallantly or menacingly, with or without a strong accent, and most roles can be played by actors of varying ethnic or physical presentations. All of these factors will cause the performance of these characters to be categorically different as different troupes perform the same script. Each of these varying performances is "true" to each audience, though. When playing video games, players are both performer and audience, and the player has just as much right to imbue the character with specific characterization as does an actor performing a script.

Games that need to be played in a very specific way to "correctly" characterize their playable cast are not written in a collaborative manner. An artist must expect a range of interactions with her work, and her job in producing the art is to cater toward this range rather than targeting exclusive, specific, instantiated enactments. Games are systemic, and though their systems can be imbued with ideology and intended messages, developers are ultimately systems designers rather than expository orators. To the degree to which developers want to evoke or communicate something specific, developers must constrict players' agential expressiveness or rebalance reward and punishment mechanisms to shape the play process toward greater likeliness of intended results.

An artist who paints an abstract, formless painting understands that viewers are likely to have a greater range of reactions to her painting than they would if she painted a realistic, crying face. The details and specificity of the second image encourage a narrower range of interpretations. Similarly, video games that wish to characterize their cast through gameplay must do so by either narrowing the field of possible performances or accepting the wider gamut of performances as narratively valid.

There are many great games that depend upon imperfect play to characterize their casts. In *Octodad: Dadliest Catch* (2014), the player controls an octopus who has contorted his legs to occupy a standard set of (human) coat and trousers in order to blend in amongst human society. Gameplay consists of performing mundane tasks without incurring suspicion from onlookers that might lead them to discover that he is not a real human. *Octodad* depends upon sub-optimal play. It is famously difficult to control. Each of his limbs is controlled through separate, unconventional controller interactions, and most players will spend much of the game wildly flailing his gangly limbs, haphazardly knocking over objects and causing a cartoonish ruckus. It is theoretically possible to play a "perfect game" of *Octodad: Dadliest Catch* and to have such adept control over the character that his ambulation is indistinguishable from that of a normal human, accomplishing all tasks perfectly and efficiently. But this is not the experience that the developers want players to have. In this case, the flawed, imperfect play of individual players is more "true" to the story they wish to tell and the characterization of the character than the theoretical "ideal" playthrough.

Though *Octodad: Dadliest Catch* is pitched as a slapstick comedy of errors, it is not an outlier with regard to player-driven characterization. Characters are often differentiated by how they "feel" to control, even if the specific actions that they perform can be described similarly: slow and heavy vs. fast and light, and any number of other possible descriptors. Through "ideal" play, many of these differences can be minimized or ignored completely, but developers want players to feel these differences. These differences guide play, encouraging natural characterization through performance.

UNCHARTED 4: A Thief's End (2016) is a globe-hopping action game starring plucky treasure hunter and historian Nathan Drake and his rotating band of adventuring comrades. The game cycles between third-person shooter gunfights against rival treasure-hunting bands, navigation/platforming segments that typically involve crossing degraded terrains or scaling ancient buildings, and action set-piece segments, such as escaping a crumbling building or engaging in a high-speed car chase through a city. Throughout the game, combat encounters are typically two-phase battles. In the first phase, Nathan Drake is undetected by enemies. As long as he stays out of sight, either by creeping through long grass or hiding behind low walls, he can freely move around the battlefield, surveilling the area and even quietly killing a few enemies unnoticed. In the second phase of the battle, the enemies are aware of Drake's presence, and a fast-paced gun battle breaks out. Drake is able to take cover behind low walls, rocks, and buildings, but he is encouraged to avoid being flanked and to get better angles on enemies.

On lower difficulty levels (as selected in the game's options menu), the quickest way to complete combat encounters is to "go in guns blazing", as they say. That is, to initiate phase two of the battle as soon as possible. Running at full speed between cover and shooting enemies from across the battlefield are fast and effective tactics, and Drake can take quite a few shots himself before dying and having to try again. Playing in this way characterizes Nathan Drake as an impulsive, improvisational action hero. On higher difficulty levels, Nathan Drake will die upon taking one or two bullets, encouraging more cautious play. In this case, players are heavily incentivized to make use of phase one of the battle condition: stealth. While Drake remains undetected, he is relatively safe from harm, so the more enemies he is able to dispatch during this first phase of the battle, the fewer he will have to defeat during the phase in which he is more vulnerable. Nathan Drake played in this manner can be described as cautious, sly, and resourceful, and the eventual breakout of phase two gun battles may be seen as desperate fights for survival rather than the super-soldier-adjacent liberty with which players on low difficulties may play, emboldened by their abundance of vitality. By adjusting one parameter (Nathan Drake's health; his ability to withstand gunfire before dying), players are encouraged to play the game in different ways. An "ideal" player could play in either mindset regardless of the difficulty level, but there is value in this diversity of player experiences prompted by the imperfections in their play.

These examples lead us to the conclusion that a game's narrative storytelling is not "most true" in instantiations that feature ideal play. In fact, ideal play may lose some of the in-built texture intended to be animated by challenge and personal flourishes. Video games are designed to be experienced with widely variable results. We should not privilege the ideal playthrough as the "canonical" telling of stories over individualized manifest content. In the same way that the tellers of folklore will embellish their stories with each telling, the truth of a video game's story does not come from how closely it adheres to a particular style of play. Rather, all playthroughs, like tellings of folktales, contribute to the grander meta-narrative, a collective of experiences.

Possible Content

While the instantiated happenings of individual play result in the manifest content of that particular playthrough, we recognize that there are potentially infinite other possible instantiations that were not enacted, latent within the story volume. And while consideration of a single playthrough or play experience must privilege the manifest content of that particular playthrough (with regard to critical reflection of the single playthrough as a narrative artifact), we recognize that the unrealized or differently ordered happenings we may have enacted had player choices, player performance, or systemic actions transpired differently are "untrue" of our particular enacted narrative but equally valid as systemic outputs. All non-instantiated, alternate occurrences are classified as *possible content*, the content that exists within the possibility space.

While the manifest content is (aggregated across the playthrough) singular, possible content is always expansively plural. It includes not only the alternate paths that could have been taken at major story branches but also the minuscule, moment-to-moment actions that differentiate play (whether the player causes Mario to jump 30 or 35 frames after hitting a platform leads to a difference in instantiated happenings, even if it is unnoticeably small).

The consideration of potential content serves two primary purposes. First, it is necessary to recognize the validity of divergent instantiations when discussing or comparing playthroughs. Returning to a previous example, if a player says of their *Super Mario Bros.* (1985) playthrough that "Mario defeated Bowser on his first attempt", it would be unproductive to assert that "no, this did not happen. Canonically, it took Mario four attempts to defeat Bowser. I saw it myself in my own playthrough". Presuming the other player was, indeed, telling the truth about her own playthrough, I must recognize both series of events as being equally valid products of *Super Mario Bros.* as a system of narrative production while retaining that each is specifically and exclusively true of our own playthroughs as individual narrative artifacts. This is not a call to unbounded open-mindedness in the evaluation of other players' gameplay accounts, though. Had the other player claimed to have defeated Bowser on her first attempt because "Mario ran him over with a car", that story does not reflect a valid potential outcome because there is no car in that game. Possible content does not mean "anything-is-possible" content; rather, that which is possible may occur.

It is the potential content in aggregate that forms the "shape" of the possibility space described earlier, from which design and narrative intention can theoretically be read. This is most often a hypothetical exercise, as it is most often impossible to accurately discern and consider the consequences of every possible gameplay occurrence. If we consider a very simple example, though, we can imagine a text adventure game that gives players the choice, at a fork in the road, of going west or going east. Going west moves the player character into a town in which she may meet a large number of NPCs and partake in a variety of quests, while going east marches the character off of a cliff where she immediately plummets to her death. If we consider the shape of a decision tree outlining this series of events, we notice that the westward direction balloons out to a great volume of potential adventures while the eastward choice terminates immediately. Reading the "shape" of the designed experience, it can be assumed that the westward choice reflects a narratively or experientially "preferred" action within the designed space.

This is an extremely simple example that likely doesn't reflect anything worthy of serious consideration with regard to the characterization, narrative, or ideology of the game, but similar principles apply to more complex situations as well. Consider the complex and multifaceted simulation of the stealth assassin game *HITMAN* (2016). A particular mission may task avatar Agent 47 with assassinating a particular person, but the method in which this assassination is accomplished is quite open-ended. The player may choose to load up on high-caliber firearms and immediately rush into the target's guarded compound, "guns blazing", as it were. The game allows but disincentivizes this approach by systemically weighing against it. Targets' compounds are awash with armed guards and security cameras, and Agent 47 cannot sustain much gunfire before collapsing (this is not said as a criticism; neither can I). Because of the danger of these locations and the frailty of the avatar, the number of successful potential branches following from this approach is relatively low, compared to the greater number of choices and chances for success available to players who engage with the game's stealth and deception mechanics to sneakily accomplish their goal.

Though the game allows multiple potential narratives to unfold, its systems are weighted to "prefer" certain types of stories, particularly those that characterize Agent 47 as a patient, professional, clever, and sneaky assassin rather than an impulsive maniac. Though all resulting instantiated narratives are valid applications of the game as a reactive system of narrative creation, developers' intent becomes more apparent when considering, as completely as possible, the multiplicity of possible systemic outworkings. From that perspective, we can observe the ways in which systemic factors nudge players toward particular types of actions, and we can hypothesize that, across all players' playthroughs, incentivized forms of play are more common than aberrant play, and we can expect most gameplay enactments to reflect aspects of this "essential" characterization.

This is how systemic stories are ultimately told. As Salen and Zimmerman (2003, p. 67) were quoted saying earlier in this chapter, narrative design in games is indirect, second-order. In encoding a system that animates a virtual world, they choose the conditions by which stories are generated. In supposing a world with particular variables, specific forms of play are incentivized and rewarded over others. However, they may leave open unanticipated synergies or affordances that undercut or bewilder intended meaning, at which point that meaning becomes interpretively valid. Players can almost always choose to "perform" their avatar characters "against" type, and these outcomes must be narratively respected, though such aberrant play will occupy the peripheries of the game's collective legacy. But the individual player's responsibility is to base her interpretations and characterizations on that which she observes from her instantiated play.

A community of players all *guessing* about what constitutes the "center" of a game's possibility space produces useless data about the expressive possibilities of a game system. It is only through collective accounts of individualized play that we can explore all that a game can mean holistically.

Glitches and the Possibility Space

Earlier, I alluded to a playthrough of *The Legend of Zelda: Ocarina of Time* (1998) that exploits a glitch to travel to a late portion of the game from an early point. This series of events produces a linear narrative artifact like any other method of play, though what it produces is of questionable narrative coherence. This represents an intentional exploitation of a technical unintended affordance. More commonly, players experience glitches unintentionally, being caught by surprise when their characters fall through the virtual world into the infinite emptiness below or get caught in the intersection between 3D objects trying to occupy the same space. Is it valid to say that "*Ocarina of Time* is about a warrior on a grand adventure who occasionally falls through the earth"?

We will examine this topic in much greater detail in Chapter 13, but to briefly touch upon the points relevant to this exploration, glitches and exploits are components of a playthrough's manifest content. Intentionally triggered or unintentionally encountered, these experiences will certainly impact a player's journey through a game. They represent expressions of the technical affordances of the system of narrative generation.

The representational game world does not exist (in the *Ocarina of Time* example, the magical land of Hyrule), but in another sense, the simulated game world *does* exist, as it is bounded by laws and variables that contain and constrain the actions that the player may take within it (Jesper Juul explores this dichotomy in much greater detail in the seminal *Half-Real* [2005]). It is governed by a series of coded mechanics and systems and even real-world physical laws (such as disc-read speed and memory limitations). Just as the constant of gravity applies to our world, mathematical parameters govern interaction between objects within the simulation, and those parameters can also be known.

In a sense, the game character exists in two worlds at once: the world of fiction (Hyrule) and the world of simulation (the game engine). This is represented in the layered literacy model that this book proposes: the mimetic perspective of play concerns the fantasy, and the diegetic and methectic perspectives concern the simulation. The world of fiction is an illusion brought about by the continuity of object behaviors and artistry, and we can only act upon the world of fiction through the avatar (player-controlled character or non-character presence such as a mouse cursor).

The game engine can be acted upon by both the actions in the fictional world and the real world. Choices made in accordance with the fictional world's narratives and laws feed back into the simulation, as do real-world occurrences, such as hard-drive failure or power surges. Philosophically speaking, this is not dissimilar to how we live concurrently in both physical and social worlds. We are primarily governed by laws of physics and biology, yet we organize ourselves within socially constructed systems to which we ascribe narrative value. Going to university and achieving a degree and having that degree honored in a workplace as a mark of qualification for a particular type of labor is a series of actions firmly rooted in bestowed meaning; consistent only in the minds and imaginations of humanity as a collective, but disconnected from any physical or biological truth that governs our existence at a more fundamental level. Yet these realities also interact; misbehaving by the standards of socially constructed laws can limit or even end our biological lives, and no amount of social-philosophizing will ultimately allow us to overcome a force of nature like a tsunami or meteor strike.

All that is to say, when playing a video game, we are ultimately controlling an avatar within the simulation, and the simulation's laws supersede those of the fictional world's. If a fictional door requires a key to unlock, yet the simulation can be exploited to bypass the key requirement, the door does not *actually* require the key. Mastering the code (methexis) is as valid a way to play a game as mastering the fiction. Likewise, falling victim to glitches in the code can be as disruptive as falling victim to designed obstacles within the fiction.

As noted previously, artistic interpretation is a reparative process. Artistic stimuli (the work of art itself) is delivered to us devoid of objective meaning. Though its images and words may communicate a coherent message, the aim of art is to evoke a second-order reaction, an intangible state, concept, emotion, or sense memory that cannot be directly communicated; it can only be indirectly activated through the interaction of the stimulus and our facilities of mental processing: memories, imagination, associations, values, involuntary responses, etc. In that sense, the artistic stimuli arrive incomplete. It only becomes "art" in its processing through this mental machine. The artistic stimuli do not "contain" this information in its presented form. As such, we apply meaning to the art as it is experienced, not how it is conceptualized. A statue damaged with time, less an arm from when it was carved, will forevermore be processed by those who view it differently than was intended, but it is not necessarily less evocative. In many cases, degraded art can be more evocative than the object in perfect repair, as evidenced by the complex feelings and intrigue evoked by abandoned and degraded theme park equipment or buildings. Similarly, glitches in video games, though incongruent with the established fiction, are true of the simulation and ultimately true of the observed artistic stimulus.

On the action-oriented level of processing our experiential narrative, glitches and exploits are additive (not always positive—often subjectively frustrating—but additive to the amount and breadth of events that occur in the course of a playthrough). On the fiction-oriented level of processing the semiotic narrative, though, glitches and exploits can be destructive. As we immerse ourselves in the fiction and form empathetic and projective bonds with characters, glitches can serve as a sudden reminder of the unreality of the world (what I call *ontological upset* in Chapter 2).

As explored in Chapter 4, players often mentally inhabit their characters through a process called projective embodiment. The reality of holding a controller and viewing a collection of moving pixels on a screen lessens. We stop visualizing the chain of commands and responses (my brain desires an action, I remember which button performs that action, my finger presses that button, the controller transmits that command to the computer, the computer registers the command and enacts it within the simulation, visual feedback is presented on-screen), and soon our impulses are seen as being enacted directly in the character, in the same way that the mechanism of a bicycle disappears once we become comfortable riding it. In this act of transparency, we view the avatar (player character) as an extension of our "self", the tool through which we can explore and act upon the simulated world. We naturally slip into first-person descriptors when describing gameplay: "I jumped on the Koopa. The Piranha Plant bit me".

When a projective link has been formed, a glitch can be momentarily frightening. It can rudely eject the player from the world into which she was immersed. Even when not projecting onto a character, the interruption of a well-crafted story by a glitch can be frustrating. At best, it is a momentary distraction from the storytelling. At worst, it can break the simulation so completely that the story is permanently unable to resume. Even after the corruption of a glitch has passed, the sense memory lingers in the player's mind, expectant of further glitches, particularly if the experienced glitch was destructive to gameplay flow or progress. Like seeing one cockroach in a hotel room, the player is awakened to the possibility that more will follow, coloring her perception of the gameplay experience and story in a way that is difficult to ever fully recover.

In these ways, glitches can be simultaneously additive and destructive to the different levels in which a game is observed and played. Experientially, glitches can cause some of the most memorable occurrences in a playthrough as the logic of the simulated world breaks for a moment. Like anything sufficiently unexpected, glitches can make for great moments of comedy or even awe. They risk breaking immersion and connection to the written story and its world, though. Video game fans often angrily insist that glitches spoil a game. They make evident the artifice and make the game feel cheap, unfinished, or amateurish. Once harmless and aesthetic glitches are fixed via software patches, another group of players (with, I suspect, some overlap with the first group) decries the effort, claiming that the ridding of bugs represents a regression toward the expected, removing some of the mystery, unpredictability, and comedy inherent in the virtual. They claim that the game has lost some of its unique personality; defining characteristics that, like a poorly considered tattoo on a friend, end up being more endearing than destructive. A common adage of "don't fix the good glitches" is often heard. These players recognize that art does not have to be intentional to be meaningful. Finding meaning in the outgrowths of oversights can often feel more personal and generative. Glitches abide by the simulation's code, exactly the same as the intended content, but their unintentionality and unknowable spirit give them the feeling of being natural, like mold growing on old food. In that sense, glitches are almost like nature reclaiming the simulation, as it does the abandoned and degraded theme park ride.

While encountering glitches usually has the connotation of unexpected or unwanted outcomes, triggering exploits has the connotation of intentionality. There is most often overlap between these two categories. Engaging an exploit is the intentional use of a glitch or oversight in game logic to provide unsanctioned early or easier access to a reward or objective. Though often thought of as poor sportsmanship in competitive settings (unless the exploit is known and adopted as a "house rule", a part of the metagame), the use of exploits can be quite constructive in the context of a single-player game, often leading to unsanctioned, player-defined objectives, such as speedrunning (trying to beat a game or level as quickly as possible, typically achieved by utilizing exploits and careful pathing to engage the minimum number of traditional challenges possible to complete the objective; see Chapter 13).

Again, the written narrative of games is a fantasy, an illusion. The characters do not truly obey the laws of the fantasy world; they obey the laws of the simulation. Goals set within the game are communicated to the player in terms of the fantasy, but they are actually goals of the simulation, unbound to the fantasy and its parameters. The player can break the laws of the fantasy to complete the objectives of the simulation, but she cannot break the laws of the simulation to complete the objectives of the fantasy (if we consider glitches and exploits to be within the strictest definition of "laws" of the simulation).

Breaking the Artifice

In terms of narrative meaning-making, exploits can be damaging to the written story but additive to the experiential narrative. If the manifest content is taken as the gospel happenings of the story, a character performing impossible actions (seemingly intentionally) can create a confusing discontinuity. The character either has a godlike ability that is otherwise never utilized, or this break in the rules of the fiction reveals the artifice of the simulation. Yet, from an experiential perspective, exploits present some of the greatest moments of creative, methectic, and expressive problem-solving in video games.

Though games vary in the amount of creativity they afford players in achieving goals (see Chapter 12 on the subject of expressivity), most creativity is sanctioned within the boundaries of developer intent. The player may choose the weapon that she uses to clear out a room of enemies, but the verbs that she chooses between are all sanctioned, planned, and tested by the developers. Utilizing exploits is truly generative. It creates additional possible solutions that are not intended and sanctioned by the developers. It is providing an answer to a question that had not been previously considered, shifting the paradigm of the question. When utilizing an exploit, the player blazes her own path, abandoning not only the expectations and parameters of the developer but also their promise of safety.

For, though players can fail within video games, failing in expected and sanctioned ways results in a "safe" failure: an opportunity to retry the challenge or journey elsewhere. When operating outside of the "graces of the gods", though, it is possible to experience utter failure—the avatar can get stuck in a place from which she cannot return, like halfway through a wall or in a void out of boundaries. The player can "soft lock" or "hard lock" the game (entering into an unwinnable state or a software freeze/crash, respectively). Consequences are rarely that dire, but the player knows that there is a gamble when she pushes outside of the established boundaries. This gamble may discourage some players from seeking out useful glitches, but for others, the risk is what makes it exciting and rewarding.

Ultimately, players who utilize exploits play a slightly (or significantly) different metagame from those who play as intended. The central question shifts from "what am I supposed to do?" to "what can I do?". Instead of seeking the next signpost in the trail through the game, players go off-trail, looking for corners that can be cut. And like going off-trail in real-world hiking, alternate social trails form. When hiking along designated trails, hikers will often see small paths of dirt linking stretches of trail, cutting corners on switchbacks, or leading to points of interest. These social trails are formed when enough people go off-trail in the same location, stepping on the same plants and soil every time until, eventually, packed dirt is all that remains, often to the disapproval of those who actually maintain the trails and care for the well-being of the forests. Like these social trails, exploits often form metagames in communities across the world.

Speedrunners will gather and share videos of their best times, challenging themselves to shave mere milliseconds off of record-holders' times. They share strategies, routes, and knowledge of these exploits until these exploits—naughty glitches when first encountered—become codified, cataloged, named, and normalized; recognized not by the developers of the games, but known and even regulated by unofficial communities. In this sense, even highly structured games can become platforms for unstructured or structured play to emerge.

Speedrunners, along with other communities that compete to play games "incorrectly" or by unsanctioned means (such as breaking sequence), play a separate metagame with separate rules within the space of the games they exploit. Speedrunning *Super Mario 64* (1996) is fundamentally different from playing *Super Mario 64* in the intended method. Speedrunners encounter most of the same locations, objects, and characters on their journey, but incentives, goals, and even available verbs are different from typical players' experiences. This is generative play. It extends the life and usefulness of games, and it empowers players with the kind of creative freedom typically reserved for game developers.

How does this kind of intentional breaking of the artifice square with games' narrative coherence? If we can ascertain the "shape" of a story by taking account of the affordances players are given, does this reckoning also take into account unintended affordances? The artistry of games is the shaping and presentation of novel agencies (Nguyen, 2020), and there is no more true and beautiful expression of the adoption of a novel agency than the use of a system's capabilities to extend beyond that which is intended. As players are a part of the game's system of meaningful generation, this is akin to *evolution* within the system of artistic production. Embedded narrative is context for experiential play, but embedded narrative coherence should never be used to limit the systemic capabilities of emergent experience.

CHARACTERIZATION

The interactive nature of video games provides a unique challenge when it comes to reading and understanding the characterization of player-controlled characters. As previously discussed, the manifest content of a playthrough should be treated as the "truth" of that particular telling of the story. It may not be "true" of other players' experiences, just as two tellers of a folk story may include different or contradictory details to describe the same event. The point is not to arrive at accurately conveyed information; rather, the intention is to engage in fiction that is reactive to the teller and receiver and that perhaps communicates a deeper truth in its accumulated multiplicity.

In previous sections, we used *The Legend of Zelda: Ocarina of Time* (1998) as an illustrative example. That game can be played in any number of ways—deftly, clumsily, slowly, maliciously, in a manner that takes advantage of known exploits—and all of these manners affect the way that Link, the player's avatar, is characterized.

Shared Custody

Much of the time, developers have a disproportionate amount of influence, compared to players, regarding how characters (even the controllable avatar character) are characterized. In most cases, developers determine characters' appearances, abilities, voice performances, actions taken during cutscenes, backstory, etc. These often enforce such a rigid construction of the character that divergent actions taken during gameplay sections do not feel like player expression and interpretation as much as they feel like active rebellion against what seems to be a very specific vision for the character's identity. Rigidly and holistically constructed characters can impress such a "closed loop" of characterization that player choices and actions can feel non-canonical, like a child playing with action figures in between the episodes of her favorite TV show—that which happens during the scripted show represents the actual course of events for those characters while the unsupervised play is frivolous make-believe. In such cases, one would presume that we should learn who a character is during scripted cutscenes or dialogue and ignore incongruent data witnessed during gameplay.

A famous example of this comes from the crime drama *Grand Theft Auto IV* (2008). Protagonist Niko Bellic is an Eastern European ex-soldier, retreating from a lifetime of war and criminality, looking for a new life in America. He moves to Liberty City, the series' equivalent of New York City, to pursue the American dream, though he finds that, for a man like himself, that dream is an unreachable fantasy, and he falls back into systems of criminality to survive. In cutscenes, he is portrayed as being reluctant to reoffend—that is the life from which he was fleeing. He is a competent criminal, but he knows that his position as a recent immigrant is tenuous, and he would prefer to keep his head down and make an honest living. Yet *Grand Theft Auto IV* is a game that empowers players with the means and rewards for causing chaos during gameplay. Player-available verbs are primarily violent; guns and ammunition are readily given to the player, and the game's city simulation is built to react to chaos in amusing and exciting ways. Driving dangerously through the crowded streets is thrilling; civilians are irritable and will start fistfights with very little provocation; performing illegal actions alerts police, and police chases are some of the most exciting moments of gameplay. Mechanical affordances and rewards incentivize a style of play that seems to contradict the embedded narrative goals, such that we can hypothesize that the violent and chaotic action sits toward the center of the story volume; its most natural and common course of play. Players are likely to play Niko in ways that contradict his expressed motivations during cutscenes, and this gives him a dissonant characterization.

The described dissonance is not between the character-as-written and head-canon (characterization as imagined by the player but not supported by textual evidence). It is not frustration that players cannot act out every whim and utterly transform the character into whomever they wish the characters to be. The dissonance arises from being allowed the ability to contribute to characterization through actions during gameplay in ways that are ignored or contradicted in cutscenes and dialogue. As stated before, these actions are a part of the manifest content—the data of a playthrough as a resulting linear narrative.

Gameplay actions are sometimes treated as if they are of secondary canonicity to the actions that take place during cutscenes, as if cutscenes and dialogue are historical artifacts that ground the story while the gameplay is an interpretation of what may have happened between these canonically true moments. This interpretation is reinforced by the often repetitive nature of gameplay. Surely, the character did not die at this point in her adventure, much less multiple times. Deaths and restarts are often intrinsically viewed as an incorrect telling of a story, and the successful run could be understood as the only one to have canonically occurred. Some games even make a joke out of this, like *Prince of Persia: The Sands of Time* (2003) and *Monkey Island 2: LeChuck's Revenge* (1991). Both games feature framing devices in which their protagonists recount their stories to companions at a point in the future, so deaths are met with a comical "Oh no, that can't be right. That's not what happened". Regardless, the idea that a death in these fictional worlds is the equivalent of a death in the real world—a singular event that ends an individual's experience of life—is questionable, as we cannot assume that fictional worlds must adhere to the rules of our own. Clever games have found ways of integrating the cycle of dying and retrying into their canonical storytelling (*Dark Souls* [2011], *BioShock* [2007]). Ultimately, whether figurative gameplay actions (including deaths as well as play choices) are acknowledged or excluded from a game's embedded narrative, they remain important within the experiential narrative of the player. The avatar character is made the center of conflict when the two narratives are at tension with one another, leading to the described difficulty in their characterization.

If playing as a character (and, thus, bestowing characterization through actions performed) is like performing a theatrical role, watching a cutscene that differently characterizes the character would be like watching an understudy fill in for a role at random points during a performance and make wildly different choices than the primary actor would have. A strong dissonance between written and performed characterization can be frustrating and disempowering. It is common to have performed optimally during gameplay only to have an obstacle that could have been easily conquered ultimately stall the protagonist's progress when control is taken away due to plot necessity. It is all too common to play through scenes in which the protagonist fights through dozens of enemies, only to be ambushed during a cutscene by five or six at once, causing the protagonist to surrender (a plot-necessary diversion but one frustrating to players who just defeated a multitude more enemies at once within the same scene). The player can feel excluded from the storytelling process when a character behaves rudely during scripted interactions when the player had extensively tried to be chivalrous during gameplay.

This dissonance is a result of the shared custody of the co-authored story. A certain amount of storytelling friction between the player and the elements of fantasy should be expected. The sign of a good storytelling system is not *absolute obedience* to the whim of the player. Most stories require conflict, and conflict requires resistance to a desired result. But a circumstantial or environmental resistance is different from an intre-personal resistance in the avatar's characterization. To the degree that the avatar is the instrumental tool for the expression of player agency within the game world, a level of transparency is beneficial to enable the projection past the layers of mediation (see Chapter 4). But it is still reasonable for a game's developers to wish to tell a story about a specific kind of character and to bestow certain characteristics—heroism, pluckiness, wryness, and fear. But characteristic choices like this must be communicated not only through the semiotic layer of embedded storytelling; they must also be supported through enactment, either by inspiring similar feelings in the player, such that her performance naturally mirrors that of the protagonist, or by limiting or incentivizing a subsection of the verbs of play available to the player.

Horror games typically do a good job of inspiring emotional congruence between players and avatar characters' narrative representation. Horror games typically feature protagonists under-equipped to manage the threats that they encounter (disempowerment) with high stakes upon failure (usually the loss of more progress than other genres, often with save points that require the expenditure of limited resources, so players are disincentivized from casting too generous of a safety net for themselves). Jump scares (the technique of startling a player or viewer with a sudden loud noise or upsetting visual) are also an example of *non-representational stimuli* in art; they act upon the audience separate from the layer of fictionality and representation in the exact same manner as similar stimuli would in a real situation. So while a zombie in *Resident Evil* (1996) may be a mortal threat to the diegetic avatar and only a threat to lost time and expended effort for the player, the precognitive startle response of an unexpected zombie jumping out from the shadows is the same between the player and (personified) avatar, encouraging congruence of performance (panicking and acting impulsively, perhaps).

Horror-themed cinematic adventure game *Until Dawn* (2015) makes the most of this performance congruence principle by featuring sections in which the player must hold the controller still (determined by the controller's inbuilt motion sensor) so as to stay quiet and not draw the attention of a killer in the room (an example of *autonomic control* outlined in Chapter 4). This challenges the same physical and emotional impulses that the character must suppress diegetically, creating a congruent experience of characterization.

Other games limit the actions afforded to the player to only those that are congruent with the avatar's characterization. This is where the *Grand Theft Auto IV* (2008) example above falters. Fighting games (such as *GUILTY GEAR -STRIVE-* [2021] and *TEKKEN 8* [2024]) and stylish character action games (such as *Bayonetta* [2009] and *Devil May Cry 5* [2019]) particularly excel at this. Kratos, from the character action game *God of War* (2005), is angry and impulsive, a wave of destruction willing to cut down anyone and anything in his way to achieving revenge upon the Greek gods, has a verb set of wide, sweeping attacks, as he swings his mythical blades attached to chains wildly at anything that moves. His powerful swings tear through pottery, bits of ruined building, and bystanders during combat. Kratos does not attack individual enemies; he obliterates everything in their immediate area. This can be contrasted to his later characterization in the series revival *God of War* (2018), in which his temper has cooled, and he is instead looking to live undisturbed with his son. His new primary weapon is an axe—a practical instrument that is deadliest at close quarters and in slower, more methodical one-on-one fights against enemies. He has matured past leaving mass destruction in his wake, choosing instead to more thoughtfully overcome individual roadblocks head-on. The change in his characterization is instinctively felt and acted out by players due to the actions afforded in each scenario.

Silent Protagonists

Another way to address the dissonance between play and narrative characterization is to minimize the details of an avatar's embedded characterization. Often, characters are presented as blank slates or silent protagonists. This is the developers ceding characterization influence almost entirely to the player. Gordon Freeman from the first-person shooter *Half-Life* (1996) is a classic example. A theoretical physicist, Freeman accidentally opens a portal to an alien dimension during a test in a giant, underground science research hub. Dangerous aliens escape this rift and terrorize the station and, in the numbered sequel, the world. Throughout the series, Freeman doesn't speak, even when directly addressed by other characters. Characters speak to and about him, hailing him as a kind of hero and "last hope for humanity" in *Half-Life 2* (2004), especially, encouraging players to assimilate other characters' perceptions of Freeman as a hero into their conceptualization of the character, but even this is presented as a legend that has grown disproportionately over time within the context of the story, so it still leaves the door open for Freeman to be played in different ways.

The implication of the silent protagonist is that she is a vessel for the player's feelings, reactions, thoughts, and curiosities. That which the player feels is what the character feels. Since Gordon Freeman does not outwardly react to the events that happen around him, the player projects onto the character and fills in the blanks with her own presumptions. Blank slate/silent protagonist characters assist with projective embodiment (the player immersing herself into the perspective of the character as an extension of her own "self", as opposed to giving orders to someone fundamentally separate; see Chapter 4) by offering little resistance and minimizing moments of disagreement between the player's thoughts and the character's actions.

Writing a silent protagonist clears the path for projective embodiment, but it leads to a number of smaller problems. Considering only the manifest content of the game, silent protagonists often appear uninvested in the worlds they inhabit. Characters will speak to them and often directly ask them questions, and there is a feeling of social discomfort and narrative contrivance that the silent protagonist will not respond or explain important information that they have witnessed. Silent protagonists will often appear cold or uninterested, not extending gestures of comfort to friends during hardship and not reacting in believable ways to life-threatening situations. This is because, if it is true that silent protagonists are vessels for the player's cognitions, then the essence of their being truly does not exist in the same world that they inhabit. They are split beings with bodies in the virtual space but minds in a super-reality (our own). As such, they cannot be fully present in their worlds.

Danger in the virtual world is not actual danger to the player, so the reactions of the player are not pitched at the level to which we would expect characters to react under the plot's circumstances. This problem is not unique to video games; other role-playing mediums, such as stage acting and tabletop games, require participation from performers who cannot fully experience and embody the stakes of the fictional characters that they portray, but while a stage actor can, through empathy, access some of those primal emotions necessary to communicate fear of dying (for example) with an understanding that the character fears death to the same degree as the actor, such empathy is more difficult when performing roles in video games. In many games, death is a common occurrence—the *de facto* failure state that prompts a retry—so it becomes mundane. The silent protagonist cannot be adequately embodied because she knows (via the player's mind that embodies her) the artifice of the world. Death is non-permanent; progress follows a predetermined path; there is little fear of injury or impediment. The player-avatar unit is motivated by excitement in engaging with the game systems or curiosity for the remaining narrative. Though curiosity is enough to prompt a reader to continue reading a book, it is not a strong enough stake to facilitate a thoroughly convincing presence and performance.

Silent protagonists will often be paired with companion characters who will speak, emote, and experience the stakes of the story on the avatar's behalf. *Half-Life 2* (2004) pairs Gordon Freeman with the expressive and fully characterized Alyx Vance, and the *Legend of Zelda* series (1986-present) typically pairs mute protagonist Link with a different companion in each game (Navi, Ezlo, Midna, Fi...). This offsets (or perhaps distracts from) the awkwardness of the avatar not behaving in believable ways, such as not responding when directly addressed.

Deterministic Characterization

With infinite capacity for choice at any moment, players could theoretically make the characters under their control express any number of personal characteristics. Player choice is never infinite, though; there are boundaries either by developer choice or necessity. The inability to perform certain actions limits players' choices for characterization. Though I can make Link in *Ocarina of Time* (1998) behave quite erratically, I cannot make him pickpocket or murder civilians. Even if I desired to characterize him as a criminal, there are certain actions that Link cannot perform, thus extents of that particular characterization that cannot be achieved. Link cannot become a serial killer. That choice is not left open to players. Mario cannot become a walnut farmer or stand-up comedian in *Super Mario 64* (1996). The text simply does not recognize those as available outcomes. Conversely, it is impossible to complete *Ocarina of Time* or *Super Mario 64* without engaging in a violent confrontation against each game's respective antagonist. Besides the player's ability to stop playing at any time, there is no way for Mario or Link to be fully pacifist in the resolution of their goals.

Even within the realm of available actions, though, developers can lead characters toward desired characterizations by tuning character abilities in ways that create natural paths-of-least-resistance toward desired outcomes. This is equivalent to what philosophers call *soft determinism*: one is not locked into a singular sequence of unchangeable actions, but certain conditions and predispositions make specific actions predictably more likely. For example, someone living in New Orleans is not any more innately suited to liking jazz music than someone living in Anchorage, but the availability and plentitude of jazz performers in New Orleans compared to those in Anchorage may make a New Orleans resident more likely to develop an affinity over time.

Well-designed characters are tuned to best represent their intended characterizations and differentiate them from other characters. Bayonetta, the titular character from the *Bayonetta* (2009) series of character action games, engages enemies in stylish hand-to-hand combat, but her defining ability is being able to magically slow time when she dodges an enemy attack at the last moment, encouraging players to play in a risky manner for access to her most powerful attacks, reinforcing her characterization as a fearless battler who is always in control of the situation, and perhaps one that likes to flirt with danger and humiliate enemies who feel like they have gotten the upper hand in battle with last-second reversals.

To contrast, *Red Dead Redemption 2* (2018), an Old West-themed, open-world action drama, stars aging member of a cowboy criminal gang, Arthur Morgan. While a proficient marksman when in gunfights, his movement and actions are effortful and slow. His years of hard living are slowly catching up to him. While Bayonetta controls in a way that is empowering to the player and graceful to spectators, Arthur Morgan is somewhat disempowering, reflecting not only his failing health but also his declining relevance within a post-frontier society. Bayonetta can be played in a slow, meticulous manner, and Arthur Morgan can be played recklessly, but their mechanical balances—their strengths and weaknesses—discourage incongruent play, meaning that players are more likely to experience the characters in a thematically resonant way while not strictly prohibiting alternative performances.

Other games outright disallow actions that interfere with intended characterization. Many protagonists of first-person shooters can fire their guns indiscriminately but will respectfully lower their guns when pointing at allies, disallowing friendly fire. Beyond fostering a good team dynamic between allies, this saves developers from having to script alternate scenarios of characters reacting to unexpected ally murder or writing paths through the rest of the game without key characters. Perhaps a more interesting example is found in the early *Assassin's Creed* (2007) games, stealth games set during various pivotal moments in human history in which the player controls one of an order of assassins. In the games' narrative, these historical assassins are accessed through a futuristic technology that uses a kind of genetic memory to look back through a person's lineage and allow her to virtually inhabit the perspective of one of her ancestors. Killing civilians causes the simulation to "desynchronize" (the equivalent of a game over), as the honorable assassin did not perform this action in the historical record that the genetic memory accesses. In practice, it justifies adherence to character-harmonious actions by narratively demanding documentary-like play while not constraining real-time control.

Permissive Characterization

Some games permissively allow and affirm any and all readings of a character through flexible systems or narratives. In some cases, such as in *Fable II* (2008), dozens of gameplay actions are invisibly tracked, feeding into a characterization engine that results in many possible "alignments", reflected in physical changes to the avatar, narrative changes, as well as differences in the way that other characters address the avatar. The game has multiple independent measures of character traits, informed by gameplay actions and narrative choices: good/evil (morality, affecting the world around the avatar), purity/corruption (morality, affecting the avatar), funny/scary (how inviting or intimidating the avatar behaves), attractive/ugly (physical appearance, affected by clothing, hairstyle, makeup, etc., relative to the tastes of each NPC), etc. The system is robust enough to feel responsive to the manners in which each player performs a diverse series of actions throughout the game. It cleverly tracks both global and personal measures, meaning that behaving uncharacteristically poorly toward one NPC will impact their opinion of you, while the rest of the world's characters will not have the knowledge of this interaction, and its global effect will be relatively minor (only contributing to a cumulative measure), and actions that might be disagreeable to one faction might be celebrated by another.

A less mechanically ambitious way of being permissive in player-initiated characterization is to write a game or a character so broadly or chaotically that any action a player can choose feels in alignment with their narrative representation. For example, the open-world gang crime farce *Saints Row: The Third* (2011) takes place in an over-the-top and cartoony caricature of a crime-ridden urban setting.

The player-created character, leader of the 3rd Street Saints gang, is empowered to enact all kinds of chaos. Being over-the-top caricatures themselves, the other characters of the game will talk to and about the avatar as an unpredictable loose cannon, never describing any specific personality trait. With such broad characterization, it is impossible for any gameplay action to fall outside of this wide target. In a form of soft determinism, as described above, the game provides players with high-powered and often quite silly weaponry and little ability to perform any action that does not lead to a violent or chaotic conclusion.

This kind of non-reactive permissiveness does not always mean that there is a lack of writing nuance, though. A different open-world crime game, *Sleeping Dogs* (2012), sees police officer Wei Shen go undercover in the criminal underworld of Hong Kong. Aiming to gain the trust of the gang members in these criminal organizations, Wei Shen must perform a number of dangerous and illegal actions, but he is disincentivized from endangering the public or incurring fatalities due to his role as an officer. While gameplay actions are tracked, increasing or decreasing his affinity with either faction, most narrative beats are written with the understanding that Wei Shen is juggling both peacekeeping and criminality as a part of his job. Any action that the player takes can be contextualized as a part of Wei Shen's personal and professional conflict. Regardless of what choices the player has yet made, characters on either side of the police/gang divide regard Wei Shen with cautious skepticism, ambiguous performances into which the player can read further and contextualize her own gameplay choices.

The Player-Avatar Being of Distributed Cognition

As described above, games have differing levels of characterization allowances, some deferential to player-guided choices and some deferential to developer-intended narrative crafting. When comparing experiences with other players, or even when just reflecting on one's own experience with a game, how does one answer the central narrative question of who a character is? It would not be accurate of a *Mass Effect* (2007) player to say, "Commander Shepard is a cool-headed negotiator always looking out for ways to de-escalate ethically challenging conflicts", because another player's experience of the game may lead her to find that Commander Shepard is instead a hot-tempered renegade who abides only by her own rules to do what she thinks is right for the galaxy. Equally, it is not quite accurate to say, "I, the player, am a cool-headed negotiator always looking for ways to de-escalate ethically-challenging conflicts", because there are elements of soft determinism built into the systems and mechanics of the game to guide Shepard's characterization; the characterization does not solely reflect the player. So if the avatar cannot be accurately described as being truly separate from the player nor a true reflection of the player's will, how should the character be understood?

Before answering that, it should be noted that other mediums of storytelling also involve participatory characterization. Though readers of a book and viewers of a film may not have direct influence over the manifest content of their respective stories, all good stories create moments of ambiguity that encourage projection and empathetic hypothesizing. When a character in a book or film shoots someone else a glance, the audience is not only seeking to determine what that glance means in that moment in time, but the audience also interjects their own feelings onto the situation, providing elements of characterization that may differ from other audience members' interpretations. Characters in stories are intended to be at times distinct, reflective, or unknowable. The way in which video games differ is that the player's interpretation guides action rather than resolving ambiguity. Or, framed differently, the actions of gameplay are the ambiguity into which players can reflect and empathetically hypothesize.

We can hypothesize that player-directed gameplay serves a similar purpose as narrative ambiguity in other mediums. It presents a precipice of multiple possibilities that the audience must expend effort to interpret. We must consider the value of multiple "interpretations" (i.e. gameplay choices) as additive rather than exclusive. In gameplay terms, this means that we should not judge gameplay actions on how closely they adhere to a singular "correct" play method (resolution of the ambiguity) but consider that all possible play methods can benefit from the knowledge and possibility of all others. A stealthy approach to *HITMAN* (2016), for instance, describes an aspect of avatar Agent 47's character, enhanced by the knowledge of alternate approaches (violent action, environmental puzzling, disguise utilization).

Though open-ended games that afford a great deal of player agency construct the complex and multi-faceted characterizations as described above, this does not mean that mastery-oriented games with relatively narrow ranges of player affordances are necessarily lesser in their characterization capacities. Remember that games concurrently convey separate written and experiential narratives. The written narrative is the story conveyed within the representational fiction, affected by story-pivotal choices, while the experiential narrative is the story of the player's actions, often not explicitly reflected in the written narrative.

For mastery-oriented games (such as games in the puzzle and rhythm genres), there are narrow allowances of possible actions that result in progression or successful completion, with all other actions (non-optimal play) resulting in failure and retrying (a narrative reset, so to speak). Even in these cases, the experiential narrative is still highly divergent. Though a puzzle in *Myst* (1993) may only have one solution, each player's method of reading and discerning the meaning of clues and arriving at the answer is an important aspect of the multitudinous experiential narratives. The player and in-game avatar share faculty with one another and are extensions of one another's being (the player thinks and motivates avatar actions, which the avatar is unable to do on her own, while the avatar performs actions within the virtual world and remembers self-oriented and world-oriented states, such as "at half health", "able to brew potions", or "holding a key", which the player is unable to directly perform). Therefore, the player's cognitive processing involved in the resolution of a puzzle is the equivalent of the avatar character arriving at an answer within the story. The performance of the player-avatar collective being, sharing the role of character within the story, holds narrative weight.

Game characters are neither entirely reflective of nor entirely separate from the player's performance. The relationship with the player is one of distributed cognition and volition (see Chapter 4). The avatar cannot act during gameplay without the cognitive presence of the player, and the player cannot act upon the game world except through the avatar. The player is the brain and the avatar the hands. Yet the avatar is often predisposed to act in ways which align with her intended narrative framing (deterministic characterization). It is incomplete to consider a character as written separate from details of player-motivated performance. Equally, the thrust of deterministic characterization will affect performance, so considering a character in terms of performed actions is not an anarchic framing of narrative, reflective only of player will. Performed actions are also allowed actions, after all (enforced by systems and mechanics). Yet, the performed actions of one playthrough should not be understood as the absolute, totalizing characterization of the avatar, as other possible (non-chosen) actions inform the chosen actions, creating a cumulative "shape" of the character's total possibility space and the holistic expression of the character. Each manifested choice and its unchosen opposite inform the characterization of the avatar (as someone who could have made either choice) but ultimately strengthen the chosen resolution of that instance of narrative ambiguity by the choice's resolution. Each moment-to-moment choice bears this narrative weight and accumulates to create individualized and valuable semiotic and experiential narratives.

To return to the reoccurring example throughout this chapter, Link in *The Legend of Zelda: Ocarina of Time* (1998) can be a great warrior, a clumsy but determined fighter, a troublemaker who throws pots at his neighbors, or a magician who exploits glitches in his world to circumvent the challenges and events of his own destined narrative. All are true but not equally likely possibilities. The reality in which Link is a skilled swordfighter depends upon the skill of the player in the cumulative player-avatar being of distributed cognition and volition, and his journey to becoming a great fighter is literalized in the player's learning and mastery of the gameplay systems. Even the glitch-exploiting playthrough is a true outcome of the total possibility space of the game. It requires a significantly greater threshold of player understanding and mastery, often requiring many hours of intentional practice to be able to execute glitches reliably, but it should not be discounted as a fundamentally incongruent reading of the story. It is allowed (by the systems and mechanics, even if not explicitly by the developers), and it requires a proportionate level of investment and mastery by the player-avatar being.

There is no immutable "truth" to an avatar to discover in a video game that excludes player performance. Examining the avatar apart from the player is examining a being without a brain, breaking a network of distributed cognition and volition. Examining the avatar character only as they appear and behave in cutscenes or marketing materials is not video game analysis and requires no video game literacy; that is cinematic or literary analysis (of incomplete artifacts). Video game analysis and, thus, video game literacy requires contending with the character as performed, additively, rather than viewing the player's performance as a corrupting factor that moves the character farther from a central "truth" with every mistake and error. In fact, each divergence embodies a greater proportion of total "truth".

The Amnesiac Protagonist

With the player taking on the role of the thoughtful mind in the collective being of distributed cognition, a problem presents. If the mind of the player *is* the mind of the avatar but the avatar, according to the narrative, existed previously and separately from the player's perspective and influence, how can the player adequately inhabit the experience of a member of that fictional world when that world is yet entirely unknown to the player? At the beginning of any *Pokémon* game (1996-present), for instance, the avatar, a child who is now old enough to venture into the world and have a monster-collecting adventure, wakes from her bed and walks downstairs to talk with her mother. The player does not know the mother; this is the player's first meeting with her, as it will be with all of the townsfolk in this opening village. The player quickly infers the relationship based on context and dialogue, but the player lacks any kind of history with the character or world.

Audiences are similarly unfamiliar with the contextual world-building information present in movies, books, and theatrical productions, requiring exposition to catch them up with the characters' histories, but these audiences do not bear the responsibility of embodied performance. They take a much more passive role in these other mediums. While a viewer can watch a film about a character who has and knows her own history, the character in a video game is performed and enacted with a fundamental absence of memory and contextual awareness that she, herself, *would* have. If the player is served literary exposition to catch her up with the history of a character, it widens the divide between player and character, striking a division between parts of the avatar's essential being (which is inclusive of the player as a cognitive and volitional function).

Some video games, like *God of War* (2005), present necessary aspects of world-building and the avatar's backstory in a cinematic video before the player is put in control of the character. Similarly, games in the CRPG genre like *Wasteland* (1988) and *Divinity: Original Sin* (2014) will present or allow players to choose from pre-written character backstories—brief flavor text that gives context without heavily altering gameplay from a mechanical perspective. Still, problems present when players do not know how to perform basic functions within the fictional world that the character presumably would have known. It leads to strange, fish-out-of-water storytelling to frame characters who ostensibly should have a history with this world, leading to adult characters being told how often they have to eat, how to operate everyday machines, and how to withdraw money from the bank.

For this reason, a significant number of video game protagonists are presented as having amnesia at the beginning of the story. This is a way to cleanly align the experiences of the player and character, so even if the character has history in the world, the character's experience (following their memory loss) is aligned with the player as they (re)discover details about the world and themselves at the same pace at which the player discovers these details for the first time. There are a number of justifications for this amnesia, from head injuries (*FINAL FANTASY V* [1992]) to drug and alcohol overuse (*Disco Elysium* [2019]) to defense against traumatic events (*Bayonetta* [2009]) to magical or science-fiction brainwashing (*Flashback* [1992]). Other characters are given practical, though not medical, "amnesia" due to being introduced to a new setting or having been separated from society for a long period of time (*High on Life* [2022] and *Half-Life 2* [2004], respectively). All of these storytelling devices are employed to better align the experiences of the player and avatar, as they compose a single composite being of extended cognition.

Information about or known by the avatar can still be effectively hidden from the player, but in these cases the game is more likely to be experienced as a story about a separate character rather than a story in which the player embodies the character. This is the *de facto* storytelling modality across all other media, so it is certainly not a *lesser* way of telling a story, but the difference should be recognized and considered for its appropriateness given the type of story being told. A greater degree of differential knowledge between avatar and character will typically result in a greater degree of perceived psychological distance between the player and character, resulting in a lesser degree of projective identification.

A DYNAMIC MEDIUM

Ultimately, the variance in manifest content and narrative-pertinent characterization between playthroughs presents a problem for interpretation and critical engagement. How do we communally understand and discuss a video game if we cannot fundamentally agree upon *what happens* within the narrative? How can we have critical discussions about characters and narrative beats if elements of characterization and narrative are player-determined and unlikely to be shared by other players? How do we discuss games critically, academically, or even interpersonally if there is not a prevailing consistency on which conversational participants can agree? Surely, an exhibit of ice sculptures that are melted down and re-carved into different shapes each day would present a problem for critical engagement, as reviews of one day's exhibit would not necessarily apply to the exhibit as seen on another, particularly if the points of deviation vary based on audience whims rather than a singular artist's vision.

Video games are fundamentally a dynamic medium, meaning that a game has no definitive form. Unlike a film, which is a complete document played back (roughly) identically for all audiences, video games are not "whole" prior to their play. While a movie can progress from scene to scene in the absence of a viewer's attention, a video game's "next scene" does not exist until it is enacted through play until the code is executed. In their fundamental form, video games exist as series of contingencies: if x input is fed into the system, the system will output y (which, itself, is often an input that may trigger a ripple of contingent actions; see the description of procedural emergence in Chapter 5). Elements of video games are pre-determined in advance: the written script is complete, voice acting is prerecorded, and cutscenes are pre-recorded or pre-planned; this is the data we previously referred to as the *protostory* (Koenitz, 2023, p. 76). Theoretically, every contingency is either expected or allowed, but unlike music physically stamped onto the ridges of a record, video games are only *fully* existent in their play. Video games have no "platonic ideal version" against which the individual instances of enacted play can be compared.

If this is so, how do we compare our experiences? Readers at a book club can jump straight into discussing and debating interpretive take-aways from a book since the text is consistent between readers. Second-order interpretations can be discussed directly without having to re-establish first-order truth. But can we have second-order conversations without first-order consistency? Can an interpretation be valid when only considering a small amount of a game's possibility space? I believe this requires a reorientation of focus to accomplish.

Specifically focusing on experiential narrative (the verb-based happenings of gameplay, as opposed to the written narrative that has less variance between players), we must orient ourselves toward experimental reading rather than discovery-based reading. This is similar to the aforementioned *reparative reading* and *paranoid reading* (Sedgwick, 1997). Again, pertaining specifically to experiential narrative, the narrative engine of a video game is the set of systems and mechanics tuned to produce a specific range of experiences. Similar to how a rollercoaster is tuned to use speed, sudden turns, and height variance to induce a series of adrenaline-producing emotions, video games tune their systems of affordances, boundaries, punishments, and rewards to generate specific types of experiential arcs.

Communally discussing and understanding video games' experiential narratives must be rooted in an experimental, personal mindset. "When I played this game in such a way, I experienced a reaction as the result of the systems responding to my actions in such a way". Ultimately, our goal should be to work toward having the literacy to be able to reflect upon the ways in which the design of the gameplay system acts upon the player's specific temperance and cognitive capacities to create a resulting experience. Further, the player's personal reactions to the happenings within the game feed back into the play and further happenings through better-informed or emotionally heightened play (for instance, our own narrative inferences may lead us to make certain gameplay choices, or our emotional state during play may become manifest in avatar performance).

This is why, even more than definite media like film or literature, critical discussion around games should primarily be rooted in subjective, personal experience. This is something for which the video game enthusiast community, as of the time of writing, does not properly prepare. Currently, a great proportion of professional video game writing that members of the community encounter are consumer reviews that, despite being based in subjective evaluation, aim to answer a question in such a way that is often misinterpreted by the community as being objectively prescriptive: whether or not a video game is worth purchasing as a consumer product. Though consumer reviews are useful, if this is the only kind of games writing that a member of the community encounters, it can lead to unhelpful archetypes for how to frame one's understanding of games as an artistic medium. The pursuit of faux-objectivity encourages the consideration of only a game's most archetypical form: what one might consider idealized play, rather than honoring it as a mode of expression that is enriched by its formal multiplicity. This is similar to evaluating the performance of actors playing a role. Variances from the "truth" of the character as written are not usually unwelcome deviations that distract from the essential story; they are separate perspectives on the same source material that bring fuller truth in their diversity.

For example, consider two pre-semiotic readings of the 2D platformer *Donkey Kong Country 2* (1995):

> I prefer to play slowly and cautiously, observant of the surroundings to find secret bonus items. Unfortunately, my standard attack accelerates me forward with such force that it breaks the slow and cautious rhythm that I typically exercise. But when I tried using this extra momentum to my favor before jumping, I found that I gained extra distance and could reach some items and bonus levels that I could not previously reach. While I still play cautiously, I find that the game rewards the moments of daring.

And separately:

> I decided to run as quickly as I could through this game's levels, reacting to threats in the moment and trying never to break my momentum. To my surprise, I found that the game seems to be designed to accommodate running through it at a full sprint. Moving enemies and objects are positioned in such a way that I almost always reach them at optimal moments to bounce on top of or harmlessly pass by. Maintaining my momentum feels like the way the game is intended to be played, and I appreciate that it rewards fearlessly barreling forward.

Both players played the game in very different ways yet arrived at similar conclusions: despite being a rather difficult game, it tends to favor bold, proactive action, and its mechanics align to encourage propelling oneself forward, out of their comfort zone.

Similarly, we can compare two semiotic readings of crime and family drama *As Dusk Falls* (2022), a cinematic adventure game with a story that can branch at dozens of points based on player decisions, often with unintended consequences that can be difficult to predict in the heat of a dangerous situation. The players discuss the ramifications of a scene in which Michelle, wife of (then) main character Vince, has been shot during a tense hostage situation standoff taking place at a remote Arizonan motel. In the previous scene (a flashback to two weeks before the hostage situation occurred), Michelle and Vince had a tense confrontation in which Vince presents evidence that seemingly indicates that she had been cheating on him with a colleague from the university where she works. Players can choose whether or not to press the issue to have the infidelity definitively confirmed or denied, which may color how they respond during the hostage situation:

> When discovering an intimate text on Michelle's phone from someone named Bruce, I could tell Vince was upset. He had been struggling with the stresses of losing his job and moving to a new state. In that situation, I would feel vulnerable and might have a short temper. When I (Vince) found the text, I confronted her immediately. Vince does not need another uncertainty hanging over his head. It is best to know for sure what did or did not happen. Upon her confession, I could not make Vince commit to preserving their

> marriage. I was upset on Vince's behalf. When she was badly injured during the hostage situation later, though, I said what I needed to say to give her hope so that she would pull through. I told her that we could work on our marriage. It was uncertain whether or not she was going to survive. That was not the time to have a tough conversation. Maybe it was a white lie. Maybe the traumatic situation brings the couple closer.

Another player:

> I suspected that Michelle was cheating on Vince, and I (Vince) brought up the topic of the text – just to let her know that I knew, but I chose not to pursue it further. Maybe I was being diplomatic and forgiving – showing that I was ready to be the bigger man and work on repairing what has been broken – but more likely, I was embarrassed on Vince's behalf and did not entirely want to know. Regardless, I chose to trust her. During the hostage situation, she was injured, but the conversation that we had made me confident that she believed in the strength of the marriage, and perhaps it would be a bit of extra motivation to fight to survive. She told Vince that she was shocked that he trusted her so quickly, and they share a genuine moment of connection. I hope that the trust reinforces their bond as a couple rather than filling her with guilt and causing her to act heroically to satisfy that guilt.

Again, the players experienced similar events with some key differences. Even the moments of ambiguity were colored by the choices that they made during non-pivotal story branches. Though some factual details were exchanged (the first player can confirm that Michelle had been cheating on Vince, a detail that the second player chose not to pursue), greater insight—personally and narratively—can be gained by comparing their interpretations of these dramatic situations and reflecting upon how their own personalities may have affected these decisions.

So, then, a multiplicity of non-privileged interpretations holistically makes for a broader understanding of the range of themes and experiences that can be evoked by a video game. How do we present a singular opinion? By nature, a critical review, museum exhibition description, or dissertation about a particular game would privilege the experience of a singular author, and it risks painting a dynamic artifact as if it is a static experience like a book or film. A singular author can present valuable insight and interpretation but also risks reducing the dimensionality of a piece.

I have found that a productive way of framing individual perspectives on games is to favor an experiential description rather than a normative, singular description. "In my experience of *The Legend of Zelda: Breath of the Wild* (2017), Link scoured the farthest regions of the map to find secrets to better empower him to challenge Calamity Ganon" vs. "*The Legend of Zelda: Breath of the Wild* is a game about scouring the farthest regions of the map to find secrets to better empower Link to challenge Calamity Ganon". In that example, even if the game pushes players in a particular direction, the game is not fundamentally *about* a particular method of play to the exclusion of alternate approaches. This is not to say that themes cannot be read from systemic alignment ("one of the themes expressed by the mechanics of *The Legend of Zelda: Breath of the Wild* is curiosity-guided exploration, reinforced by long sight lines, novelty of instanced encounters, and usefulness of hidden resources"), and themes can certainly be read into semiotic narrative construction like any other storytelling medium.

REVISITING THE THEORETICAL MODEL OF ART

At this point in the exploration of video games as forms of artistic expression, it is worth revisiting the theoretical model that underscores this exploration and considering how the information established thus far reshapes and recontextualizes the relationships and processes it describes. To review, the process-based model of artistic communication differentiates the artist-made product from the art proper by framing the latter as the result of a transformational process enacted within the audience.

The Process Model Re-Explained

The process model of artistic communication satisfies the presupposition that art is the means of intentional communication of intangible, indirectly accessible (or second-order) emotional, sensory, empathetic, or conceptual states through aesthetic craft or contextualization, designed to produce a range of reactions through the intersection with an individual's memories, emotions, knowledge, and associations. The model is conceived like a machine that receives an input and processes that input into a different form through individually unique and unpredictable mechanisms.

In the first step of the model describing typical, non-game art forms, the artistic product/craft, as created by the originating artist(s), serves as the raw material to be processed by each beholder. In most cases, the work is complete and singular as of this moment. At this point, the artistic product/craft has no *artistic meaning.* It may be laden with *literal* meaning and may invite narrowly prescriptive interpretations, but we should resist the temptation to insist that the work has *intrinsic* artistic meaning that precedes its observation by audiences. This work of craft is the *artistic artifact*, or the *artistic potentiator.*

Referring back to my definition of art, art is used to express that which cannot be directly expressed through first-order, informational conveyance. A story may have an uncontroversial *literal* meaning ("after her grandmother's funeral, she went to the casino"), but that level represents *informational conveyance.* Artistic meaning refers to what is evoked through the work indirectly. In the above example, several inferences and emotional states can be brought to the surface through the short story. One who has a propensity to gamble to distract from heartache may read and empathize with the character very differently than one who recently heard a story about someone impulsively gambling away an inheritance.

Framing an artistic artifact as being (artistically) meaning-neutral at this point resists the notion that artworks are puzzles to be solved by observers (Sedgwick [1997]'s *paranoid reading*). This paranoid perspective insists that, like prophets of the gods, they hold universal truths that observers must labor to understand. The privileging of authorial intent above all else delegitimizes alternate readings, essentially denying a work its ability to "live" beyond its time and express anything beyond that which was originally intended. This morbidly lepidopterist approach not only unnecessarily limits the power of art in evolving contexts but also presumes a perfect lucidity of intent that *any* artist would deny of herself. The complexity of the collective human experience in the context of the greater whole makes our minds, languages, symbols, and associations at least *partially* unknowable.

Step two involves decoding and meaning-making. The product is processed by each beholder and shaped and molded by her unique constellations of cognitive propensities as the sensory experience of the artifact is transformed into a cognitive experience and memory of it. This mental model is shaped by a number of factors: memories, associations, knowledge, temperament, proximal context, beliefs, mood, cultural background, etc. This process transforms the mental model from a primarily sensory experience to a primarily meaning-laden model. It is this post-transformation instance that we can call *art* (or the *artistic experience*, for greater specificity) in step three of the model diagram.

In this context, if we conceptualize the processed instance as art, then the initial artifact is not *art*, as such, but rather parameters guiding the generation/emergence of artistic experience. In this sense, this model aligns nicely with Kendall L. Walton (1990)'s assertion of representational art as a "game" of guided imaginings. The properties of the artistic artifact/craft establish reflexive parameters that act as loosely enforced "rules" in the "game" of transformational processing. The advantage of this model is that it discourages exclusive, revelatory analysis and sets the expectation for playful and imaginative divergence between beholders. As such, artists do not produce an artwork to contain a singular artistic meaning that observers must work to discern; artists set the parameters within which a desired range of reactions (and, unavoidably, undesired reactions) will necessarily conclude the process of interpretive transformation. Artists do not directly create artistic experience; they initiate the processes by which artistic experiences incubate.

Following the experience of the artifact, observers' minds continue to reflect upon the reconstructed and transformed mental instantiation. Self-guided reflection, study, and interpersonal conversation constitute post-processing, which results in insights and greater depth of meaning. These processes form a generative system, meaning that *all* artwork exhibits emergent behaviors during the process of interpretation.

Applying the Model to Video Games

Video games have an unconventional relationship with this model of artistic communication, primarily due to the unique relationship between form and player participation. Whereas a painting or film is a singular, static artifact, ostensibly "complete" at the time that it is presented to an audience (maybe not "finished", as art can be revised later, but it is at least observably *whole* in its presented state), video games take no such definite shape. Whereas a film will play out exactly the same way every time it is watched, the manifest content of video games will *always* vary in each instantiation. Whereas a roll (or multiple rolls) of film contains every frame and audio fragment that comprise the film, the contents of a video game narrative are not analogously pre-produced, such that if one decompiled the code that comprises a game to look at the irreducible "raw material" that comprises it (analogous to individual frames of a film), one would not be able to observe the exact happenings of a playthrough. One could see the parameters that set the narrative into action, and one could make informed inferences about the narrative of the game by observing the predefined materials (cutscenes, dialogue, text, visual aesthetics…), but the game does not contain the moment-to-moment record of the linear narratives it is designed to generate, much less a discernible account of its primary artistic form, as a presentation of novel forms of agency. Video games are indeterminate until the moment at which gameplay is enacted through player interaction. Elements of protostory may form points of narrative convergence between multiple or all plathroughs, but the fundamental artifact of *gameplay* is created at the moment of its enactment.

Defining analogous elements of games as systems of artistic products illuminates key formal differences between games and other mediums. Working backwards, if artistic experience is the result of a beholder's individually processed interpretation of an artifact, what constitutes the "video game artifact"? I argue that the artistic artifact of a video game is not the commercial product (protostory, parameters, and paratexts…) but *live gameplay*, which presents and manipulates novel forms of player agency in a similar manner similar to music's presentation of novel aural forms or painting's presentation of novel visual experiences. "[Games] are a method for inscribing forms of agency into artifactual vessels: for recording them, preserving them, and passing them around. […] In other words, we can use games to communicate forms of agency" (Nguyen, 2020, p. 1).

The experience of live gameplay initiates the process of personalized interpretation, but the artist (game developer) does not directly craft live gameplay like the sculptor directly carves a statue. The developer acts in proxy, by way of a designed system created and tuned to produce the artifact of live gameplay. In this sense, the game as a *commercial product* (including its protostory elements, parameters, and paratexts) acts as a proxy artist, generating the artifact of live gameplay in real time. The commercial product serves as a set of approximate instructions for the systemic generation of the gameplay artifact.

As already noted, a process of interpretive transformation generates personal and emergent artistic experiences for each beholder, and that pattern holds in the subjective interpretation of gameplay, but that *same* process *also* occurs in the transformative state between game code and live gameplay. The player's expressive agency forms a layer of mediation that shapes the gameplay artifact, personalizing and diversifying its instantiated form. Just as the beliefs, temperament, and mood of a painter affect what is ultimately manifested on canvas, the internal state of the player unavoidably affects the resulting gameplay. The player is a co-creator of the experience, bounded by affordances and restrictions (game logics) determined by developers who wish to shape the gameplay experience in particular ways.

The practical, transformational processing results from two player-centric feedback vectors. This participatory enactment loops back in on itself to produce the feedback loop of participatory gameplay, perpetually shaping and reshaping the manifest content of the instantiated narrative. The manifest content of gameplay informs the interpretive processing that results in artistic experiential meaning. The interpreted meaning *itself* loops back and informs the practical interpretation of gameplay. This second feedback vector is unique to games. While processed interpretation may affect how we understand an artistic artifact of another medium, the static work does not actually change to reflect that new understanding. Gameplay, steered by player agency, *is* internally reactive to interpreted insights and external knowledge of the game itself.

Each of these transformational points represents a change in narrative form. As the gameplay transitions from code to live gameplay (artifact), it is a multilinear system, and the experience of operating within it is the experience of crafted agency. As it transitions from gameplay (artifact) to interpretive processing (artistic experience), it becomes a linear record of that which occurred within the system.

The model can even be extended to include reflective post-processing, comparative analysis alongside other members of the community of players, the collective evolution of the community's knowledge of the game's capacities (metagame), the production of paratexts (such as retellings and fan artwork), and the evolution of the game's codebase through updates or later versions.

REFERENCES

Aarseth, E. J. (1997). *Cybertext: Perspectives on ergodic literature*. The Johns Hopkins University Press.

Aronofsky, D. (2000). *Requiem for a dream* [Film]. Thousand Words; Protozoa Pictures.

Burkinshaw, R. (2009). *Alice and Kev: The story of being homeless in The Sims 3*. Wordpress. https://aliceandkev.wordpress.com/

Burroughs, W. S. (1959). *The naked lunch*. Olympia Press.

Carter, M. (2015). Emitexts and paratexts: Propaganda in EVE Online. *Games and Culture, 10*(4), 311–342.

Chiang, T. (1998). Story of your life. In P. N. Hayden (Ed.) *Starlight 2*. Tor Books.

Coppola, F. F. (Director). (1972). *The godfather* [Film]. Paramount Pictures; Alfran Productions.

Dickens, C. (1838). *Oliver Twist; or, the parish boy's progress*. Richard Bentley.

Docter, P. (Director). (2009). *Up*. Pixar Animation Studios.

Eladhari, M. P. (2018). Re-tellings: The fourth layer of narrative as an instrument for critique. *International Conference on Interactive Digital Storytelling*, 65–78. doi:10.1007/978-3-030-04028-4_5

Everett, A. (2009). *Digital diaspora: A race for cyberspace*. State University of New York Press.

Ewick, P. & Silbey, S. S. (1995). Subversive stories and hegemonic tales: Toward a sociology of narrative. *Law & Society Review, 29*(2), 212.

Galloway, A. R. (2006). *Gaming: Essays on algorithmic culture*. University of Minnesota Press.

Genette, G. (1987). *Paratexts: Thresholds of interpretation*. Cambridge University Press.

Gray, K. L. (2020). *Intersectional tech: Black users in digital gaming*. Louisiana State University Press.

Grinblat, J. (2017). Emergent narratives and story volumes. In T. S. Short & T. Adams (Eds.), *Procedural generation in game design* (pp. 199–207). CRC Press.

Grinblat, J., Manning, C., & Kreminski, M. (2021). *Emergent narrative and reparative play*. Springer. doi:10.1007/978-3-030-92300-6_19

Handford, M. (1987). *Where's Waldo? Walker Books.*

Homer (n.d.). *Iliad.*

Hooper, T. (Director). (1974). *The Texas chain saw massacre* [Film]. Vortex Inc.

Järvinen, A. (2008). *Games without frontiers*. Tampere University Press.

Juul, J. (2003). *255,168 ways of playing tic tac toe*. The Ludologist. https://www.jesperjuul.net/ludologist/2003/12/28/255168-ways-of-playing-tic-tac-toe/

Juul, J. (2005). *Half-real: Video games between real rules and fictional worlds*. The MIT Press.

Koenitz, H. (2023). *Understanding interactive digital narrative*. Routledge. doi:10.4324/9781003106425

Kolko, B. E. (2000). Erasing @race. In B. E. Kolko, L. Nakamura, & G. B. Rodman (Eds.) *Race in cyberspace*. Routledge.

Kreminski, M., Samuel, B., Melcer, E., & Wardrip-Fruin, N. (2019). Evaluating AI-based games through retellings. *Fifteenth AAAI Conference on Artificial Intelligence and Interactive Digital Entertainment, 15*(1), 45–51. doi:10.1609/aiide.v15i1.5223

Liu, Y., Andersen, E., Snider, R., Cooper, S., & Popović, Z. (n.d.). *Feature-based projections for effective playtrace analysis*. University of Washington. https://grail.cs.washington.edu/projects/playtracer/fdg2011/

Lowery, D. (Director). (2021). *The green knight* [Film]. A24; Ley Line Entertainment; BRON Studios; Wild Atlantic Pictures; Sailor Bear.

Lynch, D. (Director). (2001). *Mulholland drive* [Film]. Asymmetrical Productions; Babbo Inc.; Le Studio Canal+; The Picture Factory.

Malick, T. (Director). (2011). *The tree of life* [Film]. River Road Entertainment; Plan B Entertainment.

Mukherjee, S. (2015). *Video games and storytelling: Reading games and playing books*. Palgrave Macmillan. doi:10.1057/9781137525055

Murray, J. H. (1997). *Hamlet on the holodeck: The future of narrative in cyberspace*. The MIT Press.

Murray, J. H. (2012). *Inventing the medium: Principles of interaction design as cultural practice*. The MIT Press.

Nguyen, C. T. (2020). *Games: Agency as art*. Oxford University Press.

Noble, S. U. (2018). *Algorithms of oppression: How search engines reinforce racism*. New York University Press.

Nolan, C. (Director). (2020). *Tenet* [Film]. Warner Bros. Pictures.

Parrish, A. (2022). *Dead by Daylight drops Leatherface cosmetics after reprts of harassment against black players*. The Verge. https://www.theverge.com/2022/1/5/22869258/dead-by-daylight-blackface-leatherface-texas-chainsaw-massacre

Pettit, H. (2020). *Sick gamers use cheats to spawn KKK characters that chase and kill black players in Red Dead Redemption*. The Sun. https://www.thesun.co.uk/tech/11887407/red-dead-redemption-2-cheats-kkk-black-players/

Ramis, H. (Director). (1993). *Groundhog day* [Film]. Columbia Pictures.

Reiner, R. (Director). (1990). *Misery* [Film]. Castle Rock Entertainment; Nelson Entertainment.

Ricœur, P. (1970). *Freud and philosophy: An essay on interpretation*. Yale UP.

Rollings, A. & Morris, D. (2000). *Game architecture and design*. Coriolis.
Ryan, J. (2018). *Curating simulated storyworlds* [Doctoral dissertation, UC Santa Cruz]. UC Santa Cruz Electronic Theses and Dissertations. https://escholarship.org/uc/item/1340j5h2#main
Salen, K. & Zimmerman, E. (2003). *Rules of play: Game design fundamentals*. The MIT Press.
Schank, R. C. (1979). Interestingness: Controlling inferences. *Artificial Intelligence, 12*(3), 273–297.
Sedgwick, E. K. (1997). *Paranoid reading and reparative reading: Or, you're so paranoid, you probably think this essay is about you*. Duke University Press. doi:10.2307/j.ctv11cw6d8.4
Shklovsky, V. (2015). Art, as device (A. Berlina, Ed. & Trans.). *Poetics Today, 36*(3). (Original work published 1919). doi:10.1215/03335372-3160709
Spielberg, S. (Director). (2001). *A.I. artificial intelligence* [Film]. Warner Bros. Pictures.
Tolkien, J. R. R. (1954). *The lord of the rings*. Allen & Unwin.
Trier, J. (Director). (2021). *The worst person in the world* [Film]. Oslo Pictures; MK Productions; Film i Väst; Snowglobe; B-Reel Films.
Vertov, D. (Director). (1929). *Man with a movie camera* [Film]. All-Ukrainian Photo; Cinema Administration.
Vyasa (n.d.). *Mahabharata*.
Walton, K. L. (1990). *Mimesis as make-believe: On the foundations of the representational arts*. Harvard Press.
Welles, O. (Director). (1941). *Citizen Kane* [Film]. RKO Radio Pictures.
Wells, H. G. (1895). *The time machine*. William Heinemann.
Zemeckis, R. (Director). (1985). *Back to the future* [Film]. Amblin Entertainment.

CHAPTER 12

Expressivity

INTRODUCTION TO EXPRESSIVITY

An important step in gaining functional literacy for video games is acquiring the language to discuss the non-semiotic, pre-linguistic differences between games and between genres. While we might be, at this point, well-prepared to formulate descriptions of the formal elements of particular games (describing the types of inputs, systemic relationships, and emergent propensities that constitute a game), describing *why* formally similar games "feel" different from one another and reliably evoke different aesthetic experiences can still be elusive.

One factor that is broadly useful in describing player agency and categorizing different types of games is *expressivity*. Linguistically representing the player's capacity for self-expression (and divergent, expressive play) in a game, expressivity is actually a property of the game itself. Expressive games are reactive to individualized play, giving players opportunities for self-expression in their systemic enactment. These games reflect the unique personalities of players in ways that are identifiable and highly individualized.

This is more than just a divergence in outcome; it specifically refers to reactivity: multitudinous divergence in response to player agency. In other words, a divergence point with a hundred different outcomes is not *necessarily* expressive; despite its plentitude of outcomes that would likely lead to highly individualized (rarely repeated) experiences, if the outcome is decided at random or in a manner that doesn't establish a clear link to player input, the outcome cannot be characterized as *expressive*. It is not reactive; it is simply active.

Whereas extensive control can be *deep*, expressive control can be described as *rich*. Expressive play is identifiable, like a person's handwriting. Someone who knows the player well should be able to identify their anonymized gameplay because it is unique in its expression or it expresses something specific about her personality. The community that has developed around fighting games—a *highly *expressive genre—can easily identify both the micro-movements and macro-tactics of well-known competitors. Beyond the patterns we might expect of a typical Guile player, for instance, fans of competitive *Street Fighter 6* (2023) can easily distinguish Daigo's Chun Li from Justin Wong's Chun Li.

We can draw three polarities in this balance: expressive games have structure and mechanics that encourage highly individualized play; prescriptive games are those that demand exacting or idealized play, and ambivalent games are those that either proceed in a predetermined path regardless of player input or express a multitude of vectors that are seemingly disconnected from the actions or choices of the player. All of these metrics are gradients rather than binaries. A game can be *more* or *less* expressive, prescriptive, or ambivalent than another game. Any seemingly totalizing claim ("*The Sims* is a highly expressive game") implies a comparison against an *average* expressivity of all games. The contextual framing allows us to make very granular comparisons rather than simply lumping games into categories. For example, one could compare whether *The Sims* (2000) or *The Sims 2* (2004) gives better affordances for player expression. We can even make inter-systemic comparisons.

DOI: 10.1201/9781003530961-12

For example, in *Halo: Combat Evolved* (2001), does the Plasma Pistol or the Needler weapon offer greater propensity for individualized play?

These polarities are not deterministic. As the speedrunning community has shown (see Chapter 13), almost *any* game can be played in an expressive manner by exploiting glitches and unconventional applications of systemic elements. Some games encode a greater propensity for expressivity into their systems, though. Players can also choose to play even highly expressive games in manners that maximize or minimize their own expression. Consider sandbox games like *The Sims* (2000) or *Grand Theft Auto V* (2013), in which players can choose to approach their systems and mimesis very playfully or to simply prioritize efficiently pursuing the games' objectives with very little flourish. As such, we can consider separately the expressivity afforded by a game's systems and, separately, the expressiveness of a particular player's gameplay. Throughout the chapter, I will use those two terms as such: expressivity refers to the game's design, and expressiveness refers to player choices.

Expressivity is also not a measure of the quality of a game. The relative levels of expressivity, prescriptiveness, or ambivalence do not inherently make a game better or worse (though particular balances of these affordances may better suit or be inappropriate for a particular game, given its goals), but it is useful to be able to understand the spectrum of expressivity. My goal is to provide a framework that can be applied across genres so that expressive games (or even expressive mechanics within games) can be identified and discussed.

WHAT MAKES A GAME EXPRESSIVE?

What makes a game expressive? To answer this question, we will develop a more comprehensive definition. As stated before, an expressive game (a game that is highly reactive to player expression) is one that encourages or allows each player to play it differently rather than requiring inflexible, "correct" play. It is reactive to the choices that players make rather than proactively defining a narrow course of progression or being random in its responses to input. Expressivity is like an essay question, as opposed to the multiple-choice question with one correct answer. This may or may not be reflected in open-ended or lax rules and objectives, though. A game can have a very narrow set of win conditions while still encouraging highly expressive play.

To frame the definition less didactically, highly expressive games allow creative self-expression from players. Watching an expressive game being played may tell the viewer something about the player in the same way that listeners can make inferences about a singer's personality from the way that she sings. Viewers familiar with particular competitive communities may begin to recognize players' signature playstyles. These levels of expressivity are similar to Hartmut Koenitz's *local agency* (interactions that result in immediate, perceivable change) and *global agency* (interactions that have an effect only at a larger scale, including affecting the game's ending) (Koenitz, 2023, p. 111).

Expressivity manifests on differing scales of interaction. We can separate micro-level expressivity, which affords highly individualized moment-to-moment play, and macro-level expressivity, which affords expressive strategy, sequencing, and configuration on longer time scales. Macro-scale expressivity may be reflected in a wide set of objectives, paths of progression, tactical decisions, or story branches, allowing players to set the course of their gameplay and narrative. Macro-expressivity provides players the opportunity to shape or choose the rules and boundaries of play. Micro-expressiveness, in contrast, is more closely associated with variations attributable to real-time control.

Game writer Justin Keenan describes a similar concept that he and his team utilized in the development of *Disco Elysium* (2019) called *micro-reactivity*, which he defines as a game remembering and reacting to "seemingly inconsequential player choices", which "ripple" outwards to create new, logical consequences and choices (Keenan, 2021). Micro-expressivity is closely associated with the diegetic perspective of play (the operation and projective embodiment of the avatar in the play environment), while macro-expressivity is more closely associated with mimetic narrative agency and methectic strategy. These, again, are not closed categories; they only reflect the most common expressions.

Micro- and macro-expressivity are also independent factors, and they should be examined together in parallel. A game (or a mechanic in a game) might be highly micro-expressive and highly macro-prescriptive, or micro-prescriptive and macro-ambivalent, etc. These separate categories provide a more well-rounded view of how a choice or series of mechanics affects affordance structure at differing levels of time and/or scale.

Macro-Expressivity

Macro-expressivity manifests in the flexibility of the rules that govern progression, objectives, and story. Macro-expressiveness usually does not affect the way that a game "feels" to play on a moment-to-moment basis, but it greatly affects the lasting impression of the game in totality. The ways in which it *can* affect moment-to-moment *game feel* tend to be contextual. For example, the highly configurable narrative structure of the cinematic horror game *Until Dawn* (2015) provides such significant macro-level consequences for moment-to-moment actions that the tension involved with enacting the desired outcome can be felt in real-time play.

Simulation and strategy games often allow for multiple valid playstyles, any of which can result in victory. For example, the turn-based, nation-building strategy series *Sid Meier's Civilization* (1991-present) allows multiple paths to victory in a particular competitive session that will be suited to different play styles and personal preferences. As multiple nations simultaneously compete for victory within the same map, players may achieve Science Victory (advancing a scientific research tree to its furthest branch), Cultural Victory (reaching a threshold of cultural influence via the construction of cultural wonders and encouragement of tourism), Religious Victory (achieving religious dominance within every competing civilization), Domination Victory (utilizing tools of war to annihilate or force the surrender of all other civilizations), and Diplomatic Victory (achieving a diplomatic threshold by researching peace-encouraging technology and forming diplomatic ties with other civilizations). Part of the challenge of playing Civilization is balancing the pursuit of your chosen path to victory with keeping track of how far opponents have progressed down any of these avenues. Moment-to-moment, micro-level play is fairly consistent regardless of the route chosen, but the variability of strategic focus makes these different objective pursuits feel quite distinct over the course of an entire gameplay session.

Similarly, simulation games like *SimCity* (1989) and *Cities: Skylines* (2015) allow players to set their own goals with regard to the types of cities they want to build, with the games either accompanied by a wide range of victory conditions rewarding different types of cities (industrial cities, tourism cities, commerce cities…) or not featuring formal victory conditions at all and allowing players to construct cities to their own taste (this can either be framed as expressivity or ambivalence), allowing them to set and achieve their own goals outside of formal direction. This is formalized in *The Sims* (2000-present) series, in which a Sim's ultimate life ambition is chosen as a personality trait when designing each character, allowing each Sim to prioritize different activities in pursuit of their individual goals (such as becoming a celebrity or a master painter).

Macro-expressivity can be achieved through highly configurable emergent content. Species evolution and civilization-building simulation *SPORE* (2008) gives players near-unlimited freedom to create unusual aliens through an open-ended creature creator that allows for creative combination and configuration of body parts that the system procedurally animates into living, operable beings. Regardless of where essential features, such as legs, arms, eyes, and mouths, are placed on the creature's body, the procedural logics "figures out" how such a creature would move, eat, mate, and dance. These creatures, configurable at early stages in their evolutionary journey, persist as the game moves from the hunt-or-be-hunted, survival-oriented stages of primordial life through the galaxy-spanning, civilization-building stage of the late game. The procedural affordances decided by the creature's biological configuration continue to affect (and evolve during) the tribe and civilization's ascendance.

Highly emergent games can sometimes ride a line between expressivity and ambivalence. Complicated simulations, such as *Dwarf Fortress* (2022), can be heavily affected by more simulated factors than a player can realistically keep track of. They can often feel the consequences of their choices echo throughout the systemic layers of simulation, blossoming into gratifying emergent narratives, but just as easily, unanticipated factors can punctuate these emergent systems. In such cases, the resulting narratives can be very *personal* (James Ryan describes the *lived-experience principle* in which a series of events feels significant and personal to a player because she experienced an unusual set of events first-hand that will never be experienced again by any other player [2018, p. 78]), even though they are not very *reactive* or *expressive* of the player's personality or intentions.

Other forms of macro-expressivity tend to follow prescribed pathways (such as choosing between multiple pre-written story branches in a narrative adventure game or choosing the order in which challenges are completed in an open-world game). In these cases, players do not necessarily create something net-new within the game's systems, but the macrostructure of the game is shaped by their choices in ways that may differ from the experiences of other players. Though the moment-to-moment play may still expect ideal play rather than creative play, these experiences can feel immensely personal when taken as a whole. Players often fondly remember their individual playthroughs of games like *As Dusk Falls* (2022) and *Until Dawn* (2015) as if their experience had been wholly their own, as opposed to the reality that every condition and story branch was one of several pre-planned possibilities. As with the example from the previous paragraph, though, a high-enough volume of prefabricated material can create highly personal and expressive scenarios for their uniqueness in their sequencing.

Metagames can also create macro-expressive gameplay. Choosing a particular route or plan of action through a game can reflect player priorities or lead to highly individualized expressions of play. Speedrunners, for instance, will choose particular sequences of challenges or exploit glitches to finish games in the shortest amount of time possible (see Chapter 13), and sometimes these routes become closely associated with their founders (as these routes, particularly those that involve glitch exploitation, require a great amount of research into the technical structure of the game). Other self-imposed metagame challenges may express the personalities and beliefs of the players who attempt them, even if they are not explicitly encouraged nor acknowledged by the software systems themselves, such as *Undertale* (2015) players who play through the game avoiding combat in favor of nonviolent resolution, or *Dark Souls* (2011) players who play with unconventional controllers, such as a dance mat or bongo drums (Lynch, 2016).

Micro-Expressivity

Micro-scale expressivity emphasizes divergent decision-making in moment-to-moment operation, allowing for highly individualized, expressive play. Micro-expressivity is typically achieved in real-time control and becomes evident in *game feel* in how the player utilizes the game's primary verb sets. As such, micro-expressivity can be most easily demonstrated by a game's movement systems, and micro-expressivity is most obvious in games in which movement is a core focus, such as platformers and fighting games.

Micro-expressivity can be achieved in a number of ways. Players may be given a long list of prefabricated verbs, used to react to moment-to-moment challenges (like the dozens of attacks available to each of a fighting game's characters), or simple player mechanics may be given versatility or high sensitivity, giving the player a simple but robust verb set that she can use to creatively achieve her goals.

Micro-expressivity can also be achieved through (and result in) emergence. Complex physics systems, for instance, procedurally individualize play in a manner and at a scale that would be difficult to replicate through bespoke programming of prefabricated choices. Consider the emergent, moment-to-moment possibilities within games like physics platformers *JellyCar* (2007) and *Getting Over It with Bennett Foddy* (2017) or competitive climbing series *Mount Your Friends* (2013). Each of these titles results in even greater emergent expressivity when their physics systems are exploited or "glitched" by expert players, who can achieve impressive feats with a methectic mastery of metagame affordances.

Micro-expressivity most often results in opportunities for improvisational play. Compare the highly micro-expressive *Super Mario Odyssey* (2017) against the comparatively more micro-prescriptive *ASTRO BOT* (2024). Mario's active affordances consist of many verbs that allow for correcting or changing course mid-action or reaching areas by numerous methods. Mario has a high degree of in-air mobility as well as the ability to throw his hat (which can be bounced upon to earn a second "jump" while in the air), and he has a robust arrangement of backflips and wall jumps that can be chained to reach areas one might assume are inaccessible, even allowing skilled players to skip past significant portions of designed challenges. When the player makes a mistake, Mario also has many tools (including his hat throw and wall jump) that allow players to make up for this, improvising around mistakes instead of resigning to failure.

On the other hand, *ASTRO BOT*'s avatar has a fairly limited move set that specializes in playing each linear course as intended (with less ability to approach platforming challenges in creative and unexpected ways). Though Astro Bot has a generous hover ability, the lack of a wall jump or a way to gain additional height mid-jump leads to a less improvisational style of play. Jumps and movements are to be planned ahead of time and executed correctly, whereas Mario gives greater leniency for "leaping before he looks". As such, *Super Mario Odyssey*'s challenges can be considered more open-ended (reflected in that game also having a higher *macro*-expressivity), whereas *ASTRO BOT*'s challenges are oriented around a narrower form of mastery. Again, this is not to say that *Super Mario Odyssey* is a *better* game than *ASTRO BOT*; this is not a measure of quality. This is just a design variable that expresses different design intentions and results in different styles of play. The level of expressivity should be thought of not in terms of "good and bad" but rather in terms of the "goodness of fit" for a particular game and its intended experience.

Differing micro-expressivity priorities produce differing gameplay aesthetics. Once a player gains confidence and skill in playing *Super Mario Odyssey*, they are rewarded with the aesthetic pleasure of creative expression. Playing Mario is like performing jazz. The skilled musician's instrument can play its notes reliably (with some freedom to bend notes with dexterous finesse), but each musician can use the same

TABLE 12.1 A comparison of the various combinations of micro- and macro-expressivity

	Macro-expressive	**Macro-prescriptive**	**Macro-ambivalent**
Micro-expressive	Open-ended sandbox play at both the character and structural levels. Players can choose their own objectives or path through the game and creatively fulfill these choices. Often produces the most interesting personal stories, as both micro- and macro-levels are oriented toward producing unique occurrences. (*Grand Theft Auto V, Super Mario Odyssey, Middle-earth: Shadow of War, Just Cause 2*)	Encourages creative solutions to predetermined challenges. Good for comparison against other players, as objectives and structure are consistent, amplifying the divergent effects of creative play. Also good for discovery-oriented games, in which creative deductive methods can be applied to determine singular answers. (*Super Mario 64, Neon White, Outer Wilds, Shadows of Doubt*)	Invites a great amount of configurability, but results of those configurations may not be obviously or predictably linked to their preceding inputs or may not be scored or valorized. May create a toy-like, creative aesthetic of free play rather than a demanding game. (*Nour: Play with Your Food, FUSER*)
Micro-prescriptive	Games that deprioritize real-time control for greater longitudinal expression. Common in story-oriented games with branching storylines or games that emphasize slow, tactical play. (*Life Is Strange, Sid Meier's Civilization VI, Pokémon, SimCity*)	Games that test mastery with narrow margins of error or games that feature largely prefabricated elements, minimizing real-time control and telling predetermined stories. This structure is common in rhythm games and adventure games/visual novels. (*Guitar Hero, Dragon's Lair, Phoenix Wright: Ace Attorney, Dance Dance Revolution, WarioWare, Inc: Mega Microgames!*)	Games that offer limited moment-to-moment affordances but tend to proceed in unpredictable or inconsequential manners, from a structural perspective. Many "artgames" fit this description. (*LSD: Dream Emulator, Luxuria Superbia*)
Micro-ambivalent	Includes games that are configured by the player and then play out in the absence of direct control, like setting up a Rube Goldberg machine and not touching it while it is in motion. (*The Incredible Machine, Bloons TD 6*)	Games that set strict objectives or scoring mechanics but present resistant control schemes, often for comedic effect. Often highly individualized but cannot be said to be "expressive" due to lack of intentionality in performance. (*QWOP, Octodad: Dadliest Catch*)	Games that produce interesting emergent outputs with or without input from the player, or games with minimal interaction (*Dwarf Fortress, Super Mario Clouds, Hey You, Pikachu!*)

instrument to significantly different effect, even when improvising around the same accompaniment (play discourse).

The particular pairings of micro- and macro- play structures can also produce different complimentary aesthetics. Prescriptive macrostructure is a good complement to micro-expressiveness, since consistent goals serve as structure around which players are free to improvise ("your goal is at the top of that building; use whatever method you can to get there"), whereas expressive macrostructure is well complemented by prescriptive moment-to-moment gameplay, since a player's macro-decision-making must be performed with reliable and predictable moment-to-moment input/output pairings. The table below features a non-exhaustive list of play aesthetics expressed in the combinations of each polarity.

THE PURPOSE OF EXPRESSIVITY

As repeated previously, expressivity is not an indication of quality. A highly expressive game is not necessarily more meaningful than a highly prescriptive or highly ambivalent game. But there are particular aesthetics that expressive games produce with regard to player agency.

Expressivity corresponds to the degree or sensitivity of control a player has within the simulation. As such, expressive control can create a strong projective link between the player and avatar if she feels that her impulses can be expressed in a broader or deeper set of actions. A greater granularity of nuanced choices will more likely present players with an expression that matches their intention. Though, conversely, there is an upper boundary to the amount of freedom that further immerses a player in a role before they again feel distanced from it. The creativity and improvisation characteristic of expressive systems are often given weight and meaning in their constraints.

For example, *Minecraft* (2011)'s Survival Mode allows players great freedom to build highly personalized structures and tools, though they can only build with that which they scavenge and harvest from the environment through their own hard work and exploration. Conversely, the less-restrictive Creative Mode allows players to fly freely around the environment and build anything they wish with unlimited resources. Players can use this additional affordance to construct more impressive structures, but the degree to which that structure is *of* and *from* that world is lessened; the wood, stone, and other materials were not obtained through exploration and risk-taking. There is not the same feeling of "using what I can find to scrap together the resources I need to survive". Whereas the Survival Mode avatar is a *character* within the diegesis, exposed to the dangers and limitations of the world, the Creative Mode avatar is more like a *cursor*, not exposed to danger nor the limitations of physics. While one might mimetically project into the former, the latter serves a primarily practical, non-narrative purpose.

Expressive games most often present challenges with multiple correct solutions or approaches. If an objective is to get to the other side of the city, it might be wholly ambivalent to the route or manner by which that is accomplished, giving players a great degree of freedom to overcome challenges in ways that suit their preferences or skills. This also circumvents the feeling that the game is railroading play toward a predetermined path, which can shatter a player's illusion of choice and agency. If a game presents a setting modeled to look like a sprawling city but prevents the player from exploring any of the city other than the narrow pathway that leads to the objective, the illusion of scale and of simulated realism is broken.

Again, the balance of expressivity, prescriptiveness, and ambivalence is not an objective measure that is correct for each and every game; it is about goodness-of-fit with a game's goals. A murder mystery *should* only have one correct answer; the joy of investigating is closing in on the singular truth. A mastery-oriented rhythm game *should* have a narrow range of acceptable inputs to preserve the demand on skillful play. Sometimes game-world simulations *should* be ambivalent to player activity to tell stories about characters who have to work hard to survive rather than being divinely awarded everything that they need to complete their destined journeys.

Therein lies the trade-off, though. Video games permit the expression of both players and developers, and as player expression takes greater precedence, developer expression often lessens. If a developer wishes to tell a story about a specific series of events that transpire in a specific manner and sequence, the player cannot be afforded influence great enough to alter or circumvent these events. Characterization is also expressed through an avatar's limitations as much as her affordances. It is necessary to the characterization of *God of War* (2005)'s Kratos that he is only capable of solving his problems with destructive violence; players are not given the option to calmly reason with his enemies, as this would portray him as a very different type of character.

However, player and developer expressions are not always in zero-sum conflict. The highly expressive movement affordances of Mario in *Super Mario Odyssey* (2017) convey the kind of brave and capable hero that he is. If he were less expressive, this nonverbal aspect of his characterization would not be properly communicated. Similarly, there is a trope of scripted losses in several pivotal RPG battles, usually demonstrating to what degree an enemy outclasses the heroes or galvanizing a necessary narrative event. When the player senses the inevitability of this loss, though, it does not emotionally register *as* a loss. It is a necessary event in the progression of the story. The only way forward is to lose, so a loss is actually a victory. Because the player is unable to express herself in this macro-level instance, the incentive structure of the moment is inverted, and emotional valence and personal responsibility are lost.

Most often, gamic elements will transition between differing levels of expressivity, prescriptiveness, and ambivalence over the course of a game, based on what is needed in each particular scene. A character with highly expressive play characterization will revert to a particular personality expression during cutscenes, or an open macro-challenge structure will bottleneck for boss fights to "quiz" the player on the skills that she has acquired thus far. These swaps might be necessary for preserving the pacing or dramatic structure of the game, but harsh or unjustified pivots may result in the experience of *ludonarrative dissonance*, a tension between play agency and embedded narrative elements.

This dissonance is sometimes avoided by making avatar characters "blank slates", being very reserved in embedded characterization. If a character does not express much personality or reaction, it is difficult to betray a player's internalized, personal characterization. For example, *HITMAN* (2016)'s Agent 47 is written and performed with a strong sense of deadpan dark comedy through the use of assassination-based double entendres. To those who play Agent 47 as a cold and calculated assassin, these lines come across as being "played straight", or like he is "playing with" his targets before moving in for the kill. For those who play in a more slapstick, comedic, or clumsy manner, the humor in these lines can feel like a gratifying acknowledgement that 47 doesn't take his job *too* seriously. As the *tabula rasa* of a character, every expressive choice is justified.

Other times, stories may be structured in such a way that the player's avatar plays a secondary narrative role to a companion or even a rival. *Half-Life 2* (2004) and *The Legend of Zelda: Ocarina of Time* (1998) feature largely expressive gameplay, reacting to varying play styles and priorities. Both games pair their silent protagonists with companion characters (Alyx and Navi, respectively) who speak and perform most plot-advancing actions on behalf of the avatar characters, allowing players freedom to define the characters during gameplay stretches without contradicting bestowed traits during cutscenes (another version of the "blank slate" character above). The characterization of the avatars is not a load-bearing element of the plot. Games may also spread this role of "carrying" the story to a wider supporting cast or even villains. The *Far Cry* games (2004-present) have had success with rather narratively blank main characters, with plot momentum kept up by eccentric allies and adversaries that interject often to reassert the effect that the player's actions have on the game world.

Alternatively, game narratives may explicitly treat avatar characters like agents of chaos, bestowing upon them the trait of erratic unpredictability and counting on players to prove that true through their expressive play. Characters like Trevor in *Grand Theft Auto V* (2013) and Crypto from *Destroy All Humans!* (2005) are wild and unpredictable during story cutscenes, meaning that any choice that players make during gameplay is ostensibly "correct". If the character is highly unpredictable, nothing is "out of character". Player expression is never contradicted. Avatar characterization is further explored in Chapter 11.

HOW IS EXPRESSIVITY ACHIEVED?

In previous sections, I've alluded to differences between games that have low and high levels of macro- and micro-expressivity. In this section, we will drill down further into how, specifically, expressivity is achieved.

Macro-Expressivity

Flexible objectives and victory conditions: As victory conditions represent the ultimate goals within games (or subsections of games therewithin, such as levels), a flexible victory condition expands the scope of possible shapes that the experience can take.

As discussed previously, the *Sid Meier's Civilization* series (1991-present) accommodates a number of victory conditions, all rewarding different goals and priorities in play. These are not exclusive victory conditions chosen at the beginning of a match, though; all victory conditions are active throughout. The player can change her goal at any time, and she must be aware of her opponents' progress down any of these pathways.

This can be seen even more clearly in the single-screen competitive strategy/platformer hybrid arcade game *Killer Queen* (2013), developed by BumbleBear Games. Players, taking on the roles of the utilitarian Worker, offense-oriented Warrior, or the highly mobile Queen, face off in 5v5 team battles to achieve one of three goals: collecting berries and returning them to the hive for an Economic Victory, defeating the opponent's powerful Queen character three times for a Military Victory, or sacrificing the productivity of a team member to ride a slow-moving snail to your team's side of the screen in a game-long tug-of-war played at the periphery of the playfield for a Snail Victory. Like in *Civilization*, all victory conditions are active concerns at all times in a game of *Killer Queen*, and even a beautifully executed game can come to ruin quickly if a team is not cognizant of the opposing team's progress toward an unexpected victory condition.

Flexibility of victory conditions is not only reserved for multiplayer games, it has also become increasingly common in single-player games as a way of allowing players to self-select the level of challenge that is appropriate for them. Increasingly, games will present a wide array of challenges and ask the player to complete a certain number of those challenges in order to progress to the next level without mandating which of those challenges must be completed, allowing players to self-select the challenges that they find most interesting or that best suit their competencies. Games like *Super Mario Odyssey* (2017) and *Tony Hawk's Pro Skater* (1999) allow players this kind of freedom.

Flexible paths of progression: Flexible paths of progression are similar to flexible victory conditions, but the variance takes place earlier in the journey of play. Allowing multiple approaches to completing fixed victory conditions gives challenges a dynamic quality that encourages individualized play.

An informal, loose genre of games called immersive sims is built with this guiding notion in mind. Games like *Deus Ex* (2000), *HITMAN* (2016), and *Dishonored* (2012) typically feature large, sprawling, intricate levels that must be infiltrated or crossed. Instead of prescribing a path through them, they are designed with many entrances, exits, routes, and obstacles. Players must utilize the affordances of the environment and skills afforded by their unique character progression choices or equipment to move through these densely layered environments. Players might choose to specialize in stealth and lockpicking, staying in the shadows and infiltrating unnoticed, or players may opt for disguises and blending in socially. The relative stability of these games' singular objectives makes the creative routes by which they are reached more interesting.

Open-world games have unique possibilities in this space. Since the world is typically designed as an environment first rather than being constructed around specific objectives, there is often a level of ambivalence in affordances for progression. In other words, instead of outlining an intended "golden path" through a set of challenges, players will be tasked with utilizing that which "naturally" exists in the world around them to overcome challenges that may or may not have been designed around that specific space. For that reason, players must internalize these games' rule systems rather than seeking indications of how something is "intended" to be done. The *Far Cry* (2004-present) and *Horizon* (2017-present) games will often routinize standard gameplay loops and add variety by placing those standardized encounters in different (often random) locations with unique environmental affordances to add to the variety and improvisational requirement of each engagement.

In microcosm, the open-world structure of *Burnout Paradise* (2008) gives each race a starting point and a finish line (usually an intersection elsewhere in the city) but does not prescribe a specific route to get there. Players are encouraged to determine which streets in the densely interweaving city will get them to the finish line first. One may consider the most direct route, given that the shortest distance between two points is a straight line. In cases in which the direct route is a diagonal line, as the crow flies, perhaps it is better to cover more distance but spend more time building extreme speed on straightaways instead of making frequent turns. Even better still, perhaps players know of slightly out-of-the-way shortcuts that may require more setup but will allow them to skip difficult portions of the city. Players are encouraged to think about their route creatively, and greater familiarity with the city will increase a player's navigational resources via acquired knowledge rather than in-game mechanical reward.

Configurability: Macro-expressivity can be achieved by allowing a great diversity of "build" options for avatar characters or adventuring parties. RPGs and even some action games feature a variety of specializations that allow for different strategic possibilities. *ELDEN RING* (2022) features a wide variety of magics and weapons that encourage a variety of playstyles, from fleet-footed, ranged play with distance-casted magic or crossbows to feet-planted, defensive play with shields and enormous hammers. Players can choose to invest combat and exploration rewards by "leveling up" particular attributes (such as strength, intelligence, or dexterity), allowing for a great amount of individuation on a tactical level. *ELDEN RING*'s configuration at the macro-expressive level actually *manifests* at the micro-expressive level in different moment-to-moment affordances, but it is still considered a strategic consideration at a large timescale. Other macro-considerations, like the party composition of one's *Pokémon* (1996) team, allow players to prepare for specific challenges and minimize anticipated vulnerabilities, with certain synergies between monsters available to advanced players. In fact, games like *Balatro* (2024) and *Slay the Spire* (2019), though most often quite constrained in the amount of choice that they offer, can be quite expressive in the metagame play of synergistic strategy.

Aesthetic configurability can also be tremendously expressive. Anyone who has spent a lot of time in character creator menus can appreciate the effect of a well-designed avatar as a medium of interaction in multiplayer games or as a conduit of player projection in single-player games. Whether the avatar is modeled to look like the player, like an imagined character, or hilariously discordant with the world in which the game is set, the choice of aesthetic configuration can be as considered a mode of expression as a person's real-world wardrobe.

Multiple prescribed branches: Though thoughtfully tuned emergent systems can create very personal stories for the players who experience them, great embedded narratives (the semiotic storytelling communicated through plot, text, and dialog) typically require human authorship.[1] As a result, macro-expressivity applied to game narratives can often feel like choosing from a menu of possibilities instead of being truly personalizable. Though in the instances of each choice, the illusion of uniqueness may not hold, over the course of an entire game or series, the compounding uniqueness of dozens of choices can still create narratives that have not been experienced exactly by others.

When thinking about expressivity, specifically, we should consider whether a game's systems governing narrative or gameplay divergences support or inhibit the goal of making the game more expressive by catering to the personal decisions of each player. I will not argue that every branch should play out exactly as the player intends it to—there should be an element of surprise and conflict in any good story—but some systems fall short of instilling narrative agency by guiding players toward optimal paths or not properly contextualizing the relationships between actions and outcomes.

Loose primary constraints: Constraints are the systems that enforce game mechanics, like the referees in a football match. By "primary constraints", I refer to the systems that directly enforce victory conditions, loss conditions, and progress toward victory. These are often checks, or "flags", that a condition has or has not been met.

If we think of a victory condition as the human-generated decision regarding what victory entails, a victory constraint is the mechanic that enforces how that victory is achieved. This can include object discrimination. For example, if a quest-giver in an RPG tasks the player character with killing ten rats, does this include swamp rats, tundra rats, flying rats, and skeletal rats, or only the normal rats native to the immediate area? Constrictive requirements dictate a specific course of play, while less discriminatory requirements allow players to be more creative in their pursuits of victory.

Micro-Expressivity

Extensive control scheme: Greater micro-expressivity (or moment-to-moment expressivity) is a result of the player having greater agency at any given moment, and this is often achieved by giving players a greater number of choices. As a writer may be able to express more complex and coherent thoughts when given a full keyboard rather than just the top row of keys, so too can a player enact a more highly individualized response to a situation when she has more tools in her toolbelt, so to speak. Perhaps the most straightforward (though sometimes inelegant) way to accomplish this is by giving the player an extensive library of control options that they may trigger at any time.

This can be seen in the fighting genre. Though fighting games in recent years (at least as of the time of writing this) have trended toward simpler, more intuitive controls, fighting games have a well-deserved reputation for requiring an almost academic level of memorization of complex control options for each character. Beyond standard attacks (low kicks, high punches, etc.), characters often have dozens of special attacks that add extra functions to their offensive and defensive capabilities, most often triggered by pairing an attack button with one or more directional motions of the control stick or pad (most commonly, a quarter-circle motion may roll from down to down-forward to forward). When paired with the punch button, it famously triggers the projectile fireball of *Street Fighter* (1987-present)'s Ryu, whereas a Z-shape motion of forward, down, and down-forward paired with the same punch button will activate his vertical Dragon Punch, useful for punishing opponents jumping toward Ryu or launching opponents from the ground into the air.

Ultimately, the hope is to give players tools to react to any given situation. Skilled players can hold all of these situationally specific attacks in their mind at once and skillfully execute them at a moment's notice as they read their opponent's behavior. Enthusiasts know not only the possibilities available to their own character but also the attacks available to their opponents, constantly gauging when it is safe to advance for a cheeky jab, when it's best to keep their distance and pelt from afar with projectiles, and when to punish a misjudged movement from the opponent. Like expert poker players, fighting game competitors read their opponent's patterns, try to bait out attacks that can be punished, and are persistently aware of the shifting dynamics of positioning, momentum, and spacing.

This entails a significant learning curve, though, and the extensiveness of these control schemes might actually *hinder* a novice player from having the capability to express herself. Player expression is an extension of agency, and having a sense of control within the system is a necessary component that creates the feeling of agency.

Versatility of simple controls: While complex and extensive controls can add options for more nuanced responses to unpredictable situations, the opposite approach is highly effective as well. Instead of dozens of highly situational options, games can offer fewer controls with greater versatility. This can be an elegant approach. Experientially, the complexities of the game's systems may reveal themselves to players more naturally over time, when compared to the "drinking from the firehose" feeling of learning an overly complex control scheme upfront. In the best circumstances, the player will feel a sense of self-guided discovery as her own curiosity prompts her to find ways in which these versatile systems interact. Players are more inclined to learn naturally about the extensions of simple but versatile control schemes, whereas they more likely need to be taught about the intricacies of complex schemes.

Versatility can manifest in a number of ways. A large number of contextual actions can be attached to a single object or core mechanic. *The Big Catch* (2025) is a fishing-themed 3D platformer in which the avatar uses a fishing rod for many actions. The rod can be used to fish, in combat (as a blunt object), and as a grappling hook to climb to or swing from distant objects. All follow logical (if quite fantastical) extensions of what a fishing rod *might* be able to do in a fantasy setting. Similarly, *Super Mario Odyssey* (2017) packs a lot of actions into Mario's cap, which can now be thrown in a boomerang fashion. The cap can collect distant objects, it can be bounced upon in the air for an additional mid-air jump, it can trigger switches, and it can be used to "capture" enemies (making them temporarily controllable while Mario's cap sits on their heads).

Versatility can also manifest in control sensitivity. Sensitivity simply refers to the number of degrees of activation of a particular input. A binary on/off button would have a low degree of sensitivity (two states), while a computer mouse has a very high degree of sensitivity (nearly unrestricted movement in large, sweeping movements as well as small, nuanced adjustments). Consider games like *Asteroids* (1979) or *Super Monkey Ball* (2001). They exceed their contemporaries in the level of sensitivity in their movement controls, allowing for players to perform creative and expressive actions without requiring extensive memorization of complex schemes.

Another way that versatility can manifest is through highly reactive *receivers* of input. If the avatar expresses players' input into the game world, the objects within the game world and the world itself receive those inputs, and they can be tuned to be receptive to a large number or a high sensitivity of inputs. The 2D tactical artillery series *Worms* (1995-present) features fully destructible environments, allowing players to carve defensive bunkers for their own units or inconveniently exposed craters for opponents' units. The fact that the whole of the environment is reactive to the weapons of war employed in competitive matchups means that a great deal of strategically salient change can be effected through the limited actions afforded to the worm units. Similarly, the *Tony Hawk's Pro Skater* series (1999-present) features action affordances that correspond with almost every type of surface in the game's virtual worlds. Regardless of what lies ahead of the player, she almost always has some kind of skateboard trick that utilizes that specific environmental feature. In that way, the play of *Tony Hawk's Pro Skater* becomes like an improvisational exercise. As author Steve Swink says, "*Tony Hawk* is a form of interpretive dance, enabled by the fact that all the objects have a very high degree of utility from just about any state or relative position" (2009, p. 309).

Loose secondary constraints: Unlike the "loose primary constraints" point in the macro-expressivity section, this refers to a looseness of game mechanics separate from primary goals, rewards, and punishments. Consider the constraints the game puts on players that do not directly contribute to high-level win/loss states. Physics and animation systems, for example, fit within this category. If we consider the strict, utilitarian, grid-based movement of Chess as one far end of the spectrum (strict secondary constraints), the free, unrestrained 3D movement of *Super Mario 64* (1996) might sit farther toward the *other* polarity (loose secondary constraints). Mario's movement is, compared to the Chess pieces, relatively unconstrained.

Farther along that spectrum, though, we might hold some of the 3D platformers of the mid-2000s–2010s, like *Psychonauts* (2005) and *Yooka-Laylee* (2017). The relative complexity of their environments compared to the simple polygons of *Super Mario 64* introduced some interesting wrinkles to platformer strategy. With an increase in environmental detail, rendered as physics objects within the game world, it became more possible than it had been before to interact with rogue physics objects and maneuver around the intended course of traversal, at times skipping significant portions of the stages. This kind of design exploitation metagame became an endearing characteristic of an era of 3D platformers, where it often became fun not only to finish a level but especially to find one's own creative way through or around its intended challenges.

This "unintended" platforming has the improvisational feeling of parkouring within abandoned buildings—knowing that everything around me was ostensibly created for human interaction but not for the purposes that I intend to use it. This route was not "gifted" to me by the developers as designed pathways are; this was a route that I created myself. This is true gameplay expressiveness: making the player's personality visible in the gameplay.

Analog control: Analog control pertains to the "versatility through sensitivity" quality detailed above. A greater degree of analogue control will almost inevitably result in more unique outcomes in a movement system. Increased sensitivity will result in increased subtlety and nuance to the player's interactions.

Analog control offers a gradation of degrees of input, contrasted with digital control, which is binary or constrained to guides/guards. When applied to character movement, consider digital movement that constrains movement to grids, offering 4 degrees of movement at any time (up, down, left, and right; as in the classic 2D *FINAL FANTASY* [1987] or early *Pokémon* games [1996]). Fully analog movement, by contrast, gives characters the ability to traverse freely across the screen with 360 degrees of movement at diagonal angles and curved trajectories, unconstrained by a grid.

Or consider the freedom to freely adjust the viewing angle and aim in a modern first-person game as opposed to the rigid clicking between predetermined angles of the classic puzzle game *Myst* (1993). Within the rhythm genre, consider the binary off/on inputs that are triggered in a game of *Dance Dance Revolution* (1998) or *PaRappa the Rapper* (1996) versus the bending of notes and nuance of performance present in *Gitaroo Man* (2001) or *Spin Rhythm XD* (2023).

Greater analog control gives *more* control, but not necessarily *greater* control. Like playing a trombone as opposed to a saxophone, there is greater capacity for gradation between notes, but there is also a greater capacity for inputs to err slightly to one side or the other of what is intended. Additionally, regardless of how analog a game's *inputs* are, if the game (or we as observers) judge actions as discrete choices, the fluidity of control might be meaningless. Like playing a game of Connect Four, the player's hand has a tremendous degree of movement when choosing where to drop the token, but once the token enters the grid, it follows a rigidly defined path to one of seven possible resting points. Brian Upton writes, "when we play an arcade driving game we choose how far to turn the steering wheel, but there is no way to meaningfully map that continuous range of motion onto 'picking a move'" (2015, p. 52).

Analog control sensitivity can also be tuned to produce moments of emergent slapstick comedy. In *Octodad: Dadliest Catch* (2014), an octopus disguised in human clothing must fool everyone around him into thinking that he is a typical human father by performing mundane tasks. The challenge and comedy come in the extremely finicky, analogue per-limb control through which players control the cephalopod. The player independently operates each limb one at a time, adding challenge to performing even the most basic of tasks, like making coffee or putting on a bow tie. The controls are intended to feel imprecise and unwieldy, mirroring the experience of the octopus—a literal fish out of water. In this way, the analogue controls are "expressive" of each player in that they are unique to each player, who may pick up individual mannerisms within the unfamiliar movement toolset, but it may fall short of being "expressive" of a player's will in playing.

One area in which analog control has become a defining cornerstone is in motion controls. Though the earliest motion controls amounted to little more than physical gestures triggering pre-programmed, canned outputs and animations, modern motion controls now often mirror player movement one-to-one. The Nintendo Wii's athletic collection, *Wii Sports Resort* (2009), used highly analog motion controls to simulate a diverse collection of activities, like playing table tennis, practicing archery, and throwing a Frisbee. Players' performance is dependent upon the slightest alterations made to their physical actions, making these highly individualized and reactive to player actions.

Similarly, motion controls took another leap forward with the introduction of modern VR. Handheld controllers are tracked one-to-one by external sensors or sensors built into the headset, giving players direct and intuitive hand-to-virtual-object control in ways more precise than ever before. The capacity for expressiveness is extremely high, as games are reactive to the subtlest of physical movements, and interaction with the objects in the game world is as intuitive as grabbing a spoon from a table. This is amplified by the fact that many VR games are social multiplayer games that can be enjoyed with others. Even if a game's systems are not programmed to "react" to particular analog actions of a player (such as feigning eating a virtual object), other players have a great capacity for recognizing and reacting to these pantomime behaviors. Even if they do not serve a gameplay function, they serve a social function.

Within the VR space, the player is an actor in each scene more directly than ever before, and gameplay is performance in those scenes. The psychological distance between player and character is at a minimum. Even new players begin quickly adding their own flourishes to the gunplay of *Half-Life: Alyx* (2020), the sword dance of *Beat Saber* (2019), or the no-wrong-answers comedy interactions of *Job Simulator* (2016).

To conclude, it should be remembered that the degree to which a control scheme may be considered analog or digital is a gradient spectrum and dependent upon that which it is being compared against. Analog control can be a challenge or an opportunity for greater mastery. In that sense, on the low ends of player skill or finesse, it can present a uniquely individualized experience (an aspect of expressiveness) while acting as a barrier to direct impulse-to-intended-action control (another aspect of expressiveness). For a highly skilled player, though, it can offer an unparalleled degree of personal expression and artistic creativity in play, with some games even offering opportunities to create bespoke pieces of art within the mechanics of the game (such as the ability to freely solo or remix on-the-fly in Harmonix's *Rock Band 4* [2015] and *Disney Fantasia: Music Evolved* [2014], respectively, or the opportunity to paint or engage in digital photography in *Passpartout: The Starving Artist* [2017] and *Umurangi Generation* [2020], respectively).

Metagame convention: A final quality that can produce micro-expressivity in this non-exhaustive list refers to behavioral conventions that accumulate within a game's communal metagame. These might include ritualized behaviors performed with a game's limited behavioral affordances, typically against or ambivalent to their intended uses. These flourish in competitive games. Certain behavioral rituals, unrecognized by the games from a mechanical perspective, may be considered signs of good or poor sportsmanship when performed. For example, players of competitive shooters and fighting games have a long tradition of "teabagging" after winning small victories—causing the avatar to repeatedly crouch while standing over a downed opponent as an act of humiliation. This is only commonly recognized because of its conventional ubiquity amidst particular competitive communities. They have used an unrelated action affordance as a means of (rude) communication.

On the more positive side, the desert exploration game *Journey* (2012) is built around such convention-based communication, this time in a manner that is supported (but not made easy) by its mechanics. *Journey* is ostensibly single-player, in that the game begins with the player on a journey to a distant mountaintop, and it resolves only once this player has reached their destination. Along the way, though, play becomes passively multiplayer. Two players will be (without it being announced) seamlessly put into the same world as one another, like encountering a stranger upon a journey. When encountering another player, they might be novices making this journey for the first time, or they might be wise veterans of the game, returning to help others along their journeys. Crucially, players have very limited means by which they can communicate. They are not afforded voice chat or expressive gestures; they are only allowed their typical movement affordances as well as a "ping" that makes a distinctive noise and instantiates a visual bubble around the communicating player (to draw attention). Players sometimes have to communicate rather complicated solutions to puzzles, and this is done using a pantomime of movements and pings, like communicating with someone who does not speak your language.

Once players become accustomed to the crude communicational conventions employed by the other randomly matched player, a more effective partnership builds up, albeit only briefly. Just as unexpectedly as players' worlds are brought together, they are also separated, and players may be randomly matched with others.

NON-RESPONSIVE EXPRESSION

While the operational definition of expressivity used in this chapter specifically refers to modes of expression to which gameplay systems are tuned to respond, it can also be useful to separately look at the means by which players can self-express to which gameplay mechanics do not directly respond. We may classify these as elements of effective ambivalence, referencing the third polarity not referenced in the previous sections as heavily as the "expressive" and "prescriptive" polarities. These moments of non-mechanical expression tend to be aesthetic or semiotic in nature, appreciable by the player or spectators. An ambivalent response is not necessarily the absence of a planned response, nor is it necessarily negative. Ambivalence can be planned and can often be a very effective choice, as will be detailed below.

In the worst moments, gameplay systems may alienate players by being ambivalent to their expressive choices. It is common for dialog scenes to present players with dialog options that are not borne out in the system's response. Often, a preferred dialog choice (necessary for advancing the conversation in the way in which the writers intended) will be presented alongside a "fake" dialog option created with the assumption that most players will be interested in furthering the intended dialog path and will pick the first. Choosing the second results in either the exact same statement that would have been given were the first option chosen or a reworded prompt that ends up expressing the same information or sentiment as if the first response had been chosen. In cases in which the player can detect that the choice is illusory, she may experience a greater psychological distance from the avatar, and the artificiality of the narrative may be harder to look past.

This type of response may be used effectively, though. For instance, if the avatar character is interrupted while speaking, say by a nearby explosion, it is realistic that the choice of dialog did not matter. The shock or frustration at the lack of narrative agency in that moment is shared by both the player and the avatar character. It is an *effective* moment in *affective* role-playing. Similarly, if another character being spoken to responds in the same way regardless of the dialogue choice selected, it can give the feeling that she is not listening to or honoring the player's choices, which can be the correct characterization choice (and elicit the proper affective response) for certain types of self-interested or neglectful characters.

Further, there are moments in which systemic ambivalence can *amplify* the effectiveness of particular expressive choices. Games that allow extensive, creative customization of player characters can allow the player to create moments of uproarious comedy with the system acting as the "straight man" in their routine. Games like *Saints Row: The Third* (2011) and *Baldur's Gate 3* (2023) feature created characters in their cutscenes, appearing exactly as players cosmetically style them. Seeing eccentrically dressed and ludicrously proportioned characters perform often quite self-serious scenes without acknowledgement feels like an amplification of the comedy. Like bending the social mores of the story world; getting one over on the narrative design. In games in which silly dress is acknowledged (like *The Sims 4* [2014]), the choice is mimetically justified as an eccentricity of the character. In games in which silly dress is *not* acknowledged, like *Dead Rising* (2006), the eccentricity becomes a property of the story logic itself, like a spoof movie in which the absurd is accepted because the story's reality is ontologically *other*.

Most cosmetic customizability is primarily for the benefit of players, either for the simple aesthetic gratification of players in a single-player setting or as a communicative tool (and even a practical affordance) in multiplayer games. Games with customizable avatars or multiple selectable "skins" or costumes, such as online multiplayer games *Fortnite* (2017) or *Street Fighter V* (2016), costume choice can communicate in-group status to other players. For instance, *Fortnite* avatars can be dressed as hundreds of characters from other media properties such as Star Wars, Marvel Comics, and Dragon Ball Z. Choice of costume communicates fandom of those properties (a desire to play that role within *Fortnite*'s "multiverse" fantasy) and may engender favor with other players who share that fandom, leading to impromptu alliances between strangers who find that they have something in common.

Ownership of rare costumes or emotes can also be a form of conspicuous consumption, indicating that the player has enough money to make frequent purchases within the *Fortnite* store or enough free time (also an expression of financial security) to dedicate to unlocking the material through play labor. This is doubly true for games that distribute items, costumes, and characters through gambling-like "gacha" systems (an onomatopoeic term adapted from the sound made by the machines that distribute surprise-prize capsules in Japanese arcades), in which desirable items are distributed at random, requiring players to purchase (most often for real money) "booster packs" that may or may not contain their desired items. Such games include *Genshin Impact* (2020), *Fire Emblem Heroes* (2017), and *Overwatch* (2016).

In the ways outlined above, cosmetic presentation *can* have a gameplay effect if we consider slight manipulations of other players' behavior to ultimately feed back into the loop of instantiated gameplay. More direct gameplay effects of cosmetic costuming can be seen in some fighting games. Because a strong character silhouette is important in "reading" fighting games, costumes that interfere with the readability of characters' physical boundaries or animations are often banned from tournaments. For example, the fighting game *Street Fighter V* (2016) features a cheerleader-themed costume for character R. Mika in which she holds pom-poms in her hands, obscuring the *true* position of her hands and making her posing and animations *slightly* harder to read. For this reason, fighting game tournaments tend to ban costumes that match the background colors of particular stages (making avatar poses indistinct against certain backgrounds), costumes that greatly exaggerate the frame of a fighter (making it difficult to identify their "hurtboxes"; areas that represent the body that can be attacked), costumes that include a significant amount of extraneous physics objects (that can add "visual noise" to their animations and silhouettes), and even costumes that are too sexy (to the point that they might be distracting for the opponent). In cases such as these, cosmetic choices may cease to be *expressive* of the player, as they are chosen primarily for competitive advantage rather than as expressions of personal taste.

A final, vital factor of mechanically non-responsive expression is in mimetic performance agency in the operation of the avatar. In scenes in which the player retains control of the avatar during dialogue or scripted narrative moments, the player may choose to utilize basic control affordances to enrich the "performance" of the scene in ways that may not be recognized by the mechanical systems that govern gameplay but are more deeply immersive for the player herself or for onlookers. The player may adopt a "panicked" affectation during scenes of danger and disarray purely for the purpose of immersing herself in the performance—for no mechanical benefit. The player may choose to have the avatar respectfully match the gait of a conversation partner in a walk-and-talk scene as a performance choice.

Perhaps the most engrossing example of this kind of unenforced performance affordance that I have seen is in the comedic adventure game *Once Upon a Jester* (2022), which tells the story about a duo of thieves-turned-performers staging semi-improvised theatrical performances in a medieval fantasy setting. During each stage performance, the player is given small mastery/timing tests to simulate the stakes of hitting one's lines and marks during a performance and may choose between several performance directions based on what the crowd may or may not want to see in a given setting. During the performance, I found myself naturally moving across the stage in order to frame action appropriately, moving downstage when my performer spoke and keeping the blocking dynamic and interesting. This was not mechanically acknowledged or rewarded, but I felt like it immersed me further as a performer of improvised theatre. In this case, I was only "performing" for my own imagination, but the imagination's capacity to reconstruct ambiguity into greater nuance and meaning proves the effectiveness of well-utilized mechanical ambivalence.

EXPRESSIVITY CONCLUSION

Expressivity is a factor of ludic expression that has not been frequently studied or consistently defined. As an experiential factor, it can be useful in identifying how and why some games feel like more fertile ground for creative expression than others. Self-expression is one of the primary outlets of ludic meaning, as argued in Chapter 8. In such capacities, games act as conduits for creative expression, amplifying the resonance of player agency through contextualization within fantasy worlds and expressive systemic response. Identifying expressivity at the micro- and macro-levels can give players important factors by which games or mechanics can be contextualized, contrasted, and considered.

NOTE

1 Early experiments in generative semiotic narratives typically involved written content with a high degree of machine reconfiguration. As of the time of writing, teams are experimenting with large language model (LLM) artificial intelligence engines that may avail generative content of this sort in the future, but, to date, produced material has been lacking in quality and has not been ethically sourced and produced.

REFERENCES

Keenan, J. (2021). *Meaningless choices and impractical advice* [Video]. GDC Vault. https://www.gdcvault.com/play/1027160/-Disco-Elysium-Meaningless-Choices

Koenitz, H. (2023). *Understanding interactive digital narrative*. Routledge. doi:10.4324/9781003106425

Lynch, K. (2016). *Video: Gamer defeats Dark Souls using guitar, drumkit, bongos and more*. Guinness World Records. https://www.guinnessworldrecords.com/news/2016/9/video-gamer-defeats-dark-souls-using-guitar-drumkit-bongos-and-more-444468

Ryan, J. (2018). *Curating simulated storyworlds* [Doctoral dissertation, UC Santa Cruz]. UC Santa Cruz Electronic Theses and Dissertations. https://escholarship.org/uc/item/1340j5h2#main

Swink, S. (2009). *Game feel: A game designer's guide to virtual sensation*. Morgan Kaufmann Publishers.

Upton, B. (2015). *The aesthetic of play*. The MIT Press.

CHAPTER 13

Glitches, Cheating, and Metagame

THROUGHOUT THIS BOOK, ATTENTION has been paid to reading video games as products of design and artifacts of communication. In our exploration of meaning-making, there has been a balance between elucidating the generative qualities of game systems, capable of constructing novel emergent narratives, sensitive to player agency, and the embedded qualities of artistic inscription and design—the invariable qualities that give games their structures and semiotic identities.

This chapter explores the emergent elements that arise *parallel* to and even *contrary* to design. The beautiful ways in which games can break and the ways in which the aspects of inflexibility within game systems can give rise to unexpected and unintended novel play. This chapter begins with an exploration of *metagame* before moving into more explicitly contrarian behaviors: the technical contrarian represented by the *glitch* and the participatory contrarian represented by the *cheater*. I argue that these aspects are not necessarily deleterious to the gameplay experience but natural and, at times, *constructive* elements of games' formal structure.

METAGAME

Rules are elements of design. They explain how play is *supposed to* operate, but they undergo translation in their substantiation as mechanics, logical parameters that the computer can directly action and enforce. Unlike human players, who self-monitor and socially enforce rules in board, card, social, and tabletop games, computers are bound, inflexibly, to their logical structures. While the administrator of a game of *Dungeons & Dragons* (Gygax & Arneson, 1974) can adapt the game to the choices of the players and respond appropriately when a player follows the letter but not the spirit of the law, the computer is only able to respond in non-nuanced terms. Rather than being a limitation of the form, though, this impersonality of rule application ends up being the stiff and inflexible skeleton around which other categories of games and culture emerge. Ultimately, this is the level on which games are played, not bound by rules but bound by possibilities. This is the layer of the metagame.

Magic: The Gathering creator Richard Garfield (2000) says that metagame is "how a game interfaces with life. A particular game, played with the exact same rules will mean different things to different people, and those differences are the metagame". It is the overlap between games and reality; the manners in which reality pushes inward into the game and the manners in which the game pushes outward into reality.

"Meta-" as a prefix refers to a self-reflective perspective by which a subject examines or elucidates something about itself, often questioning or bringing to light the core assumptions that would otherwise be unchallenged. Metacognition, for instance, is "thought about thought", conscious consideration of the manner in which thought occurs. Metaphysics is a philosophy of the core nature of reality, preceding the point at which other sciences *begin*; what are the physics *of* physics? Similarly, metagames are games that reveal the structural fundamentals of games. "Metagame" as a term was developed in the context of *game theory*, the mathematical and economic discipline studying optimal strategies in decision-dependent situations. Nigel Howard (1971) coined the term to describe the

DOI: 10.1201/9781003530961-13

play of knowledge and information in the Prisoner's Dilemma. In it, he describes how each "rational" choice in a Prisoner's Dilemma is actually contingent upon a self-reflective and reflexive "metachoice", such that each quadrant of the 2×2 Prisoner's Dilemma decision grid contains, in itself, a smaller game theory grid, a pattern that can be followed infinitely downwards.

Stephanie Boluk and Patrick LeMieux (2017) suggest four categories of metagames in the forms of prepositions that can complete the definitional clause.

Games about games. This category of metagame captures and reproduces an aspect of a particular game or its iconography in another game. The metagame played between these games is the interplay of meaning and shared context. Something familiar is re-established with a new ludic context for the purpose of parody, re-examination, or simply to call attention to a lineage of design. This can be done through the invocation of imagery (*Super Smash Bros. Ultimate* [2018] is a game about *many types* of games, homogenized into a fighting game format without losing their essential flavors) or the transfer of specific logics and *ludemes* (*Getting Over It with Bennett Foddy* [2017] extends ludemes established in Flash game *Sexy Hiking* [2002], weaving them into a new experience that pushes players to the limits of their loss tolerance).

"Deeper than recontextualizing a particular IP's iconography, some *games about games* question and prod at the fundamental nature of computer software altogether. Games like *FEZ* (2012) examine the metaphysics of two-dimensional and three-dimensional games. *Portal* (2007) explores alternate approaches to presenting and existing within three-dimensional, simulated space. "They are games not only about games, but about *aboutness* itself: games that play with the aesthetic conventions of videogames as a visual medium and intervene in software genres that emerged as a consequence of specific graphic technologies" (Boluk & LeMieux, 2017, p. 18).

Games within games. These are the standard, unavoidable type of metagame that is engaged during the play of any game. If the "rules" represent an idealized vision for how play within a game is supposed to unfold, the metagame within normal gameplay is one that considers rules not in their ideal abstract but the type of play that can occur within the material affordances of the game as specifically instantiated.

Every game was designed with means and method of play in mind. *Super Mario 64* (1996) was designed to be played with the Nintendo 64's unconventional, three-pronged controller. Playing *Super Mario 64* on Nintendo Switch using the system's more modern and conventional controller options is a form of metagame. If we consider play of *Super Mario 64* on Nintendo 64 hardware using the standard N64 controller on a period-appropriate television to represent the *standard metagame* (or *orthogame*; Carter et al., 2012), every deviation from that introduces a degree of novelty and alternative play.

This can also result in what amounts to playing an alternate game entirely. Speedrunners introduce a self-imposed objectives: finish the game (or a subsection of the game) as quickly as possible; and the speedrunning community has their own set of rules that are socially-enforced rather than computationally-enforced: allowance of particular techniques and exploits and disallowance of others. Alternate metagames within games do not need to be this organized, though. Every choice that players make in a game point them towards playing the game *in a particular manner.* A *Super Mario 64* player who enjoys collecting all of the coins in each level will have different incentives than those who prefer to only rush through levels and not bother with optional collectables.

More fundamentally, though, metagames *emerge* from the concrete constraints and affordances of mechanics. All that is possible is allowed; only what is impossible is disallowed. As such, while we can say that *rules* define *games*, *mechanics* structure *metagames.* Since *rules* and *games* are abstract concepts of design, the player *can* only play metagames. The establishment of any in-game challenge or any in-game economy is only a setting in which metagame play may occur. Richard Garfield (2000) writes, "A game without a metagame is like an idealized object in physics. It may be a useful construct but it doesn't really exist".

"Metagames transform videogames from a mass medium and cultural commodity into instruments, equipment, tools, and toys for playing, competing, spectating, cheating, trading, making, breaking, and ultimately intervening in the sensory and political economies of those technologies responsible for the privatization of play" (Boluk & LeMieux, 2017, p. 4).

Games around games. Any time that a community forms around a game, the community reshapes the "rules" that structure the game. In competitive games, knowledge of optimal strategies or situationally-specific counters is an informal mechanic of play. This form of metagame plays out over the entire lifespan of a competitive game. This can be witnessed in the evolving "tier lists" of competitive fighting games, in which some characters are thought to vastly outclass others, and players who use those characters regularly sweep competitions until, invariably, an appropriate counter-play is discovered. Once knowledge of that counter-play spreads throughout the community, playing as the previously-dominant character becomes riskier; the balance of power resettles and tier lists are adjusted.

In fact, the highest layer of strategy – that beyond the individual player's own conceptualization; held in the collective mind of the community of play – is informally called "the metagame" or "the meta" by players. To adjust to new dominant strategies as they are discovered by the community is to "follow the meta". This level of strategy does not only affect competitive, multiplayer games. As techniques and efficiencies are learned in single-player games, it affects the way that people play through those games individually. The crowd-sourcing of knowledge, strategy, and narrative is a form of metagame (one that fits nicely into the final category).

Another type of metagame that occurs *around* games involves the social element of play. Being able to read or influence the psychology of an opponent can radically upset a match; hidden information games like Poker and *Among Us* (2018) are based around these games of psychological manipulation – played interpersonally, in the ephemeral space between players rather than with the tokens and pieces of the games themselves. Games of diplomacy also hinge on how one communicates trustworthiness and dependability, at and away from the table of play (Garfield, 2000). These are truly "meta"-games, because they involve consideration of what you think the opponent thinks that you are thinking. Knowledge external to the functional mechanisms of the game are being utilized to make decisions more complex than fundamental, mechanical strategy.

We can also consider some elements of cheating to fall into this category. Distracting opponents with loud noises or tickling during a game can be a strategic consideration, though not great sportsmanship. Similarly, unplugging a router during a LAN game can disrupt the game for opponents (Terrell, 2011).

Carter et al. (2012) calls this style of metagame *paragames* – parallel games – describing activities that form alongside other games. The social management of a guild of real players in MMORPG *World of WarCraft* (2004) constitutes a paragame, itself. Conceivably, someone could derive a tremendous amount of enjoyment from the *WoW* guild paragame without having any interest in *WoW*'s RPG content.

Games without games. Finally, aspects of metagames operate even in the absence of the game itself. Maintenance or breakdown of relationships between players in the times between sessions of play has consequences that echo within the game itself. Time spent thinking about, researching, and thinking about a game in between sessions of play contributes to performance. Even in non-competitive settings, many players have the experience of solving a difficult puzzle by reviewing the components in their minds while away for the game – in bed, in the shower, on a morning commute… This, though away from the "magic circle" that designates the boundary of the game, can still be considered a form of play – of engagement with the game's puzzles.

Further, fan communities that develop around games and produce fan art, write fan fictions, spread jokes and rumors about ludic fictions, and dress as their favorite characters at conventions carry the meaning generated by the games into different social spaces. Bands and orchestras may reinterpret a game's soundtrack; characters may be incorporated into crossover titles like *Super Smash Bros. Ultimate* (2018); game stories may be adapted for film and television. These extend the ways in which players can engage with beloved games, and they reshape and influence aspects of what it means, culturally, to *play* the game.

To synthesize earlier points, human-administered games require players to adopt, abide by, and monitor others' respect of the rules; otherwise, the game will collapse. This is what philosopher Bernard Suits (1978) calls the *lusory attitude*: the acceptance and abidance of rules necessary to create the condition of play. To play a social game is to engage in a social contract with the other players: to enter into what early play theorist Johan Huizinga (1938) called the *magic circle*, the social and physical space of the real world dedicated to the play and fantasy of the game in which normal expectations and conventions are deferred for the unique behaviors and goals that drive the game.

Since video games are computationally self-governing, it relieves the player of the responsibility of adopting the lusory attitude. The player does not work toward the game's maintenance; she pushes against the boundaries of the rules, imposed impersonally like natural forces. These mechanics form a rigid structure around which metagames form.

Katie Salen (Tekinbaş) and Eric Zimmerman (2003) define *play* as "free movement within a more rigid structure", drawing a clever parallel with the concept of *mechanical* play, "the amount the steering wheel can turn before it begins to turn the tires of the car". In that sense, metagame play is a very true and direct expression of this type of play. The rules of the game, substantiated as mechanics, function as the rigid structure around which metagames are developed.

In fact, engagement with art of all kinds involves metagames in which the abstract or representative form of the piece suggests a structure that is played with, molded, and reformed in the mind of the beholder through associative resonances to produce something personal and unique. Kendall L. Walton (1990) framed artworks as props in imaginative games, suggesting that the imaginings into the fictions that works represent are a form of play, a game played within the structure that the work suggests (p. 38).

Metagame and Narrative

Following Walton's assertion that art invites beholders into games of imaginative mimesis, we can recognize an aspect of universality in the metagame. As it applies to narrative, specifically, differing levels of metagame may be at play. Some stories require only the basic aspects of metagame: extrapolation of ungiven details (closure) that comes naturally from imaginative investment. Other narratives, even among traditional, linear media, are more inherently game-like in their structure, inviting expansive metagame play.

Detective novels position the reader as a co-investigator. Though the reader does not have the same kind of instrumental agency as the narrative detective, the reader can take great pleasure from working out the clues and deducing the solution to the mystery ahead of the narrative conclusion. This is why it can be so frustrating when detective stories do not include all of the necessary clues, treating withheld information as a narrative twist—the game structurally invites metagame play but then denies the reader access to the metagame.

Similarly, there are types of films that rely more on game-like "mechanics" than conventional narrative presentation. The comedy epic *PlayTime* (Tati, 1967) eschews singular focus in most scenes for densely crowded, highly dynamic scenes through which many people and groups of people pass through, each expressing a narrative or quirk. The viewer chooses on whose stories she will focus, piecing together a portrait of the film's hyper-modern city through the stories and personalities she chose to prioritize. Though the film does not respond to this choice in the same way that a video game would, the viewer may end up with a completely dissimilar experience on a subsequent viewing if she instead chooses to attend to other characters instead. The congestion of each scene communicates the aesthetic of emergence at work in urban centers: the apparent chaos and confusion of the individual resolves to a beautiful, clockwork harmony at a higher level as the grander rhythms of the holistic "machine" of the city become apparent.

In Chapter 6, I describe three parallel perspectives that players adopt while playing video games: the *diegetic perspective* involves the sense-pleasure of embodied play within the simulation: movement, simulated "physical" interactions, the sense of being and manipulating a compelling space, and a recognition of the "real" elements of the simulation that can be directly manipulated and the toyetic joy that comes from doing so. The *mimetic perspective* involves the narrative appeal of playing a role within a fantasy story, a recognition of the artifice of the video game artifact, and an acceptance of one's role as a performer within that narrative. The *methectic perspective* involves reckoning with the game as a series of computational tasks and logical structures, stepping outside of the fantasy to form strategies to achieve objectives, a recognition of the artifice of the game, and an exploitation of that knowledge. The methectic perspective is closely aligned with metagame formation and will be the focus of the next section, but I must first contrast the ways in which metagame play fits into the player's mimetic play.

Role-playing within a fantasy involves taking on a series of self-motivated constraints pertaining to the performance of the avatar character. If we consider a stage actor, she performs a role to create a mimetic illusion *by* denying her natural impulses. She knows the script and knows what will befall her character and all others, but she presents to the audience the illusion of someone who does not know—someone who experiences these events for the first time. She limits her freedom of speech and movement to that which serves this purpose—that which is contained within the script. She temporarily defers her own identity to embody another role during the performance.

The degree to which players immerse themselves in this kind of role-playing during video game play varies (Tu et al., 2022). The deferment of the player's *total* available agency for the benefit of embedded narrative-adherent enactment may or may not be recognized or rewarded by the game's mechanical layer, but it can be rewarding in and of itself. This is most evident in its converse: playing a story-rich game in a manner that is purely logical and impersonal can feel narratively unfulfilling, like the player witnessed the procession of narrative beats from a detached perspective; the character coldly running between tasks rather than truly *existing* in the social and fantasy space defined by the game's semiotic expression. Especially in RPGs, there is a particular pleasure in treating the agents and locations in games not only as simulated physical entities and not only as tokens within games of strategic computation but as links to an imagined world of story.

Role-playing as a character rather than treating the avatar *simply* as a locus of manipulation within the virtual space is a metagame. Sometimes this type of play is rewarded in-game (for example, making "good" or "evil" moral decisions during gameplay rewards the avatar with similarly oriented abilities in games like *STAR WARS Knights of the Old Republic* [2003] or *inFAMOUS* [2009]), and sometimes it is purely for the interest and entertainment of the player (Robin Burkinshaw played *The Sims 3* [2009] as a pair of unhoused characters, a task that the game was not *built* to anticipate but was allowable within its flexible role-playing systems. The account of this playthrough can be read in retelling; Burkinshaw, 2009).

In these cases, the metagame being played has a separate objective: to explore or construct a character's personal narrative through fantasy-adherent gameplay. Every action that advances the avatar's characterization represents progress, while every action that strains narrative coherence risks breaking the immersive continuity. The value of achieving narratively immersed play is one of discovery and can result in stories that feel *personal* and *chosen* rather than *mandated* and *unavoidable*.

Striving for narrative agency, even within highly designed game spaces, is a form of metagame. The relationships between characters and narrative consequences of player choices and gameplay actions form an incentive structure parallel to progression toward a game's ludic conclusion. Games like *As Dusk Falls* (2022) and *Life Is Strange* (2015) are undemanding in terms of gameplay execution but highly configurable from a narrative perspective. The player is often presented with difficult choices that have significant narrative consequences. Some players may take equal pleasure from seeing how any series of events plays out (trusting that all routes result in well-written and satisfying stories), but some may desire particular outcomes—perhaps positive outcomes for sympathetic characters or the most interesting and chaotic series of events. Achieving these ends—and deducing the narrative choices that will lead to players' desired outcomes—is like directing the story, and it creates a metagame structure of objectives and incentives.

Since the logic of games functions to generate interesting narratives around the choices of players, it can be fascinating to see how these logics respond to unanticipated or unconventional role-playing decisions. For example, players have chosen to role-play avatar Link as a vegan in *The Legend of Zelda: Breath of the Wild* (2017; Poole, 2019) or to play games like *The Elder Scrolls V: Skyrim* (2011) as a pacifist, rejecting the game's mechanical pushes toward violence (Kelly, 2022).

In multiplayer settings, role-playing can create rich, shared fantasies through collaborative storytelling, such as *Red Dead Online* (2019) role-playing servers in which players enact their Old West fantasies with careful adherence to fictional coherence (Harris, 2020) or simply using the simulation as a stage within which to create bespoke fantasies not related to the semiotic skin of the host games (Cabubas, 2021). In such games, the simulation becomes a setting of imaginative play, giving structure to games running in parallel to or even completely separately from the designed objectives within the game.

Metagame and Methexis

Metagame play is most closely associated with the methectic perspective. To review, this perspective understands the artificiality of a game and rejects deferment of that knowledge. Strategy is built around gameplay systems as consistent, logical variables of computational behavior, even exploiting elements of design that might be *contrary* to the game's mimetic illusion. For example, many games use weighted systems of chance to convey how likely it would be for a character to successfully perform a chosen action given her present proficiency with complementary skills. For example, in the detective CRPG *Disco Elysium* (2019), avatar Harry Du Bois' ability to successfully break through a locked door is mediated by his physical fitness. Players who have chosen to invest character points (earned through game progress) in physical attributes may have an 80% chance of successfully breaking through a locked door, while those who have not invested in Du Bois' physical prowess may have a 5% chance of a successful break and enter. Presented with a 5% success rate, a player *can* choose to save the game immediately before attempting the action, reloading after every failed attempt until a successful attempt is achieved by chance. There is no disincentive for this behavior (termed "save scumming" by the gaming community). Save scumming prioritizes the methectic perspective (achievement of goals using *all* affordances of the software as an artificial construct) at the expense of narrative coherence, whereas refusing to save scum and simply playing on with the consequences of chosen actions, even if they are not preferable, represents a dedication to the mimetic perspective, a trust that an interesting story will emerge even in the case of a failed action.

From the methectic perspective, gameplay is only constrained by mechanical behavior, not by narrative or semiotic coherence. While the human game masters who administer tabletop gameplay decide operational happenings based on what makes for the most compelling narrative, acting and reacting based on a semiotic understanding of the developing story, video games are purely computational; thus, the rules suggested in the abstract are only contextual suggestions by which one can understand the mechanical logics that the game *actually* enforces. As such, *all* video gameplay is metagame play. Each objective that a game sets in front of the player is achievable, *not necessarily* how it was designed to be completed but how the player can manipulate the systems of play to satisfy its requirement.

For example, the 3D platformer *Donkey Kong 64* (1999) features a series of locked doors barring entry to each new level. To open these doors, the player must have collected a certain amount of one of the game's currencies to pay the toll that serves as the "key" to open the door. On the other side of the door is a "warp plane", a doorway that transports the avatar to a new level when the avatar crosses its threshold. One of the playable avatars, Lanky Kong, has stretchy arms, which he can use to punch enemies from afar. Arms, unlike the Kongs' bodies, do not collide with solid surfaces (so as to not interrupt attack animations in tight spaces). As such, Lanky Kong can be aligned in such a way that he punches *through* the gate (as collision is not obstructed) and touches the warp plane behind it, warping him into the level despite not possessing the requisite currency to pay the toll. This is an exploitation of a design oversight and makes no sense at the level of semiotic representation, but because it is allowed by the game's mechanics, it is a valid method by which to surpass that barrier. Instead of being a currency gate, it becomes a test of meta-knowledge and skill for players familiar with the workaround.

Even in the case of conventional play, a metagame is being enacted because the computer cannot understand and enforce the game's rules as a series of semantic ideas. Every form of play is a choice to play *in some way*; a selection of any manner of possible sequences of agential enactment around the operational core of a game's systems. It is this quality that makes gameplay personal and worthy of the kinds of stories that players derive from it. This form of play embodies the "meta" quality of metagame play. The player utilizes her outside knowledge, reflecting upon the game as a system of knowable dependencies, to guide decisions. It is gameplay empowered by the knowledge that it is gameplay; a reflective exercise in thinking about the game as a game.

Embedded Metagames

It is increasingly common for game developers to embed peripheral metagame systems within the games that they produce. Since a gameplay system is attuned to generate interesting challenges and prompt interesting decision-making from its players, it is most often an additive value to prompt alternative play with the logics and systems built to support the orthogame (the standard manner of play; Carter et al., 2012). This form of metagame, called *paragame*, can radically recontextualize game logics and ludemes (see Chapter 7) to produce interesting, alternate forms of play.

Some paragames are embedded into the structure of the game itself and run in parallel with normal play. High-score systems are common forms of paragames in otherwise progression-based titles. For example, the story-based character action game *Bayonetta* (2009) gives players scores and ordinal ranks after each fight. Though the formal structure of the game only requires players to *survive* these fights in order to advance to the next chapter of the game, the presence of a scoring system and feedback of medaled ranking prompts players to replay and perfect completed battles in order to achieve the coveted Pure Platinum medal in each. Similarly, the point-to-point racing game *Out Run* (1986) features a multilinear course that resolves to a definite ending as the player reaches the finish line, but play during the race is also scored to reward skillful and risky driving. As such, reaching the finish line (a narrative conclusion to the orthogame) becomes a precondition for engaging in the competitive paragame of high-score achievement, particularly in the arcade setting.

Some paragames are embedded into games' systems but are played separately from orthogame play. These often emerge from the discovery of mechanics of play interesting or versatile enough to stand alone or support other structured play activities. For example, the 2D tactical artillery game *Worms 2* (1997) features a diverse assortment of weapons and utilities, among which is the Ninja Rope, a grappling-hook-like item that allows a worm avatar to shoot a rope into a piece of the game world and swing on it like Spider-Man, allowing the worms to reach places that would be otherwise inaccessible. Swinging on the rope is fun in and of itself, so the player community developed what came to be known as Rope Race maps: maze-like courses in which players would non-violently race one another to a finish line using the movement techniques afforded by the Ninja Rope. Similarly, *Super Mario Odyssey* (2017) contains a paragame called Luigi's Balloon World in which players, using the game's unique movement affordances, challenge each other to reach balloons they have hidden within the world of the game. The catch is that players seeking these balloons have a strict time limit. They are only given the amount of time to retrieve them that the hider took to place them (from a designated starting point). This incentivizes both players to use the game's movement techniques to their optimal potential, taking unconventional and non-obvious routes to hiding places in order to, from the hider's perspective, create as challenging a gauntlet as possible or, from the retriever's perspective, to beat the clock.

Finally, there are designed paragames that exist at a layer external to the game's systems. Xbox Achievements, for example, reward designated in-game actions with points that accumulate at the level of the user's Xbox profile, tracking a cumulative "Gamer Score" across *all* of the games that the player has played within the Xbox ecosystem. These Achievements can encourage alternate forms of play, such as the Little Rocket Man Achievement for the first-person shooter *Half-Life 2: Episode Two* (2007), which requires players to carry a garden gnome prop found early in the game through all of the game's challenges and deposit it into a rocket ship near the game's conclusion. This action is not rewarded (or suggested) in-game; it exists only as a peripheral, optional challenge at the extradiegetic layer of play. Achievement hunting is a game that exists within other games.

ALTERNATIVE PLAY: SPEEDRUNS AND CHALLENGES

Just as developers can embed sanctioned metagames into games' systems, unofficial metagames can thrive within the rich and complex systems that games present. I have already mentioned several types of player- and community-generated metagames, and I would like to spend time focusing on two types in particular: speedrunning and self-imposed challenge play.

Speedrunning

Speedrunning is a metagame that involves completing a game (or a subsection within a game, such as a level or an arbitrary task) as quickly as possible. This can be an individual pursuit; one may simply wish to see how quickly she can complete a game with which she is familiar or challenge her previous best time. More commonly, though, it is a communal practice with both competitive and cooperative elements. Players within the speedrunning community compete for the best times within designated categories and keep surprisingly rigorous standards for recording and validating submitted times. But the community also collaborates to build knowledge of chosen games. Finding new exploitable glitches or time-saving techniques is excitedly shared across the community rather than held in competitive secrecy.

Almost any game can support a speedrunning metagame. The community sets guidelines and constraints in order to create consistent standards of evaluation. Often, this results in multiple *categories* of challenges available to players of a particular game. For example, *Super Mario 64* (1996) speedruns are divided into 120-star (100%; completing every challenge in the game), 70-star (completing the minimum number of challenges necessary to complete the game as designed), and "Any%" (reaching the game's conclusion utilizing glitches to bypass checkpoint requirements, meaning that players can finish with under 70 stars) categories. Each category has a separate world record holder and has different strategies of play.

The rules created around each category of run for each game evolve alongside the community. At what point does the timer start and stop? Does the run start as soon as the system turns on or when the player gains control over the character? Does it conclude when credits play, when the final necessary action is performed, or at another arbitrary endpoint? What kinds of glitches can be exploited? What versions of the game can be played (in cases in which, for example, a European release of a game may run slower than an American release or the more space-efficient Chinese text may progress quicker than English text)? Must games be played on original hardware, or can they be played on emulators? Are unconventional controllers allowed? What kind of proof must be submitted for a run to be considered for leaderboard placement?

Some speedruns resemble normal gameplay played at a very high level of mastery. Speedruns of rhythm games or auto-scrolling shmups designate a maximum pace of play, so time-saving is only possible with flawless play. Other speedruns render their host games almost unrecognizable for how alternative their strategies become. Some involve utilizing glitches to skip significant portions or to realize unintended affordances. Some even involve exploiting particular glitches that allow players to "reprogram" elements of game systems, altering code values with specific sequences of actions or controller inputs, as some exploits "directly [expose] the computational logic of videogames by transforming the gamespace into a programming interface capable of both pointing to specific memory addresses and replacing their values at will" (Boluk & LeMieux, 2017, p. 44)—a particular aesthetic of digital games that is always impressive, sometimes frightening.

Within the speedrunning community, glitches are not embarrassing mistakes or artifacts of technical failure—they present exciting opportunities for alternative play. The exhibition of such glitches can not only be highly entertaining and surprising; it can also be an educational tool for helping audiences understand how games function at the level of their technical logics. Boluk and LeMieux (2017) give an interesting example of a speedrunning technique for the first-person shooter *DOOM 64* (1997).

> if a Nintendo 64 is powered on with the control stick tilted, that angle will be calibrated as the default position, altering the value of stick's neutral position and [...] permitting an extra range of directional motion—a position faster than fast.
>
> *(p. 45)*

Events such as Awesome Games Done Quick/Summer Games Done Quick celebrate the speedrunning community and exhibit impressive runs with educational commentary to ensure that the audience understands what kinds of technical or conventional affordances are being utilized to produce such impressive gameplay.

Boluk and LeMieux (2017) continue:

> The ideology of speedrunning recognizes videogames exclusively in terms of a discrete state space produced by the operation of specific hardware and software [...] If videogames are agnostic to how they are played and every operation yields states of equal value, then there are no glitches, nothing is out of bounds, and the intentions of an author and audience are a completely arbitrary metagame in and of themselves.
>
> *(p. 46)*

Chapter 12 explores *expressivity* as a property of gameplay systems. Highly expressive games are reactive to unconventional or individualized play in a manner that reflects and is expressive of the player. Considering the freedom around the rigid structure of games' mechanics (to call back Salen & Zimmerman [2003]'s definition of play), speedruns can be highly transformative artistic artifacts in and of themselves. Players who push into game systems in unconventional ways to find novel affordances are artists, exploring forms of agency even beyond that which the developers had intended. This kind of artistic production *within* other artworks is an exciting extension of the postmodern philosophy of artistic reflexiveness.

Challenge Runs

While speedrunning utilizes novel technological affordances and executional techniques to optimize gameplay for *time*, other types of challenge runs explore other ways of engaging games as flexible systems of producing unconventional forms of gameplay and agency. This can involve adopting particular behavioral restrictions or modifying an aspect of the gameplay system (computer, player, or environment). For instance, some challenge runs involve playing a game blindfolded (Summoning Alt, 2022), with an unconventional controller (Colbert, 2022), or any number of other circumstances that might make the game more difficult or interesting to play.

Self-imposed challenges push past the boundaries of the orthogame in order to find other types of challenges that particular game logics can support. Blindfolded gameplay, such as the exhibition of Blindfolded *Mike Tyson's Punch-Out!!* (1987) cited above, demonstrates how the game remains legible even without visual cues—one can succeed with audio cues and knowledge of its distinctive gameplay rhythms alone. Alternative controller runs, such as the "*ELDEN RING* (2022) played with bananas" article cited above, exhibit (in their absence) how controller ergonomics contribute to the gameplay experience and how much that experience can change with ergonomically unsuited controllers. Tests of extreme mastery, such as "soul level 1" runs of *Dark Souls* (2011) or "no hit, no damage runs" of *Sekiro: Shadows Die Twice* (2019; Nightingale, 2022), exhibit through pressure tests the fairness of particular game mechanics, proving that such play is mechanically supported by the game should such heights of skill and knowledge be attained.

Like speedruns, these challenge runs are not only recreational. They are novel artistic products in and of themselves. Painting on the canvases of these games with novel expressions of agency and performance. If a game's core artistic output is the framing of a novel form and framework of *being* and *acting*, the challenge run metagame produces an equally valuable output. Novel metagame is an interpretive artifact, like pop art.

A famous example of a challenge run category is *Super Mario 64* (1996)'s "A Button Challenge". Extensively documented in a fascinating, five-and-a-half-hour documentary by YouTuber and speedrunner Bismuth (2022), the A Button Challenge is the exploration of what sounds like an impossibility. Can *Super Mario 64*—a 3D platformer—be completed without pressing (or with minimal usage of) the "A" button on the controller—the button used to make Mario jump? Jumping is Mario's primary verb—almost all of the game's challenges are built to test players' mastery of that singular mechanic. As detailed in the extensive documentary, players not only had to exhibit creativity in skillful play (finding non-obvious ways around obstacles that would typically require jumping) but also in-depth knowledge of the game's technical processing.

In the most famous part of the documentary, Bismuth explains how the community developed a technical exploit that propels Mario through "parallel universes":

> If you remember, a misalignment is a 1x1 unit square on the corner of a platform that exists because the floor detection function converts Mario's position from a 32-bit floating point number by rounding it down to a 16-bit integer. The limitations of 16-bit integers actually go both ways: both in precision and in scale. [...] Mario's actual position always remains a floating-point number. [...] If Mario's position exceeds the integer limit, when it comes to detecting if Mario has a floor under him, his position will be truncated to a number within the integer limit. Essentially, his real position and the floor detection position become disjointed. If the truncated integer position happens to line up with a floor, no matter how far Mario's actual position is, the floor detection function will say that, yes, Mario is standing on a floor. But instead of thinking about it in terms of Mario having two different positions simultaneously, it's easier to think about it as there being infinite copies of the entire map's floors 65,000 units away in every direction. [...] So long as the game *believes* there is a floor, Mario will be able to stand there. Functionally, there is no difference.
>
> *(Bismuth, 2022)*

Though unconventional and unintended from the perspective of the game's developers, this type of alternative play is beautiful. It is a product of systemic emergence: not naturally emerging from the game's *technical* systems (normal play would not trigger this highly specific behavior), but emerging from the game's players and context, important elements of a game's total system of gameplay production. The construction of the game's technical systems provides the scaffolding around which this unique occurrence of play emerged. It *is* a product of the game's design, as the complexity and specificities of the designed systems allowed (and compelled) its emergence.

GLITCHES AND THE AESTHETIC OF THE UNINTENDED

One of the conditions included in the operational definition of art used to guide the central philosophy of this book is intentionality. Artwork is designed to evoke a second-order response in the audience by the intentional use of symbolic or sensory elements. The requirement of intentionality is to differentiate human-generated artwork from naturally occurring beauty like the Grand Canyon, which can certainly evoke emotional reactions but is not intentionally created artwork (theological arguments aside). Based on the idea that art is a communicative tool (discussed in this book's introduction), naturally occurring beauty is not communicative.

Many artistic works make use of elements that are at least in part unintentional. From the Exquisite Corpse games played by the Surrealists of the 1910s and 1920s to techniques developed during the proliferation of abstract expressionism like action painting and drip painting, unintentional elements of artistic creation are often emphasized to connect with deeper, automatic, and subconscious processes in the age of Freudian and Jungian philosophies, or, in the modern age, as an assertion of humanity in an age of a higher degree of cold automation. In these cases, though, techniques with unknown outcomes are utilized (intentionally) with a desired outcome in mind in order to communicate specific feelings or ideas. The unpredictability of these methods produces the desired, communicative outcome.

Intentionality can also be read into the curation of unintentional circumstances. Though the Grand Canyon cannot, itself, be considered a piece of artwork, a photograph of the Grand Canyon can, as it is a curated perspective of the natural occurrence, captured, chosen, and shared with specific vision and intention. Similarly, dozens of films have been improved by improvised lines or a harmless accident on set causing the scene to play out differently than intended, but the choice to use the unintended scene in the final cut is an intentional choice. It could be argued that the live theatre equivalent may not be as intentional, as the performers do not always have the opportunity to choose between an accidental moment and a re-performed scene in accordance with the script, though talented performers are often able to improvise around flubbed lines and malfunctioning equipment in artful ways. Even then, though, the art form of live performance includes the possibility of accidents and flubbed lines. That is a part of what makes live performance vital and interesting. That uncertainty and risk are essential to the medium.

Within the realm of video games, there are primarily two types of "mistakes": glitches and design oversights. Even compared to the examples above, arguing for their intentionality is difficult. There are times when the visual language of glitches is intentionally evoked, such as the Psycho Mantis scene from the tactical espionage game *Metal Gear Solid* (1998) or the insanity effects from the history-spanning survival horror game *Eternal Darkness: Sanity's Requiem* (2002). Both of these instances use false reproductions of common console or television errors (such as the dreaded hard crash or accidentally changing the television's video input) to produce metatextually aware anxiety and surprises during tense encounters.

True glitches, though, are rarely intentionally utilized (else they become design choices). Whether or not they can be considered "curated" is debatable. Large-budget games typically go through extensive QA cycles to find and address glitches before the time of release, but even talented QA teams are unlikely to find every glitch that may be encountered once a game is released to the general public. Furthermore, even when QA does flag a glitch, production teams must weigh its negative impact on player experience against the cost and burden of fixing it, but leaving known glitches in a game due to scheduling or budget isn't comparable to true curation. Occasional glitch curation occurs, as some glitches are encountered during development and found to actually improve the gameplay experience (such as the unintended "Wavedash" movement technique in *Super Smash Bros. Melee* [2001]) or community-favorite glitches that are cheekily acknowledged but not "fixed" in post-launch patch notes. These instances are relatively infrequent occurrences, though.

Games are also not able to improvise around these accidental elements as easily as other mediums of performance. While stage or screen actors may turn a flubbed line or missed cue into an effective and memorable moment (much of the fun of watching *The Carol Burnett Show* (Banner & Hamilton, 1967–1978) is watching the actors cause the others to break into laughter, "ruining" the mimesis of the scene), games are absent of developer agency in the moment of the performance. Apart from checks for the most severe of freezes and crashes, games and the actors within do not "know" anything has gone wrong with the performance and cannot creatively respond unless a specific happenstance was anticipated ahead of time (players will sometimes be greeted by some cheeky lines of dialogue with messages similar to "What?! You're not supposed to be here yet!" when utilizing glitches or exploits to break the expected sequence of events when developers have the foresight to acknowledge those who intentionally or unintentionally "break" their games, but these messages are anticipatory, not reactive).

Glitches are, nevertheless, important aspects of the language of video games. Though we may not be able to ascribe artistic intent to the majority of glitches encountered in games, it is important to reckon with their presence when developing our video game literacy. Though only marginally attributable to the *artistic intent* of games, glitches have an important place in the culture surrounding games and even have an undeniable aesthetic appeal.

Before further exploring their effect on games as artistic artifacts, we must define "glitch". A broad and oft-referenced definition by Olga Goriunova and Alexei Shulgin says a glitch is "an unpredictable change in the system's behavior, when something obviously goes wrong" (Goriunova & Shulgin, 2008), though I would argue that not all glitches are necessarily unpredictable. Some are quite repeatable and exploitable, so perhaps undesirability or unintentionally is a better measure. Additionally, requiring that things have "obviously" gone wrong discounts the possibility of subtle and unnoticed errors. Though perhaps less impactful on the players' experiences, unnoticed errors are not *fundamentally* different from "obvious" errors, at least to the degree that the former should be excluded from the definition. Actual usage within gaming communities is colloquial and non-rigid, variously used to refer to "audio-visual imperfections (graphics drawing incorrectly or audio breaking up) [or] gameplay abnormalities (the ability to get stuck in certain looping sequences)" (Newman, 2005).

There are two primary forms of glitches that players may encounter: those that are the result of normal systemic performance but are discordant with the semiotic presentation and those that are caused by true malfunctions in the software or hardware. Glitches of the first type represent the game operating normally but in an undesirable manner. If collision data (the information that marks certain objects as impermeable to present the illusion of solidity) is not applied to the ground in a distant corner of the world and the player's avatar falls through the floor when stepping into this space, that represents the game operating as programmed with the error coming from an oversight of design. This is an unexpected and undesirable result of the system following its programming *correctly.* The game is only *broken* if this mistake inhibits other aspects of the designed progression. This serves as a reminder that the player is actually interfacing with the game engine and its computational affordances rather than interacting directly with the (abstract) rules and operations of the fictional world with which players are ostensibly presented.

The second type of glitch represents something *actually* behaving incorrectly within the software or hardware. Software may freeze or crash, "memory leaks" may cause cumulative resource drains during extended play sessions, and code may improperly execute if old code is run in newer iterations of the engine, among thousands of other possible problems that might manifest. On the hardware side, failure or malfunction of computer components can manifest in strange effects in-game, such as polygons being stretched in unexpected directions or failing to load entirely when the graphical processing unit experiences an electrical shortage. Though framed as largely harmful to the play experience, glitches can sometimes be comical or even advantageous to play, and the rest of this chapter endorses a predominantly value-neutral perspective on glitches.

Glitches in the Visual Language of Games

Glitches may occur in any of the systems and components from which a game is composed, but visually identifiable glitches are often the most memorable. Some glitches are purely aesthetic, like the particularly famous examples found in the early, unpatched builds of Ubisoft's historical action game *Assassin's Creed Unity* (2014), in which some characters' faces fail to load properly in some players' games, instead depicting these characters as invisible, save for their clothing, hair, and unsettling eyeballs and teeth, floating and animating where their faces should be.

Some visual glitches result from unexpected interactions of physics systems, such as the frequent occurrences in *The Elder Scrolls IV: Oblivion* (2006) in which characters' bodies somehow improperly intersect with physics objects like doors, causing the characters to spasm and flop wildly like a fish as the engine tries to reconcile two objects paradoxically occupying the same space. Others are failures in logic and memory systems, like the well-known Missingno glitch from the original *Pokémon* games (1996), in which the games, under a series of specific conditions, could be forced into loading improper data into the space in which Pokémon information should be, causing the resulting monster in the battle screen to appear as a scrambled mess of shapes and textures. There are hundreds of examples of well-known glitches that result in memorable and striking images in games of all kinds. Among these examples are patterns of glitches that reoccur and form a recognizable visual language of their own.

Like cinematic mistakes that are not noticed until after a film releases, finding and sharing evidence of some types of glitches is often a point of communal fun and even a proud part of game player identity. Most players have inadvertently fallen through virtual floors or passed through virtual walls at some point. Most games produced within the commercial industry enter communities' consciousness months or years before they are publicly available via highly tailored screenshots, trailers, and press outreach. These materials are professionally produced (and often post-processed) to give the game a pristine presentation. It is not unusual for pre-release trailers and screenshots to present the game looking and performing better than it does at the time of launch, sometimes intentionally to make the game appear more enticing than it would be if presented honestly, though other times entirely non-maliciously as a representation of how the studio expects the game will look and perform at the time of launch, which may still be months or years away at the time the trailer is produced. Post-release, though, players share videos and screenshots of glitches, sometimes framed with indignity as evidence of how marketing has lied to them, and other times with a sense of glee, reveling in the wonderful weirdness of unpredictable and breakable artwork.

Within games, glitches not only make apparent the unreality of games but also a surreality. Whereas the Surrealists of the 1910s used processes like automatic writing and art driven by chance rather than singular vision to tap into subconscious forces (exploring the then-new Freudian construction of the conscious/unconscious divide within the mind) to more fully explore our creative potential, glitches in video games are automatic (outside of human design) processes that arrive at unpredicted results that express the fuller capacities of the mechanistic *non-mind*. Glitches' intersection with the representational elements of the simulation draws stark contrast between the creative force of human design and the mediating machine that ultimately has no understanding of and is not beholden to any semiotic logic or fiction.

In that sense, glitches occupy the space of the abstract. Abstraction in the traditional arts can be a powerful tool to call upon the beholder's capacities for generative subjectivity. Whereas a realistic painting dictates a specific and literal interpretation, greater variance in meaningful interpretations is expected as works trend toward the abstract. Video games tend not to explore *true* abstraction. They are quite comfortable with the iconic and the absurd; early computer graphics could create only simple shapes, so much of the visual language of games was built on the back of a technological necessity to feature iconic representations instead of more literal or realistic models of simulated spaces and figures. Some games have embraced visual styles that evoke other abstract arts (such as *Thomas Was Alone* [2012], *Super Hexagon* [2012], *Tales from Off-Peak City Vol. 1* [2020]) or absurdist scenarios (*Super Mario Bros.* [1985] is an *Alice's Adventures in Wonderland*-like parade of dreamlike nonsense decisions), but abstraction in *gameplay* is rare. Due to games' interactivity, legibility of gameplay is necessary, so abstraction in games' artistic core (agency) is challenging.

Glitches are able to abstract the experience of play. Graphical and aural logics can be disrupted, the illusions of spatial logics are broken (the player can be "glitched" from one place to another or may fall out of the world completely, seeing the space that represents the world in abstract from the wrong side, floating in a void of nothingness), agency can be inverted (control disruption, lag, incorrectly registered actions), and the "memory" of the world can lose important variables (lost saves or incorrectly registered variables).

It is unlikely that *true* glitches will be used to produce artistic abstraction in an intentional sense because glitches are unpredictable. It is like letting a swarm of hornets loose into a movie theater to increase the experience of tension and fear in a film. But the *appearance* of (illusory) glitches is a tool that developers have used to introduce limited abstraction of form. The visual language of glitches (freezing, broken graphics, etc.) is commonly used to represent intrusions into the game space from members of higher planes of reality, such as from the real world of the developer or a parallel story world (see *There Is No Game: Lost Dimension* [2020], *The Magic Circle* [2015], *Doki Doki Literature Club!* [2017], *Pony Island* [2016]) or elements of magic or supernatural power within the digital story worlds (*INDIKA* [2024], *FEZ* [2012], *Hack 'n' Slash* [2014], *Axiom Verge* [2015], *Eternal Darkness: Sanity's Requiem* [2002]). Sometimes it is used to represent an existential threat to the stability of the game world altogether (*PAC-MAN 256* [2015], *Yume Nikki* [2004]).

The experience of glitches in video games is common, and though their unpredictability and potential to disrupt or even destroy the gameplay experience makes them a dangerous element to deliberately incorporate into a game's design, they can serve as a useful common touchpoint as a visual, aural, or operational reference. As players, we should recognize the importance of glitches in the cultural lexicon of games. Rather than mentally "editing them out" of our experience (like we might say that a scratched disc causing a stutter in the playback of a film is not representative of the cinematic experience of that film), consider how the experience of glitches can be additive. As artifacts of the digital artifice of games, the possibility of glitches is a part of the "social contract" of designing a digital game, in the same way that a sculptor of an outdoor statue knows that most who view it will see it weathered and dirty. The probability of glitches should be incorporated into a game's design considerations.

In Chapter 11, I introduced the idea of the *manifest content* of a playthrough: that which occurs on-screen is the privileged information that constructs a player's experience of a game. A player is not supposed to conform her view of a game with what she expects the "archetypical, ideal" version of a game is supposed to be. Developers know that no player will ever experience a game *as designed*; they design for a multitude of experiences. "Metagaming undermines the authority of video games as authored objects, packaged products, intellectual property, and copyrighted code by transforming single-use software into materials for making many metagames." (Boluk & LeMieux, 2017, p. 25). The player's experience, blemishes and all, *is* the product that the system of gameplay was designed to produce.

As such, players should consider glitches to be a part of games' manifest content and ultimately constructive of the total experience of a playthrough. An argument that glitches are deleterious to the logical consistency of the embedded narrative discounts that players *already* play games with parallel perspectives that "break" the illusion of embedded narrative primacy—the diegetic perspective is often at odds with the urgency of mimetic storytelling while the methectic perspective embraces a liberating understanding of games' unreality altogether. The player can hold multiple things in mind at once. Glitches contribute to the personal uniqueness of a playthrough; they are an element of unplanned emergence. And to the degree that they are damaging or sometimes catastrophic, recognizing their effect on the emotional arc of play (the tension brought about by trying to avoid game crashes or save data loss after such a glitch has been encountered) is important to understand as a player reconciles her experience with the game. It might not be fair to say, "I found the game's use of tension to be very effective; you never know when it will accidentally delete all of your saved progress", attributing it to an aspect of intentional design, but it would also be unfair to exit a game experience with an emotional memory of tension or frustration and *not* acknowledge the glitch as the part of the experience that produced that emotional reaction.

Glitches and Exploits as Metagames

Beyond being a touchpoint in gaming culture and a constructive element of a player's total experience with a game, glitches can form an important element of a metagame. In the methectic perspective of play, the holistic totality of a game's affordances becomes tools with which the player can pursue her objectives. Glitches are unintended elements of design, but they are still products of the system of play, and the ways in which they can be exploited to help the player reach her objectives are part of methectic considerations.

Early in this chapter, I noted two types of mistakes seen frequently in games: glitches and design oversights. The former of which represents unexpected technical behavior, while the latter represents unanticipated player behavior for which appropriate systemic response was not accounted. This is the video game equivalent of exercising a legal loophole. Whereas glitches are unjustifiable within the mimetic fantasy of the game, design oversights are most often exploited in such a way that is contiguous (though unusual) with the fiction.

For example, early players of *The Witcher 3: Wild Hunt* (2015) noticed that the game world's dairy farms are programmed to include cows in their fields, and cows killed are (after a short while) replaced with new, living cows, seemingly with no limit. Players found that they could kill the cows at any farm (some are found quite early in the game) and sell their hides for 27 gold each. After a two-hour meditation (which can be performed quickly; it is not beholden to actual time passage), new cows will populate the farm, allowing players to continue the cycle *ad infinitum*, accumulating tremendous amounts of virtual money with minimal risk or effort. This exploit was later patched (amusingly, by adding a high-level monster that attacks the avatar once too many cows have been killed rather than outright removing the functionality, allowing players to continue slaying cows if they think that they can best the beast), but it does not represent a glitch. All behaviors and systems are working as intended. It is simply unexpected player behavior that led to unintended results. Apart from the implication that these farmers would not become suspicious after their 27th herd of cows had been killed in the same way, there is nothing about these events that is out of alignment with players' expectations of the fictional reality.

Utilization of these oversights for player gain is typically called exploits, though the term also includes the beneficial and intentional use of glitches. Though the use of exploits may be classed as cheating in competitive settings, these are separate from what are colloquially referred to as "cheats": developer-intended, beneficial gameplay changes typically unlocked through entering codes, secret button combinations, or by completing specific gameplay challenges.

Exploits are strategic considerations, sometimes called *degenerate strategies*. "The negative connotation of the terms 'exploit' and 'degenerate' imply that players are consciously eschewing the designed experience in favor of the shortest route to victory" (Salen & Zimmerman, 2003). Certainly, if games as an art form produce the artistic experience of gameplay—tests of agency against challenges designed to necessitate clever or skillful play—the circumvention of designed challenges must represent an incomplete experience of the game, right? The struggle *is* the experience. Yes, some exploits rob a game of its texture, but more broadly, the discovery of an exploit *is* a valuable experience in and of itself, and it is only valuable within the context of a challenge to be overcome. Throughout the book, I have insisted that games are more interesting for their ability to produce highly variant experiences of play and discovery rather than producing experiences with high fidelity to their envisioned designs. So though robbing a bank may circumvent the experience of earning money in a prosocial way, robbing a bank is, itself, a story.

Clara Fernández-Vara (2014) shares a story of a famous exploit from *The Elder Scrolls II: Daggerfall* (1996):

> if the player camps out in a store until it closes, the shopkeeper will leave, so the player can pick up all the items that may fit in the inventory. What is more, the player can come back to the store to sell the shopkeeper the items back, making this strategy an easy way to obtain a large number of resources. This makes it easy to acquire items and money, in a way that the developers probably did not plan for.
>
> *(p. 212)*

This exploit produces a more interesting story than earning the money normally and purchasing the desired items. It reveals an interesting aspect of the game's system of logic; the game centralizes functions that are normally performed by the *game state* (the depersonalized system, generally) into an NPC. If the shop owner does not "see" the player stealing from the store, the game state does not "know" that a theft occurred. This decision communicates something about the game's design priorities, and the legacy of those design priorities continues to echo through the series. A decade and a half later in *The Elder Scrolls V: Skyrim* (2011), players found that they could steal from stores without consequence if they placed a bucket over the shop owner's head (covering her face), showing that, by the logic of the game, the shop owner's *presence* is not the trigger for detection of theft—it is literally the NPC's *eyes* that need to witness the crime at hand, opening up other possibilities for performing crimes while NPCs have their backs turned. These design experiences can be exploited to circumvent the challenge of the game's economy of goods, but doing so requires knowledge, cleverness, and an element of risk. The logics of the system are robust enough to produce interesting choices even in their exploitation.

Game researcher Espen J. Aarseth (2003) tells of another famous example from the fantasy World War II first-person shooter *Return to Castle Wolfenstein* (2001):

> At one point more than a year after the game was released, someone discovered that by exploiting the fact that players were invulnerable for the first seconds after they were revived by a medic, one could 'fly' over the wall if one was revived next to a live grenade about to explode. Thus, by committing suicide, one could win the game in a novel way.
>
> *(p. 4)*

This violates the game's mimetic representation, but it is a thrilling encapsulation of methectic thinking. As many of the best-known exploits are, this was discovered and iterated upon by the community. In this way, the finding of new exploits becomes a communal, cooperative metagame that takes place around the simulation itself. Particularly true in the speedrunning community, communal knowledge-sharing and exploit-testing becomes a form of meta-play aimed at overcoming challenges at a grander scale than that presented within the game's challenge structure itself. At the highest level of this metagame play, years and decades of detailed research can go into the exploration and modeling of approaches at exploiting a game's systems and discovering new technical affordances. This is an exhibition of skill and dedication that surpasses that which most put into a game played conventionally, and it is an important aspect of a game's legacy as an artistic work.

Aesthetics of the Glitch

I would like to briefly muse on the aesthetics of the glitch. What about computer glitches do we find so intriguing? Beyond video games, glitch aesthetics have found their way into many types of art. Graphic artists have developed a visual language associated with *glitch art*. Of course, codifying conventions of glitch art works against its purpose. As influential glitch artist Rosa Menkman (2011a) explains, the conventionalization of glitch aesthetics commodifies the accident; in breaking a system intentionally, the essence of the glitch is nullified. Thus, we can consider three levels of abstraction of the glitch aesthetic: the genuine, spontaneous failure of a machine with the shock and danger it entails; the tamed glitch that can be invoked by known methods of breaking and corrupting processes; and the aesthetic reproduction of conventional glitch forms (Menkman, 2011a, p. 65). The first category of genuine, unexpected breakages holds the *true* glitch but may be untenable as an art form due to the definitional impossibility of harnessing the void and expressing through an accident. The second method reveals something true and exciting about the operation and artifice of the machine but trades the glitch's danger for a docile domestication, commodifying the accidental. The last form draws upon the culture's collective memory and understanding of the glitch as an aesthetic form and represents it. The essence of the process is removed, leaving *only* the conventional, commodified form. It reminds us of the glitch in a static and inherently retro (Menkman, 2011a, p. 57) form as opposed to the procedural and active *process* that it actually is. "The procedural essence of glitch art is opposed to conservation; the shocking experience, perception and understanding of what a glitch is at one point in time cannot be preserved for a future time" (Menkman, 2011b, p. 341).

Glitch aesthetics are necessary elements of an art form's maturation. Forms and techniques such as the rayograph, decollage, and solarization represent pre-digital "glitch art", and they reveal the process operations of their respective machines. Critically, Michael Betancourt notes that it not only reveals the machinery but also the humanity of production. "The appearance of visible brush strokes, imperfections and natural variation in manufacture such as hammer marks or bubbles, that were the historical signs of unskilled labor", and indeed,

> the transition to digital capitalism is a dissolution of concerns with physicality and a denial of material basis. The glitch can act as a stoppage of this autonomous production[. …] Glitch, in this interruptive role, suggests the materiality of media, offering the potential for a transition into a critique of digital capitalism, requiring a refusal of mystification: the productive, material and historical connections between industrial capitalism and digital capitalism proceed from a matrix of precise control that connects the seemingly immaterial action of autonomous machinery to earlier protocols of industrial production that rendered their (necessary) human labor unintelligent.
>
> *(Betancourt, 2017)*

To this end, the glitch works in opposition to the transparency of the medium. The glitch reminds us of the mediation of process and, indeed, message. "The glitch does not only invoke the death of the author, but also the death of the apparatus, medium or tool" (Menkman, 2011b, p. 343).

The increasing ubiquity of digital adoption has made the experience of common glitches near universal. Representation of these glitch types has become a common form of artistic representation. Artists such as Sabato Visconti produce hypnotic displays of the visual smearing of corrupted digital video, an artifact of video compression that has become familiar due to the ubiquity of YouTube and phone-recorded video. Peder Norrby captures and curates screenshots from the 3D photo mode in iOS Maps, showcasing surreal artifacts of unreality caused by imperfections in global scanning. The types of distorted buildings and unexpected features of topography will be familiar to anyone who has used that or Google Earth.

Within the video game space, games like *Metal Gear Solid* (1998), *Eternal Darkness: Sanity's Requiem* (2002), and *Batman: Arkham Asylum* (2009) imitate common forms of video game glitches—hard crashes, data corruption, and video output disruption—to invoke what I call in Chapter 2 *ontological upset*; the "horror vacui" of witnessing the collapse of a world into which the player is immersed. Other games evoke glitches or design errors in gentler ways. Parodic 3D platformer *Conker's Bad Fur Day* (2001) resolves its final boss fight with a game freeze, after which Conker chastises the game's developers and uses the "glitch" to blackmail them into giving him more suitable weapons for defeating the game. Documentary-style fiction *The Beginner's Guide* (2015) and comedic exploration adventure *The Stanley Parable* (2013) feature moments of going "out of bounds" in the game's 3D maps, evoking the visual language of dev environments and single-sided textures that will be familiar to players who have experienced game glitches frequently. The visual style of the games of auteur developer Cosmo D does not evoke *glitch* aesthetics but specifically introduces a world that feels constructed from assets that do not stylistically cohere with one another—improperly scaled, misapplied, incorrectly rendered, or textured—but, like Dadaist art, utilizes an aesthetic of garishness composed with an eye for composition, balance, and taste. His works, like *Tales from Off-Peak City Vol. 1* (2020) and *The Norwood Suite* (2017), combine the ugliness of amateur "asset store" game making (constructing games from free or purchased assets rather than creating bespoke assets with visual cohesion) with the intentionality of collage art. His games transform an "accidental aesthetic" familiar to those who play amateur or student games into something quite transcendent and beautiful.

These games all evoke elements of the glitch or "poor design" to different aesthetic effects. *Metal Gear Solid*, *Eternal Darkness*, and *Batman* aim to create a sense of shock and panic and to suggest that the power of the diegetic enemy is great enough to push into the super-reality of the player, representing a world-altering evil by fundamentally altering the world of the avatar. *Conker* and *The Stanley Parable* use it to tell digital-native jokes. *The Beginner's Guide* also uses it to further its theme of exercising free will and pushing back against one's designed course of action—aligning its rejection of destined determinism with the confines of a digital avatar's designed being. *The Beginner's Guide* uses its glitch aesthetics to show a budding artist experimenting with the digital form, as well as a collaborator disrespecting his work by introducing unintended manners of viewing it. Cosmo D's collage of misfit assets reflects the vitality of urban life—the cohesion of the macro-level gestalt of the city despite no two pieces *feeling* like they should necessarily "fit" together—an insistent reminder that every building and every citizen has a lifetime of stories that concentrate into the dense centers of life.

To a greater degree, though, the aesthetic of the glitch is a release of the frustration caused by machine failure. To see glitches represented in the arts is an acknowledgement of a shared experience. It draws upon moments of frustration and even fear for the health of the hardware and transforms it into a moment of connection. Like a standup comic putting into words a common frustration, thereby giving the audience a framework within which to contextualize their own experiences and a broader context for the universality of it. The computer is a powerful tool capable of telling all kinds of stories, but the glitch is the more direct and identifiable artifact of the digital medium—regardless of the strength of the representational mimesis, glitches unify all games and reveal the computational machine base that unites them all.

Finding Meaning in the Glitch

I challenge readers to find value in experiences with gameplay glitches. Not only in the deferred gratification sense that a familiarity with the visual language of glitches enables us to participate in the cultural fetishization of the glitch, but for its own sake. Glitches naturally encountered can be difficult to appreciate. They often cause interruption or breakage in vital functions, resulting in wasted time or corruption of data. That is certainly annoying, but it is also a part of the experience of the game object, and it must be properly contextualized as a constitutive piece of the gestalt.

Is that a fair statement to make? On one hand, it would be difficult to justify giving a film a negative evaluation because a viewer got a speeding ticket on the way to the theater. The breakage seems external to the designed artifact. But every art form accepts risks inherent to its medium. Live music is exciting because of the unpredictability of the live environment—the risk of missing notes goes hand in hand with the benefit of improvising along with the mood of the crowd. To regard a video game as an idealized object against which glitches deviate is to undercut its essential nature. Video games are systems of generation—regarding only the "idealized object" is to not only ignore the glitch but also to marginalize the player. Glitches may be *undesirable* in the eye of the artist, but they are inevitable and true to the systemic form.

Dr. Francis O'Connor wrote about Jackson Pollock's abstract expressionist paintings,

> meaning is the sum of three things: 1. what you feel on first encountering the work, 2. what you can see of the qualities of the work that made you feel as you did, 3. what you can know about the works' imagery and intent, and the historical origins and context from which, and in which, it was created.

Regarded as an example of abstract art, we can regard that which the glitch makes us feel on first exposure, and we can interrogate that feeling to understand what about the glitch from a formal perspective evoked such a response. Glitches are usually contrary to *intent*, but they are certainly relevant to study from the perspective of history and context. Noticing similar glitches across games built within the same engine gives such titles an aspect of unintended formal unity. The frequency and severity of glitches can also grant insights about a game's development process. How much attention was paid toward quality assurance and the types of glitches that were not deemed necessary or worthy of fixing weighed against the game's budget?

Throughout the book, I have endorsed a particular skepticism toward authorial intent, particularly as it pertains to ludic artifacts. Not only is gameplay co-authored by the player in instantiated play, but the procedural nature of its computational emergence surrenders formal qualities to its machine processes. More than a canvas that records the inscription of the artist, the digital medium is an active presence in the construction of gameplay. The glitch is a "friction" of that activity, and it is best to regard it as a constructive element of gameplay. For that which reveals the artifice of the system also reveals metagame possibilities; systemic possibilities that can be incorporated into methectic strategy. As far as the glitch reveals the machine, the systemic affordances ultimately determine the shape of the possibility space.

CHEATING

Consideration of metagame prompts conversation about cheating. There are two related terms that "cheat" evokes in the context of video gaming. As a noun, "cheats" are functions included by developers that modify gameplay in permitted manners. Some games will have "cheat codes"—combinations of button presses or passwords that can be entered to enable special functions, such as infinite lives or infinite in-game currency. This has become less common in recent decades since the internet makes finding these codes trivial; they do not prompt communal sharing (spreading useful cheat codes via schoolyard rumors, for instance) or paratextual purchases (cheat codes were often revealed in the pages of gaming magazines), so the extra effort involved with leaving the game environment to gain the information no longer constitutes an interesting part of the game experience.

More recently, games tend to include "cheat" menus, either accessible by default or unlockable throughout the course of non-cheat-assisted play. For example, *UNCHARTED 4: A Thief's End* (2016) features a bonus menu, unlockable after finishing the game, which contains gameplay and cosmetic modifications such as character costumes, mechanical adjustments such as unlimited ammunition, free selection of weapons, and rendering filters (each purchasable with points awarded from game progress). These types of cheats are only labeled as such to designate them as being deviations from the intended course of play. Toggling on unlimited ammunition removes an element of tension that may be necessary for building the ludic drama of particular scenarios of play.

Of course, what one player regards as excitingly tense another might find near impossible. If the intention is to give the player an invigorating level of challenge (a subjective measure), some players may *benefit* from utilizing "cheats", and labeling them as "cheats" (implying that those who utilize them are spoilsports of sorts) can be unnecessarily judgmental. For that reason, many of the modifications previously designated "cheats" are now delivered in a more friendly and collaborative method through *accessibility* options. This is not a 1:1 replacement for cheats, as "accessibility" is really only an appropriate label for features that aid in the assistance with particular disabilities. It might seem disrespectful to the community of players with disabilities to label some of the sillier forms of cheats, like "give all characters horse heads" accessibility options. Besides that, "accessibility" is a nonjudgmental way of delivering the options that some players may find necessary to enjoy a balanced experience of play without making them feel like *cheaters*.

For the purpose of this exploration, though, the cheat code or cheat menu is not the form of "cheat" that most interests us. Metagame play prompts consideration of cheating—that is, acting in disobedience of a game's rules. As already discussed, though, video games are not like social games, in which rules are maintained through social contracts between players. Video gameplay is given structure by mechanics, impersonally enforced by the computational capacities of the computer itself. As such, one cannot "cheat" in a video game because cheating is to break *rules*, and video games (arguably) do not *have* rules (Boluk & LeMieux, 2017, p. 8). As mentioned previously, video games played in a social setting *do* have a layer of social contract and, thus, rules. Players may prohibit one another from "screen-looking" (looking at another player's portion of the screen in a split-screen multiplayer game in order to gain information about their whereabouts or strategies), while other groups may consider screen-looking a valid strategy (as focusing attention on another player's portion of the screen means risking taking attention off of her own). There are rules of fair play in social settings—do not interfere with an opponent's line of sight to the screen. Do not physically restrain a competitive opponent. Do not unplug an element of an opponent's hardware during play. But these considerations are separate from the level of computational mechanics.

In social games, cheating is typically punished in a predetermined manner. Professional sports have specific punishments befitting of differing severities of offenses, typically involving the temporary removal of offending players from the game for a set period of time or surrender of possession of the (ball, puck, token) to the opposing team. As penalties are known quantities, they can be weighed against the potential advantage of fouling an opponent. As Salen and Zimmerman (2004) explain, "players may strategically transgress rules, accepting a short-term punishment for a long-term strategic or psychological advantage". Other games sanction forms of cheating, which renders such actions not "cheating", as such, but rather creative expression beyond the specified rule set, within a loosely defined set of meta-boundaries.

As opposed to sports and social games in which rule-breaking takes particular, recognized forms and warrants predetermined penalties, cheating in video games is entirely confined to the metagame layer of play—beyond the punitive capacities of the mechanical systems. That which we may consider "cheating" must be punished by human moderators (banning someone from a server for "griefing" other players, for instance; Carter et al., 2012) or result in reputational "damage" (an experienced player who exercises mechanically legal shortcuts or enhancements not known to a less-experienced player has not broken any of the formal constraints of the game but has behaved unsportingly, considering the social asymmetry of relevant knowledge, and may be perceived as being unsporting or untrustworthy in future competitive events).

MODS

"The game, like all other digital objects, is but a vast clustering of variables, ready to be altered and modified" (Galloway, 2006, p. 112). Video games are expressive systems built around player-directed reconfiguration. The game, an incomplete artifact, serves as a structural guide for the unique metagames that the player enacts within its constructs. The bounds, conditions, and variables that the game enforces can be regarded (along with the truly static *protostory* content; see Chapter 3) as the material content of the developers' craft. So if permitted reconfiguration within the constraints of the developed game systems constitutes a *standard metagame*, we must also recognize an additional type of metagame play that stems from reconfiguration of the *systemic constructs themselves*.

Modding is a general term referring to several related practices that involve *modifying* video games at a software level in manners beyond those that are explicitly endorsed by the developers. At the very basic level, this might mean changing digits within configuration files (often .ini files) in a game's installation directory or using an in-game debug prompt in order to unlock software capabilities that may not have been included in the game's player-facing options menu. For example, playing older games on new computers and new monitors often requires manually entering custom screen resolution numbers into the game's configuration files because now-standard display resolutions may exceed those which the game's developers, at the time of the game's launch, anticipated would be needed. The game's engine is able to output at the higher display resolution, but the developer did not include the ability to select such a high resolution in the game's options. Unlocking a capability that the game's engine *already possesses* requires altering files outside of the game's interface.

Most uses of the term "modding" within the community, though, require the production or utilization of distributed (or distributable) *mods*, files that can be shared between players in order to introduce new content or functionality into games. Whereas the community might not consider altering the screen resolution values on one's own.ini file to be *modding*, such a practice might *become* modding if a player posted a preconfigured.ini file online for others to drop into their games' installation directories in order to ease the process of modernizing the game's display resolution. The distributability makes it something of a "package" that can be colloquially referred to as a *mod*.

Types of Mods

We can break mods into several categorizations based on the intent and effect of the modifications the mod performs.

Reconfigurative Mods

Reconfigurative mods change the behavior of the software rather than the representational content of the game. This can be at the nondiegetic level (such as a mod that allows the game to output at a higher resolution and framerate) or at the diegetic level (such as a mod that alters the behavior of NPCs or in-game objects). For example, the Carmageddon mod (Gipphe, 2011) for *Grand Theft Auto IV* (2008) modifies the behavior of all vehicles so that they move at ludicrous speed. As demonstrated in videos showcasing the mod, simply crossing the street becomes a perilous endeavor as cars constantly zip around (and crash) at mach speeds, creating a comical and dangerous gameplay environment.

Reconfigurative mods allow for a large variety of metagames to be developed within the systems of a game. Mods that make all NPCs in a game world instantly hostile and aggressive toward the avatar create an entirely new manner of play, like being in a zombie movie. Mods that change the graphical rendering from realistic to highly stylized can change the aesthetic cues of gameplay. Changing properties of the physics system, such as making gravity half as powerful, can change the dynamics of movement through a space. "God mode" mods make avatars impervious to damage or death, turning challenging encounters into trivial or even comical bouts. Some reconfigurative mods provide useful shortcuts or information, such as mods that improve the layout and behavior of in-game menus and UI or add a minimap to the screen.

Some reconfigurative mods do not even require the commitment of mod installation. Runtime reconfigurative mods can run "on top" of the game and can be toggled on and off freely during play. Such mods, running in programs called "trainers", allow players to modify elements of the game's execution in real-time.

Content Mods

Content mods inject new content into a game, sometimes at a purely *thematic* level (called "skinning"—applying new "skins" to existing objects, characters, and environments) and sometimes involving both theme and mechanics (such as mods that inject new actors or objects that include their own behavioral affordances).

Re-skinning in-game assets is typically regarded as an "honest" form of modding, in that the game at the level of software execution and diegetic behavior is unchanged. Skinning is perhaps most common in fighting games, in which modding communities offer alternative costumes for combatants, often based around other video games or media properties. When a player installs a new skin for a character, she only changes the character's local representation—meaning that the files on the player's local computer affect its visual presentation, but this change will *not* be visible on the computer of an online opponent since *her* computer does not contain the files that replace the character's cosmetic appearance. As such, so long as the new skin does not affect the "skeleton" (animation-rigged structure of the character) or "hit-box" (physical boundaries of the character), it can be harmlessly played online without the opponent knowing of the change. The only instance in which modding a skin might be considered "cheating" in a competitive setting would be if the mod increases the visibility or readability of an opponent, such as a mod that causes characters to glow in games of low-light stealth.

Some content mods *extend* rather than *replace* the available content in a game. Rhythm games are, at their core, sets of logics and mechanics that create interesting challenges of mastery for the library of songs that the developers have either created or licensed to be "charted" into performable challenges. Players who love the mechanics of a rhythm game and wish to extend the number and types of songs featured within it may download or create mods that feature additional tracks. Games such as *Beat Saber* (2019), *Rhythm Doctor* (2021), and *Spin Rhythm XD* (2023) are easily "moddable" to add community-charted tracks, making the amount of playable content theoretically limitless. As with the skin mods above, the "unofficial" nature of communal mod development and sharing often means that the mod community can get away with skirting legal and practical lines that a game's official developers cannot. Music that might be prohibitive to officially license or characters that might originate from rival game companies can often be modded into a game.

Content mods add value for players, most of the time for no additional cost. As such, developer companies tend to take a "collaboratively hands-off" approach to the modding community. Some companies release official modding tools (special software that makes the development of mods for their games or engines much easier), and some games even feature native mod interfaces or integrations that make installing and managing mods much easier for the community. Given the propensity of the community to inject content that bends or breaks copyright laws, the degree of comfort that different developers feel with *directly* engaging with the mod community differs. With a hands-off, "look the other way" co-existence, mods that infringe upon other companies' copyrights are difficult to *blame* on the game's official developers since *they* did not create or encourage the creation of the offending content; they only produced the platform on which *the community* broke copyright law. The more friendly the developer is with the modding community, though, the more difficult it can be to claim plausible deniability with regard to intellectual property infringement. With content mods being such a large value add for the most invested players, developers *tend to* opt for peaceful coexistence, only cracking down on mod communities when they are legally compelled, when added content replicates content they are selling *themselves* (such as replicating character costumes being sold as DLC), or when mods create unsafe or brand-damaging environments (such as the injection of erotic content into games for which that type of content is not appropriate, or the inclusion of content that is racist or otherwise hateful).

Some content mods are reconfigurative in their methods, restoring or preserving content included within the game's files but inaccessible under normal gameplay conditions. This can result in a fascinating form of "ludic archaeology", as discarded artifacts of production can sometimes be remounted and explored within the game's engine, such as unfinished environments that remain buried in code rather than deleted from the data outright. A canonical and controversial example of this was *Grand Theft Auto: San Andreas'* (2004) Hot Coffee mod (Thorsen, 2005). This mod restores a mission that was cut from the final game entitled Hot Coffee, and in the course of this mission, the avatar performs sexual acts with NPCs that cannot be performed elsewhere in the game. Sexual acts of this nature warrant a game receiving a higher age rating classification than the game (without the sex acts) received (in the United States, it would raise the game's Mature [17+] rating to an Adults Only [18+] rating that most physical retail locations refuse to stock). Mods of a sexual nature are common in games that attract older audiences, but this one drew particular attention since it restores functionality that *exists within the files of the game*, even if it is not accessible under normal circumstances. This raises the question of what constitutes the "game" that someone purchases: the files that are bestowed upon purchase or the runtime behavior of those files? If a game is the sum of its data, *GTA: SA* contained undisclosed sexual content that should have warranted a higher age classification. If a game is its runtime behavior, *GTA:SA* was appropriately rated. Given that a player would have to go out of her way to restore the cut content with a mod (the same steps that she would have to take to *inject* similarly sexual material into other games), it is difficult to tell whether or not the age rating was appropriate.

Structural Mods

Like reconfigurative mods, *structural mods* tend not to introduce net new *content* into the game, but they may introduce new back-end technology into the software that enables new features or modes of play. This can range from injecting new rendering technology into a game engine that vastly improves the way that a game looks (Razed Mods, n.d.; Moooses, 2024) to introducing entirely new forms of gameplay altogether, such as the impressive Just Cause 2 Multiplayer Mod (Savage, 2013) that adds the ability for *thousands* of players at a time to play the otherwise single-player action shooter *Just Cause 2* (2010) together.

Total Conversion Mods

A type of content mod, the *total conversion mod* builds so much on top of the game in which it ostensibly runs that it can make the game no longer recognizable. These mods can be so extensive that they essentially constitute entirely separate games (though they run on their base game's codebase). *The Elder Scrolls V: Skyrim* (2011) has a number of impressive total conversion mods that replace the land of Skyrim with new worlds featuring new characters with new quests and separate mechanics, like *Enderal: The Shard of Order* (2016) and *The Forgotten City* (2015; which was remade as a standalone game in 2021). *Half-Life 2* (2004)'s Source Engine was modified into *Garry's Mod* (2006), a creative tool in which countless metagames, amateur films, and 3D artworks have been built. Entire *genres* of games have emerged from total conversion mods, such as MOBAs and auto-battlers/auto-chess games, which were originally developed as mods of *WarCraft III: Reign of Chaos* (2002).

Sanctioned Mods and UGC

Many of the earliest video game mods were made by altering the uncompiled code of games on early PCs. Some early games were even distributed as printed programming code in magazines, which players could manually type into their own computers. Due to the exacting nature of this reproduction, many players found themselves accidentally "modifying" the code with typos that most often led to utter failure to compile and play properly but would sometimes lead to unexpected and interesting behavior.

Early modifications were not only the domain of personal computer enthusiasts. Modification was frequently found in arcade settings as well. Arcade cabinets would often have settings that arcade owners could operate, called "dip switches", that could change certain parameters of the game to make gameplay easier, more difficult, or different in some way. This allows arcade owners to choose settings ideal for their particular clientele, and it would mean that the same game might play quite differently at different arcades. Enterprising programmers and hardware fabricators would sell "speed-up kits" (or "enhancement kits") separate from the blessing or intention of the game's developers, forming a gray market of cabinet mods.

In fact, developers of *Missile Command* (1980) enhancement kit *Super Missile Attack* (1981), Doug Macrae and Kevin Curran, sold an enhanced (reverse-engineered) version of the *PAC-MAN* (1980) arcade game to rights-owners Midway, which became the esteemed sequel, *Ms. PAC-MAN* (1981; Minotti, 2016).

In the late 1980s, some computer games shipped official mod tools. The *Boulder Dash Construction Kit* (1986) and *The Bard's Tale Construction Set* (1991) gave players development tools not unlike those that were used to build the games' content in the first place, allowing them to implement their own content into these engines. The mod scene *really* took off following the release of the seminal first-person shooter *DOOM* (1993). Though *DOOM* featured then-cutting-edge technology, it was quite friendly for the development and distribution of mods, packaged as WAD files (the file type is a playful acronym for "Where's All the Data?"). As the internet became more common in players' homes, online distribution of WADs made the sharing of new content and even entire new *games*' worth of original, user-generated content easier than ever before. This aligned with the philosophies of *DOOM*'s primary creators, Johns Carmack and Romero, who were a part of hacker culture and took a permissively postmodern perspective on creatives building upon the work of others. Even 30 years later, the *DOOM* modding scene is still active, with games as innovative and divergent as the widely acclaimed *MyHouse.wad* (2023) releasing as recently as 2023 (Fenlon, 2023).

As it became more common for games to be internet-connected, the line between mods and tools for in-game creative expression blurred. Games like *LittleBigPlanet* (2008) and *Super Mario Maker* (2015) shipped with robust level-creation engines, and these games were built around not only the fun of *creating* levels in a player-friendly environment but also around the seemingly *endless* content that the community made freely available, all browsable and playable from within each respective game. *Forza Motorsport 2* (2007) introduced the ability to share custom liveries and vehicle paint jobs with the community, a feature that has become synonymous with the series moving forward. Games as diverse as *SOULCALIBUR VI* (2018) and *Miitopia* (2016) make sharing and downloading custom-created characters as easy as choosing from a menu. This content is not typically classified as "mods" but rather UGC, *user-generated content*. There is certainly overlap between UGC and mods with regard to the type of content that is typically distributed.

The scope, quality, and diversity of content distributed as UGC can constitute the designation of entirely new *games* within powerful creation engines. For instance, members of the community surrounding the creativity-oriented engine *Dreams* (2020) have produced impressive and sometimes full-scale games within the tool, such as *Ruckus - Just Another Disaster* (2019), *Kuro: A Shadow's Dream* (2020), and *Trip's Voyage* (n.d.). Game creation and distribution engine *Roblox* (2006) has become a pillar of the video game sphere in and of itself, reporting a player base of almost 80 million daily active players (though this number may be inflated, according to analysts; Roth, 2024). Similarly, robust game creation tools have been introduced to the mega-popular *Fortnite* (2017) as well.

The communities surrounding games that feature robust engines for creating and sharing UGC always impress, and the availability of such tools allows players to exercise the ability to produce games without having to learn to program or build art assets from scratch. This allows young and inexperienced players the opportunity to gain valuable experience and insight into the design tasks involved with producing a game. It also expands the range and diversity of voices of video game artists at scale. While this diversification is good, it is not a replacement for the need to push for an increase of diversity amongst formal training programs and in-industry jobs. Though a diversity of UGC artists broadens the scope of expressive messages within the medium of games, works created within particular games' frameworks will carry with them ideologies inherent to those contexts. For insofar as the mechanics and assumptions that govern these softwares are latent with ideological and ethical presumptions, these influences are likely to populate "downstream" in UGC. Greater attention is paid to this point in Chapter 14.

Mods as Distinct Works

While many mods enhance or expand the content of a particular game, modders can and regularly do create separate works that warrant exploration as works of art in their own right. Like the aforementioned *MyHouse.wad* (2023) and *The Forgotten City* (2015), some mods are so different from the games in which they ostensibly run that they can be classified as different genres of work altogether.

Post-conceptual artist Cory Arcangel created some of his best-known works by modifying video game cartridges. His 2002 art piece, *Super Mario Clouds* (2002), is a modified *Super Mario Bros.* (1985) cartridge in which all graphics except for the sky and clouds have been removed, leaving only a serene and minimal skyscape. *Tetris Screwed* (2004) is a modification of *Tetris* (1985), in which the speed at which blocks fall has been reduced dramatically; a complete game would take hours to play. These works explore some of the novel aesthetics of games, straining and decoupling elements of player interactivity and drawing attention to the aspects of these games' design that may go unnoticed otherwise.

Though highly divergent mods can create gameplay experiences that feel disconnected from the games around and within which they have been built, it is useful to note the lineage of their design. The unmodified (or *vanilla*) game provides a baseline model against which the design decisions of a modification can be assessed, giving a uniquely lucid point of comparison to elucidate differences. At the same time, design constraints of the original software will doubtlessly affect the behavior of the mod, and it can be useful to keep track of the ways in which the "root" game determines elements of the "shape" of the mod.

REFERENCES

Aarseth, E. J. (2003). Playing research: Methodological approaches to game analysis. *Game Approaches / Spil-veje, Papers from spilforskning.dk Conference.*

Banner, B. & Hamilton, J. (Executive producers). (1967–1978). *The Carol Burnett show.* Burngood Inc., Bob Banner Associates, Punkin' Productions Inc., Whacko Inc.

Betancourt, M. (2017). *Glitch art in theory and practice.* Routledge.

Bismuth. (2022, December 20). *The complete history of the A button challenge* [Video]. YouTube. https://youtu.be/yXbJe-rUNP8

Boluk, S. & LeMieux, P. (2017). *Metagaming: Playing, competing, spectating, cheating, trading, making, and breaking videogames.* University of Minnesota Press.

Burkinshaw, R. (2009). *Alice and Kev: The story of being homeless in The Sims 3.* Wordpress. https://aliceandkev.wordpress.com/

Cabubas, D. (2021). *The Dream SMP and storytelling.* Honi Soit. https://honisoit.com/2021/10/the-dream-smp-and-storytelling/

Carroll, L. (1865). *Alice's adventures in Wonderland.* Macmillan.

Carter, M., Gibbs, M., & Harrop, M. (2012). Metagames, paragrames, and orthogames. *FDG '12: Proceedings of the International Conference on the Foundations of Digital Games*, 11–17. doi:10.1145/2282338.2282346

Colbert, I. (2022). *Elden Ring player builds controller out of bananas, slays dragon.* Kotaku. https://kotaku.com/elden-ring-super-louis-64-banana-controller-emulator-bo-1848657617

Fenlon, W. (2023). *In the year Doom turned 30, nothing better captured the endless imagination and creativity of its mod scene than Myhouse.wad.* PC Gamer. https://www.pcgamer.com/in-the-year-doom-turned-30-nothing-better-captured-the-endless-imagination-and-creativity-of-its-mod-scene-than-myhousewad/

Fernández-Vara, C. (2014). *Introduction to game analysis.* Routledge. doi:10.4324/9781003355779

Galloway, A. R. (2006). *Gaming: Essays on algorithmic culture.* University of Minnesota Press.

Garfield, R. (2000). Metagames. *Proceedings of the Game Developers Conference 2000.*

Gipphe (2011). *Carmageddon mod.* ModDB. https://www.moddb.com/mods/gtaiv-carmageddon

Goriunova, O. & Shulgin, A. (2008). Glitch. In M. Fuler (Ed.) *Software studies: A lexicon* (pp. 110–119). The MIT Press.

Gygax, G. & Arneson, D. (1974). *Dungeons & Dragons.* TSR, Inc.

Harris, I. (2020). *RDR2 RP: How to get involved in some Red Dead Redemption 2 roleplay.* PCGamesN. https://www.pcgamesn.com/red-dead-redemption-2/rdr2-rp

Howard, N. (1971). *Paradoxes of rationality: Theory of metagames and political behavior.* The MIT Press.

Huizinga, J. (1938). *Homo ludens: A study of the play element in culture.* Beacon Press.

Kelly, A. (2022). *Looking for a new way to play Skyrim? Reject violence and become a pacifist.* The Gamer. https://www.thegamer.com/skyrim-pacifist-non-violent-playthrough/

Menkman, R. (2011a). *The glitch moment(um).* Institute of Network Cultures, Amsterdam.

Menkman, R. (2011b). Glitch studies manifesto. In G. Lovink & R. S. Miles (Eds.), *Video vortex reader II.* Institute of Network Cultures.

Minotti, M. (2016). *How a bunch of MIT dropouts created Ms. Pac-Man.* GamesBeat. https://venturebeat.com/games/how-a-bunch-of-mit-dropouts-created-ms-pac-man/

Moooses20 (2024). *Cyberpunk 2077 with photorealistic mods.* Reddit. https://www.reddit.com/r/BeAmazed/comments/1btvq49/cyberpunk_2077_with_photorealistic_mods/

Newman, J. (2005). Playing (with) videogames. *Convergence: The International Journal of Research into New Media Technologies, 11*(1), 48–67. doi:10.1177/135485650501100105

Nightingale, E. (2022). *Twitch streamer completes Elden Ring, Sekiro, and Soulsborne games in one no hit run.* Eurogamer. https://www.eurogamer.net/twitch-streamer-completes-elden-ring-sekiro-and-soulsborne-games-in-one-no-hit-run

Poole, N. (2019). *Hero of time, vegan of Hyrule.* Medium. https://tenderly.medium.com/hero-of-time-vegan-of-hyrule-753e84234132

Razed Mods. (n.d.). *NaturalVision evolved.* Razed Mods. https://www.razedmods.com/gta-v

Roth, E. (2024). *Roblox accused of lying to investors about user numbers by Hindenburg Research.* The Verge. https://www.theverge.com/2024/10/8/24265145/roblox-hindenburg-reseach-dau-child-safety-short-seller-report

Salen, K. & Zimmerman, E. (2003). *Rules of play: Game design fundamentals.* The MIT Press.

Savage, P. (2013). *Just Cause 2: Multiplayer Mod gets absurd launch trailer ahead of its impending release.* PC Gamer. https://www.pcgamer.com/just-cause-2-multiplayer-mod-gets-absurd-launch-trailer-ahead-of-its-impending-release/

Suits, B. (1978). *The grasshopper: Games, life and utopia.* Broadview Press.

Summoning Alt. (2022, March 10). *Blindfolded Punch-Out in 18:03.54 (world record)* [Video]. YouTube. https://youtu.be/jc9XE6zns7A

Tati, J. (Director). (1967). *Playtime* [Film]. Spectra Films; Jolly Film.

Terrell, R. (2011). *Appraising the art of combat pt. 10.* Critical-Gaming Network. https://critical-gaming.squarespace.com/blog/2011/1/24/appraising-the-art-of-combat-pt10.html

Thorsen, T. (2005). *Confirmed: Sex minigame in PS2 San Andreas.* GameSpot. https://www.gamespot.com/articles/confirmed-sex-minigame-in-ps2-san-andreas/1100-6129301/

Tu, C., Tunggal, J., & Brown, S. (2022). Character immersion in video games as a form of acting. *Psychology of Popular Media.* doi:10.1037/ppm0000435

Walton, K. L. (1990). *Mimesis as make-believe: On the foundations of the representational arts.* Harvard Press.

CHAPTER 14

Ideology and Ethics

IDEOLOGY

One of the essential tasks of any functional model of literacy involves making the beholder aware of ideological and ethical positions latent in the artwork and media that she consumes. All arts and media artifacts possess ideological values inherent to not only their content but also their construction. Even works that would not be considered "message" pieces carry with them ideological suppositions. Works carry with them shades of the hegemonies of the cultures from within which they are created, and like all hegemonic texts, they make unspoken suppositions about what is considered normal, natural, and matter of fact within the world that they depict in ways that unavoidably reflect (or react to) the cultures from which they come. At a larger scale, individual works sit within larger *media cultures,* which serve, in aggregate, as pedagogies that reinforce hegemonic norms about values, behavior, and identity (Kellner, 1995).

From an interpretive perspective, ideological frameworks can determine or influence the roles and behaviors of elements within the simulation in ways that might be unnoticeable or invisible if the player shares an ideological context with the game's developers, but they might not come as naturally for players who live in separate ideological contexts. Janet H. Murray (2012) identifies useful but non-exhaustive examples:

> ideological beliefs about the nature and appropriate social role of women may shape the way in which female avatars are constructed in virtually worlds. Other areas of contested ideological assumptions include political systems; economic systems; stereotypes of nationality, gender, race, age, and occupation; sexual morality; religious doctrines; nationalism; pacifism; vegetarianism; secularism, and so on.
>
> *(p. 424)*

Most ideological discussion concerns the "theme" layer of semiotic presentation: characters, settings, contexts, identification, dialogue, story, costuming, weaponry, etc., but there are even ideological assumptions at play in the non-semiotic layer of gameplay enactment. *Pong* (1972) takes an ideological position in its presentation of adversarial, zero-sum competition between its players. It privileges a particular modality of interaction that contributes, in a small way, to the greater contextual pedagogy of games and cultural artifacts at large. This form of *semiotically ambivalent* ideological determination is possible due to *Pong*'s simplicity; as games become more complex, consideration of their "thematic skin" (representational visual, audio, or written content) becomes more important.

To illustrate this, consider the quintessential first-person shooter, *DOOM* (1993). It presents a context in which all challenges are overcome through acts of violence. The hordes of demons the game represents are blown away by shotguns, rapidly dispatched with machine guns, or dismembered with chainsaws. How much can we attribute the "violence" of gameplay to its thematic aesthetics (the representation of powerful

DOI: 10.1201/9781003530961-14

weaponry, the rendering of blood and viscera, etc.), and would we still consider the gameplay inherently "violent" were these thematic details changed? If it were not for the chainsaws and demons and guns and blood, is there something about the behavioral pattern of "click on an enemy to remove them from the game world" that is inherently violent?

To examine that question, we can look at games that feature similar *ludemes* (see Chapter 7) but offer different thematic aesthetics. Three years after *DOOM*'s release, General Mills cereal released a game on *DOOM*'s engine entitled *Chex Quest* (1996). Gameplay is almost identical to that of *DOOM*'s, but instead of retaking an abandoned Mars station from demons, the player plays as the Chex Warrior, dressed in armor that resembles Chex cereal, using weapons that resemble remote controls and spoons to zap "Flemoids", an alien species made of slime that presents in a number of comical shapes. The game's story gives the context that Flemoids are not *killed* by the Chex Warrior; they are simply teleported back to their home world. The game contains no blood or carnage, but the range of available weapons still (euphemistically, anyways) present as gun-like. The game's Wikipedia entry ("Chex Quest", 2005) introduces it as a "non-violent first-person shooter" in the opening line of the article, but the core mechanical loop of the game is virtually the same as that of *DOOM*—shoot projectile weapons at all threats until they are removed from the simulated game world. Is there an inherent violence to the mechanic that still registers subconsciously? Does it still insist upon a logic of indiscriminate elimination?

Further abstracted, we may consider a game like *Say No! More* (2021), a game about starting a job as an intern in a big business. The avatar moves throughout the building while others block her progress to ask favors, bully her, or take credit for her work. Though at the bottom of the social order in the office, she learns to say "NO!" to her coworkers' unreasonable requests. As she says "NO!" her coworkers recoil in embarrassment and shame, allowing her to continue on her route through the office and her ascendency to a better career path. Compared to *DOOM*, *Say No! More* takes what can be seen as almost an *opposite* political ideology, with *DOOM* representing a "might makes right" approach—in a conflict, the one left standing has the final say—while *Say No! More* endorses the perspective that "regardless of the social hierarchy, every member of society has an inalienable dignity, and all it takes to overcome the adversity of those who would take advantage of their social position is a confident assertion of one's baseline dignity". But the gameplay of the latter is still framed as a matter of removing one's threats and adversaries from the playfield with deliberate and well-timed action. Does *Say No! More* frame an anti-violent philosophy in terms of mechanics that still represent a form of an eliminative violence of their own? This is not the kind of question that has a definitive answer; it is a useful type of question that can guide fruitful examination of a game's latent ideological dynamics.

As such, despite the persistent insistence of vocal groups of media-illiterate members of the video game enthusiast community, there is not a division between games that "are" and "are not political", because *every* game has layers of ideological dynamics at play. Objections to developers "injecting politics" into games typically involve the challenging of hegemony, a point that is proven by the lack of such discord over games that are *explicitly* political but uncritical of the hegemony, such as *Sid Meier's Civilization VI* (2016) and *Metal Gear Solid* (1998).

Every game makes ideological "claims" and asserts ideological assumptions. This in itself is not "bad", nor should it be minimized. It is a component of communication and particularly a component of artwork—one cannot meaningfully reflect the human spirit without reflecting an aspect of what it *means* to be human in relation to some kind of context. But players *should* be aware of the presence, context, and perspective of the ideologies at play in the games with which they engage. Players should distinguish what is *actually* natural from what reflects a social hegemony. Players should be able to identify propaganda based on appropriate contexts; for example, interrogating the manner in which *Call of Duty* (2003–present) games represent international military intervention and the necessity of violence-based rule in the context of the series' partnerships and monetary relationships the publisher shares with real-world military organizations and arms manufacturers (Robertson, 2024; People Make Games, 2024; Stanton, 2023). Empowered with this knowledge, players should be able to make up their own minds with regard to what they consider to be good and bad ideological positions, but it is *critical* for the fostering of new media literacy that these ideological pedagogies do not just *wash over* players uncritically.

Systemic Ideology

We have spoken about ideologies in terms of hegemonic assumptions. These represent what can be considered "matter of fact" within the story world of a work. The fact that they are not presented *as* points of critical discussion subtly implies that they are *above* criticism or reproach. These are simply matters of schematic framing. For example, the framing of white settlers as noble, heroic, and the center of audience perspective in Western movies, while natives of the land are presented as threats, brutal attackers, and are not empathetically framed, *implies* a rightness (almost a "naturalness") to the presence of the settlers in the American West—a self-justifying correctness of the "Manifest Destiny" philosophy of westward expansion. It does not ask the question, "were the settlers justified in moving into land that was already occupied by existing communities?". Viewed in the context of later decades in which more of the audience is familiar with the historical account from the perspective of various Native American peoples, these assumptions more obviously bristle, but the framing did not clash with the predominant American hegemony of the time of their production, and thus, many (presumably white) audiences of the time may not have noticed that a *statement of truth* was being established or furthered.

While video games contain similar types of ideological positions in the stories that they present, they also contain a deeper level of ideological transparency. Games, as simulative systems, present operative worlds in which artificial relationships play out *as* logical functions of the simulated space. Every variable, from interpersonal dynamics to simulated physics, is equally arbitrary—and equally deterministic. Players are not only *presented with* narratives in which particular actions play out as matter of fact; they *interact* with *systems* that produce matter-of-fact results in response to their own inputs. So, for instance, when a *Cities: Skylines* (2015) player observes that placing a police station in a city effectively lowers crimes in the surrounding area, this is presented as an uncomplicated mechanic of the game's urban simulation. The fact that its thematic skin represents a function of real-world society implies a generalizability of the same functional relationship into the real world. It is up to the player to recognize this as an abstraction and engage with its ideological assumption critically in order to determine the ways in which this relationship differs from the real-world analogue that it simulates.

Beyond even the intre-simulational behavior of game systems, we can also consider the ideological dynamics involved with players' participation with those systems. Raph Koster (Koster, 2005) identifies several of the ideologies that most gameplay implicitly reinforces: "Blind obedience to leaders and cultism [...] Rigid hierarchies [...] Binary thinking [...] The use of force to resolve problems [...] Like seeking like, and its converse, xenophobia" (p. 68). In fact, ideologically explorative first-person shooter *BioShock* (2007) hinges a major plot point around how the blind acceptance of ludic objectives constitutes a practice of obedience. For a medium that sells itself on liberating expressions of agency, it is notable how much time players spend in games following directives and expending "labor" (Boluk & LeMieux, 2017, p. 67) at the behest of unseen developers' direction. How might this behavioral pattern generalize in the context of a world in which an increasing proportion of our work and commerce is being "gamified"? How might these games prepare players for being obedient subjects in the context of late capitalism?

To Koster's "binary thinking" and "xenophobia", consider the ways in which the starkness of competitive orientation may generalize. Even in a game as simple as Checkers, there are "my pieces" and "my opponent's pieces", and never shall the two categories overlap. There are no star-crossed lovers in Checkers; there are no civilians in Checkers; there is no compromise in Checkers. In video games, competing teams often present as different *species* entirely—*Halo: Combat Evolved* (2001) is a contest between the humans, Covenant, and Flood. *Super Mario Bros.* (1985) presents only the unerringly good humans and Toads against the ubiquitously evil Goombas and Koopas (though, to his credit, Mario seems to have expanded his mind in the years since his first adventure, now regularly playing sports, board games, and going kart racing with his early adversaries).

The logic of xenophobia is baked into the construction of many games. Ian Bogost cites the example, originally raised in Zyda et al. (2003), of the squad-based, competitive first-person shooter *America's Army* (2002). In a stark example of the ideological privileging of the player's perspective, in its competitive multiplayer matches, *both sides* of the conflict see themselves as the United States' Army, with the opposing team always rendered as a foreign military. This asymmetrical theming not only implies a singular rightness of the American military, but, as Bogost (2007) writes,

> Perceptual equivalence reinforces the notion that military conflicts affirm a singular truth, one that is literally 'seen' as identical from both vantage points. This line of thinking accurately represents contemporary U.S. attitudes about military conflict. Our perspective is not only right, but there is no explanation for the opposition's behavior save wickedness.
>
> *(p. 78)*

Video games also express ideology in how they are positioned for use. Developers choose who is and is not able to interact with games as systems by way of accessibility settings. In deprioritizing or excluding accessibility considerations, developers indicate that certain audiences will be excluded from partaking (wholly or partially) in particular games. There are ideological and practical reasons why this choice might be made—it is not always simply negligence or lack of care and consideration—but it expresses an ideology about games as artistic artifacts: what purpose they should serve and for whom.

As systems of information, video games form sprawling architectures of links between informational nodes rather than adhering to prescriptively linear structures. As such, ideologies emerge not necessarily in the manner of a fable in which a moral is formed through allegory, proven out by illustrative, sequential events, but rather in the manner of movement *between* informational nodes and the types of transformations it makes to various kinds of information. As such, they serve not only as demonstrative fables but also as models through which players can actively test their own worldviews. Players who have never run a business, planned a city, or commanded a military can test working models of their own economic, civic, and political beliefs against the system and see success or failure. But as literate game players, we must be aware that the matter-of-fact operations of the ludic system do not represent an *actual* test of these worldviews; rather, it is a test of compatibility with the worldviews of whomever programmed it. As *Colleen Macklin* said, "*SimCity* [1989] doesn't actually simulate a real city. It simulates the inside of Will Wright's brain" (quoted in Soren Johnson's presentation, GDC [2023]).

Elucidation of latent ideologies in the systemic design of gameplay has been perhaps most thoroughly explored by Ian Bogost, who introduced the term *procedural rhetorics* to describe the use of procedural systems design to make claims or arguments about ideological positions. The term has been introduced in Chapters 5 and 8, but the most thorough exploration can be found in the book that introduced the concept, *Persuasive Games* (2007). From this basis, academics at UC Santa Cruz, led by Michael Mateas (and in collaboration with Bogost), developed the proceduralist framework, also introduced in Chapter 5. This framework is a formalized method of structuring arguments about procedural meaning, including ideological messaging.

Conceptualizing the ideological moves of gameplay *as* arguments is useful framing. Procedural arguments are not made declaratively and illustratively, like in other narrative forms, but instead by designing systems that will return relevant results when players input into them. It creates a model by which player curiosity is both aroused and sated; it not only "responds" to player "inquiries", but it creates the incentive and affordance structure that influences the types of "questions" the player will pose. The player can always prod the system with unexpected inputs and find the extents to which the simulative model can be pushed, but the player should also recognize that *she* is a "designed" aspect of the system as well—operating within narrow lanes of affordances and cued in particular directions by the game's incentive structure.

As designed actors within the system, the player must become aware of the elements of design that constrain and guide her own interaction. Participatory play involves not only the practical adoption of mechanics and logics of play but also the *practice* of such logics in embodied play. While most players can recognize and easily assess the ideological validity of representational elements presented on the semiotic level—such as the use of guns in *DOOM* (1993) or the depiction of small-town life in *Stardew Valley* (2016)—the necessary adoption and internalization of particular cause-and-effect logics poses arguments at levels that might only be subconsciously recognized.

Contextual Ideology

Every artwork contains ideological positions, even abstract or non-formic artwork. Consider monochromes—paintings that contain only one color or hue. Formally, many present as "empty" and, thus, may not obviously proclaim that they *have* ideological positions. But many fascinating dynamics are made evident when one expands her perspective beyond the scope of the painting's (non)representation. For example, an "empty" painting can be read as a formalist critique in the context of a tradition of form-based paintings. The curatorial context of a monochrome as a part of a museum's exhibit puts it in conversation with the works surrounding it and implies an intent behind its selection. A formless canvas can be used to draw attention to brush strokes and texture—evidence of the construction of painting as a craft of the hand in an age of mechanistic and digital production. It can be read as a refutation of the over-reliance on symbolism in art, as it presents a hue—an atmosphere—that the artist finds aesthetically meaningful in itself. There are any number of interpretations and valid contexts that can be drawn into such consideration (Campbell, n.d.). In the absence of form, though, most of these interpretative directions involve holding the work in the context of a system—whether it's a system of critique that contextualizes the work amongst contemporaries or a system of aesthetic experience involving the beholder. Paintings are fascinating as being (mostly) static artifacts held in the context of perpetually dynamic systems of context and meaning.

In a similar way, determining ideological positions can be easier when a game is held in comparison and contrast to works of similar genre and time period. The differences that constitute the intentional choices of its construction become apparent in their difference from the mean of conventional presentation. Chronological context (particularly considering the technological context of a game's development and release) can help identify games that are merely keeping pace with contemporaries, those that are pushing technological presentation ahead, and those that call back to design conventions of the past (such as retro-stylized games). Both innovators and retro revivalists hold ideological positions relevant to the games' enjoyment.

With a great enough perspective, ideological trends become apparent, reflecting development culture, gaming fandom culture, and mass culture at large. Being able to locate a game in time based on these ideological trends can provide useful contextual insights. Matters of preference and technique that have changed significantly over the years—such as the depiction of women as sexualized or disempowered "damsel" figures or heavy utilization of motion controls—follow clear trends, and when games significantly precede or follow the trend's peak, a game can feel "out of time", as if aspects of it were designed for another period. There is usually ideological weight to these types of decisions—be it forward-thinking innovation, countercultural backlash, satirical callback, etc.

Procedural Metaphor

Throughout this book, we have examined several aspects of game design that can be read as a form of metaphor. Control interfaces, for example, may physically emulate the actions that they represent (such as using the instrument-shaped controllers of *Guitar Hero* [2005] and *Rock Band* [2007]), or they may represent actions in a more allegorical, non-literal way (such as the disciplined memorization and input of complex strings of inputs necessary to perform certain techniques in many fighting games, which mirrors the discipline and presence of mind involved in the practice of real martial arts).

Ian Bogost (2007) identifies *procedural representation*: using a procedural system (such as gameplay) to symbolically model the operation of another existent system. Some of-kind, abstracted representations simplify complex systems into systems that are easier to operationalize, such as how the real-world phenomena of emergent road traffic patterns are simplified in games such as *Mini Motorways* (2019) and *Cities: Skylines* (2015), in which the behavior of each agent within the system is abstracted to a very simple set of rules—each driver has a destination that they wish to reach, and they will take the most direct route to that destination. This abstraction excludes factors that contribute to real traffic patterns—drivers have different behaviors (aggressive, cooperative, distracted, etc.), not all drivers *have* destinations (some just wish to drive to clear their minds or get out of the home), some drivers have medical conditions that may affect their behavior (poor eyesight, having a stroke behind the wheel, etc.), and so on.

Other kinds of procedural metaphors are not such direct representations. 3D platformer *Psychonauts* (2005) is a game in which psychic agents in training utilize magical devices to explore the minds of others, which manifests into explorable worlds populated with representations of the subject's memories, self-perceptions, and subconscious forces. The game literalizes several forms of disordered thought into semi-abstract landscapes, and the manner in which the avatar, Razputin, moves through them reflects aspects of how one might navigate those cognitive patterns in a therapeutic relationship. For example, a character presented as composed and controlled has a relatively featureless, puzzle-like mental landscape in which everything is arranged and contained logically until certain insecurities cause the pressurized architecture to rupture; the forces that represent these insecurities must be individually addressed in order to reform the composed structure of the space. In the game's most memorable example, the mind of a paranoid schizophrenic is represented as a sprawling suburban neighborhood, impossibly twisting and winding in a void of blue, sunny sky. Threats hide everywhere, and the player can often detect eyes peering from bushes, mailboxes, and from around corners, giving the sense of being perpetually watched. Buried in the deepest recess of the twisted neighborhood is an alternate representation of the mind's owner—a "person" constructed to recontextualize a violent action the mind's owner took in his real life. It is only in confrontation with this buried Doppelgänger that the two halves of the self are able to rejoin.

Both examples above are grounded in the textual details of the examined games, but if we follow the concept of procedural metaphor to its logical conclusion, it should be possible to interpret metaphors without semiotic grounding. Theoretically, the semiotic theme is only a layer of context that sits on top of the procedural *behavior* of a system. A system's primary *form* is behavioral operation. Thus, rather than viewing procedural metaphor as a more complex dressing for textual metaphor, it should be possible to draw representational parallels *solely* at the behavioral level. Regardless of the semiotic theme, systems of ludic behavior can have inherent resonances with systems of real-world behavior.

This should not be a radical suggestion, as it mirrors the way in which abstract art (and abstraction within art) is interpreted in other mediums. For example, English painter Louis Wain's cat paintings exhibit increasing levels of abstraction and proto-psychedelia later in his life after a head injury caused the onset of a formally undiagnosed condition that was most likely schizophrenia or something of the kind (Milton, 2011). Modern interpretation of his art, and particularly charting of the drastic change in style over time, mostly concerns the relationship between style and his cognitive processes. For these interpretations, the cats are unimportant; rather, the *manner* in which the cats were drawn is paramount. Interpretations of fully abstract, non-figurative art are similar—beholders are comfortable attributing the meaning of a work to the mood or process (behavior) of thought that it evokes rather than the specifics of its representation.

As such, if we consider video games to be, in their essence, the structuring and presentation of patterns of behavior or forms of novel agency (Nguyen, 2020, p. 1), it should be possible to ground interpretations of meaning and, thus, ideologies purely in their behavioral outworking. Perhaps due to the relative immaturity of the medium and practice of the tradition of its interpretation, such interpretations tend to be rejected by portions of critical, academic, and enthusiast audiences of the medium.

With respect to Mike Treanor and the other authors of the Proceduralist model overviewed in Chapter 5—framework that I find very useful, well-formulated, and influential to my own work—part of their reason for operationalizing their interpretive framework was in response to ludic interpretations that they found to be shallowly supported by the text of the games. Such interpretations "conflate action, representation and sensation. The interpretations hold only as long as the interpreter omits much of the experience of playing the game and selectively considers only the abstract experience of playing or interpretations of the game's theme" (Treanor et al., 2010). Oft-cited in Janet H. Murray (1997)'s controversial interpretation of *Tetris* (1985) as "a perfect enactment of the overtasked lives of

Americans in the 1990s" (p. 143). Murray seized upon a feeling evoked by the procedural play of the game and drew a parallel with a behavioral condition of life that evokes a similar patterning of behavior and affective response. Treanor et al.'s criticism is valid, noting that selective focus on a subset of details in a work can lead to irresponsible interpretations if posited as totalizing explanations, but I feel that there is also validity in Murray's reaction to *Tetris*. *Tetris* mounts a structure of play that evokes a particular pattern of behavior from players; recognizing this behavioral pattern in relation to other aspects of life has value. Such personal interpretations might pose a problem when framed as objective explanations of the artistic message of a work—to say that *Tetris* is *about* "the overtasked lives of Americans in the 1990s" puts words into Alexey Pajitnov's mouth that may not represent his intention in designing the game (particularly since he was neither American nor "in the 1990s" when he designed *Tetris*), but it presents an interpretive data point that, in the context of all others, starts to elucidate the interpretive and ideological volume of the game as a procedural, behavior-native work.

To this end, Treanor et al. distinguish between two types of metaphors in games: the above would be classified as an *experiential metaphor* (defined by Doris C. Rusch [2009] as "the phenomenon of understanding a gameplay experience as a physical visualization of abstract ideas such as emotional processes or mental states", concerning the experience of participating in a procedural system), and the *procedural metaphor* is more specifically grounded in Ian Bogost's work and specifically concerning the nature of the operation of and relationships between elements of systems.

Bogost gives a fascinating example of the latter in his exploration of the conflicting conservative and progressive frameworks at play in *Grand Theft Auto: San Andreas* (2004). The game requires the regular consumption of food in order to maintain the avatar, CJ's, energy. As in the real world, fatty, unhealthy foods such as hamburgers and tacos are offered at a low cost and can lead to CJ gaining weight, making effortful actions within the game world more difficult to perform, while healthier options that keep CJ in peak physical form, such as salads, are more expensive, requiring a greater amount of virtual money earned from (mostly crime-based) play labor.

> In the conservative frame, obesity and poor health are tied to self-control: the ability to assess and resist the internal temptation to eat the wrong food, or to overeat. [...] the fact that food comes only from fast food joints implies a social condition inherent to the fast food and packaged food industries, one that recalls Nestle's critique: for the less fortunate in particular, the cheap, factory-style, high-fat, low-nutrient food of the burger joint or taco hut offers the easiest and most viable way to fill a grumbling stomach. [...] Under this interpretation, *San Andreas*'s enforcement of fast food eating serves to expose the social forces that drive the poor and working-class residents of the inner city to consume fast food habitually. [...] the game's insistence that the player eat only at fast food restaurants draws attention to the social reality of poverty and its related health effects. Players of San Andreas might leave the game and make new observations about the world around them and about how social opportunity and disclosure often overshadow the issue of self-restraint:
>
> At the same time, the game seems to allow the player to overcome the social conditions of poverty and poor nutrition through hard work—a textbook example of moral strength. No matter what the player eats in the pizza place or the chicken hut, he can always build a ripped chest and six-pack for CJ by working out consistently in the game's gym. [...] Despite its apparent support for nutrition as a condition of social station, *San Andreas* allows the player to overcome that condition through relatively simple, if sometimes tedious, work and exercise. Such rules might tilt the game toward a more conservative frame, one in which discipline and hard work can overcome material conditions.
>
> *(Bogost, 2007, pp. 114–116)*

The above reading accounts for players' involvement in the systemic conditions that structure gameplay, including incentive structure and account for choice, and it frames these forces in terms of the real-world ideologies that they reflect. This type of interpretation is grounded in the variables and construction of game mechanics and systems and, thus, can be more easily argued as representing something "true" of the system as a rhetorical work. Despite its greater "objectivity", grounded in evidence, than Murray's aforementioned *Tetris* example, it is still an interpretation rather than fact, as it "tests" the procedural functioning of the system of *San Andreas*' gameplay through particular ideological frameworks. Different frameworks (such as feminist theory or Marxist theory) may reveal different valid arguments that one can make from the operational behaviors of a game system. Despite Bogost's approach being more thoroughly evidence-based than Murray's, variability of approach and result are still necessary and exciting conditions of such explorations.

Ideology and Theme

Despite operational behavior being the primary area of interest in our exploration of ludic ideology, theme has a fundamental role in ideological conveyance. Bogost's above reading of the food economy in *Grand Theft Auto: San Andreas* relies upon thematic representation that adheres with the systems of real-world economic disparity that it models. We can consider how a similar system would work if it were completely abstracted or reskinned. We could imagine a game about high school popularity in which an avatar can acquire "high-quality" friends that require more labor and effort to attract but enable a greater range of social activities vs. "low-quality" friends that are easily attracted, restrict social affordances, but can be "trained" for better social etiquette through effortful exertion (a rough approximation for the food, health, physical aptitude, currency acquisition, and gym workout elements of *San Andreas*). The experience of navigating such mechanics and incentive structures may be functionally similar, but the legibility of the metaphor (were one to still wish to relate it back to food economies in low-income neighborhoods) would be strained and potentially difficult to justify. Simulative nuance would be lost, particularly as it pertains to real-world parallels.

Thematic detail and semiotic coding modify the ways in which interactive context is read. Superficial thematic changes can alter ideological positions substantially. The aforementioned distinction between *DOOM* (1993) and *Chex Quest* (1996), in which the former frames its action as the bloody evisceration of demons and the latter as peacefully teleporting an alien species back to its home planet, reframes functionally identical activities to embody differing ideological stances.

Even separate from interactivity entirely, consider the ways in which incidental aesthetic theming expresses ideological positions. World-building in games reflects and comments upon cultural ideologies. For instance, in many real-world spaces, a disparity has been noticed between the availability of baby changing stations in public restrooms designated for male and female uses (Anthony, 2019), silently insisting upon a cultural, ideological norm in which women are seen as primary caregivers for infants and tasks of caregiving are not as often expected to perform tasks such as diaper changing. Even in a game in which diaper changing is not an interactive activity, the propagation of decorative changing stations in games that simulate spaces that include public restrooms holds ideological value—whether it *follows* cultural norms of unequal prevalence and therefore reinforces that cultural rhetoric or if it *addresses* the disparity and makes a silent refutation of the cultural norm.

All levels between the semiotic and non-semiotic presentation of video games have the capacity to express and explore ideological positions. There are particular ideologies that do not become apparent until these layers are taken in the context of one another. For example, though *Tony Hawk's Pro Skater* (1999) expresses an evocative form of freedom of movement within 3D spaces that would retain its engrossing qualities if all thematic detail was removed, it is only in its semiotic contextualization of its spaces as familiar areas from the real world in which skating is typically prohibited, such as malls, schools, and dams, that the game expresses its punk-rock ideology of reclaiming ordered spaces for the sheer joy of human movement in spite of the restrictions that might be placed upon them from economic and political owners.

ETHICS

Related to ideology is the study of ethics and/or morality. These terms are broadly used and tend to be quite fluid in their definitions. Hazard (1995) distinguishes between *law* (politically and legally enforced regulations based on adjudication), *morals* (personal and subjective notions of right and wrong), and *ethics* (norms recognized by a group on the basis of mutual benefit). Walker and Lovat (2016) take an opposite perspective, defining *ethics* as the personal, relativistic, and subjective standards by which people live their own lives and *morals* as the rules that guide the ways in which we live our lives together, with respect to the plurality of society. Rauch (2007) defines *ethics* as what concerns correctness and incorrectness, dependent upon the type and context of activity, as bounded by an explicit system of rules known to all participants, whereas *morals* concern what is right and wrong, as generalized to *all* activities and even to all *existence*.

Ethics and morals are not the area of my studied expertise, so I do not posit these definitions as being more valid or reasonable than others, but it is useful to have some consistency in the terminology used in this section in spite of the diversity of definitions posited elsewhere. For the purpose of aligning definitions within this section alone, I will use the terms as follows: *ethics* evaluate the rightness and wrongness of actions with respect to logical assessment (of help vs. harm, group cohesion vs. discord, etc.) and context-dependent, *morals* bases the rightness and wrongness of actions on opinion or tradition that is arbitrary or conventional rather than logical (commandments of a deity, respect for cultural tradition, etc.) and context-independent, and *law* enforces the permissibility and possibility of actions based on legal, political, or natural bases separate from evaluations of rightness and wrongness (including laws not enforced by human means, such as the laws of physics and thermodynamics). In my definitions, morality sits closest to *deontology*, while ethics sit closer to *consequentialism/utilitarianism*.

Each of these terms has separate relationships with one another. An action may be *ethical* but *immoral*, such as feigning happiness at an unexciting gift—it is ethical because it is a conventionally acceptable response that minimizes social discord without doing any serious harm, but it is immoral (for, say, someone whose morality is based upon an Abrahamic tradition) because it constitutes a lie, which is a universally unacceptable action, regardless of the severity or context. If one ascribes to a system of morality that requires respect for the rule of law, one may be torn by their responsibility to disobey unjust laws, such as racial segregation, which is (in certain societies) required by law, unethical (personal, interpersonal, and communal harm is committed with no reasonable benefit), and questionably moral (based on one's system of morality, respect for the dignity of all people or respect for the rule of law may take greater precedence).

Laws are formally or automatically enforced. Ethics and morals are enforced socially. In that way, we can draw an (imperfect) parallel back to the distinction between *rules* and *mechanics* introduced in Chapter 3, in which rules are social contracts that guide proper play, whereas mechanics are computationally enforced invariants that constrain play.

Design Ethics

The first layer that we must consider in the examination of game ethics involves the ethics of their design. Miguel Sicart frequently writes about games in terms of being ethical technologies, subject to ethical consideration in their own right. Games, in their design, can embody ethical principles by way of the ideological outplaying of their designed systems and in their interface with the world of the player.

Consideration of game ethics often starts and ends with judgment of player actions. Questions like "is it immoral to commit simulated murder in a game?" or "is it ethical to cheat in a cooperative game if other players are not offended by it?" should begin with an examination of the ethics of the game as a designed object. Whether or not it is "immortal" to commit virtual murder has *some* relationship to the degree to which the game mechanically incentivizes and contextualizes that simulated murder. We might conclude that the balance of culpability for whatever moral weight is assigned to the simulated murder weighs differently between the player and the system's design in games in which players are "forced" or highly incentivized into performing such actions (such as *Postal* [1997], in which virtual murder is the only afforded activity) versus games in which players have to go out of their way to perform such actions with little to no mechanical incentive (such as *The Sims* [2000]).

In the above example, though, it is not the fact that *Postal* forces players into **unethical** actions that Sicart would most strongly object to; it is the fact that *Postal* **forces** players into unethical actions. The distinction is that ethical design requires the affordance of choice—of action or reflective interpretation—rather than simply the depiction of moral actions. Sicart (2009a) identifies two modalities of ethical design: *open ethical design* gives players the ability to make ethically relevant choices in games that will reflect the results of those ethical choices, and games of *closed ethical design* constrain value choices to designated expressions and do not allow the player to operate as a free, ethical agent within gameplay. Successfully designed closed ethical play frames invariable value expressions with opportunity to reflect and come to personal, ethical conclusions without being refuted by games' systems (such as *Shadow of the Colossus* [2005], which frames the plot-necessary slaying of giant, statuesque colossi in an uncomfortable emotional ambiguity, prompting the player to consider whether or not the actions are ethically just), as opposed to games with unsuccessfully designed closed ethical systems, which frame and reward or punish players' ethical decisions in terms of predefined, narrow systems of evaluation (such as *STAR WARS Knights of the Old Republic* [2003], which features a system by which "good" actions strengthen the avatar's affinity to the light side of The Force, and evil actions move the avatar closer to the dark side, but in a manner that adheres to a specific and arbitrary ethical worldview imposed by design).

Simplifying Sicart's evaluation, we can hold the positions to be the degree to which games give players the opportunity to act as moral agents versus the degree to which games define the moral spectrum and, themselves (or the developers, by proxy), become the relevant moral agents in ethical considerations.

Another factor that contributes to the ethical design of games is legibility. To the degree that we consider players ethically responsible for choices made during gameplay (based on their agency of choice), we have to consider that agency requires *understanding* of choice. Thus, an aspect of games' ethical design is ensuring that players *understand* their capacities to make ethical decisions. Sicart (2008) writes,

> When a computer game is designed with rules that evaluate values, and that evaluation is not directly communicated to players, then the game design is unethical. A computer game must always inform players of their state according to those rules. Otherwise, players are partially deprived of their creative stewardship, of what makes them ethical players.

One may argue against that point; there are situations in which information may be withheld for the purpose of dramatic surprise or commentary. Darkly satirical military third-person shooter *Spec Ops: The Line* (2012) features numerous ethical decisions in which the most ethical option is not obvious, based on the design of the scenario. For example, the player is presented with a scene in which a group of angry, unarmed civilians approach the avatar and his military squad. The most obvious action available to the player (based on the visual language of the third-person shooter genre) is to shoot these apparent threats. The player's only method of interaction with the game world is through the barrel of his gun; a crosshair is visible on-screen at all times; threats are consistently neutralized through violent reprisal. Less obvious is the option to invoke a yet-unused mechanic and shoot into the air to disperse the crowd. The non-obviousness of this choice *may be* unethical design, but it makes its intended point about military imperialism—when all you have is a hammer, everything looks like a nail; or, more appropriately, when all you have is a gun, everything looks like a target. The game puts the player in a situation in which the ethically correct choice (the choice that is *not* a war crime) may not occur to her because she has been trained to see certain situations as inherently threatening. With reflection, this leads us to the uncomfortable realization that this dynamic mirrors aspects of *real* military deployment as well.

In that case, the game is designed (and paced, with downtime following this decision) to elicit reflection. This re-engages the player as an ethical agent (of the drama, if not the ludic choice). A similar explanation can be given to ethical choices made in story-based games like *The Walking Dead* (2012) and *The Witcher 3: Wild Hunt* (2015), in which consequences of choices are often far removed from the point in time that the choice is made in the first place. *The Walking Dead*'s signature design decision is the ominous notification that "[character] will remember that" after making ethically tinged choices without revealing at the time whether the character in question will react positively or negatively to the choice. It introduces a layer of ambiguity that elicits reflection—"what did I just do? To what degree did I consider the effect of my action on those who were watching?". Indeed, *The Walking Dead* repositions the center of ludic consequence from the fight to survive or strive to achieve of most video games to a perspective of empathetic consideration of the relationships between and needs of the characters. This prompts ethical engagement from the player even though the connection between action and consequence is temporally separated.

Morality as Mechanic

The example of ethical engagement with *The Walking Dead* above benefits from the ambiguity that its delayed consequences and naturalistic performances create. This ambiguity leaves space for the player to fill in the gaps with their own subjective interpretations of how characters might think and respond to the difficult decisions she has to make. Ultimately, though, the ambiguity *does* resolve with discrete consequential states, with the delayed consequences being either direct reactions to specific actions previously taken or cumulative assessments of multiple choices, given the weighted effect upon the *total* opinion another character has upon the player's avatar. Ultimately, because video games need to manage all information transformations in terms of mathematical and machine logic, any moral choices that are intended to feed back into the systemic enactment of gameplay must be operationalized as mechanics.

This can manifest in several ways. Like *The Walking Dead*, some games have fully designed and mapped moral choices, each with bespoke consequences. When presented with two choices, if the player does x, then a is the result, and if the player does y, then b is the result. This gives developers the greatest amount of control over the ethical storytelling, and the level of nuance reflected in these choices depends on the quality of writing. The amount of bespoke protostory content that has to be prepared for each of these predesigned branches, though, means that all moral weight in the game tends to be placed on these discrete, binary choices rather than being truly systemically represented. So, for instance, the player can choose to comfort a character who suffered a family death in a dialogue scene and then break everything in her house when gameplay resumes, and all moral weight (with regard to mechanical consequences) will be placed upon the former action and none upon the latter.

The next step toward a more systemic representation of ethical consideration is the moral "score" approach. Games like *STAR WARS Knights of the Old Republic* (2003), *Mass Effect* (2007), and *inFAMOUS* (2009) exhibit this mechanic. Plot-relevant, binary choices in the protostory layer exist, but their effects are not only directly reflected in designed, consequential branches; they also cumulatively contribute to a spectrum between good and evil, paragon and renegade, order and chaos, or however it is represented in each game. The advantage of this method is that, since there is an incremental, mechanical representation of the morality of the character, it is possible to incorporate actions taken during free play (outside of the designed, binary choices of the protostory) into the character's moral assessment. So, if a character makes saintly dialogue choices during protostory portions of the game but robs and murders NPCs during free play, the systemic representation of her morality will trend evil rather than good.

Though this approach offers greater representational nuance, it is still unsatisfying. In The Banality of Simulated Evil (2009b), Miguel Sicart writes that such systems trivialize moral thought by assigning points that incentivize maximizing a chosen approach rather than engaging with the choices reflectively. Each of the examples listed above, *Knights of the Old Republic*, *Mass Effect*, and *inFAMOUS*, offer mechanical incentives for dedicating oneself wholly to good or evil—in *KOTOR* and *inFAMOUS*, they come in the form of advanced, magical abilities that become increasingly powerful and useful as one becomes more good or evil, and in *Mass Effect*, they come in the form of specific action and dialogue affordances only available to sufficiently "paragon" or "renegade" avatars. For players who value these incentives, these games actually *minimize* moral choice and reflection by reducing *all* choices to one macro-choice made at the beginning of the game—shall I pursue good or evil in this playthrough?

When I attended university, a friend of mine and I played through the dramatic, space-faring epic *Mass Effect* trilogy at the same time, separately, often comparing our experiences and discussing the difficult ethical choices with which we were presented. I chose to role-play without alignment to either Paragon or Renegade (roughly, good or evil, respectively) polarities, instead making the decisions that *I* would actually make in each situation (certainly leaning Paragon most of the time, but not shying away from the occasional Renegade option that I found situationally justifiable). My friend pursued a perfect Paragon path (perhaps not entirely unrelated; he has since become ordained as a monk in the Catholic church, now effecting a very different kind of Mass).

Late in *Mass Effect 3* (2007), I was presented with a difficult choice between siding with one of two factions in a deadly conflict. One was a civilization of nomads whom I had allied with at several points during the series and of which one of my most trusted crew members was a citizen. On the other side of the conflict was a race of machines who only recently exhibited early signs of sentience and self-realization. They had been a consistent threat throughout much of the series, but the dawning of their nascent moral agency cast them now as thinking and feeling "people" who deserved a chance to finally pursue their own destiny.

The conflict that my character entered was the last stand in a long-running war between these two races, and my decision to side with one civilization would necessarily result in the annihilation of the other. Examining the ethical and practical consequences of this monumental choice was grueling. I had come to care about members of both civilizations, and I empathized with the justifications of both. Ultimately, with a heavy heart, I made a difficult decision that aligned with my morals and watched the destructive consequences unfold. That decision was perhaps the most memorable in the entire series for me.

Eager to see how my friend would handle the same decision, I asked him day after day if he had yet made it to that point in the game. Finally, he progressed to that point in the story, and, recapping his experience to me as I eagerly awaited his moral calculus of the same situation, he shrugged and said, "I chose the Paragon option and both civilizations survived". Apparently, if the player character's morality meter is sufficiently Paragon, a new option appears that injects an "and they all lived happily ever after" resolution to the conflict. An option that was not available to my neutrally oriented character and one that, frankly, neuters the experience by allowing my friend to sidestep a monumental choice and walk away with barely a memory of the event.

In this example, where along the way was my friend let down? Conditioned by his desire to maximize Paragon rewards, many of the series' pivotal choices were reduced from complex ethical dilemmas to "find the blue text option" tasks. In this immediate circumstance, he had been mechanically "rewarded" with the ability to forgo all consequences of a major decision, reducing it to another automatic choice that did not significantly alter the trajectory of his story. Is the mechanical reward of a third option necessarily "bad" storytelling? No. There are many justifications for a character who consistently acts benevolently to become aware of a more benevolent option that others might not recognize, from the increased empathy that comes from ethical self-discipline to the increased trust of those around a character. Arguing for the storytelling merits of this kind of decision is reasonable, but, in my opinion, this significantly flattened the moral landscape of his journey and suppressed his expressiveness as a player. Through his decision, I was not able to learn more about him and the way that he thinks. I was only able to observe him pick a maximally beneficial option when presented with one.

Some games add necessary nuance to this approach. Detective CRPG *Disco Elysium* (2019) features what resembles an RPG-standard character stats system (in which players can allocate points into tasks and character capacities that they value in order to "build" a character's unique aptitudes), but most of the stats that can be customized and leveled contribute to the character's moral reasoning. When sufficiently leveled, these aspects of himself will engage him in conversation, advocating for choices and elucidating details of investigative situations relevant to their particular faculties. In this sense, points are still allocated to meters that unlock additional ethically relevant capacities when invested in, but it adds nuance in breaking these skills into 24 separate meters against which the game checks and modifies probabilities at relevant crossroads, rather than confining all ethical considerations to a single two-sided spectrum.

Fantasy ARPG *Fable II* (2008) features a host of spectrums affected by both protostory and gameplay deeds—good vs. evil, purity vs. corruption, funny vs. scary, and love vs. hate, along with aesthetic categories that sometimes interface with gameplay mechanics as well—attractiveness vs. scariness, wealthy vs. poor, strong vs. weak, and tall vs. short. These attributes not only affect the way in which NPCs regard the player; they also physically manifest on the avatar in the form of glowing auras and halos for the good and horns and cracked skin for the wicked. The additional axes of evaluation and sensitivity to ludic action (the manner in which citizen NPCs are treated, for example) make the system feel more reactive and holistic than some of the simpler operationalizations.

Though a totalizing binary between good and evil is overly simplistic, ethical evaluation tends to feel more fair and justified when specifically embodied by NPC actors. *STAR WARS Knights of the Old Republic II—The Sith Lords* (2004) and *Baldur's Gate 3* (2023) augment or replace totalizing systems of character morality with levels of favor with the companions in the player's party. Each character has different tolerances and preferences, some valuing compassion and charity while others respect ruthlessness, for instance. Balancing one's favor with the party plays out naturalistically—in the same way that one may balance the preferences of multiple friends in a social group. Ultimately, the game does not need to holistically proclaim, "this avatar is *good* or *evil*", only "this is the kind of person who would most likely respect and follow this avatar". It is up to the player to determine whether or not this constitutes a favorable endorsement.

Other games do not alter mechanical expression but pose ethically rich conundrums separate from gameplay feedback. Choices shape the manner in which characters are understood by the player, even if gameplay is relatively unaffected by the ethics of players' actions. Though players can read and reflect upon the ethics of avatar actions in *any* game (is Mario *justified* in stomping on Koopas?), some games specifically draw attention to their ethical considerations and leave room for player reflection. Games like *Kentucky Route Zero* (2020) and *Firewatch* (2016) give players frequent opportunities to make ethically relevant choices reflected only in dialogue.

These layers of nuance are introduced to address the absurdity of the absolute polarities. The intention is to produce gameplay "in which regulation, mediation, or goals require from the player moral reflection beyond the calculation of statistics and possibilities" (Sicart, 2013, p. 24). The mechanics of ethics in games should not reduce the complexity of human morality to sheer maximization of numerical value but instead give players the opportunity to role-play as members of living narratives and gain insight into their own ethical models.

Ethics of Play

It has been observed that most players choose to be "good" or act heroically in games, at least in their first playthroughs. Experimenting with evil and chaos tends to be reserved for later playthroughs, after they have already seen the game "properly" (Lange, 2014; Pohl, 2008). In a survey of over 1,000 players, Amanda Lange (2014) found (according to player self-report) that, of players who play games more than once, only 9% of players reported making "evil" ethical choices during their first playthrough; instead, nearly two-thirds reported that they made a concerted effort to play in an ethically "good" manner during their first time through a game. We cannot conclude whether this reflects an aversion to immoral actions at a core, human level or whether this simply falls in line with the types of stories that players are primed to expect from video games and narrative media in general, but it does seem to indicate that many players see the stories that reflect positive ethics to be the "definitive" or "correct" versions of game stories.

Even if this reflects narrative preference, do players see themselves as morally *accountable* for simulated actions that they perform in-game? Should they? Certainly, one of the values of narrative fables is the ability to reflect upon morally relevant actions from afar, in a manner that gives audiences a vicarious sense of improper action and its consequences without making them morally *complicit*. From fables told in religious texts to fairy tales such as Hansel and Gretel, stories have always been used to instruct populations about proper conduct and morality. Video games shrink the layer of vicariousness, though. The actions are not those of storybook characters, written and told as if they were recitations of historical events—the player is actively involved in making ethically challenging choices. Consequences belong more specifically to the player. When the avatar shoots someone in *Grand Theft Auto V* (2013) or *Call of Duty 4: Modern Warfare* (2007), the avatar does not act independently—it is ultimately the player who pulls the trigger.

Intuitively, performing virtual murder is not ethically equivalent to committing a real-life murder. From a consequentialist perspective, no *actual* loss of life occurs. The enemies and NPCs in most video games are instanced agents that, if eliminated, will repopulate the space once it is reloaded. In this sense, it seems no more reasonable to hold video game players ethically responsible for killing NPCs than it would be to hold an actor portraying Claudius responsible for killing King Hamlet. An exception that perhaps proves the rule is the rare situation in which a ludic killing *does* have lasting consequences, such as betraying and murdering another player's character in a *Dungeons & Dragons* (Gygax & Arneson, 1974) role-playing game, with which the player may have spent months playing already. The offended player may mourn the permanent loss (as a dedicated role-player) of a fictive character to which she had grown quite attached.

On the other hand, unnecessarily severe violence in a video game *can* arouse discomfort from those observing one's play. Were a player to repeatedly run over and maim an NPC in *Grand Theft Auto V* for no reason, many would see that as taking the play action too far. Aversion to unnecessary cruelty indicates that there is *some* line to be drawn in culpability for virtual actions.

Academic philosopher Morgan Luck (2009) proposed an ethical quandary known as The Gamer's Dilemma. He asks, if virtual murder is acceptable—and, by social convention, it seems to be—because no *actual* harm is done in its performance, how do we account for the aversion most would feel toward acts of virtual pedophilia? To be clear, the latter condition is a provocative hypothetical—there are no mass-market games, to my knowledge, that *permit* or *endorse* sexual abuse of minors. Grappling with the hypothetical, the intuitive dichotomy he proposes seems accurate. Personally, I am permissive of the former and repelled by the idea of the latter. But, seizing on that repulsion and holding it in a consequentialist framework, it seems to refute the idea that virtual murder is permissible because "no one is harmed".

Luck explores several possible counterarguments. He notes the social acceptability of the former and not the latter, and if we believe that "good ethics" are defined by majority (or philosophically studied) consensus, that may be sufficient justification, but it is not much of an explanation. He asks whether acts of virtual pedophilia are more likely than acts of virtual murder to translate to real-world action but concludes that there is not significant evidence to support either perspective. He wonders if, maybe, "killing" is incidental in violent games—people enjoy the competition, and the elimination of game tokens is one of the oldest forms of keeping track of ludic action. A *Grand Theft Auto* player may not revel in the "murder" being depicted any more than a Chess player. But this argument seems intuitively false, due to the many, many games that boast of the graphicness of their violence, such as *Mortal Kombat* (1992) and *DOOM* (1993). He asks whether discomfort arises from the singling out of one group for harm, evidenced by the fact that, while virtual murder is socially acceptable, group-targeted virtual murder, such as a game that involves exclusively killing Jews or gay people, would be unacceptable. This argument seems to be refuted by the fact that a game that would let players molest *many groups* of people would *still* be more abhorrent than games involving virtual murder. Finally, he asks whether the particular aversion has to do with the special, protected role of children in society, noting that a game specifically about murdering children would also be ethically unacceptable. This still implies an arbitrary line is drawn *somewhere*, though. He playfully asks, "Do we really wish to imply stealing a child's lollipop is worse than torturing an adult?" (Luck, 2009, p. 35).

Others, such as Christopher Bartel (2012) and Garry Young (2016), have proposed alternative solutions to this quandary. My intention in bringing up this dilemma is not to offer a definitive, philosophically sound justification to resolve the dissonance altogether, though. As literate players, grappling with the ambiguity and forming our own resolutions is necessary. Whether one reflects upon the dilemma and concludes that, yes, players *are* to be held morally accountable for virtual action, or, no, an arbitrary line between acceptable and unacceptable virtual action exists *somewhere*, whether or not it can be cleanly, philosophically justified. This is contending with the moral stakes of play and is necessary in contextualizing one's own moral culpability in ludic actions.

How does one constitute or find one's own line of what "going too far" entails? What details of game design and construction can prompt actions that are acceptable in some games to be unacceptable in others? For example, the offering of non-violent "combat" options and the imbuing of personality onto the game's monsters causes many *Undertale* (2015) players to feel ethically uncomfortable with fighting in the context of that game, whereas most do not feel that same discomfort in similar JRPGs like *DRAGON QUEST XI* (2017). Understanding the ethical framework of a game requires not only studying the game's systems but also the ways in which they affect our emotional experience of play.

Perspective

We can frame The Gamer's Dilemma as complicating the diegetic perspective of play (see Chapter 6). To the degree that we project into the game world as an embodied avatar, the actions performed in that "sub-reality" are being performed by an extension of our networked selves (see Chapter 4). From that perspective, one can consider the actions performed within the virtual world as being of lesser moral "weight" than actions committed in our own world because of the "unreality" of the virtual. That is to say, we may be indignant at the sins and betrayals committed *between* members of the same reality in, say, *The Sims 4* (2014), but *the player* does not bear ethical responsibility because the Sims exist in a "lower" reality than she does. This is a similar justification that some religious scholars make to excuse the actions of gods, as it pertains to acts of warfare or damnation—a god is not held to the same standard as humans because she exists within a "higher" reality than do humans.

If this is the case, though, it is necessary to contend with the split ontology of the player's avatar. The avatar is a conduit for the player who lives in our higher reality, but the avatar is also a member of the game world. On what standard are her actions judged? Even though players live in a higher reality, is it unethical to persuade members of a lower reality to commit actions that, within that reality, would be unacceptable? This involves a great degree of personification of the unreal, obviously. Virtual NPCs do not silently resent player avatars in between gameplay sessions, as might be suggested by *Wreck-It Ralph* (Moore, 2012). Forming an ethical viewpoint of player action—even if it means picking apart our own feelings on these silly hypotheticals—encourages healthy reflection with gameplay texts in a manner necessary for truly literate play.

We can consider the role of the avatar perspective in our ethical judgments from the mimetic perspective as well. The act of avatar-based play is, to differing degrees, the act of role-playing. We can understand that the dramatic performance of a role might entail the performance of actions to which we would not typically be ethically aligned. We can contextualize these as the actions that the character performs within the story.

Being able to differentiate between point of view and ethical endorsement is a necessary skill—and one that might not come naturally. James Paul Gee writes about watching a six-year-old play *Sonic Adventure 2* (2001), a game in which the storyline is split between parallel campaigns—one following the traditionally heroic Sonic, Tails, and Knuckles, and the other following the evil or roguish Shadow, Dr. Eggman, and Rouge. Shadow the Hedgehog, an evil doppelgänger of Sonic, performs many antisocial actions throughout the game, and during a period of play as Shadow, the six-year-old remarked, "the bad guy was the good guy" (Gee, 2003, p. 140). The child not only conflated point of view with ethical endorsement—the relationship goes beyond point of view. The story is not only *shown* from the perspective of the avatar; the player's *lusory* goals (Suits, 1978) align with the antihero's *narrative* goals. In order to progress, the player must internalize the evil avatar's aims.

In a game like *Thief Simulator* (2018), the player *must* temporarily *desire* the theft of others' (virtual) goods. While antiheroes are common in other media, they are typically viewed from a detached perspective, requiring only empathy. In games, the player is given an incentive structure that aligns with that of the avatar. If the avatar's aim is to destroy the world or fight opponents to the death, so too must the player strive toward these ends. Separating one's own striving action from ethical endorsement is a more challenging task than simply observing someone perform illegitimate actions in a film or in a book.

A surprisingly lucid examination of this phenomenon can be found in the otherwise-middling *Fahrenheit/Indigo Prophecy* (2005). The player begins the game controlling avatar Lucas Kane, who has woken up in a public restroom next to a recently murdered body with no memory of what immediately preceded that moment. The player must control Kane to scramble to conceal all evidence that would point back toward him. Under a strict time limit, the sweep of the scene is intense. Though the player does not need to adopt Kane's *macro*-objective—getting away with murder—the player adopts the *micro*-objective—concealing the evidence and getting out of the room. Once the player escapes, the perspective shifts to that of a police officer examining the scene. Success in that moment requires *finding* evidence that the player missed in her first sweep of the scene (from Kane's perspective). The player is working directly against the goal from her previous perspective, yet both objectives remain compelling. This goes to prove that players do not need to internalize the entirety of a character's goals and objectives in order to assimilate the immediate goal (Treanor et al., 2010).

There is something powerful about coming to understand the actions of a despicable person through the *experience* of the incentive structures and circumstances that drive, necessitate, or complicate their actions. Katherine Isbister writes a compelling exploration of the experimental shooter *Waco Resurrection* (2003) in *How Games Move Us* (2016), a game in which players take on the role of David Koresh of the Branch Davidian cult's 1993 Waco siege. The experience of this alternate perspective, which mechanically operationalizes the hallucinatory religious delusions of the controversial figure, is thought-provoking, but it requires a literate player to understand the context in which it was developed, the purpose of its design, and the limits of its perspective transference.

Players early in the practice of this specific skill might find it useful to hold a fluid relationship with avatar perspective. Roth et al. (2018) describe how some players transition from first- to third-person pronouns in the retelling of gameplay stories once they are forced into actions with which they do not ethically agree ("I drove to the petrol station and then he robbed the clerk"). The authors note that this practice aligns with what Erving Goffman (1975) calls *role distancing*: the act of establishing distance between the self and the role that the self plays.

This concludes the examination of ideology and ethics provided in this book. My area of study is the arts; I am far from being an ethics philosopher or anything of the sort, so I recommend further reading from those who have a greater history with the discipline. As frequently cited in their respective sections, I encourage readers who seek additional (and more intelligent) context on the ideology and ethics of games to pursue the writings of Ian Bogost and Miguel Sicart, respectively. Further, beyond that which I have cited already, Soren Johnson's GDC lecture You Have No Idea How Hard It Is to Run a Sweatshop (2023) provides an interesting exploration of over-identifying with unethical perspectives and objectives. Additionally, I have frequently cited Alexander R. Galloway's *Gaming: Essays on Algorithmic Culture* (2006) throughout this book, but his perspectives on ideologies latent in game design are extremely valuable. His book is fun to read and dense with exemplary insights.

This paragraph *also* concludes the book as a whole. For those who have made it this far, I thank you for reading, and I hope that some useful insights have been gleaned. This book may not have provided answers for *simplifying* the task of sense- and meaning-making in games, but I find that engagement with the arts is enriched by asking the right questions—introducing the necessary complications to form richer relationships with the stories and experiences art has in store for its audiences. My aim is to unlock fruitful channels of inquiry that lead players toward rich interpretations, and I will be satisfied if members of the next generation of players and developers use these explorations as a starting point in more nuanced explorations of game narratives. Games empower their players to become creators, and the radical expressivity of the medium is perhaps its most exciting element. I wish you the best in your virtual adventures, and if at first you don't succeed, insert coin(s) to continue.

REFERENCES

Anthony, K. H. (2019). *Baby changing blues: The problem with changing stations*. UTNE. https://www.utne.com/community/baby-changing-blues-problem-with-changing-stations-ze0z1901zgsch/

Bartel, C. (2012). Resolving the gamer's dilemma. *Ethics and Information Technology, 14*, 11–16. doi:10.1007/s10676-011-9280-8

Bogost, I. (2007). *Persuasive games: The expressive power of videogames*. The MIT Press.

Boluk, S. & LeMieux, P. (2017). *Metagaming: Playing, competing, spectating, cheating, trading, making, and breaking videogames*. University of Minnesota Press.

Campbell, T. (n.d.). *The monochrome: A history of simplicity in painting*. Artland Magazine. https://magazine.artland.com/the-monochrome-a-history-of-simplicity-in-painting/

Chex Quest. (2005, January 7). In *Wikipedia*. https://en.wikipedia.org/wiki/Chex_Quest

Galloway, A. R. (2006). *Gaming: Essays on algorithmic culture*. University of Minnesota Press.

Gee, J. P. (2003). *What games have to teach us about learning and literacy*. St. Martin's Press.

Goffman, E. (1975). *Life as theater: A dramaturgical sourcebook*. Transaction Publishers.

Gygax, G. & Arneson, D. (1974). *Dungeons & Dragons*. TSR, Inc.

Hazard Jr., G. C. (1995). Law, morals, and ethics, *19 S. Ill. U. L.J.*, 447.

Isbister, K. (2016). *How games move us: Emotion by design*. The MIT Press.

Johnson, S. (2023). You have no idea how hard it is to run a sweatshop. *Proceedings of Game Developers Conference 2023*. https://youtu.be/YsCigLYxNYs

Kellner, D. (1995). *Media culture: Identity and politics between the modern and the postmodern*. Routledge.

Koster, R. (2005). *A theory of fun for game design*. Paraglyph Press.

Lange, A. (2014). **"You're just gonna be nice": How players engage with moral choice systems. *Journal of Games Criticism*. https://gamescriticism.org/2023/07/14/youre-just-gonna-be-nice-how-players-engage-with-moral-choice-systems/

Luck, M. (2009). The gamer's dilemma: An analysis of the arguments for the moral distinction between virtual murder and virtual pedophilia. *Ethics and Information Technology, 11*, 31–36. doi:10.1007/s10676-008-9168-4

Milton, J. (2011). *How a mental disorder opened up an invisible world of colour and pattern*. Scientific American. https://www.scientificamerican.com/blog/creatology/how-a-mental-disorder-opened-up-an-invisible-world-of-colour-and-pattern/

Moore, R. (Director). (2012). *Wreck-It Ralph* [Film]. Walt Disney Animation Studios.

Murray, J. H. (1997). *Hamlet on the holodeck: The future of narrative in cyberspace*. The MIT Press.

Murray, J. H. (2012). *Inventing the medium: Principles of interaction design as cultural practice*. The MIT Press.

Nguyen, C. T. (2020). *Games: Agency as art*. Oxford University Press.

People Make Games. (2024, September 5). *The games behind your government's next war* [Video]. YouTube. https://youtu.be/lYaDXZ2MI-k

Pohl, K. (2008). Ethical reflection and emotional involvement in computer games. *Proceedings of the Philosophy of Computer Games 2008*.

Rauch, P. E. (2007). Playing with good and evil: Videogames and moral philosophy [Master's thesis]. *Massachusetts Institute of Technology*.

Robertson, J. (2024). *Call of duty: Pentagon ops*. The Nation. https://www.thenation.com/article/society/call-of-duty-pentagon-ops-2/

Roth, C., van Nuenen, T., & Koenitz, H. (2018). Ludonarrative hermeneutics: *A Way Out* and the narrative paradox. *International Conference on Interactive Digital Storytelling*, 93–106. doi:10.1007/978-3-030-04028-4_7

Rusch, D. C. (2009). Mechanisms of the soul: Tackling the human condition in videogames. *DiGRA 2009: Breaking New Ground: Innovation in Games, Play, Practice, and Theory*.

Sicart, M. (2009a). *The ethics of computer games*. The MIT Press.

Sicart, M. (2009b). The banality of simulated evil: Designing ethical gameplay. *Ethics of Information Technology, 11*.

Sicart, M. (2013). *Beyond choices: The design of ethical gameplay*. The MIT Press.

Stanton, R. (2023). *How one gun company partnered with Call of Duty to attract 'young potential shooters'*. PC Gamer. https://www.pcgamer.com/how-one-gun-company-partnered-with-call-of-duty-to-attract-young-potential-shooters/

Suits, B. (1978). *The grasshopper: Games, life and utopia*. Broadview Press.

Treanor, M., Schweizer, B., Bogost, I., & Mateas, M. (2010). Proceduralist readings: How to find meaning in games with graphical logics. *FDG '11: Proceedings of the 6th International Conference on Foundations of Digital Games*. doi:10.1145/2159365.2159381

Walker, P. & Lovat, T. (2016). Should we be talking about ethics or about morals? *Ethics & Behavior*. doi:10.1080/10508422.2016.1275968

Young, G. (2016). *Resolving the gamer's dilemma: Examining the moral and psychological differences between virtual murder and virtual paedophilia*. Palgrave. doi:10.1007/978-3-319-46595-1

Zyda, M., Hiles, J., Mayberry, A., Wardynski, C., Capps, M. V., Osborn, B., Shilling, R., Robaszewski, M., & Davis, M. J. (2003). Entertainment R&D for defense. *IEEE Computer Graphics and Applications, 23*(1), 28–36.

Appendix: Ludography

Format:
Game title (year)
Developer, developer; publisher, publisher
Genre (subgenre)
Platforms [...] later ports or remakes (remake, remaster, or collection)

13 Sentinels: Aegis Rim (2019)
Vanillaware; Atlus, SEGA
Strategy, RPG (tactics)
PS4, NS

1942 (1984)
Capcom, Elite Systems, Micronics, Digital Eclipse; Capcom, Romstar, Williams Electronics
Shmup (vertically scrolling shmup)
ARC, NES, PC [...] GB, PSX, SS [...] PS2, XB, PSP, mobile

20 Minutes till Dawn (2023)
flanne; flanne
Shmup (bullet heaven)
PC, AND, iOS

3D Pinball for Windows – Space Cadet (1995)
Microsoft, Cinematronics; Microsoft, Maxis
Arcade (pinball)
PC

428: Shibuya Scramble (2008)
Chunsoft, Abstraction Games; SEGA, Spike, Spike Chunsoft, Ravenscourt
Adventure (visual novel)
Wii, PS3, PSP, iOS, AND [...] PS4, PC

4D Toys (2017)
mtb design works inc; mtb design works inc
Simulation
PC

720° (1986)
Atari; Atari
Sports (skateboarding)
ARC, NES [...] GB [...] PS2, GCN, XB, PC [...] PS3, X360

80 Days (2014)
Inkle; Inkle
Adventure (text adventure)
iOS, AND, PC [...] NS

911 Operator (2017)
Jutsu Games; PlayWay, Code Horizon, SONKA
Simulation (job sim)
PC, PS4, XBO, AND, NS, iOS

Aaero (2017)
Mad Fellows; Mad Fellows
Rhythm, Shmup
PC, PS4, XBO, NS

Accounting (2016)
Crows Crows Crows, Squanch Games; Crows Crows Crows
Adventure
PC, PS4, Quest

Advance Wars (2001)
Intelligent Systems; Nintendo

Strategy (TBS)
GBA […] WU […] NS (remake)

Afrika (2008)
Rhino Studios; Sony Computer Entertainment, Natsume Inc.
Simulation (photography sim)
PS3

Age of Empires II: The Age of Kings (2001)
Ensemble Studios; Microsoft, Konami
Strategy (RTS)
PC […] PS2 […] XBO (remaster)

Age of Wonders (1999)
Triumph Studios, Epic Megagames; Gathering of Developers, Take-Two Interactive
Strategy (turn-based strategy)
PC

Alan Wake (2010)
Remedy Entertainment; Microsoft Game Studios
Horror (third-person shooter)
X360, PC […] PS4, PS5, XBO, XS NS (remaster)

Alien: Isolation (2014)
Creative Assembly; SEGA
Horror (survival horror, stealth)
PS3, PS4, PC, X360, XBO […] NS […] AND, iOS

American McGee's Alice (2000)
Rogue Entertainment; Electronic Arts
Platformer (3D platformer)
PC […] PS3, X360

America's Army (2002)
United States Army; United States Army
Shooter (first-person shooter)
PC

Among Us (2018)
Innersloth; Innersloth
Party
AND, iOS, PC […] NS, PS4, PS5, XBO, XS

Angry Birds (2009)
Rovio Entertainment; Chillingo, Rovio Entertainment
Strategy, puzzle (artillery)
iOS, AND, PSN, PC

Animal Crossing (2001)
Nintendo EAD; Nintendo
Simulation (life sim)
N64, GCN […] iQue

ANIMAL WELL (2024)
Shared Memory; Bigmode
Platformer (2D platformer, metroidvania)
PC, PS5, NS

Antichamber (2013)
Demruth; Demruth
Puzzle
PC

APE OUT (2019)
Gabe Cuzzillo; Devolver Digital
Action
PC, NS

Apex Legends (2019)
Respawn Entertainment; Electronic Arts
Shooter (first-person shooter, hero shooter)
PS4, PC, XBO […] NS, PS5, XS, AND, iOS

ARK: Survival Evolved (2017)
Studio Wildcard; Studio Wildcard
Action (survival, first-person shooter)
PC, PS4, XBO, AND, iOS, NS

ARMS (2017)
Nintendo EPD; Nintendo
Fighting (3D fighting)
NS

Art of Fighting series (1992-1996)
SNK; SNK
Fighting (2D fighting)
ARC, NG, SNES, GEN, PC, PS2

As Dusk Falls (2022)
Interior Night; Xbox Game Studios, Interior Night
Adventure (visual novel)
PC, XBO, XS, PS4, PS5

Assassin's Creed (2007)
Ubisoft Montreal; Ubisoft
Action (stealth)
PS3, X360, PC

Assassin's Creed IV: Black Flag (2013)
Ubisoft Montreal; Ubisoft
Action (sandbox, stealth)
PS3, X360, PS4, PC, XBO [...] NS

Assassin's Creed Unity (2014)
Ubisoft Montreal; Ubisoft
Action
PS4, PC, XBO

Assault Android Cactus (2015)
Witch Beam; Witch Beam
Shmup (twin-stick shooter)
PC, PS4, XBO, NS

Assetto Corsa (2014)
Kunos Simulazioni; Kunos Simulazioni, 505 Games
Racing
PC, PS4, XBO [...] iOS

Asteroids (1979)
Atari; Atari
Shmup
ARC, 2600, 7800, GB

ASTRO BOT (2024)
Team Asobi; Sony Interactive Entertainment
Platformer (3D platformer)
PS5

Asura's Wrath (2012)
CyberConnect2; Capcom
Action
PS3, X360

Atari Vault (2016)
Code Mystics; Atari
Arcade (anthology)
PC

Axiom Verge (2015)
Thomas Happ Games; Thomas Happ Games
Platformer (metroidvania)
PS4, PC, PSV, WU, XBO, NS

Baba Is You (2019)
Hempuli; Hempuli
Puzzle (sokoban)
PC, NS [...] iOS, AND

Balatro (2024)
LocalThunk; Playstack
Strategy (card game, roguelite)
PC, PS4, PS5, XBO, XS, NS, AND, iOS

Baldur's Gate 3 (2023)
Larian Studios; Larian Studios
RPG (CRPG)
PC, PS5, XS

Banjo-Kazooie (1998)
Rare; Nintendo, Microsoft Game Studios
Platformer (3D platformer)
N64 [...] X360 [...] XBO (Rare Replay)

The Bard's Tale Construction Set (1991)
Interplay; Interplay
RPG (dungeon crawler)
PC

Batman: Arkham Asylum (2009)
Rocksteady Studios; Eidos Interactive, Warner Bros. Interactive Entertainment
Action
PS3, X360, PC [...] PS4, XBO [...] NS

Battlezone (1980)
Atari; Atari, SEGA, Taito
Shooter (first-person shooter)
ARC [...] 2600, PC

Bayonetta (2009)
PlatinumGames; SEGA
Brawler (character action)
PS3, X360 [...] WU [...] PC, NS [...] PS4, XBO

Beat Saber (2019)
Beat Games; Beat Games, Oculus Studios
Rhythm
PC, Quest, PS4, PS5

Beetle Adventure Racing! (1999)
Paradigm Entertainment, EA Canada; Electronic Arts
Racing (arcade racing)
N64

Before Your Eyes (2021)
GoodbyeWorld Games; Skybound Games
Adventure
PC, AND, iOS, PS5

The Beginner's Guide (2015)
Everything Unlimited Ltd.; Everything Unlimited Ltd.
Adventure
PC

Bejeweled (2001)
PopCap Games; PopCap Games, Electronic Arts
Puzzle (tile matching)
PC, Flash, mobile, iOS, AND, Xbox

Bejeweled (2001)
PopCap Games; PopCap Games, Electronic Arts
Puzzle (tile matching)
PC, Flash, mobile, iOS, AND, Xbox

Beyond: Two Souls (2013)
Quantic Dream; Sony Computer Entertainment, Quantic Dream
Adventure (cinematic adventure)
PS3 […] PS4 […] PC

The Big Catch (2025)
Filet Group; Filet Group
Platformer (3D platformer)
PC

Binary Land (1984)
Hudson Soft, Konami; Hudson Soft, Nintendo
Arcade (maze)
NES, PC […] 3DS, Wii

The Binding of Isaac (2011)
Edmund McMillen, Florian Himsl; Edmund McMillen
Shmup (roguelike)
PC […] PS4, PSV, 3DS, WU, XBO […] iOS, NS

BioShock (2007)
2K Boston, 2K Australia; 2K
Shooter (first-person shooter)
PC, X360, PS3, […] iOS […] PS4, XBO, NS (remaster; BioShock: The Collection)

Black & White (2001)
Lionhead Studios; Electronic Arts, Feral Interactive
Strategy (god game)
PC

Black Desert Online (2015)
Pearl Abyss; Pearl Abyss
RPG (MMORPG)
PC […] iOS, AND, XBO, PS4

BlazBlue Centralfiction (2015)
Arc System Works; Arc System Works, Aksys Games, PQube
Fighting (2D fighting; airdash fighting)
ARC, PS3, PS4, PC, NS

A Blind Legend (2015)
Dowino; Plug In Digital
Adventure (audio game)
AND, iOS, PC

Bloodborne (2015)
FromSoftware; Sony Computer Entertainment
RPG (ARPG)
PS4

Bloodroots (2020)
Paper Cult; Vibe Avenue
Brawler (hack and slash)
PC, NS, PS4, XS

Bloons TD 6 (2018)
Ninja Kiwi; Ninja Kiwi
Strategy (tower defense)
AND, iOS, PC, XBO, XS, PS4, PS5

blur (2010)
Bizarre Creations; Activision
Racing (arcade racing)
PC, PS3, X360

Boom Blox (2008)
EA Los Angeles; Electronic Arts
Party (physics puzzle)
Wii

Botanicula (2012)
Amanita Design; Amanita Design, Daedalic Entertainment
Adventure (point-and-click adventure)
PC […] iOS

Boulder Dash Construction Kit (1986)
First Star Software; Epyx, Databyte
Puzzle (maze)
PC

Boxyboy (1990)
NEC; NEC
Puzzle (sokoban)
PC

Braid (2008)
Number None; Number None
Platformer (2D platformer, puzzle platformer)
X360, PC, PS3 [...] PS4, PS5, NS, XBO, XS, AND, iOS (remaster)

Brawlout (2018)
Angry Mob Games; Angry Mob Games, Merge Games
Fighting (platform fighting)
PC, NS, PS4, XBO

Breakout (1976)
Atari; Atari, Namco
Arcade
ARC, 2600, PC

The Bridge (2013)
The Quantum Astrophysicists Guild; The Quantum Astrophysicists Guild
Puzzle
PC, X360, AND, XBO, PS3, PS4, PSV, WU [...] NS

Brotato (2023)
Thomas Gervraud; Blobfish
Shmup (bullet heaven)
PC, AND, iOS, NS, PS4, PS5, XBO, XS

Brothers: A Tale of Two Sons (2013)
Starbreeze Studios; 505 Games
Adventure
X360, PS3, PC, PS4, XBO, iOS, AND [...] NS [...] PS5, XS (remake)

Burnout series (2001-2018)
Criterion Games, EA UK; Acclaim Entertainment, Electronic Arts
Racing (arcade racing)
PS2, GCN, XB, X360, PSP, NDS, PS3, PC, PS4, XBO, NS, iOS

Burnout Paradise (2008)
Criterion Games; Electronic Arts
Racing (arcade racing)
PC, X360, PS3 [...] PS4, XBO, NS (remaster)

Buzz!: The BIG Quiz (2006)
Relentless Software; Sony Computer Entertainment Europe
Party (quiz / game show)
PS2

Call of Duty series (2003-present)
Infinity Ward, Treyarch, Sledgehammer Games, Raven Software; Activision
Shooter (first-person shooter)
AND, mobile, GCN, iOS, NDS, NG, PC, PS2, PS3, PS4, PS5, PSP, PSV, Wii, WU, XB, X360, XBO, XS

Call of Duty 4: Modern Warfare (2007)
Infinity Ward; Activision
Shooter (first-person shooter)
PC, PS3, X360 [...] Wii [...] PS4, XBO (remaster)

Candy Crush Saga (2012)
King; King
Puzzle (tile-matching)
PC, iOS, AND

Captain Toad: Treasure Tracker (2014)
Nintendo EAD Tokyo; Nintendo
Puzzle (puzzle platformer)
WU [...] 3DS, NS

Carcassonne (2007)
Sierra Online Seattle; Vivendi Games
Strategy (board game)
X360 [...] NS

Castlevania: Symphony of the Night (1997)
Konami Computer Entertainment Tokyo; Konami
RPG (ARPG, metroidvania)
PSX, SS [...] PSP, X360, PS3, PSV [...] PS4, AND, iOS

Celeste (2018)
Maddy Makes Games; Maddy Makes Games
Platformer (2D platformer, precision platformer)
PC, NS, PS4, XBO

Centipede (1981)
Atari; Atari, Sanritsu, Kiwako
Shmup (stationary shmup)
ARC, PC, 2600, 5200, ITV, 7800 [...] GB

Chants of Sennaar (2023)
Rundisc; Focus Entertainment
Puzzle
NS, PS4, PC, XBO

Chex Quest (1996)
Digital Café; General Mills
Shooter (first-person shooter)
PC [...] NS (remake)

Chicory: A Colorful Tale (2021)
Wishes Ultd.; Finji
RPG (ARPG)
PC, NS, PS4, PS5, XBO, XS

Chip's Challenge (1989)
Epyx; Atari, U.S. Gold, Epyx, Microsoft Home, Pixel Games UK
Puzzle (sokoban)
PC, Lynx [...] NS

Chrono Trigger (1995)
Square; Square
RPG (JRPG)
SNES [...] PSX [...] NDS [...] iOS, AND (remaster) [...] PC (remaster)

Cities: Skylines (2015)
Colossal Order; Paradox Interactive
Simulation (city builder)
PC, NS, PS4, PS5, XBO, XS

Clicker Heroes (2014)
Playsaurus; Playsaurus
Simulation (clicker game)
PC, iOS, PS4, XBO

The Climb (2016)
Crytek; Crytek
Sports (rock climbing)
PC [...] Quest

Colossal Cave Adventure (1976)
William Crowther; William Crowther
Adventure (text adventure)
PC

The Complex: Found Footage (2022)
pgWave.; pgWave.
Horror (exploration horror)
PC

Conker's Bad Fur Day (2001)
Rare; Rare, THQ
Platformer (3D platformer)
N64 [...] XB (remake) [...] XBO (Rare Replay)

Contra (1987)
Konami; Konami
Shmup (run and gun)
ARC, PC, NES [...] PS2 [...] Wii, X360, PS3, NDS [...] WU [...] PS4 [...] XBO, NS

Control (2019)
Remedy Entertainment; 505 Games
Shooter (third-person shooter)
PS4, PC, XBO, NS, PS5, XS

Cookie Clicker (2013)
Julien Thiennot; DashNet, Playsaurus
Simulation (clicker game)
PC [...] AND

Counterfeit Monkey (2012)
Emily Short; Emily Short
Adventure (text adventure)
PC

Cow Clicker (2010)
Ian Bogost; Ian Bogost
Simulation (clicker game)
PC

Crash Bandicoot 2: Cortex Strikes Back (1997)
Naughty Dog; Sony Computer Entertainment
Platformer (3D platformer)
PSX [...] PS4, NS, PC, XBO (remake; Crash Bandicoot N. Sane Trilogy)

Crash Team Racing (1999)
Naughty Dog; Sony Computer Entertainment
Racing (kart racing)
PSX [...] PS3, PSV [...] NS, PS4, XBO (remake)

Crazy Taxi (1999)
SEGA AM3; SEGA
Racing (arcade racing)
ARC, DC, PS2, GCN, PC [...] PS3, X360, iOS, AND (remaster)

Crime O'Clock (2023)
Bad Seed; Just for Games
Puzzle (hidden object game)
PC, NS

Crimzon Clover (2011)
Yotsubane; Yotsubane, Degica
Shmup (bullet hell)
PC [...] ARC [...] NS

Cruis'n USA (1994)
TV Games Inc., Williams Entertainment; Nintendo, Midway Games
Racing (arcade racing)
ARC […] N64

Crusader Kings (2004)
Paradox Development Studio; PAN Vision AB, Koch Media, Paradox Interactive
Strategy (4X)
PC

Crysis (2007)
Crytek; Electronic Arts, Crytek
Shooter (first-person shooter)
PC […] X360, PS3 […] NS, PS4, XBO (remaster)

Cuphead (2017)
Studio MDHR; Studio MDHR
Shmup (run and gun)
PC, XBO, NS, PS4

Cut the Rope (2010)
ZeptoLab; Chillingo
Puzzle (physics puzzle)
iOS, AND, NDS, PC, 3DS

Cyberpunk 2077 (2020)
CD Projekt Red; CD Projekt
RPG (ARPG, first-person shooter)
PC, PS4, XBO, PS5, XS

Dance Central (2010)
Harmonix; MTV Games
Rhythm (dancing game)
X360

Dance Dance Revolution (1998)
Bemani; Konami
Rhythm (dancing game)
ARC, PSX

Danganronpa: Trigger Happy Havoc (2010)
Spike; Spike
Adventure (visual novel)
PSP, AND, iOS, PSV […] PC, PS4 […] NS, XBO

Darfur Is Dying (2006)
Susana Ruiz; mtvU
Simulator (newsgame)
Flash

Dark Echo (2015)
RAC7 Games; RAC7 Games
Adventure (audio game)
AND, iOS, PC

Dark Souls (2011)
FromSoftware; FromSoftware, Namco Bandai Games
RPG (ARPG)
PS3, X360, PC […] PS4, XBO, NS (remaster)

Dark Souls II (2014)
FromSoftware; FromSoftware, Bandai Namco
RPG (ARPG)
PS3, X360, PC, PS4, XBO

Dead by Daylight (2016)
Behaviour Interactive; Behaviour Interactive, 505 Games, Deep Silver, NetEase Games, Starbreeze Studios
Horror
PC, PS4, XBO […] NS, AND, iOS, XS, PS5

Deadly Creatures (2009)
Rainbow Studios; THQ
Action
Wii

Deadly Premonition (2010)
Access Games; Ignition Entertainment, Marvelous Entertainment, Rising Star Games, Aksys Games, Numskull Games
Horror (survival horror)
X360, PS3, PC […] NS

DEAD OR ALIVE 6 (2019)
Team Ninja; Koei Tecmo
Fighting (3D fighting)
PS4, PC, XBO, ARC

Dead Rising (2006)
Capcom Production Studio 1; Capcom
Action (sandbox, horror, brawler)
X360, PC […] PS4, XBO […] PS5, XS (remaster)

Dead Space (2008)
EA Redwood Shores; Electronic Arts

Horror (survival horror; third-person shooter)
PS3, X360, PC […] PS5, XS (remake)

Dead Space: Extraction (2009)
EA Redwood Shores, Eurocom; Electronic Arts
Horror (on-rails shooter)
Wii, PS3

Dear Esther (2012)
The Chinese Room; The Chinese Room, Curve Digital, Secret Mode
Adventure (exploration adventure)
PC […] PS4, XBO […] iOS

Death Stranding (2019)
Kojima Productions; Sony Interactive Entertainment, 505 Games
Action
PS4, PC, PS5 […] iOS

Defender (1981)
Williams Electronics; Williams Electronics, Taito, Atari
Shmup (horizontally scrolling shmup)
ARC, PC, 2600, 5200, ITV

Def Jam Vendetta (2003)
AKI Corporation, EA Canada; EA Sports BIG, EA Games
Fighting, sports (wrestling)
PS2, GCN

Demon's Souls (2009)
FromSoftware; Sony Computer Entertainment, Atlus, Namco Bandai
RPG (ARPG)
PS3 […] PS5 (remake)

Desperados III (2020)
Mimimi Games; THQ Nordic
Strategy (real-time strategy, tactics, stealth)
PC, PS4, XBO

Destroy All Humans! (2005)
Pandemic Studios; THQ
Shooter (third-person shooter)
PS2, XB […] PS4 […] PC, XBO, NS (remake)

Detroit: Become Human (2018)
Quantic Dream; Sony Interactive Entertainment
Adventure (cinematic adventure)
PS4, PC

Deus Ex (2000)
Ion Storm; Eidos Interactive
Shooter (first-person shooter, immersive sim)
PC, PS2

Devil Daggers (2016)
Sorath; Sorath
Shooter (first-person shooter, boomer shooter)
PC

Devil May Cry (2001)
Capcom Production Studio 4; Capcom
Brawler (character action)
PS2 […] PS3, X360 (remaster) […] PS4, PC, XBO, NS (remaster)

Devil May Cry 5 (2019)
Capcom; Capcom
Brawler (character action)
PS4, PC, XBO, XS, PS5

Devil World (1984)
Nintendo R&D1, Intelligent Systems; Nintendo
Arcade (maze)
NES

Diablo IV (2023)
Blizzard Team 3, Blizzard Albany; Blizzard Entertainment
RPG (ARPG)
PS4, PS5, PC, XBO, XS

Diddy Kong Racing (1997)
Rare; Rare, Nintendo
Racing (kart racing)
N64 […] NDS (remake)

DIG DUG (1982)
Namco; Namco, Atari
Arcade
ARC, 2600, 5200, PC, NES, 7800, GB, GBA, mobile

Disco Elysium (2019)
ZA/UM; ZA/UM
RPG (CRPG)
PC, PS4, PS5, NS, XBO, XS

Disgaea 4 (2011)
Nippon Ichi Software; Nippon Ichi Software, NIS America
Strategy (tactics)
PS3 […] PSV […] PS4, NS, PC […] AND, iOS

Dishonored (2012)
Arkane Studios; Bethesda Softworks
Action (stealth, immersive sim)
PC, PS3, X360 […] PS4, XBO

Disney Fantasia: Music Evolved (2014)
Harmonix; Disney Interactive Studios
Rhythm
X360, XBO

Divinity: Original Sin (2014)
Larian Studios; Larian Studios, Focus Home Interactive, Spike Chunsoft
RPG (CRPG)
PC, PS4, XBO

DNF DUEL (2022)
Arc System Works, Eighting, Neople; Bandai Namco, Nexon
Fighting (2D fighting)
PC, PS4, PS5, NS

DoDonPachi (1997)
Cave, SPS; Atlus
Shmup (bullet hell)
ARC, PSX, SS […] PS3

Doki Doki Literature Club! (2017)
Team Salvato; Team Salvato, Serenity Forge
Horror (visual novel)
PC […] NS, PS4, PS5, XBO, XS (expansion)

Donkey Kong (1981)
Nintendo R&D1; Nintendo
Platformer, arcade (2D platformer)
ARC, G&W, 2600, ITV, PC, NES […] 7800 […] GBA […] Wii […] 3DS […] WU

Donkey Kong 64 (1999)
Rare; Nintendo
Platformer (3D platformer)
N64 […] WU

Donkey Konga (2003)
Namco; Nintendo
Rhythm
GCN

Donkey Kong Country (1994)
Rare; Nintendo
Platformer (2D platformer)
SNES […] GBC […] GBA […] Wii […] WU, 3DS

Donkey Kong Country 2: Diddy's Kong Quest (1995)
Rare; Nintendo
Platformer (2D platformer)
SNES […] GBA […] Wii […] 3DS […] WU

Donkey Kong Country Returns (2010)
Retro Studios; Nintendo
Platformer (2D platformer)
Wii […] 3DS […] NS

Donkey Kong Country: Tropical Freeze (2014)
Retro Studios; Nintendo
Platformer (2D platformer)
WU […] NS

Donkey Kong Jungle Beat (2004)
Nintendo EAD; Nintendo
Platformer (2D platformer)
GCN […] Wii

DOOM (1993)
id Software; id Software
Shooter (first-person shooter)
GEN, JAG, PC, SNES, PSX, 3DO, SS […] GBA […] X360 […] iOS […] PS3 […] AND, NS, PS4, XBO […] PS5, XS

DOOM 64 (1997)
Midway Studios San Diego; Midway Games, GT Interactive
Shooter (first-person shooter)
N64 […] NS, PS4, PC, XBO

DOOM Eternal (2020)
id Software; Bethesda Softworks
Shooter (first-person shooter)
PC, PS4, XBO, NS, PS5, XS

Doshin the Giant (1999)
Param; RandnetDD, Nintendo
Strategy (god game)
N64 […] GCN

Dota 2 (2013)
Valve; Valve
MOBA
PC

Dota Auto Chess (2019)
Drodo Studio; Drodo Studio
Strategy (auto battler)
PC

Dota Underlords (2020)
Valve; Valve
Strategy (auto battler)
AND, iOS, PC

Double Dragon (1987)
Technōs Japan, Arc System Works, Software Creations; Taito, Tradewest, Nintendo, Mastertronic
Brawler (beat-em-up)
ARC, NES, MS

Downwell (2015)
Ojiro Fumoto, Red Phantom Games; Devolver Digital
Platformer (2D platformer, precision platformer, roguelike)
iOS, PC, AND, PS4, PSV […] NS

DRAGON BALL FighterZ (2018)
Arc System Works, Ecole Software; Bandai Namco
Fighting (2D fighting; airdash fighting)
PS4, XBO, PC, NS […] PS5, XS

Dragon's Crown (2013)
Vanillaware; Atlus, NIS America
Brawler (hack and slash)
PS3, PSV […] PS4

Dragon's Lair (1983)
Advanced Microcomputer Systems; Cinematronics, Atari, Universal
Adventure (cinematic adventure)
ARC, 3DO, JAG […] GEN, PC […] iOS, PS3, X360

DRAGON QUEST XI: Echoes of an Elusive Age (2017)
Square Enix; Square Enix
RPG (JRPG)
3DS, PS4, PC, NS, PS4, XBO

Dragon Spirit (1987)
Namco; Namco, Atari
Shmup (vertically scrolling shmup)
ARC, PC

Dream Daddy: A Dad Dating Simulator (2017)
Game Grumps; Game Grumps
Adventure (dating sim, visual novel)
PC, PS4, NS, AND, iOS

Dreams (2020)
Media Molecule; Sony Interactive Entertainment
Simulation
PS4

Driver: San Francisco (2011)
Ubisoft Reflections; Ubisoft
Racing
PS3, Wii, X360, PC

Dr. Mario (1990)
Nintendo R&D1; Nintendo
Puzzle (falling block puzzle)
GB, NES, ARC […] SNES […] GBA […] Wii […] 3DS […] WU

Duck Hunt (1984)
Nintendo R&D1, Intelligent Systems; Nintendo
Shooter (light gun shooter)
NES, ARC […] WU

Duke Nukem 3D (1996)
3D Realms, Lion Entertainment, General Arcade, Gearbox Software, Nerve Software; FormGen, MacSoft, U.S. Gold, Eidos Interactive, GT Interactive, King Records, SEGA, TecToy, Piko Interactive, Microsoft Game Studios, MachineWorks Northwest, Devolver Digital, Gearbox Publishing, 2K Games
Shooter (first-person shooter)
PC, SS, N64, PSX, GEN […] X360, iOS […] AND […] PS3, PSV, PS4, XBO, NS

Duke Nukem Forever (2011)
Gearbox Software; 2K
Shooter (first-person shooter)
PC, PS3, X360

Dungeon Master (1987)
FTL Games, Victor Musical Industries; FTL Games, Victor Musical Industries
RPG (dungeon crawler)
PC […] SNES

Dwarf Fortress (2022)
Bay 12 Games; Bay 12 Games
Simulation
PC

Dynasty Warriors 8 (2013)
Omega Force; Tecmo Koei
Action (musou)
PS3, X360, PS4, PC, XBO, PSV […] NS

EARTH DEFENSE FORCE 6 (2022)
Sandlot; D3 Publisher
Shooter (musou, third-person shooter)
PS4, PS5, PC

EA SPORTS FC 25 (2024)
EA Vancouver, EA Romania; EA Sports
Sports (football)
NS, PS4, PS5, PC, XBO, XS

echochrome II (2010)
Japan Studio; Sony Computer Entertainment
Puzzle
PS3

ELDEN RING (2022)
FromSoftware; Bandai Namco Entertainment, FromSoftware
RPG (ARPG)
PC, PS4, PS5, XBO, XS

The Elder Scrolls II: Daggerfall (1996)
Bethesda Softworks, MediaTech West; Bethesda Softworks
RPG (ARPG)
PC

The Elder Scrolls IV: Oblivion (2006)
Bethesda Game Studios; Bethesda Softworks, 2K, Ubisoft
RPG (ARPG)
PC, X360, PS3

The Elder Scrolls V: Skyrim (2011)
Bethesda Game Studios; Bethesda Softworks
RPG (ARPG)
PC, PS3, X360, PS4, XBO […] NS, PS5, XS

Elite Beat Agents (2006)
iNiS; Nintendo
Rhythm
NDS

El Paso, Elsewhere (2023)
Strange Scaffold; Strange Scaffold, Frosty Pop
Shooter (third-person shooter)
PC, XBO, XS, iOS, PS5

Enderal: The Shards of Order (2016)
SureAI; Nicolas Samuel Lietzau
RPG (ARPG)
PC

Enter the Gungeon (2016)
Dodge Roll; Devolver Digital
Shmup (twin-stick shooter, roguelike)
PC, PS4, XBO, NS

Escape from Tarkov (2017)
Battlestate Games; Battlestate Games
Shooter (first-person shooter, extraction shooter, tactical shooter)
PC

Eternal Darkness: Sanity's Requiem (2002)
Silicon Knights; Nintendo
Horror (survival horror)
GCN

Etrian Odyssey (2007)
Atlus, Lancarse; Atlus, Nintendo, SEGA
RPG (dungeon crawler)
NDS […] NS, PC

Europa Universalis IV (2013)
Paradox Development Studio; Paradox Interactive
Strategy (4X)
PC

Euro Truck Simulator 2 (2012)
SCS Software; SCS Software

Simulator (job sim)
PC

EVE Online (2003)
CCP Games; Simon & Schuster Interactive, Crucial Entertainment, CCP Games, Atari
RPG (MMORPG)
PC

EverQuest (1999)
Verant Interactive, 989 Studios; Sony Online Entertainment, Ubisoft
RPG (MMORPG)
PC

Everybody's Golf (1997)
Camelot Software Planning; Sony Computer Entertainment
Sports (golf)
PSX

Everybody's Gone to the Rapture (2015)
The Chinese Room; Sony Computer Entertainment
Adventure (exploration adventure)
PS4, PC

Excitebike (1984)
Nintendo R&D4, Hudson Soft, Arika; Nintendo, Hudson Soft
Racing (arcade racing)
NES, ARC, PC […] GBA […] Wii […] 3DS […] WU

Fable II (2008)
Lionhead Studios; Microsoft Game Studios
RPG (ARPG)
X360

Façade (2005)
Procedural Arts; Procedural Arts
Simulation (life sim)
PC

Face Raiders (2011)
HAL Laboratory; Nintendo
Shooter (first-person shooter)
3DS

Fahrenheit / Indigo Prophesy (2005)
Quantic Dream; Atari
Adventure (cinematic adventure)
PS2, PC, XB […] X360 […] AND, iOS, PS4

Fall Guys (2020)
Mediatonic; Devolver Digital, Epic Games
Party (3D platformer)
PS4, PC, NS, PS5, XBO, XS […] AND, iOS

Fallout 2: A Post Nuclear Role Playing Game (1998)
Black Isle Studios; Interplay Productions
RPG (CRPG)
PC

Fallout: New Vegas (2010)
Obsidian Entertainment; Bethesda Softworks
RPG (ARPG)
PC, PS3, X360

FantaVision (2000)
Japan Studio; Sony Computer Entertainment
Puzzle
PS2, mobile

Far Cry series (2004-present)
Crytek, Ubisoft Montreal, Ubisoft Toronto; Ubisoft
Shooter (first-person shooter)
PC, XB, X360, Wii, ARC, PS3, PS4, XBO, XS, PS5

Farming Simulator 22 (2021)
Giants Software; Giants Software
Simulation (job sim)
PC, XBO, XS, PS4, PS5

Fatal Frame (2001)
Tecmo; Tecmo, Microsoft Game Studios
Horror (survival horror)
PS2, XB

FEZ (2012)
Polytron Corporation; Trapdoor
Platformer, puzzle
X360, PC, PS3, PS4, PSV […] iOS […] NS

Fighters Megamix (1996)
SEGA AM2; SEGA, Tiger Electronics
Fighting (3D fighting)
SS

FINAL FANTASY (1987)
Square; Square
RPG (JRPG)

NES […] PSX, GBA […] PSP […] iOS […] AND […] 3DS […] PC, NS, PS4 (remake)

FINAL FANTASY V (1992)
Square; Square, Sony Computer Entertainment, Square Enix, Nintendo
RPG (JRPG)
SNES […] PSX […] GBA […] iOS, AND, PC […] NS, PS4, XS (remaster)

FINAL FANTASY VI (1994)
Square; Square, Sony Computer Entertainment, Square Enix, Nintendo
RPG (JRPG)
SNES […] PSX […] GBA […] AND, iOS, PC […] NS, PS4, XS (remaster)

FINAL FANTASY VII (1997)
Square; Square, Sony Computer Entertainment, Eidos Interactive, Square Enix
RPG (JRPG)
PSX, PC […] iOS, PS4, AND (remaster) […] NS, XBO (remaster)

FINAL FANTASY VII REMAKE (2020)
Square Enix Business Division 1; Square Enix
RPG (ARPG)
PS4, PS5, PC

FINAL FANTASY XIV (2013)
Square Enix Business Division 5; Square Enix
RPG (MMORPG)
PS3, PC, PS4 […] PS5, XS

Fire Emblem Awakening (2012)
Intelligent Systems; Nintendo
Strategy (tactics)
3DS

Fire Emblem Heroes (2017)
Intelligent Systems; Nintendo
Strategy (tactics, turn-based strategy)
AND, iOS

Fire Pro Wrestling World (2017)
ZEX Corporation; Spike Chunsoft
Sports (wrestling)
PC, PS4

Firewatch (2016)
Campo Santo; Panic, Campo Santo
Adventure
PC, PS4, XBO […] NS

Five Nights at Freddy's (2014)
Scott Cawthon; Scott Cawthon
Horror, strategy (tower defense)
PC, AND, iOS […] NS, PS4, XBO

Flashback (1992)
Delphine Software International, Tiertex, Chui; U.S. Gold, JoshProd, Microids
Platformer (2D platformer, cinematic platformer)
PC, GEN, SNES, 3DO, CDi, JAG […] DC […] iOS, NS, PS4, XBO

Foldit (2008)
University of Washington Center for Game Science, Department of Biochemistry; University of Washington
Simulation, puzzle
PC

Football Manager 2024 (2024)
Sports Interactive; SEGA
Simulation, sports (business management)
PC, PS5, XBO, XS

The Forgotten City (2015)
Modern Storyteller; Modern Storyteller
Adventure
PC (mod for *The Elder Scroll V: Skyrim*) […] PS4, PS5, XBO, XS, NS (standalone remake)

Fortnite (2017)
Epic Games; Epic Games
Shooter (third-person shooter, battle royale)
PC, PS4, PS5, XBO, XS, iOS, NS, AND

Forza Horizon 5 (2021)
Playground Games; Xbox Game Studios
Racing
PC, XBO, XS

Forza Motorsport (2005)
Turn 10 Studios; Microsoft Game Studios
Racing (simulation racing)
XB

Forza Motorsport 2 (2007)
Turn 10 Studios; Microsoft Game Studios
Racing (simulation racing)
X360

The Free Culture Game (2008)
Molleindustria; Molleindustria
Arcade
PC

From Dust (2011)
Ubisoft Montpellier; Ubisoft
Strategy (god game)
X360, PC, PS3

Frostpunk (2018)
11 bit studios; 11 bit studios
Simulation (city-builder)
PC, PS4, XBO [...] iOS, AND

FUSER (2020)
Harmonix; NCSoft
Rhythm
PC, NS, PS4, XBO

F-Zero GX (2003)
Amusement Vision; Nintendo
Racing (arcade racing)
GCN

GALAGA (1981)
Namco; Namco, Midway Manufacturing
Shmup (stationary shmup)
ARC, PC, NES, 7800, GB [...] GBA [...] mobile, X360 [...] iOS, XBO, PS4

Galaxian (1979)
Namco; Namco, Taito, Midway Manufacturing
Shmup (stationary shmup)
ARC, 2600, 5200, PC, ITV, NES, GB [...] GBA

Game Dev Tycoon (2012)
Greenheart Games; Greenheart Games
Simulation (business management)
PC [...] iOS, AND, NS

Gang Beasts (2017)
Boneloaf; Double Fine Presents, Boneloaf
Party (physics competition)
PC, PS4, XBO [...] NS

GAROU: MARK OF THE WOLVES (1999)
SNK, DotEmu, Code Mystics, Bandai Namco; Agetec, SNK, Hamster Corporation
Fighting (2D fighting)
ARC, NG, DC [...] PS2 [...] X360 [...] mobile, PS4, PSV, PC

Garry's Mod (2006)
Facepunch Studios; Valve
Shooter (sandbox, first-person shooter)
PC

Gears of War (2006)
Epic Games; Microsoft Game Studios
Shooter (third-person shooter)
X360, PC [...] XBO (remaster)

Gears Tactics (2020)
Splash Damage, The Coalition; Xbox Game Studios
Strategy (tactics)
PC, XBO, XS

Genshin Impact (2020)
miHoYo; HoYoverse, miHoYo, Funtap, Nijigen Games
RPG (ARPG)
AND, iOS, PS4, PC, PS5 [...] XS

Geometry Wars: Retro Evolved (2003)
Bizarre Creations; Microsoft Game Studios
Shmup (twin-stick shooter)
XB [...] X360, PC

Getting Over It with Bennett Foddy (2017)
Bennett Foddy; Bennett Foddy
Platformer
PC, iOS, AND

Gex: Enter the Gecko (1998)
Crystal Dynamics; Crystal Dynamics, Midway, GT Interactive, Ubisoft
Platformer (3D platformer)
PSX, N64, PC

GigaBash (2022)
Passion Republic Games; Passion Republic Games
Fighting (3D fighting)
PC, PS4, PS5, NS, XBO, XS

Gitaroo Man (2001)
iNiS; Koei, THQ

Rhythm
PS2 […] PSP

God of War (2005)
Santa Monica Studio; Sony Computer Entertainment
Action (character action)
PS2 […] PS3, PSV (remaster; God of War Collection)

God of War (2018)
Santa Monica Studio; Sony Interactive Entertainment
Action
PS4 […] PC

God of War II (2007)
Santa Monica Studio; Sony Computer Entertainment
Action (character action)
PS2 […] PS3 (remaster)

Golden Axe (1989)
SEGA; SEGA
Brawler (hack and slash)
ARC, GEN, PC, MS

GoldenEye 007 (1997)
Rare, Nintendo
Shooter (first-person shooter)
N64 […] XBO, XS (remaster; Rare Replay)

Golden Tee Golf (1989)
Incredible Technologies; Incredible Technologies
Sports (golf)
ARC

Gone Home (2013)
The Fullbright Company, BlitWorks; The Fullbright Company, Majesco Entertainment, Annapurna Interactive
Adventure (exploration adventure)
PC […] PS4, XBO […] NS, iOS

Gorf (1981)
Midway, Rokland Corporation, CBS Electronics; Midway, Roklan, CBS Electronics, Commodore, Handic Software, Doctorsoft, Coleco
Shmup (stationary shmup)
ARC, PC, 2600, 5200

Gorogoa (2017)
Jason Roberts; Annapurna Interactive
Puzzle
PC, iOS, NS, PS4, XBO, AND

Grand Theft Auto IV (2008)
Rockstar North; Rockstar Games
Action (sandbox, third-person shooter)
PS3, X360, PC

Grand Theft Auto: San Andreas (2004)
Rockstar North; Rockstar Games
Action (sandbox, third-person shooter)
PS2, PC, XB […] iOS, AND, mobile, X360, PS3 […] NS, PS4, PS5, XBO, XS (remaster; Grand Theft Auto: The Trilogy — The Definitive Edition)

Grand Theft Auto V (2013)
Rockstar North; Rockstar Games
Action (sandbox, third-person shooter)
PS3, X360, PS4, XBO, PC […] PS5, XS

Grand Theft Auto: Vice City (2002)
Rockstar North; Rockstar Games
Action (sandbox, third-person shooter)
PS2, PC, XB […] iOS, AND […] NS, PS4, PS5, XBO, XS (remaster; Grand Theft Auto: The Trilogy — The Definitive Edition)

Gran Turismo 3: A-Spec (2001)
Polyphony Digital; Sony Computer Entertainment
Racing (simulation racing)
PS2

Gran Turismo 7 (2022)
Polyphony Digital; Sony Interactive Entertainment
Racing (simulation racing)
PS4, PS5

Grindstone (2019)
Capybara Games; Capybara Games
Puzzle (tile-matching game)
iOS, PC, NS, PS4, PS5, XS

Grounded (2022)
Obsidian Entertainment; Xbox Game Studios
Action (survival)
PC, XBO, XS, NS, PS4, PS5

Grow Home (2015)
Ubisoft Reflections; Ubisoft

Platformer (3D platformer)
PC, PS4

Guild Wars 2 (2012)
ArenaNet; ArenaNet, NCSoft, Tencent Games, Kongzhong
RPG (MMORPG)
PC

GUILTY GEAR -STRIVE- (2021)
Arc System Works, Monolith Soft; Arc System Works, Bandai Namco, SEGA, Andamiro, Nintendo
Fighting (2D fighting)
PC, PS4, PS5, ARC, XBO, XS, NS

GUILTY GEAR Xrd -SIGN- (2014)
Arc System Works; SEGA, Arc System Works, Aksys Games, Sony Computer Entertainment
Fighting (2D fighting)
ARC, PS3, PS4, PC

Guitar Hero series (2005-2015)
Harmonix, Neversoft, Budcat Creations, Vicarious Visions, Aspyr, Beenox, FreeStyleGames, Exient Entertainment, Underground Development; RedOctane, Activision, Aspyr
Rhythm
PS2, X360, PS3, Wii, PC, ARC, NDS, mobile, PS4, WU, XBO, iOS

Guitar Hero (2005)
Harmonix; RedOctane
Rhythm
PS2

Gunpoint (2013)
Suspicious Developments; Suspicious Developments
Action
PC

Gunstar Heroes (1993)
Treasure; SEGA
Shmup (run and gun)
GEN, GG […] 3DS […] PC

Hack 'n' Slash (2014)
Double Fine Productions; Double Fine Productions
RPG
PC

Hades (2020)
Supergiant Games; Supergiant Games
Brawler (roguelite)
PC, NS, PS4, PS5, XBO, XS […] iOS

Half-Life (1998)
Valve; Sierra Studios
Shooter (first-person shooter)
PC, PS2

Half-Life 2 (2004)
Valve; Valve
Shooter (first-person shooter)
PC, XB, X360, PS3 […] AND

Half-Life 2: Episode Two (2007)
Valve; Valve
Shooter (first-person shooter)
PC, PS3, X360

Half-Life: Alyx (2020)
Valve; Valve
Shooter (first-person shooter)
PC

Halo: Combat Evolved (2001)
Bungie; Microsoft Game Studios
Shooter (first-person shooter)
XB, PC, […] X360 […] XBO (remaster) […] XS (remaster)

Handshakes (2022)
Pet Pumpkin, Damaskino, Trumpetguy; Pet Pumpkin
Puzzle (sokoban)
PC

A Hat in Time (2017)
Gears for Breakfast; Humble Bundle, Gears for Breakfast
Platformer (3D platformer)
PC, PS4, XBO, NS

Hatoful Boyfriend: A School of Hope and White Wings (2011)
PigeoNation Inc., Mediatonic; Mist Psi Press, Devolver Digital
Adventure (dating sim, visual novel)
PC, PS4, PSV, iOS, AND

Haunted House (1982)
Atari; Atari
Horror (exploration horror)
2600 [...] PC

Heart of Darkness (1998)
Amazing Studio; Infogrames Multimedia, Interplay Productions
Platformer (2D platformer, cinematic platformer)
PSX, PC

Helldivers 2 (2024)
Arrowhead Game Studios; Sony Interactive Entertainment
Shooter (third-person shooter, extraction shooter)
PS5, PC

Her Story (2015)
Sam Barlow; Sam Barlow
Adventure
PC, iOS, AND

Herzog Zwei (1989)
Technosoft; SEGA, Technosoft
Strategy (MOBA)
GEN [...] NS

Hexcells (2014)
Matthew Brown Games; Matthew Brown Games
Puzzle (number puzzle)
PC, iOS

Hey You, Pikachu! (1998)
Ambrella; Nintendo
Simulation (virtual pet)
N64

Hidden Cats in New York (2023)
Nukearts; Nukearts
Puzzle (hidden object game)
PC, NS, PS4, PS5, XBO, XS

Hidden through Time (2020)
Crazy Monkey Studios; Crazy Monkey Studios
Puzzle (hidden object game)
AND, PC, NS, PS4, XBO

Hi-Fi RUSH (2023)
Tango Gameworks; Bethesda Softworks
Brawler (character action)
PC, XS, PS5

High on Life (2022)
Squanch Games; Squanch Games
Shooter (first-person shooter)
PC, XBO, XS, PS4, PS5

The Hitchhiker's Guide to the Galaxy (1984)
Infocom; Infocom
Adventure (point-and-click adventure)
PC

HITMAN (2016)
IO Interactive; Square Enix
Action (stealth)
PC, PS4, XBO

Hollow Knight (2017)
Team Cherry; Team Cherry
Platformer (2D platformer, metroidvania)
PC, NS, PS4, XBO

The Hong Kong Massacre (2019)
Vreski; Vreski, Untold Tales
Shmup (twin-stick shooter)
PC, PS4, NS [...] XBO, XS

Horizon series (2017-present)
Guerrilla Games; Sony Interactive Entertainment
Action
PS4, PS5, PC

Hotline Miami (2012)
Dennaton Games; Devolver Digital
Shmup (twin-stick shooter)
PC, PS3, PSV, PS4 [...] NS, XBO, PS5, XS (Hotline Miami Collection)

The House of the Dead (1997)
SEGA AM1; SEGA
Shooter, horror (first-person shooter, on-rails shooter, light gun shooter)
ARC, SS, PC

HuniePop (2015)
HuniePot; HuniePot
Adventure (dating sim, visual novel, tile matching)
PC

Hunt: Showdown (2019)
Crytek; Crytek, Koch Media
Shooter (first-person shooter, extraction shooter)
PC, XBO, PS4 […] PS5, XS

Hyperbolica (2022)
CodeParade; CodeParade
Adventure
PC, Quest

Hypnagogia 無限の夢 Boundless Dreams (2021)
sodaraptor; sodaraptor
Adventure (exploration adventure)
PC

Hyrule Warriors (2014)
Omega Force, Team Ninja; Koei Tecmo, Nintendo
Brawler (musou)
WU, 3DS, NS

I Am Your Beast (2024)
Strange Scaffold; Strange Scaffold, Frosty Pop Games Inc.
Shooter (first-person shooter)
PC, iOS

i commissioned some bees (2022)
Follow the Fun; Follow the Fun
Puzzle (hidden object game)
PC

Ikaruga (2001)
Treasure; Treasure, Entertainment Software Publishing, Infogrames, Nicalis
Shmup (bullet hell)
ARC, DC, GCN […] X360 […] PC […] NS, PS4

IMMORTALITY (2022)
Sam Barlow; Half Mermaid Productions
Adventure (cinematic adventure)
PC, XS, AND, iOS […] PS5

The Incredible Machine (1993)
Jeff Tunnell Productions; Sierra On-Line, Dynamix
Puzzle
PC

INDIKA (2024)
Odd Meter; 11 bit studios
Adventure
PC, PS5, XS

Inertial Drift (2020)
Level 91 Entertainment; PQube
Racing (arcade racing)
PC, NS, PS4, PS5, XBO, XS

inFAMOUS (2009)
Sucker Punch Productions; Sony Computer Entertainment
Action (sandbox)
PS3

Inscryption (2021)
Daniel Mullins Games; Devolver Digital
Strategy (card game)
PC, PS4, PS5, NS, XBO ,XS

Insurgency: Sandstorm (2018)
New World Interactive; Focus Home Interactive
Shooter (first-person shooter, tactical shooter)
PC […] PS4, XBO […] PS5, XS

Into the Breach (2018)
Subset Games; Subset Games, Netflix
Strategy (tactics)
PC, NS […] iOS, AND

Ion Fury (2019)
Voidpoint, General Arcade; 3D Realms
Shooter (first-person shooter, boomer shooter)
PC, NS, PS4, XBO

The Jackbox Party Pack (2014)
Jackbox Games; Jackbox Games, Telltale Games
Party (quiz)
PS3, PS4, XBO, PC, X360, NS

JellyCar (2007)
Walaber; Walaber
Platformer (physics platformer)
iOS, X360, PC

Jet Lancer (2020)
Code Wakers; Armor Games Studios
Shmup
PC, NS

Jet Set Radio (2000)
Smilebit, BlitWorks; SEGA
Action (rollerblading)
DC […] PC, PS3, X360, PSV, iOS, AND (remaster)

Job Simulator (2016)
Owlchemy Labs; Owlchemy Labs
Puzzle (physics puzzle)
PC […] PS4, Quest […] PS5, AVP

Journey (2012)
thatgamecompany; Sony Computer Entertainment, Annapurna Interactive
Platformer; adventure
PS3 […] PS4 […] PC, iOS

Joust (1982)
Williams Electronics; Williams Electronics
Arcade
ARC, PC, 2600, 5200, 7800, Lynx, NES

Jumping Flash! (1995)
Exact, Ultra; Sony Computer Entertainment
Platformer (3D platformer)
PSX

Just Cause 2 (2010)
Avalanche Studios; Square Enix
Action (sandbox, third-person shooter)
PC, X360, PS3

Just Dance (2009)
Ubisoft Paris; Ubisoft
Rhythm (dancing game)
Wii

Katamari Damacy (2004)
Namco; Namco
Arcade
PS2 […] PC, NS, PS4, XBO (remaster)

Kane & Lynch: Dead Men (2007)
IO Interactive; Eidos Interactive
Shooter (third-person shooter)
PC, PS3, X360

Kaze and the Wild Masks (2021)
PixelHive; SOEDESCO Publishing
Platformer (2D platformer)
PC, NS, PS4, XBO

Keep Talking and Nobody Explodes (2015)
Steel Crate Games; Steel Crate Games
Puzzle
Gear, PC, PS4, NS, XBO, Quest, iOS, AND

Kentucky Route Zero (2020)
Cardboard Computer; Annapurna Interactive
Adventure (point-and-click adventure)
PC, NS, PS4, XBO, AND, iOS, PS5, XS

Killer Queen (2013)
BumbleBear Games; BumbleBear Games
Arcade (RTS)
ARC […] PC, NS, XBO

Kingdom Rush (2011)
Ironhide Game Studio; Armor Games
Strategy (tower defense)
PC, iOS, AND […] NS […] XBO, XS

The King of Fighters XIII (2010)
SNK Playmore, Safari Games; SNK, Atlus, Rising Star Games
Fighting (2D fighting)
ARC, PS3, X360, AND, PC […] PS4, NS

King's Quest: Quest for the Crown (1984)
Sierra On-Line; IBM, Sierra On-Line
Adventure (point-and-click adventure)
PC, MS

Kirby's Dream Course (1994)
HAL Laboratory, Nintendo EAD; Nintendo
Sports (golf)
SNES […] Wii […] WU

Knotwords (2022)
Zach Gage, Jack Schlesinger, Noodlecake Studios; Zach Gage, Jack Schlesinger
Puzzle (word puzzle)
AND, iOS, PC

Kuro: A Shadow's Dream (2020)
Bawnanable; Bawnanable
Platformer (2D platformer)
PS4 (Dreams)

Kuru Kuru Kururin (2001)
Eighting; Nintendo
Arcade (maze)
GBA […] WU

The Last of Us (2013)
Naughty Dog; Sony Computer Entertainment
Horror (third-person shooter, survival horror)
PS3, PS4 […] PS5, PC (remaster)

The Last of Us Part II (2020)
Naughty Dog; Sony Interactive Entertainment
Horror (third-person shooter, survival horror)
PS4 […] PS5 (remaster)

Later Alligator (2019)
Pillow Fight; Pillow Fight
Adventure (point-and-click adventure)
PC, NS

League of Legends (2009)
Riot Games; Riot Games
Strategy (MOBA)
PC

Legacy of Kain: Soul Reaver (1999)
Crystal Dynamics; Eidos Interactive
Action
PSX, PC, DC

Legend of Grimrock (2012)
Almost Human; Almost Human
RPG (dungeon crawler)
PC […] iOS […] NS

The Legend of Zelda series (1986-present)
Nintendo EAD, Capcom, Flagship, Grezzo, Nintendo EPD; Nintendo
RPG (ARPG)
NES, G&W, SNES, GB, CDi, N64, GBA, GCN, Wii, NDS, 3DS, WU, NS

The Legend of Zelda (1986)
Nintendo R&D4; Nintendo
RPG (ARPG)
NES […] GBA […] Wii […] 3DS […] WU

The Legend of Zelda: A Link to the Past (1991)
Nintendo EAD; Nintendo
RPG (ARPG)
SNES […] GBA […] Wii […] WU […] 3DS

The Legend of Zelda: Breath of the Wild (2017)
Nintendo EPD; Nintendo
RPG (ARPG)
NS, WU

The Legend of Zelda: Link's Awakening (1993)
Nintendo EAD; Nintendo
RPG (ARPG)
GB […] 3DS […] NS (remake)

The Legend of Zelda: Ocarina of Time (1998)
Nintendo EAD; Nintendo
RPG (ARPG)
N64 […] GCN, iQue […] Wii […] 3DS (remaster)

The Legend of Zelda: The Wind Waker (2002)
Nintendo EAD; Nintendo
RPG (ARPG)
GCN […] WU (remaster)

Lemmings (1991)
DMA Design; Psygnosis, SEGA, Atari, Ocean Software, Philips Media
Strategy
PC, SNES, GEN, GG, SMS, NES, 3DO, Lynx, GB, CD-i

Lethal League (2014)
Team Reptile; Team Reptile
Sports, arcade, fighting
PC […] PS4, XBO

Libble Rabble (1983)
Namco; Namco
Arcade
ARC, PC, SNES […] PS4, NS

Life Is Strange (2015)
Dontnod Entertainment; Square Enix
Adventure
PC, PS3, PS4, X360, XBO, iOS, AND, NS

LIMBO (2010)
Playdead; Microsoft Game Studios, Playdead
Platformer (cinematic platformer)
X360, PS3, PC, PSV, XBO, AND, PS4 [...] NS

LittleBigPlanet (2008)
Media Molecule; Sony Computer Entertainment
Platformer (2D platformer)
PS3

Little Computer People (1985)
Activision; Activision
Simulation (life sim)
PC

Little Nightmares (2017)
Tarsier Studios; Bandai Namco Entertainment
Platformer, horror (cinematic platformer)
PC, PS4, XBO, NS [...] AND, iOS

Llamasoft: The Jeff Minter Story (2024)
Digital Eclipse; Digital Eclipse
Arcade
PC, NS, PS4, PS5, XBO, XS

Lonely Mountains: Downhill (2019)
Megagon Industries; Thunderful
Sports, racing (mountain biking)
PS4, PC, XBO, NS

Lorelei and the Laser Eyes (2024)
Simogo; Annapurna Interactive
Puzzle
PC, NS

LovePlus (2009)
Konami; Konami
Adventure (dating sim)
NDS [...] 3DS (expansion)

LSD: Dream Emulator (1998)
Asmik Ace Entertainment; Asmik Ace Entertainment
Adventure (exploration adventure)
PSX [...] PC (remake)

LUFTRAUSERS (2014)
Vlambeer; Devolver Digital
Shmup
PC, PS3, PSV, AND

Luigi's Mansion (2001)
Nintendo EAD; Nintendo
Horror, adventure
GCN [...] 3DS

Lumines: Puzzle Fusion (2004)
Q Entertainment; Bandai, Ubisoft
Puzzle, rhythm (falling block puzzle)
PSP [...] PS2, mobile, PC [...] NS, PS4, XBO

Luxuria Superbia (2013)
Tale of Tales; Tale of Tales
Shmup, rhythm
AND, iOS, PC

Mafia III (2016)
Hangar 13; 2K
Action (sandbox, third-person shooter)
PC, PS4, XBO

The Magic Circle (2015)
Question; Question
Adventure
PC, PS4, XBO

Manhunt (2003)
Rockstar North; Rockstar Games
Action (stealth)
PS2, PC, XB

Manifold Garden (2019)
William Chyr Studio; William Chyr Studio
Puzzle (exploration puzzle)
iOS, PC, NS, PS4, XBO, XS, PS5

Manor Lords (2025)
Slavic Magic; Hooded Horse
Simulation (city builder)
PC, XBO, XS

Marble It Up! (2018)
The Engine Company; Alvios
Platformer (3D platformer, marble game)
PC, NS [...] PS4, PS5, XBO, XS

Marble Madness (1984)
Atari; Atari
Platformer (marble game)
ARC, PC […] GB, GG, GEN, MS, NES […] GBA

Mario + Rabbids Kingdom Battle (2017)
Ubisoft Milan, Ubisoft Paris; Ubisoft
Strategy (tactics)
NS

Mario Golf (1999)
Camelot Software Planning; Nintendo
Sports (golf)
N64 […] Wii […] WU

Mario Kart 8 (2014)
Nintendo EAD, Nintendo EPD; Nintendo
Racing (kart racing)
WU […] NS

Mario Kart 64 (1996)
Nintendo EAD; Nintendo
Racing (kart racing)
N64 […] iQue […] Wii […] WU

Mario Kart Wii (2008)
Nintendo EAD; Nintendo
Racing (kart racing)
Wii

Mario Paint (1992)
Nintendo R&D1, Intelligent Systems; Nintendo
Simulation
SNES

Mario Party (1998)
Hudson Soft; Nintendo
Party (board game)
N64

Mario Tennis (2000)
Camelot Software Planning; Nintendo
Sports (tennis)
N64 […] Wii […] WU

Mark of the Ninja (2012)
Klei Entertainment; Microsoft Studios, Klei Entertainment
Action (stealth, 2D platformer)
X360, PC […] NS, PS4, XBO (remaster)

Marvel's Spider-Man 2 (2023)
Insomniac Games; Sony Interactive Entertainment
Action
PS5

Marvel: Ultimate Alliance (2006)
Raven Software; Activision
Brawler (hack and slash)
XB, PC, PS2, X360, GBA, PSP, Wii, PS3 […] PS4, XBO

Marvel vs. Capcom 2: New Age of Heroes (2000)
Capcom; Capcom
Fighting (2D fighting)
ARC, DC […] PS2, XB […] X360, PS3 […] iOS […] NS, PS4, PC, XBO (MARVEL vs. CAPCOM Fighting Collection: Arcade Classics)

Marvel vs. Capcom 3: Fate of Two Worlds (2011)
Capcom, Eighting; Capcom
Fighting (2D fighting)
PS3, X360 […] PSV (expansion) […] PS4, PC, XBO (expansion)

Mass Effect (2007)
BioWare; Microsoft Game Studios
RPG (ARPG)
X360, PC […] PS3 […] PS4, XBO (remaster; Mass Effect Legendary Edition)

Mass Effect 3 (2012)
BioWare; Electronic Arts
RPG (ARPG, third-person shooter)
PS3, PC, X360, WU […] PS4, XBO (Mass Effect Legendary Edition)

Max Payne (2001)
Remedy Entertainment; Gathering of Developers, Rockstar Games
Shooter (third-person shooter)
PC, PS2, XB, GBA […] iOS, AND

Mayor Munch (2010)
Arcade (maze game)
Flash

MELTY BLOOD: TYPE LUMINA (2021)
French-Bread; Lasengle
Fighting (2D fighting; airdash fighting)
NS, PS4, XBO, PC

Metal Gear Solid (1998)
Konami Computer Entertainment Japan; Konami
Action (stealth)
PSX, PC [...] GCN (remake) [...] PS3 [...] NS, PS4, PS5, XS (Metal Gear Solid: Master Collection)

Metal Gear Solid 4: Guns of the Patriots (2008)
Konami Digital Entertainment; Konami
Action (stealth)
PS3

Metal Slug (1996)
Nazca Corporation; SNK
Shmup (run and gun)
ARC, NG, PSX, SS, PC

Metroid Prime Pinball (2005)
Fuse Games; Nintendo
Arcade (pinball)
NDS

Microsoft Flight Simulator (2020)
Asobo Studio; Xbox Game Studios
Simulation (flight sim)
PC, XS

Microsoft Solitaire (1990)
Microsoft; Microsoft
Strategy (card game)
PC

Middle-earth: Shadow of Mordor (2014)
Monolith Productions; Warner Bros. Interactive Entertainment
Action
PS4, PC, XBO, PS3, X360

Middle-earth: Shadow of War (2017)
Monolith Productions; Warner Bros. Interactive Entertainment
Action
PC, PS4, XBO

Miegakure (n.d.)
mtb design works inc.; mtb design works inc.
Platformer, puzzle
PC, PS4

Miitopia (2016)
Nintendo EPD; Nintendo
RPG (JRPG)
3DS [...] NS (remaster)

Mike Tyson's Punch-Out!! (1987)
Nintendo R&D3; Nintendo
Sports (boxing)
NES [...] Wii, 3DS, WU

Minecraft (2011)
Mojang Studios; Mojang Studios, Xbox Game Studios
Simulation (sandbox)
PC, AND, iOS, X360 [...] PS3, PS4, PSV, WU, NS, 3DS

Mini Metro (2015)
Dinosaur Polo Club; Dinosaur Polo Club, Playdigious
Puzzle, simulation
PC, AND, iOS, NS, PS4

Mini Motorways (2019)
Dinosaur Polo Club; Dinosaur Polo Club
Puzzle, simulation
iOS, PC, NS

Mirror's Edge (2008)
DICE; Electronic Arts
Platformer (3D platformer, first-person platformer)
PS3, X360, PC

Missile Command (1980)
Atari; Atari, SEGA, Taito, Nintendo
Shmup (stationary shmup)
ARC, 2600, PC, 5200 [...] GB

Monaco: What's Yours Is Mine (2013)
Pocketwatch Games; Pocketwatch Games
Action (stealth)
PC, X360 [...] NS

Monkey Island 2: LeChuck's Revenge (1991)
LucasArts; LucasArts, U.S. Gold
Adventure (point and click adventure)
PC [...] iOS, PS3, X360 (remake)

Monster Hunter series (2004-present)
Capcom; Capcom
RPG (ARPG)
PS2, PS3, PS4, PS5, PSP, PSV, PC, Wii, WU, 3DS, NS, X360, XBO, XS, AND, iOS

Monster Hunter: World (2018)
Capcom; Capcom
RPG (ARPG)
PS4, XBO, PC

Monster Prom (2018)
Beautiful Glitch; Those Awesome Guys
Adventure (dating sim, visual novel)
PC […] NS, PS4, XBO

Mortal Kombat (1992)
Midway, Probe Software, Sculptured Software; Midway, Acclaim, Virgin Interactive Entertainment, Jakks Pacific
Fighting (2D fighting)
ARC, GEN, SNES, GG, GB, MS, PC

Mosa Lina (2023)
Stuffed Wombat; Stuffed Wombat
Platformer (2D platformer, physics competition)
PC

Moss (2018)
Polyarc; Polyarc
Platformer (3D platformer)
PS4, PC, Quest, PS5

Mother 3 (2006)
Brownie Brown, HAL Laboratory; Nintendo
RPG (JRPG)
GBA

Mount Your Friends (2013)
Stegersaurus Software Inc.; Stegersaurus Software Inc.
Party (physics competition)
PC, X360

The Movies (2005)
Lionhead Studios; Activision, SEGA, Feral Interactive
Simulation (business management)
PC

Moving Out (2020)
DevM Games, SMG Studio; Team17
Party (physics competition)
PC, NS, PS4, XBO

Ms. PAC-MAN (1981)
General Computer Corporation, Midway; Midway
Arcade (maze)
ARC, 2600, 5200, 7800, PC, GEN, MS, NES, SNES, GB, GG, Lynx, XBO, PS4

MTV Music Generator (1999)
Jester Interactive; Codemasters
Rhythm (music-making)
PSX, PC

Museum of Mechanics: Lockpicking (2022)
Dim Bulb Games; Dim Bulb Games
Arcade
PC

Mushroom 11 (2015)
Untame; Untame
Platformer
PC, iOS

MyHouse.wad (2023)
Veddge; Veddge
Shooter (first-person shooter)
PC

Myst (1993)
Cyan; Broderbund, Sunsoft, Acclaim Entertainment, SoftBank, Psygnosis, Micro Cabin, Paanasonic, Red Orb Entertainment, Atari, Philips Media, SEGA, Midway, Empire Interactive, Storm City Games, Maximum Family Games, Funbox Media, Noodlecake Games
Puzzle
PC, 3DO, SS, JAG, PSX, CD-i […] PSP, NDS (remake) […] iOS, 3DS, AND (remake) […] Quest, NS, XBO, XS (remake)

n++ (2015)
Metanet Software; Metanet Software
Platformer (2D platformer, precision platformer)
PS4, PC, XBO, NS

NARUTO SHIPPUDEN: Ultimate Ninja STORM 3 (2013)
CyberConnect2; Namco Bandai
Fighting (3D fighting)
PS3, X360, PC […] PS4, XBO, NS

NBA Jam (1993)
Midway; Midway, Acclaim Entertainment

Sports (basketball)
ARC, GG, GEN, SNES, GB, PSX, SS

Need for Speed: Most Wanted (2005)
EA Canada, EA Black Box; Electronic Arts
Racing
GCN, PS2, PC, XB, X360

Neon White (2022)
Angel Matrix; Annapurna Interactive
Platformer (3D platformer, first-person platformer)
PC, NS, PS4, PS5, XBO, XS

Nevermind (2015)
Flying Mollusk; Flying Mollusk
Horror
PC, XBO

Nex Machina (2017)
Housemarque; Housemarque
Shmup (twin-stick shooter)
PS4, PC

Nickelodeon All-Star Brawl (2021)
Ludosity, Fair Play Labs; GameMill Entertainment, Maximum Games, Just for Games
Fighting (platform fighting)
NS, PS4, PS5, PC, XBO, XS

NieR:Automata (2017)
PlatinumGames; Square Enix
RPG (ARPG)
PS4, PC, XBO […] NS

Night in the Woods (2017)
Infinite Fall, Secret Lab; Finji
Adventure
PC, PS4, XBO, NS […] iOS

Nintendo Land (2012)
Nintendo EAD; Nintendo
Arcade, party (anthology)
WU

No More Heroes (2007)
Grasshopper Manufacture; Marvelous Entertainment, Ubisoft, Rising Star Games, Xseed Games
Brawler (character action)
Wii […] NS, PC

The Norwood Suite (2017)
Cosmo D; Alliance
Adventure (exploration adventure)
PC

Nour: Play with Your Food (2023)
Terrifying Jellyfish; Panic
Simulation
PC, NS, PS4, PS5

Octodad: Dadliest Catch (2014)
Young Horses; Young Horses
Adventure (physics puzzle)
PC, PS4, PSV, XBO, WU, AND […] NS

OCTOPATH TRAVELER II (2023)
Square Enix, Acquire; Square Enix
RPG (JRPG)
NS, PS4, PS5, PC, XBO, XS

Oddworld: Abe's Oddysee (1997)
Oddworld Inhabitants, Digital Dialect, Saffire; GT Interactive
Platformer (2D platformer, cinematic platformer)
PSX, PC, GB […] PS4, XBO, PS3, PSV WU, AND, iOS (remake) […] NS (remake)

Oddworld: Stranger's Wrath (2005)
Oddworld Inhabitants, Just Add Water, Square One, Ouya; EA Games, Oddworld Inhabitants, Microids
Shooter (first-person shooter)
XB […] PC, PS3, PSV (remaster) […] iOS, AND (remaster) […] NS (remaster) […] PS4, XBO (remaster)

Ōkami (2006)
Clover Studio; Capcom
RPG (ARPG)
PS2, Wii […] PS3 (remaster) […] PC, PS4, XBO, NS (remaster)

OlliOlli (2014)
Roll7; Roll7, Devolver Digital, Curve Digital
Sports (skateboarding)
PSV, PC, PS3, PS4, AND, 3DS, WU, XBO […] NS

Once Upon a Jester (2022)
Bonte Avond; Crunching Koalas
Adventure
PC, NS

Orbo's Odyssey (2023)
Feverdream Johnny; Feverdream Johnny
Platformer (3D platformer)
PC

Ori and the Blind Forest (2015)
Moon Studios; Microsoft Studios
Platformer (2D platformer, metroidvania)
PC, XBO [...] NS

Outer Wilds (2019)
Mobius Digital; Annapurna Interactive
Adventure
PC, XBO, PS4 [...] PS5, XS, NS

The Outfoxies (1995)
Namco; Namco
Fighting (platform fighting)
ARC

Outlast (2013)
Red Barrels; Red Barrels
Horror (exploration horror)
PC, PS4, XBO [...] NS

Out Run (1986)
SEGA; SEGA, U.S. Gold
Racing
ARC, SMS, GEN, GG, SS [...] GBA [...] 3DS, PC, NS

Overcooked! (2016)
Ghost Town Games; Team17
Party
PS4, PC, XBO, NS [...] XS, PS5

Overwatch (2016)
Blizzard Entertainment; Blizzard Entertainment
Shooter (first-person shooter, hero shooter)
PS4, PC, XBO [...] NS

PAC-MAN (1980)
Namco; Namco, Midway
Arcade (maze)
ARC, 2600, 5200, NES, PC [...] GB, GG, GBC, NGPC [...] mobile, GBA, iOS [...] X360 [...] PS4, XBO

PAC-MAN 256 (2015)
3 Sprockets, Bandai Namco Studios Vancouver, Hipster Whale; Bandai Namco Enteratinment
Arcade (maze)
iOS, AND, PC, PS4, XBO

Paladins: Champions of the Realm (2018)
Evil Mojo Games; Hi-Rez Studios
Shooter (first-person shooter, hero shooter)
PC, PS4, XBO, NS

Panel de Pon (1995)
Intelligent Systems; Nintendo
Puzzle (falling block puzzle)
SNES, GB

Papa Sangre (2010)
Somethin' Else; Somethin' Else
Horror (audio game)
iOS

Paper Mario: The Thousand Year Door (2004)
Intelligent Systems; Nintendo
RPG (JRPG)
GCN [...] NS (remake)

Papers, Please (2013)
3909 LLC; 3909 LLC
Simulation (job simulation)
PC, iOS [...] PSV [...] AND

PaRappa the Rapper (1996)
NanaOn-Sha; Sony Computer Entertainment
Rhythm
PSX [...] PSP (remaster) [...] PS4

Passpartout: The Starving Artist (2017)
Flamebait Games; Flamebait Games
Simulator
PC, iOS, NS

Patrick's Parabox (2022)
Patrick Traynor; Patrick Traynor
Puzzle (sokoban)
PC, NS, PS5

Peggle (2007)
PopCap Games; PopCap Games
Arcade
PC, NDS, X360, PS3, iOS, PSP, AND

Perfect Dark (2000)
Rare; Rare
Shooter (first-person shooter)
N64 […] X360 (remaster)

Persona series (1996-present)
Atlus, P-Studio; Atlus, SEGA, ASCII Corporation, Deep Silver, Koei, Square Enix, THQ, NIS America
RPG (JRPG)
PSX, PC, PS2, PSP, PSV, NS, PS4, XBO, XS, PS5

Persona 5 (2016)
P-Studio; Atlus, Deep Silver, SEGA
RPG (JRPG)
PS3, PS4 […] PS4 […] NS, PS5, PC, XBO, XS

Persona Q: Shadow of the Labyrinth (2014)
P-Studio; Atlus, NIS America
RPG (dungeon crawler)
3DS

Phoenix Wright: Ace Attorney (2001)
Capcom Production Studio 4; Capcom
Adventure (visual novel)
GBA […] NDS, PC […] Wii, iOS […] AND, 3DS, NS, PS4, XBO (remaster; Phoenix Wright: Ace Attorney Trilogy)

Picross DS (2007)
Jupiter; Nintendo
Puzzle (number puzzle)
NDS

Pikmin 4 (2023)
Nintendo EPD, Eighting; Nintendo
Strategy (real-time strategy)
NS

Pinball FX 3 (2017)
Zen Studios; Zen Studios
Arcade (pinball)
PC, PS4, XBO, NS

PixelJunk Shooter (2009)
Q-Games, Double Eleven; Q-Games, Sony Computer Entertainment, Double Eleven
Shmup
PS3 […] PC, PS4, PSV, PC

Pizza Tower (2023)
Tour de Pizza; Tour de Pizza
Platformer (2D platformer)
PC, NS

Planescape: Torment (1999)
Black Isle Studios; Interplay Entertainment
RPG (CRPG)
PC […] AND, iOS (remaster) […] NS, PS4, XBO (remaster)

Planet Coaster (2016)
Frontier Developments; Frontier Developments
Simulation (business management)
PC […] PS4, XBO, XS, PS5

Planet Zoo (2019)
Frontier Developments; Frontier Developments
Simulation (business management)
PC […] PS5, XS

Plants vs. Zombies (2009)
PopCap Games; PopCap Games
Strategy (tower defense)
PC, iOS, NDS, PS3, AND, PSV

Point Blank (1994)
Namco; Namco, Sony Computer Entertainment Europe
Shooter (light gun shooter)
ARC […] PSX

Pokémon series (1996-present)
Game Freak; Nintendo, The Pokémon Company
RPG (JRPG)
GB, GBA, NDS, 3DS, NS

Pokémon GO (2016)
Niantic; Niantic
RPG
iOS, AND

Pokémon: Red Version / Pokémon: Green Version / Pokémon: Blue Version (1996)
Game Freak; Nintendo
RPG (JRPG)
GB […] GBA (remake) […] 3DS […] NS (remake)

Pokémon Snap (1999)
HAL Laboratory; Nintendo
Simulation (photography sim)
N64 […] Wii […] WU

Pokémon Unite (2021)
TiMi Studio Group; The Pokémon Company
Strategy (MOBA)
AND, iOS, NS

Pole Position (1982)
Namco; Namco, Atari
Racing
ARC, 2600, 5200, Vectrex […] IV, PC

Poly Bridge (2016)
Dry Cactus; Dry Cactus
Puzzle (physics puzzle)
PC, iOS, NS, AND

Pong (1972)
Atari; Atari
Arcade, sports
ARC

Pony Island (2016)
Daniel Mullins Games; Daniel Mullins Games
Platformer
PC

Populous (1989)
Bullfrog Productions, Infinity, Alfa System, Code to Go, Enigma Variations; Electronic Arts, Krisalis Software, Imagineer, Acclaim Entertainment, SEGA, Hudson Soft
Strategy (civilization sim)
PC, GB, MS, GEN, SNES

Portal (2007)
Valve; Valve
Puzzle
PC, X360, PS3 […] AND […] NS

Postal (1997)
Running with Scissors; Ripcord Games, Loki Software, Running with Scissors, Wave Game Studios
Shmup (twin-stick shooter)
PC […] AND […] DC

Power Stone 2 (2000)
Capcom, Klein Computer Entertainment; Capcom, Eidos Interactive
Fighting (3D fighting, platform fighting)
ARC, DC […] PSP […] NS, PS4, XBO, PC (Capcom Fighting Collection 2)

PowerWash Simulator (2022)
FuturLab; Square Enix
Simulation (job sim)
PC, XBO, XS, NS, PS4, PS5, Quest

Predator: Hunting Grounds (2020)
IllFonic; Sony Interactive Entertainment, IllFonic
Shooter
PS4, PC […] PS5, XS

Prey (2017)
Arkane Austin, Bethesda Softworks
Shooter (first-person shooter, immersive sim)
PS4, XBO, PC

Prince of Persia (1989)
Brøderbund; Brøderbund
Platformer (2D platformer, cinematic platformer)
PC

Prince of Persia: The Sands of Time (2003)
Ubisoft Montreal; Ubisoft
Platformer, action
PS2, XB, GCN, PC

Prodeus (2022)
Bounding Box Software; Humble Games
Shooter (first-person shooter, boomer shooter)
PC, NS, PS4, PS5, XBO, XS

Project X Zone (2012)
Banpresto, Monolith Soft; Namco Bandai Games
Strategy (tactics)
3DS

Psychonauts (2005)
Double Fine Productions; Majesco Entertainment
Platformer (3D platformer)
PC, XB, PS2

P.T. (2014)
Kojima Productions; Konami
Horror (exploration horror)
PS4

Puyo Puyo (1991)
Compile, CRI Middleware, Lavastorm, Tokuma Shoten, Winkysoft; Compile, Banpresto, Bothtec, CRI Middleware, NEC Avenue, SPS, Tokuma Shoten, SEGA
Puzzle (falling block puzzle)
NES, ARC, GEN, GG, PC, SNES, GB [...] mobile, NDS, Wii [...] 3DS [...] NS

Puzzle & Dragons (2012)
GungHo Online Entertainment; GungHo Online Entertainment
Puzzle, RPG (tile-matching game)
iOS, AND

Quake (1996)
id Software; GT Interactive
Shooter (first-person shooter)
PC, SS, N64 [...] NS, PS4, XBO, PS5, XS (remaster)

Quake III Arena (1999)
id Software; Activision, Loki Entertainment, SEGA, EA Games, Bethesda Softworks
Shooter (first-person shooter)
PC, DC, PS2 [...] X360

Quantum Break (2016)
Remedy Entertainment; Microsoft Studios
Shooter (third-person shooter)
PC, XBO

QWOP (2008)
Bennett Foddy; Bennett Foddy, Noodlecake Studios
Sports (physics puzzle)
PC, Flash [...] iOS [...] AND

Radiant Silvergun (1998)
Treasure; Treasure, ESP, Microsoft Studios, Live Wire
Shmup
ARC, SS [...] X360 [...] NS, PC

Rampart (1991)
Atari; Atari, Namco
Strategy (tower defense)
ARC, PC

Rare Replay (2015)
Rare; Microsoft Studios
Arcade (anthology)
XBO

Ratchet & Clank series (2002-present)
Insomniac Games, Handheld Games, High Impact Games, Sanzaru Games, Idol Minds, Tin Giant, Mass Media Games; Sony Interactive Entertainment
Platformer, shooter (third-person shooter, 3D platformer)
PS2, PSP, PS3, PSV, iOS, AND, PS4, PS5, PC

Rayman Legends (2013)
Ubisoft Montpellier; Ubisoft, Nintendo
Platformer (2D platformer)
WU, PC, PS3, X360, PSV, PS4, XBO [...] NS

Red Dead Online (2019)
Rockstar Games; Rockstar Games
Action (sandbox, third-person shooter)
PS4, XBO, PC

Red Dead Redemption 2 (2018)
Rockstar Games; Rockstar Games
Action (sandbox, third-person shooter)
PS4, XBO, PC

Red Faction: Guerrilla (2009)
Volition; THQ
Action (third-person shooter)
PS3, X360, PC [...] PS4, XBO (remarstered) [...] NS (remarstered)

The Red Strings Club (2018)
Deconstructeam; Devolver Digital
Adventure
PC, NS

République (2016)
Camouflaj; GungHo Online Entertainment, NIS America
Action (stealth)
iOS, AND, PC, PS4 […] NS

Resident Evil (1996)
Capcom; Capcom, Virgin Interactive Entertainment, SEGA, Nintendo Australia
Horror (survival horror)
PSX, PC, SS […] GCN (remake) […] NDS […] Wii (remake) […] PS3, PS4, X360, XBO (remake) […] NS (remake)

Resident Evil 4 (2005)
Capcom Production Studio 4; Capcom
Horror (third-person shooter)
GCN, PS2, PC, Wii […] iOS, Zeebo […] PS3, X360, AND […] PS4, XBO […] NS […] Quest […] PS5, XS (remake)

Resident Evil Village (2021)
Capcom; Capcom
Horror (first-person shooter)
PS4, PS5, PC, XBO, XS, NS, iOS

Resogun (2013)
Housemarque, Climax Studios; Sony Computer Entertainment
Shmup (horizontally-scrolling shmup)
PS4, PS3, PSV

Return of the Obra Dinn (2018)
3909 LLC.; 3909 LLC.
Puzzle
PC, NS, PS4, XBO

Return to Castle Wolfenstein (2001)
Gray Matter Studios; Activision, Aspyr
Shooter (first-person shooter)
PC, XB, PS2

Rez (2001)
United Game Artists; SEGA, Sony Computer Entertainment, Microsoft Game Studios, Enhance Games
Shooter, rhythm (on-rails shooter)
DC, PS2 […] X360 (remaster) […] PS4, PC, AND (remaster) […] Quest (remaster) […] PS5 (remaster)

Rhythm Doctor (2021)
7th Beat Games; 7th Beat Games, indienova
Rhythm
PC

Rhythm Heaven Fever (2011)
Nintendo SPD, TNX Music Recordings; Nintendo
Rhythm
Wii

Rhythm Heaven Megamix (2015)
Nintendo SPD; Nintendo
Rhythm
3DS

Ridiculous Fishing (2013)
Vlambeer; Vlambeer
Sports (fishing)
iOS, AND

Rivals of Aether (2017)
Aether Studios; Aether Studios
Fighting (platform fighting)
PC, XBO […] NS

Riven: The Sequel to Myst (1997)
Cyan, Sunsoft, Cyan Worlds; Red Orb Entertainment, Acclaim Entertainment, SEGA, Mean Hamster Software, Noodlecake Studios, Cyan Worlds
Puzzle (exploration puzzle)
PC, PSX, SS […] iOS […] AND […] Quest (remake)

River City Ransom (1989)
Technōs Japan, SPS, KID, Million; Technōs Japan, Sharp Corporation, Infogrames, Naxat Soft, Atlus
Brawler (beat-em-up)
NES, PC […] GBA […] Wii […] 3DS […] WU

Roadwarden (2022)
Moral Anxiety Studio; Assemble Entertainment
Adventure (text adventure)
PC

Roblox (2006)
Roblox Corporation; Roblox Corporation
Action (MMO, game creator)
PC […] iOS […] AND, XBO […] Quest, PS4

Rock Band series (2007-2015)
Harmonix, Pi Studios, TT Fusion, Backbone Entertainment, EA Montreal; MTV Games, Warner Bros. Interactive Entertainment, EA Mobile, Harmonix, Mad Catz, Performance Designed Products, Oculus Studios
Rhythm
PS2, PS3, PS4, PSP, X360, XBO, Wii, NDS, iOS, PC

Rock Band (2007)
Harmonix; MTV Games
Rhythm
X360, PS2, PS3, Wii

Rock Band 4 (2015)
Harmonix; Harmonix
Rhythm
PS4, XBO

Rocket League (2015)
Psyonix; Psyonix
Sports (football)
PS4, PC, XBO, NS

Rogue (1980)
A.I. Design; Epyx, Mastertronic
RPG (roguelike)
PC

RollerCoaster Tycoon (1999)
Chris Sawyer; Hasbro Interactive, Infogrames Interactive
Simulation (business management)
PC […] XB

Rome: Total War (2004)
Creative Assembly; Activision, SEGA, Feral Interactive
Strategy PC […]
iOS, AND

The Room (2012)
Fireproof Games; Fireproof Games, Team17
Puzzle (exploration puzzle)
iOS, AND, PC […] NS

Ruckus - Just Another Natural Disaster (2019)
HeartFactory-KW; HeartFactory-KW
Action
PS4 (Dreams)

Rust (2018)
Facepunch Studios, Double Eleven; Facepunch Studio
Action (survival)
PC […] PS4, XBO

Saints Row: The Third (2011)
Volition; THQ
Action (sandbox, third-person shooter)
PS3, X360, PC […] NS […] PS4, XBO, PS5, XS (remaster)

Sam & Max Hit the Road (1993)
LucasArts; LucasArts, Disney Interactive
Adventure (point-and-click adventure)
PC

Samurai Gunn (2013)
Beau Blyth, Doseone; Beau Blyth
Fighting (platform fighting)
PC

Say No! More (2021)
Studio Fizbin; Thunderful Publishing
Arcade (rail shooter)
iOS, PC, NS

Sayonara Wild Hearts (2019)
Simogo; Annapurna Interactive
Shooter, rhythm (on-rails shooter)
iOS, PC, XBO

Schildmaid MX (2021)
HitP Studio; HitP Studio
Shmup (horizontally scrolling shmup)
PC

Scorched Earth (1991)
Wendell Hicken; Wendell Hicken
Strategy (artillery)
PC

The Secret of Monkey Island (1990)
Lucasfilm Games; Lucasfilm Games, U.S. Gold, The Software Toolworks
Adventure (point-and-click adventure)
PC […] iOS, PS3, X360 (remake; Special Edition)

SEGA Bass Fishing (1997)
SEGA, SIMS Co., Cavia; SEGA

Sports (fishing)
ARC, DC, PC […] Wii […] X360, PS3 […] iOS

Sekiro: Shadows Die Twice (2019)
FromSoftware; Activision, FromSoftware
RPG (ARPG)
PC, PS4, XBO

Sexy Hiking (2002)
Jazzuo; Jazzuo
Platformer (2D platformer, physics puzzle)
PC

Shadow Man (1999)
Acclaim Studios Teesside, Nightdive Studios; Acclaim Entertainment, Nightdive Studios
Action
PC, N64, PSX, DC […] PS4, XBO, NS (remaster)

Shadow of the Colossus (2005)
Japan Studio, Team Ico; Sony Computer Entertainment
Action
PS2 […] PS3 (remaster) […] PS4 (remake)

Shadows of Doubt (2024)
ColePowered Games; Fireshine Games
Adventure (immersive sim)
PC, XS, PS5

Shenmue (1999)
SEGA AM2; SEGA
RPG
DC […] PC, XBO, PS4

Shenmue II (2001)
SEGA AM2; Microsoft Game Studios, SEGA
RPG
DC, XB […] X360 […] PC, XBO, PS4

Shovel Knight (2014)
Yacht Club Games; Yacht Club Games
Platformer (2D platformer)
3DS, WU, PC, PS3, PS4, PSV, XBO, NS

Sid Meier's Civilization series (1991-present)
MicroProse, Activision, Fireaxis Games; MicroProse, Activision, Hasbro Interactive, Infogrames, 2K Games
Strategy (TBS, 4X)
PC, SNES, PSX, SS, X360, PS3, iOS, AND, NDS, PSV, NS, PS4, XBO

Sid Meier's Civilization (1991)
MicroProse; Asmik Ace, Koei
Strategy (TBS, 4X)
PC, SNES, PSX, SS

Sid Meier's Civilization VI (2016)
Firaxis Games; 2K, Aspyr Media
Strategy (turn-based strategy, 4X)
PC, iOS, NS, PS4, XBO, AND

Silent Hill 2 (2001)
Team Silent; Konami
Horror (survival horror)
PS2, XB, PC […] PS3, X360 (remaster) […] PS5 (remake)

SimAnt (1991)
Maxis; Maxis
Simulation (life sim)
PC […] SNES

SimCity (1989)
Maxis; Infogrames, Acornsoft, Fujitsu, Nintendo, Interplay Productions
Simulation (city builder)
PC, SNES […] Wii […] iOS

The Sims series (2000-present)
Maxis; Electronic Arts
Simulation (life sim)
PC, PS2, GCN, XB, GBA, NDS, PSP, mobile, PS3, X360, Wii, 3DS, PS4, XBO, iOS, AND

The Sims (2000)
Maxis; Electronic Arts
Simulation (life sim)
PC […] PS2, GCN, XB

The Sims 2 (2004)
Maxis; Electronic Arts
Simulation (life sim)
PC, GBA, GCN, NDS, PS2, XB, PSP

The Sims 3 (2009)
Maxis Redwood Shores; Electronic Arts

Simulation (life sim)
PC, X360, PS3, NDS, Wii, 3DS

The Sims 4 (2014)
Maxis; Electronic Arts
Simulation (life sim)
PC [...] PS4, XBO

The Sims Online (2002)
Maxis; Electronic Arts
Simulation (life sim)
PC

Sin & Punishment: Star Successor (2009)
Treasure; Nintendo
Shooter (third-person shooter, on-rails shooter)
Wii

Sinistar (1983)
Williams Electronics; Williams Electronics
Shmup
ARC, 2600, 5200, PC

Sins of a Solar Empire (2008)
Ironclad Games; Stardock
Strategy (4X)
PC

Skullgirls (2012)
Reverge Labs; Autumn Games
Fighting (2D fighting)
PS3, X360, PC, PS4, ARC, PSV [...] NS [...] XBO, XS

Slay the Spire (2019)
Mega Crit; Humble Games, Mega Crit
Strategy (card game)
PC, PS4, NS, XBO, iOS, AND

Sleeping Dogs (2012)
United Front Games; Square Enix
Action (sandbox)
PS3, X360, PC [...] PS4, XBO

Smash TV (1990)
Williams Electronics, Probe Software, Beam Software, Probe Software; Williams Electronics
Shmup (twin-stick shooter)
ARC, PC [...] NES, MS, GEN, GG

SOCOM U.S. Navy SEALs (2002)
Zipper Interactive; Sony Computer Entertainment
Shooter (third-person shooter, tactical shooter)
PS2

Sokoban (1982)
Hiroyuki Imabayashi; Hiroyuki Imabayashi
Puzzle (sokoban)
PC

SOMA (2015)
Frictional Games; Frictional Games
Horror (exploration horror)
PC, PS4, XBO

Sonic & All-Stars Racing Transformed (2012)
Sumo Digital; SEGA
Racing (kart racing)
PS3, X360, WU, PSV, PC, 3DS, iOS, AND

Sonic Adventure (1998)
Sonic Team; SEGA
Platformer (3D platformer)
DC [...] GCN, PC [...] X360, PS3

Sonic Adventure 2 (2001)
Sonic Team USA; SEGA
Platformer (3D platformer)
DC, GCN [...] PS3, X360, PC

Sonic R (1997)
Traveller's Tales, Sonic Team; SEGA
Racing (arcade racing)
SS, PC [...] GCN, PS2

Sonic Spinball (1993)
SEGA Technical Institute, SEGA InterActive; SEGA
Arcade (pinball)
GEN, GG, MS [...] PC [...] GBA

SoulCalibur II (2002)
Project Soul; Namco, Electronic Arts, Nintendo, Namco Bandai
Fighting (3D fighting)
ARC, GCN, PS2, XB [...] PS3, X360

SOULCALIBUR VI (2018)
Bandai Namco Studios, Dimps; Bandai Namco Entertainment

Fighting (3D fighting)
PS4, PC, XBO

Space Harrier (1985)
SEGA; SEGA
Shooter (third-person shooter, on-rails shooter)
ARC, MS, PC, NES […] GG […] SS […] PS2 (remake) […] 3DS

Space Invaders (1978)
Taito; Taito, Midway, Leisure & Allied Industries, Atari
Shmup (stationary shmup)
ARC

Spec Ops: The Line (2012)
Yager Development; 2K
Shooter (third-person shooter)
PS3, PC, X360

Spelunky 2 (2020)
Mossmouth, BlitWorks; Mossmouth
Platformer (2D platformer, roguelike)
PS4, PC, NS, XBO, XS

Spin Rhythm XD (2023)
Super Spin Digital; Super Spin Digital
Rhythm
PC, NS, PS5

Spiritfarer (2020)
Thunder Lotus Games; Thunder Lotus Games
Adventure
PC, NS, PS4, XBO […] AND, iOS

Splatoon 2 (2017)
Nintendo EPD; Nintendo
Shooter (third-person shooter)
NS

Split/Second (2010)
Black Rock Studio; Disney Interactive Studios
Racing (arcade racing)
PC, PS3, X360, iOS, PSP

SPORE (2008)
Maxis; Electronic Arts
Simulation, strategy (life sim, RTS)
PC

S.T.A.L.K.E.R. 2: Heart of Chornobyl (2024)
GSC Game World; GSC Game World
Shooter (first-person shooter, survival horror)
PC, XS

The Stanley Parable (2013)
Galactic Cafe; Galactic Café
Adventure (exploration adventure)
PC […] iOS, NS, PS4, PS5, XBO, XS (expansion)

StarCraft (1998)
Blizzard Entertainment; Blizzard Entertainment
Strategy (real-time strategy)
PC […] N64

Stardew Valley (2016)
ConcernedApe; ConcernedApe
Simulation (life sim)
PC, PS4, XBO, NS, PSV, iOS, AND

Star Fox Guard (2016)
Nintendo EPD, PlatinumGames; Nintendo
Strategy (tower defense)
WU

Starseed Pilgrim (2013)
droqen; droqen
Puzzle, platformer (puzzle platformer)
PC

STAR WARS Battlefront (2004)
Pandemic Studios; LucasArts
Shooter (third-person shooter)
PC, PS2, XB […] NS, PS4, PS5, XBO, XS (remaster)

STAR WARS Galaxies (2003)
Sony Online Entertainment; LucasArts
RPG (MMORPG)
PC

STAR WARS Knights of the Old Republic (2003)
BioWare Edmonton; LucasArts
RPG (CRPG)
XB, PC […] iOS, AND […] NS

STAR WARS Knights of the Old Republic II - The Sith Lords (2004)
Obsidian Entertainment; LucasArts

RPG (CRPG)
XB, PC […] AND, iOS, NS

STAR WARS X-Wing vs TIE Fighter (1997)
Totally Games; LucasArts
Shmup
PC

State of Decay 2 (2018)
Undead Labs; Xbox Game Studios
Action (survival, third-person shooter)
PC, XBO

SteamWorld Heist (2015)
Image & Form; Image & Form
Strategy (turn-based strategy)
3DS, PC, PS4, PSV, WU, iOS, NS

the static speaks my name (2015)
the whale husband; the whale husband
Horror (exploration horror)
PC

Steel Battalion (2002)
Nude Maker, Capcom Production Studio 4; Capcom
Action
XB

Steins;Gate (2009)
5pb., Nitroplus; 5pb., Nitroplus, Kadokawa Shoten, JAST USA, PQube, Mages, Spike Chunsoft
Adventure (visual novel)
X360, PC, PSP, PS3, PSV, AND, PS4 […] NS, iOS (remake)

Stellaris (2016)
Paradox Development Studio; Paradox Interactive
Strategy (4X)
PC […] PS4, XBO

Stephen's Sausage Roll (2016)
Increpare Games; Increpare Games
Puzzle (sokoban)
PC

Storyteller (2023)
Daniel Benmergui; Annapurna Interactive
Puzzle
PC, NS, iOS, AND

Street Fighter series (1987-present)
Capcom, Dimps, Arika; Capcom
Fighting (2D fighting)
ARC, PC, SNES, PSX, GB, SMS, SS, DC, PS2, PS3, X360, iOS, AND, PSV, PS4, PS5, XS

Street Fighter 6 (2023)
Capcom; Capcom, Taito
Fighting (2D fighting)
ARC, PS4, PS5, PC, XS

Street Fighter Alpha: Warriors' Dreams (1995)
Capcom; Capcom, Virgin Interactive Entertainment
Fighting (2D fighting)
ARC, PSX, SS, PC, GBC […] PS2 (Street Fighter Alpha Anthology) […] NS, PS4, PC, XBO (Street Fighter 30th Anniversary Collection)

Street Fighter II: The World Warrior (1991)
Capcom; Capcom
Fighting (2D fighting)
ARC, SNES, PC, GEN, 3DO […] GB […] GBA, PS2, XB […] Wii, PS3, X360 […] WU […] NS, PS4, XBO (Street Fighter 30th Anniversary Collection)

Street Fighter V (2016)
Capcom, Dimps, Taito; Capcom, Taito
Fighting (2D fighting)
PS4, PC, ARC

Streets of Rage (1991)
SEGA; SEGA
Brawler (beat 'em up)
GEN, GG, MS, ARC […] Wii […] iOS, PC […] 3DS

Strider (1989)
Capcom, SEGA, Tiertex Design Studios; Capcom, SEGA, U.S. Gold
Brawler (hack and slash)
ARC, PC, GEN, MS […] PSX

Subnautica (2018)
Unknown Worlds Entertainment; Unknown Worlds Entertainment
Action (survival)
PC, PS4, XBO […] NS, PS5, XS

Suika Game (2021)
Aladdin X; Aladdin X

Puzzle (falling block game)
NS […] iOS, AND

Sunset Overdrive (2014)
Insomniac Games; Microsoft Studios
Shooter (third-person shooter)
XBO […] PC

Super Hexagon (2012)
Terry Cavanagh; Terry Cavanagh
Arcade
iOS, PC, AND, mobile

Superliminal (2019)
Pillow Castle Games; Pillow Castle Games
Puzzle
PC, NS, PS4, XBO […] PS5, XS, AND, iOS

Super Mario 3D World (2013)
Nintendo EAD Tokyo; Nintendo
Platformer (3D platformer)
WU […] NS

Super Mario 64 (1996)
Nintendo EAD; Nintendo
Platformer (3D platformer)
N64 […] iQue […] NDS (remake) […] NS (Super Mario 3D All-Stars)

Super Mario Bros. (1985)
Nintendo R&D4; Nintendo
Platformer (2D platformer)
NES, ARC […] SNES (remake; Super Mario All-Stars) […] 3DS, Wii, WU

Super Mario Clouds (2002)
Cory Arcangel; Cory Arcangel
Simulation
NES, PC

Super Mario Galaxy 2 (2010)
Nintendo EAD Tokyo; Nintendo
Platformer (3D platformer)
Wii

Super Mario Maker (2015)
Nintendo EAD, Nintendo EPD, Nintendo Software Technology; Nintendo
Platformer, simulation (2D platformer)
WU, 3DS

Super Mario Odyssey (2017)
Nintendo EPD; Nintendo
Platformer (3D platformer)
NS

Super Mario World (1990)
Nintendo EAD; Nintendo
Platformer (2D platformer)
SNES […] GBA […] Wii […] WU, 3DS

Super Meat Boy (2010)
Team Meat; Team Meat
Platformer (2D platformer, precision platformer)
X360, PC […] PS4, PSV, WU, NS

Super Metroid (1994)
Nintendo R&D1, Intelligent Systems; Nintendo
Platformer (2D platformer, metroidvania)
SNES […] Wii […] 3DS […] WU

Super Missile Attack (1981)
General Computer Corporation; General Computer Corporation
Shmup (stationary shmup)
ARC

Super Monkey Ball (2001)
Amusement Vision; SEGA
Platformer (marble game)
ARC, GCN […] NS, PS4, PS5, PC, XBO, XS (remake; Super Monkey Ball Banana Mania)

Super Smash Bros. (1999)
HAL Laboratory; Nintendo
Fighting (platform fighting)
N64 […] iQue […] Wii

Super Smash Bros. Melee (2001)
HAL Laboratory; Nintendo
Fighting (platform fighting)
GCN

Super Smash Bros. Ultimate (2018)
Bandai Namco Studios, Sora Ltd.; Nintendo
Fighting (platform fighting)
NS

Super Time Force (2014)
Capybara Games; Capybara Games
Shmup (run and gun)
X360, XBO, PC, PS4, PSV

Sunset Riders (1991)
Konami; Konami
Shmup (run and gun)
ARC, GEN, SNES [...] PS4, NS

Sweet Home (1989)
Capcom; Capcom
Horror (survival horror)
NES

System Shock 2 (1999)
Irrational Games, Looking Glass Studios, Nightdive Studios; Electronic Arts, Nightdive Studios
Shooter (first-person shooter, immersive sim)
PC [...] PS4, PS5, XBO, XS (remake)

Tales from Off-Peak City Vol. 1 (2020)
Cosmo D; Cosmo D
Adventure (exploration adventure)
PC

The Talos Principle (2014)
Croteam; Devolver Digital
Puzzle
PC, AND, PS4 [...] iOS, XBO, NS

tapestry (2024)
mut / moochi; mut / moochi
Platformer (plunderludic)
PC

Teamfight Tactics (2019)
Riot Games; Riot Games
Strategy (auto battler)
PC, AND, iOS

Team Fortress 2 (2007)
Valve; Valve
Shooter (first-person shooter)
PC, X360, PS3

Teardown (2022)
Tuxedo Labs; Tuxedo Labs, Saber Interactive
Action
PC, PS5, XS

Teenage Mutant Ninja Turtles: Shredder's Revenge (2022)
Tribute Games; Dotemu
Brawler (beat-em-up)
PC, NS, PS4, XBO, PS5, AND, iOS

TEKKEN 8 (2024)
Bandai Namco Studios, Arika; Bandai Namco Entertainment
Fighting (3D fighting)
PS5, PC, XS

Tetris (1985)
Alexey Pajitnov; Mirrorsoft
Puzzle (falling block puzzle)
PC [...] PS4, PS5, XBO, XS (Tetris Forever)

Tetris Effect (2018)
Monstars, Resonair, Stage Games; Enhance Games
Puzzle (falling block puzzle)
PS4, PC, Quest, XS, NS [...] PS5

Tetris Screwed (2004)
Cory Arcangel; Cory Arcangel
Puzzle (falling block puzzle)
NES, PC

Thank Goodness You're Here! (2024)
Coal Supper; Panic Inc.
Adventure
PC, NS, PS4, PS5

theHunter: Call of the Wild (2017)
Expansive Worlds; Avalanche Studios
Sports, shooter (hunting)
PC, PS4, XBO

There Is No Game: Wrong Dimension (2020)
Draw Me a Pixel; Draw Me a Pixel
Adventure, arcade
AND, iOS, PC, NS

Thief Simulator (2018)
Noble Muffins; PlayWay S.A.
Action (stealth)
PC, NS, PS4

Thief: The Dark Project (1998)
Looking Glass Studios; Eidos Interactive
Action (stealth)
PC

Thirsty Suitors (2023)
Outerloop Games; Annapurna Interactive
RPG (JRPG)
PC, NS, PS4, PS5, XBO, XS, AND, iOS

Thomas Was Alone (2012)
Mike Bithell; Mike Bithell
Platformer (2D platformer)
PC, PS3, PSV, iOS, AND, XBO, PS4, WU […] NS

Thumper (2016)
Drool; Drool
Rhythm
PC, PS4, NS, XBO, iOS, AND, Quest […] PS5

Time Crisis 4 (2006)
Nex Entertainment; Namco Bandai Games, Sony Computer Entertainment Europe
Shooter (first-person shooter, on-rails shooter, light gun shooter)
ARC, PS3

TimeSplitters 2 (2002)
Free Radical Design; Eidos Interactive
Shooter (first-person shooter)
PS2, XB, GCN […] PC, PS4, XBO (Homefront: The Revolution)

Tiny Glade (2024)
Pounce Light; Pounce Light
Simulation
PC

Tinykin (2022)
Splashteam; tinyBuild
Platformer (3D platformer)
NS, PS4, PS5, XBO, XS, PC

Tiny Lands (2021)
Hyper Three Studio; Maple Whispering Limited
Puzzle (hidden object game)
PC, NS

Titanfall 2 (2016)
Respawn Entertainment; Electronic Arts
Shooter (first-person shooter)
PC, PS4, XBO

Tokimeki Memorial (1994)
Konami; Konami
Adventure (dating sim)
PC, PSX, SNES, SS […] GBC […] mobile, PSP […] NS

Toki Tori 2 (2013)
Two Tribes B.V.; Two Tribes B.V., Rainy Frog
Platformer (puzzle platformer)
WU, PC […] PS4 […] NS

Tom Clancy's Ghost Recon (2001)
Red Storm Entertainment; Ubisoft
Shooter (third-person shooter, tactical shooter)
PC, XB, PS2, GCN

Tom Clancy's Rainbow Six (1998)
Red Storm Entertainment, Saffire, Rebellion Developments, Crawfish Interactive, Pipe Dream Interactive; Red Storm Entertainment, Take-Two Interactive, Majesco Sales, Swing! Entertainment
Shooter (first-person shooter, tactical shooter)
PC, N64, PSX, GB, DC

Tom Clancy's Splinter Cell (2002)
Ubisoft Montreal; Ubisoft
Action (stealth)
XB, PC, PS2, GCN […] PS3

Tony Hawk's Pro Skater series (1999-present)
Neversoft, Vicarious Visions, Robomodo; Activision
Sports (skateboarding)
PSX, N64, GBC, GBA, DC, PS2, GCN, XB, NG, PSP, PS3, X360, Wii, mobile, iOS, AND, NDS, PS4, XBO, NS, PC, XS, PS5

Tony Hawk's Pro Skater (1999)
Neversoft; Activision
Sports (skateboarding)
PSX, N64, DC […] NG, mobile […] X360, PS3, PC (remake) […] PS4, PC, XBO, PS5, XS, NS (remake; Tony Hawk's Pro Skater 1+2)

Tony Hawk's Pro Skater (2000)
Natsume; Activision
Sports (skateboarding)
GBC

Tony Hawk's Pro Skater 1 + 2 (2020)
Vicarious Visions; Activision
Sports (skateboarding)
PS4, PC, XBO, PS5, XS, NS

Toodee and Topdee (2021)
dietzribi; dietzribi
Platformer
PC, NS, PS4, PS5, XBO, XS

To the Moon (2011)
Freebird Games; Freebird Games
Adventure
PC […] AND, iOS […] NS […] PS5, XS

Townscaper (2021)
Oskar Stålberg; Oskar Stålberg
Simulation (city builder)
PC, NS, iOS, AND, XBO, XS

Tricky Towers (2016)
WeirdBeard; WeirdBeard
Puzzle (falling block, physics puzzle)
PC, PS4, XBO, NS

Trine 2 (2011)
Frozenbyte; Frozenbyte, Atlus USA, Nintendo
Platformer (puzzle platformer)
PC, PS3, X360, WU, PS4 […] NS, XBO

Triple Play 2000 (1999)
EA Canada; EA Sports
Sports (baseball)
PSX, N64, PC

Trip's Voyage (n.d.)
Eupholace; Eupholace
Platformer (3D platformer)
PS4 (Dreams)

TUNIC (2022)
Isometricorp Games; Finji
RPG (ARPG)
PC, XBO, XS, NS, PS4, PS5

TwinBee (1985)
Konami, Arika, SPS; Konami, Sharp, Nintendo
Shmup (vertically scrolling shmup)
ARC, NES, PC […] mobile, GBA […] Wii […] 3DS […] WU […] PS4, NS

Two Point Hospital (2018)
Two Point Studios; SEGA
Simulation (business management)
PC, NS, PS4, XBO

UFO 50 (2024)
Mossmouth; Mossmouth
Arcade (anthology)
PC

Ultimate Chicken Horse (2016)
Clever Endeavour Games; Clever Endeavour Games
Platformer (2D platformer, precision platformer)
PC, PS4, XBO, NS

Ultima Underworld: The Stygian Abyss (1992)
Blue Sky Productions; Origin Systems
RPG (immersive sim)
PC […] PSX […] mobile

Umurangi Generation (2020)
Origame Digital; Origame Digital, Playism
Simulation, adventure (photography sim)
PC, NS, XBO, PS4, PS5, Quest

UNCHARTED 2: Among Thieves (2009)
Naughty Dog; Sony Computer Entertainment
Action (third-person shooter)
PS3 […] PS4 (remaster; UNCHARTED: The Nathan Drake Collection)

UNCHARTED 4: A Thief's End (2016)
Naughty Dog; Sony Computer Entertainment
Action (third-person shooter)
PS4 […] PS5, PC

UNDER NIGHT IN-BIRTH (2012)
French-Bread, Ecole Software; SEGA, Arc System Works, Aksys Games, NIS America, PQube
Fighting (2D fighting)
ARC, PS3, PS4, PSV, PC, NS, PS5

Undertale (2015)
tobyfox; tobyfox
RPG (JRPG)
PC, PS4, PSV, NS, XBO

Universal Paperclips (2017)
Frank Lantz; DecisionProblem
Simulation (clicker)
PC, iOS, AND

Unreal Tournament (1999)
Epic Games, Digital Extremes; GT Interactive, Epic Games, MacSoft, Infogrames
Shooter (first-person shooter)
PC, PS2, DC

Until Dawn (2015)
Supermassive Games; Sony Computer Entertainment

Horror (cinematic adventure)
PS4 […] PS5, PC (remaster)

Untitled Goose Game (2019)
House House; Panic
Puzzle (stealth)
PC, NS, PS4, XBO

Use Your Words (2017)
Smiling Buddha Games; Screenwave Media
Party
PC, PS4, XBO, WU, NS

The Vale: Shadow of the Crown (2021)
Falling Squirrel; Falling Squirrel
RPG (audio game)
NS, PC, XBO

Valheim (n.d.)
Iron Gate Studio, Fishlabs; Coffee Stain Publishing
Action (survival)
PC, XBO, XS

Valiant Hearts: The Great War (2014)
Ubisoft Montpellier; Ubisoft
Adventure
PC, PS3, PS4, X360, XBO, iOS, AND […] NS

Valkyria Chronicles (2008)
SEGA, Media.Vision; SEGA
Strategy (tactics)
PS3 […] PC, PS4 (remaster) […] NS (remaster)

VALORANT (2020)
Riot Games; Riot Games
Shooter (first-person shooter, hero shooter)
PC, PS5, XS

Vampire Survivors (2022)
Poncle Ltd.; Poncle Ltd.
Shmup (bullet heaven)
PC, XBO, XS, iOS, AND, NS, PS4, PS5

Vanquish (2010)
PlatinumGames; SEGA
Shooter (third-person shooter)
PS3, X360 […] PC […] PS4, XBO

Venineth (2020)
Venineth Team; Monad Rock
Platformer (marble game)
PC

Victoria 3 (2022)
Paradox Development Studio; Paradox Interactive
Strategy (4X)
PC

Viewfinder (2023)
Sad Owl Studios; Thunderful Publishing
Puzzle
PS5, PC, PS4

Viva Piñata (2006)
Rare, Climax Group; Microsoft Game Studios
Simulation (life sim)
X360, PC […] XBO

VOEZ (2016)
Rayark, Esquadra; Rayark, PM Studios, Flyhigh Works, Circle Entertainment
Rhythm
iOS, AND, NS

Waco Resurrection (2003)
Team Waco; Team Waco
Shooter (third-person shooter)
PC

Walkabout Mini Golf (2020)
Mighty Coconut; Mighty Coconut
Sports (golf)
PC, Quest […] PS5, AND, iOS

The Walking Dead (2012)
Telltale Games; Telltale Games
Adventure (cinematic adventure)
PS3, PC, X360, iOS, PSV, PS4, XBO […] NS

WarCraft III: Reign of Chaos (2002)
Blizzard Entertainment; Blizzard Entertainment
Strategy (RTS)
PC

WarioWare, Inc.: Mega Microgames! (2003)
Nintendo R&D 1; Nintendo

Arcade (anthology)
GBA, WU, 3DS

Wasteland (1988)
Interplay Productions, inXile Entertainment, Krome Studios; Electronic Arts, inXile Entertainment, Xbox Game Studios
RPG (CRPG)
PC [...] XBO (remake)

Watch_Dogs 2 (2016)
Ubisoft Montreal; Ubisoft
Action (sandbox)
PS4, XBO, PC

Webbed (2021)
Sbug Games; Sbug Games
Platformer (2D platformer)
PC, NS, PS4, XBO

West of Loathing (2017)
Asymmetric Publications; Asymmetric Publications
RPG (JRPG)
PC, NS [...] iOS

What Remains of Edith Finch (2017)
Giant Sparrow; Annapurna Interactive
Adventure (exploration adventure)
PS4, PC, XBO, NS [...] iOS, PS5, XS

WHAT THE GOLF? (2019)
Triband; Triband
Arcade, sports (golf)
iOS, PC, NS [...] PS4, PS5

Wii Sports Resort (2009)
Nintendo EAD; Nintendo
Sports
Wii

Windjammers (1994)
Data East; SNK
Sports, arcade
ARC, NG [...] PS4, PSV, NS

The Witcher (2007)
CD Projekt Red; Atari, CD Projekt
RPG (ARPG)
PC

The Witcher 3: Wild Hunt (2015)
CD Projekt Red; CD Projekt
RPG (ARPG)
PC, PS4, XBO [...] NS [...] PS5, XS

The Witness (2016)
Thekla, Inc.; Thekla, Inc.
Puzzle
PS4, PC, XBO, iOS

Wolfenstein 3-D (1992)
id Software; Apogee Software, FormGen
Shooter (first-person shooter)
PC, ARC, SNES, JAG [...] GBA, XB [...] iOS, X360, PS3 [...] AND

Wordle (2021)
Josh Wardle; Josh Wardle, The New York Times Games
Puzzle (word puzzle)
PC, iOS, AND

World of Goo (2008)
2D Boy; 2D Boy, Nintendo, Brighter Minds Media, Tomorrow Corporation, Microsoft Game Studios
Puzzle (physics puzzle)
Wii, PC [...] iOS, AND, mobile [...] NS

World of WarCraft (2004)
Blizzard Entertainment; Blizzard Entertainment
RPG (MMORPG)
PC

Worms series (1995-present)
Team17; Team17, Ocean Software, MicroProse, Ubisoft, SEGA, Codemasters, THQ, Electronic Arts
Strategy (TBS, artillery)
PC, JAG, GB, PSX, GEN, SS, SNES, GB, N64, DC, GCN, PS2, XB, GBA, mobile, NDS, PSP, X360, PS3, iOS, Wii, AND, PS4, NS, XBO, XS, PS5

Worms 2 (1997)
Team17; Team17, MicroProse
Strategy (turn-based strategy, artillery)
PC

Worms Armageddon (1999)
Team17, Infogrames Lyon House; Team17, Hasbro Interactive, Infogrames

Strategy (turn-based strategy; artillery)
PC, DC, PSX, N64, GB […] XBO, XS, PS4, PS5, NS (remaster)

WWE SmackDown! vs. Raw 2006 (2005)
Yuke's; THQ, Yuke's
Sports (wrestling)
PS2, PSP

XCOM 2 (2016)
Firaxis Games; 2K
Strategy (tactics)
PC, PS4, XBO […] NS, iOS, AND

Xybots (1987)
Atari; Atari
Shooter (third-person shooter)
ARC, PC, Lynx

Yakuza 0 (2015)
Ryu Ga Gotoku Studio; SEGA
RPG, brawler (JRPG, beat-em-up)
PS3, PS4, PC, XBO

Yakuza 6: The Song of Life (2016)
Ryu Ga Gotoku Studio; SEGA
RPG, brawler (JRPG, beat-em-up)
PS4 […] PC, XBO

Yakuza: Like a Dragon (2020)
Ryu Ga Gotoku Studio; SEGA
RPG (JRPG)
PS4, PC, XBO, XS, PS5

Year Walk (2013)
Simogo; Simogo, Nintendo
Horror (point and click adventure)
iOS, PC, WU

Yellow Taxi Goes Vroom (2024)
Panik Arcade; Those Awesome Guys
Platformer (3D platformer)
PC

Yooka-Laylee (2017)
Playtonic Games; Team17
Platformer (3D platformer)
PC, PS4, XBO, NS

You Don't Know Jack (1995)
Jellyvision, Berkley Systems, Starsphere Interactive; Sierra On-Line
Party (quiz / game show)
PC, PSX

Yume Nikki (2004)
Kikiyama; Kikiyama, Playism
Adventure, horror
PC

Zero Escape: Virtue's Last Reward (2012)
Chunsoft; Chunsoft, Aksys Games, Rising Star Games, Spike Chunsoft
Adventure (visual novel)
3DS, PSV […] PC, PS4 […] XBO

Zero Time Dilemma (2016)
Chime; Aksys Games, Spike Chunsoft
Adventure (visual novel)
3DS, PSV, PC, PS4 […] XBO

Zork (1977)
Infocom; Personal Software, Infocom
Adventure (text adventure)
PC

Index

abstract art 3, 7, 20–22, 96, 118, 121, 169, 232, 333, 338–339, 348, 350
achievement 42, 72, 167, 327–328
actum *see* ludic framework
aesthetics 39–42, 134, 138, 141–143, 151, 156, 204–208, 227–229, 336–337
affective matching 257–259
agency 5, 7, 10, 11, 38, 73, 119–122, 124–125, 128, 132–133, 192, 196–202, 208–213, 215, 222, 303–304, 307, 315, 354
alternate reality (AR) 43; *see also* virtual reality (VR)
analog 43–44, 98, 316–318; *see also* digital
anamorphism 261–262
approachability 20–22
argument *see* semiotics
artificial intelligence (AI) 75, 80, 162, 195–196
audio games 33, 35
authorial intent 39, 137, 219, 302, 338
autonomic control 123
avatar 11–12, 24, 32–33, 40, 43, 73, 81, 98–114, 120, 129–131, 146, 154–155, 163–166, 173, 176, 182–185, 195–199, 236, 254–257, 260–261, 264, 268–269, 275, 283, 289–299, 311–312, 314, 320, 325

black box 69, 75, 91–93
Bogost, I. 35, 127, 136–138, 144, 150, 230–231, 240, 347–352
Boluk, S. 31, 77–78, 180, 201, 262, 322–323, 328–329, 334–337, 347
branches (narrative) 133, 200, 241, 251–253, 270, 272, 277–278, 286–287, 300–301, 307, 309, 314, 355
breadcrumbing 84–87, 247
bumper *see* controller
button *see* controller

Caillois, R 27–29, 77
challenge run *see* speedrun
characterization 199–200, 237, 246, 284–287, 291–299, 311–312
cheating 74–75, 77, 321, 323, 335, 338–339, 341
choice *see* agency
cinematic *see* cutscene
code 31–32, 37–39, 65–72, 77, 79, 93, 115–116, 138–140, 145–146, 149, 162, 235, 288–289, 303, 342
context (culture) 1–10, 19–20, 22–23, 47–49, 62, 99, 116–117, 119, 127–128, 143, 145, 148–150, 158–160, 187, 190, 216–220, 227, 231–232, 241, 338, 345, 349
context (of gameplay) / environment 98, 127, 132, 142, 172, 175–179, 189–190, 201, 229, 244, 267, 283
controller 21–23, 32–33, 40, 43–45, 66, 71–73, 80–81, 95–99, 102, 108–123, 130, 166–167, 173, 181–185, 189–192, 198, 210–211, 222–224, 261, 288–289, 309, 316–318, 322, 328–330, 349
conversation 73, 81–91, 98, 153, 156, 195
Crawford, C. 29–30
culture *see* context (culture)
curationism 155, 199, 237, 273–274
cutscene 12, 70, 103–104, 125, 127–128, 242, 284, 291–292, 299, 312, 319

Dadaism 3, 337
Deleuze, G. 134–135, 145, 213
design 31, 66–68, 353–355
dicisign *see* semiotics
diegesis 67, 99, 110, 129, 147, 158–169, 175–177, 182–185, 189–190, 194–201, 204, 207, 212–215, 224–225, 228–229, 231, 233, 236–237, 248, 254, 268–269, 275, 282–283, 325
  extradiegesis 42, 166–167, 174, 182, 190–192, 248
  interdiegesis 165–167, 174, 177, 185, 194–196
disability 20–21, 96, 101, 118, 121, 131, 339
D-pad *see* controller
dynamics 93, 128–129, 138, 140–143, 149, 175, 188–196, 206–207, 240, 243, 346

Ebert, R. 6–8, 12
embodiment 12, 19, 40, 67–68, 73, 81, 92, 99–113, 129, 161, 165–169, 179, 183–185, 196–200, 206–207, 211–217, 222–225, 233, 244, 256, 259–264, 268, 270–275, 288–289, 293–294, 325, 359
emergence 69–72, 78–83, 128–132, 137–140, 149, 171, 188–192, 273–280, 299, 302, 308–310
emitext *see* paratext
engine 44–45, 71, 109, 288, 332, 340–343
ethics 19–20, 110, 198, 343, 352–360
expressionism 3
expressivity 41–42, 72–73, 76, 196, 204, 207, 211–212, 219, 225, 229, 232–235, 263–264, 274–279, 282, 284, 290, 303, 306–320, 329
  macro-expressivity 122, 233, 307–313, 320
  micro-expressivity 123, 233, 307, 309–311, 314–318, 320
extradiegesis *see* diegesis

factum *see* ludic framework
feedback 3, 6, 32–35, 71–73, 99–100, 107, 111–113, 132, 182–188, 193, 196, 198, 210–212, 215, 241, 274–275, 303
Fernández-Vara, C. 15, 155–156, 335

flow 40, 142–143, 197, 265
forces 77–78

game feel 139, 142–143, 151, 308–309
Game of Life 79–80
game state 29, 32–34, 97–99, 146, 153, 171–182, 186, 202, 209–210, 335
gamification 2–5, 13, 192, 218, 347
gating 87–91
genre 40, 45–61
  action 49
  adventure 50
  arcade 51
  brawler 51
  fighting 52
  horror 52
  party 52
  platformer 53
  puzzle 54
  racing 54
  rhythm 55
  role-playing game (RPG) 55
  shmup 57
  shooter 58
  simulation 59
  sports 60
  strategy 60
glitch 36, 41–42, 62, 76, 82, 97, 162, 166, 181, 234, 245, 278, 287–290, 297, 309, 328–338
goal *see* victory condition

icon *see* semiotics
identification 255–257, 259–260
ideology 5, 12–13, 19–20, 93, 136–138, 204, 217–220, 230–233, 345–352
immersion 110–111, 193, 262–266
index *see* semiotics
input 32–33, 38, 43, 72–73, 80–81, 98–99, 109–110, 118–123, 130, 154, 176–189
inscription 65–66, 128–129, 133–134, 151, 169, 194, 207–208
insight 236–237
instantiation 114, 138, 194, 232, 236, 267, 272–286
instrumental providence 83–84
intentionality *see* agency
interdiegesis *see* diegesis

Järvinen, A. 155, 172–174, 228

Kanaga, D. 30

Laban, R. v. 156
Labanotation 156
legisign *see* semiotics
LeMieux, P. 31, 77–78, 180, 201, 262, 322–323, 328–329, 334–337, 347
linearity 10, 38, 127, 236–237, 240, 242, 251–253, 267–274, 277, 279–282, 348
literacy 13, 17–20
lore 70, 240, 246–247
ludeme 76–77, 186–188, 202, 213, 222–223, 226–227, 322, 346
ludic framework 152–155, 172, 213
ludomotif 134–136, 150, 213, 215, 225–227

manifest content 200, 211, 232–235, 283–287, 334
Mateas, M. 69, 80, 127, 144, 151, 155, 215, 348
MDA model 39–42, 127, 138–145, 151, 158, 188, 193, 204
meaning-making 134, 151–152, 169, 203
mechanics 78, 130, 138–140, 147–148, 173–174, 180–181, 355–357
metagame 31–32, 39, 68, 76–77, 80, 114, 118, 143–144, 180–181, 185, 191, 201, 212–213, 229, 231, 234, 248, 274, 277–278, 289–290, 309, 318, 321–329, 334–336, 339
metaphor 103, 113, 163, 220–224, 349–352
methexis 68, 162, 166–167, 179, 184–185, 190–191, 200–201, 207–208, 212–213, 225, 231, 233, 325–327, 334
middleware 71–72
mimesis 40, 68, 159–162, 167, 174, 184–185, 190–191, 199–201, 212–213, 225, 231, 233, 237, 254, 288, 320, 324–326
mods 339–343
motivation *see* agency
multilinearity/multisequentiality *see* linearity
Murray, J. H. 33, 65, 70, 72, 98, 106, 139, 144, 193, 230, 240, 262, 270, 345, 350–352

narrative 41, 142, 212, 240–253, 324–326
  embedded narrative 70, 125, 194, 199, 200, 240–247, 279, 291, 314
  emergent narrative 70, 200, 206, 237, 240–246, 308
narrativization 155, 196–200, 237, 248–251, 273–274
non-player character (NPC) 44, 80–81, 96–97, 133, 146, 154–155, 172–173, 195–196, 221, 229, 254, 359

objectives 6, 28, 34, 40, 82–83, 86, 179, 192–193, 196, 212, 217, 310, 313, 322
ontological upset 41, 263, 288, 337
ontology 35–39, 114–115

paragame 323, 327
paratext 247, 273–274, 304
Peirce, C. S. 65, 153–154
personification 254–255, 259–260
perspective 103–104, 260–262, 359–360
  perspective transformation 136
playtrace *see* recording/retelling
pointer/cursor 43, 99–100
polish 184
port 44, 70–71
possibility space/possible content 208, 211–213, 233–234, 251, 276–279, 284–289
post-processing 236–237
presence 40, 207; *see also* embodiment
proceduralism 127, 144–152, 171–172, 193, 207, 350–352
procedural rhetoric 136–138, 158, 227–231
projection/projective embodiment *see* embodiment
proprioception 100–107, 163–164, 215, 275
protostory 70, 80, 239–241, 246, 279–280, 299

qualisign *see* semiotics

recording/retelling 236–237, 240, 249, 267, 272–274
remake/remaster 37, 44–45
resonance 213–218
  associative resonance 222–223
  circumstantial resonance 215–216
rheme *see* semiotics
roguelike/roguelite 56, 191
rules 71, 73–77, 130, 139, 148, 173–174, 180–181
Ryan, J. 155, 202, 206, 237, 273–276, 308–309

schema 65, 109, 186–187, 216, 239
score 3, 32, 45, 147, 177–178
second-order state 9–12, 134, 150, 214–215, 224–225, 301–302, 330
Sedgwick, E. K. 199–200, 269–270, 302
semiotics 12–15, 65, 152–154
  semiotic vs. non-semiotic 12, 128, 133–134
sensation 40, 111–113, 136, 142, 164, 183–185, 204, 207–208, 275; *see also* vicariosensation
Seraphine, F. 127, 152–156, 172, 213
sign *see* semiotics
sinsign *see* semiotics
Sleep No More 4, 95
speedrun 33, 62, 234, 245, 289–290, 309, 322, 328–330, 335–336
sprite 42, 45, 115, 118–119, 156
state 175–180, 183–184, 234–236
  state machine 32, 175–176

stimmung 46, 129
story volume 200, 279–284
strategy 162–163, 185, 190–191, 196, 200–201, 208, 212, 307, 323, 326; *see also* methexis
structuralism 186, 268, 282–283
surrealism 3
Swink, S. 73–74, 99, 106–107, 139, 156, 183, 316
symbol *see* semiotics
systemic framework 96–99, 170–180, 194
  information system 170–171

tactum *see* ludic framework
telepresence *see* embodiment; presence
theme 144–151, 158, 174, 179, 207, 219–221, 231, 352
threshold object *see* controller
thumbstick *see* controller
transparency 73, 109–114, 190, 197–198, 210–211, 224, 336
Treanor, M. 127, 144–152, 171–172, 207, 350–352
trigger *see* controller
2D/3D 42, 45, 262

vertigo 40, 204, 207–208, 228
vicariosensation 40, 112, 183–185, 275; *see also* sensation
victory condition 34, 146, 171, 192, 201, 308, 313–314
video (output) 17, 33, 35, 65, 99, 118–119, 165, 188
virtual reality (VR) 15, 23, 32, 42, 45, 101, 109, 123, 140, 263–264, 317; *see also* alternate reality (AR)

Walton, K. S. 11, 159–160, 164, 261, 302, 324